ALSO BY SYLVIA NASAR

A Beautiful Mind

SYLVIA
NASAR

GRAND PURSUIT

THE STORY OF
ECONOMIC GENIUS

SIMON & SCHUSTER

NEW YORK   LONDON   TORONTO   SYDNEY   NEW DELHI

Simon & Schuster
1230 Avenue of the Americas
New York, NY 10020

First Simon & Schuster hardcover edition September 2011

SIMON & SCHUSTER and colophon are registered
trademarks of Simon & Schuster, Inc.

For information about special discounts for bulk purchases,
please contact Simon & Schuster Special Sales at
1-866-506-1949 or business@simonandschuster.com.

The Simon & Schuster Speakers Bureau can bring authors to your live event.
For more information or to book an event, contact the Simon & Schuster Speakers
Bureau at 1-866-248-3049 or visit our website at www.simonspeakers.com.

Designed by Ruth Lee-Mui

Manufactured in the United States of America

1   3   5   7   9   10   8   6   4   2

Library of Congress Cataloging-in-Publication Data
Nasar, Sylvia.
Grand pursuit : the story of economic genius / Sylvia Nasar
p.   cm.
Includes bibliographical references and index.
1. Economics—History.   2. Economists.   3. Economic history.   I. Title.
HB75.N347 2011
330.15092'2-dc23   2011024751

ISBN 978-0-684-87298-8
ISBN 978-1-4391-9861-2 (ebook)

The photo credits appear on pages 557–58.

For my parents

Contents

ACT III: CONFIDENCE

Preface

The Nine Parts of Mankind

The experience of nations with well-being is exceedingly brief.
Nearly all, throughout history, have been very poor.

John Kenneth Galbraith, The Affluent Society, *1958*[1]

In a Misery of this Sort, admitting some few Lenities, and those
too but a few, nine Parts in ten of the whole Race of Mankind
drudge through Life.

Edmund Burke, A Vindication of Natural Society, *1756*[2]

The idea that humanity could turn tables on economic necessity—mastering rather than being enslaved by material circumstances—is so new that Jane Austen never entertained it.

Consider the world of Georgian opulence that the author of *Pride and Prejudice* inhabited. A citizen of a country whose wealth "excited the wonder, the astonishment, and perhaps the envy of the world" her life coincided with the triumphs over superstition, ignorance, and tyranny we call the European Enlightenment.[3] She was born into the "middle ranks" of English society when "middle" meant the opposite of average or typical. Compared to Mr. Bennett in *Pride and Prejudice* or even the unfortunate Ms. Dashwoods in *Sense and Sensibility,*[4] the Austens were quite impecunious. Nonetheless, their income of £210 a year exceeded that of 95 percent of English families at the time.[5] Despite the "vulgar economy" that Austen was required to practice to prevent "discomfort, wretchedness and ruin,"[6] her family owned property, had some leisure, chose their professions, went to school, had books, writing paper, and newspapers at their disposal. Neither Jane nor her sister Cassandra were forced to hire themselves out as governesses—the dreaded fate that awaits Emma's rival Jane—or marry men they did not love.

The gulf between the Austens and the so-called lower orders was, in the words of a biographer, "absolute and unquestioned."[7] Edmund Burke, the philosopher, railed at the plight of miners who "scarce ever see the Light of the Sun; they are buried in the Bowels of the Earth; there they work at a severe and dismal Task, without the least Prospect of being delivered from it; they subsist upon the coarsest and worst sort of Fare; they have their Health miserably impaired, and their Lives cut short."[8] Yet in terms of their standard of living, even these "unhappy wretches" were among the relatively fortunate.

The *typical* Englishman was a farm laborer.[9] According to economic historian Gregory Clark, his material standard of living was not much better than that of an average Roman slave. His cottage consisted of a single dark room shared night and day with wife, children, and livestock. His only source of heat was a smoky wood cooking fire. He owned a single set of clothing. He traveled no farther than his feet could carry him. His only recreations were sex and poaching. He received no medical attention. He was very likely illiterate. His children were put to work watching the cows or scaring the crows until they were old enough to be sent into "service."

In good times, he ate only the coarsest food—wheat and barley in the form of bread or mush. Even potatoes were a luxury beyond his reach. ("They are very well for you gentry but they must be terribly costly to rear," a villager told Austen's mother).[10] Clark estimates that the British farm laborer consumed an average of only 1500 calories a day, one third fewer than a member of a modern hunter-gatherer tribe in New Guinea or the Amazon.[11] In addition to suffering chronic hunger, extreme fluctuations in bread prices put him at risk of outright starvation. Eighteenth-century death rates were extraordinarily sensitive to bad harvests and wartime inflations.[12] Yet the typical Englishman was better off than his French or

German counterpart, and Burke could assure his English readers that this "slavery with all its baseness and horrors that we have at home is nothing compared to what the rest of the world affords of the same Nature."[13]

Resignation ruled. Trade and the Industrial Revolution had swelled Britain's wealth, as the Scottish philosopher Adam Smith predicted in *The Wealth of Nations* in 1776. Still, even the most enlightened observers accepted that these could not trump God's condemnation of the mass of humanity to poverty and "painful toil . . . all the days of your life." Stations in life were ordained by the Deity or nature. When a loyal retainer died, he or she might be praised for "having performed the duties of the Station of life in which he had been pleased to place her in this world."[14] The Georgian reformer Patrick Colquhoun had to preface his radical proposal that the state educate the children of the poor with assurances that he did not mean that they "should be educated in a manner to elevate their minds above the rank they are destined to fill in society" lest "those destined for laborious occupations and an inferior situation in life" become discontented.[15]

In Jane Austen's world everybody knew his or her place, and no one questioned it.

A mere fifty years after her death, that world was altered beyond recognition. It was not only the "extraordinary advance in wealth, luxury and refinement of taste"[16] Or the unprecedented improvement in the circumstances of those whose condition was assumed to be irremediable. The late Victorian statistician Robert Giffen found it necessary to remind his audience that in Austen's day wages had been only half as high and "periodic starvation was, in fact, the condition of the masses of working men throughout the kingdom fifty years ago . . ."[17] It was the sense that what had been fixed and frozen through the ages was becoming fluid. The question was no longer if conditions could change but how much, how fast, and at what cost. It was the sense that the changes were not accidental or a matter of luck, but the result of human intention, will, and knowledge.

The notion that man was a creature of his circumstance, and that those circumstances were not predetermined, immutable, or utterly impervious to human intervention is one of the most radical discoveries of all time. It called into question the existential truth that humanity was subject to the dictates of God and nature. It implied that, given new tools, humanity was ready to take charge of its own destiny. It called for cheer and activity rather than pessimism and resignation. Before 1870 economics was mostly about what you couldn't do. After 1870, it was mostly about what you could do.

"The desire to put mankind into the saddle is the mainspring of most economic study," wrote Alfred Marshall, the father of modern economics. Economic possibilities—as opposed to spiritual, political, or military ones—captured the popular imagination. Victorian intellectuals were obsessed with economics and an extraordinary number aspired to produce a great work in that field. Inspired by advances in natural sciences, they began to fashion a tool for investigating the "very ingenious and very powerful social mechanism" that is creating not just unparalleled material wealth, but a wealth of new opportunities. Ultimately, the new economics transformed the lives of everyone on the planet.

Rather than a history of economic thought, the book in your hands is the story of an idea that was born in the golden age before World War I, challenged in the catastrophic interwar years by two world wars, the rise of totalitarian governments, and a great depression, and was revived in a second golden age in the aftermath of World War II.

Alfred Marshall called modern economics an "Organan," ancient Greek for tool, not a body of truths but an "engine of analysis" useful for discovering truths and, as the term implied, an implement that would never be perfected or completed but would always require improvement, adaptation, innovation. His student John Maynard Keynes called economics an "apparatus of the mind" that, like any other science, was essential for analyzing the modern world and making the most of its possibilities.

I chose protagonists who were instrumental in turning economics into an instrument of mastery. I chose men and women with "cool heads but warm hearts"[18] who helped build Marshall's "engine" and innovated Keynes's "apparatus." I chose figures whose temperaments, experiences and genius led them, in response to their own times and places, to ask new questions and propose new answers. I chose figures that took the story from London in the 1840s around the world, ending in Calcutta at the turn of the twenty-first century. I tried to picture what each of them saw when they looked at their world, and to understand what moved, intrigued, inspired them. All of these thinkers were searching for intellectual tools that could help solve what Keynes called "the political problem of mankind: how to combine three things: economic efficiency, social justice and individual liberty."[19]

As Keynes's first biographer Roy Harrod explained, that protean figure considered the artists, writers, choreographers, and composers he loved and admired to be "the trustees of civilization." He aspired to a humbler but no less necessary role for economic thinkers like himself: to be "the trustees, not of civilization, but of the possibility of civilization."[20]

Thanks in no small part to such trustees, the notion that the nine parts of mankind could free itself from its age-old fate took hold during the Victorian era in London. From there it spread outward like ripples in a pond until it had transformed societies around the globe.

It is still spreading.

Act I

HOPE

Mr. Sentiment Versus Scrooge

It was the worst of times.

When Charles Dickens returned from his triumphant American reading tour in June 1842, the specter of hunger was stalking England.[1] The price of bread had doubled after a string of bad harvests. The cities were mobbed by impoverished rural migrants looking for work or, failing that, charity. The cotton industry was in the fourth year of a deep slump, and unemployed factory hands were forced to rely on public relief or private soup kitchens. Thomas Carlyle, the conservative social critic, warned grimly, "With the millions no longer able to live . . . it is too clear that the Nation itself is on the way to suicidal death."[2]

A firm believer in education, civil and religious liberty, and voting rights, Dickens was appalled by the upsurge in class hatred.[3] In August a walkout at a cotton mill turned violent. Within days the dispute had escalated into a nationwide general strike for universal male suffrage, called by leaders of a mass movement for a "People's Charter."[4] The Chartists had taken up the principal cause of middle-class Radicals in Parliament—one man, one vote—into the streets. The Tory government of Prime Minister Robert Peel promptly dispatched red-coated marines to round up the agitators. Rank-and-file strikers began drifting back to their factories, but Carlyle, whose history of the French revolution Dickens read and reread, warned darkly that "revolt, sullen, revengeful humor of revolt against the upper classes . . . is more and more the universal spirit of the lower classes."[5]

In the glittering London drawing rooms where lords and ladies lionized him, Dickens's republican sympathies were as hard to overlook as his garish ties. After running into the thirty-year-old literary sensation for the first time, Carlyle described him patronizingly as "a small compact figure, *very* small," adding cattily that he was "dressed a la D'Orsay rather than well"—which is to say as flash as the notorious *French* count.[6] Carlyle's best friend, the Radical philosopher John Stuart Mill, was reminded of Carlyle's description of a Jacobin revolutionary with "a face of dingy blackguardism radiated by genius."[7] At fashionable midnight suppers the Chartist "uprising" provoked bitter arguments. Carlyle backed the Prime Minister who insisted that harsh measures were necessary to keep radicals from exploiting the situation and that the truly needy were already getting help. Dickens, who swore that he "would go farther at all times to see Carlyle than any man alive,"[8] nonetheless maintained that prudence and justice both demanded that the government grant relief to the able-bodied unemployed and their families.

The Hungry Forties revived a debate that had raged during the famine years, 1799 to 1815, of the Napoleonic Wars. At issue was the controversial law of population propounded by the Reverend Thomas Robert Malthus. A contemporary of Jane Austen and England's first professor of political economy, Malthus was a shy, softhearted Church of England clergyman with a harelip and a hard-edged mathematical mind. While still a curate, he had been tormented by the hunger in his rural parish. The Bible blamed the innate sinfulness of the poor. Fashionable French philosophers like his father's friend the Marquis de Condorcet blamed the selfishness of the rich. Malthus found neither explanation compelling and felt bound to search for a better one. *An Essay on the Principle of Population,* published first in 1798 and five more times before his death in 1834, inspired Charles Darwin and the other founders of evolutionary theory and prompted Carlyle to dismiss economics as the "dismal science."[9]

The fact that Malthus sought to explain was that, in all societies and all epochs including his own, "nine parts in ten of the whole race of man-kind" were condemned to lives of abject poverty and grinding toil.[10] When not actually starving, the typical inhabitant of the planet lived in chronic fear of death by hunger. There were prosperous years and lean ones, richer and poorer regions, yet the standard of life never departed for long from subsistence.

In attempting to answer the age-old question "Why?" the mild-mannered minister anticipated not only Darwin but Freud. Sex, he argued, was to blame. Whether from observing the wretched lives of his parishion-ers, the influence of natural scientists who were beginning to regard man as an animal, or the arrival of his seventh child, Malthus had concluded that the drive to reproduce trumped all other human instincts and abili-ties, including rationality, ingenuity, creativity, even religious belief.

From this single provocative premise, Malthus deduced the principle that human populations tended always and everywhere to grow faster than the food supply. His reasoning was deceptively simple: Picture a situation in which the supply of food is adequate to sustain a given population. That happy balance can't last any more than could Adam and Eve's tenure in paradise. Animal passion drives men and women to marry sooner and have bigger families. The food supply, meanwhile, is more or less fixed in all but the very long run. Result: the amount of grain and other staples that had just sufficed to keep everyone alive would no longer be enough. Inevitably, Malthus concluded, "the poor consequently must live much worse."[11]

In any economy where businesses compete for customers and workers for jobs, an expanding population meant more households contending for the food supply, and more workers competing for jobs. Competition would drive down wages while simultaneously pushing food prices higher. The average standard of living—the amount of food and other necessities available for each person—would fall.

At some point, grain would become so expensive and labor so cheap that the dynamic would reverse itself. As living standards declined, men and women would once again be forced to postpone marriage and have fewer children. A shrinking population would mean falling food prices as fewer households competed for the available food. Wages would rise as fewer workers competed for jobs. Eventually, as the food supply and population moved back into balance, living standards would creep back to their old level. That is, unless Nature's "great army of destruction"[12]—war, disease, and famine—intervened to hurry the process, as happened, for example, in the fourteenth century, when the Black Plague wiped out millions, leaving behind a smaller population relative to the output of food.

Tragically, the new balance would prove no more durable than the original one. "No sooner is the laboring class comfortable again," Malthus wrote sadly, "than the same retrograde and progressive movements with respect to happiness are repeated."[13] Trying to raise the average standard of living is like Sisyphus trying to roll his rock to the top of the hill. The faster Sisyphus gets almost there, the sooner he triggers the reaction that sends the boulder tumbling down the slope again.

Attempts to flout the law of population were doomed. Workers who held out for above-market wages wouldn't find jobs. Employers who paid their workers more than their competitors did would lose their customers as higher labor costs forced them to raise prices.

For Victorians, the most objectionable implication of Malthus's law was that charity might actually increase the suffering it was intended to ease—a direct challenge to Christ's injunction to "love thy neighbor as thyself."[14] In fact, Malthus was extremely critical of the traditional English welfare system, which provided relief with few strings attached, for rewarding the idle at the expense of the industrious. Relief was proportional to family size, in effect encouraging early marriage and large families. Conservative and liberal taxpayers alike found Malthus's argument so persuasive that Parliament passed, virtually without opposition, a new Poor Law in 1834 that effectively restricted public relief to those who agreed to become inmates of parish workhouses.

"Please, sir, I want some more." As Oliver Twist discovers after making his famous plea, workhouses were essentially prisons where men and women were segregated, put to work at unpleasant tasks, and subjected to harsh discipline—all in return for a place to sleep and "three meals of thin gruel a day, with an onion twice a week, and half a roll on Sundays."[15] The fare in most workhouses probably wasn't as meager as the starvation diet Dickens described in his novel, but there is no doubt that these institutions topped the list of working-class grievances.[16] Like most reform-minded middle-class liberals, Dickens considered the new Poor Law morally repulsive and politically suicidal and the theory on which it was based a relic of a barbaric past. He had recently returned from America with its "thousands of millions of acres of land yet unsettled and uncleared" and where the inhabitants were in "the custom of hastily swallowing large quantities of animal food, three times a-day,"[17] and found the notion that abolishing the workhouse would cause the world to run out of food absurd.

Bent on striking a blow for the poor, Dickens began early in 1843 to write a tale about a rich miser's change of heart, a tale that he liked to think of as a sledgehammer capable of "twenty times the force—twenty thousand times the force" of a political pamphlet.[18]

A Christmas Carol, argues the economic historian James Henderson, is an attack on Malthus.[19] The novel is bursting with delicious smells and tastes. Instead of a rocky, barren, overpopulated island where food is scarce, the England of Dickens's story is a vast Fortnum & Mason where the shelves are overflowing, the bins are bottomless, and the barrels never run dry. The Ghost of Christmas Past appears to Scrooge perched on a "kind of throne," with heaps of "turkeys, geese, game, poultry, brawn, great joints of meat, sucking-pigs, long wreaths of sausages, mince-pies, plum-puddings, barrels of oysters, red-hot chestnuts, cherry-cheeked apples, juicy oranges, luscious pears, immense twelfth-cakes, and seething bowls of punch, that made the chamber dim with their delicious steam." "Radiant" grocers, poulterers, and fruit and vegetable dealers invite Londoners into their shops to inspect luscious "pageants" of food and drink.[20]

In an England characterized by New World abundance rather than Old World scarcity, the bony, barren, anorexic Ebenezer Scrooge is an anachronism. As Henderson observes, the businessman is "as oblivious to the new spirit of human sympathy as he is to the bounty with which he is surrounded."[21] He is a diehard supporter of the treadmill and workhouse literally and figuratively. "They cost enough," he insists, "and those who are badly off must go there." When the Ghost of Christmas Past objects that "many can't go there; and many would rather die," Scrooge says coldly, "If they would rather die, they had better do it, and decrease the surplus population."

Happily, Scrooge's flinty nature turns out to be no more set in stone than the world's food supply is fixed. When Scrooge learns that Tiny Tim is one of the "surplus" population, he recoils in horror at the implications of his old-fashioned Malthusian religion. "No, no," he cries, begging the Spirit to spare the little boy. "What then?" the Spirit replies mockingly. "If he be like to die, he had better do it, and decrease the surplus population."[22] Scrooge repents, resolves to give his long-suffering clerk, Bob Cratchit, a raise, and sends him a prize turkey for Christmas. By accepting the more hopeful, less fatalistic view of Dickens's generation in time to alter the course of future events, Scrooge refutes the grim Malthusian premise that "the blind and brutal past" is destined to keep repeating itself.

The Cratchits' joyous Christmas dinner is Dickens's direct riposte to Malthus, who uses a parable about "Nature's mighty feast" to warn of the unintended consequences of well-meaning charity. A man with no means of support asks the guests to make room for him at the table. In the past, the diners would have turned him away. Beguiled by utopian French theories, they decide to ignore the fact that there is only enough food for the invited guests. They fail to foresee when they let the newcomer join them that more gatecrashers will arrive, the food will run out before everyone has been served, and the invited guests' enjoyment of the meal will be "destroyed by the spectacle of misery and dependence."[23]

The Cratchits' groaning board, wreathed with the family's beaming faces, is the antithesis of Malthus's tense, tightly rationed meal. In contrast to Nature's grudging portions, there is Mrs. Cratchit's pudding—"like a speckled cannon-ball, so hard and firm, blazing in half of half-a-quartern of ignited brandy, and bedecked with Christmas holly stuck into the top"—not large enough for seconds perhaps, but ample for her family. "Mrs. Cratchit said that now the weight was off her mind, she would confess she had had her doubts about the quantity of flour. Everybody had something to say about it, but nobody said or thought it was at all a small pudding for a large family. It would have been flat heresy to do so. Any Cratchit would have blushed to hint at such a thing."[24]

The Christmas spirit was catching. By the story's end, Scrooge had even stopped starving himself. Instead of slurping his customary bowl of gruel in solitude, the new Scrooge surprises his nephew by showing up unannounced for Christmas dinner. Needless to say, his heir hastens to set a place for him at the table.

Dickens's hope that *A Christmas Carol* would strike the public like a sledgehammer was fulfilled. Six thousand copies of the novel were sold between the publication date of December 19 and Christmas Eve, and the tale would stay in print for the rest of Dickens's life—and ever since.[25] Dickens's depiction of the poor earned him satirical labels such as "Mr. Sentiment,"[26] but the novelist never wavered in his conviction that there was a way to improve the lot of the poor without overturning existing society.

Dickens was too much a man of business to imagine that schemes for bettering social conditions could succeed unless they could be paid for. He was a "pure modernist" and "believer in Progress" rather than an opponent of the Industrial Revolution. Wildly successful while still in his twenties, he had gone too far on his own talent to doubt that human ingenuity was climbing into the driver's seat. Having escaped poverty by making his way in the new mass-media industry, Dickens was impatient with conservatives such as Carlyle and socialists such as Mill who refused to admit that, as a society, "we have risen slowly, painfully, and with many a hard struggle out of all this social degradation and ignorance" and who "look back to all this blind and brutal past with an admiration they will not grant to the present."[27]

Dickens's sense that English society was waking up, as if from a long nightmare, proved prescient. Within a year of the Chartist "uprising," a new mood of tolerance and optimism was palpable. The Tory prime minister admitted privately that many of the Chartists' grievances were justified.[28] Labor leaders rejected calls for class warfare and backed employers' campaign to repeal import duties on grain and other foodstuffs. Liberal politicians responded to parliamentary commissions on child labor, industrial accidents, and other evils by introducing the Factory Acts of 1844, legislation regulating the hours of women and children.

Dickens never imagined that the world could get along without the calculating science of economics. Instead, he hoped to convert political economists as the Ghost of Christmas Future had converted Scrooge. He wanted them to stop treating poverty as a natural phenomenon, assuming that ideas and intentions were of no importance, or taking for granted that the interests of different classes were diametrically opposed. Dickens was especially eager for political economists to practice "mutual explanation, forbearance and consideration; something . . . not exactly stateable in figures."[29] When he launched his popular weekly, *Household Words,* he did so with a plea to economists to humanize their discipline. As he wrote in his inaugural essay, "Political economy is a mere skeleton unless it has a little human covering, and filling out, a little human bloom upon it, and a little human warmth in it."[30]

Dickens was not alone. There were—and would be—men and women in London and all over the world who reached the same conclusion. Having overcome formidable obstacles, they too saw man as a creature of circumstance. They too realized that the material conditions of life for the "nine parts in ten of the whole race of mankind" were no longer immutable, predetermined by the "blind and brutal past," and utterly beyond human control or influence. Convinced that economic circumstances were open to human intervention yet skeptical of utopian schemes and "artificial societies" imposed by radical elites, they devoted themselves to fashioning an "engine of analysis"[31] (or, as a later economist put it, an "apparatus of the mind")[32] that they could use to understand how the modern world worked and how humanity's material condition on which its moral, emotional, intellectual, and creative condition depended—could be improved.

Chapter I

Perfectly New: Engels and Marx in the Age of Miracles

The exact point is that it has not gone on a long time. [It is] perfectly new. . . .

Our system though curious and peculiar may be worked safely . . . if we wish to work it, we must study it.

—*Walter Bagehot,* Lombard Street [1]

"See to it that the material you've collected is soon launched into the world," the twenty-three-year-old Friedrich Engels wrote to his corevolutionist, Karl Marx. "It's high time. Down to work, then, and quickly into print!" [2]

In October 1844, continental Europe was a smoldering volcano threatening to erupt. Marx, the son-in-law of a Prussian nobleman and editor of a radical philosophy journal, was in Paris, where he was supposed to be writing an economic treatise to prove with mathematical certainty that revolution must come. Engels, the scion of prosperous Rhenish textile merchants, was at his family's estate, up to his eyebrows in English newspapers and books. He was drafting a "fine bill of indictment" against the class to which he and Marx belonged. [3] His only anxiety was that the revolution would arrive before the galleys.

A romantic rebel with literary aspirations, Engels was already an "embryonic revolutionary" and "enthusiastic communist" when he met Marx for the first time two years earlier. Having spent his adolescence freeing himself from his family's strict Calvinism, the slender, fair, severely near-sighted Royal Prussian artillerist had trained his sights on the twin tyrannies of God and Mammon. Convinced that private property was the root of all evil and that a social revolution was the only way to establish a just society, Engels had yearned to live the "true" life of a philosopher. To his infinite regret, he was predestined for the family trade. "I am not a Doctor," he had corrected the wealthy publisher of a radical newspaper who mistook him for a scholar, adding that he could "never become one. I am only a businessman." [4]

Engels Senior, a fervid Evangelical who clashed frequently with his freethinking son, wouldn't have it any other way. As a proprietor, he was quite progressive. He supported free trade, adopted the latest British spinning equipment in his factory in the Wuppertal, and had recently opened a second plant in Manchester, the Silicon Valley of the industrial revolution. But as a father he could not stomach the notion of his eldest son and heir as a professional agitator and freelance journalist. When the global cotton trade collapsed in the spring of 1842, followed by the Chartist strikes, he insisted that the young Engels report to work at Ermen & Engels in Manchester as soon his compulsory military service was over.

Bowing to filial duty hardly meant the death of Engels's dream of becoming the scourge of authority in all forms. Manchester was notorious for the militancy of its factory hands. Convinced that the industrial strife was a prelude to wider insurrection, Engels had been only too delighted to go where the action was and to use the opportunity to advance his writing career.

En route to England in November, he had stopped in Cologne, where he visited the grubby offices of the prodemocracy newspaper *Rheinische Zeitung,* to which he had been contributing occasional articles under the byline *X.* The new editor was a brusque, cigar-smoking, exceedingly myopic philosopher from Trier who treated him rudely. Engels had taken no offense and had been rewarded with an assignment to report on the prospects for revolution in England.

· · ·

When Engels arrived in Manchester, the general strike had petered out and the troops had returned to their London barracks, but there were unemployed men hanging around street corners, and many of the mills were still idle. Despite his conviction that the factory owners would rather see their employees starve than pay a living wage, Engels could not help noticing that the English factory worker ate a great deal better than his counterpart in Germany. While a worker at his family's textile mill in Barmen dined almost exclusively on bread and potatoes, "Here he eats beef every day and gets a more nourishing joint for his money than the richest man in Germany. He drinks tea twice a day and still has enough money left over to be able to drink a glass of porter at midday and brandy and water in the evening."[5]

To be sure, unemployed cotton workers had had to turn to the Poor Law and private soup kitchens to avoid "absolute starvation," and Edwin Chadwick's just-published *Report on the Sanitary Condition of the Labouring Population of Great Britain* revealed that the average male life span in Manchester was seventeen years, half that of nearby rural villages, and that just one in two babies survived past age five. Chadwick's graphic descriptions of streets that served as sewers, cottages damp with mold, rotting food, and rampant drunkenness demonstrated that British workers had ample grounds for resentment.[6] But while Carlyle, the only Englishman Engels admired, warned of working-class revolt, Engels found that most middle-class Englishmen considered the possibility remote and looked to the future with "remarkable calm and confidence."[7]

Once settled in his new home, Engels resolved the conflict between his family's demands and his revolutionary ambitions in a characteristically Victorian fashion. He lived a double life. At the office and among his fellow capitalists, he resembled the "sprightly, good humored, pleasant" Frank Cheeryble, the "nephew of the firm" in Dickens's *Nicholas Nickleby* who "was coming to take a share in the business here" after "superintending it in Germany for four years."[8] Like the novel's attractive young businessman, Engels dressed impeccably, joined several clubs, gave good dinners, and kept his own horse so that he could go fox hunting at friends' estates. In his other, "true" life, he "forsook the company and the dinner-parties, the port-wine and champagne" to moonlight as a Chartist organizer and investigative journalist.[9] Inspired by the exposés of English reformers and often accompanied by an illiterate Irish factory girl with whom he was having an affair, Engels spent his free time getting to know Manchester "as intimately as my native town," gathering materials for the dramatic columns and essays he filed to various radical newspapers.

Engel's twenty-one months as a management trainee in England led him to discover economics. While German intellectuals were obsessed by religion, the English seemed to turn every political or cultural issue into an economic question. It was especially true in Manchester, a stronghold of English political economy, the Liberal Party, and the Anti–Corn Law League. To Engels, the city represented the interconnections between the industrial revolution, working class militancy, and the doctrine of laissez-faire. Here "it was forcibly brought to my notice that economic factors, hitherto ignored or at least underestimated by historians, play a decisive role in the development of the modern world," he later re-called.[10]

Frustrated as he was by his lack of a university education, particularly his ignorance of the works of Adam Smith, Thomas Malthus, David Ricardo, and other British political economists, Engels was nonetheless perfectly confident that British economics was deeply flawed. In one of the last essays he wrote before leaving England, he hastily roughed out the essential elements of a rival doctrine. Modestly, he called this fledgling effort "Outlines of a Critique of Political Economy."[11]

Across the English Channel in St. Germain-en-Laye, the wealthiest suburb of Paris, Karl Marx had buried himself in histories of the French Revolution. When Engels's final piece arrived in the post, he was jolted back to the present, electrified by his correspondent's "brilliant sketch on the critique of economic categories."[12]

Marx too was the prodigal (and profligate) son of a bourgeois father. He too was an intellectual who felt trapped in a philistine age. He shared Engels's sense of German intellectual and cultural superiority, admired all things French, and bitterly resented British wealth and power. Yet he was in many ways Engels's opposite. Domineering, impetuous, earnest, and learned, Marx had none of the other man's glibness, adaptability, or cheerful bonhomie. Only two and a half years older, Marx was not only married and the father of a baby girl but also a doctor of philosophy who insisted on being addressed as such. A short, powerfully built, almost Napoleonic figure, he had thick jet-black hair that sprouted from cheeks, arms, nose, and ears. His "eyes glowed with an intelligent and malicious fire," and, as his assistant at the *Rheinische Zeitung* recalled, his favorite conversation starter was "I am going to annihilate you." [13] One of his biographers, Isaiah Berlin, identified Marx's "belief in himself and his own powers" as his "single most outstanding characteristic." [14]

While Engels was practical and efficient, Marx was, as George Bernard Shaw pointed out, "without administrative experience" or any "business contact with a living human being." [15] He was undeniably brilliant and erudite, but he had never acquired Engels's work ethic. Whereas Engels was ready at any hour to roll up his sleeves and start writing, Marx was more likely to be found in a café, drinking wine and arguing with Russian aristocrats, German poets, and French socialists. As one of his backers once reported, "He reads a lot. He works with extraordinary intensity . . . He never finishes anything. He interrupts every bit of research to plunge into a fresh ocean of books . . . He is more excitable and violent than ever, especially when his work has made him ill and he has not been to bed for three or four nights on end." [16]

Marx had been forced to turn to journalism when he failed to obtain an academic post at a German university and his long-suffering family finally cut him off financially. [17] After just six months at his newspaper job in Cologne—"the very air here turns one into a serf"—he picked a fight with the Prussian censor and quit. Luckily, Marx was able to convince a wealthy Socialist to finance a new philosophical journal, the *Franco-German Annals,* and appoint him to run it in his favorite city, Paris.

Engels's reports from Manchester emphasizing the link between economic causes and political effects made a powerful impression on Marx. Economics was new to him. The terms *proletariat, working class, material conditions,* and *political economy* had yet to crop up in his correspondence.

As his letter to his patron shows, he had envisioned an alliance of "the enemies of philistinism, i.e. all thinking and suffering people," but his goal was
reforming consciousness, not abolishing private property. His contribution
to the first and only issue of the *Franco-German Annals* makes clear that
Marx meant to hurl criticisms, not paving stones, at the powers that be:
"Every individual must admit to himself that he has no precise idea about
what ought to happen. However, this very defect turns to the advantage of
the new movement, for it means that we do not anticipate the world with
our dogmas but instead attempt to discover the new world through the
critique of the old."

He went on, "We shall simply show the world why it is struggling . . .
Our program must be: the reform of consciousness . . . the self-
clarification . . . of the struggles and wishes of the age." The philosopher's
role was like that of a priest: "What is needed above all is a *confession*, and
nothing more than that. To obtain forgiveness for its sins, mankind needs
only to declare them for what they are."

Marx and Engels had their first real encounter in August 1844 at the
Café de Regence. Engels stopped in Paris on his way home to Germany expressly to see the man who had earlier rebuffed him. They talked, argued,
and drank for ten straight days, discovering again and again that each had
been thinking the other's thoughts. Marx shared Engels's conviction of
the utter hopelessness of reforming modern society, and the need to free
Germany from God and traditional authority. Engels introduced him to
the idea of the proletariat. Marx felt an immediate sense of identification
with that class. He saw the proletariat not only, as one might expect, as
the "naturally arising poor" but also as the "artificially impoverished . . .
masses resulting from the drastic dissolution of society,"[18] aristocrats who
had lost their lands, bankrupt businessmen, and unemployed academics.

Like Carlyle and Engels, Marx seized on hunger and rebelliousness
as evidence of the bourgeoisie's unfitness for rule: "absolutely imperative
need" will drive the proletariat to overthrow its oppressors, he predicted.[19]
By abolishing private property, the proletariat would free not only itself
but the entire society. As the historian Gertrude Himmelfarb observes,
Engels and Marx were hardly the only Victorians who were convinced that

modern society was suffering from a terminal illness.[20] They differed from Carlyle and other social critics chiefly in their emphasis on the inevitability of the demise of the existing social order. Even as they struggled to free themselves from Protestant dogma, they became convinced that the economic collapse and violent revolution they predicted were fates from which there was no escape—so to speak, predestined. While Carlyle's doomsday message was meant to inspire repentance and reform, theirs was meant to urge their readers to get on the right side of history before it was too late.

In *The Condition of the Working Class in England in 1844,* Engels had made a compelling, if not necessarily accurate, case that England's industrial workforce normally lived in a state of semistarvation and that famine had driven it to violence against factory owners in 1842. What his journalistic account could not establish was that workers' precarious existence was immutable and that no solution existed short of the overthrow of English society and the imposition of a Chartist dictatorship. This is the argument that Engels had kept losing with his English acquaintances and the problem he had urged Marx to take up. He explained to Marx that in England, social and moral problems were being redefined as economic problems, and social critics were being forced to grapple with *economic* realities. Just as the disciples of the German philosopher Georg Hegel had used religion to dethrone religion and expose the hypocrisy of Germany's ruling elite, they would have to use the principles of political economy to eviscerate the hateful English "religion of money."

When the new friends parted, Engels went home to Germany to pour out his charges of "murder, robbery and other crimes on a massive scale" against the British business class (and, by implication, Germany's as well).[21] Working in his family's cotton thread factory had confirmed Engels's feeling that business was "filthy."[22] He had "never seen a class so deeply demoralized, so incurably debased by selfishness, so corroded within, so incapable of progress, as the English bourgeoisie." These "bartering Jews," as he called the businessmen of Manchester, were devotees of "Political Economy, the Science of Wealth," indifferent to the suffering of their workers as long as they made a profit and, indeed, to all human values except money. "The huckstering spirit" of the English upper classes was as repugnant as the "Pharisaic philanthropy" that they dispensed to the poor after "sucking out their very life-blood." With English society increasingly "divided into millionaires and paupers," the imminent "war of the poor against the rich" would be "the bloodiest ever waged." [23] As fast and fluent a writer as he was a talker, Engels finished his manuscript in less than twelve weeks.

All the while, Engels badgered Marx to "Do try and finish your political economy book . . . It must come out soon." [24] His own book was published in Leipzig in July 1845. *The Condition of the Working Class in England* drew favorable reviews and sold well even before the economic and political crises that the author correctly forecast for "1846 or 1847" gave it the added cache of successful prophecy. *Das Kapital,* the grandiose treatise in which Marx promised to reveal the "law of motion of modern society," took twenty years longer.[25]

In 1849, when Henry Mayhew, a *London Morning Chronicle* correspondent, climbed to the Golden Gallery atop St. Paul's Cathedral to get a bird's-eye view of his hometown, he found that "it was impossible to tell where the sky ended and the city began." [26] At nearly 20 percent a decade, the city's growth "seemed to obey no known law." [27] By the middle of the century, the population had swelled to two and one half million. There were more than enough Londoners to populate two Parises, five Viennas, or the eight next-largest English cities combined.[28]

London "epitomized the 19th century economic miracle." [29] The pool of London was the world's biggest and most efficient port. As early as 1833, a partner in the Barings Brothers Bank observed that London had become the "center upon which commerce must turn." London's wet docks covered hundreds of acres and had become a prime tourist attraction—not least because of a twelve-acre underground wine cellar that gave visitors a chance to taste the Bordeaux. The smells—pungent tobacco, overpowering rum, sickening hides and horn, fragrant coffee and spices—evoked a vast global trade, an endless stream of migrants, and a far-flung empire.

"I know nothing more imposing than the view which the Thames offers during the ascent from the sea to London Bridge," Engels had confessed in 1842 after seeing London for the first time. "The masses of buildings, the wharves on both sides, especially from Woolwich upwards, the countless ships along both shores, crowding ever closer and closer together, until, at last, only a narrow passage remains in the middle of the river, a passage through which hundreds of steamers shoot by one another; all this is so vast, so impressive, that a man cannot collect himself."[30]

London's railway stations were "vaster than the walls of Babylon ... vaster than the temple of Ephesus," John Ruskin, the art historian, claimed. "Night and day the conquering engines rumbled," wrote Dickens in *Dombey and Son*. From London, a traveler could go as far north as Scotland, as far east as Moscow, as far south as Baghdad. Meanwhile, the railroad was pushing London's boundaries ever farther into the surrounding countryside. As Dickens related, "The miserable waste ground, where the refuse-matter had been heaped of yore, was swallowed up and gone, and in its frowsy stead were tiers of warehouses, crammed with rich goods and costly merchandise. Bridges that had led to nothing, led to villas, gardens, churches, healthy public walks. The carcasses of houses, and beginnings of new thoroughfares, had started off upon the line at steam's own speed, and shot away into the country in a monster train."[31]

The financial heart of world commerce beat in the "City," London's financial center. The financier Nathan Mayer Rothschild, not given to exaggeration, called London "the bank of the world."[32] Merchants came there to raise short-term loans to finance their global trade, and governments floated bonds to build roads, canals, and railways. Although the London stock exchange was still in its infancy, the City's merchants and bill discounters attracted three times the amount of "borrowable money" as New York and ten times as much as Paris.[33] Bankers', investors', and merchants' hunger for information helped make London into the world's media and communications center. "Anyone can get the news," a Rothschild complained in 1851 when the advent of the telegraph made his carrier pigeon network obsolete.[34]

London, not the new industrial towns in the north, boasted the big-

gest concentration of industry in the world, employing one in six manufacturing workers in England, nearly half a million men and women.[35]
That was roughly ten times the number of cotton workers in Manchester.
The "dark satanic mills" in William Blake's *Jerusalem* probably weren't
in the Coketowns of northern England. Like the monster Albion flour
mill, which employed five hundred workers and was powered by one
of James Watt's gargantuan steam engines, they were more likely on the
Thames in London.[36] A popular 1850s travel guide refers to "water works,
gas works, shipyards, tanning yards, breweries, distilleries, glass works the
extent of which would excite no little surprise in those who for the first
time visited them."[37] True, London had no single dominant industry such
as textiles, and most of its manufacturing firms employed fewer than ten
hands,[38] but entire industries—printing in Fleet Street, paint, precision
instruments in Camden, and furniture making around Tottenham Road—
were concentrated in London. The vast shipyards at Poplar and Millwall
employed fifteen thousand men and boys to build the biggest steamships
and armor-plated warships afloat. But while factory towns like Leeds and
Newcastle supplied the bulk of England's exports, most of London's manufacturers catered to the needs of the city itself. Wandsworth had its flour
mills, Whitechapel its sugar refiners, Cheapside its breweries, Smithfield
its cattle markets, and Bermondsey its tanneries, candle and soap makers.
Mayhew called London the world's "busiest hive."[39]

Above all, London was the world's biggest market. Here one could get
"at a low cost and with the least trouble, conveniences, comforts, and amenities beyond the compass of the richest and most powerful monarchs."[40]
In the prosperous West End of London "everything shines more or less,
from the window panes to the dog collars" and "the air is colored, almost
scented, by the presence of the biggest society on earth."[41] Regent Street
displayed the greatest collection of "watchmakers, haberdashers, and photographers; fancy stationer, fancy hosiers, and fancy stay makers; music
shops, shawl shops, jewelers, French glove shops, perfumery, and point
lace shops, confectioners and milliners" the world had ever seen.[42]

Mayhew astutely attributed "the immensity of . . . commerce" in the
city to "the unparalleled prevalence of merchant people in London, and

the consequent vastness of wealth." [43] The *Economist* boasted, "The richest persons in the Empire throng to her. Her scale of living is most magnificent; her rents highest; her opportunities of money-making widest." [44] One in six Britons lived in London, but London accounted for an even bigger share of national income. Incomes were, on average, 40 percent higher than in other English cities, not only because London had more wealthy residents but also because London wages were at least one-third higher than elsewhere. Her huge population and vast income made London by far the greatest concentration of consumer demand in the world. The economic historian Harold Perkin argues that "Consumer demand was the ultimate economic key to the Industrial Revolution," providing a more powerful impetus than the invention of the steam engine or the loom. [45] London's needs, passion for novelty, and growing spending power supplied entrepreneurs with compelling incentives to adopt new technologies and create new industries.

If London attracted some of the richest individuals on earth, it was also a magnet for a large number of the poorest. When Mayhew referred to "the unprecedented multitude of individuals attracted by such wealth to the spot," he meant not only the shopkeepers, tradesmen, lawyers, and doctors who catered specifically to the rich, but also the legions of unskilled migrants from the surrounding rural counties who came to work as servants, seamstresses, shoemakers, carpenters, dockhands, casual laborers, and messengers, or, failing that, as petty criminals, scavengers, and prostitutes. [46] The juxtaposition between rich and poor was rendered more striking by the exodus of the middle classes to the suburbs and, more significant in the minds of observers, by the universal assumption that London presaged the future of society. Poverty was not, of course, new. But in the country, hunger, cold, disease, and ignorance appeared to be the work of nature. In the great capital of the world, misery seemed to be manmade, almost gratuitous. Wasn't the means to relieve it at hand, actually visible in the form of elegant mansions, elaborate gowns, handsome carriages, and lavish entertainments? Well, no. It only looked that way to unsophisticated observers who had no idea that letting the poor eat cake for a day or two would hardly solve the problem of producing enough bread,

clothing, fuel, housing, education, and medical care to raise most Englishmen out of poverty. Mayhew was not alone in naïvely supposing that
the rows of brick warehouses, "vast emporia," contained wealth "enough,
one would fancy, to enrich the people of the whole globe." [47]

Journalists, artists, novelists, social reformers, clergymen, and other
students of society were drawn to London as "an epitome of the round
world" where "there is nothing one cannot study at first hand." [48] They
came there to see where society was heading. While eighteenth-century
visitors were apt to focus on sin, crime, and filth, those who flocked to
Victorian London were more often struck by its extremes of poverty and
wealth.

November was the worst month for air quality in the world's biggest and
richest metropolis, observed Charles Dickens in *Bleak House*. [49] On the
twenty-ninth of that month in 1847, Friedrich Engels and Karl Marx
struggled up Great Windmill Street toward Piccadilly, heads bowed and
trying their best to avoid slipping in the ankle-deep mud or being tram-
pled by the human throng. Their extreme myopia and the sulfurous yellow
London fog obscured everything more than a foot ahead.

Engels, still as erect as a cadet, and Marx, still with a jet-black mane
and magnificent whiskers, were in London to attend a congress of the
Communist League, one of many tiny groups comprised of Central European utopians, Socialists, and anarchists, as well as the odd Chartist
and occasional Cockney clerk in favor of male suffrage, that flourished in
the relative safety of English civil liberties and lenient immigration law.
When the recent collapse of a railroad boom spread financial panic in
London and on the Continent, the league had hastily convened a meeting
to hammer out its hitherto somewhat nebulous goals. Engels had already
convinced the league to drop its insipid slogan, "All Men Are Brothers,"
in favor of the more muscular "Proletarians of All Countries Unite!" He
had composed two drafts of a manifesto that he and Marx meant for the
league to adopt. They had discussed how they could shoulder aside those
in the leadership who were convinced that workers' grievances could be

addressed without overthrowing the existing order. "This time we shall have our way," Engels had sworn in his most recent letter to Marx.[50]

They finally found their way to Soho and the Red Lion pub. The headquarters of the German Workers' Educational Union, a front for the illegal league, was on the second floor. The room had a few wooden tables and chairs and, in one corner, a grand piano meant to make refugees from Berlin and Vienna stranded in "unmusical" London feel at home.[51] The air smelled of wet woolens, penny tobacco, and warm beer. For ten days, Engels and Marx dominated the proceedings, navigating the atmosphere of conspiracy and suspicion like fishes in water.

At one point, Marx read Engels's draft manifesto out loud. One delegate recalled the philosopher's relentless logic as well as the "sarcastic curl" of his mouth. Another remembered that Marx spoke with a lisp, which caused some listeners to hear "eight-leaved clovers" when he actually said "workers."[52] Some delegates repudiated Engels and Marx as "bourgeois intellectuals." At the end of the ten days, however, "all opposition . . . was overcome."

The congress voted to adopt their manifesto and agreed to declare itself in favor of "the overthrow of the bourgeoisie, the abolition of private property, and the elimination of inheritance rights." Marx, who had already burned through several family bequests but was, as usual, broke again, was commissioned to draft the final version of the league's call to arms.[53]

Engels had wanted the pamphlet to be a "simple historical narrative" and proposed that it be called *The Communist Manifesto*. He thought it important to tell the story of modern society's origins in order to show why it was destined to self-destruct. He envisioned the *Manifesto* as a sort of Genesis and Revelation rolled into one.[54]

Three years after Engels introduced Marx to English political economy, Marx was already calling himself an economist.[55] He had also absorbed the evolutionary theories that were beginning to pervade the sciences. Like other left-wing disciples of Hegel, he viewed society as an evolving organism rather than one that merely reproduced itself from one generation to another.[56]

He wanted to show that the industrial revolution signified more than the adoption of new technologies and the spectacular leap in production. It had created huge cities, factories, and transport networks. It had launched a vast global trade that made universal interdependence, not national self-sufficiency, the rule. It had imposed new patterns of boom and bust on economic activity. It had torn old social groups from their moorings and created entirely new ones, from millionaire industrialists to poverty-stricken urban laborers.

For a dozen centuries, as empires rose and fell and the wealth of nations waxed and waned, the earth's thin and scattered population had grown by tiny increments. What remained essentially unchanged were man's material circumstances, circumstances that guaranteed that life would remain miserable for the vast majority. Within two or three generations, the industrial revolution demonstrated that the wealth of a nation could grow by multiples rather than percentages. It had challenged the most basic premise of human existence: man's subservience to nature and its harsh dictates. Prometheus stole fire from the gods, but the industrial revolution encouraged man to seize the controls.

Engels and Marx perceived more clearly than most of their contemporaries the newness of the society in which they came of age, and tried to work out its implications more obsessively. Modern society was evolving faster than any society in the past, they believed. The consciousness of change and changeability was a breach in the firmament of traditional truths and received wisdom. In Marx's memorable phrase, "All that is solid melts into air."[57] Surely the vividness of their perceptions owes something to the fact that they came to England as foreign correspondents, so to speak, and that they came from a country that had yet to go through its industrial revolution. The trips from Trier and Barmen in Germany to London were journeys forward in time. Hardly anyone, except perhaps Charles Dickens, was as simultaneously thrilled and revolted by what they witnessed. They professed to despise England's "philistine" commercial culture while envying her wealth and power. Their observations convinced them that in the modern world, political power grew not from the barrels of guns but out of a nation's economic superiority and the energy of its business class.

England was the colossus astride the modern world. "If it is a question of which nation has *done* most, no one can deny that the English are that nation," Engels admitted.[58] Industry and trade had made her the world's richest nation. Between 1750 and 1850, the value of goods and services produced in Britain every year—her gross domestic product— had quadrupled, growing more in a hundred years than in the previous thousand.[59] The *Manifesto* emphasized the unprecedented explosion of productive power that Engels and Marx believed would determine political power in the modern world:

> The bourgeoisie, during its rule of scarce one hundred years, has created more massive and more colossal productive forces than have all preceding generations together . . . It has been the first to show what man's activity can bring about. It has accomplished wonders far surpassing Egyptian pyramids, Roman aqueducts, and Gothic cathedrals; it has conducted expeditions that put in the shade all former Exoduses of nations and crusades.[60]

Marx and Engels had no doubt that England's capacity to produce would continue to grow by multiples. But they were convinced that the distributive mechanism was fatally flawed and would cause the whole system to collapse. Despite the extraordinary accession of wealth, the abysmally low living standards of the three-fourths of the British people who belonged to the laboring classes had improved only a little. Recent estimates by Gregory Clark and other economic historians suggest that the average wage rose by about one-third between 1750 and 1850 from an extremely low level.[61] True, the laboring classes were now far more numerous, the English population having trebled. And they were not as miserable as their German or French counterparts.

But advances in some areas were balanced by retrogressions elsewhere. For one thing, most of the gain in pay occurred after 1820, and the lion's share went to skilled craftsmen and factory operatives. Any improvement in the wages of unskilled laborers, including farmworkers, was marginal and was offset, as Malthus had feared, by bigger families. Employment was less secure because manufacturing and construction were subject to booms and busts. Hours were longer, and wives and children were more liable to work as well.

Living standards of urban workers were further undermined by the degradation of the physical environment. The mass migration from the country to the city was taking place before the germ theory of disease had been discovered and before garbage collection, sewers, and clean water supplies were commonplace. Despite the greater poverty of rural England, life expectancy in the countryside was about forty-five versus thirty-one or thirty-two in Manchester or Liverpool. Filth and malnutrition simply weren't as deadly in less-contagious circumstances. At a time when cities like Liverpool were expanding at rates between 31 and 47 percent every decade, epidemics posed a constant threat. The richest of the rich were not immune—Prince Albert, Queen Victoria's husband, was carried off by typhoid—but the risks were magnified by poor nutrition and crowding. As the influx of migrants into cities accelerated in the first half of the nineteenth century, the health of the average worker stopped improving with income or actually deteriorated. Life expectancy at birth rose from thirty-five to forty between 1781 and 1851, but raw death rates stopped falling in the 1820s. Infant mortality rose in many urban parishes, and adult height—a measure of childhood nutrition, which is affected by disease as well as diet—of men born in the 1830s and 1840s fell.[62]

Reactionaries and radicals alike wondered if England was suffering from a Midas curse. "This successful industry of England, with its plethoric wealth, has as yet made nobody rich; it is an enchanted wealth," thundered Carlyle.[63] The economic historian Arnold Toynbee argued that the first half of the nineteenth century was "a period as disastrous and as terrible as any through which a nation has ever passed. It was disastrous and terrible, because side by side with a great increase of wealth was seen an enormous increase in pauperism; and production on a vast scale, the result of free competition, led to a rapid alienation of classes and the degradation of a large body of producers."[64]

True, as England's leading philosopher, John Stuart Mill, pointed out, the gradual removal of laws, levies, and licenses that tied the "lower orders" to particular villages, occupations, and masters had increased social mobility: "Human beings are no longer born to their place in life . . . but are free to employ their faculties and such favorable chances as offer, to achieve the lot which may appear to them most desirable."[65] But even Mill, a libertarian with strong Socialist sympathies, could see little improvement in the well-being of most Englishmen: "Hitherto it is questionable if all the mechanical inventions yet made have lightened the day's toil of any human being."[66]

Thus, in the second year of the potato famine in Ireland, the authors of *The Communist Manifesto* repeated Engels's earlier claim that as the nation grew in wealth and power, the condition of its people only worsened: "The modern labourer . . . instead of rising with the progress of industry, sinks deeper and deeper below the conditions of existence of his own class. He becomes a pauper, and pauperism develops more rapidly than population and wealth. And here it becomes evident that the bourgeoisie is unfit any longer to be the ruling class in society. . . . The proletarians have nothing to lose but their chains. They have the world to win. WORKING MEN OF ALL COUNTRIES, UNITE!"[67]

Having been ejected from France for publishing a satirical sketch of the Prussian king, Marx, his growing family, and the family retainer had been living in Belgium on a publisher's advance for his economics treatise. At the end of his month-long stay in London, Marx had returned to his suburban villa in Brussels, where he promptly put off the task of writing the final version and threw himself into a lecture series . . . on the economics of exploitation. In January, after league officials threatened to hand the assignment to someone else, he finally picked up his pen. Just before news of fighting in Paris between Republicans and the municipal guard reached Great Windmill Street, his partially finished final draft arrived in the mail.

On February 21, the league had one thousand copies of the *Manifesto*, written in German, printed and delivered to the German border with France. All but one copy was promptly confiscated by the Prussian authorities.

Marx and Engels waited impatiently for Armageddon. Like many nineteenth-century romantics, they "saw themselves as living in a general atmosphere of crisis and impending catastrophe" in which *anything* could happen.[68] John of Patmos, the author of the book of Revelation, had supplied them with the perfect finale for modern society and their *Manifesto*: society splits into two diametrically opposed camps, there is a final battle, Rome falls, the oppressed receive justice, the oppressors are judged, and the end of history comes.

History did not end in 1848. The French revolution of that year led not to Socialism or even universal male suffrage, but to the reign of Napoléon III. The declaration of the French Republic resulted in Marx's summary ejection from Belgium and, a few weeks after he had found a new bolt-hole in Paris, persecution by the French authorities. When the Paris police threatened to banish him to a swampy, disease-ridden village hundreds of miles from the capital, Marx objected on grounds of health and began to look around for a country that would take him. In August 1849 he moved to London, that "Patmos of foreign fugitives" and home of the former French king Louis Philippe and countless other political exiles.[69] It would be for only a short time, he consoled himself.

Marx's arrival in London coincided with one of the worst cholera epidemics in the city's history. By the time it had run its course, 14,500 adults and children had died.[70] The outbreak encouraged Henry Mayhew, the journalist, to undertake a remarkable series of newspaper stories about London's poor.[71] A scientist manqué who had a terrible relationship with his father, Mayhew was plump, energetic, and engaging, but absolutely hopeless about money. At thirty-seven, the former actor and cofounder of the humor magazine *Punch* was still recovering from a humiliating bankruptcy that had cost him his London town house and nearly landed him in jail. After months of grinding out pulp fiction with self-mocking titles such as *The Good Genius That Turned Everything into Gold,* Mayhew saw a chance for a comeback.

Mayhew's eighty-eight-part series took *Chronicle* readers on a house-by-house tour in the "very capital of cholera."[72] Jacob's Island was a particularly noxious corner of Bermondsey on the south side of the Thames immortalized by Dickens in *Oliver Twist.* Mayhew promised readers a sensational portrait of the district's inhabitants "according as they will work, they can't work, and they won't work."[73] He assured the audience that he was no "Chartist, Protectionist, Socialist, Communist," which was perfectly true, but a "mere collector of facts."[74] With a team of assistants and a few cabmen more or less on retainer, he plunged into the houses with "crazy wooden galleries . . . with holes from which to look upon the slime beneath; windows, broken and patched, with poles thrust out, on which to dry the linen that is never there; rooms so small, so filthy, so confined, that the air would seem to be too tainted even for the dirt and squalor which they shelter."[75]

Mayhew found that London's working population was by no means a single monolithic class but a mosaic of distinct and highly specialized groups.[76] He ignored the city's single biggest occupation—150,000 domestic servants—whose numbers demonstrated how large the rich loomed in the city's economy. Nor did he take an interest in the 80,000 or so construction workers employed in building railroads, bridges, roads, sewers, and so on. Instead Mayhew concentrated on a handful of manufacturing trades. As the historian Gareth Stedman Jones explains, London's labor market was a marriage of extremes. On the one hand, the city attracted highly skilled artisans who catered to the wealthy and who earned one-fourth to one-third more than in other towns, as much as the clerks and shopkeepers who comprised the "lower" middle class. On the other hand, it thrived on an uninterrupted influx of unskilled labor. Laborers also earned higher wages than their counterparts in the provinces, but their living conditions were apt to be worse because of the overcrowded, decrepit housing in areas like Whitechapel, Stepney, Poplar, Bethnal Green, and Southwark, which had been exhaustively documented by parliamentary commissions of the 1840s. Clerks, salespeople, and other white-collar workers could afford the new omnibuses or trains and were escaping to the fast-growing suburbs. Unskilled workers had no choice but to stay within walking distance of their places of employment.

Competition from provincial towns and other countries was a constant source of pressure to find ways to save on labor costs. The system of "sweating" or piecework, often performed in the worker's own lodging, was tailor-made to keep industries such as dressmaking, tailoring, and shoe manufacturing that would otherwise have migrated out of London on account of its high rents, overheads, and wages. Thus, Stedman Jones concludes, London's poverty, with its sweatshops, overcrowding, chronic unemployment, and reliance on charity, was, in fact, a by-product of London's wealth. The city's rapid growth led to rising land prices, high overheads, and high wages. High wages attracted more waves of unskilled newcomers but also created constant pressure on employers to find ways to replace more expensive labor with cheap labor.

London's needlewomen epitomized the phenomenon, and they were the subjects of Mayhew's most sensational stories. "Never in all history was such a sight seen, or such tales heard," he promised.[77] Using census figures, Mayhew calculated that there were 35,000 needlewomen in London, 21,000 of whom worked in "respectable" dressmaking establishments that ranged from the bespoke to those that catered to the lower middle class. The other 14,000, he wrote, worked in the "dishonorable" or sweated sector.[78] Mayhew contended that piecework rates "of the needlewomen generally are so far below subsistence point, that, in order to support life, it is almost a physical necessity that they must either steal, pawn, or prostitute themselves."[79]

On this occasion, Mayhew was more impresario than observer. In November, with the help of a minister, he organized "a meeting of needlewomen forced to take to the streets." He promised strict privacy of the assembly. Men were barred. Two stenographers took verbatim notes. Under dimmed lights, twenty-five women were given tickets of admission. They mounted the stage and were encouraged to share their sorrows and sufferings. The minister exhorted them to speak freely. To Mayhew's amazement, they did:

The story which follows is perhaps one of the most tragic and touching romances ever read. I must confess that to myself the mental and bodily agony of the poor Magdalene who related it was quite overpowering. She was a tall, fine-grown girl, with remarkably regular features. She told her tale with her face hidden in her hands, and sobbing so loud that it was with difficulty I could catch her words. As she held her hands before her eyes I could see the tears oozing between her fingers. Indeed I never remember to have witnessed such intense grief.[80]

Mayhew's account in the *Morning Chronicle* confirmed Thomas Carlyle's worst fears about modern industrial society, inspiring a choleric rant against economists:

Supply-and-demand, Leave-it-alone, Voluntary Principle, Time will mend it; till British industrial existence seems fast becoming one huge poison-swamp of reeking pestilence physical and moral; a hideous *living* Golgotha of souls and bodies buried alive; such a Curtius' gulf, communicating with the Nether Deeps, as the Sun never saw till now. These scenes, which the Morning Chronicle is bringing home to all minds of men, thanks to it for a service such as Newspapers have seldom done— ought to excite unspeakable reflections in every mind.[81]

Among these unspeakable reflections was the image of a volcano on the verge of eruption. "Do you devour those marvelous revelations of the inferno of misery, of wretchedness, that is smoldering under our feet?" Douglas Jerrold, then editor of *Punch* and Mayhew's father-in-law, asked a friend. "To read of the sufferings of one class, and the avarice, the tyranny, the pocket cannibalism of the others, makes one almost wonder that the world should go on."[82]

Mayhew's series in the *Morning Chronicle*, "Labour and the Poor," ran for the entire year of 1850. When about half of the articles had run, he revealed his larger ultimate aim. He wanted to invent, he confessed, "a new Political Economy, one that will take some little notice of the claims of labour." He justified his ambition by suggesting that an economics that did "justice as well to the workman as to the employer, stands foremost among the desiderata, or the things wanted, in the present age." [83]

Carlyle's friend John Stuart Mill had given precisely the same reason for embarking on his *Principles of Political Economy,* published in 1848, only two years earlier, and already the most-read tract on economics since Adam Smith's *The Wealth of Nations.*

"Claims of Labor have become the question of the day," Mill wrote during the Irish potato famine in 1845, when he conceived the idea for the book.[84] At the time, the thirty-nine-year-old Mill had long been in love with Harriet Taylor, an unhappily married intellectual whom Carlyle described as "pale . . . and passionate and sad-looking" and a "living Romance heroine." [85] As Mill's frustration over Harriet's husband's refusal to grant her a divorce grew, so did his sympathy with her Socialist ideals.

In taking up political economy, Mill hoped to overcome Carlyle's objection that the discipline was "dreary, stolid, dismal, without hope for this world or the next" [86] and Taylor's that it was biased against the working classes. Agreeing with Dickens, Mill saw a particular need to "avoid the hard, abstract mode of treating such questions which has brought discredit upon political economists." He blamed them for enabling "those who are in the wrong to claim, & generally to receive, exclusive credit for high & benevolent feeling." [87]

Mill no doubt had in mind David Ricardo, the brilliant Jewish stockbroker and politician who took up economics as a third career at age thirty-seven. Between 1809 and his untimely death in 1823, Ricardo not only recast the brilliant but often loosely expressed ideas of Adam Smith as an internally consistent, precisely defined set of mathematical principles but also proposed a remarkable number of original ideas concerning the benefits of trade for poor as well as rich nations and the fact that countries prosper most when they specialize. Nonetheless, many potential readers of his *On the Principles of Political Economy and Taxation* were as repelled by Ricardo's tendency to convey his ideas in abstract terms as by his dour conclusions. His iron law of wages—stating that wages may go up or down based on short-run fluctuations in supply and demand but always tend toward subsistence—incorporated Malthus's law of population and ruled out any meaningful gains in real wages.[88]

Mill noted that Ricardo, Smith, and Malthus were all vocal champions of individual political and economic rights, opponents of slavery, and foes of protectionism, monopolies, and landowner privileges. He himself favored unions, universal suffrage, and women's property rights. In response to the economic crisis and social strife of the Hungry Forties, he advocated the repeal of the 50 percent tax on imported grain. The typical laborer spent at least one-third of his meager pay on feeding himself and his family. Mill correctly predicted that once the tax on imports was abolished food prices would decline and real wages would rise. Yet even he remained profoundly pessimistic about the scope of improvements in the lives of workers. Like Carlyle, he was convinced that the repeal of the Corn Laws would only buy time, as the invention of the railroad, the opening up of the North American continent, and the discovery of gold in California had. Such developments, while beneficial, could not repeal the immutable laws by which the world was governed.

Malthus's law of population and Ricardo's iron law of wages and law of diminishing returns—the notion that using more and more labor to farm an acre would produce less and less extra output—all dictated that population would outrun resources and that the nation's wealth could be enlarged only at the expense of the poor, who were doomed to spend "the great gifts of science as rapidly as . . . [they] got them in a mere insensate multiplication of the common life."[89] Government could do no more than create conditions in which enlightened self-interest and laws of supply and demand could work efficiently.

For Mill, economies are governed by natural laws, which couldn't be changed by human will, any more than laws of gravity can. "Happily," Mill wrote as he was finishing *Principles* in 1848, "there is nothing in the laws of Value which remains for the present or any future writer to clear up; the theory of the subject is complete."[90]

Henry Mayhew, for one, refused to accept this conclusion. By his lights, Mill had failed in his attempt to turn political economy into a "gay science," that is, a science capable of increasing the sum of human happiness, freedom, or control over circumstances.[91] The fact that Mill had not jettisoned the iron law of wages was all the more reason for trying again. Ultimately, Mayhew did not succeed in mounting a challenge to the classical wage doctrine, and neither did anyone else of his generation. Still, his landmark series on London labor became the unofficial Baedeker for a younger generation of "social investigators" who were inspired by his reporting and shared his desire to learn how much improvement was possible without overturning the social order.

In August 1849, less than two years after Karl Marx had arrived in London amid a cholera epidemic, the whole world seemed to be descending upon his sanctuary to see the Great Exhibition. The first world's fair was the brainchild of another German émigré, Queen Victoria's husband, Prince Albert, but Marx, who was by then living with his wife, Jenny, their three young children, and their housekeeper in two dingy rooms over a shop in Soho, wanted nothing to do with it. He fled to seat G7 in the high-domed reading room of the British Museum with its cathedral-like gloom and refreshing quiet. Ignoring breathless newspaper accounts about the construction of the Crystal Palace in Hyde Park, Marx filled notebook after notebook with quotations, formulas, and disparaging comments as he pored over the works of the English economists Malthus, Ricardo, and James Mill, the father of John Stuart Mill. Let the philistines pray in the bourgeois Pantheon, he told himself. He would have no truck with false idols.

In May 1851, Karl Marx was no longer the dreamy young university student who spent days holed up in his dressing gown writing sonnets to a baron's daughter, or the louche journalist who drank all night in Paris cafés. In the ten years since he had obtained his mail-order doctorate from the University of Jena, he had squandered a surprise inheritance of 6,000 francs from a distant relative. He had started three radical journals, two of which had folded after a single issue. He had never held a job for more than a few months. While his erstwhile protégé, Engels, had produced a best seller, his own magnum opus remained unwritten. He had published, but mostly long-winded polemics against other Socialists. At thirty-two, he was just another unemployed émigré, the head of a large and growing family, forced to beg and borrow from friends. Luckily for him, his guardian angel, Engels, had promised to pursue a career at his family's firm expressly so that Marx could focus on his book full-time.

Meanwhile, as heads of state and other dignitaries swooped into town, Scotland Yard was keeping a close eye on radicals. Judging by a report from a Prussian government spy, the main threat posed by Marx was to Mrs. Beeton's standards of housekeeping:

> Marx lives in one of the worst, therefore one of the cheapest quarters of London. He occupies two rooms. The one looking out on the streets is the salon, and the bedroom is at the back. In the whole apartment there is not one clean and solid piece of furniture. Everything is broken, tattered and torn, with a half inch of dust over everything and the greatest disorder everywhere. In the middle of the salon there is a large old fashioned table covered with an oil cloth, and on it lie manuscripts, books and newspapers as well as the children's toys, the rags and tatters of his wife's sewing basket, several cups with broken ribs, knives, forks, lamps, an inkpot, tumblers, Dutch clay pipes, tobacco ash—in a word everything is topsy-turvy and all on the same table. A seller of second hand goods would be ashamed to give away such a remarkable collection of odds and ends.[92]

The Exhibition season represented a new nadir in Marx's affairs. Though he adored his wife, he had carelessly gotten Helen Demuth, her personal maid and the family housekeeper, pregnant. Jenny, who was pregnant as well, was beside herself. Three months after she gave birth to a sickly girl, the family's housekeeper delivered a bouncing baby boy. To quash the "unspeakable infamies" about the affair already circulating around gossipy émigré circles, Marx had his newborn son whisked off to foster parents in the East End, never to see him again. "The tactlessness of some individuals in this respect is colossal," he complained to a friend.[93] The boy's mother stayed behind to care for the Marx family as before. With home more unbearable than ever, Marx hurried to seat number G7 every morning and stayed until closing.

By the time the Great Exhibition opened on May Day of 1851, Marx had already begun to doubt that the modern Rome would be overthrown by her own subjects. Instead of Chartists storming Buckingham Palace, four million British citizens and tens of thousands of foreigners invaded Hyde Park to attend the first world's fair. The human wave helped launch Thomas Cook in the tour business and brought people of all backgrounds together. "Never before in England had there been so free and general a mixture of classes as under that roof," crowed one of the many accounts of the fair published at the time.[94] For Marx, the fair resembled the games Roman rulers staged to keep the mob entranced. "England seems to be the rock which breaks the revolutionary waves," he had written in an earlier column for the *Neue Rheinische Zeitung.* "Every social upheaval in France . . . is bound to be thwarted by the English bourgeoisie, by Great Britain's industrial and commercial domination of the world."[95] The Exhibition was meant to encourage commercial competition, which Prince Albert and some of its other sponsors hoped would foster peace. Marx had prayed for war: "Only a world war can break old England . . . and bring the proletariat to power."[96] The worse things got, he reasoned, the better the odds of revolution.

Still, he was not willing to totally discount the possibility that "the great advance in production since 1848" might lead to a new and more deadly crisis. Dismissing the Exhibition as "commodity fetishism," he predicted the "imminent" collapse of the bourgeois order.[97] As he and Engels had written in their *Manifesto:* "What the bourgeoisie therefore produces, above all, are its own grave-diggers."[98]

Racing against time so as not to be overtaken by the "inevitable" revolution—if not in England, then on the Continent—Marx began working furiously on his own book of Revelation, a critique of "what Englishmen call 'The Principles of Political Economy.'"[99] Marx spent most days scouring the reading room at the British Museum for material for his great work. To the contemporary questions "How much improvement in living standards was possible under the modern system of private property and competition?" and "Could it endure?" Marx *knew* the answers had to be negative. His challenge now was to prove it.

When he took up economics in 1844, Marx did not set out to show that life under capitalism was awful. A decade of exposés, parliamentary commissions, and Socialist tracts, including Engels's, had already accomplished that. The last thing Marx wanted was to condemn capitalism on moral (that is to say Christian) grounds, as utopian Socialists such as Pierre-Joseph Proudhon, who claimed that "private property is theft," had done. Marx had no intention of converting capitalists as his favorite novelist, Dickens, dreamed of doing with his *Christmas Carol.* In any case, he had long repudiated the notion of any God-given morality and insisted that man could make up his own rules.

The point of his great work was to prove "with mathematical certainty" that the system of private property and free competition couldn't work and hence that "the revolution must come." He wished to reveal "the law of motion of modern society." In doing so, he would expose the doctrines of Smith, Malthus, Ricardo, and Mill as a false religion, just as radical German religion scholars had exposed biblical texts as forgeries and fakes. His subtitle, he decided, would be *A Critique of Political Economy.*[100]

Marx's law of motion did not spring Athena-like from his powerful, brooding mind, as his doctor friend Louis Kugelmann supposed when he sent Marx a marble bust of Zeus as a Christmas present. It was Engels, the journalist, who supplied Marx with the rough draft of his economic theory. Marx's real challenge was to show that the theory was logically consistent as well as empirically plausible.

In the *Manifesto*, Marx and Engels had offered two reasons for capitalism's dysfunction. First, the more wealth that was created, the more miserable the masses would become: "In proportion as capital accumulates, the lot of the laborer must grow worse." Second, the more wealth that was created, "the more extensive and more destructive" the financial and commercial crises that broke out periodically would become.[101]

While the *Manifesto* referred to "ever-decreasing wages" and "everincreasing burden of toil" as matters of historical fact, in *Das Kapital,* Marx argued that the "law of capitalist accumulation" *requires* wages to fall, the length and intensity of the working day to rise, working conditions to dete-

riorate, the quality of goods consumed by workers to decline, and the average life span of workers to fall. He did not, however, fall back on the second
of his arguments about ever-worsening depressions.[102]

In *Das Kapital,* Marx specifically rejected Malthus's law of population,
which, as it happens, is also a theory of how the level of wages is determined. In formulating his law, Malthus had assumed that pay was strictly
a function of the size of the labor force. More workers meant more competition among them, hence lower wages. Fewer workers meant the opposite. Engels had already identified the primary objection to Malthus in his
1844 "Outlines of a Critique of Political Economy," namely that poverty
could afflict any society, including a Socialist one.

Marx's edifice rests on the assumption that all value, including surplus
value, is created by the hours worked by labor. "There is not a single atom
of its value that does not owe its existence to unpaid labor." In *Das Kapital,*
he cites Mill to support his claim:

> Tools and materials, like other things, have originally cost nothing but
> labour . . . The labour employed in making the tools and materials being
> added to the labour afterwards employed in working up the materials by
> aid of the tools, the sum total gives the whole of the labour employed in
> the production of the completed commodity . . . *To* replace capital, is to
> replace nothing but the wages of the labour employed.[103]

Mark Blaug, a historian of economic thought, points out that if
only labor hours create value, then installing more efficient machinery,
reorganizing the sales force, hiring a more effective CEO, or adopting a
better marketing strategy—rather than hiring more production workers—
necessarily causes profits to fall. In Marx's scheme, therefore, the only way
to keep profits from shrinking is to exploit labor by forcing workers to
work more hours without compensating them. As Henry Mayhew detailed
in his *Morning Chronicle* series, there are many ways of cutting the real
wage. It is crucial for Marx's argument, writes Blaug, that trade unions and
governments—"organizations of the exploiting class"—can't reverse the
process.[104]

A surprising number of scholars deny that Marx ever claimed that wages would decline over time or that they were tethered to some biological minimum. But they are overlooking what Marx said in so many words on numerous occasions. The inability of workers to earn more when they produce more—or more-valuable products—is precisely what made capitalism unfit to survive.

By asserting that labor was the source of all value, Marx claimed that the owner's income—profit, interest, or managerial salary—was unearned. He did not argue that workers did not need capital—factories, machines, tools, proprietary technology, and the like—to produce the product. Rather he argued that the capital the owner made available was nothing more than the product of *past* labor. But the owner of any resource—whether a horse, a house, or cash—could use it herself. Arguing, as Marx does, that waiting until tomorrow to consume what could be consumed today, risking one's resources, or managing and organizing a business have no value and therefore deserve no compensation is the same as saying that output can be produced without saving, waiting, or taking risks. This is a secular version of the old Christian argument against interest.

The trouble is, as Blaug points out, that this is just another way of saying that only labor adds value to output—the very statement that Marx set out to prove in the first place—and not an independent proof.

Marx compiled an impressive array of evidence, from Blue Books, newspapers, the *Economist,* and elsewhere, to show that the living standards of workers were wretched and working conditions horrendous during the second half of the eighteenth and first half of the nineteenth centuries. But he did not succeed in showing either that average wages or living standards were declining in the 1850s and 1860s, when he was writing *Das Kapital,* or, more to the point, that there was some reason for thinking that they would *necessarily* decline.

Had Marx stepped outside and taken a good look around like Henry Mayhew, or engaged brilliant contemporaries such as John Stuart Mill who were grappling with the same questions, he might have seen that the world wasn't working the way he and Engels had predicted. The middle class was growing, not disappearing. Financial panics and industrial slumps weren't getting worse.

When the Great Exhibition of 1862 closed, the "great festival" refused to disband. A businessman bought the Crystal Palace, had it disassembled and carted to Sydenham in South London, and rebuilt it on an even more monstrous scale. Much to Marx's disgust, the new Crystal Palace opened as a kind of Victorian Disney World. Worse, the economy boomed. As Marx had to admit, "It is as if this period had found Fortunatas' purse." There had been a "titanic advance of production" even faster in the second ten years than in the first:

> No period of modern society is so favorable for the study of capitalist accumulation as the period of the last 20 years . . . But of all countries England again furnishes the classical example, because it holds the foremost place in the world-market, because capitalist production is here alone completely developed, and lastly, because the introduction of the Free-trade millennium since 1846 has cut off the last retreat of vulgar economy.[105]

More fatal to Marx's theory, real wages weren't falling as capital accumulated in the form of factories, buildings, railroads, and bridges. In contrast to the decades before the 1840s, when increases in real wages were largely limited to skilled workers, and the effect on living standards was offset by more unemployment, longer hours, and bigger families, the gains in the 1850s and 1860s were dramatic, unambiguous, and widely discussed at the time. The Victorian statistician Robert Giffen referred to the "undoubted" nature of the "increase of material prosperity" from the mid 1840s through the mid-1870s.[106] Robert Dudley Baxter, a solicitor and statistician, depicted the distribution of income in 1867 with an extinct volcano that rose twelve thousand feet above sea level, "with its long low base of laboring population, with its uplands of the middle classes, and with the towering peaks and summits of those with princely incomes."[107] The Peak of Tenerife struck Baxter as a perfect metaphor for describing who got what. Still, his data show that by 1867, labor's share of national income was rising.

Scholars have since corroborated these contemporary observations. As early as 1963, Eric Hobsbawm, the Marxist economic historian, admitted that "the debate is entirely about what happened in the period which *ended* by common consent sometime between 1842 and 1845."[108] More recently, Charles Feinstein, an economic historian on the "pessimist" side of a long-running debate on the effects of the industrial revolution, concluded that real wages "at last started an ascent to a new height" in the 1840s.[109]

Marx never did step outside. He never bothered to learn English well.[110] His world was restricted to a small circle of like-minded émigrés. His contacts with English working-class leaders were superficial. He never exposed his ideas to people who could challenge him on equal terms. His interaction with economists—"commercial travelers for the great firm of Free-trade"[111] as he called them—whose ideas he wished to demolish, was nonexistent. He never met or conducted a scientific correspondence with the geniuses—John Stuart Mill, the philosopher; Charles Darwin, the biologist; Herbert Spencer, the sociologist; George Eliot, the writer; among them—who lived (and debated) a mile or two from him. Astonishingly for the best friend of a factory owner and the author of some of the most impassioned descriptions of mechanization's horrors, Marx never visited a single English factory—or any factory at all until he went on a guided tour of a porcelain manufactory near Carlsbad, where he took the waters toward the end of his life.[112]

At Engels's insistence, in 1859 Marx reluctantly published a preview of his unfinished magnum opus. The thin volume, called *A Contribution to the Critique of Political Economy*, was greeted with surprise, embarrassment, and virtually no reviews except ones that Engels wrote anonymously at Marx's behest.[113]

Marx had frequently justified his decision to remain in England— and even to seek British citizenship—by pointing to the advantages of

London, capital of the modern world, for studying the evolution of society and glimpsing its future. But Isaiah Berlin, himself an émigré, wrote that "he might just as well have spent his exile in Madagascar, provided that a regular supply of books, journals and government reports could have been secured." By 1851, when he started to work seriously on the critique that he boasted would demolish English economics, Marx's ideas and attitudes were "set and hardly changed at all" over the next fifteen or more years.[114]

When Marx took up the idea of "providing a complete account and explanation of the rise and imminent fall of the capitalist system,"[115] his eyesight was so bad that he was forced to hold books and newspapers a few inches from his face. One wonders what effect his myopia had on his ideas. Democritus, the subject of his doctoral dissertation, was said to have blinded himself deliberately. In some versions of his legend, the Greek philosopher is motivated by a desire to avoid being tempted by beautiful women. In others, he wants to shut out the messy, confusing, shifting world of facts so that he can contemplate the images and ideas in his own head without these bothersome distractions.

One might think that his family's climb from renters of rooms over a store to rate-paying owners of a London town house would have made Marx uneasy about his theory. In the twenty years since he had set out to prove that capitalism could not work, Marx himself had evolved from bohemian to bourgeois. He no longer favored the immediate abolition of the rights of inheritance in the Communist program.[116] The Marxes used one of several legacies to trade their "old hole in Soho" for an "attractive house" in one of the new middle-class developments near Hampstead Heath. It was so new that they found there was no paved road, no gas street lights, and no omnibuses; only heaps of rubbish, piles of rock, and mud.

Marx often said that there was something rotten about a system that increased wealth without reducing misery, yet it did not seem to strike him that misery can sometimes increase with wealth. He assumed that London's slums, which were becoming more Dickensian with each passing decade, were proof that the economy couldn't deliver a decent standard of living for ordinary people. On the contrary, explains Gareth Stedman Jones, the housing crisis was an unwelcome by-product of London's helter-skelter growth, growing prosperity, and voracious demand for unskilled labor. The key fact is that the mid-Victorian building frenzy involved an orgy of demolition. Between 1830 and 1870, thousands of acres in central London were cleared, mostly in the poor districts where land was cheap, to expand the London docks, lay railway lines, build New Oxford Street, dig the sewers and water pipes, and, in the 1860s, excavate the first stretches of the London tube. So, just as tens of thousands of migrants were flocking to the city in search of work, the supply of housing within walking distance of London's industrial areas was plummeting. As a result, workers were crowded into ever more dilapidated, ever tighter, ever more expensive quarters. Once the demolition stopped and white-collar workers began to commute from the suburbs by rail, the housing crisis began to ease.

The Exhibition season of 1862 coincided with another low point in Marx's financial affairs. Horace Greeley, the publisher of the *New York Tribune*, had dropped his column, which, though entirely ghostwritten by Engels, had supplied Marx with extra cash. At one point, his money woes became so dire that he applied for a job as a railway clerk, only to be rejected for "bad handwriting" and not speaking English, and briefly considered immigrating to America. Luckily, he was like an oyster that needed a bit of grit to make his pearls. With his mind on money, he was soon writing a long essay on economics and filling up notebooks again, complaining all the while that he felt like "a machine condemned to devour books and then throw them, in a changed form, on the dunghill of history."[117] He also decided on a title for his great work: *Das Kapital*.[118]

The hoopla surrounding the Exhibition continued to depress Marx. He would have sympathized with Fyodor Dostoyevsky's reaction; the Russian novelist called the glass palace "a Biblical sight, something to do with Babylon, some prophecy out of the Apocalypse being fulfilled before your very eyes."[119] Yet within a year or two, Marx's fortunes turned up again. Thanks to several unexpected legacies as well as a £375 annual subsidy from Engels, he was able to move his family to an even bigger and more imposing town house and was soon spending £500 to £600 a year, something that more than 98 percent of English families could not afford to do.[120]

Marx had almost forgotten about the Day of Judgment when it dawned.

The launch of the eleven-thousand-ton warship the HMS *Northumberland* on April 17, 1866, ought to have been a day of pride, a reminder of Great Britain's industrial and commercial domination of the world. Instead it was a fiasco. The *Northumberland* had been on the slips in the Millwall Iron Works yard for nearly five years. On the day of the launch, her unusually heavy weight caused her to slip off the railing—a portent, people understood later, of the precarious condition of the shipping firms and shipbuilders.

Less than a month later, on Thursday afternoon, May 10, in the first week of the London boating season, a frightful rumor swirled through the city. The Rolls-Royce of merchant banks, Overend, Gurney & Company, considered by the average citizen to be as solid as the Royal Mint, had failed. "It is impossible to describe the terror and anxiety which took possession of men's minds for the remainder of that and the whole of the succeeding day," wrote the London *Times*'s financial correspondent. "No man felt safe." By ten o'clock the following morning, a horde of "struggling and half frantic creditors" of both sexes and seemingly all stations of life invaded the financial district. "At noon the tumult became a rout. The doors of the most respectable Banking Houses were besieged . . . and throngs heaving and tumbling about Lombard Street made that narrow thoroughfare impassable."[121]

The *New York Times* bureau chief dashed off a telegram to his editors to convey that this was "a more fearful panic than has been known in the British metropolis within the memory of man." Before an extra battalion of constables could be called out to control the crowd and before the Chancellor of the Exchequer could authorize the suspension of the Bank Charter Act, the Bank of England had lost 93 percent of its cash reserves, the British money market was frozen solid, and scores of banks and businesses that lived on credit were facing ruin. "Englishmen have been running mad on speculation . . . The day of reckoning has arrived and blank panic and blue dismay sit on the faces of all our bankers, capitalists and merchants." [122]

Among the first victims of the panic were the owners of the Millwall shipyard. The boom in shipbuilding, fueled by a worldwide arms race and trade, had more than doubled employment in London shipyards between 1861 and 1865. [123] "The magnates of this trade had not only over-produced beyond all measure during the overtrading time, but they had, besides, engaged in enormous contracts on the speculation that credit would be forthcoming," Marx gloated. [124]

By the time of the Overend collapse, new orders were drying up. In fact, Overend may have been pushed over the edge because "they covered the seas with their ships" and "were incurring huge losses on their fleet of steamships." Other casualties included the legendary railway contractors Peto and Betts. True, the most immediate victims of the panic were gullible investors and "countless swindling companies" that had sprung up to take advantage of cheap money. But the crisis of confidence forced the Bank of England to raise its benchmark interest rate from 6 percent to a crushing 10 percent, "the classic panic rate," [125] which persisted through the summer. A play called *One Hundred Thousand Pounds* closed after a brief run. The *Times* didn't even bother to review it. The boom was over.

When news of Black Friday reached Marx via his afternoon paper, he was in his study in North London pondering a financial crisis closer to home. One Modena Villas, where he and his family had recently moved, was a pretentious affair of the kind sprouting up all over London's periphery, far too pricey for an unemployed journalist who had long since stopped accepting assignments in order to finish his book. Marx had rationalized the extravagance as necessary for his teenage daughters "to establish themselves socially." Now, alas, he was broke again and his rent was overdue. So, unfortunately, was *Das Kapital*.

For nearly fifteen years, Marx had been assuring his best friend and patron that his grandiose "Critique of Political Economy" was "virtually finished," that he was ready to "reveal the law of motion of modern society," that he would drive a stake through the heart of English "political economy." Now Engels, who had kept his nose to the grindstone in Manchester for fifteen years to support him, was becoming restive.

In truth, the glitter of England's prosperity had cast a pall on Marx's project. He had written very little since 1863. A series of windfalls had purchased temporary spells of independence, but now he was back on Engels's dole, and, for the first time, the angelic Engels was showing signs of impatience. Marx had been putting him off with graphic descriptions of a series of afflictions worthy of Job: rheumatism, liver trouble, influenza, toothache, impudent creditors, an outbreak of boils of truly biblical proportions—the list went on and on. In April 1866, Marx confessed, "Being unwell I am unable to write." On the day after Christmas, he complained of "not writing at all for so long." Around Easter, writing from the seaside in Margate, he admitted to having "lived for my health's sake alone" for "more than a month." [126]

Engels suspected, accurately as it turns out, that the real source of Marx's troubles was "dragging that damned book around" for too long: "I hope you are happily over your rheumatism and faceache and are once more *sitting diligently* over the book," he wrote on May 1. "How is it coming on and when will the first volume be ready?" [127] Since *Das Kapital* was *not* coming on, Marx retreated into a sulky silence.

Like a shot of adrenaline, Black Friday had a galvanizing effect that no amount of nagging by Engels had ever achieved. Within days, the prophet was back at his desk writing furiously. In early July, he was able to report to Engels, "I have had my nose properly to the grindstone again over the past two weeks," and to predict that he would be able to deliver the tardy manuscript "by the end of August." [128]

Who can blame the author of an apocalyptic text holding back until the time was right? By the time Marx was composing it, his melodramatic prophecy, "The death knell of capitalist private property sounds. The expropriators will be expropriated," sounded almost plausible. Yet when he composed his famous penultimate chapter on "The General Law of Capitalist Accumulation," he felt forced to fudge in order to make his case that the poor had gotten poorer. Quoting Gladstone on the "astonishing" and "incredible" surge in taxable income between 1853 and 1863, Marx has the liberal prime minister referring to "this intoxicating augmentation of wealth and power . . . entirely confined to classes of property." [129] The text of the speech, printed in the *Times of London*, shows that Gladstone actually said the opposite:

"I should look with some degree of pain, and with much apprehension, upon this extraordinary and almost intoxicating growth, if it were my belief that it is confined to the class of persons who may be described as in easy circumstances," he said, adding that, thanks to the rapid growth of untaxed income, "the average condition of the British laborer, we have the happiness to know, has improved during the last 20 years in a degree which we know to be extraordinary, and which we may almost pronounce to be unexampled in the history of any country and of any age." [130]

Marx's prediction that his manuscript would be finished by the end of the summer proved wildly optimistic, but fifteen months after Black Friday, in August 1867, he was able to report to Engels that he had put the final set of galleys in the mail to the German publisher. In his note, he alluded in passing to a famous short story by the French novelist Honoré de Balzac. An artist believes a painting to be a masterpiece because he has been perfecting it for years. After unveiling the painting he looks at it for a moment before staggering back. "'Nothing! Nothing! After ten years of work.' He sat down and wept." [131] Alas, as Marx feared, "The Unknown Masterpiece" was an apt metaphor for his economic theory. His "mathematical proof" was greeted by an eerie silence. And in the worst economic crisis of the modern age, the great twentieth-century economist John Maynard Keynes would dismiss *Das Kapital* as "an obsolete economic textbook which I know to be not only scientifically erroneous but without interest or application to the modern world." [132]

Chapter II

Must There Be a Proletariat?
Marshall's Patron Saint

The horseman serves the horse,
The neat-herd serves the neat,
The merchant serves the purse,
The eater serves his meat;
'Tis the day of the chattel,
Web to weave, and corn to grind;
Things are in the saddle,
And ride mankind.

—*Ralph Waldo Emerson,*
from "Ode, Inscribed to William H. Channing"[1]

The desire to put mankind into the saddle is the mainspring of most economic study.

—*Alfred Marshall*[2]

During the severe winter of 1866–1867, as many as a thousand men congregated daily at one of several buildings in London's East End. When the doors parted, the crowd surged forward, shoving and shouting, to fight for tickets. From the frenzied assault and the bitter expressions of those who were unsuccessful, a passerby might have assumed that a boxing match or dogfight was starting. But there was no brightly lit ring inside, only the muddy courtyard of a parish workhouse. The yard was divided

into pens furnished with large paving stones. A ticket entitled the bearer
to sit on one of these slabs, seize a heavy hammer, and break up the grime-
encrusted granite. Five bushels of macadam earned him three pennies and
a loaf of bread.[3]

The men who besieged the workhouses that January were not typical of the sickly, ragged clientele ordinarily associated with these despised
institutions. They were sturdy fellows in good coats. Until a few months
earlier, they had been earning a pound or two a week in the shipyards or
railway tunnels and highways—more than enough to house a family of
five, eat plenty of beef and butter, drink beer, and even accumulate a tiny
nest egg.[4] That was before Black Friday brought building on land and sea
and underground to an eerie standstill and an avalanche of bankruptcies
deprived thousands of their jobs; before a cholera epidemic, a freak freeze
that shut down the docks for weeks, and a doubling of bread prices; before
the savings of a lifetime were drained away, the last of the household objects pawned, and help from relatives exhausted.

The poorest parishes were turning away hundreds every day while
hard-pressed taxpayers like Karl Marx worried that the rising poor rates
would ruin them too. Despite an outpouring of donations, private charities were overwhelmed. "What that distress is no one knows," wrote Florence Nightingale, the heiress and hospital reformer, to a friend in January
1867:

> It is not only that there are 20,000 people out of employment at the East
> End, as it is paraded in every newspaper. It is that, in every parish, not
> less than twice and sometimes five times the usual number are on the
> Poor Law books. It *is* that all the workhouses are hospitals. It *is* that the
> ragged schools instead of being able to give one meal a day are in danger
> of being shut up. And this all over Marylebone, St. Pancras, the Strand,
> and the South of London.[5]

Bread riots broke out in Greenwich, and bakers and other small shopkeepers threatened to arm themselves against angry mobs.[6] In May, thousands

of East End residents battled mounted police in Hyde Park, ostensibly to show their support for the Second Reform Act and the workman's right to vote, but mostly to vent their frustration and fury at the rich.[7]

Middle-class Londoners could hardly avoid knowing of the distress in their midst, for they were living in the new information age, bombarded by mail deliveries five times a day, newspapers, books, journals, lectures, and sermons. A new generation of reporters inspired by the examples of Henry Mayhew, Charles Dickens, and other journalists of the 1840s filled the pages of the *Daily News*, the *Morning Star*, the *Pall Mall Gazette*, the *Westminster Review, Household Words*, the Tory *Daily Mail*, and the liberal *Times* with sensational eyewitness accounts and firsthand investigations in the East End. Reporters disguised themselves as down-and-out workmen and spent nights in the poorhouse in order to describe its horrors. Robert Giffen, editor at the liberal *Daily News*, was becoming one of the foremost statisticians of his day. His first major academic article had celebrated the tripling of national wealth between 1845 and 1865, but his second, written in 1867, was markedly different in tone and point of view, an attack on harshly regressive tax proposals that fell on the "necessaries of the poor." What upset Giffen about the 1866–67 depression, writes his biographer Roger Mason, is that its chief victims had mostly worked, had saved, and had obeyed the law while the more fortunate had donated generously to charity. But virtue had not sufficed to prevent widespread misery.[8]

The resurgence of hunger, homelessness, and disease in the midst of great wealth radicalized the generation that had grown up during the boom and had taken affluence and progress for granted. Playwrights wrote dramas with proletarian heroes. Poets published works of social criticism. Professors and ministers used their pulpits to denounce British society. Typical of such jeremiads was that of the blind Liberal reformer Henry Fawcett, who held a chair in political economy at the University of Cambridge:

> We are told that our exports and imports are rapidly increasing; glowing
> descriptions are given of an Empire upon which the sun never sets, and
> of a commerce which extends over the world. Our mercantile marine

is ever increasing; manufactories are augmenting in number and in magnitude. All the evidences of growing luxury are around us; there are more splendid equipages in the parks and the style of living is each year becoming more sumptuous . . . But let us look on another side of the picture; and what do we then observe? Side by side with this vast wealth, closely contiguous to all this sinful luxury there stalks the fearful specter of widespread poverty, and of growing pauperism! Visit the greatest centres of commerce and trade, and what will be observed? The direst poverty always accompanying the greatest wealth![9]

Filled with Christian guilt and the desire to do good, university graduates who had earlier anticipated becoming missionaries in remote corners of the empire were discovering that a great deal of good needed to be done at home. William Henry Fremantle, the author of *The World as the Subject of Redemption*, became the vicar in one of London's poorest parishes, St. Mary's, that year. A walk through the East End during the cholera epidemic convinced Thomas Barnardo, a member of an evangelical sect, to build orphanages for pauper children instead of going to China to convert the Chinese. A similar experience inspired "General" William Booth, the author of *In Darkest England and the Way Out*, to organize a Salvation Army. Samuel Barnett, an Oxford scholar, founded the University Settlers Association to encourage university students to live among the poor running soup kitchens and evening classes.

Missionaries in their own land, these young men and women strove to be scientific rather than sentimental. Their vocation was not dispensing charity but converting the poor to middle-class values and habits. As Edward Denison, an Oxford graduate, remarked in 1867: "By giving alms you keep them permanently crooked. Build school-houses, pay teachers, give prizes, frame workmen's clubs; help them to help themselves."[10]

A young man with delicate features, silky blond hair, and shining blue eyes boarded the Glasgow-bound Great Northern Railway at London's Euston Station. It was early June 1867. He was carrying only a walking stick and a rucksack crammed with books. His fellow passengers might have taken

him for a curate or schoolmaster on a mountaineering holiday. But when
the train reached Manchester, the young man put his rucksack on, jumped
down onto the platform, and disappeared in the crowd.

Before resuming his journey north to the Scottish highlands, Alfred
Marshall, a twenty-four-year-old mathematician and fellow of St. John's
College in Cambridge, spent hours walking through factory districts and
the surrounding slums "looking into the faces of the poorest people." He
was debating whether to make German philosophy or Austrian psychology his life's work. These were his first steps away from metaphysics and
the beginning of a dogged pursuit of social reality. He later said that these
walks forced him to consider the "justification of existing conditions of
society."[11]

In Manchester, Marshall found the smoky brown sky, muddy brown
streets, and long piles of warehouses, cavernous mills, and insalubrious
tenements—all within a few hundred yards of glittering shops, gracious
parks, and grand hotels—that novels such as Elizabeth Gaskell's *North and
South* had led him to expect. In the narrow backstreets he encountered sal-
low, undersized men and stunted, pale factory girls with thin shawls and
hair flecked with wisps of cotton. The sight of "so much want" amid "so
much wealth" prompted Marshall to ask whether the existence of a proletariat was indeed "a necessity of nature," as he had been taught to believe.
"Why not make every man a gentleman?" he asked himself.[12]

Marshall, who lacked the plummy accent and easy manners of other fellows of St. John's College, sometimes compared his discovery of poverty to
that of original sin and his ultimate embrace of economics to a religious
conversion. But although poverty first occurred to him as a subject of
study after the panic of 1866, the implication that he had had to wait until
then to look into the faces of poor people was grossly misleading.[13] His
maternal grandfather was a butcher and his paternal grandfather a bankrupt. His father and uncles started life as penniless orphans. William Marshall had put down "gentleman" as his occupation on his marriage license,
but he had never risen above the modest position of cashier at the Bank of
England. His son Alfred was born not, as he later intimated, in an upscale

suburb but in Bermondsey, one of London's most notorious slums, in the shadow of a tannery. When the Marshalls moved to the lower-middle-class Clapham, they took a house opposite a gasworks.

Thanks to his precocious intelligence and his father's efforts to convince a director of the bank to sponsor his education, Marshall was admitted to Merchant Taylors', a private school in the City that catered to the sons of bankers and stockbrokers. From the age of eight, he commuted daily by omnibus, ferry, and foot through the most noxious manufacturing districts and slums bordering the Thames. Marshall had been looking into the faces of poor people all his life.

In Charles Dickens's *Great Expectations*, published in 1861, the year Marshall graduated from Merchant Taylors', the diminutive orphan hero, Pip, makes what he describes as a "lunatic confession." After swearing his confidante to absolute secrecy three times over, he whispers, "I want to be a gentleman." [14] His playmate Biddy is as nonplussed as if Pip, on the verge of being apprenticed to a blacksmith, had expressed ambitions to become the Pope. Indeed, to make his hero's mad dream come true, Dickens had to invent convicts on a foggy moor, a haughty heiress, a haunted mansion, a mysterious legacy, and a secret benefactor. Even in an age that celebrated the self-made man, the notion that a boy like Pip—never mind the whole mass of Pips—could join the middle class was understood to be the stuff of pure fantasy or eccentric utopian vision, as divorced from real life as Dickens's phantasmagoric novel. As an editorialist for the *Times* observed dryly in 1859, "Ninety-nine people in a hundred cannot 'get on' in life but are tied by birth, education or circumstances to a lower position, where they must stay." [15]

Yet there were signs of motion and upheaval. The question of who could become a gentleman, and how, became one of the great recurring themes of Victorian fiction, observes Theodore Huppon. A gentleman was defined by birth and occupation and by a liberal, that is to say non-vocational, education. That excluded anyone who worked with his hands, including skilled artisans, actors, and artists, or engaged in trade (unless on a very grand scale). Miss Marrable in Anthony Trollope's *The Vicar of Bullhampton* "had an idea that the son of a gentleman, if he intended to maintain his rank as a gentleman, should earn his income as a clergyman, or as a barrister, or as a soldier, or as a sailor."[16] The explosion of white-collar professions was blurring the old lines of demarcation. Why else would Miss Marrable have needed to lay down the law? Doctors, archi-tects, journalists, teachers, engineers, and clerks were pushing themselves forward, demanding a right to the label.[17]

A working gentleman's occupation had to allow him enough free time to think of something other than paying the bills, and his income had to suffice to provide his sons with educations and his daughters with gentle-men husbands. Yet exactly what such an amount might be was also a mat-ter of much debate. The paupers in Trollope's *The Warden* are convinced that £100 a year was enough to transform them all into gentlemen, but when the unworldly warden threatens to retire on £160 a year, his practi-cal son-in-law chides him for imagining that he could live decently on such a mere pittance.[18] Alfred Marshall's father supported a wife and four children on £250 per annum,[19] but Karl Marx, admittedly no great man-ager of money, couldn't keep up middle-class appearances on twice that amount.[20] In 1867 gentlemanly incomes were few and far between. Only one in fourteen British households had incomes of £100 or more.[21]

Yet even Miss Marrable might have agreed that a fellow of a Cam-bridge college qualified. All fifty-six fellows of St. John's College were en-titled to an annual dividend from the college's endowment that rose from about £210 in 1865 to £300 in 1872—as well as rooms and the services of a college servant.[22] A daily living allowance covered dinner at "high table," which usually consisted of two courses, including a joint and vegetables, pies and puddings, followed by a large cheese that traveled down the table on castors. Twice a week a third course of soup or fish was added. Most fellows supplemented their fellowship income with exam coaching fees or specific college jobs such as lecturer or bursar. For a single man with no wife and children—fellows were required to remain celibate—college duties still left many hours for research, writing, and stimulating con-versation and an income that permitted regular travel, decent clothes, a personal library, and a few pictures or bibelots—the requisites, in short, of a gentleman's life.

. . .

Alfred Marshall's metamorphosis from a pale, anxious, underfed, badly dressed scholarship boy into a Cambridge don was nearly as remarkable as Pip's transformation from village blacksmith's apprentice into partner in a joint stock company. His father had gone to work in a City brokerage at sixteen. His brother Charles, just fourteen months his senior, was sent to India at seventeen to work for a silk manufacturer. His sister Agnes followed Charles to India, in order to find a husband but died instead.

Like many frustrated Victorian fathers, Marshall's tried to live vicariously through his gifted son. Committed to educating Alfred for the ministry, William Marshall got his employer to foot the tuition at a good preparatory school. He was "cast in the mould of the strictest Evangelicals, bony neck, bristly projecting chin,"[23] a domestic tyrant who bullied his wife and children. A night owl, he often kept Alfred up until eleven, drilling him in Hebrew, Greek, and Latin.[24]

Not surprisingly, the boy suffered from panic attacks and migraines. A classmate remembered that he was "small and pale, badly dressed, and looked overworked." Shy and nearly friendless, Marshall revealed "a genius for mathematics, a subject that his father despised," and acquired a lifelong distaste for classical languages. "Alfred would conceal Potts's Euclid in his pocket as he walked to and from school. He read a proposition and then worked it out in his mind as he walked along."[25]

Merchant Taylors' School was relatively cheap and heavily subsidized, but even with a salary of £250, William Marshall could barely afford the £20 per annum required to cover his son's out-of-pocket expenses as a day student.[26] Yet the senior Marshall was willing to endure—and impose—the strictest economies to send Alfred there, because success at Merchant Taylors' guaranteed a full scholarship to study classics at Oxford, no small prize at a time when a university education was a luxury that only one in five hundred young men of his son's generation could afford. Even more important, under soon to be abolished statutes, the Oxford scholarship came with a virtual guarantee of a lifetime fellowship in classics at one of its colleges or entrée into the church, the civil service, or the faculty of the most prestigious preparatory schools.

When Marshall announced his intention of turning down the Oxford scholarship and studying mathematics at Cambridge instead, his father raged, threatened, and cajoled. Only a substantial loan from an uncle in Australia and a mathematics scholarship enabled Marshall to defy parental authority and pursue his dream. When the seventeen-year-old went up to take his scholarship exam, he walked along the river Cam shouting with joy at his impending liberation.

At the end of three years at St. John's, there was another race to run, namely a grueling sporting event known as the Mathematical Tripos. Leslie Stephen, who was Marshall's contemporary at Cambridge and the future father of Virginia Woolf, estimated that a second-place finish such as Marshall's was worth as much as a £5,000 inheritance—one-half million dollars in today's money—more than enough to get a leg up in life.[27] Marshall's reward was immediate election to a lifetime fellowship at his college, which gave him the right to live at the college and to collect coaching and lecture fees (worth another £2,500 in Stephen's reckoning). After a year of moonlighting at a preparatory school to repay his uncle's loan, Marshall was, for the first time in his life, truly financially independent and free to do as he liked.

How to best use his freedom was the great question. Mathematics was beginning to bore him. As Marshall sat high up in the pure Highland air reading Immanuel Kant ("The only man I ever worshipped"[28]), the world below was hidden in mist. Yet the faces of the poor and images of drudgery and privation continued to haunt him. Like Pip, Alfred Marshall had shot up but could not forget those left behind.

Marshall had returned to Cambridge from Scotland in October 1867, "brown and strong and upright."[29] As an undergraduate he had been excluded from all the social clubs and private gatherings in dons' rooms that constituted the most valuable parts of a Cambridge education. But now that he had achieved intellectual distinction, he was invited to join the Grote Club, a group of university radicals who met regularly to discuss political, scientific, and social questions. Their leader was Henry Sidgwick, a charismatic philosopher four years Marshall's senior who quickly spotted

Marshall's talent and took him under his wing. "I was fashioned by him," Marshall acknowledged. His own father had almost squeezed the life out of him, but Sidgwick "helped me to live." [30]

With Sidgwick as intellectual guide, Marshall plunged into German metaphysics, evolutionary biology, and psychology, rising at five to read every day. He spent some months in Dresden and Berlin, where, according to biographer Peter Groeneweger, he "fell under the spell of Hegel's *Philosophy of History*." [31] Like the young Hegel and Marx, he found Hegel's message that individuals should govern themselves according to their own conscience, not in blind obedience to authority, compelling. He absorbed an evolutionary view of society from Charles Darwin's *On the Origin of Species*, which appeared in 1859, and Herbert Spencer's *Synthetic Philosophy*, published in 1862. An interest in psychology was stimulated by the possibility of "the higher and more rapid development of human faculties." [32] The young man whose chances in life had turned on access to first-rate education was coming to the conclusion that the greatest obstacles to man's mental and moral development were material.

He began to think of himself as a "Socialist." In the 1860s, the term implied an interest in social reform or membership in a communal sect, while the equally expansive label of "Communist" encompassed everyone who thought that things couldn't get better unless the whole system of private property and competition was torn down. [33] When Marshall questioned Sidgwick about overcoming class divisions, his mentor used to gently chide him, "Ah, if you understood political economy you would not say that." Marshall took the hint. "It was my desire to know what was practical in social reform by State and other agencies that led me to read Adam Smith, Mill, Marx and LaSalle," he later recalled. He began his education by reading John Stuart Mill's *Principles of Political Economy*, then in its sixth edition, and "got much excited about it." [34]

His interest was intensified by the unexpected passage of the Reform Act of 1867, which, in a single stroke, turned England into a democracy. The act did more than double the size of the electorate by extending the franchise to some 888,000 adult men, mostly skilled craftsmen and shopkeepers, who paid at least £10 a year in rent or property tax. It brought

the working classes into the political system and made democratic government the only acceptable form of government. Though it ignored the
3 million factory operatives, day laborers, and farm workers—and, of
course, the entire female sex—twentieth-century historian Gertrude Himmelfarb emphasizes that the Reform Act nonetheless lent the notion of
universal suffrage an aura of inevitability.[35] Marshall was troubled, though,
by the contrast between the ideal of full citizenship and the reality of
material squalor and deprivation that prevented most of his countrymen
from taking full advantage of their civic freedoms.

"Shooting up," as Marshall had done, can provoke feelings of guilt
or a sense of obligation. Victorian fiction is populated by the "double"
who shares the hero's attributes and aspirations but is condemned to
stay put while the other shoots up. When the American journalist and
writer Henry James explored London on foot in 1869, Hyacinth Robinson, the protagonist of James's 1886 novel about terrorists, seemed to
jump "out of the London pavement." James was watching the parade of
brilliantly dressed figures, carriages, brilliantly lit mansions and theaters,
the clubs and picture galleries emitting agreeable gusts of sound with a
sense of doors that "opened into light and warmth and cheer, into good
and charming relations," when he conceived a young man very much
like himself "watching the same public show . . . I had watched myself,"
including "all the swarming facts" that spoke of "freedom and ease,
knowledge and power, money, opportunity and satiety," with only one
difference: the bookbinder turned bomber in *The Princess Casamassima*
would "be able to revolve around them but at the most respectful of distances and with every door of approach shut in his face."[36]

Having been admitted to the rarified world of freedom, opportunity,
knowledge, and ease, if not power or great wealth, Marshall kept the face
of his double where he could see it every day:

> I saw in a shop-window a small oil painting [of a man's face with a
> strikingly gaunt and wistful expression, as of one "down and out"] and
> bought it for a few shillings. I set it up above the chimney piece in my

room in college and thenceforward called it my patron saint, and devoted myself to trying how to fit men like that for heaven.[37]

As Marshall studied the works of the founders of political economy, "economics grew and grew in practical urgency, not so much in relation to the growth of wealth as to the quality of life; and I settled down to it." The "settling" took a while. He found "the dry land of facts" intellectually unappetizing and socially unappealing. When he was asked to take over some lectures on political economy, Marshall agreed reluctantly. "I taught economics . . . but repelled with indignation the suggestion that I was an economist . . . 'I am a philosopher straying in a foreign land.'"[38]

When Marshall began to study economics seriously in 1867, his mentor Sidgwick was convinced that the "halcyon days of Political Economy had passed away."[39] After the success of the 1846 Corn Law repeal, which was followed by a period of low food prices, political economy had a brief turn as "a true science on par with astronomy."[40] But the economic crisis and political upheavals of the 1860s revived the old animus against the discipline among intellectuals. Going a step beyond Carlyle's epithet "the dismal science," John Ruskin, the art historian, dismissed political economics as "that bastard science" and, like Dickens, called for a new economics; "a real science of political economy."[41] The fundamental problem, observed Himmelfarb, was that "the science of riches" clashed with the evangelicalism of the late Victorian era.[42] Victorians were repelled by the notion that greed was good or that the invisible hand of competition guaranteed the best of all possible outcomes for society as a whole.

With the advent of the franchise for working men, both political parties were courting the labor vote. But "political economy" was invoked to oppose every reform—whether higher pay for farm laborers or relief for the poor—on the grounds that it would slow down the growth of the nation's wealth. While the founders of political economy had been radical reformers in their day, championing women's rights, the abolition of slavery, and middle-class interests versus those of the aristocracy, their theories pitted their disciples against labor. As Virginia Woolf's father, Leslie Stephen, remarked: "The doctrine . . . was used to crush all manner of socialist schemes. . . . Political economists were supposed to accept a fatalistic theory, announcing the utter impossibility of all schemes for social regeneration."[43]

For example, when Henry Fawcett, the reform-minded professor of political economy at Cambridge, addressed striking workers, he told them that they were cutting their own throats. Such advice outraged Ruskin, who said, after a builders' strike in 1869, "The political economists are helpless—practically mute; no demonstrable solution of the difficulty can be given by them, such as may convince or calm the opposing parties."[44] Mill was an even more dramatic example than Fawcett. Now a Radical member of parliament, Mill called himself a Socialist, and had championed the Second Reform Act and the right of workers to unionize and strike. Yet Mill's view of the future of the working classes was scarcely less dour than that of Ricardo or Marx. J. E. Cairnes, a professor at University College London who published a famous indictment of slavery as an economic system, echoed Mill's position a few years later:

> The margin for the possible improvement of their lot is confined within narrow barriers which cannot be passed and the problem of their elevation is hopeless. As a body, they will not rise at all. A few, more energetic or more fortunate than the rest, will from time to time escape . . . but the great majority will remain substantially where they are. The remuneration of labor, as such, skilled or unskilled, can never rise much above its present level.[45]

At the heart of Mill's pessimism lay the so-called wages fund theory. According to this theory, ultimately disowned by Mill but never replaced by him, only a finite amount of resources was available to pay wages. Once the fund was exhausted, there was no way to increase the aggregate amount of pay. In effect, the demand for labor was fixed, so that only the supply of labor had any effect on wages. Thus, one group of workers could obtain higher wages only at the expense of lower wages for others.

If unions succeeded in winning a wage rate in excess of the rate of the wages fund, unemployment would result. If the government intervened by taxing the affluent to subsidize wages, the working population would increase, causing more unemployment and even higher taxation. Moreover, the use of taxes to subsidize pay would reduce efficiency by removing competition and the fear of unemployment. Eventually, Mill warned, "taxation for the support of the poor would engross the whole income of the country."[46] Unless the working classes acquired prudential habits of thrift and birth control, the author of a popular American textbook claimed, "they will people down to their old scale of living."[47] In her political economy primer, Millicent Fawcett cited the Corn Law repeal as proof that wages were tethered to a physiological minimum. Referring to the worker, she wrote:

> Cheap food enabled him, not to live in greater comfort, but to support an increased number of children. These facts lead to the conclusion that no material improvement in the condition of the working classes can be permanent, unless it is accompanied by circumstances that will prevent a counter-balancing increase of population.[48]

By the time the Second Reform Act passed however, the theory that wages could not rise in the long run no longer looked tenable, and not only because of the dramatic increase in average pay. The conquest of nature by the railway, steamship, and power loom suggested that society was not yet close to natural limits to growth. The fact that emigrants were prospering abroad and that a middle class of skilled artisans and white-collar workers was shooting up at home contradicted the notion that a mass escape from poverty was ruled out by the biological laws. Poverty that had once appeared to be a natural and near-universal feature of the social landscape began to look more and more like a blemish.

Was there an ingenious mechanism that could lift wages until the average wage sufficed for a middle-class life? Mill acknowledged that the wages fund theory was flawed, but neither he nor his critics could propose a satisfactory alternative. An extraordinary number of Victorian intellectuals—from Charles Dickens, Henry Mayhew, and Karl Marx to John Ruskin and Henry Sidgwick—attempted to fashion one. Since none had so far succeeded, no one could say whether hopes for social betterment really could be reconciled with economic reality, or whether the palpable gains of the 1850s and 1860s were doomed to be reversed. Tories such as Ruskin and Carlyle, an anti-Abolitionist, predicted disaster if the old feudal bonds were not restored. Socialists argued that without sweeping societal changes, the condition of workers was "un-improvable and their wrongs irremediable." [49] The standard-of-living debate, as it became known, boiled down to one question: How much improvement was possible under existing social arrangements?

As he stood before "70 to 80 ladies" in a borrowed Cambridge college lecture hall on a spring evening in 1873, Alfred Marshall's handsome face was lit with an inner flame, and he spoke with great force and fluency without notes. He addressed the women in plain, direct, homely terms as if he were speaking to his sister, urging them to stop "tatting their tatting and twirling their thumbs" and counseled them to resist the demands of their families. Instead he wanted them to get jobs as social workers and teachers like "Miss Octavia Hill." Most of all, he insisted that they learn "what difficulties there are to be overcome, and . . . how to overcome them." [50]

Like his mentor Henry Sidgwick and other university radicals of the 1860s and 1870s, Marshall came to see education as a weapon in the struggle against social injustice, and like other admirers of Mill's *The Subjection of Women,* published in 1869, he considered the educated woman society's principal change agent. For Marshall, the existential problem for women and for the working classes was essentially the same: both lacked the opportunity to lead independent and fulfilling lives. Workers were condemned by low wages to lives of drudgery that prevented all but the most exceptional from fully developing their moral and creative faculties. Middle-class women were condemned by custom to ignorance and drudgery of a different sort. Inspired by the novels of contemporaries such as George Eliot and Charlotte Brontë, Marshall was particularly sensitive to the plight of women who were prevented from developing their intellects and regretted society's loss of their talents. He was convinced that the task of liberating the working classes required the energies of middle-class women as well as a more scientific economics. On the topic of "the intimate connection between the free play of the full and strong pulse of women's thought and the amelioration of the working classes," Marshall was "a great preacher." In an age that celebrated "the angel of the hearth," Marshall taught extension courses for women, acted as an unpaid examiner, and personally financed an essay-writing prize in economics for female students, as well as, later on, contributing a substantial £60 to the construction fund for Newnham Hall, the nucleus of one of Cambridge's first women's colleges. In 1873, Marshall joined Sidgwick, other members of the Grote Club, and Millicent Fawcett—whose sister Elizabeth Garrett was attempting to study medicine—to found the General Committee of Management of the Lectures for Women.[51]

Marshall's lectures focused on the central paradox of modern society: poverty amid plenty. He taught by posing a series of questions: Why hadn't the Industrial Revolution freed the working class "from misery and vice?" How much improvement is possible under current social arrangements based on private property and competition? His answers reflected how far he had distanced himself from the specific assumptions and conclusions of his predecessors. He told the women that philanthropy and political economy were not, as Malthus had supposed and latter-day Malthusians continued to believe, irreconcilable.

Even as he contradicted the conclusions of the founders of political economy, Marshall insisted that the science itself was indispensible. The problem of poverty was far more complicated than most reformers admitted. Economic science, like the physical sciences, was nothing more or less than a tool for breaking down complex problems into simpler parts that could be analyzed one at a time. Intervention based on faulty theories of causes could easily make the problem worse. Marshall cited Adam Smith, David Ricardo, Thomas Malthus, and John Stuart Mill to demonstrate the power of the "engine of analysis" they had constructed, as well as to show

how it had to be improved. Without such a tool, he told them, discovering truths would always be a matter of accident and the accumulation of knowledge with time wholly impossible.

Marshall agreed with Mill that the industrial revolution hadn't liberated him from the tyranny of economic necessity or supplied the material requisites for a "higher life." "Our rapid progress in science and arts of production might have been expected to have prevented to a great extent the sacrifice of the interests of the laborer to the interests of production . . . It has not done so."[52] What he strenuously disputed was the assertion by political economists that it *could* not do so, that the remuneration of labor as such, skilled or unskilled, could never rise much above its present level.[53]

He did not doubt that the chief cause of poverty was low wages, but what caused wages to be low? Radicals claimed that it was the rapacity of employers, while Malthusians argued that it was the moral failings of the poor. Marshall proposed a different answer: low productivity. He cited as evidence the fact that, contrary to Marx's claim that competition would cause the wages of skilled and unskilled workers to converge near subsistence level, skilled workers were earning "two, three, four times" as much as unskilled laborers. The fact that employers were willing to pay more for specialized training or skill implied that wages depended on workers' contribution to *current* output. Or, put another way, that the demand for labor, not only the supply, helped to determine pay. If that was the case, the average wage wouldn't be stationary. As technology, education, and improvements in organization increased productivity over time, the income of the workers would rise in tandem. The fruits of better organization, knowledge, and technology would, over time, eliminate the chief cause of poverty. Activity and initiative, not resignation, were called for.

Arnold Toynbee the historian later described the significance of Marshall's insight: "Here is the *first great hope* which the latest analysis of the wages question opens out to the laborer. It shows him that *there is another mode of raising his wages besides limiting his numbers.*"[54] Workers themselves could influence their own and their children's ability to earn better wages. "The chief remedy, then, for low wages is better education," Marshall told his audience.

He took great pains to demolish Socialists' claim that but for oppression by the rich, the poor could live in "absolute luxury." England's annual income totaled about £900 million, he told the women. The wages paid to manual workers amounted to a total of £400 million. Most of the remaining £500 million, Marshall pointed out, represented the wages of workers who did not belong to the so-called working classes: semiskilled and skilled workers, government officials and military, professionals, and managers. In fact, an absolutely equal division of Britain's annual income would provide less than £37 per capita. Reducing poverty required expanding output and increasing efficiency; in other words, economic growth.

The chief error of the older economists, in Marshall's view, was to not see that man was a creature of circumstances and that as circumstances changed, man was liable to change as well. The chief error of their critics—but, ironically, one that the founders of political economy shared—was a failure to understand the cumulative power of incremental change and the compounding effects of time.

> There are I believe in the world few things with greater capability of poetry in it than the multiplication table . . . If you can get mental and moral capital to grow at some rate per annum there is no limit to the advance that may be made; if you can give it the vital force which will make the multiplication table applicable to it, it becomes a little seed that will grow up to a tree of boundless size.[55]

Ideas mattered when the past was not simply being reproduced but something new was being created. "An organon" or instrument for discovering truths—truths that depended, like all scientific truths, on circumstances—would be an independent force. "The world is moving on," Marshall said, "but the pace at which it moves, depends upon how much we think for ourselves."[56]

· · ·

A year later, Marshall was deep in conversation with Henry Sidgwick in Anne Clough's sitting room on Regent Street, discussing "high subjects" when he felt someone staring at him.[57] The young woman who sat with her sewing untouched in her lap looking toward them had a "brilliant complexion," "deep set large eyes," and masses of mahogany hair "which goes back in a great wave and is very loosely pinned up behind."[58] Later, someone said of the twenty-year-old Mary Paley, "She *is* Princess Ida." The eponymous heroine of the Gilbert and Sullivan opera had "forsworn the world, / And, with a band of women, shut herself / Within a lonely country house, and there / Devotes herself to stern philosophies!" Mary had just broken off her engagement to a handsome but stupid army officer to join a handful of female pioneers seeking a Cambridge education. Her part in this "outrageous proceeding" was not a rejection of men, or of the usual terms of marriage. "He who desires to gain their favor must / Be qualified to strike their teeming brains, / And not their hearts! / They're safety matches, sir. / And they light only on the knowledge box."[59]

Mary went to one of Marshall's lectures at the coach house at Grovedodge and listened, enchanted, as he rhapsodized over Kant, Bentham, and Mill. "I then thought I had never seen such an attractive face," she confessed, captivated by his "brilliant eyes." She went to a dance at Marshall's college, and, emboldened by his "melancholy" look, she asked him to dance "the Lancers." Ignoring his protestations that he didn't know how, she led him through the complex steps only to be "shocked at my own boldness."[60] Before long she was among the regular guests at his "Sunday evening parties" in his rooms at St. John's, where he served her tea, crumpets, sandwiches, and oranges and showed her his "large collection of portraits arranged in groups of Philosophers, Poets, Artists . . ."

Possibly Mary reminded Marshall of Maggie Tulliver, the intelligent but math-phobic heroine of George Eliot's *The Mill on the Floss*, who wanted to learn "the Euclid" like her brother, Tom.[61] At the time, Eliot's novel was Marshall's favorite. Meeting Mary Paley and her best friend, Mary Kennedy, in the street one day, Marshall proposed—not marriage, but something more outrageous. The young professor wanted his two best

students to take the Moral Sciences Tripos, the final examination in political economy, politics, and philosophy that male undergraduates had to
take to get a degree. This was a far more ambitious project than acquiring
"general cultivation" by attending lectures in literature, history, and logic,
Mary's original object in coming to Cambridge.

The suggestion was also bolder than anything proposed by other education reformers whose main interest lay in raising the level of secondary-
school teaching. "Remember, so far you have been competing with cart
horses," Marshall warned, "but for the Tripos it will be with racehorses."
He promised that he and Sidgwick would coach her. According to Mary
Kennedy, "He explained that this would mean at least three years' study,
specializing in one or two subjects. We accepted the challenge lightly, not
realizing what we were undertaking."

Like Marshall, the young woman who would accept the challenge
came from a strict evangelical household. Mary Paley's great-grandfather
was William Paley, the archdeacon of Carlisle and author of *The Principles
of Moral and Political Philosophy*. Mary's father was the rector of Ufford,
near Stamford, about forty miles northwest of Cambridge. A "staunch
Radical" who opposed fox hunting, horse racing, and High Church ritual,
he refused to talk to neighboring clergymen and forbade his daughters
Dickens and dolls. Mary recalled, "My sister and I were allowed dolls until
one tragic day when our father burnt them as he said we were making
them into idols and we never had any more."

Mary's father was nonetheless a more tolerant, better-educated, and
more affluent man than William Marshall. Mary grew up in a "rambling
old house, its front covered with red and white roses and looking out on a
lawn with forest trees as a background, and a garden with long herbaceous
borders and green terraces." The Paley household was a hive of activity:
rounders, archery, croquet, excursions to London, summer holidays in
Hunstanton and Scarborough. "We had a father who took part in work
and play and who was interested in electricity and photography," Mary recalled. Her mother "was full of initiative and always bright and amusing."
In 1862 Mary was taken to London to tour the Second Great Exhibition.
Although Charles Dickens was taboo, Mary read *Arabian Nights, Gulliver's*

Travels, the *Iliad* and the *Odyssey*, Greek and Shakespearean plays, and the novels of Sir Walter Scott, also favorites of Marshall's.

When the Cambridge Higher Local Examination for Women over Eighteen was established in 1869, Tom Paley encouraged Mary to take it over the objections of her mother. After she succeeded brilliantly and broke off her engagement to the army officer, her father allowed her to go to Cambridge to live "when such a thing had never been done before." Anne Jemima Clough, a friend of Sidgwick's and one of the leaders of the women's education movement, was opening a residence for a handful of female students. Mary later wrote, "My father was proud and pleased and his admiration for Miss Clough overcame his objections to sending his daughter to Cambridge (in those days an outrageous proceeding)."[62]

In October 1871, Mary joined Miss Clough and four other young women at 74 Regent Street. The Cambridge community was wholly unprepared for coeducation. Since mixed classes were "improper," sympathetic dons had to be recruited to repeat their regular lectures separately for the women, and Miss Clough, as chaperone, had to sit through them all. The "strong impulse towards liberty among the young women attracted by the movement" and the "unfortunate appearance" of the pretty ones were chronic sources of anxiety. Mary, who was just entering her "pre-Raphaelite period" and had papered her rooms in William Morris designs, was especially troublesome. She dressed as if she were a figure in an Edward Burne-Jones painting, in sandals, capes, and flowing gowns. An amateur watercolorist, she favored jewel tones and once covered her tennis dress with Virginia creeper and pomegranates.

Mary began to go regularly. Earnest as well as artistic, with a quick facility for "curves," the graphs that Marshall employed to illustrate the interactions of supply and demand, Mary surprised herself by winning the essay prize. She was thrilled by Marshall's bold proposal that she take the Tripos, and the long comments he wrote on her weekly papers in red ink became "a great event."

Mary Paley took the Moral Sciences Tripos in December 1874. Until the eve of the examination, it was unclear whether the university examiners would be willing to let her sit for it. One was considered "very obdu-rate." Although they grudgingly agreed to grade her examination, they refused to grant her the highest mark. "At the Examiners' Meeting there was at that time no chairman to give a casting vote, and as two voted me first class and two second class I was left hanging, as Mr. Sidgwick said, 'between heaven and hell,'" she later recalled. Still, her triumph turned Paley into a local celebrity.

Her time at Cambridge seemingly having run out, Mary returned to the family home in Ufford. There she promptly organized a series of ex-tension lectures for women—"off my own bat!"—in nearby Stamford. She also agreed, at the suggestion of a Professor Stuart at Cambridge, to write a textbook on political economy for use in the extension courses. Then she got a letter from Sidgwick asking whether she could take over Marshall's economics lectures at Newnham, where Miss Clough had assembled about twenty students.

At thirty-two, Marshall was one of the "advanced liberals" at Cambridge University. He wore his hair fashionably long, sported a handlebar mus-tache, and no longer dressed like a buttoned-up young minister. He had joined the recently founded Cambridge Reform Club and read the *Bee Hive*, a radical labor magazine.

In the spring of 1874, a farmworkers' strike provoked a bitter quarrel between radicals and conservatives at Cambridge. Trade unions were then relatively novel, having only just been legalized. The National Agricul-tural Laborers' Union, a radical new organization under the leadership of Joseph Arch, had sprung up in dozens of East Anglian villages the previ-ous fall. The laborers demanded higher wages and shorter hours as well as the franchise and reform of the land laws.[63] Strikes erupted all around Cambridge. Determined to "crush the rebellion," farmers banded together in "Defense Committees," firing and evicting men with union cards and importing scab labor from as far away as Ireland. The Tory *Cambridge Chronicle* suggested that the farmers "do not make a stand so much against an increase of wage as against the cunning tactics and insufferable dicta-

tion of the union through demagogue delegates."[64] By mid-May, the lockout was two and a half months old and had become the subject of national
controversy.

At the university, where a large subscription had just been undertaken
for famine victims in Bengal, opinion was sharply divided. Middle-class
sympathies for the plight of the laborers had been awakened by a number
of inquiries, most notably a Royal Commission report by the bishop of
Manchester, who had exposed the long hours, low wages, horrific accidents, and diets of "tea kettle broth, dried bread and a little cheese" endured by agricultural workers.[65] During the lockout, the *Times* of London
ran stories calculated to horrify Victorian readers, including one description of a cottage whose single bedroom was shared by "the laborer, and his
wife, a daughter aged 24, and a son aged 21, another son of 19, and a boy
of 14, and a girl of 7."[66] Novelists seized on the subject as well. In George
Eliot's *Middlemarch*, which had appeared three years earlier, Dorothea
Brooke tells her uncle, a well-to-do landlord, that she cannot bear the
"simpering pictures in the drawing-room . . . Think of Kit Downes, uncle,
who lives with his wife and seven children in a house with one sitting-
room and one bedroom hardly larger than this table!—and those poor
Dagleys, in their tumble-down farmhouse, where they live in the back-
kitchen and leave the other rooms to the rats! That is one reason why I did
not like the pictures here, dear uncle."[67]

Among conservatives, however, the unrest raised the specter of
the Bread Riots of 1816–17 and the burning of hayricks in the 1830s.
Most opposed the idea of unionization on principle. In the spring
a leading member of the university community, who was of "recognized social position . . . occupying an influential position in one of
[Cambridge's] . . . colleges," wrote several lengthy "Notes of Alarm" in the
Cambridge Chronicle urging the farmers to stand fast. He labeled the union
leaders "professional mob orators" and their liberal sympathizers "sentimental busybodies." The writer—possibly a Cambridge don named William Whewell—signed himself only "CSM," an acronym probably chosen
to provoke his liberal opponents because it stood for Common Sense Morality. On the matter of wages and unionization, CSM invoked the laws of

political economy, claiming, "It is simply a question of supply and demand, and ought to have been allowed to settle itself on ordinary principles without the interference of paid agitators and demagogues."[68]

The overflowing crowd of union supporters that squeezed into the Barnwell Workingmen's Hall on Cambridge's scruffy north side on Tuesday, May 11, 1874, was thus somewhat bemused to find an unlikely set of allies standing on the stage clad in caps and gowns. One of the leaders, the fiery George Mitchell, confessed, amid much laughter, that "when he saw all those gentlemen with their wide-awake hats and tippets he thought he was going to have some put on him."[69] Sedley Taylor, a former Trinity College fellow and prominent reformer, spoke first, proposing a resolution condemning the farmers' efforts to break the union as "prejudicial to the general interests of the country," delivering a broadside at his fellow collegian CSM in the process.

Then it was Marshall's turn. Seconding a motion put forward by a dissident farmer supporting the locked-out laborers, he called for donations: "Let us sympathize with our hearts and with our purses."

Addressing the farmworkers, Marshall denied that political economy could "direct decisions of moral principle," which it must instead "leave to her sister, the Science of Ethics." Writing in the *Bee Hive,* he argued that "political economy is abused when any one claims for it that it is itself a guide in life. The more we study it the more we find cases in which man's own direct material interest does not lie in the same direction as the general well being. In such cases we must fall back on duty."[70]

The following Saturday, the *Cambridge Chronicle* dismissed Marshall's speech as "ingenious sophistry." In fact, he had successfully demonstrated why labor markets do not always produce fair wages, and why unions can lead to greater efficiency as well as equity. He'd "been asked to speak of the laws of supply and demand," Marshall began. He poured scorn on the union's opponents who held wages were at their "natural level" because, if they weren't, other employers would have offered the workers more, and if a worker's "wages be raised artificially they will come down again." This was Ricardo's iron law of wages, accepted even by many who sympathized with the plight of the workers. The argument was "excellent," Marshall admitted, but the assumptions false. No farmer would offer a neighbor's hired hands more to come and work for him. What's more, higher wages would make the workers more productive by allowing them to be better fed. Admitting that "unions have their faults," Marshall said that "a union gives men interests and sympathies beyond the boundaries of their parish; it will cause them to feel their need of knowledge, and to vow that their sons shall be educated . . . Wages will rise . . . poor rates will dwindle . . . England will prosper."[71]

Despite the support of the university and much of the media, the strike ultimately failed. The farmers held out by acquiring more machinery and employing more boys and girls. When the strike fund ran out in early June, the union called on the workers to return to the fields. Marshall took from the episode that new ideas would prevail over old doctrines only after a carefully plotted, patient campaign to win the hearts and minds of practical men.

Five weeks out of New York City and bound for San Francisco, Marshall stared down on the Horseshoe Falls with a frown. From the Goat Island suspension bridge where he stood, the cataract looked nowhere near as mighty as his Baedeker guide had promised. As a mathematician, he knew that perspective was to blame and engaged in some mental calculations to reassure himself that the falls were truly as colossal as advertised. But the numerical exercise did little to dispel his feeling of having been badly let down. "Niagara is a great humbug," he wrote to his mother on July 10, 1875. "It takes longer for a man to discover how much greater Niagara is than it seems than it does to discover that an Alpine Valley which appears to be only a mile broad is really six miles broad."[77]

Marshall had come to America to study its social and economic landscape. He had left Manhattan on a paddle steamer headed for Albany. In a letter, he recalled how "disgusted and savage" Alexis de Tocqueville had been forty years earlier when he discovered that the finest of the "villas built in Greek style of marble, shining from the banks of the Hudson" were actually made of wood. He, by contrast, "did not find anything like as much sham as I expected."[73]

Indeed, everywhere Marshall looked, he seemed to discover more, not less, than met the eye: American architects displayed "daring & strength," their buildings being of "uniform thoroughness & solidity."[74] An "American drink called 'mint-julep'" was "luxurious." American preachers gave sermons that were "way out of sight ahead of us," having achieved "startling improvements" on Anglican liturgy.[75] American workers were full of "go."[76] As he reported to the Moral Sciences Club on his return to Cambridge in the fall, "I met no man or woman in America whose appearance indicated an utterly dull or insipid life."[77] By the time Marshall reached Cleveland in mid-July, he was convinced that "nine Englishmen out of ten would be themselves more happy & contented in Canada than in the U.S.; though I myself if I had to emigrate should go to the U.S."[78]

Marshall's magnum opus, *Principles of Economics,* would not appear for another fifteen years, but he had already worked out the chief tenets of his "new economics"—an alternative to both the old laissez-faire doctrines of Smith, Ricardo, and Mill and the newly ascendant Socialist gospels of Marx. He had spent a decade "laying the foundations of his subject but publishing nothing."[79] His travels in America gave him confidence that he was on the right track.

Marshall's relations had scoffed at his plan to use a £250 legacy from the same uncle who had financed his university education to tour the United States. He justified himself by saying that he was gathering material for a treatise on foreign trade. While this was perfectly true, the economic historian John Whitaker observes that his actual purpose was broader, part of a growing, "almost obsessive attempt to apprehend in all its aspects an ever-changing economic reality."[80] Like other European observers, including Tocqueville, Marshall thought of the United States as a great social laboratory. Dickens, William Makepeace Thackeray, and Trollope had been occupied by old questions, now settled, of democracy, slavery, and the survival of the union. Marshall wanted to know where the rise of industry, the growth of global commerce, and the decline of traditional morality were leading. These were advancing more rapidly in America than anywhere else. "I wanted to see the history of the future in America," he told an audience when he returned to Cambridge.[81]

Marshall sailed to America during the biggest transatlantic tourism boom in history. Sales of the most popular North American guide were climbing toward the half-million mark. The North Atlantic was now a virtual highway of the sea. No fewer than ten steamship companies offered weekly departures from Liverpool to New York, and English travelers were advised to book berths as much as a year in advance.[82] Marshall's trip aboard the SS *Spain,* one of the fastest and most luxurious of the big liners, took a mere ten days, in contrast to the miserable three-week crossing Dickens had endured in 1842. Travel in America was expensive, owing to the immense distances. Marshall had to budget £60 a month versus £15 a month when he spent summers climbing in the Alps. But afterward, according to Mary, he felt that "he had never spent money so well. It was not so much what he learnt there as that he got to know what things he wanted to learn."[83]

His experiences convinced him that "economic influences play a larger part in determining the higher life of men and women than was once considered." In particular, he believed, "there are no thoughts or actions, or feelings, which occupy a man and which thus have the opportunity of forming the man . . . as those thoughts and actions and feelings which make up his daily occupation."[84] He spent some of his time in churches and drawing rooms, especially in Boston, where he met leading American intellectuals, including the poet Ralph Waldo Emerson and the art historian Charles Eliot Norton. He lingered for several days at communes run by Shakers and disciples of Robert Owen in New England. But mostly he toured factories, filling notebooks with interviews with businessmen and workers and drawings of machinery. At Chickering and Sons piano factory near Boston, he observed that "care & judgment were required from many of the workers in a very high degree" and that the workers there had "able, almost powerful & artistic faces." On a visit to an organ factory, he wondered whether "the work of each individual being confined to a very small portion of the whole operation" did not "prevent the growth of intelligence?"[85] He found that it did not.

The business traveler of that time was always something of a tourist. Marshall was no exception. He could not resist the lure of the recently completed transcontinental railroad. In his hotel in Niagara, he plotted his westward route on an advertising map provided by the Union Pacific, marking it with pinpricks so that his mother back home in London could follow his progress toward San Francisco by holding the map up to a light.

Chicago was the best place to catch a train for the Pacific coast. The new railway system was like a giant hand whose palm lay atop the Great Lakes and whose fingers stretched all the way to Seattle, Portland, San Francisco, and, in the case of the two southernmost routes, Los Angeles. Most travelers took the North Western from Chicago due west across Illinois and Iowa to Council Bluffs. Marshall took the Great Northern line to St. Paul and then sailed back down on a Mississippi riverboat, the kind "more famous for their propensity to blow up than for the magnificence of their fittings." [86] He met up with the North Western at the Iowa border and was in Council Bluffs a day later. From there he crossed the river to Omaha and transferred to the Union Pacific train. From Omaha it was a straight shot west to Cheyenne and Granger, in Wyoming, where the line dipped down toward Ogden, Utah; Reno; and Sacramento before making the final 125-mile jog south to San Francisco. In Cheyenne, Marshall boarded a stagecoach for a twenty-four-hour side trip to Denver. In Ogden, he stopped to explore the Mormon capital, Salt Lake City. On the return trip, he got off in Reno for a look at "the wild population of Virginia City." He was conscious throughout of witnessing something extraordinary and unprecedented. From his railway car he was seeing what another young Briton had earlier described as "the unrolling of a new map, a revelation of a new empire, the creation of a new civilization." [87]

Marshall was bowled over by the constant motion he witnessed. "Many things have changed since [Tocqueville's] time . . . many things which were nearly stationary then are not stationary now," he wrote in a letter home. [88] The first thing to catch his eye after he checked in at the Fifth Avenue Hotel was "a steam lift which *without ever stopping* from 7 a.m. until midnight goes up & down [emphasis his]." He was captivated by the lobby's unmanned telegraph machine spewing paper ribbons of stock quotations. Business travelers staying uptown "are as well posted as if they were on the Exchange itself," he wrote. [89]

Mobility was the preeminent fact of American life, Marshall decided. It wasn't just the railway and telegraph, the successive waves of new immigrants, or the movement of the population from the manufacturing centers of the Northeast to the "mushroom towns" of the West, sprouting so fast that one "can only suppose that, the soil being so fruitful, buildings grow spontaneously."[90] The most interesting freedom of motion was economic, social, and psychological. Marshall was astonished by ordinary Americans' readiness to leave family and friends for new towns, to switch occupations and businesses, to adopt new beliefs and ways of doing things. He reported, "If a man starts in the boot trade and does not make money so fast as he thinks he ought to do, he tries, perhaps, grocery for a few years and then he tries books or watches or dry goods." He was delighted by the independence of young people: "American lads . . . abhor apprenticeships . . . The mere fact of his being bound down to a particular occupation is sufficient in general to create in the mind of an American youth that he will do something else as soon as he has the power."[91]

Americans' welcoming attitude toward growing urbanization also struck him powerfully: "The Englishman Mill bursts into unwonted enthusiasm when speaking . . . of the pleasures of wandering alone in beautiful scenery," he noted dryly, adding that "many American writers give fervid descriptions of the growing richness of human life as the backwoodsman finds neighbors settling around him, as the backwoods settlement develops into a village, the village into a town, and the town into a vast city."[92]

Like his favorite novelists, Marshall was less interested in the material and technological advances, impressive as these were, than in their consequences for how people thought and behaved. What guarantee was there that individual choices added up to social good? Would all the up and down movement of individuals and the attendant loosening of traditional ties lead, as pessimists such as Marx and Carlyle predicted, to social chaos? Or did mobility imply a "movement towards that state of things to which modern Utopians generally look forward." That was the question.[93]

Marshall's visceral reactions put him squarely on the other, optimistic side. In Norwich, Connecticut, he went on an evening drive with a Miss

Nunn, who told him she was prepared to take the reins and wound up steering. Marshall found the experience "very delicious." He observed that young American women are "mistresses of themselves . . . [with] thorough freedom in the management of their own concerns." Such freedom, he admitted, "would be regarded as dangerous license by the average Englishman," but he found it "right and wholesome."[94]

The absence of rigid class distinctions delighted him. When a clerk in a hat shop removed the bowler Marshall was wearing and tried it on his own head in order to gauge the correct size, Marshall noted approvingly, "My friend was such a perfect democrat that it did not occur to him that there was any reason why he should not wear my hat: his manner was absolutely free from insolence. May the habit become general!"[95] When he reached California, he was pleased to report that the farther west he traveled, the more American society resembled its egalitarian ideal. "I returned on the whole more sanguine with regard to the future of the world than when I set out," he noted.

Striking a prophetic note, he envisioned a new type of society:

In America, mobility was creating an equality of condition . . . Where nearly all receive the same school education, where the incomparably more important education which is derived from the business of life, however various in form it be, yet is for every one nearly equally thorough, nearly equally effective in developing the faculties of men, there cannot but be true democracy. There will of course be great inequalities of wealth; at least there will be some very wealthy men. But there will be no clearly marked gradation of classes. There will be nothing like what Mill calls so strongly marked line of demarcation between the different grades of laborers as to be almost equivalent to the hereditary distinction of caste.

Explaining how individual choices might add up to social good—the very thing that Carlyle denied was possible—Marshall defined two types of moral education. One was characteristic of England, where, he claimed, "the peaceful molding of character into harmony with the conditions by which it is surrounded, so that a man . . . will without conscious moral effort be impelled on that course which is in union with the actions, the sympathies and the interests of the society amid which he spends his life." In America, by contrast, mobility had opened up a second route to moral evolution, namely, "the education of a firm will by the overcoming of difficulties, a will which submits every particular action to the judgment of reason." [96]

Most Victorian social commentators, including Karl Marx, feared that the industrial system was not merely destroying traditional social relations and livelihoods but deforming human nature through "ignorance, brutalization, and moral degradation." [97] In America, Marshall saw another possibility: "It appears to me that on the average an American has the habit of using his own individual judgment more consciously and deliberately, more freely and intrepidly, with regards to questions of Ethics than an Englishman uses his."

Marshall seemed to be talking about mankind in general, but he was also talking about himself. *He* had developed a firm will by overcoming all sorts of difficulties—a tyrant of a father, genteel poverty, and the oppressive strictures of class. *He* had broken with authority—by losing his religious belief and defying his father's wishes that he enter the ministry. Now he felt that his own independence would lead not to his downfall but to great things. What he witnessed in America filled him with hope. "Such a society may degenerate into licentiousness and thence into depravity. But in its higher forms it will develop a mighty system of law, and it will obey law . . . Such a society will be an empire of energy." [98]

"I have been rather spoilt" when it comes to "go" and a "strong character" in women," Marshall had written in a letter from America. In another, he described his "riveting evening" with Miss Nunn, confessing that he found her naïveté "mingled with enterprise" charming. But he added that "for steady support I would have the strength that has been formed by daring and success." [99] Apparently he was thinking of Mary Paley, who had triumphed over the Tripos in his absence.

When they got engaged on his return to Cambridge, Marshall was thirty-four and Mary twenty-six. He was a rising star of the "New Economics." She was a college lecturer. Marshall's view of marriage was inspired by intellectual partnerships such as those of George Eliot and George Lewes and Thomas and Jane Carlyle. "The ideal of married life is often said to be that husband and wife should live for each other. If this means that they should live for each other's gratification it seems to me intensely immoral," Marshall wrote in an essay. "Man and wife should live, not for each other but with each other for some end." [100] For Mary, who had entered her first engagement "out of boredom," this was a thrilling vision. Like the other unusual, idiosyncratic Victorian marriages Phyllis Rose describes in *Parallel Lives: Five Victorian Marriages*, the secret of Alfred Marshall and Mary Paley's alliance lay in their "telling the same story." [101] The couple immediately decided to make Mary's textbook a joint project and spent most of their engagement working on it.

They were married at the Parish Church in Ufford, next to the "rambling old house, its front covered with red and white roses," where Mary had grown up. Mary wore no veil, only jasmine in her hair. In a gesture that proclaimed their untraditional views and high expectations, bride and groom contracted themselves out of the "obey clause." [102]

By marrying, Marshall forfeited his fellowship at St. John's. He and Mary flirted briefly with the notion of teaching at a boarding school, but when the principalship of a newly founded redbrick college in Bristol—the first experiment in coeducation in Britain—suddenly became vacant, they leapt at the opportunity. When they moved to Bristol in 1877, Mary had a tennis court installed and most of the rooms papered with Morris while Marshall chose the secondhand furniture and piano. But she was soon back in the classroom, lecturing on economics and tutoring women students.

Underwritten by Bristol's business community, University College was to provide "middle and working class men and women with a liberal education." [103] Though strapped for funds, the college managed, during the Marshall's tenure, to offer day and evening classes to some five hundred students, sponsor public lectures in working-class neighborhoods, provide technical instruction to textile workers, and run a work-study program jointly with local businesses for engineering students. Marshall's administrative duties were heavy and so was his teaching load. His regular classes, attended by a mix of small businessmen, trade unionists, and women, were "less academic than those at Cambridge . . . a mixture of hard reasoning and practical problems illuminated by interesting sidelights on all sorts of subjects," a student recalled.[104] Marshall "spoke without notes and his face caught the light from the window while all else was in shadow. The lecture seemed to me the most wonderful I had ever heard. He told of his faith that economic science had a great future in furthering the progress of social improvement and his enthusiasm was infectious."[105] The couple continued to work on *The Economics of Industry* most afternoons, took long walks, and played many games of lawn tennis. One friend referred to "their perfect happiness."[106]

Marshall later said that reading Marx convinced him that "economists should investigate history; the history of the past and the more accessible history of the present."[107] But it was Dickens and Mayhew who inspired him to go into factories and industrial towns to interview businessmen, managers, trade union leaders, and workers. "I am greedy for facts," he used to say.[108] He wanted to write for men and women engaged in the "ordinary business of life."[109]

He was convinced that he would have to blend theory, history, and statistics, as Marx had done in *Das Kapital*. But he was instinctively aware that his audience would require useful practical conclusions and a generous sprinkling of direct observation. He was too much of a scientist to theorize without verifying facts, or to rely on secondhand descriptions.

Marshall made a commitment to study the particulars of every major industry. He gathered data on wage rates by occupation and skill level. He paid a great deal of attention to Mill's "arts of production"[110]—manufacturing techniques, product design, management—although he admitted that the constant effort of business owners to improve their products, production methods, and suppliers was hard to capture in formal theories. He was particularly interested in how the family-owned, privately held firm functioned versus the increasingly important joint stock company or corporation. Marshall participated in commissions and learned societies and sat on the board of a London charity, carried on a huge scientific correspondence, and, with Mary as an active partner, devoted several weeks each summer to fieldwork.

On one such quest, Mary's notes refer to "14 different towns, mines, iron and steel works, textile plants, and [the] Salvation Army."[111] The itinerary was extraordinarily ambitious: Coniston copper mines, Kirby slate quarries, Barrow docks, iron and steel works, Millom iron mines, Whitehaven coal mines close to the sea, Lancaster, and Sheffield. Marshall invented a device for organizing and retrieving information from his personal database. His "Red Book" was a homemade notebook sewn together with thread. Each page contained data on a variety of topics, ranging from music to technology to wage rates, arranged in chronological order. Marshall had only to stick a pin through one of the points on a page to see what other developments had occurred simultaneously.

In contrast to the majority of Victorian intellectuals, Marshall admired the entrepreneur and the worker. Carlyle, Marx, and Mill considered modern production to be an unpleasant necessity, labor to be degrading and debilitating, businessmen to be predatory and philistine, and urban life to be vile. Mill considered Communism superior to competition in every respect but two (motivation and tolerance for eccentricity) and looked forward to a stationary, Socialistic state in the not very distant future. But none of these intellectuals could claim the familiarity with business and industry that Marshall was acquiring. Of course, as Burke's phrase "drudging through life" implied, much of human labor had and was having such effects. But, once again, Marshall's reliance on firsthand observation suggested that at least some work in modern firms expanded horizons, taught new skills, promoted mobility, and encouraged foresight and ethical behavior, not to mention provided the savings to go to school or into business. What was more, he observed, that sort of work was growing while the other was becoming less common. In short, the business enterprise could be and often was a step toward controlling one's destiny.

Although Dickens is often thought of as a chronicler of the industrial revolution, almost the only factory scene in Dickens is phantasmagorical. The Coketown factory in *Hard Times* is a Frankenstein, seen only from a distance, that turns men into machines and re-creates the natural and social environment in its own monstrous image; noisy, dirty, monotonous, its air and water poisoned.

> It was a town of red brick, or of brick that would have been red if the smoke and ashes had allowed it; but, as matters stood it was a town of unnatural red and black like the painted face of a savage. It was a town of machinery and tall chimneys, out of which interminable serpents of smoke trailed themselves for ever and ever, and never got uncoiled. It had a black canal in it, and a river that ran purple with an ill-smelling dye, and vast piles of building full of windows where there was a rattling and a trembling all day long, and where the piston of the steam-engine worked monotonously up and down, like the head of an elephant in a state of melancholy madness.[112]

Coketown is inhabited by an army of "people equally like one another, who all went in and out at the same hours, with the same sound upon the same pavements, to do the same work." Significantly, Dickens imagines that inside the factory they "do the same work" and that "every day was the same as yesterday and to-morrow, and every year the counterpart of the last and the next." Production, in other words, involves never creating anything new.

Marx's description of the factory in *Das Kapital* stresses the same features as Dickens's but lacks all detail, not surprising given that Marx had never been inside even a single one. Again, men are transformed into a "mere living appendage" of the machine, work becomes "mindless repetition," and automation "deprives the work of all interest."[113]

Marshall's descriptions of factories and factory life are more specific, nuanced, and varied. He spends hours observing. He records manufacturing techniques and pay scales and layouts. He questions everyone, from the owner to the foremen to the men on the shop floor. When he encounters the same problematic phenomenon as Dickens or Marx—the effects of the assembly line on workers—he doesn't necessarily draw the same inferences.

> The characteristic of the firm is the way in which every operation is broken up into a great number of portions, the work of each individual being confined to a very small portion of the whole operation. Does this prevent the growth of intelligence? I think not . . . If a man has no brains we get rid of him: There is plenty of opportunity for this in consequence of the fluctuations of the market. If a man has some brains, he stays on at his work; but if he has any ambition, he must get to know all that goes on in the shop in which he is working: otherwise he has no chance of becoming foreman of that shop . . . Most improvements in detail are made by the foremen of the several shops: & improvements on a very large scale are made by a man who does nothing else . . . Their improvements were in small details as regards manufacture e.g. numerous contrivances for securing that certain parts should be airtight, that certain others should work easily. The Englishman had invented the harp stop.[114]

For Dickens and Marx, firms existed to control or exploit the worker. For Mill they existed solely to enrich their owners. For Marshall, the business firm was not a prison. Management wasn't just about keeping the prisoners in line. Competing for customers (or workers) required more than mindless repetition. Marshall's business enterprises were forced to evolve in order to survive. Of course, Marshall did not deny that businessmen pursued profits. His point was that to make profits competitive, firms had to generate enough revenue to still have something left over after paying workers, managers, suppliers, landlords, taxes, and so on. To do that, managers had to constantly seek out ways to do a little more with the same or fewer resources. In other words, higher productivity, the long-run determinant of wages, was a by-product of competition.

The British publisher Macmillan & Co. brought out *The Economics of Industry* in 1879. A slim volume purporting to contain nothing new and written in simple and direct prose suitable for a primer, it contained the essentials of Marshall's New Economics. Its message was summarized in the following passage:

> The chief fault in English economists at the beginning of the century was not that they ignored history and statistics . . . They regarded man as so to speak a constant quantity and gave themselves little trouble to study his variations. They therefore attributed to the forces of supply and demand a much more mechanical and regular action than they actually have; But their most vital fault was that they did not see how liable to change are the habits and institutions of industry.[115]

Marshall's obsessive effort to understand how businesses worked led to his most important discovery. The economic function of the business firm in a competitive market was not only or even primarily to produce profits for owners. It was to produce higher living standards for consumers and workers. How did it do this? By producing and distributing more goods and services of better quality and at lower cost with fewer resources. Why? Competition forced owners and managers to constantly make small changes to improve their products, manufacturing techniques, distribution, and marketing. The constant search to find efficiency gains, economize on resources, and do more with less resulted over time in doing more with the same or fewer resources. Multiplied over hundreds of thousands of enterprises throughout the economy, the accumulation of incremental improvements over time raised average productivity and wages. In other words, competition forced businesses to raise productivity in order to stay profitable. Competition forced owners to share the fruits of these efforts with managers and employees, in the form of higher pay, and with customers, in the form of higher quality or lower prices.

The implication that business was the engine that drove wages and living standards higher ran counter to the general condemnation of business by intellectuals. Even Adam Smith, who famously described the benefits of competition in terms of an invisible hand that led producers to serve consumers without their intending to do so, had not suggested that the role of butchers, bakers, and giant joint stock companies was to raise living standards. Although Karl Marx had recognized that business enterprises were engines of technological change and productivity gains, he could not imagine that they might also provide the means by which humanity could escape poverty and take control of its material condition.

A serious crisis followed the publication of the Marshalls' book. Marshall was diagnosed with a kidney stone in the spring of 1879. Surgery and drugs were not options at that time. His doctor said, "There must be no more long walks, no more games at tennis, and that complete rest offered the only chance of cure," Mary recalled later. "This advice came as a great shock to one who delighted so in active exercise." [116] The painful, debilitating condition revived Marshall's old fears of impending annihilation, still lurking from childhood. Only a few weeks earlier, he had spent a vacation hiking alone on the Dartmouth moors. Now he had become a housebound invalid who took up knitting to pass the time. A Bristol acquaintance recalled seeing Marshall and thinking that he must be seventy or so:

> He . . . looked to me very old and ill. I was told he had one foot in the grave and I quite believed it. I can see him now, creeping along Apsley Road . . . in a great-coat and soft black hat . . . The next time I saw him was . . . in 1890 . . . I was astonished to find him apparently thirty or forty years younger than I remembered him a dozen years before. [117]

It made him more dependent on Mary and caused him to cast her ever more into the role of nurse rather than intellectual companion. Illness concentrated his mind. Marshall always had a tendency toward writer's block. Now he realized he had to focus his energies and get on with his book. His hopes for writing a work that would eclipse Mill's (and perhaps also Marx's)—a synthesis of new theory and freshly distilled reports from the real world—were matched by fears that he was not up to the task. As his vision grew in scope and complexity, he grew proportionately less satisfied with what he had written. He had decided to drop plans to publish his volume on trade well before his illness flared. "I have come to the conclusion that it will never make a comfortable book in its present shape," he wrote in the summer of 1878.[118] And he quickly grew to dislike the book he had written with Mary. But in 1881, on a rooftop in Palermo, Sicily, he began to compose *Principles of Economics*.

Of all the panaceas advanced during the Great Depression of the early 1880s, the American journalist Henry George's land tax attracted by far the most popular attention and support. George's best seller, *Progress & Poverty,* had made him an instant celebrity, and his lectures drew huge crowds. George's premise was that poverty was growing faster than wealth and that landlords were to blame. He claimed that landlords were collecting fabulous incomes not for rendering a service to the community but merely because they were lucky enough to own real estate. What was more, rising rents were depressing profits and real wages by depriving businessmen of needed investment funds. Having identified rental income as the cause of poverty, he proposed a massive tax on land as a cure. The land tax would not only eliminate the need for all other taxes, he claimed. It would also "raise wages, increase the earnings of capital, extirpate pauperism, abolish poverty, give remunerative employment to whoever wishes it, afford free scope to human powers, lessen crime, elevate morals and taste and intelligence, purify government, and carry civilization to yet nobler heights."[119]

Marshall was still working on *Principles* when he was drawn once again into the long-simmering standard-of-living controversy. The early 1880s, a period of financial and economic crisis, witnessed a resurgence of radicalism and demands for social reform, as well as growing skepticism about the extent to which economic growth was benefiting the majority of citizens. The term unemployment was coined during the recession that followed the Panic of 1893 during a heated debate over whether real wages were rising or falling in the long run.

At issue in the debate was the dominant effect of competition. Did competition result in a race to the bottom in which employers matched one another's wage cuts? Or was it the case, as optimists insisted, that competition put pressure on companies to make constant efforts to increase efficiency and push up the average level of productivity and wages while reducing the number of poor?

The first formal confrontation between Marshall and Henry George took place at the Clarendon Hotel in Oxford in 1884.[120] Catcalls, clapping, and hissing repeatedly drowned out the debaters. At one point, an undergraduate felt it necessary to primly remind the chairman that "ladies were present." By eleven o'clock, the uproar was so deafening that George declared the meeting to be "the most disorderly he had ever addressed" and refused to answer any more questions. Amid "great noise" and groans of "Land Nationalization" and "Land Robbery," the meeting "was brought to a rather abrupt conclusion."

If Marshall's support for the agricultural lockout in 1874 signaled his rejection of the "dogmas" of classical economy, his confrontation with George a decade later showed that he also objected to trendy new dogmas.

On other occasions when he had criticized George's proposal to cure poverty with a tax on land, Marshall had called George a "poet" and praised "the freshness and earnestness of his view of life." But at the Clarendon, Marshall was decidedly less polite, accusing George of using his "singular and almost unexampled power of catching the ear of the people" to "instill poison into their minds." By "poison," he meant George's cure-all for poverty.

In his Bristol lectures, Marshall stuck to his stated intention to "avoid talking very much about George: but to discuss his subject," "George's subtitle includes an inquiry into" the increase of want with the increase of wealth," Marshall said. "But are we sure that with the increase of wealth want has actually increased? . . . Let us then enquire what the facts are of the case." [121]

Citing statistical evidence—much of it collected in the Red Book that he and Mary had compiled—Marshall argued that only the "lowest stratum" of the working classes were being pushed downward and that that stratum was far smaller—less than half the size, in proportion to the population—than it had been earlier in the century. As for the working classes as a whole, their purchasing power had tripled. "Nearly one half of the whole income of England goes to the working classes . . . [So] a very large part of all the benefit that comes from the progress of invention must fall to their share." [122]

Marshall drew on his growing command of economic history. He was confident that, whatever the vices of the current age, they paled in comparison to the past. "The working classes are in no part of the world, except new countries, nearly as well off as they are in England." What makes Marshall's optimism all the more noteworthy is that he was speaking during what historians would later call the Great Depression.

In his second lecture, Marshall challenged George's contention that employers who paid low wages were to blame for poverty. For one thing, employers could not set the price of labor any more than they could dictate the price of cotton or machinery. They paid the market rate, which could be high if a worker was very productive and low if he was not. "Many of the English working classes have not been properly fed, and scarcely any of them have been properly educated." Low productivity was the cause of "low wages of a large part of the English people and of the actual pauperism of no inconsiderable number." And although Marshall did not deny that "there is any form of land nationalization which, on the whole, would benefit," he argued that "there is none that contains a magic and sudden remedy for poverty. We must be content to look for a less sensational cure." [123]

That cure, Marshall said, was to raise productivity. One way was to:

educate (in the broadest sense) the unskilled and inefficient workers out of existence. On the other hand—and this sentence is the kernel of all I have to say about poverty—if the numbers of unskilled laborers were to diminish sufficiently, then those who did unskilled work would have to be paid good wages. If total production has not increased, these extra wages would have to be paid out of the shares of capital and of higher kinds of labor . . . But if the diminution of unskilled labor is brought about by the increasing efficiency of labor, it will increase production, and there will be a larger fund to be divided up.

He did not object to unions or even to some fairly radical proposals for land reform or progressive taxation. He merely noted that none of these could produce "more bread and butter." This required "competition," time, and the cooperation of all parts of society, government, and the poor themselves.[124]

He accused George of promoting a quack cure. The problem wasn't just that "Mr. George said, 'If you want to get rich, take land,'" but that it would divert from education and training, hard work, and thrift. George's scheme would yield "less than a penny in the shilling on their income . . . For the sake of this, Mr. George is willing to pour contempt on all the plans by which workingmen have striven to benefit themselves." [125]

When Marshall's *Principles of Economics* finally appeared in 1890, it breathed new life into a faltering discipline. It established him as its intellectual leader and the authority to whom governments turned for advice.

Principles embodied Marshall's rejection of Socialism, embrace of the system of private property and competition, and optimism about the improvability of man and his circumstances. The book portrayed economics not as a dogma but as "an apparatus of the mind." As Dickens hoped, Marshall had managed, while placing the discipline on a more sound scientific footing, to humanize economics by injecting "a little human bloom . . . and a little human warmth."

But the chief insight reflected the lesson he learned in America. Under a system of private property and competition, business firms are under constant pressure to achieve more with the same or fewer resources. From society's standpoint, the corporation's function is to raise productivity and, hence, living standards.

Of all social institutions, the business firm was more central, enjoyed a higher status, and did more to shape the American mind and civilization than elsewhere. The company was not only the principal creator of wealth in America but also the most important agent of social change and the biggest magnet for talented individuals. It made Dickens's depictions of businessmen as cretins or predators, workers as zombies, and successful manufacture as rigid repetition look ridiculous. The undisputed fact that American productive power was growing at an unimaginably rapid rate meant that businesses must be doing more, at least in the aggregate, than exploiting Peter to line Paul's pockets or merely repeating the same operations from one year to the next. On his visits to factories, Marshall was especially struck by managers' constant search for small improvements and workers' equally constant search for better opportunities and useful skills. Both seemed obsessed with making the most of the resources at their command.

Naturally, Marshall recognized that companies also exist to generate profits for owners, managerial salaries for executives, and wages for workers. Adam Smith had pointed out that to maximize their own income in the face of competition, firms had to benefit consumers by producing as much and as cheaply as possible. But Marshall introduced the element of time into his analysis. Over time, firms could remain profitable and continue to exist only if they became more and more productive. Survival in the face of competition not only implied incessant adaptation. Competition for the most productive workers meant that, over time, firms had to share gains from productivity improvements.

This is precisely what Mill and the other founders of political economy had denied. They had maintained that advances in productivity were of little or no benefit to the working classes. In their imaginary firms, productivity might grow by leaps and bounds, but wages never rose for long above some physiological maximum. Working conditions, if anything, worsened over time. Marshall saw not only that this was not so in fact, but also that it could not be so. Competition for labor forced owners to share the benefits of efficiency and quality improvements with workers, first as wage earners, then as consumers. The evidence confirmed that Marshall was right. The share of wages in the gross domestic product—the nation's annual income from wages, profits, interest, and proprietors' income—was rising, not falling, and so were the levels of wages and working-class consumption—as they had been in most years since 1848, when *The Communist Manifesto* and Mill's *Principles of Political Economy* appeared.

Chapter III

Miss Potter's Profession:
Webb and the Housekeeping State

She yearned for something by which her life might be filled with
action at once rational and ardent; and since the time was gone
by for guiding visions . . . what lamp was there but knowledge?

—*George Eliot,* Middlemarch [1]

Every year in March, the "upper ten thousand" descended on London like
a vast flock of extravagantly plumed and exotic migratory birds.[2] During
the three or four months of the London "season," Britain's elite devoted
itself to an elaborate mating ritual. Mornings were spent riding along Rotten Row or the Ladies' Mile in Hyde Park. Afternoons were for repairing
to Parliament or to clubs for the males of the species, shopping and paying
social calls for the wives and daughters. In the evenings everyone met at
operas, dinner parties, and balls that provided opportunities for magnificent displays. Every few days, an obligatory race, regatta, cricket match, or
gallery opening introduced a slight variation to the schedule.

As with so much else in Victorian high society, this frenetic and seemingly frivolous pursuit of pleasure was serious business: during the season,
which began when Parliament resumed its session, London became the
epicenter of the global marriage market. Wealthy parents thought of giving a daughter two or three London seasons in the same way as sending
a son to Oxford or Cambridge. The expense and effort of participating
in this extraordinarily intricate mating dance were certainly comparable.

If the family had no permanent "town" house, an imposing mansion had to be found at a fashionable address. A vast quantity of expensive items had to be purchased and conveyed, what with "the stable of horses and carriages . . . , the elaborate stock of garments . . . , [and] all the commissariat and paraphernalia for dinners, dances, picnics and weekend parties" considered de rigueur. Needless to say, socializing on so ambitious a scale demanded an executive to oversee "extensive [plans], a large number of employees and innumerable decisions"—in other words, the lady of the household.[3]

These were the reflections that occupied Beatrice Ellen Potter, Bo or Bea to her family, the eighth of nine daughters of a rich railway tycoon from Gloucester named Richard Potter. The carriage she was sharing with her father on a raw February afternoon in 1883 rolled to a stop in front of an imposing terrace of tall, cream-colored Italianate villas. The slender young woman with an air of command surveyed number 47 Princes Gate coolly. It was meant to serve as the social headquarters of the sprawling Potter clan, which included her six married sisters and their large families, for the season. The five-story mansion had a sumptuous façade with Ionic columns, Corinthian pilasters, tall windows, and swags of fruit and flowers, and it faced Hyde Park. At the back, visible through French doors, was an expanse of terraced lawn furnished with classical statues and enormous pots with masses of scarlet pelargoniums tumbling over their sides. The houses on either side of theirs were similarly grand. Her father had chosen Princes Gate precisely so they would be flanked by neighbors as wealthy and powerful as he. Junius Morgan, the American banker, leased number 13. Joseph Chamberlain, a Manchester industrialist turned Liberal politician and the father of Neville Chamberlain, had taken number 40 for the season. It was a perfect setting for Potter's brilliant daughter.

At twenty-five, Beatrice was the veteran of more than half a dozen London seasons but had never been in love. Until now, her duties had consisted of enjoying herself at some fifty balls, sixty parties, thirty dinners, and twenty-five breakfasts before society packed up and retreated to the country in July.[4] She'd had nothing whatsoever to do with "all that elaborate machinery"[5] that was required backstage. This year would be different. Beatrice had been the only one of the Potter sisters, except for thirteen-year-old Rosie, who was still living at home in Gloucester when their mother died the previous spring. Suddenly she was promoted to lady of her father's house.

Before leaving Gloucester, Beatrice had made a solemn vow "to give myself up to Society, and make it my aim to succeed therein."[6] By "succeed," she meant marry an important man, as each of her older sisters had done, although her use of "give myself up" suggests that the price of success was self-immolation. The latest to do so had been her favorite sister, Kate, who had waited until the advanced age of thirty-one to marry a prominent Liberal economist and politician, Leonard Courtney, currently serving as Treasury secretary. Her father did not doubt that Bo would follow suit. Besides beauty, breeding, and a large fortune, she had the gift of commanding attention. Her long, graceful neck, fiercely intelligent eyes, and glossy black hair made people seeing her for the first time across a crowded room think of a beautiful, slightly dangerous black swan. Men were charmed by her, especially when they realized that she refused to take them seriously.

For a while after the Potters' arrival, all was chaos and confusion. More retainers, extra horses, and additional carriages appeared. When the servants finally withdrew and her father had gotten some supper, Beatrice went upstairs and found the bedroom in the back of the mansion that she had determined would be hers. Now she could think of something besides seating plans and menus—namely, the books that she had brought to read; the things she meant to learn. Beatrice saw nothing inherently contradictory in her various desires and duties. After all, a happily married woman sat on the throne, and George Eliot reigned as the most successful writer of the day. When Beatrice was eighteen, she had spent more time studying Eastern religions than preparing for her "coming out."

Her bedroom window overlooked the Victoria and Albert Museum. It suddenly struck her that the great monument to human ingenuity stood in the very center of London yet managed to remain wonderfully "undisturbed by the rushing life of the great city."[7] Beatrice wondered whether she might do the same, maintaining a Buddhist-like detachment in crowded drawing rooms and theaters. Might she not she fulfill society's expectations while still cultivating the "thoughtful" part of her life, the part that drove her to constantly to ask herself, "How am I to live and for what object?"[8]

The question of her destiny had preoccupied Beatrice since her fifteenth birthday. Her mother and sisters had always regarded her obsession as unhealthy. Wasn't it enough to simply be "one of the fashionable Miss Potters who live in grand houses and beautiful gardens and marry enormously wealthy men?"[9] Had Beatrice been the heroine of a Victorian novel, its author would have felt obliged to offer some justification for making the question of her destiny the "center of interest." In *The Portrait of a Lady*, published in 1881, Henry James had done exactly that: "Millions of presumptuous girls, intelligent or not intelligent, daily affront their destiny, and what is it open to their destiny to be, at the most, that we should make an ado about it?" James asked in his preface.[10] Before middle-class women had viable alternatives to early marriage and motherhood, and the Married Women's Property Act of 1882 gave them the right to their own incomes, the recurring question in *The Portrait of a Lady*—"Well, what will she do?"—could hardly have merited a reader's interest.

"You are young, pretty, rich, clever, what more do you want?" Beatrice's cousin Margaret Harkness, the novelist daughter of a poor country parson, had asked with a trace of exasperation when they were at school together. "Why cannot you be satisfied?"[11] Like James's heroine Isabel Archer, Beatrice had been brought up with an unusual freedom to travel, read, form friendships, and satisfy her "great desire for knowledge" and "immense curiosity about life." Beatrice preferred the company of men and took it for granted that most would fall under her spell, but like Isabel she had no desire to "begin life by marrying."[12] She was as interested in winning recognition for her intellectual achievements as for her feminine charms. Each passing year made her longing for a "real aim and occupation" more urgent.[13] She was conscious of "a special mission" and believed with all her heart that she was meant to live "a life with some result."[14] Like

Dorothea in *Middlemarch*, Beatrice yearned for principles, "something by which her life might be filled with action at once rational and ardent." [15]

Beatrice's identity was shaped by having been born into Britain's "new ruling class," [16] and her mind by having been "brought up in the midst of capitalist speculation" and "the restless spirit of big enterprise." [17] As the historian Barbara Caine notes, Beatrice distinguished her class not by wealth but by the fact that it was "a class of persons who habitually gave orders, but who seldom, if ever, executed the orders of other people." [18] Her grandfathers were both self-made men. Her father had lost the lion's share of his inheritance in the crash of 1848, only to quickly recoup his losses by supplying tents to the French army during the Crimean War. By the time Beatrice was born in 1858, Richard Potter had amassed a third fortune from timber and railways and had become a director (and future chairman of the board) of the Great Western Railway. More entrepreneur and speculator than hands-on manager, Potter once toyed with a scheme to build a waterway to rival the Suez Canal. His business interests were scattered from Turkey to Canada, and he and his family were constantly traveling. The Potters' Gloucester estate, Standish, as grand and impersonal as a hotel, was filled with an ever-changing contingent of visiting relatives, guests, employees, and hangers on.

Though Richard Potter began to vote Conservative in middle age, he was never a stereotypical Tory plutocrat. His father, a wholesaler in the cotton industry, was for a time a Radical member of Parliament and had helped found the *Manchester Guardian* [19] ("our organ," as Beatrice used to say). [20] Intellectually engaged, broad-minded, and convivial, he counted scientists, philosophers, and journalists among his closest friends. Herbert Spencer, the most lionized intellectual in England in the 1860s and 1870s and a former railway engineer and *Economist* editorialist, called Richard Potter "the most lovable being I have yet seen." [21] Even the latter's cheerful indifference to Spencer's philosophical interests could not squelch Spencer's lifelong adoration.

It is almost axiomatic that behind every extraordinary woman there is a remarkable father. Potter encouraged Beatrice and her sisters to read and gave them free run of his large library. He made no effort to restrict their discussion or friendships. He enjoyed their company so much that he rarely took a business trip without one or another as a companion. Beatrice claimed that "he was the only man I ever knew who genuinely believed that women were superior to men, and acted as if he did."[22] She gave him credit for her own "audacity and pluck and my familiarity with the risks and chances of big enterprises."[23]

In some ways, Laurencina Potter was even more unusual than her husband, bearing even less resemblance to the plump and placid mothers that populate Trollope novels than her husband did to the stereotypical businessmen. When Spencer met the Potters for the first time shortly after their marriage, he thought they were "the most admirable pair I have ever seen."[24] As he got to know them better, he was surprised to learn that Laurencina's perfectly feminine, graceful, and refined personage hid "so independent a character."[25] In contrast to her easygoing husband, Laurencina was cerebral, puritanical, and discontented. Born Heyworth, she came from a family of liberal Liverpool merchants who educated her no differently from her brothers; that is, trained her in mathematics, languages, and political economy. As a young woman, she became a local celebrity and the subject of newspaper articles as a result of the zeal with which she canvassed against the Corn Laws. Decades later, Beatrice was used to seeing pamphlets on economic issues appear on her dressing table.

Laurencina was a very unhappy woman. The cause of her frustration was not hard for her daughter to divine. She had envisioned a married life of "close intellectual comradeship with my father, possibly of intellectual achievement, surrounded by distinguished friends."[26] Instead, for the first two decades after her marriage, she was almost always pregnant or nursing an infant and banished to the company of women and children while her husband traveled on business and dined with writers and intellectuals. Her real ambition had been to write novels, and she did publish one, *Laura Gay*, before the demands of family life overwhelmed her.

When Laurencina's ninth child and only son, Dickie, was born, she devoted herself completely to him. But when the boy died of scarlet fever at age two, she became severely depressed and withdrew from her other children. Beatrice, who was seven at the time, recalled her mother as "a remote personage discussing business with my father or poring over books in her boudoir." As a consequence of her mother's coldness, Beatrice came to believe that "I was not made to be loved; there must be something repulsive about my character." Moody, self-dramatizing, and inclined to fib and exaggerate, she had also inherited the Heyworths' tendency to Weltschmerz and suicide. Two of Laurencina's relatives had died by their own hand. "My childhood was not on the whole a happy one," reflected Beatrice as an adult. "Ill-health and starved affection and the mental disorders which spring from these, ill temper and resentment, marred it . . . Its *loneliness* was absolute."[27] Beatrice herself had toyed with bottles of chloroform even as a child.

Rebuffed by her mother, a biographer says, Beatrice sought affection "below stairs" among the servants who helped keep the Potter household running. She and her older sisters were especially close to Martha Jackson, or Dada as they called her, who took care of the children. Dada, Beatrice learned much later, was actually a relative from a branch of her mother's family who were poor but respectable Lancashire hand-loom weavers. Caine credits Dada with planting in Beatrice the notion of original sin that gave her the determination to do good and the identification she felt all her life with the "respectable" working poor. But it was Laurencina's example that inspired her to write. On her fifteenth birthday, Beatrice began a journal that she kept until her death. "Sometimes I feel as if I must write, as if I must pour my poor crooked thoughts into somebody's heart, even if it be into my own."[28]

Among the intellectuals who frequented the Potter house were the biologist Thomas Huxley; Sir Francis Galton, a cousin of Charles Darwin's; and other proponents of the new "scientific" point of view that was undermining traditional beliefs. By the time Beatrice was in her teens, Spencer, who shared the Potters' background as dissenting Protestants, had become Laurencina's closest confidant and the dominant intellectual influence in the household.

Spencer, who coined the term "survival of the fittest," was a bigger

celebrity in the 1860s than Charles Darwin. His notion that social institutions, like animal or plant species, were evolving—and therefore could be
observed, classified, and analyzed like plants or animals—had captured
the public's imagination. One of the earliest exponents of evolution,
Spencer was a radical individualist who opposed slavery and supported
women's suffrage. His antipathy toward government regulation and high
taxes appealed to the upwardly mobile middle and lower-middle classes.
His popularity was further bolstered by his refusal to rule out absolutely
the existence of God.

Fame, however, had not agreed with Spencer. In uncertain health and
prone to hypochondria, he had grown increasingly reclusive and eccentric
with age. When not at his club or alone in his rooms, he turned to the
company of the Potters and their children. A frequent guest at the Potters' Gloucester estate, he delighted in liberating the Potter sisters from
their governesses while chanting, "Submission *not* desirable."[29] Often he
would lead them off to gather specimens to illustrate one or another of
his ideas about evolution. In the summers, when the Potters were at their
Cotswold retreat, he would lead the way through beech groves and old
pear orchards, dressed in white linen from head to toe, carrying a parasol.
Trailing behind would be a "very pretty and original group"[30] of tall,
slender girls with boyishly short black hair, dressed in pale muslins and
carrying buckets and nets. From time to time, the party stopped to dig for
fossils. The old railway cuts or limestone quarries of Gloucester once lay
under shallow, warm seas and thousands of years later yielded a choice
collection of ammonites, crinoids, trilobites, and echinoids. The girls did
not take their hyperrational friend too seriously. "Are we descended from
monkeys, Mr. Spencer?" they would chorus amid giggles. His unvarying
reply—"About 99 percent of humanity have descended and one percent
have ascended!"—elicited more peals of mirth as well as, occasionally,
volleys of decaying beech leaves aimed at the philosopher's "remarkable
headpiece."[31]

The most bookish and moodiest of the sisters, Beatrice developed a
lasting fascination with the workings of Spencer's remarkable mind. Spencer encouraged Beatrice by telling her that she was a "born metaphysician,"

comparing her to his idol, George Eliot, drawing up reading lists, and urging her to pursue her intellectual ambitions. Without his support, Beatrice might have submitted to the kind of life that convention—and at times her own heart—demanded.

Beatrice's formal education was shockingly skimpy. Like that of many upper-class young women, it was limited to a few months at a fancy finishing school, in part because of her own frequent illnesses, both imaginary and real, and in part because even Richard Potter, liberal as he was by the standards of the time, never thought of sending her to university. She was therefore largely educated at home—that is to say, self-taught and free to read even books that had been banned from public libraries. "I am, as Mother says, too young, too uneducated, and worst of all, too frivolous to be a companion to her," she wrote in her diary. "But, however, I must take courage, and try to change." [32] Penny-pinching in most things, Laurencina was openhanded when it came to buying newspapers and magazines. Beatrice plunged into religion, philosophy, and psychology, her mother's interests. Her schoolgirl reading included George Eliot and the fashionable French philosopher and pioneering sociologist Auguste Comte.

Because Beatrice was given unlimited access to her father's library and her mother's journals, she was exposed in a way few girls were to the religious and scientific controversies that dominated the late Victorian era. "We lived, indeed, in a perpetual state of ferment, receiving and questioning all contemporary hypotheses as to the duty and destiny of man in this world and the next," she recalled. By the time Beatrice was eighteen and about to come out, she had substituted for the old Anglican faith Spencer's new doctrine of "harmony and progress." She had also embraced her mentor's libertarian political creed and his ideal of the "scientific investigator." The image of the latter aroused her "domineering curiosity in the nature of things" and "hope for a 'bird's eye view' of mankind" as well as her secret ambition to write "a book that would be read." [33]

After three weeks at Princes Gate, Beatrice was suffering from the "rival pulls on time and energy." [34] After a particularly tedious dinner party, she fumed that "Ladies are so expressionless." [35] She no longer understood why "intelligent women wish to marry into the set where this is the social regime." [36] She poured her discontents into her diary: "I feel like a caged animal, bound up by the luxury, comfort, and respectability of my position." [37]

Beatrice longed for work as well as love, but she was beginning to wonder whether her chances of having it all were any better than poor Laurencina's. When Isabel Archer insisted that "there are other things a woman can do," she was thinking, presumably, of the small but growing ranks of self-supporting female professionals who could befriend whomever they pleased, talk about whatever they liked, live in lodgings, and travel on their own.

But such women gave up a great deal, Beatrice realized upon reflection. When she encountered the daughter of the notorious Karl Marx in the refreshment room of the British Museum, Eleanor Marx was "dressed in a slovenly picturesque way with curly black hair flying about in all directions!" Beatrice was taken by Eleanor's intellectual self-confidence and romantic appearance but repelled by the latter's bohemian lifestyle. "Unfortunately one cannot mix with human beings without becoming more or less *connected* with them," she told herself.[38] She adored her cousin Margaret Harkness, the future author of *In Darkest London, A City Girl,* and other social novels. Maggie lived on her own in a seedy one-room flat in Bloomsbury and had tried teaching, nursing, and acting before discovering her talents as a writer. Her family was horrified, and Maggie had been forced to break off all contact with them, something Beatrice could no more imagine than she could picture immigrating to America. She wished that she could be more contented. "Why should I, wretched little frog, try to puff myself into a professional? If I could rid myself of that mischievous desire to achieve . . ." [39]

Once again Spencer came to the rescue by suggesting that Beatrice take her older sister's place as a volunteer rent collector in the East End. She could prepare for a career of social investigation while continuing her private studies. Like Alfred Marshall a generation before, Beatrice found herself drawn to London. She went off to a meeting of the Charity Organization Society, a private group dedicated to "scientific" or evidence-based charity and the gospel of self-help. "People should support themselves by their own earnings and efforts and . . . depend as little as possible on the state."[40] Women had traditionally been responsible for visiting the poor, but by the 1880s social work was becoming a respectable profession for spinsters and married women without children. The attractions were manifold. Beatrice observed: "It is distinctly advantageous to us to go amongst the poor . . . We can get from them an experience of life which is novel and interesting; the study of their lives and surrounding gives us the facts whether with we can attempt to solve the social problems."[41] Shortly afterward she thought, "If I could only devote my life to it . . ."[42] Yet, as of a few months earlier, Beatrice had made only two or three visits to the Katherine Houses in Whitechapel. "I can't get the training that I want without neglecting my duty," she sighed.[43]

One night that same month, Beatrice lay awake until dawn, too excited to sleep. Her partner at a neighbor's dinner party had been Joseph Chamberlain, the most important politician in England and the most commanding and charismatic man she had ever met.

Chamberlain was twenty-two years older than Beatrice and twice widowed, but he radiated youthful vigor and enthusiasm. Powerfully built with thick hair, a piercing gaze, and a curiously seductive voice, he was a natural leader. He had made a large fortune as a manufacturer of screws and bolts before moving into politics as the reform-minded mayor of Birmingham. For four years, he "parked, paved, assized, marketed, Gas and Watered and *improved*"[44] the grimy factory town into a model metropolis. After spending several years rebuilding the Liberal Party's crumbling political machine, he was rewarded with a cabinet post.

By the time Beatrice met Chamberlain, he had become the bad boy of English politics. His studied elegance—contrived with a monocle, a bespoke suit, and a fresh orchid on his lapel—hardly fit his rabble-rouser image. But in the stormy debates of that year, Chamberlain had focused voters' attention on the twin issues of poverty and voting rights. He had used his cabinet post to campaign for universal male suffrage, cheaper housing, and free land for farm laborers. He infuriated Conservatives by inviting the party's leader, Lord Salisbury, to visit Birmingham—only to serve as the keynote speaker at a rally protesting his presence. His rivals called him the "English Robespierre" and accused him of fomenting class hatred. Queen Victoria demanded that Chamberlain apologize after insulting the royal family at a working-class demonstration. Herbert Spencer told Beatrice that Chamberlain was "a man who may mean well, but who does and will do, an incalculable amount of mischief." [45]

As a disciple of Spencer's, Beatrice disapproved of virtually everything Chamberlain stood for, especially his populist appeals to voters' emotions. Nonetheless, he excited her. "I do, and don't, like him," she wrote in her diary. Sensing danger, she warned herself sternly that "talking to 'clever men' in society is a snare and delusion . . . Much better read their books." [46] She did not, however, follow her own advice.

Given that the Potters and Chamberlain were neighbors at Princes Gate, it was inevitable that the controversial Liberal politician and the fashionable, if slightly unconventional, Miss Potter should be constantly thrown together. The second time they met was that July, at Herbert Spencer's annual picnic. After spending the entire evening in conversation with Chamberlain, Beatrice admitted, "His personality interested me." [47] A couple of weeks later, she found herself seated between Chamberlain and an aristocrat with vast estates. "Whig peer talked of his own possessions, Chamberlain *passionately* of getting hold of other people's—for the masses," she joked. Though she found his political views distasteful, she was captivated by his "intellectual passions" and "any amount of *purpose.*" Beatrice thought to herself: "How I should like to study that man!" [48]

Beatrice was fooling herself. The social investigator and detached observer had already lost her footing and slipped into the "whirlpool" of emotions to which she was irresistibly drawn but that she could neither comprehend nor control. She agonized over whether or not she would be happy as Chamberlain's wife. Used to charming the men around her, she was unsatisfied by easy conquests. Starved for affection as a child, she longed to capture the attention of a man who was focused not on her but on some important pursuit. Chamberlain, who wanted to be prime minister, demanded blind loyalty from followers and family alike, and seduced crowds the way other men seduced women. He was the most powerful personality Beatrice had ever encountered. Might he not relish a strong mate?

She tried to analyze his peculiar fascination for her: "The common-places of love have always bored me," she wrote in her diary.

> But Joseph Chamberlain with gloom and seriousness, with his absence of any gallantry or faculty for saying pretty nothings, the simple way in which he assumes, almost asserts, that you stand on a level far beneath him and that all that concerns you is trivial; that you yourself are with-out importance in the world except in so far as you might be related to him; this sort of courtship (if it is to be called courtship) fascinates, at least, my imagination.[49]

Beatrice half expected Chamberlain to declare himself before the end of the London season, but no offer of marriage was forthcoming. Disappointed, Beatrice returned to Standish, where she "dreamt of future achievement or perchance of—love."[50] In September, Chamberlain's sister, Clara, invited her to visit Chamberlain's London house. Again Beatrice assumed that Chamberlain would propose. "Coming from such honest surroundings he surely *must* be straight in intention," she told herself.[51] Again, he did not, even though his intentions had become a topic of dis-cussion within the Potter family. Beatrice tried to lower her own and her sisters' expectations: "If, as Miss Chamberlain says, the Right Honorable gentleman takes 'a very conventional view of women,' I may be saved all temptation by my unconventionality. I certainly shall not hide it."[52]

In October, while Beatrice was at Standish obsessing over Chamberlain, the Liberal *Pall Mall Gazette* excerpted a first-person pamphlet about London's East End by a Congregational minister.[53] The series exposed deplorable housing conditions in gruesome detail that scandalized and galvanized the middle classes. Like Henry Mayhew's eyewitness accounts of poverty in the 1840s and 1850s, "The Bitter Cry of Outcast London" chronicled crowding, homelessness, low wages, disease, dirt, and starvation. But as Gertrude Himmelfarb points out, its shock value depended even more on its hints of promiscuity, prostitution, and incest:

> Immorality is but the natural outcome of conditions like these. . . . Ask if the men and women living together in these rookeries are married, and your simplicity will cause a smile. Nobody knows. Nobody cares. . . . Incest is common; and no form of vice and sensuality causes surprise or attracts attention.[54]

The immediate effect of the sensational expose was to goad Lord Salisbury, the prime minister, and Joseph Chamberlain into a debate over the cause of the crisis and the government's response. The Tory leader and major landowner in the East End blamed London's infrastructure boom for overcrowding, while Chamberlain placed the blame on urban property owners, whom he wanted to tax to pay for worker housing. Significantly, both the Tory and the Radical assumed that the responsibility for the housing crisis belonged to the government.

Beatrice dismissed the *Pall Mall* series as "shallow and sensational" and joined Spencer in regretting its political impact.[55] She recognized, however, that its first-person testimony and personal observations accounted for the extraordinary reception. She had, as she reminded herself, been led into tenements not by the spirit of charity but by the spirit of inquiry. The stupendous reaction to "The Bitter Cry"—and Spencer's hope that someone who shared his views would produce an effective rebuttal—made her eager to test her own powers of social diagnosis.

Beatrice decided to begin on relatively familiar ground by visiting her mother's poor relations in Bacup, in the heart of the cotton country. These included her beloved Dada, who had married the Potters' butler. It is a measure of the independence Beatrice enjoyed that she could undertake such a project. To avoid embarrassing her family and rendering her interviewees speechless, she went to Lancashire not as one of the "grand Potters" but merely as "Miss Jones." After a week, she wrote to her father, "Certainly the way to see industrial life is to live amongst the workers."[56]

She found what she had prepared herself to find: "Mere philanthropists are apt to overlook the existence of an independent working class and when they talk sentimentally of 'the people' they mean really the 'ne'er do weels.'" [57] She decided to write a piece about the independent poor. When she saw Spencer at Christmas, he urged her to publish her Bacup experiences. Actual observation of the "working man in his normal state" was the best antidote to "the pernicious tendency of political activity" on the part of Tories as well as Liberals toward higher taxes and more government provision.[58] Spencer promised to talk to the editor of the magazine *The Nineteenth Century*. Naturally, Beatrice, was extremely gratified, but she was also secretly amused that "the very embodiment of the 'pernicious tendency'" had not only captured his protégé's heart but was also about to invade the Potter family circle.[59]

Beatrice had invited Chamberlain and his two children to Standish at the New Year. She could see no way to resolve her divided feelings without a face-to-face meeting and she was sure that he must feel the same way: "My tortured state cannot long endure," she wrote in her diary. "The 'to be or not to be' will soon be settled." [60] Instead, the visit proved horribly awkward. The more Beatrice resisted Chamberlain's political views, the more forcefully he reiterated them, leading him to complain after one heated match that he felt as if he had been giving a speech. "I felt his curious scrutinizing eyes noting each movement as if he were anxious to ascertain whether I yielded to his absolute supremacy," Beatrice noted. When Chamberlain told her that he merely desired "intelligent sympathy" from women, she snidely accused him in her mind of really wanting "intelligent servility." Once again, he left without proposing.[61]

"If you believe in Herbert Spencer, you won't believe in me," Chamberlain had flung at Beatrice during their last exchange.[62] If he hoped to convert her, he was mistaken.

When Beatrice was a girl, her father used to tease Spencer for his habit of "walking against the tide of churchgoers" in the village near the Potter estate. "Won't work, my dear Spencer, won't work," Richard Potter would murmur.[63] But for two decades or more, Spencer had an entire generation of thinking men and women following his lead. His *Social Statics,* published within three years of the revolutions of 1848 throughout Europe, had celebrated the triumph of new economic and political freedoms over aristocratic privilege and made minimal government and maximum liberty the creed of middle-class progressives. Alfred Marshall imbibed more evolutionary theory from Spencer than from Darwin. Karl Marx sent Spencer a signed copy of the second edition of *Das Kapital* in the hopes that the philosopher's endorsement would boost its sales.[64]

By the early 1880s, however, Spencer was again walking against the tide. His latest book, *The Man Versus the State,* was a sweeping indictment of the steady growth of government regulation and taxation:

> Dictatorial measures, rapidly multiplied, have tended continually to narrow the liberties of individuals; and have done this in a double way. Regulations have been made in yearly-growing numbers, restraining the citizen in directions where his actions were previously unchecked, and compelling actions which previously he might perform or not as he liked; and at the same time heavier public burdens, chiefly local, have further restricted his freedom, by lessening that portion of his earnings which he can spend as he pleases, and augmenting the portion taken from him to be spent as public agents please.[65]

His brief for laissez-faire struck the reading public as a last-ditch defense of an outmoded, reactionary, and increasingly irrelevant doctrine. As Himmelfarb explains, not only were most thinking Victorians moving away from, or at least questioning, laissez-faire, but many now regretted that they had ever embraced it. She cites Arnold Toynbee, the Oxford economic historian, who apologized to a working-class audience: "We—the middle classes, I mean not merely the very rich—we have neglected you; instead of justice we have offered you charity."[66]

When Spencer's book appeared in 1884, he and Beatrice were closer than ever, spending several hours a day together. "I understand the working of Herbert Spencer's reason; but I do not understand the reason of Mr. Chamberlain's passion," she admitted.[67] She sent her signed copy of

The Man Versus the State to the mistress of Girton College at Cambridge with a note that shows that she remained the most ardent of Spencer's disciples. Referring to relief for the jobless, public schools, safety regulations, and other instances of large-scale "state intervention," she wrote, "I object to these gigantic experiments ... which flavor of inadequately— thought-out theories—the most dangerous of all social poisons ... the crude prescriptions of social quacks."[68]

Yet, she was ambivalent. Chamberlain had forced her to recognize that "social questions are the vital questions of today. They take the place of religion."[69] So while she was not prepared to embrace the new "time spirit" overnight, she was not ready to dismiss it out of hand, much less give up its virile and forceful proponent.[70]

When Chamberlain's sister invited her to visit Highbury, his massive new mansion in Birmingham, Beatrice went at once, assuming that the invitation originated with her chosen lover. But as soon as she arrived she was struck by the incompatibility of their tastes. She found nothing to praise about the "elaborately built red-brick house with numberless bow windows" and could barely repress a shudder when confronted with its vulgar interior of "elaborately-carved marble arches, its satin paper, rich hangings and choice watercolors ... forlornly grand. No books, no work, no music, not even a harmless antimacassar, to relieve the oppressive richness of the satin-covered furniture."

On Beatrice's first day there, John Bright, an elder statesman of the Liberal Party, regaled her with reminiscences of her mother's brilliance as "girl-hostess" to the teetotalers and Anti–Corn Law League enthusiasts who visited the Heyworth house forty years earlier, recalling Laurencina's political courage during the anti–Corn Law campaign. The old man's expression of admiration for her mother's political faculty and activism made Chamberlain's insistence that the women in his house have no independent opinions seem even more despotic. But Chamberlain's egotism attracted Beatrice. That evening at the Birmingham Town Hall, she watched him seduce a crowd of thousands and dominate it completely. Beatrice mocked the constituency as uneducated and unquestioning, hypnotized by Chamberlain's passionate speaking and not his ideas, but

seeing "the submission of the whole town to his autocratic rule," she admitted that her own surrender was inevitable. Chamberlain would rule the
same way at home and even her own feelings would betray her. ("When
feeling becomes strong, as it would do with me in marriage, it would
mean the absolute subordination of the reason to it.") Even knowing that
Chamberlain would make her miserable, Beatrice was caught. "His personality absorbs all my thought," she wrote in her diary.

The next morning, Chamberlain made a great point of taking Beatrice
on a tour of his vast new "orchid house." Beatrice declared that the only
flowers *she* loved were wildflowers, and feigned surprise when Chamberlain appeared annoyed. That evening, Beatrice thought she detected in his
looks and manner an "intense desire that I should *think and feel like him*"
and "jealousy of other influences." She took this to mean that his "suscep-
tibility" to her was growing.[71]

In January 1885, Chamberlain was launching the most radical and flamboyant campaign of his career. He enraged his fellow Liberals by warning
his working-class constituents that the franchise wouldn't lead to real
democracy unless they organized themselves politically. He scandalized
Conservatives by ratcheting up the rhetoric of class warfare with the famous phrase "I ask what ransom property will pay for the security which
it enjoys?"[72] Having administered Birmingham on the bold principle of
"high rates and a healthy city," Chamberlain took advantage of his cabinet
position to demand universal male suffrage, free secular education, and
"three acres and a cow" for those who preferred individual production
on the land to work for wages in the mine or the factory. These were to
be paid for by higher taxes on land, profits, and inheritances. Once again
Beatrice went to Birmingham and sat in the gallery while he delivered a
fiery peroration, and the next day, she again experienced the humiliation
of rejection. He did not propose.

Beatrice's obsessive, conflicted passion continued to torment her. She
despised herself for being infatuated with a domineering man, but also for
failing to conquer him. She had dared to hope for a life combining love
and intellectual achievement. She had, at different times, been ready to

sacrifice one for the sake of the other. Now it seemed to her that she had been deluded about her own potential from the start. "I see clearly that my intellectual faculty is only mirage, that I have no special mission" and "I have loved and lost; but possibly by my own willful mishandling, possibly also for my own happiness; but still lost."[73]

In her dejected state, she marveled that she had ever aspired to win an extraordinary man like Chamberlain and tortured herself with what might have been: "If I had from the first believed in that purpose, if the influence which formed me and the natural tendency of my character, if they had been different, I might have been his helpmate. It would not have been a happy life; it might have been a noble one."[74] On the first of August, she made her will: "In case of my death I should wish that all these diary-books, after being read (if he shall care to) by Father, should be sent to Carrie Darling [a friend]. Beatrice Potter."[75]

Somehow, she recovered from the blow. By the general election in early November 1885, suicide no longer dominated her thoughts, and she could feel a bit of her energy returning. As she watched her father set off for the polls to cast his vote, she was once again plotting her career as social investigator. That is when fate landed her another blow that threatened to bring independent action "to a sudden and disastrous end."[76] Richard Potter was brought back to Standish from the polls, having suffered a devastating paralytic stroke that did not, however, kill him.

As always, Beatrice poured her despair into her diary. "Companionizing a failing mind—a life without physical or mental activity—no work. Good God, how awful."[77] On New Year's Day, she drafted another will, begging the reader to destroy her diary after her death. "If Death comes it will be welcome," she wrote bitterly. "The position of an unmarried daughter at home is an unhappy one even for a strong woman: it is an impossible one for a weak one."[78]

Now, her old obsession with how she was to live, what purpose she would achieve, and whom she would love seemed like the purest hubris. "I am never at peace with myself now," she wrote in early February 1886. "The whole of my past life looks like an irretrievable blunder, the last two years like a nightmare! . . . When will pain cease?"[79]

• • •

The answer came a few days later in the form of a mighty roar that seemed to come from society's hidden depths. By noon on Monday, February 8, a crowd of ten thousand had braved fog and frost to assemble in Trafalgar Square. Some 2,500 police ringed the square's perimeter. They estimated that two-thirds of the crowd consisted of unemployed workmen, the rest radicals of every conceivable stripe. A Socialist speaker, chased off the base of Admiral Nelson's statue earlier that morning, clambered back up unhindered by the authorities. He waved a red flag defiantly and fired up the crowd with denunciations of "the authors of the present distress in England."[80] On behalf of his listeners, he demanded that Parliament provide public works jobs for "the tens of thousands of deserving men who were out of work through no fault of their own."[81] The audience cheered and swelled throughout the afternoon until it had grown fivefold.

The rally ended peacefully, but then the demonstrators began pouring into the main streets of the West End—Oxford Street, St. James Street, the Pall Mall—"cursing the authorities, attacking shops, sacking saloons, getting drunk, and smashing windows." The police were not only caught off guard but grossly outnumbered. For three hours or more, a "hooting howling mob" ruled the West End. Hundreds of shops were looted, anyone who looked like a foreigner was beaten, a Lord Limerick was pinned to the railings of his club, and carriages in Hyde Park were overturned and robbed. In addition, all street traffic in central London came to a standstill, Charing Cross Station was completely paralyzed, and by nightfall, St. James Street and Piccadilly were rivers of broken glass in which bits of jewelry, boots, clothing, and bottles bobbed.[82]

The riot sent a shudder of fear through London's wealthy West End. Though not a single life was lost in the riot and only a dozen rioters were arrested, most store owners complied with a police warning to keep their shops shuttered on Tuesday. A New York Times reporter derided the police's lack of preparedness—by Wednesday they were in a position to stop further riots should they occur, "what the police in Boston or New York would have promptly done—Monday afternoon"—sympathetically noting that this was the worst rioting London had seen since the infamous anti-Catholic riots of 1780.[83] Londoners agreed that there had not been looting on such a scale since Victoria took the throne nearly fifty years before, just after the first Reform Act passed.[84] The queen pronounced the riot "monstrous."[85]

The queen's assertion that the riot constituted "a momentary triumph for socialism" was almost certainly untrue.[86] But the episode did stimulate a good deal of activism and calls for action. Worried and conscience-stricken Londoners poured £79,000 into the Lord Mayor's relief fund for the unemployed and demanded that the money be dispensed. Beatrice's cousin Maggie Harkness began to plot a novel that she planned to call *Out of Work*.[87] Joseph Chamberlain, now a member of Prime Minister William Gladstone's new cabinet, set off a heated controversy by floating a public works scheme for the East End. Beatrice, exiled to the Potters' country estate and responsible not only for her father's care but also for a troubled younger sister and her father's equally troubled business affairs, was jolted out of her depression long enough to fire off a letter to the editor of the Liberal *Pall Mall Gazette* challenging the prevailing view of the causes and likely remedies for the crisis.

Beatrice braced herself for polite rejection. A letter from the journal's editor arrived by return post—too soon, she was sure, to contain any other message. But when she tore it open, she found a request for permission to publish "A Lady's View of the Unemployed" as an article under her byline. Beatrice shouted for joy. Her first real "bid for publicity" was a success; her thoughts and words had been judged worth listening to.[88] She had to believe that it was "a turning point in my life."[89]

Ten days after the riot, Beatrice had the pleasure of reading her own words in print for the first time: "I am a rent collector on a large block of working-class dwellings situated near the London Docks, designed and adapted to house the lowest class of working poor." She had tried to make just two points. Her first was that, contrary to what most philanthropists and politicians supposed, unemployment in the East End, "the great centre of odd jobs and indiscriminate charity," was the result not of "the national depression of trade" but of a dysfunctional and lopsided labor market. As traditional London trades such as shipbuilding and manufacturing had moved away, record numbers of unskilled farm laborers and foreign immigrants had been attracted by false or exaggerated reports of sky-high wages and jobs going begging. Her second point followed from the first: advertising public works jobs would inevitably attract more unskilled newcomers to the already overcrowded labor market, swelling the ranks of the jobless and depressing the wages of those who had work.[90]

One week after her piece appeared, she was reading another letter that made her heart pound and her hands shake. Chamberlain complimented her article and wanted to solicit her advice. As president of the Local Government Board, he was now responsible for poor relief. Would she meet to advise him on how to modify his plan to eliminate its pitfalls?[91] Her pride still hurt and fearing further humiliation, Beatrice refused to meet Chamberlain and instead sent him a critique of his plan. Chamberlain's response was a repetition of his "ransom" argument. As he put it, "the rich must pay to keep the poor alive."[92] He had taken from his experiences as the employer of thousands of workers the belief that government inaction in the face of widespread distress was no longer an option. The rules of governing were changing, irrespective of which party was in power. As wealth grew in tandem with the political power of the impoverished majority, a moral and political imperative to act where none had existed previously had emerged. Once the means to alleviate distress were available—and, more important, once the electorate knew that such means existed—doing nothing was no longer an option. Laissez-faire might have defined the moral high ground in the poorer, agrarian England of Ricardo's and Malthus's day, but any attempt to follow the precepts articulated in *The Man Versus the State* in this day and age was immoral, not to mention politically suicidal. He wrote: "My Department knows all about Paupers . . . I am convinced however that the suffering of the industrious non-pauper class is very great . . . What is to be done for them?"[93]

Beatrice was unmoved. "I fail to grasp the principle that something must be done," she persisted. Instead of proposing modifications, she advised him to do nothing. "I have no proposal to make except sternness from the state, and love and self-devotion from individuals," she wrote. She could not resist adding, half mockingly, half flirtatiously, that

> It is a ludicrous idea that an ordinary woman should be called upon
> to review the suggestion of her Majesty's ablest Minister, . . . especially
> when I know he has a slight opinion of even a superior woman's
> intelligence . . . and a dislike to any independence of thought.[94]

Chamberlain defended himself against her charges of misogyny and acknowledged that some of her objections were sound. Still, he did not disguise how repellent he found her underlying attitude:

> On the main question your letter is discouraging; but I fear it is true. I
> shall go on, however, as if it were not true, for if we once admit the im-
> possibility of remedying the evils of society, we shall all sink below the
> level of the brutes. Such a creed is the justification of absolute, unadul-
> terated selfishness.[95]

Chamberlain did as he promised, ignoring Beatrice's advice and embarking on one of the "gigantic experiments" of which Spencer so disapproved. The public works program that Chamberlain pushed through
was relatively modest in scale and lasted only a few months, but some
historians judge it to have been a major innovation.[96] For the first time,
government was treating unemployment as a social calamity rather than
an individual failure and taking responsibility for aiding the victims.

When Chamberlain indicated that he was tired of their epistolary bick-
ering, Beatrice impulsively fired off an angry confession that she loved
him—to her instant and bitter regret. "I have been humbled as far down
as a woman can be humbled," she told herself.[97] A doctor's suggestion that
she take her father to London during the season saved her life. Instead
of slipping back into her old depression and reaching for the laudanum
bottle, she moved her household to York House in Kensington. Toward
the end of April 1886, Beatrice joined her cousin Charlie Booth, a wealthy
philanthropist, in the most ambitious social research project ever carried
out in Britain.

Beatrice's cousin was in his forties, a tall and gawky figure with "the

complexion of a consumptive girl" and a deceptively mild manner.[98]
People who didn't know Charles Booth took him for a musician, professor, or priest—almost anything except what he was, the chief executive
of a large transatlantic shipping company. By day he busied himself with
share prices, new South American ports, and freight schedules. By night
he turned to his real passions, philanthropy and social science. He and his
wife, Mary, a niece of the historian Thomas Babington Macaulay, were an
unpretentious, active, and intellectually curious couple. Political Liberals
like the Potters and Heyworths, they were part of the "British Museum"
crowd of journalists, union leaders, political economists, and assorted
activists. Though Beatrice sometimes wrinkled her aquiline nose at the
Booths' casual housekeeping and odd guests, she spent as much time at
their haphazard mansion as she could.

The Like other civic-minded businessmen, Booth had long been active in
his local statistical society and shared the Victorian conviction that good
data were a prerequisite for effective social action. When Chamberlain was
mayor of Birmingham, he had done a survey at his behest and they had
become friends. His finding that more than a quarter of Birmingham's
school-age children were neither at home nor in school had led to a spate
of legislation. In the early 1880s, when poverty amid plenty was again becoming the rallying cry for critics of contemporary society, he was struck
by the widespread "sense of helplessness" that well-intentioned people felt
in the face of an apparently intractable problem and a bewildering array of
conflicting diagnoses and prescriptions. The trouble, he thought, was that
political economists had theories and activists had anecdotes, but neither
could supply an unbiased or complete description of the problem. It was
as if he had been asked to reorganize South American shipping routes
without the benefit of maps.

The previous spring, Booth had been outraged by an assertion by
some Socialists that more than one-quarter of London's population was
destitute. Suspecting but unable to prove that the figure was grossly exaggerated, he had been goaded into taking action. He determined that he
would survey every house and workshop, every street and every type of
employment, and learn the income, occupation, and circumstances of

every one of London's 4.5 million citizens. Using his own money, he would create a map of poverty in London.

Unlike Henry Mayhew, whom Beatrice admired, Booth had the vision, managerial experience, and technical sophistication to carry out this extraordinary plan. His first step, after consulting friends such as Alfred Marshall, who was teaching at Oxford at the time, and Samuel Barnett of the settlement house Toynbee Hall, was to recruit a research team. Beatrice accepted his invitation to attend the first meeting of the Board of Statistical Research at the London branch of his firm. She was, of course, the only woman. Booth explained that he aimed to get a "fair picture of the whole of London society" and presented them with an "elaborate and detailed plan" that involved the use, among other things, of truant officers as interviewers and census returns and charity records as cross-checks.[99] He wanted to start with the East End, which contained 1 million out of London's 4 million inhabitants:

> My only justification for taking up the subject in the way I have done is that this piece of London is supposed to contain the most destitute population in England, and to be, as it were, the focus of the problem of poverty in the midst of wealth, which is troubling the minds and hearts of so many people.[100]

Beatrice was deeply impressed that Booth had launched the ambitious undertaking singlehandedly. She could imagine herself taking on a similarly pioneering role in the future. This was, she realized, "just the sort of work I should like to undertake . . . if I were free."[101] She decided to apprentice herself to her cousin, so to speak, devoting as much time and absorbing as much knowledge as caring for her family would allow. Her role was not going to be collecting statistics. Instead she was to go into workshops and homes, make her own observations, and interview workers—starting with London's legendary dockworkers.

When the Potters returned to their country estate, Beatrice took advantage of her enforced isolation to fill a gap in her education. Augmenting statistics with personal observation and interviews seemed essential to her, but she grasped that good observation was impossible without some theory to separate the wheat from the chaff. Mayhew had failed to produce lasting insights because he had gathered facts indiscriminately. The need for some sort of framework made her eager to learn some economics and especially to learn how economic ideas had evolved, since "each fresh development corresponded with some unconscious observation of the leading features of the contemporary industrial life." [102]

After a day or two of fitful reading, Beatrice complained that political economy was "most hateful drudgery." [103] A mere two weeks later, however, she was satisfied that she had "broken the back of economical science." [104] She had finished—or at least skimmed—Mill's *A System of Logic* and Fawcett's *Manual of Political Economy* and was convinced that she had "gotten the gist" of what Smith, Ricardo, and Marshall had to say. By the first week of August, she was putting the finishing touches on a critique of English political economy. Except for Marx, whose work she read in the fall, the leading political economists were guilty of treating assumptions as if they were facts, she argued, chiding them for paying too little attention to collections of facts about actual behavior. She sent her indictment to Cousin Charlie, hoping that he would help her get it published. To her chagrin, Booth wrote back suggesting that she put the piece away and return to it in a year or two.

A year later, after she had completed her study of dockworkers, Booth took Beatrice to an exhibition of pre-Raphaelite artists in Manchester. Beatrice was so moved by the paintings that she resolved to turn her next study—of sweatshops in the tailoring trades—into a "picture" too. It occurred to her that if she wanted to "dramatize" her account, she would have to go underground. "I could not get at the picture without living among the actual workers. This I think I could do." [105]

Preparing for her debut role as a working girl took months. She spent the summer at Standish, immersed in "all the volumes, Blue Books, pamphlets and periodicals bearing on the subject of sweating that I could buy or borrow." [106] In the fall, she lived in a small East End hotel for six weeks while she spent eight to twelve hours a day at a cooperative tailoring workshop, learning how to sew. At night, when she wasn't too exhausted to fall into her bed, she went out to fashionable West End dinner parties.

By April 1888, she was ready to begin her underground investigation. She moved to a shabby East End rooming house. The next morning she threw on a set of shabby old clothes and went off on foot "to begin life as a working woman." In a few hours, she got her first taste of job hunting.

It gave her, she confessed, "a queer feeling." As she wrote in her diary, "No bills up, except for 'good tailoress' and at these places I daren't apply, feeling myself rather an imposter. I wandered on, until my heart sank with me, my legs and back began to ache, and I felt all the feeling of 'out o' work.' At last I summoned up courage." [107]

"It don't look as if you have been 'customed to much work," she heard again and again. Still, twenty-four hours later, in spite of her fear that everyone saw through her disguise and her awkward attempts to drop her *h*'s, Beatrice was sitting at a large table making a clumsy job of sewing a pair of trousers. Her fingers felt like sausages, and she had to rely on the kindness of a fellow worker, who, though she was paid by the piece, took the time to teach Beatrice the ropes, and of the "sweater" who sent out a girl to buy the trimmings that workers were expected to supply themselves.

The woman whose motto was "A woman, in all the relations of life, should be sought," gleefully transcribed the lyrics of a work girls' song:

> *If a girl likes a man, why should she not propose?*
> *Why should the little girls always be led by the nose?* [108]

As soon as the gas was lit, the heat was terrific. Beatrice's fingers were sore and her back ached. "Eight o'clock by the Brewery clock," cried out a shrill voice.

For this she received a shilling, the first she had ever earned. "A shilling a day is about the price of unskilled women's labor," she recorded in her diary when she got back to the rooming house.

She was back at 198 Mile End Road at eight thirty the next morning. She sewed buttonholes on trousers for a couple of days before "leaving this workshop and its inhabitants to work on its way day after day and to become to me only a memory." [109]

News of Beatrice's exploit spread quickly. In May, a House of Lords committee that was conducting an investigation of sweatshops invited her to testify. The *Pall Mall Gazette,* which covered the hearing, described her in glamorous terms as "tall, supple, dark with bright eyes" and her manner in the witness chair as "quite cool." [110] In the hearing, Beatrice slipped into her childhood habit of fibbing and claimed that she had spent three weeks instead of three days in the sweatshop. Fear of exposure kept her in an agony of suspense for weeks afterward. But when "Pages of a Workgirl's Diary" was published in the liberal journal the *Nineteenth Century,* in mid-October, its success was delicious. "It was the originality of the deed that has taken the public, more than the expression of it." [111] All the same, Beatrice admitted, an invitation to read her paper at Oxford made her ridiculously happy. ("If I have something to say I now know I can say it and say it well." [112]) Just before New Year's, despite a bad cold that kept her in bed, Beatrice was luxuriating in mentions in the daily papers and "even a bogus interview . . . telegraphed to America and Australia." [113]

Beatrice now felt emboldened to embark on a project that was hers alone. Ever since her week as "Miss Jones" in Bacup among the hand-loom weavers, she had been drawn to the idea of writing a history of the cooperative movement. Even the shock of reading in the *Pall Mall Gazette* that Joseph Chamberlain had been secretly engaged to a twenty-five-year-old American "aristocrat"—"a gasp—as if one had been stabbed—and then it was over" [114]—did not prevent Beatrice from plunging into Blue Books once more. Her cousin Charlie tried to convince her to write a treatise about women's work instead. So did Alfred Marshall, whom she met for the first time at Oxford and who invited her to lunch with him and Mary. He greatly admired her "Diary," he said. When she seized the opportunity to ask him what he thought of her new project, he told her dramatically that "if you devote yourself to the study of your own sex as an industrial factor, your name will be a household word two hundred years hence; if you write a history of Co-operation, it will be superseded or ignored in a few years."[115]

Beatrice, who preferred spending her time with men rather than with other women, and who suspected that Marshall thought her unqualified to write about one of his favorite subjects, had no intention of taking such advice. The matter was clinched when she impulsively joined with other socially prominent women in signing a petition opposing female suffrage. "I was at that time known to be an anti-feminist," she later explained.[116]

In fact, Beatrice was changing her mind about a great many things. Notwithstanding her spirited defense to Chamberlain of her laissez-faire philosophy, she was beginning to have doubts about her parents' and Spencer's libertarian creed. She and the old philosopher still saw each other often, but their disagreements were now so violent that they talked less and less about politics. In any case, she was spending more and more of her time with her cousin Charlie.

When Booth published the first volume of *Labour and Life of the People* in April 1889, the *Times* said it "draws the curtain behind which East London has been hidden from view," and singled out Beatrice's chapter on the London dockworkers for praise.[117] In June of that year, Beatrice attended a cooperative congress, where she became convinced that "the democracy of Consumers must be complemented by democracies of workers" if workers could ever hope to enforce hard-won agreements on pay and working hours.[118] The dramatic and wholly unexpected victory in August 1889 of striking London dockworkers, universally believed to be too egotistical and desperate to band together, impressed her greatly. "London is in ferment: Strikes are the order of the day, the new trade unionism with its magnificent conquest of the docks is striding along," Beatrice wrote in her diary.

> The socialists, led by a small set of able young men (Fabian Society) are manipulating London Radicals, ready at the first check-mate of trade unionism to voice a growing desire for state action; and I, from the

peculiarity of my social position, should be in the midst of all parties, sympathetic with all, allied with none."[119]

Instead of witnessing these stirring sights firsthand, Beatrice was far away in a hotel in the country, tethered to her semicomatose father, "exiled from the world of thought and action of other men and women." She worked on her book, but without any conviction that she could ever complete it. She was "sick to death of grappling with my subject. Was I made for brain work? Is any woman made for a purely intellectual life? ... The background to my life is inexpressibly depressing—Father lying like a log in his bed, a child, an animal, with less capacity for thought and feeling than my old pet, Don."[120]

As her frustration grew at being unable to sustain a career while nursing her father, Beatrice was more and more inclined to identify the plight of women with the oppression of workers. She thought about the houses of "all those respectable and highly successful men" and her sisters, to whom she remained close, had married:

> Then ... I struggle through an East End crowd of the wrecks, the waifs and strays, or I enter a debating society of working men and listen to the ever increasing cry of active brains doomed to the treadmill of manual labor—*for a career in which ability tells*—the bitter cry of the nineteenth century working man and the nineteenth century woman alike.[121]

The previous fall, when her father had told her, "I should like to see my little Bee married to a good strong fellow," Beatrice wrote in her journal, "I cannot, and will never, make the stupendous sacrifice of marriage."[122]

Beatrice became aware of Sidney Webb months before she met him. She read a book of essays published by the Fabian Society, a Socialist group that intended to win power the same way a Roman general named Fabius had won the Carthaginian war; gradually and with guerrilla tactics rather than head-on battles. She told a friend that "by far the most significant and interesting essay is by Sidney Webb."[123] Sidney returned the compliment in a review of the first volume of the Booth survey: "The only con-tributor with any literary talent is Miss Beatrice Potter."[124]

Their first encounter took place in Maggie Harkness's rooms in Bloomsbury. Beatrice had asked her cousin if she knew of any experts on cooperatives, and Maggie immediately thought of a Fabian who seemed to know everything. For Sidney, it was love at first sight, though he left their first meeting more despondent than euphoric. "She is too beauti-ful, too rich, too clever," he said to a friend.[125] Later he comforted himself with the thought that they belonged to the same social class—until Bea-trice corrected him. True, blue-collar men amused her. She enjoyed talking and smoking with union activists and cooperators in their cramped flats. But the self-importance of working men who, having "risen . . . within their own class," show up at London dinners and "introduce themselves as such without the least uneasiness for their reception" provoked her inner snob.[126] Beatrice thought Sidney looked like a cross between a Lon-don cardsharp and a German professor and mocked his "bourgeois black coat shiny with wear" and his dropped *h*'s. Unaccountably, she found that something about this "remarkable little man with a huge head on a tiny body" appealed to her.[127]

As his "huge head" indicated, Sidney was indeed a great brain. Like Alfred Marshall, he was very much a son of London's lower-middle class and had risen on the tide that was lifting white-collar workers. Born three years after Beatrice, he grew up over his parents' hairdressing shop near Leicester Square. His father, who moonlighted as a freelance bookkeeper in addition to cutting hair, was a radical democrat who had supported John Stuart Mill's parliamentary campaign. Sidney's mother, who made all the important decisions in the family, was determined that Sidney and his brother would grow up to be professionals. With a prodigious memory, a head for numbers, and a talent for test taking, Sidney excelled in school, got hired by a stockbroker at sixteen, and was offered a partnership in the firm at twenty-one. Instead of accepting, he took a civil service examina-tion and won an appointment in the Colonial Office. By then he had been bitten by the political bug and realized that he was more interested in power than in money. He continued to collect scholarships and degrees including one in law from the University of London, according to the Webbs' official biographer, Royden Harrison. By the time of the Trafalgar Square Riot and the subsequent Tory electoral victory, Sidney had found his true vocation as the brains of the Fabian Society.

The Fabians were odd ducks. Sidney embraced "collective ownership where ever practicable; collective regulation everywhere else; collective provision according to need for all the impotent and sufferers; and collective taxation in proportion to wealth, especially surplus wealth." But Fabian Socialism was associated mostly with local government and small-scale projects such as dairy cooperatives and government pawnshops. The Fabians' strategy differed from that of most other Socialist groups as well. Eschewing both electoral politics and revolution, they sought to introduce Socialism gradually by "impregnating all the existence of forces of society with Collectivist ideals and Collectivist principles." [128]

When Sidney was elected to the Fabian steering committee in 1887, the society had sixty-seven members, an annual income of £32, and a reputation for being a good place for pretty women to meet brilliant men and vice versa. The English historian G. M. Trevelyan described the Fabians as "intelligence officers without an army." They did not aspire to become a political party in Parliament. Instead, they hoped to influence policies, "the direction of the great hosts moving under other banners." [129] Sidney, who had concluded that "nothing in England is done without the consent of a small intellectual yet practical class in London not 2,000 in number" and that electoral politics was a rich man's game, called the Fabian strategy of infiltrating the establishment "permeating." [130]

Sidney's best friend and partner in crime was George Bernard Shaw, a witty Irish sprite of a man who dashed off theater reviews and acted as the Fabians' chief publicist. By the mid-1890s, the former Dublin rent collector and City of London stockbroker was convinced that social problems had economic origins. He proceeded to devote the second half of the 1880s to "mastering" economics. He and Sidney were both trying to work out what they believed and where to direct their energies. They attended regular meetings of a group organized by several professional economists at City of London College. Their studies led them to reject both utopian

Socialism and Marxist Communism. They called their goal Socialism, but it was Socialism with property, Parliament, and capitalists and without Marx or class warfare. They wished to tame and control the "Frankenstein" of free enterprise rather than to murder it, and to tax the rich rather than to annihilate them.[131]

Within a few weeks of meeting Sidney for the first time, Beatrice was beginning to think that "a socialist community in which there will be individual freedom and public property" might be viable—and attractive. "At last I am a socialist!" she declared.[132] Beatrice had caught the spirit of the times that prompted William Harcourt, a Liberal MP, to exclaim during the 1888 budget debate, "We are all socialists now."[133] As for Sidney, she was beginning to think of him as "one of the small body of men with whom I may sooner or later throw in my lot for good and all."[134]

At first, Beatrice had taken Sidney's obvious infatuation for granted and had been happy to let her intellectual dependence on him grow. When he confessed that he adored her and wanted to marry her, she had responded with a lecture against mixing love with work. She had insisted on being his collaborator, not his wife, and had banned any further allusion to "lower feelings."[135]

In 1891, Beatrice was again living in London for the season, nervously waiting for her book on cooperatives to appear in print and worrying about a series of lectures she had agreed to deliver. Sidney announced that he was quitting the civil service. He had no life other than work and felt "like the London cabhorse who could not be taken out of his shafts lest he fall down."[136] He once again brought up the forbidden topic, promising that if she relented he would let her live the outdoorsy, abstemious, hardworking, intensely social life she wanted. He suggested they write a book on trade unions together. After a year of telling Sidney "I do not love you," Beatrice finally said "yes."[137]

When Sidney sent Beatrice a full-length photograph of himself, she begged him to "let me have your head only—it is your head only that I am marrying . . . It is too hideous for anything."[138] She dreaded telling her family and friends. "The world will wonder," Beatrice wrote in her diary.

On the face of it, it seems an extraordinary end to the once brilliant Beatrice Potter . . . to marry an ugly little man with no social position and
less means, whose only recommendation so some may say is a certain
pushing ability. And I am not "in love," not as I was. But I see something
else in him . . . a fine intellect and a warmheartedness, a power of self-
subordination and self-devotion for the common good.[139]

Beatrice insisted that the engagement was to be a secret as long as her
father was alive. Only her sisters and a few intimate friends were told.
The Booths reacted coolly, and Herbert Spencer promptly dropped her as
literary executor, a position that had once been a source of great pride to
Beatrice.

Richard Potter died a few days before Beatrice's thirty-fourth birthday
on New Year's Day, 1892. He bequeathed his favorite daughter an annual
income of £1,506 a year and "incomparable luxury of freedom from all
care."[140] After the funeral, Beatrice spent a week at her prospective mother-
in-law's "ugly and small surroundings" in Park Village near Regents Park.
On July 23, 1892, Beatrice and Sidney were married in a registry office in
London. Beatrice recorded the event in her diary: "Exit Beatrice Potter.
Enter Beatrice Webb, or rather (Mrs.) Sidney Webb for I lose alas! both
names."[141]

When George Bernard Shaw paid his first extended visit to the newlyweds
more than a year later, in the late summer of 1893, Beatrice sized him up
as vain, flighty, and a born philanderer, but "a brilliant talker" who "liked
to flirt and was therefore a delightful companion." While Sidney was the
"organizer" of the Fabian junta, she put Shaw down as its "sparkle and
flavour."[142]

Shaw's first play, *Widowers' Houses*, had been put on at the Royalty
Theatre the previous December, and now he was at work on a new play
that operated on the same formula: taking one of Victorian society's "unspeakable subjects," in this case a reviled profession, and turning it into a
metaphor for the way the society really worked.[143]

All the past year the press had been full of stories about the Continent's legal brothels—high-end men's clubs where business was conducted—in which English girls were lured into sexual slavery. As usual, Shaw was recasting a social problem as an economic problem, and he wrote to another friend that "in all my plays my economic studies have played as important a part as knowledge of anatomy does in the works of Michael Angelo." [144] His character Mrs. Warren, who runs a high-end brothel in Vienna, is a practical businesswoman who understands that prostitution isn't about sex but about money. Just as he had wanted the audience to see that the slumlord of *Widowers' Houses* was not a villain but a symptom of a social system in which everyone was implicated, he now wished them to understand that in a society that drives women into prostitution, there were no innocents. "Nothing would please our sanctimonious British public more than to throw the whole guilt of Mrs. Warren's profession on Mrs. Warren herself," wrote Shaw in a preface, "Now the whole aim of my play is to throw that guilt on the British public itself." [145]

It was Beatrice who suggested that Shaw "should put on the stage a real modern lady of the governing class" rather than a stereotypical sentimental courtesan. [146] The result was Vivie Warren, the play's heroine and Mrs. Warren's Cambridge-educated daughter. Like Beatrice, Vivie is "attractive . . . sensible . . . self-possessed." Like Beatrice, Vivie escapes her class and sexual destiny. In the Guy de Maupassant story "Yvette," which supplied Shaw with his plot, birth is destiny. "There's no alternative," says Madame Obardi, the prostitute mother to Yvette, heroine of the story, but in the world that Vivie Warren inhabits—late Victorian England—there *is* an alternative. The discovery of Mrs. Warren's real business and the true source of the income that had paid for her daughter's Cambridge education shatter Vivie's innocence. But instead of killing herself or resigning herself to following in her mother's footsteps, Vivie takes up . . . accounting. "My work is not your work, and my way is not your way," she tells her mother. As with Beatrice, the choice not to repeat history was hers. In the final scene of *Mrs. Warren's Profession*, Vivie is alone onstage, at her writing desk, buried luxuriously in her "actuarial calculations."

Meanwhile, the real-life Vivie was living with her husband in a ten-room house a stone's throw from Parliament. She was joined in the library nearly every morning by Sidney and Shaw. The three of them drank coffee, smoked cigarettes, and gossiped while they edited the first three chapters of her and Sidney's book on trade unions.

Herbert George Wells, the wildly popular science-fiction writer, turned the Fabian trio into a quartet for a while before falling out with the Webbs. Afterward he satirized them in his 1910 novel *The New Machiavelli*, as Altiora and Oscar Bailey, a London power couple who steadfastly acquire and publish knowledge about public affairs in order to gain influence as the "centre of reference for all sorts of legislative proposals and political expedients." Having grown up among the ruling class like Beatrice, Altiora "discovered very early that the last thing influential people will do is work." Indolent but brilliant, she marries Oscar for his big forehead and industrious work habits, and under her steerage they become "the most formidable and distinguished couple conceivable." "Two people . . . who've planned to be a power—in an original way. And by Jove! They've done it!" says the narrator's companion.[147]

The term *think tank,* which connotes the growing role of the expert in public policy making, wasn't coined until World War II. Even then, according to the historian James A. Smith, *think tank* referred to a "secure room in which plans and strategies could be discussed."[148] Only in the 1950s and 1960s, after Rand and Brookings became familiar names, was *think tank* used to evoke private entities employing researchers, presumably independent and objective, that dispensed free, nonpartisan advice to civil servants and politicians. Yet a think tank is exactly what Beatrice and Sidney were—perhaps the very first and certainly one of the most effective—from the moment they married. "Of this they were unselfconsciously proud," mocked Wells. "The inside of the Baileys' wedding rings were engraved 'P.B.P., Pro Bono Publico.'"

The Webbs shrewdly realized that experts would become more indispensable the more ambitious democratically elected governments became. They shared the vision of a new mandarin class: "From the mere necessities of convenience elected bodies *must* avail themselves more and more of the services of expert officials ... We want to suggest that these expert officials must necessarily develop into a new class and a very powerful class ... We consider ourselves as amateur unpaid precursors of such a class." [149] This insight led them to found the London School of Economics, intended as a training ground for a new class of social engineers, and the *New Statesman* weekly newspaper.

Their "almost pretentiously matter-of-fact and unassuming" house at 41 Grosvenor Road, chosen by Beatrice, advertised their priorities. To stay fit, their daily regimen was Spartan. Middle-class comfort was sacrificed for the sake of books, articles, interviews, and testimony. In an era of coal scuttles and cold running water, the Webbs generally employed three research assistants but only two servants. "All efficient public careers," says Altiora in Wells's novel, "consist in the proper direction of secretaries." [150] Beatrice set for herself the task of converting England from laissez-faire to a society planned from the top down. To this end, they plotted ambitious research projects and organized their lives almost entirely to meet deadlines. The Webbs' friends debated "as to which of the two is before or after the other," but according to Wells, "[S]he ran him." [151] She was the CEO of the Webb enterprise; part visionary, part executive, and part strategist. Wells was sure that their joint career as idea brokers was "almost entirely her invention." In his view, Beatrice was "aggressive, imaginative, and had a great capacity for ideas" while Sidney "was almost destitute of initiative and could do nothing with ideas except remember and discuss them." [152]

Standing with her back to the fire, Beatrice glowed with "a gypsy splendor of black and red and silver all her own." Even while caricaturing her in his novel, Wells was forced to admit that Beatrice was beautiful, elegant, and "altogether exceptional." The other women he had met at Grosvenor House were either "severely rational or radiantly magnificent." [153] Beatrice was the only one who was both. Even as she talked of budgets, laws, and political machinations, she signaled her femininity by wearing outrageously expensive, flirty shoes.

A daddy's girl, Beatrice had always adored powerful men, flirting, and political gossip. The Fabians' strategy of permeation gave her an excuse to indulge all three. "I set myself to amuse and interest him, but seized every opportunity to insinuate sound doctrine and information" is a typical account of dining with a prime minister. Past, present, and future prime ministers were among her regular celebrity guests. Not in the slightest partisan, she was as happy to entertain a Tory as a Liberal. "But all of these have certain usefulness," she observed pragmatically.[154]

The think tank became a political salon at night. Once a week, the Webbs had a dinner for a dozen or so people. Once a month, they had a party for sixty or eighty. Guests did not come for the food. The Webbs practiced strict household economy to afford more research assistants, and Beatrice took more satisfaction in disciplining than in indulging her appetite.[155] Like Altoria, Beatrice fed her guests "with a shameless auster-ity that kept the conversation brilliant."[156] The price of attendance, said R. H. Tawney, an economic historian and frequent guest, was "participa-tion in one of the famous exercises in asceticism described by Mrs. Webb as dinners."[157] Yet everyone angled for invitations, and 41 Grosvenor Road was a center for quite an astonishing amount of political and social activ-ity. One "brilliant little luncheon" that Beatrice regarded as "typical of the 'Webb' set . . . in its mixture of opinions, classes, interests" included the Norwegian ambassador to London, a Tory MP, a Liberal MP, George Ber-nard Shaw, Bertrand Russell, the philosopher and future Nobel laureate, and a baroness who entertained every major politician and writer of the time.[158] Wells's novel identified Beatrice's singular skill as a hostess and its importance to the Webbs' career. "She got together all sorts of interesting people in or about the public service. She mixed the obscurely efficient with the ill-instructed famous and the rudderless rich, and got together in one room more of the factors in our strange jumble of a public life than had ever met easily before."[159]

A first-time visitor to the Baileys' tells the friend who has brought him, "'It's the oddest gathering.'"

"'Every one comes here,'" says the regular. "'Mostly we hate them like poison—jealousy—and little irritations—Altiora can be a horror at times—but we *have* to come.'"

"'Things are being done?'" asks the first man.

"'Oh!—no doubt of it. It's one of the parts of the British machinery—that doesn't show.'"[160]

Winston Churchill was one of those who *had* to come during the 1903 London season. He had been seated next to Beatrice at a Liberal dinner the previous year. Then the scion of an old aristocratic family, the Spencers, and son of a famous former Tory politician, and now a Tory member of Parliament, Churchill was thought to be at odds with the Conservative government. But he irritated Beatrice by declaring his opposition not just to trade unions but to public elementary school education. Worse, he talked about himself without pause from drinks to dessert, addressing Beatrice only to ask whether she knew someone who could get him statistics. "I never do my own brainwork that anyone else can do for me," he said breezily. "Egotistical, bumptious, shallow-minded and reactionary," Beatrice scrawled angrily in her diary that night. There is no record of his reaction to her.[161]

By the time Churchill reappeared chez Webb, he had defected to the Liberal opposition. The mood of the electorate was changing. After the costly and futile war against the Boers in South Africa, British voters were disillusioned with imperialism abroad and anxious about poverty at home. The Tories, who had been the ruling party for nearly a decade—first under the Marquess of Salisbury, then Arthur Balfour—proposed a protectionist plank but succeeded only in alienating working-class voters who feared higher food prices and lost jobs in export industries; Joseph Chamberlain, who drafted the Tory tariff "reform" program, was making the final speeches of his political career to virtually empty halls. Alfred Marshall, who had come out of retirement to blast Chamberlain and the protectionists, wondered if the distress of becoming entangled in a public controversy had even been necessary. Churchill was quick to sense the Tories' growing irrelevance and thought that the Liberals were ready to move to the left with the rest of the nation. He took this to mean that they had to address the social question . . . somehow. Without trade union votes, he reasoned, the Liberals had no chance of remaining in power, presuming they could get voted in to begin with.

At dinner, Beatrice sat Churchill to her right. He managed to make almost as bad an impression as the first time. The woman who had just decided to forswear not only alcohol but coffee and tobacco (tea remaining her "one concession to self-indulgence") came away convinced that "he drinks too much, talks too much, and does no thinking worthy of the name." She discussed the idea of a guaranteed "national minimum" standard of living with Churchill. He merely trotted out what she called "infant school economics." Her verdict: "He is completely ignorant of all social questions . . . and does not know it . . . He is evidently unaware to the most elementary objections to unrestricted competition." [162]

Near the end of his magisterial history of nineteenth-century England, the French historian Élie Halévy mentions several pieces of legislation of "almost revolutionary importance . . . passed on Churchill's initiative." [163] Among these measures was the "first attempt to introduce a minimun wage into the Labor code of Great Britain, which formed part of the Webbs' formula for the 'National Minimum.'"

Although Churchill found Beatrice overbearing—"I refuse to be shut up in a soup kitchen with Mrs. Sidney Webb," he later said—he was in fact aware of his own ignorance and soon began "living with Blue Books and sleeping with encyclopedias." [164] While he and Beatrice saw little of each other, Churchill plowed through most of the Fabian syllabus, from Booth's *Life and Labours* and Seebohm Rowntree's *Poverty: A Study of Town Life* to Beatrice and Sidney's *History of Trade Unionism* and *Industrial Democracy*. H. G. Wells, whose subject matter was shifting from science fiction to social engineering, became his favorite novelist. "I could pass an examination in them," Churchill boasted.[165] A great fan of Shaw's, he attended the opening of *Major Barbara*. At one point, he and his personal secretary, Eddie Marsh, spent hours wandering through some of Manchester's worst slums, just as Alfred Marshall had a generation earlier. "Fancy living in one of these streets—never seeing anything beautiful—never eating anything savory—*never saying anything clever!*" Churchill said to Marsh afterward.[166]

Such was Churchill's shock, reports his biographer William Manchester, that before long the former archconservative had become "a thunderer on the left." His inspirations were numerous, and political calculation played a role, but the specific arguments and remedies were mostly borrowed from Beatrice. By early 1906, when the Liberals won a majority by a landslide, Churchill was preaching what he called the "cause of the left-out millions" and urging "drawing a line" below which "we will not allow persons to live and labor"—precisely the policy that Beatrice had been urging on him.[167]

That October, Churchill gave a remarkable speech in Glasgow that not only went far beyond what the leaders of the Liberal Party had in mind but, according to the Churchill biographer Peter de Mendelssohn, "contained the nucleus of many essential elements of the programme with which the Labour Party obtained its overwhelming mandate for the 'silent revolution' of 1945–50."[168] In one of his most brilliant rhetorical performances, Churchill argued that the "whole tendency of civilization was towards the multiplication of the collective functions of society," which he believed rightly belonged to the state rather than private enterprise:

> I should like to see the State embark on various novel and adventuresome experiments. . . . I am of opinion that the State should increasingly assume the position of the reserve employer of labour. I am very sorry we have not got the railways of this country in our hands . . . and we are all agreed . . . that the State must increasingly and earnestly concern itself with the care of the sick and the aged, and above all, of the children. I look forward to the universal establishment of minimum standards of life and labour, and their progressive elevation as the increasing energies of production may permit . . . I do not want to see impaired the vigor of competition, but we can do much to mitigate the consequences of failure. . . . We want to have free competition upwards; we decline to allow free competition downwards. We do not want to pull down the structure of science and civilizations; but to spread a net over the abyss.[169]

No one has a greater claim to the invention of the *idea* of a government safety net—indeed, the modern welfare state—than Beatrice Webb. Looking back shortly before her death in 1943, she noted with satisfaction, "We saw that to the Government alone could be entrusted the provision for future generations . . . In short, we were led to the recognition of a new form of state, and one which may be called the 'house-keeping state,' as distinguished from the 'police state.'" [170]

The germ of the idea grew out of her and Sidney's study of trade unions. In their 1897 book *Industrial Democracy,* they had proposed sweeping national health and safety standards. A "national minimum" would shelter the entire workforce except for farm laborers and domestic servants. The most radical component was a national minimum wage. Arguing that "in the absence of regulation, the competition between trades tends to the creation and persistence in certain occupations of conditions of employment injurious to the nation as a whole," they insisted that a government-imposed floor under pay and working conditions was not, as Marx and Mill had assumed, inherently incompatible with the unimpeded productivity growth on which gains in real wages and living standards depended.[171] Indeed, they claimed, the cost to business of the regulations would be more than offset by fewer industrial accidents and a better-nourished, more alert workforce. Still, they admitted that the huge expansion of government power over private enterprise went far beyond anything that the trade union leaders, who mainly wanted a free hand to fight for higher pay and better working conditions, had in mind.

But the more ambitious idea of "a new form of state" didn't seize Beatrice until nearly a decade later. At the end of 1905, in the last days of the Tory Balfour government, she was appointed to a royal commission to reform the Poor Laws. The commission continued for three years under the new Liberal government. From the beginning, Webb clashed with the other commissioners. Seizing on Alfred Marshall's suggestion that "the cause of poverty is poverty," she defined the problem in absolute rather than relative terms. Inequality, and therefore poverty in the sense of having less than others, is inevitable, she reasoned, but destitution, "the condition of being without one or other of the necessaries of life, in such a way that health and strength, and even vitality, is so impaired as to eventually imperil life itself," is not.[172] Eliminating destitution would prevent the poverty of one generation from passing automatically to the next.

From her East End days, she could speak authoritatively about families in which "now in one and now in another of its members, sores, indigestion, headaches, rheumatism, bronchitis and bodily pains alternate almost ceaseless, to be periodically broken into by serious disease, and cut short by premature death"; or families where the father is out of work, "meaning as it does lack of food, clothing, firing, and decent housing conditions"; or about those who could not work: widows with little children, the aged, or the lunatic.[173]

Webb dismissed the notion that destitution could always be traced to a moral defect. Instead she listed five causes that corresponded to the main groups of destitute individuals and families: the sick, widows with young children, the aged, and people suffering from a variety of mental afflictions, from low intelligence to lunacy. The most troubling group were the able-bodied destitute. Their destitution, Beatrice argued, was the result of unemployment and chronic underemployment.

She made it clear that the urgent need to eliminate destitution didn't arise "from any sense that things are getting worse, but because our standards are, in all matters of social organization, becoming steadily higher," by which she meant both that the working classes now had the vote and that Britain's main international competitor, Germany, had adopted a variety of social welfare measures.[174]

The problem of Britain's existing policy was that it offered relief only to those desperate enough to seek it and did nothing to prevent destitution and dependency in the first place. As Beatrice put it, "all these activities of the Poor Law Authority in relieving the destitution of the sweated worker, did nothing to prevent sweating" or "saving men and women from being thrown out of work or in warding off the oncoming of illness . . . [stopping] the unnecessary killing and maiming of the workers by industrial accidents, or the wanton destruction of their health by insanitary housing and preventable industrial diseases." [175]

She wanted the government as much as possible to get out of the business of dispensing welfare and into the business of eliminating poverty's causes. "The very essence of the Policy of Prevention that what has to be supplied in every case is not relief but always treatment and the treatment appropriate to the need." [176] She never questioned whether the government or its experts knew how to treat the "disease of modern life" or worried about its cost. Inevitably, her ambitious vision of a "housekeeping state" that prevented rather than merely relieved poverty clashed with the more limited aims of the other commission members. As she had planned all along, she refused to sign the commission's report. Instead, she and Sidney spent the first nine months of 1908 pouring her vision into a document called *The Minority Report,* which she convinced three other commissioners to sign. Their "great collectivist document," as she called it,[177] envisioned a cradle-to-grave system designed to "secure a national minimum of civilized life . . . open to all alike, of both sexes and all classes, by which we meant sufficient nourishment and training when young, a living wage when able-bodied, treatment when sick, and a modest but secure livelihood when disabled or aged." [178]

Webb conceded that the idea would be regarded as utopian by other reformers and amounted to a repudiation of traditional, limited government. In contrast to the Socialist state, she believed, the household state was perfectly compatible with free markets and democracy. Indeed, she presented the welfare state as merely the next stage in the natural evolution of the liberal state. Yet the notion that the basic welfare of citizens was the responsibility of the state and that the government was obliged to guarantee a minimum standard of living to every citizen who could not provide it for himself was not only a departure from Spencer's ideal of a minimal state. Beatrice's idea broke with the whole tradition of Gladstonian liberalism that promised equality of opportunity but left results up to the individual and the market and went far beyond anything being discussed at the time by anyone except the Socialist fringe.

"It may make as great a difference in sociology and political science as Darwin's *Origin of Species* did in philosophy and natural history," her friend George Bernard Shaw predicted in his review of *The Minority Report.* "It is big and revolutionary and sensible and practical at the same time, which is just what is wanted to inspire and attract the new generation." He went on: "His right to live and the right of the community to his maintenance in health and efficiency are seen to be quite independent of his commercial profit for any private employer." That is, the objectives went far beyond Marshall's notion of increasing productivity and pay. "He is a cell of the social organism, and must be kept in health if the organism is to be kept in health." [179]

Ideas such as the minimum wage or minimum standards for leisure, safety, and health for all workplaces, the safety net, employment offices, fighting cyclical unemployment by shifting the timing of large government projects—basically, the whole notion that not only are the conditions that produce chronic poverty, or the more acute condition Webb called destitution, preventable, but it is the government's job to prevent them, and in order to prevent them the government must acquire new capabilities—have multiple authors. But nobody expressed these ideas so clearly, so systematically, or so often directly to the "mendicants of practicable proposals." And no one else found a phrase that made revolutionary changes seem evolutionary, even inevitable.

Making radical change seem evolutionary was Beatrice's genius. Even she, however, was surprised at how quickly ideas she and Sidney had thought were utopian in the 1890s seemed practical, or at least politically relevant, a decade later. Looking back at *Industrial Democracy* years later, she remarked with some measure of satisfaction, "What, in fact has characterized the social history of the present century has been the unavowed and often perfunctory adoption, in administration as well as in legislation of the policy of the National Minimum, formulated in this book." [180]

The year 1908 was a pivotal one for the new Liberal government. With unemployment and trade union militancy on the rise, an overwhelming Liberal majority in Parliament, and the "social problem" at the top of the political agenda, there was a general "scramble for new constructive ideas," Beatrice reported in her diary. The Webb's stock was soaring. "We happen just now to have a good many [ideas] to give away, hence the eagerness for our company," Beatrice continued happily. "Every politician one meets wants to be 'coached.' It is really quite comic. It seems to be quite irrelevant whether they are Conservatives, Liberals or Labor Party men—all alike have become mendicants for practicable proposals."[181] This justified a splurge, she decided, and ordered a new evening gown.

"Winston has mastered the Webb scheme," Beatrice crowed in October 1908 and remarked that they had "renewed our acquaintance." Having risen to her challenge, Churchill could now be classified as "brilliantly able—more than a phrase monger" in Beatrice's diary.[182]

For the first two years of the Liberal government led by Herbert Henry Asquith, Churchill's reforms had amounted to little more than rhetoric. Despite their electoral landslide in 1906, the Liberals had managed to push through very little of their program beyond restoring certain protections to trade unions. The logjam was broken in April 1908 when the thirty-three-year-old Churchill succeeded Lloyd George as president of the Board of Trade, a cabinet-level appointment. Beatrice found the cabinet shuffle "exciting."[183] The position, which combined many of the duties of the U.S. Departments of Labor and Commerce, entailed a grab bag of responsibilities: patent registration, company regulation, merchant shipping, railways, labor arbitration, and advising the foreign office on trade matters. Ultimately, Lloyd George's biographer points out that the president's responsibilities boiled down to ensuring "the smooth, orderly working of capitalism."[184] But Churchill proceeded to use the post to introduce radical social reforms. Remarked one of his friends at the time: "He is full of the poor whom he has just discovered. He thinks he is called by Providence to do something for them. 'Why have I always been kept safe within a hair's breadth of death,' he asked, 'except to do something for them?'"[185]

For the next two years, Churchill and Lloyd George, now Chancellor of the Exchequer, formed a partnership that ended, once and for all, "the old Gladstonian tradition of concentrating on libertarian political issues and leaving 'the condition of the people' to look after itself."[186] The new president of the Board of Trade did not wait to be sworn in before sitting up an entire night and writing the prime minister a long letter outlining his personal policy wish list. After the briefest of rhetorical flourishes—

"Dimly across gulfs of ignorance I see the outline of a policy which I call the Minimum Standard" [187]—Churchill defined his minimum in terms of five elements and listed them as his legislative priorities: unemployment insurance, disability insurance, compulsory education to age seventeen, public works jobs in road building or state afforestation in lieu of poor relief, and nationalization of the railways.

The recession that followed the panic of 1907 gave Churchill's proposals immediacy. Unemployment among trade union members, which was 5 percent at the end of 1907, doubled within a year. Alfred Marshall had shown that rising unemployment was usually caused by falling business activity. Now Beatrice demonstrated that unemployment, in turn, was a major cause of poverty. There was, however, no consensus that the government should, or could, intervene. Churchill intended to challenge the conventional wisdom. Aware that what he proposed far exceeded anything Asquith, the prime minister, had in mind, he urged the Liberal government to follow Germany's example and introduce unemployment and health insurance: "I say—thrust a big slice of Bismarckianism over the whole underside of our industrial system, & await the consequences whatever they may be with a good conscience." [188] He "is definitely casting in his lot with the [cause of] constructive state action," [189] Beatrice exulted, while concluding that "Lloyd George and Winston Churchill are the best of the [Liberal] party." [190] She appreciated Churchill's "capacity for quick appreciation and rapid execution of new ideas, whilst hardly comprehending the philosophy beneath them." [191]

Eventually the whole reform effort was swallowed up by the Liberals' struggle to wrest the veto from the House of Lords. What is remarkable is how much of it was passed, remarks William Manchester: "Before the ascendancy of Churchill and Lloyd George, all legislative attempts to provide relief for the unfortunate had failed." [192]

Webb lost the battle over social insurance, which was far less expensive than direct provision of services. But ultimately she won the war of the welfare state. She and Sidney had provided the rationale for the "assumption by the state of responsibility for an increasing number of services, administered by a growing class of experts, and supported by an expanded apparatus of the state." [193] *The Minority Report* was one of the first descriptions of the modern welfare state. Lord William Beveridge, the eponymous author of the 1942 Beveridge Plan who worked on *The Minority Report* as a researcher, later acknowledged that his design for the post–World War II British welfare state "stemmed from what all of us had imbibed from the Webbs." [194]

Chapter IV

Cross of Gold:
Fisher and the Money Illusion

These dear people, always starting their new experiments in such
deadly earnest; taking themselves so seriously; really believing
that they are getting better and better, wiser and wiser—certain
that they are getting richer and richer—every year, every month,
every day . . . Oh! It is fine, Mrs. Webb: it is fine.

—*H. Morse Stephens*[1]

"To America . . . when they might go to Russia, India or China. What
taste!" a Tory acquaintance sneered when Beatrice and Sidney announced
that they were off to New York in the spring of 1898.[2] As the putdown
implied, the Webbs were traveling not as tourists but social investigators.
Nonetheless, Beatrice went on a shopping spree, scooping up "silks and
satins, gloves, underclothing, furs and everything a sober-minded woman
of forty can want to inspire Americans and colonials with a true respect for
the refinements of collectivism."[3] If she was going to tour the world's social
laboratory, she intended to dazzle the locals.

The Americanization of the World did not become a best seller for another year or two, but the Webbs were surely familiar with the views of its
author, William Stead, editor of the *Pall Mall Gazette*. Stead was convinced
that Britain's economic future was tied to its former colony. The two
economies were more intertwined than in the eighteenth century, when
America was a British dominion, or in the 1860s, when the Union block-

ade of Southern ports during the American Civil War led to the terrible cotton famine in Lancashire. In the last quarter of the nineteenth century, imperial preferences notwithstanding, Britain imported more raw materials from the United States than from her own colonies.[4] The term "American invasion" was coined by British journalists more than half a century before the French revived it in the 1960s.[5]

In 1902, a London newspaper complained:

> The average citizen wakes in the morning at the sound of an American alarum clock; rises from his New England sheets, and shaves with his New York soap, and Yankee safety razor. He pulls on a pair of Boston boots over his socks from West Carolina, fastens his Connecticut braces, slips his Waterbury watch into his pocket and sits down to breakfast . . . Rising from his breakfast table the citizen rushes out, catches an electric tram made in New York, to Shepherds Bush, where he gets into a Yankee elevator, which takes him on to the American-fitted railway to the city. At his office of course everything is American. He sits on a Nebraska swivel chair, before a Michigan roll-top desk, writes his letter on a Syracuse typewriter, signing them with a New York fountain pen, and drying them with a blotting sheet from New England. The letter copies are put away in files manufactured in Grand Rapids.[6]

William Gladstone, the Liberal prime minister, had long predicted that the United States would inevitably wrest commercial supremacy from Britain. "While we have been advancing with this portentous rapidity," he observed in 1878, "America is passing us by as if in a canter."[7] In 1870, the most basic yardstick of average living standards, national income (GDP per person), was 25 percent higher in Britain. But for the next thirty years, the most basic measure of an economy's productive power and the key determinant of the average level of wages, nation income GDP per worker, rose nearly twice as fast in the United States.[8] One reason was that British citizens invested more than half their annual savings in America each year, more than at home and many times as much as in neighboring European countries.[9] The earnings from these investments added to Britain's national income in any given year, while the investments themselves enabled American business to modernize. Another reason was that the United States was the chosen destination of more than half of all British and an even larger fraction of Irish emigrants, almost 8 million men, women, and children over three decades. Canada, by contrast, attracted fewer than 15 percent of British emigrants even though its culture felt more "English."[10] Average incomes and living standards in the two countries had converged in the 1890s, prompting Gladstone, the British prime minister, to refer to Britain and the United States as a "momentous" example "to mankind for the first time in history of free institutions on a gigantic scale."[11]

The speed with which the United States had transformed itself from a predominantly rural, agrarian society to a predominantly industrial, urban one, and had become the global symbol of economic success, could not help but astonish. When Alfred Marshall toured the country in 1875, farming and, to a lesser extent, mining were the principal sources of American income. By the time the Webbs visited, wages and profits from manufacturing had grown to three times those from agriculture. Between 1880 and 1900, the annual income generated by America's largest industries quadrupled. Income from printing and publishing in the United States jumped fivefold, machinery and malt whisky, fourfold; iron and steel and men's clothing, threefold. Electrification, refrigeration, new cigarette making, milling, distilling and other machinery, entirely new industries based on products derived from oil and coal, the extension of rail, and telegraph links to virtually every community produced a revolution in the scale, structure, and reach of American firms. Remington (1816), Singer (1851), Standard Oil (1870), Diamond Match (1881), and American Tobacco (1890) were born. The era of mass distribution, mass production, and scientific management—big business, in short—had arrived.[12]

Beatrice and Sidney were more interested in the machinery of American government than in the operations of American business. Their first stop was Washington, D.C., an unfortunate choice given that the capital was gripped with war fever. An uprising in Cuba, Spanish repression, and the sinking of the USS *Maine* in Havana Bay, blamed on Spain, had ignited a powerful grassroots movement in favor of military intervention. Prowar sentiment wore down opposition by business and religious leaders and the Republican president, William McKinley. Beatrice and Sidney sat with more than a thousand spectators in the visitors' gallery of the House of Representatives when President McKinley signaled his change of heart. Beatrice was appalled by the House and unimpressed by the Senate. She formed a more favorable opinion of Teddy Roosevelt, undersecretary of the navy, who was a leading proponent of war. She found his talk "deliciously racy" when he was telling stories of life on a Western ranch, though she was disappointed that he spent most of their lunch "breathing forth blood and thunder" and seemed utterly indifferent to local government, the subject of her next book with Sidney.[13]

New York did not suit Beatrice any better.

> Noise noise nothing but noise . . . In the city your senses are disturbed, your ears are deafened, your eyes are wearied by a constant rush; your nerves and muscles are shaken and rattled in the streetcars; you are never left for one minute alone on the road, whether you travel by ordinary car or Pullman; doors are opened and slammed, passengers jump up and down, boys with papers, sweets, fruits, drinks, stream in and out and insist on your looking at their wares or force you to repel them rudely; conductors shut and open windows; light and put out the gas; the engine bell rings constantly, and now and again the steam whistle (more like a fog-horn than a whistle) thunders out warning of the train's approach.[14]

She shared none of Marshall's or the Americans' love of technology and the mobility that modern technology implied. Not only the trains and sky-scrapers but the "perfectly constructed telephones, skilled stenographers, express elevators, electric signals of all descriptions" left her cold. She was forced to acknowledge the "all-pervading and all-devouring 'executive' capacity of the American people" but attributed it to Americans' ready acceptance of "pecuniary self-interest as the one and only propelling motive." She quickly decided that a short attention span ("impatience") was the greatest flaw in the national character and was inclined to think that

the speed of travel, of communication, and of American life in general—
the "noise, confusion, rattle and bustle"—were merely so much wasted
energy. "All this appreciation of mechanical contrivances seems to us a
symptom of the American's disinclination to think beforehand," she commented.[15] She did not connect, as Marshall had, "nervous energy" with the
zeal to manage, organize, and get things done or the love of risk with innovation or social mobility.

When Beatrice and Sidney went west a few weeks later, their first stop
was in Pittsburgh. At Carnegie Steel, the "vast wealth-producing machine"
that eventually became U.S. Steel, she was struck by the extent to which
the technology had replaced labor. Henry Clay Frick gave Beatrice a tour
of the Homestead, Pennsylvania, steel plant. He told her that Carnegie
Steel had tripled its output while cutting the payroll from 3,400 to 3,000 in
the space of a few years. She described

> acres of shops filled with the most powerful and newest machinery.
> The place seemed almost deserted by human beings. The great engines,
> cranes and furnaces were struggling and panting, seemingly without the
> aid of man. It was only now and again that one espied a man enclosed
> in a little cabin, swinging midway between the ground and the rafts of
> the shed, and working some kind of electrical machine whereby millions
> of horse power was set in motion and directed . . . We gathered that the
> great technological advances in labour-saving had been made in the past
> ten years, largely in the application of electric power to work new auto-
> matic machinery. The "traveling buggies" which replaced labour in mov-
> ing the great masses of steel in and out of the rolling mills; the automatic
> machinery by which a single man swinging on a moving arm, opened
> the furnace door, lifted out the heated mass of steel, and swung it on to
> the buggy; and the automatic charging of the furnaces themselves with
> cradles of scrap steel also by a single man, were all introduced within the
> last six years.

She shrewdly attributed the phenomenal success of the Carnegie business
less to "the mechanical contrivances"—which were accessible to steelmak-

ers anywhere in the world—than to superior management and organization. She noted that all the owners were working members of the privately held firm that displayed "a lavishness towards all the brain-workers," who were provided with "elegant homes . . . outings to Europe, and endless treatings at home."[16]

The city, on the other hand, was

> a veritable Hell . . . which combines the smoke & dirt of the worst part of the Black country with the filthy drainage system of the most archaic Italian city. The people are a God-forsaken lot . . . tenements built back to back—crazy wooden structures crammed in between offices 20 stories high, streets narrow & crowded with electric trains rushing through at 20 miles an hour—altogether a most diabolic place with the corruptest of corrupt American governments.[17]

She saw what Charles Philip Trevelyan had warned her about before she arrived: Andrew Carnegie, whom she called "the reptile," and other Pittsburgh tycoons may have "given a Park or two, a free library or so," but had otherwise left the city "severely alone."[18] From Pittsburgh, Beatrice rushed to Chicago, Denver, Salt Lake City, and San Francisco. By the time she sailed to Hawaii on her way to New Zealand and Australia, she was convinced that the rest of the world had very little to learn from America's social experiment.

Before leaving New York, Beatrice had sought out a number of educators and economists. With the sole exception of Woodrow Wilson, later the president of Princeton University, American academics impressed her unfavorably. After a lunch at Columbia University, she compared one economics professor to "a superior elementary school teacher" and described the campus as "something between a hospital and the London polytechnic." Yale was nothing more than "a pretty little conventional university." About the economist who would become the author of the Sherman Antitrust Act, she grumbled that "from his appearance, manner and speech I should have taken him for a pushing and enterprising manager of a store in a Western city."[19]

. . .

Irving Fisher, the newest member of the economics faculty at Yale, was by no means mediocre or dull. His eyes sparkled with intelligence, his handshake was firm, he had the build and bearing of an athlete, and his face was boyishly handsome. At thirty years old, he was the only American economic theorist that Cambridge and the rest of England and the Continent took seriously. Alfred Marshall and Leon Walras, the French mathematical economist, considered him a genius.[20]

Named after Washington Irving, the author of "The Legend of Sleepy Hollow," Fisher was born in Saugerties, a farming community in New York's Hudson Valley, two years after the end of the Civil War. His grandfather was a farmer. His father, George Fisher, was a high-minded Evangelical minister. His mother, Ella Fisher, a former pupil of George Fisher's, was a strong-willed, devout young woman. When Irving was one year old, his father, who had recently graduated from Yale's divinity school, was offered a pulpit in Peace Dale, Rhode Island.

Peace Dale was a smaller, more picturesque version of Henry James's imaginary New England mill town in *The Ambassadors*. Like Woollett, Massachusetts, the town in which Irving Fisher spent his childhood was prosperous, paternalistic, and steeped in New England Evangelicalism. The town's leading citizen and benefactor was Rowland Hazard III, a Quaker, who had inherited the woolen mills his father had established and had founded a chemical company himself. Hazard was considered a progressive employer, having instituted profit sharing for his employees, and, on handing the reins of his business to his sons, he plunged into a second career as a political reformer. One of his daughters, Caroline, eventually became the president of Wellesley College. Hazard built the Congregational church and invited George Fisher to become its first pastor. Thanks to Hazard's patronage, Irving grew up in a rambling parsonage within sight of the Atlantic among "plain terms" and "honest minds."[21]

When Irving was thirteen, his father abruptly left his congregation and his family for a Wanderjahr in Europe, visiting great universities and cathedral towns. When he returned, a spirit of restlessness impelled him to take up temperance with great zeal, and he soon plunged his parish into bitter controversy. When his flock refused to support him, he resigned and moved his family into a cramped tenement in New Haven, Connecticut, where he enrolled Irving in a public school. For two years, the Fisher family relied on relatives for support.

When George Fisher finally found a new pulpit, it was 1,200 miles away on the Missouri-Kansas border. Missouri, Alfred Marshall wrote in 1875, was "full of swamps, negroes, Irishmen, agues, wildly luxuriant flowers & massive crops of . . . Indian corn" and St. Louis was a singularly "unhealthy town."[22] But neither heat nor humidity had deterred waves of migrants from the East who were attracted by rising wheat prices and appreciating farmland. Cameron, Missouri, was a jumble of rail yards, warehouses, feed lots, a few wide streets bordered by large houses, and at least one dozen churches. In the fall of 1883, when George Fisher left New Haven, he expected to send for his wife and younger son the following spring. Irving, now sixteen, went with his father as far as St. Louis, where he was to live with George Fisher's sister and brother-in-law, a professor at Washington University. Fisher had arranged for his son to finish high school at an elite Congregational preparatory school. His fervent hope was that his gifted older son would attend Yale and ultimately train for the ministry there.

When George Fisher continued his journey, father and son were separated for only the second time in their lives. They had expected to visit each other, but the distance between Cameron and St. Louis, three hundred or so miles, proved much too far in sleet, snow, and bitter cold. By the end of the first winter in Cameron, George Fisher was complaining of a strange lassitude, perpetual fever, and sinking spirits. These, it was quickly determined, were the classic symptoms of tuberculosis. In May, George, who was now very ill, made the long journey back east. He rejoined his wife and younger son in New Jersey at the home of a second brother-in-law, a physician who took the family in and cared for the dying man. Irving stayed behind. George Fisher insisted that he finish high school in St. Louis and take his college entrance examinations. By the time Irving graduated with honors, won a scholarship to Yale, and was reunited with his parents and younger brother in July 1884, his father was near death. He left behind a penniless widow, a ten-year-old, and seventeen-year-old Irving.

Fisher's grief was compounded by his disappointment at almost certainly having to postpone college, if not give it up altogether. The only prospect he could think of was to return to Missouri and look for a job on a farm that belonged to a classmate's family, where he had worked the previous summer.

A $500 legacy that his father had invested with a friend in Peace Dale and designated for Irving's education was discovered. If Fisher lived with his mother and brother in a three-room apartment near Yale, his mother could rent out the second bedroom to another student and he could tutor. Together with his scholarship and the legacy from his father, this measure would just suffice to allow him to enroll at Yale as planned in the fall of 1884.

J. Willard Gibbs, one of Yale's "great men," had observed that if the masses were going to run the world, they would need a lot of instruction. Few pursuits in that era required a university education, and the sacrifice of four years' wages was beyond the means of all but 1 to 2 percent of young men. But by the 1880s, a growing number of small-town American boys "longing to escape from the inferiorities of childhood" began to view college as a promising exit strategy. In America's new industrial and urban economy, opportunities for engineers, accountants, lawyers, and teachers, not to mention managers in the new corporate concerns, were multiplying fast enough to become a means other than the usual "grind of moneymaking"—that path being a long, uncertain, and arduous affair—to achieve distinction.[23]

A poor but ambitious boy like Fisher was lucky that family money was so commonplace an asset among Yale undergraduates that its social value was greatly depreciated. Popularity and fame required prowess as an athlete, an orator, a debater, a wit, or even a scholar. Fisher rowed for college, dazzled the faculty in the Junior Exhibition debating competition, won coveted prizes in mathematics and other subjects, and graduated first in his class of 124.[24] But the acme of his college career came the day he was tapped to become a member of the elite secret society Skull and Bones.

Muriel Rukeyser, the poet, observes in her biography of Gibbs that this was "the season for the young sciences" in America.[25] The 1880s saw an explosion of scientific activity in the United States and rising popular interest in science. Charles Darwin, Herbert Spencer, and Alfred Russel Wallace, the independent discoverer of evolution by natural selection, became household names; zoos and natural history museums proliferated; and the science-fiction novel was born. Edward Bellamy's *Looking Backward: 2000–1887*, which fast-forwarded readers to Boston in the year 2000, depicted a golden age of phonographs, credit cards, and radios.[26] New professional societies, scientific publications, and laboratories were popping up like mushrooms after a rain, while universities shifted their focus from training young men in the classics to turning out scientific and technical workers. The Brooklyn Bridge, which opened in Fisher's senior year in high school, symbolized the power of science to transform society. The rise of huge enterprises and entrepreneurial fortunes and the role of railroads in economic growth stimulated interest in finding new "instruments of mastery."[27] In the popular imagination, science was increasingly being seen as a way to get rich and, at the same time, a vehicle for solving the myriad social ills of poverty, disease, and ignorance.

Gibbs was a physicist, chemist, and mathematician, who was the first to apply the second law of thermodynamics to chemistry. The function of the scientist, he once said, was "to find the point of view from which the subject appears in its greatest simplicity."[28] He was a great champion of the mathematization of science. Mathematics was a lingua franca as well as a tool of analysis, so mathematics could promote the global exchange of ideas among scientists, just as Latin had done for centuries among botanists and anatomists. Gibbs almost never spoke at faculty meetings. But at the end of a fractious debate over whether mathematics could substitute for Greek or Latin to fulfill Yale's classical language requirement, he rose, coughed politely, and was heard to murmur as he left the room: "Mathematics *is* a language."[29]

By the time Fisher was a senior, he considered himself a mathematician but longed for more. "I want to know the truth about philosophy and religion."[30] He had rejected the idea of becoming a minister like his best friend from St. Louis, Will Eliot. At different times, he thought of the law, railways, public service, and science. "How much there is I want to do! I always feel that I haven't time to accomplish what I wish. I want to read much," he wrote in a letter to Eliot. "I want to write a great deal. I want to make money."[31] Ultimately, Fisher chose the "science of wealth."

American economics of the Progressive Era is typically described as utterly divorced from the British evolution toward collectivism and the welfare state. Except for a few so-called institutionalists such as Thorstein Veblen who were critical of commercial society, academic economics is supposed to have been dominated by Social Darwinists who defended laissez-faire and the rich and wanted to trample the poor.

It simply wasn't so. Virtually every founding member of the American Economic Association got his training and worldview at Berlin, Göttingen, or Munich and shared the values of the German "historical school," which, in opposition to English economics, explicitly condemned unfettered competition and championed the welfare state. Arthur Hadley, who held a chair in political economy at Yale, once referred snidely to American economists as "a large and influential body of men who are engaged in extending the functions of government."[32] The economics department at Yale was no exception, but for its most notorious member, William Graham Sumner. Warning that contemporary political labels— conservative versus liberal, left versus right—fit nineteenth-century intellectuals poorly if at all, the historian Richard Hofstadter once asked rhetorically about Sumner "whether, in the entire history of thought, there was ever a conservatism so utterly progressive?"[33] The son of an English immigrant laborer and an Episcopalian minister, Sumner was both a political economist and America's first sociologist. Austere and satirical with clipped, grizzled hair, Sumner taught himself "two Scandinavian tongues, Dutch, Spanish, Portuguese, Italian, Russian, and Polish" when he was in his late forties and turned "New Haven into a kind of Social-Darwinian pulpit" for his libertarian views. His lectures were described by contemporaries as "dogmatic," his manner "frigid," and his voice like "iron." [34] But his passionate delivery and fearless espousal of contrarian views made him the most popular lecturer at Yale.

Sumner was a great admirer of Charles Darwin and Herbert Spencer. He objected not only to bigger government but also to the activities of most private charities. His economics were thoroughly Malthusian, that is to say, deeply pessimistic, and, like Malthus, Ricardo, and Mill, he dismissed all schemes to speed up society's evolution as snake oil, stupidity, special pleading, or "jobbery." Yet, like the economic thinkers he admired, he was by no means a defender of the status quo. Trained as a minister, Sumner was as likely to condemn war as welfare, to defend striking unions as well as the banker Andrew Mellon's right to his millions, and to praise working women in the same breath as free trade. When Yale's president tried to forbid, on theological grounds, his use of Spencer's *Principles of Sociology* as a text, Sumner threatened to resign. Around the time of the Webbs' visit, Sumner enraged Yale's Republican alumni into calling for his dismissal, by publicly condemning the Monroe Doctrine and the Spanish-American War.

According to his son, Irving Norton Fisher, Fisher signed up for every course Sumner gave. He approached economics as a mathematician or an experimental scientist, describing himself to Eliot at one point as "your cold analytical mathematical friend." [35] Not long after Sumner introduced him to the subject, he concluded that a great deal might be accomplished by someone trained to think like a scientist—that is, coldly, analytically, mathematically.

When Fisher consulted Sumner about a dissertation topic in the spring of 1890, the latter's personal interests were shifting away from classical political economy to "the science of society." Already deep into his extraordinary spurt of late-life language acquisition, and busy collecting ethnographic data, Sumner wished to put sociology on a more rigorous footing. In this spirit, he suggested that Fisher write his doctoral thesis on mathematical economics, a subject that was both new and beyond the technical capability of most older economists, including himself. He lent

Fisher a volume by William Stanley Jevons, one of the pioneers of a new method involving calculus for analyzing consumer choice by focusing on marginal changes.

The impulse to make their respective fields more scientific was spurring ambitious young humanists to seize scientific knowledge as their special tool. The psychologist and philosopher William James, just back from Europe, wrote to a friend that year, "It seems to me that perhaps the time has come for psychology to begin to be a science." [36] Fisher already considered mathematics an ideal global currency that encouraged trade in ideas. He was intrigued by the prospect of strengthening the theoretical foundation of political economy, as Gibbs had done for that of chemistry:

> Before an engineer is fit to build the Brooklyn Bridge or to pronounce on it after it is built it is necessary to study mathematics, mechanics, the *theory* of stress and of the natural curve of a hanging rope, etc., etc. So also before applying political economy to railway rates, to the problems of trusts, to the explanation of some current crisis, it is best to develop the *theory* of political economy in general. [37]

Crude social Darwinists and their Socialist opponents identified competition as the distinctive feature of the modern economy, comparing the operation of markets to the laws of the jungle. But, like Marshall, Fisher was more impressed by the high degree of interdependence and cooperation among economic agents—households, firms, governments—and the large number of channels through which a given cause produced its ultimate effect.

Fisher occasionally went into New York City from New Haven, and on several occasions he visited the stock exchange. The operations of the market for securities were very much on his mind when he read the books Sumner had given him. He was struck that economists had evidently borrowed much of their vocabulary from the older science of physics; they spoke of "forces," "flows," "inflations," "expansions," and "contractions." But, as far as he knew, no one had actually tried to construct an actual

model of the process that resulted in "that beautiful and intricate equilibrium which manifests itself on the exchanges of a great city but of which
the causes and effects lie far outside." [38]

Marshall had conceived of modern economics as an "engine of analysis" and used graphs to trace the effects of external influences on individual markets. Fisher decided to construct a mathematical model of an
entire economy. He wanted to be able to trace how a market "calculated"
the prices that equated supply and demand. A practical Yankee, he wanted
a model that could spit out numerical solutions, not just mathematical symbols. Almost as soon as he started working on his model, Fisher
decided to take his project a step further and build a physical analog of
the equations in the form of a hydraulic machine. That is something that
probably would only have occurred to a tinkerer who had spent hundreds
of hours in a laboratory performing tedious and repetitive physical experiments. Fisher asked Gibbs, who was far more able than Sumner to grasp
what he was trying to accomplish, to read his manuscript.

In Fisher's model, everything depends on everything else. How much
of a commodity each consumer wants depends on how much of every
other commodity he wants. Fisher acknowledged that the bulky contraption, with its cisterns, valves, levers, balances, and cams applied "imper-
fectly at best" to the exchanges of "New York or Chicago" but he was in
no way apologetic. "Ideal suppositions are unavoidable in any science,"
wrote the doctoral candidate in his thesis. "The physicist has never fully
explained a single fact in the universe. He approximates only. The economist cannot hope to do better." [39]

The marvelous physical contraption let someone visualize the elements whose interplay produced prices. It also permitted someone to
"employ the mechanism as an instrument of investigation" of complicated and distant interconnections. For example, one could see how an
external shock to demand or supply in one market affected all the prices
and amounts produced in ten interrelated markets, altered prices and
quantities in all markets, and changed the incomes and choice of products purchased by various consumers. Fisher's hydraulic machine was
the precursor of the simulation and forecasting models with thousands

of equations that were developed in the 1960s to run on huge mainframe computers and that today's undergraduates can use to calculate a country's GDP on a notebook computer. Alas, both Fisher's original model and a replacement constructed in 1925 when the first was destroyed en route to an exhibition have been lost to posterity.

Fisher wrote his thesis over the summer of 1890. He showed his enthusiasm for mathematical methods by including an exhaustive survey and bibliography of applications. The economist Paul Samuelson called "Mathematical Investigations in the Theory of Value and Prices" "the greatest doctoral dissertation in economics ever written."[40] When it was published, the *Economic Journal,* founded by Alfred Marshall and other members of the newly inaugurated British Economic Association, greeted it as a work of genius. The reviewer, Francis Ysidro Edgeworth, an Oxford professor and one of the founders of mathematical economics, wrote, "We may at least predict to Dr. Fisher the degree of immortality which belongs to one who has deepened the foundations of the pure theory of Economics."[41] In the third edition of his *Principles,* Marshall, who could be stingy when acknowledging the contributions of other scholars, included not one but three highly flattering references to Fisher's "Investigations," referring to it as "brilliant," classing Fisher with "some of the profoundest thinkers in Germany and England."[42]

Fisher's picture of economic reality—especially his awareness of interdependence and mutual causation—affected how he thought on a great many other subjects. Just before he received his doctorate, he read a paper to the Yale Political Science Club proposing an international body representing all the nations of the world and dedicated to the peaceful settlement of international conflicts. According to the historian Barbara Tuchman, this paper later inspired the formation of the League to Enforce Peace, which, in turn, is credited with stimulating President Wilson's interest in forming a League of Nations.[43]

By the early 1890s in America, the post–Civil War railway, mining, and land boom had stalled, exposing the shaky nature of much of the finance. The panic of 1893 and the collapse of the stock market was followed by the worst depression in American history to date. Fisher's letters to his friend Will Eliot are as free of any mention of these calamities as Jane Austen's novels are of references to the Napoleonic Wars. Possibly his reason was similar to the author's: his mind was on love, courtship, and marriage.

Characteristically, Fisher deferred a return to Peace Dale, the scene of childhood happiness, until he could ride into town decked in a hero's laurels. When he left, he had been thirteen and deeply unhappy. When he returned, he was wrapped in the cloak of a "brilliant career at Yale, as prizeman, valedictorian, instructor and now professor of mathematics."[44] Like the hero of a Victorian three-decker novel, his object was to claim the heiress—or, since this was America, the boss's daughter. The way it happened was purely providential. It took little more than a glance for Irving to fall in love with a former childhood playmate; Margaret Hazard, or Margie, as she was called.

Margie Hazard was blessed with a sheltered upbringing, a serene temperament, and an unusually sweet nature. Her sister was the intellectual, Margie the creative, maternal one. Her faith in Irving was complete and unwavering. She was a wealthy heiress while he was penniless, yet she was convinced that she was the luckiest of women. They married in June 1893 with the entire population of Peace Dale there to witness the ceremony and take part in the festivities. The vows were read by no fewer than three ministers, and the wedding cake weighed fifty pounds. At a time when every day brought news of a fresh bankruptcy or bank run, some were scandalized by this display of conspicuous consumption. So it was just as well that the bridegroom and bride slipped away to New York, boarded an ocean liner, and sailed to Europe for a yearlong honeymoon.[45]

"All educated Americans, first or last, go to Europe," Ralph Waldo Emerson noted sourly. The rich went on the obligatory "grand tour" of capitals; the intellectually ambitious, on a "grand tour" of universities.[46] Zigzagging across England and the Continent by rail in 1893 and 1894, Fisher found it possible to exchange ideas with virtually every prominent member of the small, if growing, economics fraternity. His "little book . . . made a small path" for him through Europe, giving him instant entree to a cosmopolitan fraternity of economic thinkers. Fisher lunched in Vienna with Carl Menger, the founder of Austrian economics. He dined in Lausanne, Switzerland, with Leon Walras. Walras's brilliant student Vilfredo Pareto joined them, and Pareto's wife shocked Fisher by lighting up at tea. He stopped in Oxford to confer with the tongue-tied and absentminded Ysidro Edgeworth, and made a pilgrimage to Cambridge to pay his respects to Alfred Marshall, whose recently published *Principles* had cemented his stature as the world leader of theoretical economics.

Despite the hectic pace of his travels, Fisher still had plenty of time to attend the lectures of the mathematician Henri Poincaré in Paris and the German physicist Hermann Ludwig von Helmholtz in Berlin. When northern Europe got too cold for his now pregnant bride, he hired another student to take notes for him and took her to the French Riviera. Hiking in the Alps alone, he experienced an epiphany as he watched water tumble over rocks and gather in a pool below. "It suddenly occurred to me that while looking at a watering trough with its in-flow and out-flow, that the basic distinction needed to differentiate capital and income was substantially the same as the distinction between the water in that trough and the flow out of it."[47] After Fisher gave a talk at Oxford, Edgeworth told Margie, who had joined her husband, "Professor Fisher is soaring."[48]

By the time Fisher and his wife returned to New Haven and a brand-new, fully furnished mansion, thoughtfully provided by the Hazards, the mood of the nation was grim. By 1895, more than five hundred banks had failed. Fifteen thousand companies had declared bankruptcy. Unemployment had idled one in seven workers.[49] The fiery blast furnaces and behemoth textile mills were still standing, the vast railroads were still capable of hauling freight, and the prairies were still golden with wheat and corn. Yet amid this potential feast, there was a kind of famine. "Never within my memory have so many people literally starved to death as in the past few months," a Reverend T. De Witt Talmage told his congregation. "Have you noticed in the newspapers how many men and women here and there have been found dead, the post mortem examination stating that the cause of the death was hunger?"[50]

Popular anger against "money men" was ubiquitous. James J. Hill, the founder of the Great Northern Railway, wrote to a friend that "lately the people of the country are fixing their minds on social questions ... For ten years it has been 'railroads, monopolies and trusts' but now it shows up as those who have nothing against those who have something."[51] That year, a melodrama by Charles T. Dazey called *The War of Wealth* opened on Broadway.

The depression aggravated longstanding social and political conflicts. These were not primarily between classes: the 1894 Pullman strike notwithstanding, the number of strikes had drifted down each year. Rather, they were clashes between regions, between the representatives of different industries, between small and big business. Western silver miners blamed the collapse of metal prices on Washington. Farmers blamed their debt troubles on voracious eastern bankers and pitiless railroad monopolies. Of all constituencies, they were the angriest. The boom had passed them by, and the bust was driving them to despair. Amid a general slide in prices, those of wheat and corn and sugar had plunged two and three times more, on average, than other prices. Everyone connected with agriculture was drowning in debt, oppressed by high interest rates, and terrified of foreclosure.

The presidential campaign of 1896 became a referendum on the country's economic direction. The Democratic incumbent, Grover Cleveland, was repudiated by his own party. William Jennings Bryan, the thirty-six-year-old Democratic nominee, promised his western constituents that he would "nationalize the railroads, sweep away the tariff, and, most of all, rid them of financial tyranny." He called eastern bankers "the most merciless unscrupulous gang of speculators on earth," the "money monopoly."[52] His critics returned the compliment by calling him an anarchist, a Benedict Arnold, an Antichrist, "a mouthing, slobbering demagogue."[53] His Republican opponent, handpicked by James J. Hill and other tycoons, was William McKinley.

Six weeks before the election, Bryan had already nailed Wall Street onto his cross of gold when he took his presidential campaign up to the doors of one of the Jerichos of money power. At Yale University on the first day of the fall semester, the "Great Commoner" faced one thousand undergraduates and professors. Wild boos and cheers erupted as soon as the handsome bear of a man with flowing dark hair wearing a black felt hat and a string tie mounted the platform.

"The great paramount issue" of the 1896 election, he told them, was the seemingly obscure question of the nation's monetary standard. In a deep, slightly hoarse voice, Bryan inveighed against "a gold standard which starves everybody except the money changer and the money owner." The embrace of gold in the 1873 act banning the free coinage of silver had produced a money drought that he said was far more devastating to the nation's biggest industry, agriculture, than any act of nature. "If you make money scarce you make money dear," Bryan told the crowd. "If you make money dear you drive down the value of everything and when you have falling prices you have hard times." [54]

According to Bryan, the only way to revive the economy was to make money cheap again, that is, by tying the dollar to a more expansive standard than gold "that permits the nation to grow." He accused McKinley, and the "Gold Democrats" who supported him, of perversely trying to restore prosperity by continuing the disastrous "sound money" policies of the Democratic incumbent. In the fourth year of the depression, McKinley and the sound money clubs his supporters had organized were more worried about inflation and the London money market than the suffering at home. What was bad for the farmer was bad for America, including its small businessmen, professionals, and factory workers—and the students of New Haven. If the silver standard could ruin businessmen "with more rapidity than the gold standard has ruined them, my friends, it will be bad indeed," Bryan told the crowd, adding that the political "party that declares for a gold standard in substance declares for a continuation of hard times." [55]

At the mention of the Republican Party, the students began yelling, jeering, and bellowing McKinley's name. Uncharacteristically, Bryan lost his temper: "I have been so used to talking to young men who earn their own living," he shouted, "I hardly know what language to use to address myself to those who desire to be known, not as creators of wealth, but as the distributers of wealth which somebody else created." [56] A sophomore later recalled Bryan's next words, later denied by the candidate: "Ninety-nine out of a hundred students in this university are sons of the idle rich." The word *ninety-nine* had the effect of a starter gun at a race. "Ninety-Nine! Nine, Nine, Ninety-Nine!" the class of '99 chanted until Bryan abandoned the stage in disgust, leaving the money changers still in possession of their temple. [57] The *New York Times* crowed the next day: "YALE WOULD NOT LISTEN; Derisive Applause and a Brass Band Too Much for the Boy Orator—He Spoke Only About Twenty Minutes and Retired in Disgust." [58]

"I was never so *morally* aroused, I think, as against the 'silver craze,'" Irving Fisher confided to his friend Will Eliot in a letter. [59] "Social science is very immature and . . . it will be a very long time before it reaches the "therapeutic stage." [60]

Fisher had recently switched from Yale's Department of Mathematics to its Department of Political Economy, largely out of a desire to "make direct contact with the living age," although he privately was of the opinion that its members were "eaten with conceit" and overly confident that they knew how to fix the world's ills. He was as trim and upright as ever, keeping in shape with a regular regimen of jogging, rowing, and swimming, and was unflaggingly energetic. The only mark of time's passage was blindness in his left eye, the unhappy consequence of a squash accident. [61]

Fisher had few strong political convictions but found that, as a professor, "I am expected to have an opinion." [62] Misguided reform was likely to make matters worse, he warned. Sumner had expressed profound misgivings about populist measures in a pamphlet provocatively titled *The Absurd Effort to Make the World Over.* [63] In the depression that followed the panic of 1893, Fisher had written to his friend Will:

> Concerning social reform, I feel that the effort of philanthropists to apply therapeutics too soon is more likely to lead to evil than good. The very best the exhorter can do is to work *against* the "something must be done" spirit, and beg us to wait patiently until we know enough to base

action upon and meantime confine philanthropic endeavor to the narrow limits in which it has been proved successful—chiefly education . . .
There is so much *specific* reform at hand to be done—in city government, suppression of vice, education—that the hard workers of humanity need not and ought not talk, until "little" things are done, on broad
schemes for "society." [64]

As it turned out, Fisher did not follow his own advice. At a meeting of the
American Economic Association in November 1895, he was scandalized
at the "too lighthearted way" that some of his colleagues were willing to
"tamper with the currency" and delivered a stinging critique of the sil-
verite argument. "The effect of bimetallism, if silver is the cheaper metal,
must be a depreciation of the currency. . . . A system whose claim to recognition is based on considerations of justice has no excuse when beginning
with such a glaring injustice. Honest men must regard with horror the
proposal to reintroduce a ratio of 15½ to 1." Not surprisingly, the speech
attracted the gratified attention of the anti-Bryan forces. Fisher let himself
be recruited to the New York Reform Club's sound money committee and
the anti-Bryan campaign. [65]

How money became the paramount issue of the 1896 presidential campaign requires some explanation. Historically, money had been seen as
powerful, desirable, very likely evil, and mysterious, like natural calamities
or epidemics. Interest was traditionally treated with hostility by Christi-
anity as well as by Islam. Financial crises—from stock market crashes, to
bank runs, to hyperinflations—sparked popular rage against bankers. The
subject was shrouded in myth, superstition, and emotion.

In the 1880s and 1890s, both sides in the populist debate mytholo-
gized their metal of choice and demonized their opponents. The evil
speculator became a stock figure of fiction in the 1880s, his way paved by
the Nibelungs in Richard Wagner's opera *The Ring of the Nibelungs* and
Auguste Melmotte in Anthony Trollope's novel *The Way We Live Now.* The
historian Harold James comments:

The stories that the nineteenth century told about the global world built on a secular concept of original sin. The remedy that many thinkers then provided to the illegitimacy of the system echoed Luther's quite precisely (in a secular manner). Strong public authority was needed to overcome the legacy of that sin. There was a natural community that had been broken apart by creative greed, but the state could create its own order and community, and thus channel the destructive forces of dynamic capitalism. This strategy would offer the only way of avoiding the apocalyptic crisis prophesied by a Marx or Wagner or a Lord Salisbury." [66]

American economists were always more obsessed by "the money question" than their English counterparts were. But this was largely an accident of history, resulting partly from long-standing American suspicion of federal power and partly from the decision to issue unconvertible greenbacks during the Civil War and to allow them to be redeemed for gold twenty years later. More compelling, bank runs, financial panics, crises, and depressions occurred with dangerous frequency. The English financial writer Bagehot had observed in 1873:

> It is of great importance to point out that our industrial organisation is liable not only to irregular external accidents, but likewise to regular internal changes; that these changes make our credit system much more delicate at some times than at others; and that it is the recurrence of these periodical seasons of delicacy which has given rise to the notion that panics come according to a fixed rule—that every ten years or so we must have one of them. [67]

In the face of such traditional fatalism, it seems entirely plausible that an idealistic young scientist protested that the real problem was that money had not been sufficiently or rigorously studied and that a better understanding of money's role in economic affairs would minimize irrational decisions and unnecessary conflicts.

In his PhD thesis, which had been published in 1892, Fisher commented that "money, which is used to measure value and therefore affects all perception of economic values, is little studied and the mystery that surrounds money is at the root of many misunderstandings and miscalculations." Although the focus in that investigation was how prices were "computed" through the interaction of supply and demand, Fisher treated money first and foremost as a unit of measurement. The gold standard was a primitive mechanism for tying down its value. But even as he wrote his thesis, he developed a potentially better way. He saw that it might be possible to stabilize prices by tying the dollar's value in terms of gold to an index of consumer prices. Fisher saw equilibrium as a reference point and monetary disturbances as the source of instability. In *Mathematical Investigations,* he stressed that "the ideal statical condition assumed in our analysis is *never* satisfied in fact," which convinced him that "panics show a lack of equilibrium." [68]

Interest is the price that those with savings charge to let others use their capital, a real and valuable service. The value of capital, in turn, is determined by expectations on the part of savers and investors about the future stream of interest payments. Inflation and deflation produce large and arbitrary shifts in income and are the effects of the fluctuating value of the monetary standard—a rubber yardstick rather than a constant one—not conspiracies by demagogues and mobs on the one hand or Wall Street bankers on the other.

Having come to economics via the monetary debates that dominated American politics in the 1880s and 1890s, Fisher was concerned primarily with justice for debtors and lenders and with avoiding social conflicts that were exacerbated by unexpected changes in the value of money. As a practical matter, it was difficult for an individual businessman to distinguish between a change in the price of his product and an overall rise or fall in prices, and to adjust his contracts accordingly. Citizens who didn't understand that the value of their currency wasn't fixed tended to blame scapegoats—easterners, Jews, foreigners—for inflation or deflation.

The United States had followed Britain, Germany, and France by adopting the gold standard—a system in which each country's currency is pegged to a fixed amount of gold and hence to fixed amounts of other currencies. Think of it as a single world currency, the existence of which is a great convenience to those engaged in exporting and importing. Kansas farmers who sold wheat to British merchants wanted dollars with which to pay the men, railroads, seed suppliers, and so forth. So the British merchants were obliged to buy dollars with pounds. Obviously, knowing that £1 can always be exchanged for $5 is the next best thing, from the point of view of the importer, to a single currency.

Unfortunately, fixing exchange rates did not mean, as many supposed, that the value of the currency in terms of domestic goods was constant. Indeed, while the United States pegged the dollar to a certain amount of gold, the gold's and therefore the dollar's domestic purchasing power fluctuated by as much as 50 or 100 percent. In the 1880s the dollar's value rose sharply as a result of a worldwide shortage of gold, producing price deflation and a raging debate between those who wanted to remain on the gold standard and those who wanted to return to a silver standard.

American farmers, who tended to speculate in land and to use mortgages to finance land purchases, were net debtors. They argued that maintaining gold parity had restricted the supply of money and caused interest rates to rise and crop prices and farm income to fall. That meant that more tons of corn or wheat or bales of cotton were needed to pay off or service a given amount of debt than the farmer or bank had anticipated when the mortgage was issued. Fisher had some firsthand knowledge of western farming, thanks to his friendships with the sons of Missouri farmers during his two years in St. Louis and his summer jobs on their farms during college.

The free-silver movement reached its apogee in William Jennings Bryan's presidential campaign of 1896, and so did Fisher's defense of the gold standard. His monograph *Appreciation and Interest* had just been published. For him, the issue was distributive justice. Fisher conceded that the "silverites" were right in claiming that deflation had enriched lenders at the expense of debtors. But the argument for switching to a silver standard was faulty all the same. In fact, he claimed, declining interest rates automatically offset the rise in the real value of their debt. The market compensated . . . Bryan lost the election. Ironically, right around the time of his "Cross of Gold" speech, gold discoveries and other developments produced a spurt in the gold supply and led to a monetary expansion that brought the deflation of the 1880s and 1890s to an end without the United States abandoning the gold standard.

At thirty, Irving Fisher was the author of several books and monographs, a rising factor in the academic world, and the father of a growing family. He was stronger, handsomer, and more energetic than at twenty. He cycled, walked, and lifted weights. His favorite sport was swimming, and he let nothing—not even the chilly water off Maine or Margaret's anxiety—keep him out of the water in the summer.

In August 1899, Fisher was swimming off the family's summer estate when he nearly drowned. In the weeks that followed, he developed lassitude, a low fever, and a deepening depression, symptoms ominously reminiscent of the initial signs of his father's deadly illness. Shortly after his thirty-first birthday and his promotion to full professor, he received a death sentence in the form of a diagnosis of tuberculosis.

Tuberculosis was the nineteenth-century AIDS, writes historian Katherine Ott. At the turn of the twentieth century, one in three deaths in major cities was due to consumption, and most of the victims of the "white plague" were young adults. The course of the illness was ghastly, and recovery rates were depressingly low. Victims dreaded the loss of work and ostracism that inevitably followed a positive diagnosis. One man wrote that when the doctor told him it was tuberculosis, the words "might just as well have been followed by 'The Lord have mercy on your soul,'" for he felt himself a dead man.[69] Fisher remembered his dying father, shrunken and skeletal, totally deaf, unable to swallow anything but driblets of milk and barely capable of speech. George Fisher had lingered in this state for several agonizing weeks. When he died he was just fifty-three.

Most treatments involved rest, fresh air, and a rich diet. The "mind cure" blamed the disease on the stresses of modern life and coincided with a craze for all things Japanese or Chinese. Its practitioners urged individuals to take responsibility for their own health and advocated "calming one's fractious thoughts so that one might connect with the powerful and

invisible spirit of God, humanity or some other force."[70] This was the era
of positive thinking. In a speech at a local boys' school, Fisher explained
his personal philosophy:

> All greatness in this world consists largely of mental self control. Na-
> poleon compared his mind to a chest of drawers. He pulled one out,
> examined its contents, shut it up, and pulled out another. Mr. Pierpont
> Morgan is said to have a similar control. . . . What we call the *life* of a
> man consists simply of the stream of consciousness, of the succession of
> images which he allows to come before his mind. . . . It is in our power to
> so direct and choose our stream of consciousness as to form our charac-
> ter into whatever we desire.[71]

For the next six years, Fisher struggled to recover his health, natural
energy, and normal high spirits. He spent nearly half a year at the Ad-
irondack Cottage Sanitarium in Saranac, New York. The hospital was
operated by Dr. Edward L. Trudeau and modeled on the Alpine sanitaria
described by the German novelist Thomas Mann in *The Magic Mountain*.
The children were dispatched to their grandparents, and Margie accompanied Fisher to Saranac. They bought a raccoon coat and a copy of John
Greenleaf Whittier's long poem *Snow-Bound* to read aloud. "The doctors
fully expect me to get well but it takes time," Fisher wrote to Will Eliot in
December 1898. "I am sitting out on the porch, the thermometer is twenty
and the snow is two feet deep. I find ink freezes and so use pencil."[72] By
January 1901, Fisher's doctors told him that he was fully recovered, but it
took him three more years to regain his former energy.

Surviving tuberculosis awakened the latent preacher in Fisher. He became a crusader for public health and an advocate for healthy living and
mind control, to which he believed he owed his recovery. His triumph over
tuberculosis convinced Fisher that the extraordinary—such as the doubling of average life spans by the year 2000—was possible. When he met
Dr. John Harvey Kellogg, the crusader for "biologic living," Fisher told him
that he was "on a quest not like Ponce de León for the fountain of youth
but for ideas which may help us to lengthen and to enjoy youth."[73] Influ-

enced by Kellogg, Fisher conducted experiments on vegetarian diets with Yale athletes as subjects, applied for the job of secretary of the Smithsonian, and lobbied for the creation of a cabinet-level health department. In 1908, after the assassination of President McKinley, Fisher was appointed by his successor, Theodore Roosevelt, the youngest president of the United States, to the National Conservation Commission. The idea of conservation "has its center of gravity in our sense of obligation to posterity." It is hard for us in America, he noted, enjoying the present plenty, to realize that "we are scattering the substance that belongs to future generations."[74]

In 1906, the year of the San Francisco earthquake, Fisher declared Homo economicus, economic man, defunct and laissez-faire a dead ideology. At a plenary address at the American Association for the Advancement of Science, he called the acceptance of government regulation and welfare measures "the most remarkable change which economic opinion has undergone during the last fifty years."[75] Experience, he said, proved that the basic tenets of liberal theory—that individuals were the best judges of self-interest and that the pursuit of self-interest would produce the maximum good for society—were wrong. Government regulation and voluntary reform movements—the nineteenth-century equivalent of today's NGOs—were not merely not harmful, but necessary. Indeed, he said, they had already done much to preserve the natural environment and to improve public health. He said that if he had to choose between Sumner's extreme libertarianism or Socialism, he would choose the latter, and he enumerated many instances in which what is good for the individual is not good for society and, therefore, laissez-faire is not the right policy.

The Nature of Capital and Income, published in 1906, reflected Fisher's growing understanding of capital as a stream of future services and interest in conservation. Fisher was convinced that economic interdependence—epitomized by urbanization, economic specialization, and globalization—implied a greater need for data, education, coordination, and intervention on the part of the government. He argued that concern for the future required prevention and conservation. His near-death experience gave his concern for economic efficiency and prevention of waste even greater urgency. Perry Mehrling, a historian of economic thought, says that Fisher was influenced by a contemporary of Adam Smith, John Rae, to define "interest"—including profits, rents, and wages—as the value of the stream of services from the machines, land, and human capital accumulated in the past. All of Fisher's reforms, observes Mehrling, from increasing life spans to preventing depressions and wars, were directed at increasing current national wealth.[76]

Today, economists talk of bounded rationality, externalities, and market failures. Fisher spoke of ignorance and lack of self-control. More radically, he argued that even when individuals behaved totally rationally, the combined effect of their actions might reduce collective well-being. "Not only is it false that men, when let alone, will always follow their best interests, but it is false that when they do, they will always thereby best serve society."[77] One special kind of ignorance, he explained, involved treating the present as if it was the norm. Life spans were only half as long as they could be, he thought. Productivity was just half as great. His most intriguing insight was that the mind plays tricks. He called it the money illusion. For Fisher, inflation and deflation—all changes in the overall level of prices—were evils because they misled people into making bad decisions. At the level of the economy, the money illusion meant that it took a long time for businesses and consumers to adjust to changes in prices and interest rates.

He drew two conclusions from the recognition that Homo sapiens were not Homo economicus, hyperrational calculating machines. First, there was a strong case for compulsory education. Second, there was an even stronger case for regulating individual behavior, whether via fire regulations in tenements or the prohibition of gambling or alcohol and other drugs: "It is not true that ignorant parents are justified in imposing their ideas of education upon their children; hence the problem of child-labor, instead of concerning only the individual, as was at one time thought, has important and far-reaching relations to society as a whole."[78]

Fisher went much further than Marshall in pointing out the limits of the competitive model. In this he anticipated the entire arc of economic theory after World War II. "Even when government intervention is impracticable or inadvisable, there will still be good reason for attempting betterment of conditions through the influence of one class upon another, hence come social agitations."[79]

Even if everyone were perfectly rational, the pursuit of self-interest wouldn't necessarily add up to socially desirable results. "Individual action would never give rise to a system of city parks, or even to any useful system of streets," he said. Hence, he rejected privatizing either the money supply, as Spencer advocated, or the "still more astonishing suggestion [is] that even the police function of government should be left to private hand, that police corps should be simply voluntary vigilance committees, somewhat like the old-fashioned fire companies, and that rivalry between these companies would secure better service than now obtained through government police!"[80]

Fisher's illness was followed by an extraordinary burst of creativity. In the space of five or six years, he poured out ideas that had germinated during his enforced exile, in which he had embraced Indian philosophy and meditation practices.

> Last night at sunset I sat out there like an Indian, thinking of nothing, but *feeling* the serenity and power of the Universe . . . Those subconscious impressions of three years or more of depression, fear and worry are still in my mental storehouse, but buried, I hope permanently. It has been only by hard work and the application of auto-suggestion that the blue devils have been crowded down at all. I have to confess that the chief thing the matter with me after the first year was fear . . . Optimism is not a question of what evil exists nor of what we may expect of the future. A man may believe the world unhappy and that the earth will grow cold and dead, that he himself is to have pain, loss of friends, honor, wealth—and yet be an optimist.[81]

The year 1907 was an unsettled one in the financial markets. Fisher was hurrying to finish a new book, *The Rate of Interest*, that he subtitled "Its Nature, Determination and Relation to Economic Phenomena."

For the first time, he explicitly couched his theory in terms of a lack of foresight: periods of speculation and depression are the result of inequality of foresight. "A panic is always the result of unforeseen conditions and among those unforeseen conditions and partly as a result of other unforeseen conditions is scarcity of money on loan." [82]

If inflation or deflation were correctly anticipated, explains Perry Mehrling, interest rates in money markets would adjust instantly and perfectly. If lenders expected the overall price level to rise, they would require borrowers to pay a commensurately higher interest rate. If they expected the overall price level to fall, they would be willing to accept a commensurately lower interest rate. By the same reasoning, if borrowers expected higher inflation, they would realize that paying nominally higher interest rates would not affect their real rate of return. If borrowers expected deflation, they would realize that they could afford to pay only a commensurately lower nominal interest rate. In short, if anticipations were correct, changes in the price level would have no effect on real output or employment. The trouble, of course, is that such perfect foresight is impossible: "Their failure to [correctly anticipate deflation] results in an unexpected loss to the debtor and an unexpected gain to the creditor." [83]

Now Fisher reversed his earlier position that changes in the value of money have a negligible effect in real economic activity and decided that interest rates didn't adjust that smoothly or completely after all to compensate for the effects of changes in the dollar purchasing power, so stable prices are necessary for a fair and transparent monetary system:

> The bimetallists were partially right in their claim that the creditor class were gainers during the period of falling prices in the two decades 1875–1895. The situation has been the exact opposite during the decade 1896–1906. We must not make the mistake, however, of assuming that the enrichment of the debtor-class during the last decade atones for the impoverishment of that class during the previous two decades; for the personnel of social classes changes rapidly. Nor must we make the mistake of assuming that the debtor-class consists of the poor. *The typical debtor of to-day is the stockholder, and the typical creditor, the bondholder.*[84]

Under the prevailing monetary standard, the U.S. dollar was fixed in terms of gold *weight* but not in terms of gold *value* or purchasing power. That guaranteed that the dollar's domestic purchasing power would rise and fall with the supply and demand for money. Most people, even the most sophisticated investors and businessmen, viewed the dollar as a measure of value, and found it difficult or impossible to track or anticipate changes in value. Inflation and deflation were harmful because investors, consumers, and businessmen couldn't predict them perfectly—or even accurately gauge their magnitude in the present and recent past. Decisions made on the basis of faulty expectations necessarily resulted in faulty investment decisions and, from the vantage point of the economy as a whole, too much investment in some areas and too little in others: "reckless wastefulness, for which there must be a day of reckoning in the form of a commercial crisis."[85]

Consider what had happened in a period of sixty years. First, Charles Dickens, Henry Mayhew, and Karl Marx described a world in which the material conditions that had condemned mankind to poverty since time immemorial were becoming less fixed and more malleable. In 1848, Karl Marx showed how competition drove businesses to produce more with the same resources, but argued that no means existed for converting production increases into higher wages and living standards.

Then, in the 1880s, Alfred Marshall discovered that an ingenious mechanism of competition encouraged business owners to make constant, incremental improvements in productivity that accumulated *over time* and, simultaneously, compelled them to spread the gains in the form of higher wages or lower prices, again, over time. As long as productivity determined wages and living standards, people could alter material conditions individually and collectively by becoming more productive.

Beatrice Webb invented the *welfare state* as well as her own vocation as social investigator. Sociologist Mill argued that a welfare state would eventually absorb the entire tax revenue, and Marx insisted that such a state was a non sequitur. Webb, on the other hand, showed that destitution was preventable and that providing education, sanitation, food, medical, and other forms of in-kind assistance would increase private sector productivity and wages more than taxing would decrease it. In other words, helping the poor become literate, better fed, and less disease-ridden was more likely to raise rather than be a drag on economic growth.

Irving Fisher was the first to realize how powerfully money affected the real economy and to make the case that government could increase economic stability by managing money better. By pinpointing a single common cause for the seemingly opposite ills of inflation and deflation, he identified a potential instrument—control of the money supply—that government could use to moderate or even avoid inflationary booms or deflationary depressions.

Chapter V

Creative Destruction:
Schumpeter and Economic Evolution

Historical development which would normally take centuries
[was] compressed into two or three decades.

—*Rosa Luxemburg,* The Accumulation of Capital, *1913*[1]

On November 4, 1907, news of a run on the Knickerbocker Trust Company in New York set off a stampede on the London Stock Exchange. Frightened investors seeking safety overwhelmed the Bank of England with demands for gold bullion. Threatened with a massive outflow of reserves, the bank responded by raising the interest rate it charged other banks for overnight loans. In the midst of the panic, Joseph Alois Schumpeter, gentleman, and Gladys Ricarde-Seaver, spinster, quietly tied the knot in a registry office near Paddington Station. By the time the discount rate reached 7 percent for the first time in forty years,[2] the newlyweds had left for Cairo, Egypt.

At twenty-four, Schumpeter was already a man of the world. He was born in a small factory town in what is now the Czech Republic, the only son of a third-generation textile manufacturer. After his father's untimely death in a hunting accident at the age of thirty-one, his mother, Johanna, who was and would remain the most important person in Schumpeter's life, resolved to go to any lengths to ensure a brilliant future for her four-year-old son. Largely for his sake, she contrived to move to Graz, a pleasant university town. When her darling turned eleven, she married a retired general thirty years her senior, and convinced her husband to relocate the family to Vienna to a luxurious apartment off the Ringstrasse. Thanks to his stepfather's aristocratic connections, Schumpeter attended an ancient academy for the sons of nobles. At the Theresianum he acquired, in addition to skill in fencing and riding, fluency in no fewer than five classical and modern foreign languages, and invaluable social connections—as well as the flowery manners, promiscuous habits, and extravagant tastes of the titled set. His elite education came at an emotional price. The alter ego of the young social climber was the solitary and driven scholar who read philosophy and sociology texts. In a school where "to be a bit stupid" implied an aristocratic lineage, his brains and obsessive middle-class work habits only underscored his parvenu status.[3] Short, slight, and swarthy, with an unusually high forehead and penetrating, slightly protuberant eyes, his exotic appearance provoked sly taunts about "eastern" (read Jewish) origins. He compensated by excelling in riding, fencing, and verbal wit, and learned to bury his private anxieties under a blasé, ironic, world-weary, manner.

By 1901, the eighteen-year-old Schumpeter had succeeded in graduating from the Theresianum with top honors and gaining admission to the University of Vienna—the first step in what he and his mother hoped would be a rapid climb to the most rarefied reaches of Viennese society. True, Vienna's "first society" was essentially limited to the emperor and his court. But the occupant of a university chair or a cabinet post could breach the "second society," where the clever and capable mingled with aristocrats and plutocrats. By the time Schumpeter was a first-year law student, he already pictured himself as the empire's youngest university professor and the emperor's most trusted economic advisor.

Belle époque Vienna is often depicted by historians as a decadent, complacent, ossified society, and the Austro-Hungarian Empire as hopelessly backward compared with England, France, or Germany. Oszkár Jászi called Austria-Hungary "a defeated empire from the economic point of view."[4] Carl Schorske described the bourgeoisie as politically passive.[5] Erich Streissler bemoaned the dearth of entrepreneurship and the tendency of the sons of businessmen—Ludwig Wittgenstein and Franz Kafka, among others—to choose the arts over industry.[6] In Joseph Roth's 1932 decline-and-fall novel about the Hapsburg monarchy, *The Radetzky March*, a Viennese aristocrat, Count Chojnicki, attributes the empire's seemingly moribund state to the fact that "this is the age of electricity, not of alchemy." Pointing to a brilliantly lit electrical chandelier, he exclaims, "In Franz Joseph's castle they still burn candles!"[7]

In reality, Vienna was infatuated by modernity. As early as 1883, tens of thousands of visitors were being whisked by electric train to the Prater, the vast "people's park" on the Danube, to witness the biggest display of light and power the world had ever seen, the International Electricity Exhibition. Six hundred exhibitors, including America's Westinghouse and GE, Germany's AEG, and Sweden's Ericsson, displayed fifteen accumulators, fifty-two boilers, sixty-five motors, and one hundred and fifty electrical generators. In the "telephonic music room" visitors could "hear the music and singing going on in the opera without moving one step."[8] In another exhibit they could listen to the latest bulletin from a Budapest-based news service for telephone subscribers. The bravest could let themselves be whisked to the top of a 220-foot rotunda, blazing with 250,000 candlepower, in a glass-enclosed hydraulic elevator. At the opening ceremony, Crown Prince Rudolf spoke proudly of "a sea of light" that would "radiate" from Vienna to the rest of the world."[9]

In the race to electrify, Vienna compared favorably to London. Telephone service began in 1881. Trams replaced horse-drawn buses in 1897. By 1906, when the opera *Die Elektriker* opened, the ten inner districts of the city had power. "Elektrokultur" became the slogan of Vienna's entrepreneurs. Every housewife dreamed of an electric hookup that could banish soot and fumes from her kitchen. Factory owners wanted state-of-the-art factories with electric lighting and electric power–driven machinery. Physicians such as Sigmund Freud were eager to try electroshock therapy on their patients. Ludwig Wittgenstein's grandmother took his cousin, the six-year-old Friedrich Hayek, out for a spin in her new electric car.

While it was true that Emperor Franz Joseph spurned elevators and electric lighting, his son, Crown Prince Rudolf, was a staunch supporter of modern industry. Austria had the fourth-largest concentration of commerce and manufactures in Europe, producing steel, textiles, paper, chemicals, and cars. Vienna served as the administrative, trade, and financial center for a vast hinterland that provided the new megalopolises of Europe with food, fuel, and raw materials. The economic upswing of the late 1870s through the mid-1880s had created a boom in exports of sugar and textiles as well as in railway construction. By the late 1880s, electrification had displaced the railroads as the principal magnet for new investment.

The city's architecture reflected not only imperial but also bourgeois aspirations. The Ringstrasse, the wide boulevard that encircled the inner city with its neoclassical parliament building and baroque opera house, interspersed with the mansions of the "Boulevard Barons," reflected the stupefying progress of the times. The luxury rental apartment, or *Mietpalais*, rather than the villa, attracted the nouveau riche, the parvenu, the social climber. Middle-class, multiethnic, and determinedly monoculturally German, Vienna was the destination of choice for refugees from the rest of the empire—especially after 1867, when liberals in the cabinet promoted Jewish emancipation along with economic modernization. Many of the recent immigrants became peddlers or small shopkeepers. Their sons mostly went into professions such as law or medicine that didn't require attendance at an elite prep school, or banking, journalism, or the arts where a university degree was not needed. The preponderance of Jews in law, medicine, banking, journalism, and the arts stoked resentment, especially in bad times. As one historian put it, "Anti-Semitism rose as the stock market fell." [10]

Economic data contradict the stereotype of economic decadence. Not only did the economy grow three times as fast between 1870 and 1913 compared with the previous forty years, but per capita income doubled in real terms in that period, even as the population surged. True, Vienna suffered the same chronic shortage of housing, sewers, clean drinking water, and paved streets as Victorian London. But the economic historian David

Good cites "overwhelming" evidence that "the Empire's problems were not ones of economic failure but of economic success."[11]

By 1901, when Schumpeter began his legal studies at the University of Vienna, it had become one of Europe's great research centers in mathematics, medicine, psychology, physics, philosophy, and economics faculties. While German economics was dominated by a "historical school"—led by Gustav Schmoller at the University of Berlin—that despised abstraction and worshipped the imperial state, Carl Menger had established Vienna as the ideological and intellectual antipode of Berlin and the Continental leader in theoretical economics.

Law occupied a loftier status and connoted a more liberal education in German-speaking universities than in English or American ones. Along with canon and Roman law, Schumpeter took courses in history, philosophy, and economics. Schumpeter soon decided that economics, especially theoretical, interested him more than the law. Menger was now too old and infirm to lecture, but the intellectual battle he had long waged against the historical school was now led by two brilliant disciples, Eugen von Böhm-Bawerk and Friedrich von Wieser. Schumpeter attended their seminars where he distinguished himself from older classmates such as Ludwig von Mises, a prominent liberal; and Otto Bauer and Rudolf Hilferding, two of Europe's leading Marxists, by his "cool, scientific detachment" and "playful" manner.[12] In his final year at university, the twenty-two-year-old succeeded in publishing no fewer than three articles in Böhm-Bawerk's statistical monthly. By the time he was awarded his doctor of laws degree in early 1906, he had identified himself as a firm supporter of modern economy theory, or "English economics" as it was known in Berlin despite its well-known Austrian, French, and American contributors. His first postgraduate publication was a long and provocative essay, "On the Mathematical Method in Theoretical Economics."

Having declared his colors, so to speak, Schumpeter embarked on the intellectual "grand tour" so beloved by university graduates in the German-speaking world. Nursing an unspoken ambition to reconcile the

warring schools of economic thought and perhaps eventually to breach
the Continent's most important university, he spent the spring term at
the University of Berlin, getting to know the chief representatives of the
German Historical School. In the summer, he spent several weeks in Paris,
where he heard the mathematician Henri Poincaré lecture on physics. His
ultimate destination was England, the country he admired as "the apo-
theosis of the civilization of capitalism" and whose economists he had
studied exhaustively.[13]

Arriving in London in early fall, Schumpeter proceeded to live the
strangely double life for which his education had prepared him. His public persona was that of a gregarious, slightly flamboyant, pleasure-loving
Continental aristocrat. Finding English manners, customs, and institutions "completely congenial," he affected the routines of London's fashionable set. He rented a flat on Princes Square, near Hyde Park. He ordered
his suits on Savile Row. He kept his own hunter for daily rides on Rotten
Row. He spent evenings at plays and dinners, weekends at house parties in
the country.

His other, equally elegant persona divided his waking hours between
the austere and deliberately plebeian precincts of the London School of
Economics, and the British Museum's hushed, high-ceilinged reading
room, where he made a point of working at the same table where the over-
weight, sloppily attired Karl Marx had composed *Das Kapital.* Convinced
that truly original thinkers had their best ideas before turning thirty,
and intent on reaching the first rung of his projected academic career
as quickly as possible, the twenty-four year old Schumpeter was racing
against a self-imposed deadline.

Before leaving Vienna, he had outlined two books that he intended to
write. In the first he would introduce "English" or theoretical economics
to a hostile, ill-informed German audience. The second would be reserved
for a groundbreaking contribution that he confidently expected to revolutionize economic theory. Like most intellectuals of his generation, Schumpeter was fascinated by the implications for society of Darwin's theory of
natural selection. Was it not ironic, he thought, that while constant change

was a hallmark of modern times, economic theory ignored the process that was making the economy more productive, specialized, and complex. Economic evolution was elusive, like "certain natural processes" to which Marcel Proust would allude in *Swann's Way* that were "so gradual that . . . even if we are able to distinguish successively, each of the different states, we are still spared the actual sensation of change." [14] Economists made do with the assumption that the economy merely cloned itself year after year, becoming marginally bigger over time, but remaining essentially unchanged in all other particulars. True, if the economist wished to analyze how a small change in one economic variable affected all the others, "static" theory fit reality like a well-tailored suit. But existing theory fit badly or not at all if the change in question was large, or the timeframe too long to safely ignore structural changes in technology, the labor force, or institutions. And, contrary to the claims of German economists, economic history could do no better. Science, unlike history, was general. History concerned itself with what did happen, science with what could or could not happen under specific circumstances. That's what made science an instrument of mastery. If economics was to be science it too had to be general.

What was needed was a theory of economic development and the new university graduate intended to produce it. Schumpeter's ambition was to replace static with dynamic economic theory, just as Darwin had swept aside traditional with evolutionary biology. As he would observe years later, he thought that his idea was "exactly the same as the idea . . . of Karl Marx," who had also had a "vision of economic evolution as a distinct process generated by the economic system itself." [15]

On at least one occasion, Schumpeter took the train to Cambridge to seek Alfred Marshall's advice. Now sixty-five and in poor health, Marshall was still recovering from a confrontation over Britain's free trade policy with Joseph Chamberlain, the present colonial secretary, and was on the verge of relinquishing his Cambridge chair. Nonetheless, he gave the brash young man breakfast at Balliol Croft and listened tolerantly as he described his plans for constructing a theory of economic evolution.

As Schumpeter was well aware, such a theory had been one of the older man's unfulfilled dreams. Although Marshall had borrowed tools from physics to analyze the interplay of supply and demand in individual markets, he had always insisted that economic phenomena more closely resembled biological than mechanical processes, and criticized earlier economists for assuming that institutions, technology, and human behavior were fixed. Indeed, he introduced the latest edition of his *Principles of Economics* with the claim that "The Mecca of an economist lies in economic biology." [16] Nonetheless, Marshall had stopped short of developing a theory of economic development as Schumpeter proposed to do. Evidently the English Oracle expressed some skepticism in the course of the hour-long conversation because Schumpeter told him in parting that their exchange had cast him as "an indiscreet lover bent on an adventurous marriage and you a benevolent old uncle trying to persuade me to desist." Marshall had replied good-humoredly, "And this is as it should be. For if there is anything to it, the uncle will preach in vain." [17]

Possibly Schumpeter had been hinting that he was about to embark on adventure of a more personal nature. He was having an affair with a woman twelve years his senior. Gladys Ricarde-Seaver was English, upper class, and "stunningly beautiful," the daughter of a "high Anglican church official" who had grown up in a spacious villa in the shadow of St. Peter's Cathedral near Harrow. Although biographers have been able to agree on very little else about her, including her age, public records strongly suggest that she was one of Webb's "glorious spinsters[s]" living the "British museum life." Thirty-six years old and never married, Ricarde-Seaver probably met Schumpeter at the LSE, which catered to women like her who were interested in feminism, social reform, and the popular Fabian cause of eugenics. The decision to marry was sudden, and neither bride nor groom seems to have anticipated parental approval, if indeed they notified their parents in advance. Gladys's brother was the only witness at the civil ceremony in Piccadilly. While Anglophilia and the prospect of an aristocratic alliance might have accounted for Schumpeter's impulsive decision, a pregnancy scare would seem to be a plausible motive. Later Schumpeter hinted to friends that Ricarde-Seaver had taken advantage of his youthful naïveté and when Ricarde-Seaver died in 1933 she left what was by then a considerable estate to a birth control society.[18]

By breaking his private rule against wedlock before the end of the "sacred decade," Schumpeter had forced the issue of how he would support himself. A fragment of a novel found among his papers after his death revolves around an Austrian aristocrat who marries "an English girl with a great pedigree and absolutely no money," a clue that Gladys's income was, at least at the time, too modest to support them both.[19] Obtaining a professorship in Austria would necessarily be a tortuous and uncertain affair. He briefly toyed with the idea of joining the London bar, but that too would have taken years.

This was the age in which enterprising young men with expensive tastes, limited incomes, and brides to support went east to make their fortunes. Possibly Ricarde-Seaver suggested that Cairo might offer more moneymaking opportunities than London or Vienna for someone with legal training but no experience. The Englishwoman in Schumpeter's unfinished novel "had connections which she resolutely exploited for her darling," and various Ricarde-Seavers were involved in large-scale business ventures from North America to North Africa. One uncle, for example, had been a close associate of Cecil Rhodes and the first prominent railroad engineer to support Rhodes's scheme for building a "Cape to Cairo" transcontinental railroad.

However the decision was made, the newlyweds wasted no time after exchanging their vows and headed south to Egypt with the swallows of winter.

Travel let Edwardians see that currents of change were unsettling the whole world. In a rapidly shrinking globe, even ancient civilizations such as Egypt's were not immune. For someone who had hitherto thought of economic development as a European phenomenon, Egypt was bound to challenge the notion, not so much of limits to growth, but of limits on *who* could grow. Had Schumpeter not gone to Cairo he might very well have merited the historian of economic thought W. W. Rostow's unfair appellation as "a rather parochial economist of the advanced industrial world."[20]

Hard as it is to imagine today, Egypt was the China of the turn of the twentieth century. Anthony Trollope had visited Cairo on post office business in 1859. In *The Bertrams,* composed on the way home, he commented drily:

> Men and women, or I should rather say ladies and gentlemen, used long
> ago, when they gave signs of weakness about the chest, to be sent to the
> south of Devonshire; after that, Madeira came into fashion; but now they
> are all dispatched to Grand Cairo. Cairo has grown to be so near home
> that it will soon cease to be beneficial.[21]

Napoléon I's slaughter of the Mamluks in 1798 began the conquest of Egypt by the West, but Egypt's transformation from an Ottoman fiefdom into a British dependency was mostly the work of entrepreneurs, bankers, and lawyers in the second half of the 19th century.

The American Civil War and the resulting cotton famine turned Cairo into a Klondike on the Nile. Egypt's ruler, the khedive Ismail Pasha, seized the opportunity to turn the whole country into a giant state-owned cotton plantation. As British trade with India grew, he saw a way to exploit that too, hence, the construction of the Suez Canal. Colossal amounts of foreign capital, mostly in the form of loans, flowed into Egypt. For Rosa Luxemburg, the Polish revolutionary, Egypt was a microcosm of the "madness" of modern imperialism:

> One loan followed hard on the other, the interest on old loans was de-
> frayed by new loans, and capital borrowed from the British and French
> paid for the large orders placed with British and French industrial
> capital. While the whole of Europe sighed and shrugged its shoulders at
> Ismail's crazy economy, European capital was in fact doing business in
> Egypt on a unique and fantastic scale—an incredible modern version
> of the biblical legend about the fat kine which remains unparalleled in
> capitalist history.[22]

Inevitably, the debts piled up to complete Suez, and a host of other grandiose projects proved unsustainable. Within six years, the khedive was bankrupt, forced to sell his 44 percent stake in the canal and obliged to let his government be placed in what was essentially receivership. Had he invested more cautiously and avoided debt, some historians speculate, Egypt might have entered in the twentieth century as another, if smaller, Japan.

A period of de facto British rule commenced in 1883. Evelyn Baring, the 1st Earl of Cromer, scion of the banking family and one of the great imperialists of the age, was installed as the power behind the khedive's throne. Baring's top priority was restoring Egypt's solvency. He placed British officials at the helm of Egyptian bureaucracies, paid interest on the debt, balanced the budget, and spent what money remained on irrigation and infrastructure. An Anglo-French agreement reached in 1904 extended British rule indefinitely, sparking another, even more spectacular investment boom. Not much bigger than Holland, Egypt attracted as much British capital as India. Within three years, the nominal value of Egyptian equities had grown fivefold, and more than 150 companies with £43 million of capital had been formed. Lord Rathmore, a director of the Bank of Egypt, described the speculative mania that overtook investors: "People were apparently mad; I do not know what other word to use; they seemed to think that every company that came out was worth double its value before it had even started business." [23]

Nonetheless, the flood of foreign capital was transforming Egypt's feudal economy. Historian Niall Ferguson argues that while old empires extracted tribute, modern ones injected capital and promoted economic growth. In 1900 Egyptian manufacturing had consisted of two salt factories, two textile mills, two breweries, and a cigarette factory. Sugar refining had been by far the most important industry, employing 20,000 workers. By 1907, brand-new industries such as ginning and pressing cotton, cottonseed oil, and soap manufacture employed 380,000 workers. Wages rose along with cotton prices and Sultan Hussein Kamel, who had succeeded his father as khedive, marveled at the rapidity with which Egyptians were acquiring European culture: "I have seen in our factories the most intricate machines handled by Egyptians." [24]

Egypt's foreign colony—expats as well as Jews, Copts, and Greeks who had settled there hundreds of years earlier helped make Egypt "almost the most cosmopolitan country in the world." Cairo swarmed with fortune hunters, bankers, brokers, and entrepreneurs who invested in tourism, railways, banking, sugar, and, of course, cotton. Thomas Cook and Son tamed the Nile and provided English tourists with a "little piece of the West floating along the African river." John Aird & Company completed the Aswan High Dam in 1902. Cecil Rhodes promoted his dream of a transcontinental African railway. Not all the entrepreneurship was for profit. J. P. Morgan, an acknowledged "Egyptomaniac," was only one of several American millionaires—including John D. Rockefeller, the founder of Standard Oil—who were financing archeological digs along the Nile.

Egypt became the poster child for the new imperialism. Speaking to a Liberal Party club in London after his retirement, Baring boasted, "History, so far as I am aware, records no other instance of so sudden a leap from poverty and misery to affluence and material well-being as that which has taken place in Egypt."[25] Over-Baring, as he was known, was, of course, a self-interested promoter. Yet as hostile a critic of British imperialism as Luxemburg did not contradict him.

When William Jennings Bryan, the three-time Democratic presidential candidate, stopped in Cairo on his way back from India in 1906, he found the first sight of the city disconcertingly, even disappointingly modern. Instead of crumbling stones and "picturesque Oriental wonders," he found bright lights, electric trams, automobiles, hydraulic bridges designed by Alexandre-Gustave Eiffel, bottled water, and as many high rises as minarets. It was no harder to buy a cold Bass Ale or a copy of the *Daily Mail* than in New York or London. The business district, with its towering glass and cast-iron department stores, pharaonic luxury hotels, multitude of banks, and telephone and telegraph offices, gave Cairo the appearance of a European city. Its pastel-colored belle époque apartment buildings, wide boulevards, and outdoor cafés reminded Bryan of Paris.[26]

Nile cruises were a particular favorite among affluent honeymoon couples, but Schumpeter arrived in Cairo with more pressing matters on his mind than holding hands with Gladys on the deck of a Cook's steamer. As they made their way to Egypt, by train to Marseilles, steamboat to Alexandria, and again train to Cairo, news of the global financial crisis had followed them. In each capital that experienced a violent stock market collapse, the wave of bank runs and bankruptcies was called by a different name. Many businessmen assumed that the trouble in their community was the worst and that its causes were primarily local. In fact, identical symptoms erupted in half a dozen countries both before and after the panic in New York. The links in a chain that stretched around the globe were popping.

In Cairo the trouble began when Sir Douglas Fox & Partners, the British engineering firm that had built the first leg of Rhodes's transcontinental railroad, had tried to obtain a concession to build a "funicular railway from the base to the summit of the pyramid of Cheops." Perhaps the gods of the underworld took offense, wrote economic historian Alexander Noyes, or else investors saw the proposal as a sign of how crazy speculation had become.[27] In any case, the Egyptian stock market plunged. Brokers and businessmen dismissed the decline as temporary. Within a month a fancy dress ball drew such a huge "rollicking, pleasure-seeking and picturesque crowd" that the dance floor was too crowded for dancing. But in April the market crashed a second time and, this time, kept going down. As the *Economist* reported from London:

> Piles of shares were waiting to be sold, though the market was so satiated with paper that the offer of threescore shares in any security sent down quotations whole points. It was equally difficult at one time to buy. It was well known that a number of small houses were tottering, and when the crisis became most acute, one of these firms suspended payments.[28]

This time full-scale panic erupted. In a matter of weeks, nearly one-quarter of the value of the companies listed on the Cairo exchange had vanished like a mirage. The effect on the real estate boom was immediate. The "great staircase of unsound values" constructed with borrowed money came tumbling down. In May, rumored difficulties at several Cairo banks triggered a bank run. "The total diminution in Egyptian interests, other than Governments, appears to represent about a billion dollars since the completion of the Assouan Dam," reported the *New York Times*'s correspondent grimly.[29] It hardly helped matters that the political situation had suddenly become, in the words of a senior British diplomat, "simply damnable," nationalist agitation having turned "intensely virulent."[30]

Baring and other British officials tried to put the best face on the situation. Repeating the conventional mantra that depressions were the economic equivalent of fasting after a binge, they insisted that the "crisis must in the end be extremely beneficial to Egypt and Egyptian finance, as it will purge the financial arteries of much that is unhealthy."[31] But when credit dried up completely, the Bank of England was forced to send an "instantaneous shipment of $3,000,000 gold." A leading Egyptian expressed familiar regrets when he admitted, "We have been working beyond our means, by using capital which was not ours."[32]

The Egyptian crash was, however, part of a worldwide phenomenon, just as Cairo was a link in a chain that stretched from San Francisco to Santiago, London to Bombay, New York to Hamburg and Tokyo. The chain had been forged not just by ships, railroads, and telegraph cables, but by bills, notes, bank transfers, and gold and the boom that had appeared unique to Cairenes had in fact been almost universal. As a London banker observed after the fact, "beginning about the middle of 1905, a strain on the whole world's capital supply and credit facilities set in, which increased at so portentous a rate during the next two years that long before October, 1907, thoughtful men in many widely separated markets were discussing, with serious apprehension, what was to be the result."[33] The event that triggered the chain reaction had taken place on the far side of the world. Besides practically leveling the city, the great San Francisco earthquake and fire of 1906 resulted in enormous claims to insurance companies in London. As insurers were forced to sell pounds in order to buy dollars to settle them, the pound started to fall in terms of its gold price. To stem the outflow of gold, the Bank of England raised its discount rate to 6 percent in October 1906. The result was a credit squeeze for borrowers.

Under the gold standard, when England sneezed, the United States caught cold. The New York stock market plummeted in March 1907, and in May economic activity began to decline. The recession set the stage for the last and worst banking panic—the panic of 1907—that focused on the New York trusts. The resulting credit freeze forced thousands of banks and businesses around the United States into bankruptcy. A severe economic downturn continued for more than a year, and business conditions did not fully recover until 1910. In England, and on the Continent, the slump was even deeper and longer. In Cairo, on the other hand, the Panic of 1907 was only a pause.

One week after departing from Paddington Station, Schumpeter and his bride were sitting on the elegant terrace of the legendary Shepheard's Hotel overlooking bustling Al Kamel street, flicking flyswatters, listening to "a hundred different propositions from guides and traders,"[34] and imbibing "the peculiar colonial atmosphere of Cairo" along with their drinks.[35] Young and beautiful, they blended perfectly in a cosmopolitan scene where, as the London *Traveler* explained, "Americans, Britishers, Germans, Russians are assorted with Japanese, Indians, Australians, South Africans, well-to-do, well-dressed and handsome specimens of what we call civilization."[36]

The collapse of stock and real estate prices had left a mountain of civil lawsuits in its wake. Schumpeter joined an Italian law firm and was soon representing European businessmen before Egypt's peculiar Mixed Court, a relic of Ottoman administration. The court building overlooked Ataba-el-Khadra, where all the electric trams converged. Cairo's noisiest square was filled with "the raucous shouting of the pedlars, the rattling of the water-carriers' tiny brass trays, the blowing of motor car trumpets and the ringing of tram bells . . . the uproar heightened by the voices of men and women in passionate controversy."[37]

Schumpeter found that his legal practice, though lucrative, hardly required all his time. Instead of going straight to the country club when he left the court, he often ducked into a favorite coffeehouse—for Cairo, like Vienna, was a city of coffeehouses. These male-only retreats served as chess parlors, offices, literary salons, and, increasingly, headquarters for

Islamic fundamentalists and anti-imperialist conspirators. Sipping Turkish coffee and puffing on a hookah that was passed around in the same manner as in Vienna, Schumpeter composed quickly and neatly, his pen flying over the sheets of paper.

"German economics does not really know what 'pure' economics is all about," the twenty-four-year-old author opined. Schumpeter intended his book to be a plea to critics, especially German economists, "to understand not fight; learn, not criticize; analyze and find what is correct . . . not just simply accept or dismiss" economic theory, and a rebuttal of the view, popular in German universities, that "English" or theoretical economics was a dying discipline.[38] True, "Economics, like mechanics, gives us a stationary system, not like biology, a narrative of evolution."[39] It could shed no light on the dynamic process that had transformed, first Britain, then France, Germany, and Austro-Hungary, and now Egypt. But this gap in economic theory was an argument for constructing a new, dynamic theory, not for abandoning theoretical economics.

Schumpeter closed his book's final chapter on the future of economics by posing two questions: Could one prove the existence of *economic* development in the sense that growth could be traced to *economic* rather than demographic, political, or other external causes? Was it possible to devise a plausible narrative of economic evolution under the assumption that existing social arrangements—capitalism and democracy—would persist? His provisional answer to both was a strong affirmative.

Schumpeter had only just sent his 600-page manuscript off to a publisher in Germany in early March 1908, when the sirocco began blowing from the south and he was stricken with Malta fever, a debilitating, often fatal bacterial infection. The omnipresent dust, furnace-like heat, and the threat of complications convinced him that it was time to return to London. He had achieved his twin objectives in coming to Cairo. Besides finishing his first book, he was now, if not rich, at least back in funds. His law practice had prospered and he had been lucky, having ingratiated himself with one of the khedive's daughters and become her investment manager. Having succeeded in doubling the rental income from her estates, as he later recalled, and overseen the reorganization of a sugar refinery, he had earned a substantial sum.[40] By October 1908, he was back in London recuperating at his brother-in-law's house, plotting his return to Vienna.

He had recovered sufficiently by February 1909 to deliver his "Habilitation" lecture on *The Nature and Essence of Economic Theory* at the University of Vienna. His performance on the podium won rave reviews and the title of Privatdozent. The reviews of his book were more mixed, although even the critics were impressed. To his chagrin, his alma mater did not make him an offer. Instead of a prestigious appointment in one of Europe's great capitals, he had to accept an associate professorship in a remote outpost of the Empire not dissimilar to his place of birth.

Cernowitz was a polyglot town of transients, and its university was new and undistinguished. The inhabitants were divided among German Protestants, Jews who spoke German, and Romanian Catholics, most of whom had arrived relatively recently and many of whom were itching to move on to Vienna, Paris, or New York. Partly because few had deep roots there, no single ethnic or religious group dominated the rest, engaged in proselytizing, or had much impulse to do anything but mind their stores and businesses and take a stroll through the city park on Sunday. Schumpeter expressed his resentment by being unfaithful to Gladys, snubbing his colleagues, and thumbing his nose at decorum. He scandalized the faculty by sauntering into meetings in his jodhpurs. On one occasion, he challenged the university librarian to a duel.

Reflecting on the years he spent in the Bern patent office from 1902 to 1909, Albert Einstein observed that the solitude and monotony of his country life stimulated his "creative mind." He recommended similar periods of enforced isolation to other scholars bent on producing works of genius, by taking up temporary occupation as a lighthouse keeper, for example. It gave one time to think one's thoughts and, of course, to write them down. It also cut down on the distracting buzz of other people's ideas.

Cernowitz proved to be Schumpeter's lighthouse. In the two years he spent there, he distilled what he had absorbed, observed, imagined, and thought between the ages of twenty-four and twenty-six when he was living abroad, and poured the resulting combination into *The Theory of Economic Development.*

For Schumpeter, the process of development not only implied that the economy was getting bigger, but also that its structure was evolving, its workers becoming more productive, its industries more specialized, its financial system more sophisticated. He took for granted that the aim of all production was "the satisfaction of wants,"[41] and that a rising living standard was the result of development. But development was not the "mere growth of population or wealth." A nation with a rapidly growing population could produce more output without delivering higher average wages or consumption. Predatory empires like ancient Egypt's could enrich themselves at the expense of weaker powers without achieving ever higher levels of productivity. New, sparsely populated territories could be opulent without having developed a capacity for specialization or a high degree of interdependence.

A nation's ability to provide its citizens with a high standard of living depended first and foremost on its productive power, which enabled the economy to produce more and more with the same resources, like the porridge pot in the Grimm brothers' fairy tale. Output per worker had doubled or tripled in his own lifetime after more or less stagnating for nearly two thousand years between the births of Christ and Victoria. In the same spirit as Mark Twain had ventured in 1897 that "the world has moved farther ahead since the Queen was born than it moved in all the rest of the two thousand put together,"[42] Schumpeter treated economic development as a fact rather than a theoretical possibility. By contrast, Malthus and Mill had

> lived at the threshold of the most spectacular economic developments ever witnessed. Vast possibilities matured into realities under their very eyes. Nevertheless, they saw nothing but cramped economies, struggling with ever-decreasing success for their daily bread. They were convinced that technological improvement . . . would . . . fail to counteract the fateful law of decreasing returns . . . and that a stationary state . . . was near at hand.[43]

It was no longer possible to dispute, as it had been possible in 1848 or even in 1867, that the living standards of ordinary people had improved. In the rich countries, consumption of food as well as clothing, tobacco, meat, and sugar had risen sharply. Better nutrition was reflected in demographic trends. Infant mortality began to plummet after 1845, life expectancy at birth to rise after 1860, and average height, which fell between 1820 and 1870, to increase after 1870. The twin blights of homelessness and begging began to disappear. "The capitalist process, not by coincidence but by virtue of its mechanism, progressively raises the standard of life of the masses," Schumpeter wrote. Even the normally cautious Alfred Marshall had insisted in 1907 that "The Law of Diminishing Return is almost inoperative . . . just now."[44]

If development were being driven mainly by globalization, as Marx had hypothesized, and local conditions mattered little, average living standards should have become more, not less, similar. But anyone who had recently lived in Cairo as well as in London, Cernowitz, and Vienna had to be struck by the stunning differences in the level and rate of economic development of different countries. In 1820, the average standard of living in the world's richest country—still Holland—was roughly three and a half times that of the poorest nations of Africa and Asia. By 1910, however, the lead of the richest over the poorest had grown to more than eight-fold.[45] These differences in living standards primarily reflected differences in productive power rather than in territory, natural resources, or populations. For any given amount of capital and labor, the most efficient economies could produce many times as much as the least efficient ones.[46] What's more, the productivity of some economies was growing several times as fast as others. So the question was not just what process could increase productive power by multiples in the course of two or three generations, but why the process operated so much faster in some countries than others.

The traditional answer would have been that a nation's development depended on its resources. Schumpeter took the opposite view. What mattered was not what a nation had, but what it did with what it had. He identified three *local* elements of "industrial and commercial life" that

drove the process: innovation, entrepreneurs, and credit. The distinctive
feature of capitalism, he believed, was "incessant innovation," the famous
"perennial gale of creative destruction."[47] Marx too had observed that
"The bourgeoisie cannot exist without constantly revolutionizing the
instruments of production" but he had had in mind primarily factory
automation.[48] Schumpeter took a broader view. "Innovation," by which he
meant the profitable application of new ideas rather than invention per se,
could involve many types of change, he pointed out: a new product, production process, supply source, market, or type of organization.

Marshall, whose motto was that nature took no leaps, had stressed
continual incremental improvements by managers, and skilled workers
that accumulated over time.[49] Schumpeter stressed innovative leaps that
were dramatic, disruptive, and discontinuous. "Add successively as many
mail coaches as you please, you will never get a railway thereby," he insisted, ". . . the essence of economic development consists in a different
employment of existing services of labor and land."[50] But new technologies alone could not explain why some economies were developing and
others were not, since new machines and methods could be, and were,
transferred globally. Marx had explicitly ruled out any role for the individual in his economic drama. Webb once complained that Marx's "automaton owner" was driven by forces over which he had no control, and
into which he had no insight, blindly pursuing "profit without even being
conscious of the existence of any desire to be satisfied."[51] Schumpeter focused on the human element. For him, development depended primarily
on entrepreneurship. He shared the obsession of late nineteenth-century
German culture with leadership. Having heard Sidney Webb expound on
the Fabian theory of hereditary genius as the cause of unequal incomes,
he had also become interested in the work of Francis Galton, Darwin's
cousin, and Karl Pearson, a professor at the LSE, on hereditary genius and
the role of elites.

The central character in Schumpeter's narrative was the visionary
leader. The entrepreneur's function was "to revolutionize the pattern of
production by exploiting an invention or, more generally, an untried

technological possibility." [52] This might mean new products like cars or telephones, new processes like the cyanide method for extracting South African gold, new organizations such as the trust, new markets such as Egypt for rail cars and cotton ginning machinery, or new sources of supply such as India for cotton. In contrast to Marx's automaton capitalist or Marshall's owner-engineer, the entrepreneur distinguished himself by a willingness to "destroy old patterns of thought and action" and redeploy existing resources in new ways. Innovation meant overcoming obstacles, inertia, and resistance. Exceptional abilities and exceptional men were required. "Carrying out a new plan and acting according to a customary one are things as different as making a road and walking along it," Schumpeter wrote. [53]

His entrepreneurs are motivated less by the love of money than by a dynastic urge—"the drive and will to found a private empire," as well as the urge to dominate, fight, and earning others' respect. Finally there was "the joy of creating, getting things done, or simply exercising one's energy and ingenuity." [54] While Marx had cast the bourgeois as a parasite whose activities would ultimately destroy society, Schumpeter took up and developed Friedrich von Wieser's notion that "growth was the result of the "heroic intervention of individual men [who] appear as leaders toward new economic shores." [55] He never grew tired of pointing out "the creative role of the business class that the majority of the most 'bourgeois' economists so persistently overlooked." Science and technology were not independent forces, he insisted, but "products of the bourgeois culture" just like "business performance itself." [56] Though many did realize great fortunes, entrepreneurs did more to eliminate poverty than any government or charity.

Despite his energy, vision, and domineering nature, the entrepreneur could thrive only in certain environments. Property rights, free trade, and stable currencies were all important, but the key to his survival was cheap and abundant credit. To carry out his plans, Schumpeter argued, the entrepreneur had to divert land, labor, and machines from their existing uses to his projects. His enablers are "bankers and other financial middlemen who mobilize savings, evaluate projects, manage risk, monitor managers, acquire facilities and otherwise redirected resources from old to new channels."[57] True, the financial sector's peculiar dependence on confidence and trust made it vulnerable to panics and crashes. But without well-functioning credit markets and a robust banking system, an economy would be deprived of the low interest rates and abundant credit needed for innovation. What distinguished successful economies was not the absence of crises and slumps, but, as Irving Fisher also stressed, the fact that they more than made up lost ground during investment booms.

The highest interest rates in the world were found in the poorest countries. As the economic historian David Landes writes, "In these 'underdeveloped' countries, where the civilizing rays of capitalism had not yet exercised their mysterious faculties of enlightenment, there were few banks but many money-lenders, little investment but much hoarding, no credit but much usury."[58] In Egypt, entrepreneurs faced huge obstacles because of the backward state of local banking and the primitive facilities of credit and exchange. Interest rates were twice or three times as much as in the West. The best securities paid interest of 12 to 20 percent. The poor peasant, meanwhile, paid 5 to 6 percent a month.

Having shown that economic theory had been designed for a "system essentially without development," Schumpeter succeeded in formulating a new one for a body in motion, while building on existing theory. He showed how an economy could produce more with the same resources while evolving a new, more specialized structure. What's more, his theory implied that any nation could do it. By emphasizing the local business environment instead of natural resources, Schumpeter's theory suggested that nations made their own destinies. Governments that wished to see their citizens prosper should give up territorial ambitions and focus on fostering a favorable business climate—strong property rights, stable prices, free trade, moderate taxes, and consistent regulation—for entrepreneurs at home. There were no intrinsic limits to growth. Human wants were infinite. Rising incomes and new desires provided just as much opportunity for profitable ventures as opening up new territories. As long as trade was possible, innovation could offset the constraints of population, territory, and resources. It was a beguiling, romantic, even a heroic narrative. His was an equal opportunity, optimistic, and, not coincidentally, unwarlike formula for economic success.

Schumpeter completed the manuscript of *The Theory of Economic Development* in May 1911. By then he was back in Vienna, staying at his mother's apartment, and waiting to hear whether he had been chosen to fill an empty chair at the University of Graz. The city, where he had spent part of his childhood, was a pleasant provincial town and its university was not especially distinguished. Nonetheless, it had the advantage of being just two and a half hours by train from the capital. The faculty proved to be anything but amenable, deemed his work "barren, abstract and formalistic," and voted to appoint another candidate. Only intervention at the education ministry by his mentor Böhm-Bawerk succeeded in overturning the decision, fulfilling Schumpeter's ambition to become the empire's youngest full professor at the age of twenty-eight.

When Schumpeter started teaching in Graz in fall of 1911, he got a chilly reception from students, who boycotted his classes, as well as from his new colleagues. But it was nowhere as frigid as that accorded to his magnum opus, which appeared that fall. It was, he later testified, "Met with universal hostility."[59] Even Böhm-Bawerk was sharply critical, so much so that he devoted sixty pages to an attack on Schumpeter's book the following year. More discouraging, his mentor was one of the few economists to review it at all.

When Schumpeter got an invitation to spend the academic year 1913–1914 as the first Austrian exchange professor at Columbia University, he accepted with alacrity. Gladys, however, made it clear that she did not intend to accompany him. Their marriage had soured soon after it had begun, perhaps because an English feminist and Fabian and a Viennese prince were hardly likely to be compatible or simply because both were, at least on Schumpeter's testimony, promiscuous. Accepting that the marriage had been a mistake, he made no effort to dissuade her. In August 1913, he sailed alone from Liverpool on the RMS *Lusitania*, while Gladys resumed her former life in London.

Schumpeter's sabbatical was a great success. He adored New York and was adored in turn by Americans who were charmed by his sparkling conversation and astonished by his personal habits, such as taking an hour every day to complete his toilette. One colleague at Columbia called his inaugural lecture at the university "a remarkable performance . . . and . . . very unusual—both brilliant and profound."[60]

The triumph was crowned by a note from the president of Columbia informing him that the trustees had voted to give him an honorary degree. Lecture invitations from Princeton, Harvard, and other universities poured in. Irving Fisher invited him to New Haven for Thanksgiving. At dinner they talked about the possibility of a European war. Like the English politician Norman Angell, Fisher was convinced that economic integration made the possibility remote. Many nations were now so dependent on foreign capital, he said, that they could no longer afford to misbehave. Schumpeter listened skeptically.

Before leaving the United States, he could not resist touring the country by train as Marshall had done. He did not return to Vienna until August 1914.

Act II

FEAR

War of the Worlds

The world will seek the greatest possible salvage out of the wreck.

—*Irving Fisher, 1918*[1]

"Sidney had refused to believe in the probability of war among the great European powers," Beatrice Webb later commented in the margin next to her original diary entry for July 31, 1914.[2] Investors didn't see the Great War coming either, judging by the stock and bond markets that hovered near all-time highs. Surely war was economic suicide and therefore unthinkable. One week after Germany overran Belgium, George Bernard Shaw predicted in the *New Statesman,* his venture with the Webbs, that the war would be over in a few weeks. As Webb observed in early August, the war seemed like "a terrible nightmare sweeping over all classes, no one able to realize how the disaster came about."[3]

For Webb, the war was "a blank and dismal time." Her political stock had been falling since before 1914 and continued to decline. She hoped that she and Sidney would be given some important role in the Liberal-led wartime coalition government of David Lloyd George. No offer materialized, and the Webbs eventually went off on a somewhat desultory world tour. When Beatrice was finally appointed to a commission to study the gap between women's and men's wages in 1918, she regretted accepting the assignment almost immediately. "I am not the least interested in the subject," she complained. She was too preoccupied by fears of "the kind of world we shall live in when the peace has come."[4]

• • •

A Cambridge don, civil servant, speculator, and art patron, John Maynard Keynes was rather homely and quite rude. He made up for these short-comings with cleverness, a charming voice, and efficiency in practical matters. His best friends, who invariably called him Maynard, were the artists, writers, and critics known collectively as "the Bloomsbury Group." They counted on him to buy their paintings, advise them on real estate, and invest their trust funds—all while they debated whether he was or wasn't a hopeless philistine.

When Britain declared war in August 1914, Bloomsbury immediately agreed with Shaw that war was madness and would "benefit only a few capitalists."[5] Keynes pledged to seek conscientious objector status, but then dismayed his friends by changing his mind. He upset them further by accepting the invitation of the then Chancellor of the Exchequer, David Lloyd George, to serve on the Treasury staff. Keynes argued that while the war was undoubtedly bad, his presence in the government would make it less so.

The Treasury's task was not only to achieve "maximum slaughter for minimum expense" but also to finance the war without debauching the world's safest currency or jeopardizing Britain's supremacy as the world's banker.[6] As the war dragged on, Britain loaned massive sums to her European allies and was obliged to borrow even more massive sums from the United States. Because the loans were so colossal, writes Keynes's biographer Robert Skidelsky, the "headache of inter-allied debt . . . became the chief source of irritation, misunderstandings and almost constant squabbling within the Alliance." Within a few months, Keynes became "the go-to official for inter-Allied (read American) loans."[7] Communication within Whitehall was by memorandum, and Keynes was a wizard with a pen. His energy, confidence, and nerve never seemed to flag.

An episode toward the end of the war captures Keynes's uncanny ability to stay focused on the big picture. In the early spring of 1918, the Germans caught the Allies off guard and smashed through the western front. Tens of thousands of German troops were soon encamped a few miles from the Arc de Triomphe, and Paris was being shelled day and night. The

Big Bertha howitzers were sowing terror as far away as London. If Paris were to fall, anxious Britons reasoned, the Germans could move them to the channel beaches and bombard the southern counties.

Keynes was too tantalized by a suggestion from one of his Bloomsbury friends to indulge in such anxious speculation. The painter and critic Roger Fry had given him a heads-up about an extraordinary collection of modernist paintings that was about to go on sale. Edgar Degas, who had been an art dealer before he devoted himself full-time to painting, had amassed hundreds of works by Manet, Corot, Ingres, Delacroix, and other contemporary artists over his long career, rarely parting with a single canvas. This treasure trove was to be auctioned off at the Galerie Roland in Paris on March 26 and 27.

Recognizing a chance to save a piece of the civilization he loved and for which his country was fighting, Keynes did not hesitate. He immediately contacted Charles Holmes, director of the National Gallery, to urge him to lobby the war cabinet for a £20,000 war chest. Judging that his superiors at the Treasury would react with disapproval to such extravagance at a time of national sacrifice, Robert Skidelsky relates that Keynes recast the scheme as an insurance policy against default: "Under our agreements with the French Treasury we are entitled to set off British government expenditure in France against our loans to them," he began his memorandum to the Chancellor. At that point in the war, France owed Britain such gargantuan sums that the likelihood of collecting interest on the debt, never mind the principal, looked exceedingly remote. How much better, Keynes argued, to collect "priceless pictures than dubious French bonds."[8]

A few days later, Keynes sent the painter Duncan Grant, his former—and Vanessa Bell's current—lover, a triumphant telegram: "Money secured for pictures."[9] Meanwhile, he had contrived to get himself and Holmes invited to an Allied conference in Paris. They crossed the channel escorted by "destroyers and a silver airship watching overhead" and traveled to Paris by train.[10] To avoid tipping off French dealers and inquisitive British reporters, Holmes disguised himself with a false mustache and whiskers, and both he and Keynes used aliases. The ruse was so successful that at the close of the auction two days later, Keynes wrote gleefully to his mother, "I bought myself four pictures and the nation upwards of twenty."[11]

In fact, he came home with one of Cézanne's still lifes of apples and two Delacroix, while Sir Charles Holmes returned to the National Gallery with twenty-seven drawings and paintings, including a Gauguin still life and Manet's *Woman with a Cat*. Prices had slumped under the threat of German occupation, and Keynes was especially pleased that Holmes had had to use only half of his budget. Of his return from France, Vanessa Bell wrote to Roger Fry that "Maynard came back suddenly and unexpectedly late last night having been dropped at the bottom of the lane . . . and said he had left a Cezanne by the roadside! Duncan rushed off to get it."[12]

An Anglophile and constitutional monarchist, Joseph Schumpeter was horrified when Austria and Germany entered the war as allies. When he got a draft notice in December 1914, he promptly applied for a permanent exemption on the grounds that he was the only professor of economics at the University of Graz. According to his biographer Robert Lorie Allen, he hoped for an advisory role in the government and spent as much time as possible in Vienna cultivating politicians of all parties. (He was equally promiscuous in his private life, Gladys having announced her intention of remaining in England for good, even though she had not consented to a formal divorce.) But Schumpeter proved too radical for his own party, the conservative Christian Socials, and too conservative for the Socialists. The longer the war dragged on, the more frustrated he became at being "totally cut off from any possibility of being effective."

Having opposed the war, Schumpeter lobbied the emperor and his advisors to make a separate peace with the Allies—which, in fact, Franz Joseph nearly did—as well as to seek a postwar alliance with England. On the eve of surrender, Schumpeter was waging a personal campaign on two fronts: against the increasingly popular notion of a postwar economic and political union or "Anschluss" with Germany, and against the increasingly fatalist attitude on the part of the Austrian middle class toward the future of democracy and private enterprise in Europe. He spent the final year of the war anticipating the problems that the Austrian government would face after the war.

Six months before the armistice, at a public lecture at the University of Vienna, Schumpeter proposed a blueprint for postwar economic recovery. Like Keynes, he was an optimist. In *The Crisis of the Tax State,* based on his lecture, he argued against the inevitability of Socialism and predicted that the capitalist welfare state, which he called the *"Steuerstaat"* or "tax state," would survive the war. The crisis he foresaw would result not from the triumph of Socialism, he argued, but rather from a gap between the voters' expectations and their willingness to pay taxes. The major challenge for democratic governments would be avoiding chronic budget deficits and inflation.

Even young men who had experienced the triumph of "brutality, cruelty and mendacity" over civilization assumed that civilization would eventually reassert itself.[13] On August 31, 1918, hundreds of soldiers waited on a train platform in the Alpine resort where the emperor had declared war on Serbia four years earlier. A remarkable-looking man—short, taut, radiating nervous energy, with gaunt features, graying hair, and cold blue eyes wearing a K.u.K. uniform—strode through the crowd toward a skinny young corporal. "Aren't you a Hayek?" he asked him. "Aren't you a Wittgenstein?" the other shot back.[14]

The Hayeks and the Wittgensteins were among Vienna's leading families. The former were senior civil servants and academics; the latter, wealthy industrialists and art collectors. Friedrich von Hayek and Ludwig Wittgenstein were cousins, although the latter was old enough to be Hayek's uncle. They had never exchanged more than a few words at family gatherings, but both had volunteered within a few weeks of each other, having welcomed the war partly out of the hope that facing death would make them better men. Both had endured months of semistarvation, grossly inadequate clothing, nonexistent shelter, influenza, malaria, and intensifying ethnic tensions. Both had taken part in the disastrous Piave offensive, the final desperate gesture of the hopeless Austro-Hungarian army. They had witnessed their comrades in arms wading through the mosquito-infested salt-water marshes, rifles held over their heads, until they fell. Unlike one hundred thousand other members of the K.u.K. army, they had survived.

Hayek was anxious to get home to Vienna to learn whether his application to the air force had been accepted. Wittgenstein had taken leave from his unit in order to see a publisher who had expressed an interest in a manuscript he was carrying in his rucksack, the *Tractatus Logico-Philosophicus,* soon to be recognized as one of the most important works of twentieth-century philosophy. When the train for Vienna came, the two men got into the same compartment, and as it rolled eastward through the night, they talked.

Wittgenstein went on and on about Karl Kraus, whose antiwar journal, *Die Fackel,* satirized the mendacious Austrian media and emphasized "the duty of genius" to seek and tell the truth. Hayek was troubled by Wittgenstein's gloom about the future, but at the same time was profoundly impressed by his "radical passion for truthfulness." [15] When they arrived in Vienna, he and Wittgenstein went their separate ways. In another world war, Hayek would fulfill his own duty to the truth by writing *The Road to Serfdom.*

The best and brightest of the generation that had been too young to fight was Frank Ramsey, a protégé of Maynard Keynes. Like Keynes, Ramsey came from an old Cambridge family. His father was the head of a college and his younger brother the future archbishop of Canterbury. An awkward but brilliant great bear of a boy, Ramsey helped to translate Wittgenstein's *Tractatus* when he was sixteen. At age nineteen he wrote a criticism of Keynes's thesis on probability so devastating that Keynes gave up any notion of a mathematic career. He was drafted to revise the *Principia Mathematica,* Bertrand Russell and Albert North Whitehead's prewar attempt to reduce all of mathematics to a few logical principles.

Ramsey was eleven when war was declared, and the war radicalized him, as it did many of the boys at his school. He upset his headmaster by threatening to switch from mathematics to economics, which he considered more likely to make the world a better place. Instead of specializing in either mathematics or economics, Ramsey became a philosopher who contributed original ideas to both disciplines. He published only two papers in the *Economic Journal* before his tragic death from a botched operation at age twenty-six, but both became classics as Keynes accurately predicted.

A free spirit with a passion for literature, psychoanalysis, and the many women who adored him, Ramsey personified Keynes's attitude that whatever the limitations of formal logic, imaginative solutions could be found for social problems. Even as an undergraduate, he was indifferent to the notion, seemingly proven by the world war, that vast, impersonal forces beyond human control would determine society's future. In a talk delivered at a meeting of the Apostles, the Cambridge secret society to which Keynes and Russell had also belonged as undergraduates, Ramsey announced that the "the vastness of the heavens" did not intimidate him. "The stars may be large, but they cannot think or love; and these are qualities which impress me far more than size does," he said, adding, "My picture of the world is drawn in perspective, and not like a model to scale. The foreground is occupied by human beings and the stars are all as small as three-penny bits." [16]

Appalled by the colossal waste of human life and capital in the war, Irving Fisher redoubled his efforts on behalf of public health and a postwar League of Peace. Between 1914 and 1918, he helped to found the Life Extension Institute, whose purpose was to promote best practices in individual hygiene and so further "the preservation of health . . . and increase vitality" [17]; coauthored a best seller, *How to Live,* on what today would be called wellness; and started campaigning in earnest for alcohol prohibition. Even as he argued for America to enter the war against Germany, he deplored the negative "eugenic" effects of sending the cream of the younger generation to be slaughtered and maimed on the battlefield. He became president of a labor group that lobbied for safety legislation, automatic cost-of-living wage increases, and universal health insurance. Oddly, the war seemed to strengthen rather than weaken his belief in modern science and man's improvability.

Before it was over, though, he suffered a grievous blow that might have caused a less confident man to question whether his certitude was justified. In the late spring of 1918, after months of nagging anxiety, he was forced to confront the agonizing possibility that his twenty-four-year-old daughter Margaret, to whom he was extremely close and who had recently become engaged, might be incurably insane. Shortly after her fiancé received his officer's commission, she began to talk incessantly about strange portents, God and immortality, and her conviction that her fiancé would be killed.[18] When it became obvious that she had begun hearing voices, and her behavior became more and more bizarre, Fisher took her to the Bloomingdale Asylum in upper Manhattan. The diagnosis, dementia praecox, was devastating. Unable to accept that Margaret was unlikely to recover, he tapped his contacts in the medical community in search of a more hopeful prognosis.

He soon discovered Henry Cotton, the medical director of the New Jersey State Hospital at Trenton, who had been reporting extraordinary success in treating schizophrenia. A prominent psychiatrist and medical reformer, Cotton was convinced that mental illnesses were due to "focal infections." What distinguished him from researchers with similar views was his willingness to apply his theory to his patients by aggressive removal of infected teeth, tonsils, colons, and reproductive organs. He claimed that he had completely cured hundreds of hopeless cases since the start of the war.

This is what Fisher, a parent desperate to save his child and a true believer in modern medical miracles, wanted to hear. Elated at having found someone who promised a cure, Fisher had his daughter transferred to Cotton's care in March 1919. When the doctor reported the presence of "pure colon bacillus," Fisher assented to his recommendations for treatment. Cotton had two of Margaret's wisdom teeth removed immediately. When she remained suspicious, delusional, apathetic, and perplexed, he had her cervix removed. Before and after the surgery, she was inoculated repeatedly with her own streptococcus bacilli, the last time in September. Later, Cotton had to admit to a Princeton audience that Patient Number Twenty-four was a "treatment failure." Margaret died of septicemia on November 19, 1919, at the age of twenty-five.[19]

Fisher was devastated. Yet he never questioned the wisdom of Cotton's "treatment" or his conclusion that the origin of Margaret's psychosis, and the indirect cause of her death, was her parents' failure to deal in a timely fashion with her impacted wisdom teeth and her tendency to constipation. Nor was his boundless faith in medical science shaken. If anything, Fisher's campaigning grew more frenetic. He told himself over and over that some good would come out of the twin calamities of Margaret's death and the war. In his mind, the two became inextricably linked. He predicted that society would enter "a period of life conservation" and use science to extend life and improve health: "The war has for a time withdrawn much of the world and destroyed and maimed a large part of that which it has withdrawn," he said. "The world will seek the greatest possible salvage out of the wreck." [20]

The wreck was beyond calculation: 8.5 million dead, 8 million permanently disabled, mostly young men. Ninety percent of the Austro-Hungarian army and nearly three-fourths of the French army was killed, wounded, imprisoned, or missing. "The toll of the war for our family is three killed and four others wounded, two seriously injured, out of a total of seventeen nephews and nephews in law in khaki," Webb recorded. "Every day one meets saddened women, with haggard faces and lethargic movements, and one dare not ask after husband or son." [21]

World War I destroyed globalization, disrupted economic growth, severed physical, financial, and trade links, bankrupted governments and businesses, and led weak or populist regimes to rely on desperate measures that were supposed to head off revolutions but just as often hastened them. When the war was over, the victors as well as the vanquished were crippled by colossal debts and subject to vicious attacks of inflation and deflation. Poverty, hunger, and disease, those Malthusian scourges, once again seemed to have the upper hand. In London and Paris as well as Berlin and Vienna, citizens of the great capitals of Europe were forced to realize that they and their nations were now a great deal poorer. Virginia Woolf could not stop brooding about the war and its devastating effects. In her novel *The Voyage Out,* published in 1915, a sheltered West End matron discovers that "after all it is the ordinary thing to be poor and that London is a city of innumerable poor people." In *Mrs. Dalloway*, a decade later, "the war was over" except for victims like the suicidal working-class veteran Septimus Smith and the impoverished and crazed Socialist Doris Kilman, who continue to suffer five years on. In *To the Lighthouse*, Mrs. Ramsay and her family are haunted by the threat of tuberculosis, another of the war's legacies.

The war had dealt a blow to the legitimacy of private property, free markets, and democracy while providing an impetus to violent revolutionary movements from Moscow to Munich. "The people are everywhere rejoicing," observed Beatrice Webb anxiously on Armistice Day. "Thrones are everywhere crashing and men of property are secretly trembling."[22] From their respective positions in Austria and England, Joseph Schumpeter and Maynard Keynes tried to convince their countrymen that political healing would depend on economic recovery, as would any dampening of dangerous revolutionary ardor. Reviving the world economy would require the Allies to draw political boundaries that made economic sense, they argued; and, more important, to give up the fantasy that exacting reparations from the losers would make up their own losses. Both men pleaded for stabilizing national currencies, restoring the flow of credit, and eliminating trade barriers.

Bertrand Russell, the philosopher, was among the many Western intellectuals who were convinced that "The Great War showed that something is wrong with our civilization."[23] His initial reaction to news of the Bolshevik Revolution was cautious optimism. He was prepared to believe that if not the promised land, Soviet Russia was at least a grand futurist experiment. But unlike many others who let themselves be swept away by their own hopes and fears, he made up his mind to reserve judgment until he had a chance to examine the new society that the revolutionaries claimed they were building—firsthand.

Chapter VI

The Last Days of Mankind:
Schumpeter in Vienna

The hour of socialism has not yet struck.

—*Joseph Schumpeter, 1918*[1]

If Austria was a pathetic ruin . . . there was plenty of material,
I thought, with which to rebuild the ruins.

—*Francis Oppenheimer, British Treasury Representative, 1919*[2]

When the armistice was announced on November 11, 1918, Webb reported, London exploded in "a pandemonium of noise." In Paris, there was "a wild celebration" until dawn. Even Berlin was "elated," its citizens glad to be rid of the war and the dynasty that had dragged them into it.[3] Of the four great European capitals, only Vienna was silent. An enormous gray crowd gathered in the Ringstrasse in front of the parliament building. A few soldiers stripped the imperial eagle from their uniforms and forced others to do the same. A mile or so away in the Berggasse, Sigmund Freud sat in his study and jotted in his pocket diary: "End of war." Significantly, he avoided the word *peace*.[4]

The disintegration of the multinational Austro-Hungarian Empire had been a fait accompli for weeks. A city with a population as large as Berlin's, Vienna suddenly found itself the capital of a "mutilated and impoverished republic" of 6 million, one-tenth the size of the old empire. After a final session of the imperial parliament in which legislators hurled inkwells and briefcases at speakers' heads, Czechoslovakia, Hungary, and Yugoslavia had seceded, taking many German-speaking lands with them. As a result, Austria's eastern and northern frontiers now lay just beyond Vienna's outer suburbs.[5] And Austria's new neighbors challenged even these borders and constantly threatened to invade. Meanwhile, Austria was in no position to defend itself or issue counterthreats. By November 12, after the emperor and his family had slipped into exile and the new republican government was formally proclaimed, the 4-million-man Austro-Hungarian army had completely dissolved. In the interval between the armistice offer in November and its signing a few days later, hundreds of thousands of soldiers had been imprisoned in Italian POW camps. Most wouldn't find their way home for several years.

The revolutionary firestorm that had been ignited by defeat and hunger in St. Petersburg in February 1917 was now spreading west to Budapest, Berlin, and Vienna. Two Marxists dominated Austria's provisional government. Most observers had taken the inevitability of a Communist putsch for granted since January 1918. The week after New Year's, militants at the Daimler-Benz works had struck to protest a halving of the flour ration. Half a million men and women who had been drafted by the imperial authorities to work in munitions plants had abandoned their factories. Rumors were circulating of an imminent uprising in Hungary and revolution in Germany.

The city was bracing for the return of Austria-Hungary's defeated troops. In *The Last Days of Mankind*, Karl Kraus, the antiwar satirist, warned that embittered, half-starved, armed hordes would turn Austria into a battlefield. "The war . . . will be child's play compared to the peace that will not break out."[6] Hundreds of thousands of men, including the nineteen-year-old Friedrich Hayek, had abandoned their units on the Venetian plain and joined a "hungry, disorganized and undisciplined" mass exodus to the north. Along the way, they exchanged military horses, cars, and artillery for food and looted shops or set them ablaze. By early November, the mass was trying to squeeze through the single, narrow exit from Italy over the Brenner Pass and into Innsbruck. Gun-wielding soldiers commandeered trains. "Roofs, platforms, buffers, steps of carriages, even the engines themselves, swarmed with soldiers," reported one correspondent. "Seen from a distance each train looked like a madly rushing swarm of bees."[7] Hundreds were thrown to their deaths when the trains roared into tunnels und under bridges, and their bodies littered the embankments on either side of the tracks.

Determined to avoid Austria's destruction by "bloody anarchy," the civil servants of the now defunct empire simply tried to keep the trains moving. At one point, a British businessman reported, the Trieste-Vienna line was carrying off between seventy thousand and one hundred thousand men every twenty minutes or so. Worried about anarchy and Communist takeover, the bureaucrats set up depots at the outskirts of Vienna where soldiers turned in their arms before they entered the city. Inside the city, the police continued to report for duty. After an incident in which some Red Guards "liberated" some food and weapons depots, the Social Democratic government hastily recruited unemployed factory workers into a peoples' militia. Thanks to such measures, as well as to the overwhelming desire of Hungarian, Czech, and Yugoslav soldiers to get home as fast as possible, Vienna remained relatively calm.

The returning soldiers found a city under siege. In this most middle-class of European cities, there was hardly any food or fuel. Virtually from the moment the new republic was announced, no more manufactured goods left Vienna and no shipments of beef, milk, potatoes, or coal arrived. Not since 1683, when the city was briefly encircled by the Ottoman Turks, had Vienna been so cut off from the outside world. Travel to Munich, Zurich, or nearby Budapest became difficult, if not impossible. Mail service was fitful. Telegrams took two or three weeks to reach their destinations, if they ever did. Packages arrived without their contents or not at all. "Don't feed the customs officials or railway workers," Freud warned relatives in England.[8]

It hardly needs saying that a city of 2 million must buy food from elsewhere in order to eat. Before the war, Vienna and the Alpine provinces had relied on imports from the non-German-speaking parts of the empire for nearly all of their potatoes, milk, and butter, one-third of their flour, and two-thirds of their meat.[9] But Hungary had suspended exports to Austria in the middle of the war. Now Austria's other new neighbors—mainly Czechoslovakia and Yugoslavia—imposed blockades. As the British high commissioner put it, "For hundreds of years trade has followed certain channels and lines of communication have developed accordingly. These channels and lines have been suddenly blocked . . . The result is districts that are starving close to districts having a superfluity of food-stuffs."[10]

Austria also had plenty of arms, salt, timber, and manufactures to sell; Czechoslovakia had sugar, potatoes, vegetables, and coal; Hungary and Yugoslavia had milk. But despite efforts by the provisional government to work out barter deals with the new states, nationalist politics and anxiety over the latter's own potential shortages prevented the exchanges from taking place.

That was not all. The Allies announced that their wartime blockade of Germany would continue until the Central Powers had signed the peace terms proposed by the victorious Entente. That meant that the only country still willing to sell food to Austria had none to sell. Herbert Hoover, who had come to Europe on a fact-finding mission for the American government, commented bitterly, "The peacemakers had done about their best to make [Austria] a foodless nation."[11]

Making matters immeasurably worse, Austria's rural provinces created an informal blockade of Vienna. Several were, indeed, threatening to pursue union with Germany or Switzerland. In the farm districts, the war had wrecked domestic agriculture. The men were not at home to plant fields. Livestock, the chief source of fertilizer, was slaughtered to supply the military. And the government's policy of forcing farmers to sell food at controlled prices led to less planting and more hoarding. As food shortages worsened, especially in the war's final year, rural districts began to act independently by enacting local export bans on food, passing laws prohibiting tourists from visiting, and organizing stop-and-search operations to prevent anyone from taking food out of the district.

The new government had inherited crushing war debts but no gold reserves with which to buy food for its citizens. The governments of

Hungary and Czechoslovakia had seized the last of the gold deposited in the central bank. Hoover arrived in Paris in mid-December to set up a program for reviving food trade and, if necessary, delivering food aid. He was shocked by the state of Austrian finances: "The citizenry that paid the taxes to pay the army and the bureaucracy had seceded. The state—which paid the salaries of the army, the railway workers—was bankrupt." [12]

Serious food shortages had cropped up almost as soon as the war began. As early as 1915, Vienna's airy white rolls had been replaced by leaden *"Kriegsbrot,"* and "meatless" weeks had become routine as early as 1915. Everything became ersatz: not only was bread made "of anything but flour," wrote Stefan Zweig, an Austrian journalist and novelist, but "coffee was a decoction of roasted barley, beer yellow water, chocolate colored sand." [13] The government's requisitioning and distribution efforts drove a growing share of what food supplies there were underground into the black market. And now, despite the end of hostilities, the city's supplies continued to dwindle. Ludwig von Mises, Austria's leading business economist, recalled that "at no time during the first nine months of the Armistice did Vienna have a supply of food for more than eight or nine days." [14] Government depots, the only legal source of food, had absurdly small amounts of pickled cabbage and "war bread" to hand out to housewives who had stood on a queue for hours. The bread ration was six ounces a week per person, less than one-fourth of average prewar consumption. The meat ration had fallen to 10 percent of the prewar level. There was no milk ration for children over the age of one. But one expert estimated that average daily calorie consumption had fallen to little more than a thousand calories—not enough to sustain life for more than a few weeks.

Crowds on the street were wan and listless, while children looked three years younger than they were. "Now we are really eating ourselves up," Freud wrote to a friend. "All four years of the war were a joke compared to the bitter gravity of these months, and surely the next ones, too." [15] Franz Kafka, a clerk in an insurance office, wrote a short story, "Ein Hungerkünstler," about the art of starving. Tuberculosis was common in middle-class neighborhoods, where it had virtually disappeared before the war. By early 1920, the prewar burial rate of forty to fifty corpses per day would climb to two thousand per day. Felix Salten, an Austrian theater critic and novelist best known for *Bambi* (1923), remembered "hearing of lions, of panthers, of elephants, of giraffes that died in the drawn-out agony of starvation in their cages in the zoological gardens, people shrugged their shoulders. How many human beings lay in their beds in the throes of death, and dragged on, emaciated, wracked by suffering, to the bitter end." [16]

The city itself began to waste away. The population was displaying the classic symptoms of starvation—lassitude, indifference, and passivity, alternating with bouts of mania. Despite the influx of demobilized soldiers, imperial civil servants, and several thousand Jewish refugees fleeing pogroms in the east, the city's population, which had expanded rapidly during the early 1900s boom, shrank by several hundred thousand people. Like a body deprived of food that begins to absorb its own muscle, the whole country began living off its accumulated possessions. At one point, the government announced that Austria was willing to pawn "anything"— castles, palaces, shooting boxes, game preserves, and chateaus owned by the Hapsburgs.[17]

The misery of the food blockade was multiplied by a "cold blockade." One week after the armistice, there was no coal for heating apartments and just one week's worth of supplies for cooking. The weekly fuel ration consisted of one twenty-five-watt lightbulb per apartment, one candle, and a little more than a cup of fuel. Even for middle-class households, baths and laundry became unaffordable luxuries. Schools, which had already been closed due to the influenza pandemic, now announced Kaltferien, or cold vacations. Stores had to close by four in the afternoon. Cafés were required to kick out their patrons before nine o'clock. People chopped up their doors, stripped bark off the trees, and cut down trees in city parks. Entire tracts of the Vienna Woods were denuded. The telephone poles and trees that had lined Vienna's elegant boulevards disappeared. Wooden crosses vanished from cemeteries. A visitor wrote, "The whole life of Vienna is haunted by this lack of fuel." [18]

Any number of maddening Catch-22s cropped up, as the Social Democratic *Die Arbeiter-Zeitung* pointed out: "People need wood because they have no coal, but no wood can be shipped because there's no coal for the locomotives." [19] According to the historian Charles Gulik, the Austrian Republic had inherited 30 percent of the former empire's factory workers, 20 percent of its steam-generating capacity, and only 1 percent of its coal supplies. No fuel meant that factories; blast furnaces; bakeries; brick, lime, and cement works; and power plants had to be shut down, choking off industrial production, homebuilding, and power generation. Half of Vienna's sixteen industrial concerns with more than one thousand workers shut down for good. In the city that had been a pioneer of electrification, blackouts became routine, even on Christmas Day. Tram service, which depended on electricity, had to be suspended. Railroad traffic was restricted to freight trains carrying food shipments. In turn, the energy shortage, the falloff in arms production, and demobilization continued to swell the ranks of the unemployed.

On Christmas Eve 1918, just before midnight, Thomas Cuninghame, the official British representative in the former Hapsburg Empire, drove up one of Vienna's stateliest streets, Mariahilferstrasse. "There was not a soul stirring and hardly a light in the streets," he wrote in his diary. "The beautiful old city had become 'Die Tote Stadt.'" [20] William Beveridge was mobbed on Boxing Day by desperate housewives at a market "twittering around us like ghosts in Hades, saying that they wanted food." [21] One of the great European capitals seemed to be on the verge of death.

Joseph Schumpeter's latest ambition—to become commerce secretary in the monarchy's last cabinet—had come to naught a few weeks before the armistice. Since then he had been cooling his heels in Graz, halfheartedly preparing his lectures for the spring term. With the first national election imminent and the Social Democrats and right-wing Christian Social Party expected to form a coalition government, he put feelers out to the Left about the possibility of being appointed finance minister. A Burkean liberal who favored maximum individual freedom and minimum government intervention, he was on generally good terms with Socialists. The two Social Democrats who were temporarily in charge of the country were old friends from his university days. Otto Bauer, a middle-class Jew with pan-German sympathies, was the party leader and interim foreign secretary. Karl Renner, the bluff, portly eighteenth child of a Moravian peasant, was chancellor. Though both were Marxists, their politics had more in common with Fabianism than with Bolshevism. Nonetheless, another man got the job.

Early in the New Year, a fresh political opportunity presented itself. Another university pal, a German Socialist who would soon become the Weimar Republic's first finance minister, wrote to Schumpeter from Berlin with an interesting proposal. Would he join a group of Socialist luminaries assembled that December to advise the new German government on the transition to Socialism; in particular, the possible nationalization of the coal industry?

Strange as it might seem, the Socialist politicians now in charge of the well-being of 60 million citizens had never given any serious thought to how a socialist economy might operate. Marx had expressly forbidden his followers to indulge in what he dismissed as utopian "fantasizing." The leading German Marxist would admit only that such leaps of the imagination might be "a good mental exercise."[22] But the growing radicalization of German workers had forced the issue. Since the armistice in November, there had been mutinies and strikes, extortionist wage demands, physical intimidation, and "spontaneous expropriations" of firms by their employees. The German working class had sacrificed for more than four years. Now they wanted to be compensated. The leaders of the Left parties had been promising for years to wrest control from employers and put workers in charge. Yet now that they were in power, they realized that no government could survive unless it could revive production. The commission's job was to suggest a way out of the dilemma.

Schumpeter accepted the invitation with alacrity. The shortest road to Vienna might lie through Berlin, he saw. With Socialists in power in both Austria and Germany, the likelihood that the two German-speaking states would merge was growing, and Bauer, the Austrian foreign secretary, was a member of the commission. Besides, Schumpeter expected the commission to adopt a gradualist view. Later, Schumpeter justified his willingness to get involved in a Socialist project by saying, "If someone insists on committing suicide, it's better for a doctor to be present."[23] But at the time, most investors, bankers, and industrialists did not expect the commission to propose any such thing. Eduard Bernstein, a prominent German Socialist on the panel, had recently warned, "We cannot seize the wealth of the rich people for then the whole system of production would become paralyzed."[24] Bauer, who wanted to replace boards of directors with representatives of management, workers, and consumers, had stressed that socialized and private enterprises would function side by side "for generations."[25]

Schumpeter lost no time in applying for a leave of absence from the University of Graz, which the provost promptly granted. The journey to Berlin took four days instead of the usual two, but when he arrived in the Prussian capital, he was in a city that no one could possibly describe as "dead" even in these desperate times.

Berlin, January 1919: The city had been spared Allied occupation and had emerged from the war structurally intact, if shabby, woefully short of supplies, and expensive. But each wave of demobilized soldiers—embittered, excitable, and by now addicted to violence—threatened to overwhelm the city. Any stray spark could start a conflagration.

The explosion occurred between Christmas and New Year's. The Communist Spartacists called a general strike, and a full-scale civil war ensued. Mass demonstrations stretched from Alexanderplatz to the Reichstag. Trains were paralyzed, banks barricaded, the university closed, stores boarded up. Spartacists seized virtually every factory, power plant, government building, newspaper, and telegraph office. Tanks rumbled through the streets, and, after the revolutionaries rained grenades and machine-gun fire on government troops, the German chancellor authorized the use of flamethrowers and field artillery. Terrified citizens jammed the train stations in a vain attempt to flee. Berlin's most famous citizen, Albert Einstein, had already withdrawn to Zurich: "Glorious reading about events in Berlin here, under sunny skies, eating chocolate," he wrote to a friend.[26] Schumpeter, however, relished being in the thick of things.

The Socialist brain trust had been meeting for several weeks in the basement of the Reichsbank, which had been spared a takeover by alert civil servants who barricaded the building. Despite the chaos and blood-shed, the commission continued to conduct its proceedings like a university seminar, calmly and deliberately considering alternatives ranging from nationalization to laissez-faire, and addressing practical questions such as how enterprises could be socialized without undermining efficiency gains or innovation.

Schumpeter adopted the same supercilious, cynical attitude he had displayed in Böhm-Bawerk's seminar at the University of Vienna. "I have no idea whether socialism is possible, but if it is, one has to be consistent," he would say flippantly. "In any case it would be an interesting experiment to try it once."[27] He treated the issue of nationalization as a technical one, a banker recalled: "'If one wanted, at the end of a war, to socialize large firms, one had to proceed in a certain way.'"[28]

In the end, as expected, the commission rejected both laissez-faire and Soviet-style state ownership and opted for a combination of public owner-ship and private management. When the report was drafted, two liberal commission members refused to sign it and issued a minority report. Schumpeter, however, added his name to the majority report. His stint on the commission paid off exactly as he had hoped. Impressed by his coop-erative attitude and technical expertise, Hilferding urged Bauer to consider Schumpeter for the position of finance minister of Austria, and by the time the commission report was published on February 15—the day before the Austrian parliamentary elections—the Viennese press was already hinting that Schumpeter would be asked to join the government. Two weeks later, Bauer was back in the German capital for four days of secret Anschluss talks with Weimar's foreign minister, Ulrich von Brockdorff-Rantzau. (Union with Germany was Bauer's top priority. He had already enlisted Robert Musil, the writer, who was "officially charged with the task of in-dexing newspaper clips . . . In reality, assigned to promote union with Ger-many in various newspapers."[29]) At that point, "Schumpeter was in a hurry to leave," recalled another commissioner.[30] On the eve of another general strike and bloody uprising, he left Berlin in Bauer's company.

. . .

The post of finance minister was one of two or three in the new coalition government so unrewarding that no career politicians could be found to take them.

How was one to prevent the currency of a bankrupt nation from falling, buy food from abroad without gold or dollars, or cobble together a budget when every variable from borders to reparations was being decided by the Allies in Paris? As soon as Renner floated his name, Schumpeter's own party, the conservative Christian Socials, hastily agreed. They did not necessarily trust him. In an anti-Semitic culture, the party of landowners and aristocrats considered Schumpeter a Judenfreund because he associated with Rothschilds and other Jewish bankers and businessmen. He had also shown a woeful lack of party loyalty by blocking the promotion of the Christian Social whip, who was on the faculty at Graz. But the Socialists considered Schumpeter, who was regarded as "something of a genius in the economic sciences," the right man to take charge of the republic's shaky finances.[31] Since Austria's fortunes depended on the Allies, Renner and Bauer reasoned, his pro-Western sentiments and early opposition to the war were welcome assets, as was his experience living abroad, his American honorary degree, and his fluency in English and French.

Pamphleteers on the left and right instantly labeled Schumpeter as an opportunist: "How delightful it must be to have three souls in one," liberal, conservative, and Socialist, *Die Morgen* began. Karl Kraus called him an "exchange professor in his convictions."[32] But Schumpeter's desire to join the government was hardly discreditable. If the fledgling Austrian Republic failed to deliver bread along with peace, democracy was doomed. He had an economic recovery plan. For Schumpeter, becoming finance minister in a time of revolution was an opportunity to save his country from ruin.

In some ways, the new finance minister and the Viennese housewife faced similar challenges. To pay for food and fuel for her family, Anna Eisenmenger, whose extraordinary diary provides a window onto day-to-day life in those catastrophic times, had three options: to earn, to borrow, or to sell her belongings. To keep the trains running, the militia on patrol, and the soup kitchens open, Schumpeter had the same choices. To survive, Eisenmenger and her family wound up applying for pensions, renting out rooms, working for an American relief organization, and, as a last resort, selling off Dr. Eisenmenger's precious stash of prewar cigars. Schumpeter could collect taxes, cajole bankers into buying government bonds, dip into the country's reserves of cash and gold, if these existed, and, in a pinch, sell assets belonging to the state.

Of course, if an individual had to buy things from abroad—or even take a trip to next-door Geneva—he had to get his hands on foreign currencies. If he had a Swiss bank account he could tap it, as did Max von Neumann, a banker in Budapest who took his family, including his son John, into temporary exile after Béla Kun's Communist coup. If he had no such reserves, the foreign currency had to be earned or borrowed. Sigmund Freud and his fellow psychoanalysts took in English patients, such as James Strachey and his wife, Alix, who paid him in pounds. Eisenmenger borrowed dollars from a cousin in America. Most of the time, the individual had to use krone to buy pounds or dollars.

Because so much of what Austria needed to stay alive had to be imported, the Austrian finance minister had to find foreign currencies or gold with which to buy it. If he couldn't, he had to arrange a foreign loan or hope for a gift. But his principal job was to defend the krone's value vis-à-vis other currencies. Every uptick in the exchange value of the krone meant that Austria could pay less for coal or pork. Every downward movement meant that Austria had to pay more. That is why housewives stood outside the windows of currency shops waiting for the latest report on the krone's value with "constricted chests." For the finance minister, the value of the currency was of even greater consequence, because he was also responsible for the government's budget. Every decline in the krone's value caused the government's deficit to rise. The finance minister's most important single task was to prevent the currency from collapsing. Ultimately it was a confidence game. People took one's money if they believed that they could settle their debts with it. What gave them this confidence was, of course, the knowledge that they could settle their debts with it. So every finance minister had to be bullish on his currency, and if he had no gold or foreign currency reserves, he had to use air to keep it afloat.

Schumpeter, the youngest finance minister in Austria's history, was delivering his maiden speech in a gilded marble palazzo tucked in a narrow lane—Heaven's Gate—in the city center. Pacing back and forth, waving his hands, enunciating in his best Theresianum accent, he alternated between playfulness and passion. Success in modern politics, he was aware, depended on a leader's ability to "fascinate," "impress," and "engage" the public. And economic stabilization required "a popular government and a credible leader of brilliance, will, power and words that nations can trust." [33] In the gloomy, frigid hall full of black-coated officials, he radiated energy, optimism, and hope.

The war had saddled all the combatants, including England and France, with unprecedented debts, but Austria's case was extreme. The imperial government had not dared to raise taxes during the war. In 1919, as a result, tax receipts covered only two-thirds of government spending. The government owed huge interest payments on its war debt, a disproportionate share of which was inherited by the new Austrian Republic. It had also promised relief for the unemployed, principally the cost of sustaining the militia. It had to pay civil servants, including thousands who flocked to Vienna from outposts of the old empire. Finally, it had to provide food subsidies to cover the difference between the price paid by the government and that charged to consumers. The old imperial government had assumed that the lion's share of the huge debts they were accumulating would be paid by the losers. This, of course, only postponed the day of reckoning.

Most Austrians could imagine only two alternatives now: to be adopted by Germany or to become a permanent ward of the Entente. Otto Bauer was an enthusiastic supporter of Anschluss with Germany. He saw nothing wrong, either, with a little inflation, regarding it as "a means of animating industry and raising the standard of life of the workers." [34] Bankers and industrialists leaned toward an alliance with the Entente. They shared

the fondest wishes of British Treasury officials, in particular those of Maynard Keynes, that "Austria will never be allowed to go under. The Entente
will put her finances straight. A large loan in sterling is all that is needed." [35]

Schumpeter took a different view. He believed that a shrunken Austria
had the means to recover economically. His deepest conviction was that
nations' resources matter less than what they did with what they had. As
long as entrepreneurs were allowed to create new enterprises, the financial
system was functioning efficiently, and there were not too many barriers
to trade, society could regenerate itself. He rejected the popular assumption that economic viability depended on vast territories, huge populations, and natural resources. In an extraordinary essay on the sociology
of imperialism written in 1919 with Germany in mind, he described how
ancient Egypt's military-industrial complex impoverished the empire by
chronic warfare: "Created by wars that required it, the machine now created the wars it required." [36] England became the richest country before
she acquired an empire. Switzerland, whose per capita income rivaled
that of Britain, was no bigger than Scotland. And before the war, Vienna
had been the most important financial, transportation, and trading center in Central Europe. As long as the Allies or her neighbors did nothing
to prevent Austria from trading freely or its government from restoring
her creditworthiness, he saw no reason why Vienna could not resume her
prewar economic role and once again earn a good living, provided no insuperable obstacles were placed in her way. "People so often say that German Austria is not viable," Schumpeter admitted. But, he added forcefully,
"I believe in our future . . . One must not think that a country in order to
survive economically must possess all essential raw materials within its
own frontiers . . . The neighboring countries cannot exist without us or
without our financial mediation." [37]

To be sure, the nation had to deal with its massive war debt. The historian Niall Ferguson points out that there are five, and only five, ways
to ease such burdens: de jure repudiation, as practiced by Lenin in 1918
and Hitler in 1938, and varying degrees of de facto repudiation involving
changing the repayment terms, lowering the value of the money in which
the debt is repaid (inflation), or achieving such rapid economic growth

that income rises faster than interest payments. The most respectable, of course, is simply to pay it off.

Reflecting his faith that Austria could help itself, Schumpeter told his audience that he strongly favored the last option. It was the fastest way to restore investor confidence in Austria's creditworthiness and revive production. But no postwar government would get away with raising taxes on farmers and the middle class to compensate wealthy bondholders. Jacking up income taxes would also discourage investment just when the economy desperately needed an infusion of fresh capital. Schumpeter's preferred solution was to force the rich to shoulder Austria's war debt by levying a steep, one-time tax on *property*. In effect, he wanted to pay wealthy bondholders off with their own money by seizing a big chunk of their liquid assets, including cash, bonds, and stock.

The genius of Schumpeter's plan, which reflected the priorities he had set out in his theoretical treatise *The Crisis of the Tax State*, was that while the ownership of business enterprises, farms, and other property would be reshuffled, it would remain in private hands. Taxing existing property rather than future income had the further advantage of not discouraging investors from making fresh capital available for investment or businessmen from expanding production. To reduce the risk the government would inflate its way out of debt, Schumpeter also proposed creating a central bank that, like the Bank of England, was independent of the Treasury. At the same time, he favored stabilizing the krone at its current value rather than its prewar parity. These measures would bolster the confidence of foreign investors, on whom Schumpeter pinned his hopes, and ensure that Austrian investments would be bargains for them.

Schumpeter's recovery program required two conditions in order to work: peace terms that did not impose insuperable obstacles to a renewal of trade, and a sustained effort to raise enough taxes to cover the government's spending. "At the moment we cannot get any credit even abroad because foreigners have no faith in our future," he told his staff. Eliminating or even dramatically reducing the government's deficit would require heroic measures, he admitted. He favored sin taxes on "conspicuous consumption" of such proletarian indulgences as beer and tobacco, as well as sales taxes on "luxury foods, luxury entertainment, luxury textiles, luxury stores, servants, luxury clothing."[38] It was not a plan designed to win friends on either the right or the left. His own party was dead set against a tax on property, especially if it included farms. The Socialists considered the notion of taxing beer a hilarious example of Schumpeter's political cluelessness.

By the third day of Schumpeter's tenure as finance minister, the krone was in free fall. Communist guerrillas, led by a former Austro-Hungarian army corporal who had been trained and armed by Moscow, were riding around Budapest in open trucks festooned with red flags. A Red Guard of demobilized Austrian soldiers immediately set off for the Hungarian capital to express solidarity. The Bolshevik victory was widely interpreted as Hungary's having thrown herself into Moscow's arms rather than submit to the Entente. It prompted Lloyd George, the British prime minister and something of a hawk on reparations, to issue a warning to the peace conference. While the Entente, no less "tired, bleeding and broken" than the losers, were intent on making the Germans and their allies pay for reconstruction, Lenin's disciples were busy trying to seduce Germans with promises of "a fresh start," that is, as Lloyd George explained, a chance "to free the German people from indebtedness to the Allies and indebtedness to their own richer classes" that had lent the Reich the resources with which to fight the war. If the Allies insisted on imposing overly harsh terms on Germany, the inevitable result would be "Spartacists from the Urals to the Rhine."[39]

As if on cue, Lloyd George's gloomy prophecy proceeded to unfold. On April 7, in Munich, a band of anarchists declared a Bavarian Soviet Republic. Within a week the homegrown mob was replaced by professional revolutionaries—Russian émigrés with ties to the Internationale—who promptly unleashed a reign of terror. A Russian document captured in a police raid suggested that Lenin's army was poised to march into Germany via Poland to join the insurrectionists. The word in Paris was that Vienna, now flanked by two red capitals, would be the next domino to fall. In a Parliamentary debate on whether or not to leave British troops in Russia to help defeat the Bolsheviks, Winston Churchill warned that "Bolshevism is a great evil, but then it has arisen out of great social evils." Six weeks later, the British cavalry officer in Russia, General Briggs, wrote to Churchill arguing for British support: "starvation means Bolshevism."[40]

Béla Kun's emissaries did appear in working-class districts of Vienna to make dramatic pledges to supply food to the proletarians—but not the bourgeoisie—in the future Soviet Republic of Austria. They painted fantastic pictures of life in Budapest, of prices in first-class hotels now on a par with those of rough taverns, workers' families living like royalty in confiscated palaces, and social equality between the bourgeoisie and the proletarians. In his memoir, Bauer recalled:

> As soon as [Béla Kun] realized that we had no intention of [proclaiming the Austrian Soviet] he embarked upon a campaign against us. The Hungarian Embassy in Vienna became a centre of agitation. Large supplies of money came from Hungary to the Communist Party of Austria, which not only served to strengthen its propaganda, but which was also expended for the purpose of bribing trusted individuals among the workers and soldiers. The communist propaganda sought to persuade the workers that there were large supplies of food in Hungary which were sufficient to meet all the requirements of Austria.[41]

To counter such propaganda, Herbert Hoover sent cables from his Paris headquarters at 51 Avenue Montaigne urging his deputies to plaster Vienna's city walls with fliers warning that "any disturbance of public order will render food shipments impossible and will bring Vienna face to face with absolute famine."[42] Meanwhile, he stepped up relief operations in a race against Communism and death. In Vienna, the government ordered half a company of the Socialist militia, the Volkswehr, to take up residence in the courtyard of 7 Herrengasse, where the cabinet held its meetings.

Fears of a coup may explain a curious incident related by the food minister, Hans Loewenfeld-Russ. Apparently, Schumpeter had telephoned him on the last day of March, invited himself to dinner, and asked him to invite Ludwig Paul, the transportation minister, as well. As soon as the three men were alone, Schumpeter asked the others abruptly whether, in the event of a coup, they would be willing to join the new Bolshevik government with him. "Not even in my dreams," retorted Paul sharply.[43] Loewenfeld-Russ nodded angrily in agreement. Schumpeter immediately backtracked, chiming in that he too wouldn't dream of joining such a government.

When Loewenfeld-Russ demanded that Schumpeter explain why he had wanted a private meeting and had asked such a peculiar question, Schumpeter replied that he was merely sounding out the only two cabinet members besides himself who had been appointed not by the chancellor but by a political party.

He was probably telling the truth. At around that time, Cuninghame reported that one of his sources had submitted a "long circumstantial report . . . detailed plan, worked out by the Socialist Party, for establishing a Socialist form of government." According to Cuninghame's informant, this government was supposed to be a decoy, "Soviet in appearance rather than reality."[44] Supposedly Renner and other moderates in the cabinet were ready to adopt this ruse, although the more left-leaning members like Bauer refused to have anything to do with it. Cuninghame was instructed by the British Foreign Office to inform the Austrian defense minister that a Bolshevik government, phony or genuine, would mean a suspension of food aid and a resumption of arms shipments to Poland, which was harassing Austria with territorial demands.

As the Austrian republic hovered between life and death, the cabinet was in permanent session. Sessions typically started hours after the end of the normal work day. Around the time that the opera let out, the fifteen ministers and their undersecretaries converged by car or on foot on the Palais Modena at 7 Herrengasse, one of the finest streets in Vienna, dating from the late Middle Ages. Anxious, sleep-deprived men trudged past the disheveled Volkswehr guards camped in the courtyard and climbed the imposing stairway to the once brilliantly lit, elegant rooms where emperors had met with their councilors and where Karl Renner had set up his chancellery. They had to take care to avoid tripping over the machine guns haphazardly positioned at the windows and were forced by the cold and damp to keep their heavy overcoats on. The meetings usually lasted well past midnight, and the prime minister sometimes sent out to a nearby restaurant for a meager meal and a glass of beer to keep them all going.

On April 17, the ministers had barely begun to tackle the "unimaginably long" agenda when thousands of gaunt and ragged men with "pinched and yellow" faces came marching along the Ringstrasse, now strewn with litter, past luxury high rises with boarded-up windows, to gather in front of parliament a few blocks away. Most were unemployed factory workers and demobilized soldiers, many with missing limbs or other visible war wounds. Scattered among them was a small cadre of armed Communist Party members and foreign agitators. After a few hours, they succeeded in whipping the crowd into a sufficient frenzy to storm the parliament building and, once inside, set it ablaze. When shooting started, the Volkswehr rushed in. In retaking the building, the "peoples' militia" shot some fifty demonstrators dead and wounded several hundred, or so the first reports claimed.

One episode shocked the public even more than the attempted putsch. At the height of the fighting, a horse was shot out from under a policeman in the street in front of the parliament. As the animal lay dead in the street, a hungry mob tore it to pieces and carried off hunks of bloody meat. For ordinary Viennese, who adored the emperor's white show horses the way Americans loved boxing champions, the incident seemed to prove that civilization was reverting inexorably to barbarism. No one could have been more appalled than the republic's newly installed finance minister, who, even in these desperate times, kept several thoroughbreds.

In Budapest, the opinion on the street was that revolution was imminent in Vienna, but by midafternoon the insurrection had petered out. Friedrich Adler, the recently released assassin of the monarchy's penultimate prime minister and a popular Socialist politician, had arrived to urge calm. The Communist leaders themselves could not agree on whether to proclaim a Soviet republic. The next day, the heads of the workers' councils declined to call a general strike. Ellis Ashmead-Bartlett, the *Daily Telegraph*'s war correspondent, rushed to the Austrian capital from Budapest. "Instead of finding Vienna in flames, I found the town absolutely quiet."[45]

Hotel Sacher, across from the opera and famous for its voluptuous chocolate cake, was the preferred trysting place for Vienna's diplomats, spies, and counterrevolutionaries. Madame Sacher was said to be an ardent monarchist. Schumpeter lunched there often. On May 2, Sir Thomas Cuninghame discovered Schumpeter in one of the "salles privees" at the rear of the hotel, huddled with four other men, including Ellis Ashmead-Bartlett, the British correspondent who had broken the story of the slaughter at the battle of Gallipoli. Halfway through their meal, Cuninghame, who had apparently heard that Ashmead-Bartlett was in town, joined them.

Ashmead-Bartlett was trying to raise money on behalf of about 150 Hungarian officers who were hanging around Vienna, terrified of being deported on the one hand and eager to organize a counterrevolution against Bela Kun on the other. Their trouble was the complete lack of money or credit with which to hire as much as a train, beyond that extended by the sympathetic Madame Sacher. Von Neumann, the Budapest banker, was in Vienna to help in the fund-raising effort. Other rich sympathizers were afraid to lend them cash for fear that such a loan would reach the ears of Austria's Socialist government. Louis Rothschild, on whom the plotters had pinned their hopes, was changing his conditions daily. Finally, Cuninghame had suggested that Ashmead-Bartlett see Schumpeter, known to the British as a bitter opponent of union with Germany, which Britain also opposed.

The journalist was impressed by Schumpeter's intelligence, lively manner, and flawless command of English. He noted approvingly that Schumpeter was not yet forty and betrayed none of the caution typical of Treasury men. "We discussed the future of Austria," he recalled. Schumpeter had immediately declared himself in favor of a constitutional monarchy such as Britain's and agreed that "the only way to eliminate the Red danger from Vienna was to drive the Soviet Government out of Hungary." After saying that he would gladly advance the revolutionaries money from the Treasury were it not for the need to account for every kroner to parliament, he offered to assure Rothschild that if he lent the money, the Treasury would look the other way. "This was good news," said Ashmead-Bartlett, "as it did away with Louis Rothschild's main objection . . . namely his fear of being asked awkward questions by the Austrian government."

As it turned out, when the monarchists seized the Hungarian embassy in Vienna on May 4, they unearthed a large cache of the money—reportedly 135 million krone and 300,000 thousand Swiss francs—earmarked for fomenting revolution in Vienna. So, just as the negotiations with Rothschild were winding up, Schumpeter sent his secretary to inform the banker, "There is no need for him to advance any money, as it has been raised elsewhere."[46] When Béla Kun tried to retrieve his war chest and get the aristocratic officers extradited, Schumpeter intervened on their behalf. Before the matter went any further, the Béla Kun government was overthrown by the right-wing Admiral Miklós Horthy and his followers.

Over the next few weeks, the Austrian government went on a spending spree. The Socialists dominated the coalition government formed in March 1919 because they were the only ones who could control the unemployed, soldiers, workers' councils, and radicals. Arguing that the large conservative peasant majority would not permit a Socialist revolution and that any putsch would result in Allied intervention, Bauer pressed for a variety of social welfare measures. Aware that they might have only a narrow window in which to act, the Socialists succeeded in laying the groundwork of the Austrian welfare state in a few short weeks. In Vienna alone, sixty thousand war invalids, dependents of POWs, and officials of the former empire and their families qualified for relief. Within a year, one-sixth of the population would be on welfare and not producing any salable goods.

Meanwhile, Schumpeter's efforts to gather support for his tax proposals stalled. No loans were forthcoming from the Allies. Reserves of gold and hard currencies were minuscule. The government had little choice but to finance its deficit by printing more money.

The government looked for ways to shift the burden onto business via what Bauer called a "far reaching encroachment on the rights of private enterprise, originally conceived as emergency regulation for a few months." In May the cabinet passed a decree requiring large companies to boost employment by 20 percent. It was soon followed by others compelling employers to recognize trade unions and give workers paid holidays, and forbidding layoffs without government approval. Not surprisingly, the law resulted in a sharp decline in productivity, complaints about *"Arbeitsunlust"* or absenteeism, and a further slump in tax receipts.

Nonetheless, the Renner cabinet forged ahead with socialization. In mid-May, Otto Bauer announced a program of partial nationalization of mining, iron foundries, power stations, forests, and timber. Schumpeter objected that as long as the government administration got its finances in order and stabilized the krone, business owners would once again invest and expand. After alienating conservatives by proposing that the rich bear the burden of the war debt, he alienated his Social Democratic colleagues by claiming that socializing private enterprises would make it impossible to attract foreign investors and smother any recovery.

Schumpeter's Social Democratic colleagues trusted him no more than his own party did and called him "vain," "conceited," and "affected" behind his back. The other ministers wore shabby clothes and shoes with holes in their soles. Schumpeter dressed like an English banker or diplomat. The cut of his Savile Row suit was impeccable. The silken handkerchief that he tucked under his heavy gold watch was snowy. Newspaper caricatures invariably depicted him in jodhpurs, high boots, and a Homburg. He carried a riding crop under his arm as if to suggest that he intended to whip his ministry, the cabinet, or the whole country into shape. The other ministers lived in modest flats with their frumpy wives. Separated from Gladys, apparently for good, Schumpeter flaunted his lavish bachelor lifestyle. He rented a suite at the posh Hotel Astoria around the corner from the ministry, an apartment on Strudlhofgasse, and half of a palais belonging to a count, where he threw teas and dinners for the likes of the Rothschilds, Wittgensteins, and other plutocrats, as well as foreign diplomats, journalists, and politicians. He often pulled up to the ministry in an ostentatious horse-drawn carriage. He ate in the best restaurants, drank the finest French champagne, and often had a call girl or two on his arm or sitting beside him in his carriage. It was a manner of living far beyond a cabinet officer's pay grade, and it was obvious that Schumpeter was running up debts to his wealthy friends. Even his old mentor Friedrich von Wieser got the impression that Schumpeter did "not really care about the general misery" or suspected that "as soon as his vanity is no longer satisfied . . . he will retire."[47] Schumpeter made matters worse by pretending to be indifferent to criticism. He would tell reporters, "Do you think that I want to remain Minister of a State that goes bankrupt?"[48]

Anschluss, which Otto Bauer regarded as Austria's only chance for economic revival and Schumpeter was the only cabinet member to oppose, was another major source of friction. In late May, the local correspondent for *Le Temps* discovered Le Docteur Schumpeter, seated at his desk in the yellow ballroom. The sumptuous baroque palace in the heart of a starving city, the lavish gold leaf decorating the Treasury's empty vaults, and the floor-to-ceiling frescoes glorifying Austria's past military triumphs amid anarchy and defeat struck the reporter as highly ironic. And then to come upon Schumpeter, the "bourgeois whipping boy" in the cabinet, sitting "at the feet" of a portrait of Ferdinand I was too much![49] *Le Temps* readers would have gotten the joke: the famously feeble-minded and sexually impotent Austrian emperor had been forced to abdicate in 1848, another year of revolution. Such a fate seemed likely for the similarly weak and helpless Austrian Republic and its minister, even one as strong-willed, brilliant, and notoriously libertine as Le Docteur Schumpeter.

The Austrian government was trying to influence the terms of a peace treaty that would be dictated by the Entente by waging a propaganda war for "the right to union with Germany."[50] When the *Le Temps* interview appeared quoting Schumpeter, Bauer accused him at the next cabinet meeting of secretly lobbying the French and English to forbid the merger. As Bauer complained in his memoir, "The French statesmen were able to answer us that the leading men of Austria, the bankers and the industrial magnates daily assured the Entente diplomats at Vienna that Austria did not need union and could get along pretty well by herself, provided the peace conditions were relatively favorable."[51]

Bauer's accusation was largely true. Schumpeter had been giving anti-Anschluss speeches for weeks. He had also proposed the idea of a monetary union with France to Henry Allize, head of the French Military Mission to Vienna. His contention that the new Austrian state could avoid bankruptcy was based on an expectation that France would give a higher priority to establishing a non-German-dominated common market in Central Europe. As late as the end of June, Schumpeter declared publicly that he was hopeful that the Entente would ensure an "equitable distribution of the burden" of war debts and would not insist on the confiscation of Austrian assets in Czechoslovakia, Hungary, and Yugoslavia. As he put it, "In the case of Germany, the peace terms were drafted to check recovery; in the case of Austria, they must encourage it."[52]

At the end of May, Schumpeter once again attacked the Anschluss policy in a "sensational" interview with *Neues 8 Uhr Blatt*, warning, "Our safety lies in our peaceful intercourse with all states, and especially with our immediate neighbors."[53] Bauer wrote him a furious letter, but instead of heeding his warning, Schumpeter tried to engineer a secret side deal with the British. He gave Francis Oppenheimer, Keynes's emissary to Vienna, the draft of a "secret" plan involving Allied control of Austria's finances and central bank in exchange for long-term loans. As Oppenheimer reported in a cable to his boss warmly supporting Schumpeter's plan, the Austrian foreign minister

> does not share the general opinion that Anschluss to Germany was Austria's only salvation. He wanted, if possible, a strong Allied Finance Commission to take charge of Austria on the lines of the British financial administration in Egypt, but whatever form the control might take, it would have to safeguard Austria's amour propre. He insisted that a single currency throughout the successor states, with Vienna remaining the banker of them all, was perhaps the most important item in the program of Austria's recovery.

He added, "Suffice it to say that it was a rare and fortunate privilege to have had to deal with such a genial, open-minded expert."[54] The two continued to meet frequently. Among other things, Schumpeter was actively trying to help the British acquire the Austrian companies that controlled shipping on the Danube. As Oppenheimer had informed Keynes, "Dr. Schumpeter had agreed to facilitate the transfer of this company, possibly of the other three as well, into British ownership on exceptional terms for cash, and he promised to maintain for us a first refusal until we had either accepted or declined the offer." [55] Naturally, nothing in Vienna stayed secret for long. "Schumpeter carries on with his intrigues," Bauer wrote to Renner. "I shall do nothing for the time being, but after the conclusion of the peace treaty it will be inevitable to force his resignation." [56]

Almost as soon as the Allied treaty terms had been presented to the Germans on May 7 in Versailles, the Austrian delegation, with the prime minister Karl Renner at its head, left Vienna for France. On June 2, 1919, after spending two weeks cooling their heels in the old royal chateau in Saint-Germaine-en-Lay, relishing the French food and wine, they learned the Entente's terms for Austria. "It was a terrible document," Otto Bauer recalled. Large chunks of German-speaking Austria were parceled out to the Czechs, Yugoslavs, and Italians. "Equally harsh were the economic provisions . . . They were simply a copy of the German Peace Treaty." [57] The draft Treaty of Saint-Germaine acknowledged that the Austro-Hungarian Empire had broken up but penalized only Austria for its crimes. Three million German-speaking Austrians were to live under Czech rule. The private property of Austrian citizens was to be confiscated. Austria's government was to pay reparations for thirty years. The coup de grâce, at least from Bauer's point of view: union with Germany was expressly forbidden.

In Vienna, the reaction was shock mingled with disbelief. Schumpeter told a reporter that "the Allies' motivation can only be to destroy German Austria." [58] On June 30, he said, "It is not easy to kill a people. In general it is impossible. But here we have one of the few cases in which it is possible . . . fiscal collapse inevitably brings with it social collapse." [59] When the foreign exchange market issued its verdict on the treaty, the krone collapsed once more. As Friedrich Wieser told a London conference on relief and reconstruction at which Keynes was present a few months later, the currency markets have declared thereby that they do not consider the Austrian Republic, with boundaries as fixed by the Peace Treaty, and with the burdens laid upon her therein, as capable of life. The Austrian who loves his country will do everything in order to keep her alive. But it is not surprising that the outside world, to whom her existence is a matter of indifference, has declared that she is incapable of life.[60]

By treating Austria as harshly as Germany, the Allies not only destroyed the viability of the new state but also shredded what little was left of Schumpeter's credibility. He was forced to admit that his political judgment had been naïve. He was, as he confided to his diary, a man without an intuitive feel for political reality, "a man without any antennae."[61]

Schumpeter's political demise was agonizingly drawn out. At the July 15 cabinet meeting, Bauer hurled yet another accusation at him, this time of sabotaging the "socialization" of basic resource industries by conniving to deliver a major Austrian mining and timber concern into the hands of Italy's Fiat company, making it impossible for the government to take it over. Schumpeter tried vainly to defend himself by portraying a series of transactions with a foreign exchange trader named Kola as an attempt to raise gold and hard currencies with which to defend the krone.[62] Two weeks later, Schumpeter had the humiliating task of defending the government's plan to sell or mortgage several of the nation's "immortal works of art," including the emperor's prized Gobelin tapestries. There was no other way to raise the requisite foreign currencies for buying food abroad, he argued, warning dryly, "This process cannot be often repeated." He begged the lawmakers one final time to pass his budget: "The greatest problem of the State would be to get through the next three years without Government bankruptcy and without the issue of new notes," he pleaded, knowing that his arguments were falling on deaf ears.[63] It was Schumpeter's last appearance in front of parliament.

In mid-October, utterly isolated and constantly ridiculed in the media, Schumpeter was finally dismissed. The manner and circumstances were so brutal that one liberal newspaper accused Renner of character assassination. Nor was that the end, for several of his actions as finance minister resulted in investigations that continued for months. Felix Somary, the banker, observed that "Schumpeter made light of everything" and attributed his cool manner to his training at the Theresianum, "where the students learned to cultivate self-control and under no circumstances to show emotion. One should master the rules of the game of all parties and ideologies, but avoid commitments."[64] Inwardly, though, Schumpeter was shattered. He was convinced that he lacked "the quality of leadership,"[65] and his public humiliation was made more painful by his mother's disappointed hopes. The fact that subsequent Allied stabilization programs for Austria were modeled on his or that the government that sacked him was judged to be "incapable of governing the country" failed to ease the sting of failure. When asked about his experiences, he rarely said more than "I held the minister-ship in a time of revolution, and it was no pleasure, I may assure you."[66]

In November, when Wieser returned from London, his acquaintances were still talking about Schumpeter's fall. The older man observed, "It seems that Schumpeter is utterly ruined in the eyes of all the Parties. Even the young economists, who regarded him as their leader, have written him off. No one has any more expectations of him."[67] His former admirers had sold him short. After two terms at the University of Graz, where he licked his wounds, Schumpeter did what many former public servants do. He joined the private sector.

His timing was impeccable. The destruction of Austria's hopes for the future coincided with a stock market boom and deal-making frenzy. As one observer recalled,

> Stock quotations began to adapt themselves from day to day to the falling value of money. The capitalists sought to preserve their capital from depreciation by investing it in securities and bills . . . The Stock Exchange speculated upon a continuous fall in the Krone. The Krone's exchange

value vis a vis other currencies fell faster than its internal purchasing power. As a result, Austrian prices were far below the level of world market prices and large profits could be realized by exporting Austrian products.[68]

In a last-minute expression of appreciation, parliament had awarded Schumpeter a golden parachute in the form of a banking license, and by 1921 Schumpeter had parlayed it into the presidency of a small but old, highly respected bank. He had run through his savings and borrowed heavily to live far beyond the means of a professor and politician. Now he needed to make money.

Chapter VII

Europe Is Dying: Keynes at Versailles

Expert opinion is being ignored.

Keynes has been too splendid about the Austrian treaty. He is going to fight. He says he's going to resign.

—*Francis Oppenheimer, 1919*[1]

Vienna was not unique. In January 1919, famine and pestilence raged from St. Petersburg to Istanbul. To the Britons and Americans who came to Europe to survey the damage, the whole continent seemed to be on the verge of dying. After a ten-hour drive from the coast to Lille, in eastern France, one observer wrote in his diary that he could recall seeing no "human being not connected with the Army . . . or any animal . . . or really any living thing except rank grass or any inhabited house." In Ypres, Belgium, where some of the worst fighting had taken place, "the colors of the bricks and stone are mellowed; grass and moss are beginning to grow over the ruins."[2]

Eight weeks after the signing of the armistice, the restoration of peaceful conditions had proved impossible. The blockade was still in effect. The Allies dared not give up their most effective weapon against Germany too soon. Fighting involving hundreds of thousands of troops continued as dozens of small wars erupted. Pogroms, expulsions, and mass murder were under way. Eight and a half million men had lost their lives. Nearly as many were left physically disabled or psychologically maimed. An entire generation of children in Central Europe—the Kriegskinder, or children of war—was growing up underfed and undersized.

In the aftermath of the war, the "universal age" and its economic achievements seemed as unreal as a dream. In addition to the staggering loss of life and property, the prewar channels of trade and credit were in ruins. Everywhere new barriers to exports and imports were springing up. Those who possessed something to sell were often reluctant to part with it for paper currencies issued by bankrupt governments; a large share of trade reverted to barter. Winners and losers alike had mortgaged themselves to the hilt to fight the costliest war in history, exhausting not only their reserves but also their limited powers of taxation. As late as 1916, France, Germany, and Russia had no income tax. Now there was no credit to feed the population, fuel the furnaces, repair the damaged factories, or finance renewed trade. The threat of bankruptcy as much as the thirst for revenge was making shaky governments determined to make someone else foot the bill.

"The economic mechanism of Europe is jammed," wrote David Lloyd George, Britain's wartime prime minister, to Woodrow Wilson.[3] Everything depended on economic revival, but the heads of victorious states gathering in Paris seemed incapable of paying attention. This, in any case, was the gloomy view from the third floor of the magnificent Hotel Majestic near the Place d'Etoile, where the British delegation was housed and where Maynard Keynes, the rising Treasury star, was dashing off a letter to Vanessa Bell, assuring her that she would "really be amused by the amazing complications of psychology and personality and intrigue which make such magnificent sport of the impending catastrophe of Europe."[4]

Keynes had arrived at the Hotel Majestic on the tenth of January, the wettest, most depressing month of the year. President Woodrow Wilson had been in Paris for a month, prime minister Lloyd George was not due for another day. The city, which had managed to avoid falling to the kaiser's troops despite heavy bombardment, was now an occupied zone. American Express branches had sprouted like chanterelles. Giant British printing presses were groaning in the Champs de Mars. Black sedans carrying diplomats and drab military vehicles clogged the streets while young men and women wearing the uniforms of some twenty-seven countries jammed the sidewalks. The whole world was in Paris, it seemed.

A mini-Whitehall and a mini–White House constituted themselves on the Seine. Winston Churchill, Britain's minister of munitions, accompanied as always by his faithful secretary, Eddie Marsh, shuttled back and forth between the two. On the far end of the Champs-Elysees were President Woodrow Wilson and a team of advisors that included Bernard Baruch, the financier; John Foster Dulles, counsel to the American team; and Felix Frankfurter, the former secretary of war. The delegations brought their own fleets of cars and airplanes, set up their own telephone and telegraph networks, and operated their own trains.

Keynes was not a member of Lloyd George's inner circle. Accordingly, while the prime minister and his mistress, Frances Stevenson, were installed in a luxury flat, Keynes was bunking in the Hotel Majestic with the rest of the British delegation. The hotel, which had been undergoing preparations since shortly after the armistice, had its own physician, a chaperone for the female staff, and a security detail of Scotland Yard detectives who were supposed to forestall leaks. As a result, it was easy to get out of, but "extremely difficult to get in," recalled Harold Nicolson, a British diplomat in the delegation who was married to the writer Vita Sackville-West and was an old friend of Keynes's. The hotel was "staffed from attic to cellar with bright British domestics from our own provincial hotels. The food, in consequence, was of the Anglo-Swiss variety," Nicolson added.[5] Oddly, no one thought of replacing the French staff in the Hotel Astoria next door, where the British delegation had its offices and kept its confidential maps and papers.

The most extraordinary people floated in and out of the Majestic. Ho Chi Minh, the future leader of the Viet Cong, washed dishes in the kitchen. T. E. Lawrence, aka Lawrence of Arabia, was often in the lobby, as were Jean Cocteau, the playwright; and Marcel Proust, "white, unshaven, grubby, slip-faced, wearing a fur coat and white kid gloves." Nicolson described their encounters:

He asks me questions. Will I please tell him how the Committees work? I say, "Well, we generally meet at 10:00, there are secretaries behind . . ." "No, no, you're going too much too fast. Start over. You took the official car. You got out at the Quai d'Orsay. You climbed the stairs. You entered the room. And, then? What happened? Be precise, my dear, precise!" So I tell him everything. The sham cordiality of it all; the handshakes; the maps; the rustle of papers; the tea in the next room; the macaroons. He listens enthralled, interrupting from time to time—"Be more precise, my dear man, don't go too fast." [6]

Journalists outnumbered diplomats. Frederick Maurice, a former major general, was in Paris on assignment for the London *Daily News*. He had nearly brought down the government by accusing the prime minister of lying to Parliament about British troop strength late in the war. His favorite child, Nancy, was in Paris too, the brand-new secretary of the married, middle-aged, conservative Major General Edward Louis Spears, who would one day become her husband—one of countless young female assistants whose khaki uniforms inspired several mildly salacious chansons. Her younger sister, Joan, a precocious fifteen-year-old student at St. Paul's Girls School in London, who showed no sign of becoming one of the century's most famous economic thinkers, would have given anything to be in Paris too. She had to content herself with Nancy's patchy, pompous bulletins to their mother.

Maynard Keynes was considered "one of the most influential men behind the scenes" in Paris. Even his critics acknowledged that he was "clear headed, self confident, with an unerring memory." [7] He complained, with justification, of overwork, but his dinner companions wryly noted his "unsurpassable digestion" and capacity for champagne. At thirty-six, Keynes was still as thin and lanky as an undergraduate. His upturned nose and fleshy lips had earned him the nickname Snout in his school days and he had the hungry look of someone who was, as Lady Ottoline Morrell, one of Bertrand Russell's lovers, remarked disparagingly, "greedy for work, fame, influence, domination, admiration." [8] Keynes's arrogance could be breathtaking, his manners appalling, his dress sloppy. Yet his luminous eyes, animated features, and aura of confidence made him attractive. Men and women alike found his silky, melodious voice irresistible.

Born in 1883, the same year as Joseph Schumpeter, Keynes was the favorite son of a highly successful, close-knit Cambridge academic family, at home with, and in some cases related by marriage to, other intellectual dynasties, including the Darwins, Ramseys, Maurices, Stephens, and Stracheys. Neville Keynes, his father, was a professor of moral philosophy and a close friend of Alfred Marshall. His mother, Florence, who became mayor of Cambridge in 1932, was active in local politics and philanthropy. They were bright, attentive, affectionate parents to Keynes and his two younger siblings.

Recognized as a genius in adolescence, Keynes was groomed to be a Cambridge fellow virtually from the cradle. Neville Keynes encouraged his gifted son to pursue mathematics. After graduating with honors from Eton in 1902 and obtaining a top score on the Cambridge entrance examination, Keynes entered one of the oldest Cambridge colleges, King's, on a scholarship. The publication of the philosopher G. E. Moore's *Principia Ethica* at the end of Keynes's freshman year was the great event of his undergraduate career, all the more so because Moore was a former member of the Apostles, which served as a link between generations of Cambridge intellectuals. *Principia Ethica* was concerned with defining a good life. The Victorian preoccupation with striving, moneymaking, and obeying rules was the target. Rejecting the utilitarian values and do-good moralism of Alfred Marshall's generation, as well as its sexual mores, Moore espoused a kind of radical individualism and aestheticism tempered by the Golden Rule. "Nothing mattered except states of mind, our own and other people's, of course, but chiefly our own," Keynes recalled in 1938. "These states of mind were not associated with action or achievement or with consequences. They consisted in timeless, passionate states of contemplation and communion."[9]

Such reflections give no hint of Keynes's devotion to boating, riding, tennis, and especially golf, his passion for public debate, and his commitment to the Liberal Party or the prestigious social or intellectual student societies that he was invited to join or lead. His college career showed Keynes to be a natural leader as well as a brilliant intellect. Though rarely in bed before three in the morning, he graduated with first-class honors on the eve of his twenty-first birthday. Assuming that he would follow in Neville's footsteps, he spent a year studying for the mathematics Tripos. By 1905, the queen of sciences was significantly harder to subdue than when Marshall had scored his second place. Keynes's twelfth-place finish was hardly embarrassing, but it was not good enough to win a fellowship at King's. To give an idea of the competition, the great number theorist G. H. Hardy, best known as the author of *The Mathematician's Apology,* was still waiting for a university lectureship after finishing in fourth place on the Tripos in 1900.

Keynes escaped to hike in the Alps with a copy of Marshall's *Principles of Economics.* He was back in Cambridge in the fall, sufficiently intrigued to attend Marshall's lectures while preparing to take the civil service examination. "Marshall is continually pestering me to turn professional Economist and writes flattering remarks on my papers," Keynes wrote to his close friend Lytton Strachey. "Do you think there is anything in it? I doubt it." [10]

Nonetheless, the subject grew on Keynes, and he began to think that he might like to "manage a railway or organize a Trust, or at least swindle the investing public." [11] With an academic appointment off the table, Keynes set his sights on the Treasury. But a second-place finish in the civil service examination resulted in a temporary exile to the Colonial Office, where he was assigned to work involving the Indian rupee. Unlike Cecily in Oscar Wilde's *The Importance of Being Earnest,* Keynes found the rupee more fascinating than not. He took the view that the currency—any currency, actually—was a clue to the state of a nation's economy and, since countries were connected to one another through trade and investment, the world's economy.

Everybody was willing to accept British pounds in return for goods or services, but not everyone was willing to take rupees. The value of money—whether the giant millstones favored by ancient Micronesians, gold coins, or entries on a bank balance sheet—depended strictly on people's willingness to accept it. So a nation's currency must reflect the world's confidence in its economic prospects, solvency, and willingness to make good on its promises. In that sense, a currency was like a pulse, a vital sign that could signal anything from disease or injury to a momentary rush of excitement or fear. The challenge for a doctor was to find the cause of a racing pulse before the patient went into shock or made him look foolish by hopping off the gurney in apparently perfect health. If the patient was thousands of miles away and more details about his condition were impossible to obtain, the challenge was that much greater. With his nimble mind, knack for spotting connections, and gift for synthesis, Keynes not only relished such conundrums but proved to be a natural diagnostician.

Keynes dispatched his official duties vis-à-vis the rupee with such ease that he had ample time in the office to write a treatise on probability, which he hoped would win him the elusive college fellowship. It also left him with free evenings and weekends in which to cultivate his social life. He lived in London, where he rented a flat at 46 Gordon Square in a fashionably louche part of town. His upstairs neighbors were the beautiful, intimidating, wildly talented Stephen sisters, the future Vanessa Bell and Virginia Woolf. Keynes got on especially well with Vanessa, a painter who loved to gossip and talk dirty. Keynes's sex diary, as meticulously detailed as the notebooks in which he recorded his expenses and golf scores, indicates that his love life blossomed too. In contrast to the period from 1903 to 1905, when the number of his sex partners was "nil," by 1911 there were eight, and in 1913 they peaked at nine. Among them were lovers and lifelong friends Duncan Grant, Lytton Strachey, and J. T. Sheppard, the openly gay provost of King's.[12] Still, he rarely missed Sunday lunch in Cambridge with the large Keynes clan.

For most of his twenties, Keynes was Britain's resident expert on obscure currencies. Thinking about currencies got him into the habit of thinking about economies holistically instead of focusing on "trade" or "labor" or "industry" in isolation, and taught him how to draw salient conclusions from a handful of indicators. It also gave him a feeling for which government actions exerted systemic effects, like those of the moon on tides, instead of effects only on a particular industry or group. By 1908, however, he had quit the India Office. Arthur Pigou, the successor to Al-fred Marshall's chair at Cambridge, and Keynes's father offered to support him for up to a year while he finished his treatise. When in 1909 the com-pleted work failed to win him the coveted King's fellowship—a license, essentially, to take on paying students and dine at high table—Marshall personally financed an economics lectureship at Cambridge for Keynes. At that point, the fellows of King's College elected him as one of their own.

In his first communication to his parents after arriving at King's College as a freshman, the eighteen-year-old Keynes had announced, "I've taken a good look around the place and come to the conclusion that it's pretty in-efficient."[13] As his biographer Robert Skidelsky points out, the institutions would vary over his life, but never Keynes's view of them or, indeed, of the world as he found it. They were badly run and in need of more competent management. Though given to fits of "ungovernable anger,"[14] especially when confronted by stupidity, Keynes was on the whole more exasperated than outraged, more impatient than self-righteous. He parted company with his Bloomsbury friends in that he had none of the artist's disdain for worldly success or people in power. Like Winston Churchill, who con-fessed to his wife that even when "everything tends towards catastrophe and collapse. I am interested, geared up and happy,"[15] Keynes was more invigorated than depressed by the world's problems and could not repress his impulse to make the bad slightly less so or the good a little better.

His response to the war was a characteristic blend of patriotism, op-portunism, and pragmatism. When England declared war on Germany in August 1914, he had not known what to think. An incorrigible opti-mist, he shared the general view that the fighting would be over in a few months, if not weeks. The first time that the Chancellor of the Exchequer, David Lloyd George, had asked for his advice was before the fighting broke out. He spent a day trying to convince Lloyd George not to cave in to pres-sure from City bankers to suspend gold convertibility of the pound until absolutely necessary. Keynes's optimism evidently exceeded that of City bankers.

He was formally drafted by the Treasury in January 1915 and assigned to war finance. The military draft, introduced in 1916 for males ages eighteen to forty-one, raised the personal stakes considerably, for Keynes had become part of the British war machine. At least a half dozen of his closest friends and former lovers were pacifists who had resolved not to fight. They constantly pressed him to end his complicity in a war that he professed to despise. On one occasion he found a note from Strachey on his dinner plate: "Dear Keynes, Why are you still at Treasury? Yours, Lytton." [16] As long as he was on the Treasury staff, Keynes was not actually at risk of being drafted, since the military exempted men who were "engaged in work of national importance." Under intense pressure from his friends to take a stand against the war, Keynes constantly threatened to quit, and in February 1916 he alarmed his parents by going so far as to apply formally for conscientious objector status. In his application, he made it clear that he objected to the coercion of the draft rather than to the war, that is, on libertarian rather than pacifist grounds. After he informed the draft board that he would be too busy at the Treasury to attend his hearing, his application was rejected and he pursued the matter no further. His friends eventually forgave him, especially after he began using his Whitehall connections to protect them when he could. Still, most of Keynes's biographers prior to Skidelsky had considered the episode so potentially damaging to his reputation that they had covered it up, just as they had avoided mentioning his homosexuality.

Keynes's job was to help the Treasury borrow dollars from the Americans on the cheapest possible terms while lending pounds to the French and Britain's other Continental allies on the most lucrative ones, all while protecting the foreign exchange value of the pound sterling. Rounding up scarce currencies such as Spanish pesetas in emergencies was another of his duties, one that gave him hands-on experience as a foreign exchange trader and left him addicted to that risky but thrilling game of betting on one currency's rise, another's fall. Ultimately, writes Skidelsky, all matters of war finance—and many related to postwar finance—passed through Keynes's hands.

Toward the end of the war, as popular hopes that its staggering cost could be recouped from Germany soared, Keynes was increasingly drawn into the vexing debate over reparations. Lloyd George, who had become prime minister of a wartime coalition government at the end of 1916, asked the Treasury to estimate how much the Germans could pay. He had taken it for granted that "the Treasury experts naturally had their mind primarily set on securing some source of revenue which would reduce the crushing burden of taxation by the payment of interest on our gigantic war debt for the next two generations."[17] But other considerations weighed on Keynes, who was ultimately assigned to draft the Treasury position paper. When he delivered his report on reparations to the incoming Treasury chief, Austen Chamberlain, Joseph's son, on the heels of the December 14, 1918, general election, it was a bombshell.

An Allied reparations commission headed by a former governor of New York, Charles Evans Hughes, had already recommended that Germany should be made to pay $40 billion, or roughly one-third of the Allies' war expenditures. Keynes concluded that the most that could be extracted from Germany was £3 billion or $15 billion, less than the amount Britain and France owed the United States. Pointing out that the Allied commission's figure was twice the estimated prewar value of Germany's gold reserves, securities, ships, raw material inventories, factories, and machinery, Keynes warned that placing too high a figure on reparations would ultimately undermine British economic interests by increasing the risk that Germany would ultimately repudiate her debt.

The report caused a furor. Most Britons felt that since the Germans had started the war, they should bear its cost. After all, as Lloyd George pointed out, the burden had to be carried by someone. Prewar tax revenues would not have sufficed to pay *interest* on the war debt. The French national debt had multiplied tenfold; the British, fourfold since 1914. If the Germans didn't pay, then innocent Britons and Frenchmen would have to shoulder higher taxes in order to pay it down. One reason that the British electorate was so passionate on the subject was that nearly 40 percent of the British population owned government securities. British business was also in the pro-reparations camp. They wanted German firms, not British industry, to be taxed in order to repay the debt.

Keynes refused to backtrack, insisting that his £3 billion figure was probably too high. In the furious row that erupted inside the Treasury, he stood his ground, consistently representing the low end of estimates. Lloyd George started referring to him as "the Puck of economics," after Shakespeare's mischief maker and speaker of the immortal phrase "Lord, what fools these mortals be!"[18]

While journalists, politicians, and the public were fixated on the amount Germany should pay, Keynes drew attention to *how* the indemnity might be collected. The easiest method was the oldest and the one that Germany had planned to use to extract reparations from Britain, France, and Belgium had she prevailed on the western front. It was the method proposed by the Hughes commission and involved stripping Germany of her portable public and private property, from stock certificates and gold reserves to ships and machinery. Keynes favored the second alternative, which was to leave Germany's existing wealth more or less intact, supply her with raw material, and levy an annual tribute on her future export earnings. "Having thus nursed her back to a condition of high productivity," Keynes explained, the Allies could "compel her to exploit this product under conditions of servitude for a long period of years."[19]

According to Skidelsky, Keynes went to Paris with twin objectives that were not easily reconciled; namely, reviving the European economy without damaging British export prospects. Two conditions were essential for his strategy to work: a relatively low German indemnity and the willingness of Americans to forgive Britain's war debt. That was the only way Germany could avoid running huge trade surpluses—that is, export more than she imported in order to earn pounds or francs—and that Britain could avoid head-to-head competition with the German export juggernaut. Keynes refused to be daunted by the fact that neither part of his plan was remotely acceptable to the American, French, and British public, something their elected representatives could not possibly ignore.

Ten days after the German surrender, Keynes boasted to his mother, "I have been put in principal charge of financial matters for the Peace Conference."[20] This was an overstatement. His formal role at the conference involved relief, not the political tar baby of reparations. His immediate brief was to help Herbert Hoover work out the financial arrangements required for Europe's transition from war to peace, especially the provision of food.

The armistice called for continuing the blockade of Germany and Austria but permitted exceptions for needed food and medicine. The French had subsequently placed a lien on Germany's remaining gold, hard currencies, and other liquid assets, arguing that they had to be set aside for reparations. With her accounts frozen, Germany could buy no food and faced slow starvation. Keynes was determined to overcome the obstacles placed by the French.

Within a few days of his arrival in France, Keynes was on his way to an "extraordinary adventure" in occupied Germany. He had been asked to join a team of American and French financial experts in Trier, the ancient town on the Mosel River at the intersection of France, Germany, and Luxembourg, where Karl Marx had grown up. Adjacent to the headquarters of Marshal Ferdinand Foch of France and currently occupied by the US Army, Trier had been chosen as the site for renegotiating the November armistice. Though curious "whether the children's ribs would be sticking out," the Allied experts had hardly ventured from the train for three entire days except for a little shopping spree to buy wartime scrip, paper clothing, and other souvenirs.[21] A bridge foursome had formed the first night, and Keynes played more or less around the clock.

Keynes's mission involved finance as well as food. Like Hoover, he was appalled at the blockade and, like President Wilson, convinced that "so long as hunger continued to gnaw, the foundations of government would continue to crumble."[22] He was in Trier ostensibly to find a way to get food trains rolling into Germany. Typical of all negotiations during the Peace Conference, however, things were not quite that simple. As an entirely separate matter, the Allies were determined to get hold of Germany's merchant fleet, now anchored off the city of Hamburg, but were at somewhat of a loss about how to accomplish the takeover. They had not stipulated the surrender of the ships in the armistice, and sending the navy to seize them seemed politically unwise. So it occurred to Allied leaders that the food crisis might provide a convenient opportunity for getting the Germans to strike a deal. Keynes's job was to convince them that "ships against food was . . . a reasonable bargain." As he later admitted, there was an element of bluff involved, not to speak of the difficulty of making it clear to "bewildered, cowed, nerve-shattered and even hungry" financiers "to comprehend how the ground really lay."

In Trier, Keynes watched curiously as the German financiers, dressed like undertakers, approached their train. They walked "stiffly and uneasily," lifting their feet "like men in a photograph or a movie." After they climbed into the railway carriage, they did not extend their hands but only bowed stiffly. They were a sad lot "with drawn, dejected faces and tired staring eyes, like men who had been hammered on the Stock Exchange."[23]

The head of the Reichsbank looked like "an old, broken umbrella." The "sly Corps type" from the Foreign Office had a "face cut to pieces with dueling." The spokesman for the German team was a third figure, "a very small man, exquisitely clean, very well and neatly dressed, with a high stiff collar which seemed cleaner and whiter than an ordinary collar" and with "eyes gleaming straight at us, with extraordinary sorrow in them, yet like an honest animal at bay." This was Carl Melchior, a Jewish banker from Hamburg. He was a liberal, a critic of submarine warfare, and a partner of the banker Max Warburg who had extensive connections in the United States.

Keynes spoke first and asked whether everyone understood English. In his memoir, Max Warburg described Keynes's face as an expressionless mask but said that his voice and his phrasing of questions conveyed sympathy. When it was Melchior's turn to speak, he did so in "moving, persuasive, almost perfect English." The banker used ingenious arguments to plead for a loan, while Keynes endeavored "clearly and coldly" to communicate the idea that a loan was politically out of the question.[24] They managed to agree that the Germans would immediately hand over £5 million in gold and hard currencies in exchange for milk and butter, but that was all.

When Keynes next met the Germans a month later, again in Trier, a stalemate had developed on the question of ships for food. The Germans were determined to hold on to their ships as long as possible, because they

saw them as their best bargaining chip in the upcoming peace negotiations and were determined not to give them up without a quid pro quo.
What's more, the Germans were under the impression that the United
States would be willing to advance them the funds needed to purchase the
first few installments of food—a sizeable chunk of which was to consist of
surplus American pork.

By the end of the second meeting, the Germans had declared that
large-scale food imports couldn't be financed without a loan. If an Allied
loan should prove politically impossible, as Keynes had warned would
likely be the case, then they would not deliver the ships. If the negotiations
broke down and Germany couldn't get food, no one could prevent "the
flooding of Bolshevism over the whole of Europe."[25] The negotiators had
reached an impasse. Nothing could be done except by the Big Four—the
leaders of the United States, England, France, and Italy—but the Big Four
were busy arguing over the number of members of the Brazil delegation
and hearing proposals from "Copts, Armenians, Slovaks and Zionists."
T. E. Lawrence, ostensibly the interpreter for Emir Faisal of Saudi Arabia, took advantage of the Emir's decision to quote several passages from
the Koran to propose a scheme for Arab self-rule in the old Ottoman
territories.[26]

The next meeting between Keynes and Melchior took place at the
beginning of March in Spa, in Belgium, at the former headquarters of the
German high command amid hills covered in black pines "far also from
the starved cities and growling mob."[27] But the talks again went nowhere,
and Keynes was feeling desperate that two months had passed since the
first meeting in Trier with no progress toward freeing up gold to pay for
food. He sensed that Melchior might feel the same way and asked for permission to sound him out. Getting past Melchior's sullen clerks, Keynes
caught him alone and, quivering with excitement, asked if they could
speak privately. He recalled:

> Melchior wondered what I wanted . . . I tried to convey to him what I
> was feeling, how we believed his prognostications of pessimism, how we
> were impressed, not less than he, with the urgency of starting food sup-

plies, how personally I believed that my Government and the American Government were really determined that the food should come, but that . . . if they, the Germans, adhered to their attitude of the morning a fatal delay was inevitable; that they must make up their minds to the handing over the ships.[28]

Melchior promised that he would do his best but held out little hope. "German honor and organization and morality were crumbling; he saw no light anywhere; he expected Germany to collapse and civilization to grow dim; we must do what we could; but dark forces were passing over us."[29] Keynes's meetings with Melchior confirmed his own pessimism about the war's devastating consequences, and, not surprisingly given the uprisings in Berlin and elsewhere in Germany, he shared Melchior's fears that Germany would succumb to Bolshevism if the treaty terms were too onerous.

By the next evening, it was obvious that Melchior's effort had come to nothing and that the new German government in Weimar was digging in its heels. At times, Keynes seemed more anxious than the Germans about the threat of revolution and the glacial pace of the negotiations. He couldn't be sure whether Germany's food supplies were really as depleted as the British thought. Convinced that a dramatic gesture was required to break the logjam, Keynes proposed a public rupture and convinced the team to order its train back to Paris in the middle of the night so that the Germans would awaken in the morning to find them gone. Back in Paris, Keynes found that his ploy had succeeded in capturing the attention of the Big Four. As Lord Riddell, newspaper baron and Britain's wartime press secretary, wrote in his diary on March 8, 1919:

The Council decided to victual the Germans, provided they hand over their ships and pay for the food in bills of exchange on other countries, goods or gold. The French strongly opposed this. LG said to me afterwards that the French are acting very foolishly, and will, if they are not careful, drive the Germans into Bolshevism. He told me that he had made a violent attack on Klotz, the French Minister of Finance, in which he said that if a Bolshevist state is formed in Germany, three statues will be erected—one to Lenin, one to Trotsky, and the third to Klotz. Klotz made no reply . . . The Americans are pleased . . . All the commercial people, British and American, favor abolishing the blockade and urge an early settlement with Germany so that the world may again get to work.[30]

Four days later, Keynes was on a train bound for Trier in the company of the British admiral Rosslyn Wemyss, whom the Big Four had deputized to deliver the ultimatum to the Germans. The French had succeeded on one point: the Germans had to agree unconditionally to hand over the ships before they were to be told about the food. "D'you think you could see to it that they don't make any unnecessary trouble?" the admiral asked Keynes. So Keynes once again sought out Melchior in private and told him that if the Germans declared their willingness unconditionally, there would be a quid pro quo. "Can you assure me von Braun will do this?" Keynes asked, referring to the head of the German delegation. Melchior paused for a moment before "he looked at me again with his solemn eyes. 'Yes,' he replied, 'there shall be no difficulty about that.'" The next day, everyone stuck to their script: "All was settled now and the food trains started for Germany."[31]

With considerably less difficulty, Keynes also convinced the Allies to approve a loan to pay for British food shipments to Austria by early 1919. After this small triumph, Keynes had the Germans installed at the Château de Villette outside Paris. A plan was afoot to collect financiers from many countries to discuss reconstruction. As it turned out, Keynes visited the chateau only once or twice. Not long after the Germans moved in, the Peace Conference turned away from the issue of reconstruction and became terminally entangled in the matter of reparations.

"The subject of reparations caused more trouble, contention, hard feeling, and delay at the Paris Peace Conference than any other point in the Treaty," Thomas Lamont, the US Treasury representative, wrote afterward.[32] Harold Nicolson remarked that while the conference was often portrayed as a duel between the forces of darkness and light—Wilson versus Georges

Clemenceau of France, Carthaginian versus Wilsonian peace, Keynes versus Klotz—in fact, it was "not so much a duel as a general melee."[33]

The Allies were at loggerheads among themselves. President Wilson opposed saddling Germans with the entire cost of the war. It was reasonable to demand that Germany pay for the damage inflicted by her troops, he argued, but that was all. Then there was the tricky question of what share of the levy on Germany each of the victors would be entitled to and how long. When Lloyd George suggested that payments cease after thirty years, Clemenceau said they should extend for a thousand years if necessary. As late as March 1919, the Allies could not agree over the issue. The French were calling for £25 billion while the United States refused to countenance any figure over £5 or £6 billion. The official British figure was £11 billion. In early March, Keynes finally suggested leaving the total amount of reparations to be paid out of the treaty. That solution was ultimately adopted.

Lloyd George, annoyed by constant press leaks, suggested that the Big Four meet privately. Thus, the second half of the Peace Conference, from mid-March to mid-May, took place in Woodrow Wilson's "tiny study." At first alone except for one interpreter, the heads of state of the United States, UK, France, and Italy—Woodrow Wilson, David Lloyd George, Georges Clemenceau, and Vittorio Orlando—sat around a fire in overstuffed chairs, recalled Nicolson, "with maps spread out on the floor which they were sometimes obliged to crawl about on their hands and knees to study, the big Four managed to hammer out what was, in effect, the penultimate version of the settlement."[34]

April turned out to be the cruelest month. As the weather turned warm, the formerly festive atmosphere in Paris suddenly became frenetic. The reservations that many participants had had about holding the conference in Paris were confirmed: bedbugs, medieval plumbing, and price gouging were the least of it. The press had turned vituperative. "The constant clamour of their newspapers, the stridency of their personal attacks, increased in volume," observed British diplomat Harold Nicholson. "The cumulative effect of all this shouting outside the very doors of the Conference produced a nervous and as such unwholesome effect."[35] Lloyd

George had to face down a rebellion in Parliament, where conservatives feared he was not being tough enough on Germany. Clemenceau became the bête noir of the French press, which was convinced that he was being outmaneuvered by the English and Americans. Orlando left the conference. And Woodrow Wilson became terribly ill with either food poisoning or influenza. By May the fights among the four grew so bitter that on one occasion Wilson was forced to intervene physically between Lloyd George and Clemenceau.

The conference within the conference not only froze out the representatives of the smaller countries but left experts like Keynes in the cold too. The Big Four made far-reaching economic decisions on the fly with hardly any input. President Wilson considered the British plea for debt forgiveness for a few minutes before summarily rejecting it. The British prime minister consulted Keynes when he wanted "to wriggle out of his commitments," observed Lloyd George's biographer, but "he never thought of taking his advice." [36] After twelve-hour days climbing in and out of drafty cars and racing from one overheated room to another, Keynes often had dinner with Jan Smuts, a South African member of the British war cabinet and strong proponent of the League of Nations and reconciliation with Germany.

> Poor Keynes often sits with me at night after a good dinner and we rail against the world and the coming flood . . . Then we laugh, and behind the laughter is Hoover's horrible picture of thirty million people who must die unless there is some great intervention. But then again we think things are never really as bad as that; and something will turn up, and the worst will never be. [37]

On May 7, 1919, Herbert Hoover, who was solid and square and struck most Europeans as gratuitously pugnacious in his day-to-day dealings, was heading down the Champs-Elysees before dawn. The streetlights still glimmered, and the avenue was deserted. He walked slowly and kept his head down, like a pugilist after a losing match. He did not expect to meet anyone he knew. Except for a few ascetic French generals, the delegates at the Peace Conference liked to linger over their *Times* of London and En-

glish marmalade at breakfast. So he was surprised to see two familiar figures in bowlers crossing the boulevard in his direction. Keynes and Smuts
were talking animatedly, heads together and seemingly oblivious to his
presence. What were those two doing out at this hour?

When they got close enough to recognize him, they too gave little
starts of surprise. It dawned on all three at once: each had been up since
at least four in the morning, when the freshly printed draft treaty was
delivered to their rooms by messenger. None had seen the treaty in its en-
tirety before, although Keynes had read, with mounting dismay, parts of
the draft as early as May 4. Despite their insider's knowledge and Keynes's
and Smuts's cynicism about the proceedings, they were shocked. Each had
been driven out of doors by anger, disbelief, and awful premonitions. After
this flash of telepathy, Hoover, Keynes, and Smuts all began to talk at once.
As Hoover recalled, "We agreed that it was terrible."[38]

Within two weeks, the incorrigible optimist had moved out of his
room at the Majestic, rented an apartment with cook and valet on the edge
of the Bois de Boulogne, and crawled into bed, too depressed to get up
except when the PM summoned. By May 14, feeling like "an accomplice
in all this wickedness and folly," Keynes had made up his mind to resign.
"The Peace is outrageous and impossible and can bring nothing but misfortune," he wrote to his mother, Duncan Grant, and others.[39]

Keynes's final intervention was a protest against "murdering Vienna."[40] The negotiations over Austria had been postponed until the
German terms were settled. He was getting regular reports from Francis
Oppenheimer, the Treasury's emissary on the scene, who had been in constant touch with Joseph Schumpeter, who, in turn, was supplying data on
Austrian assets, tax revenues, and the like. On May 29, Keynes sent Lloyd
George a memorandum pleading the case that Austria should pay no
reparations. On the thirtieth, he attended a meeting of the Austrian reparations commission and won a major concession, getting a demand for
10 billion gold crowns in reparations dropped. Quoting ghastly statistics
about children dying of TB and malnourishment, he was partly successful
in modifying a demand from the French that Austria surrender her milk
cows.

Keynes agreed with one Viennese newspaper's harsh criticism of the treaty:

> Never has the substance of a treaty of peace so grossly betrayed the intentions which were said to have guided its construction as is the case with this Treaty . . . in which every provision is permeated with ruthlessness and pitilessness, in which no breath of human sympathy can be detected, which flies in the face of everything which binds man to man, which is a crime against humanity itself, against a suffering and tortured people.[41]

Although he must have known that it was a lost cause, Keynes continued to plead with Bernard Baruch for the US Treasury to endorse "my Grand Scheme for putting everyone on their legs."[42] Lloyd George called a special meeting of the British delegation and promised to refuse the services of the British Army to advance into Germany, or the services of the British Navy to enforce the blockade of Germany in order to obtain eleventh-hour changes in the treaty. But, as Keynes predicted in a letter to his mother, it really was too late for grand gestures. The French were furious, and President Wilson, who should have been sympathetic, had grown increasingly suspicious of British intentions. He vetoed Lloyd George's proposal as peremptorily as he had rejected Keynes's proposal for debt forgiveness a month earlier. Lloyd George did not press the case further, possibly because of an intelligence report that the German cabinet had already secretly decided to sign the treaty. Nonetheless, he predicted gloomily, "We shall have to do the whole thing over again in twenty five years at three times the cost."[43]

By the time the Germans actually signed the Treaty of Versailles on June 28, Keynes had been back in England for nearly a month. He had retreated to Charleston, Virginia and Vanessa Stephen's house in the country, where he spent long hours weeding furiously to distract himself. He had dashed off a letter of resignation to Austen Chamberlain, the Chancellor of the Exchequer, on June 5. On the same day, he had also written to Lloyd George, "The battle is lost. I leave the twins [the judge Lord Sumner

and financier Lord Cunliffe, head of the British reparations commission]
to gloat over the devastation of Europe and to taste what remains for the
British taxpayer." [44]

Austin Robinson, son of an Anglican minister, war pilot, and Cambridge
undergraduate, dated his "conversion to the faith of the economists"
to October 1919, when he attended one of Keynes's last lectures for the
term. [45] Keynes read from his half-finished manuscript about the peace
treaty in front of a large audience. Robinson was incredibly moved by "the
very obvious depth of his dedication to the problems of the world and his
hatred of failure to avert foreseeable disaster." [46] For Robinson's generation, which wanted to put the war behind it by doing something to heal its
wounds, Keynes's argument that getting the economics right was essential
for preventing future wars was a genuine revelation. He was intrigued
by Keynes's conviction that ideas mattered as much as, if not more than,
competing economic and political interests.

Keynes had begun writing almost as soon as he returned to Cambridge
from Paris. He plucked his theme for *The Economic Consequences of the
Peace* from a clever remark by Jan Smuts's mistress: "Mrs. Gillett, referring
to the Anti–Corn Law League, had reminded Smuts that economic reform
had preceded franchise reform in the nineteenth century, and that 'now
it seems as though in the same way the political and territorial questions
won't be solved 'til the economic world is righted.'" Smuts reported this
remark to Keynes, who said "how true it was and he had never thought of it
that way." [47] Margot Asquith, the amusing wife of the former prime minister,
had suggested to Keynes that he include portraits of the major personalities.
In August, Macmillan's in London agreed to publish the book, although
Keynes had to agree to pay the printing costs. Felix Frankfurter, with whom
he had become friendly in Paris, arranged for an American edition.

Keynes blasted the treaty as a rank betrayal by the older generation of
political leaders. Not only had the Big Four done nothing to restore the
prewar European economy, but they had not seriously considered the need
to do so. They had simply assumed that the restoration of broken ties and
rebuilding would happen spontaneously.

The Treaty includes no provisions for the economic rehabilitation of
Europe, nothing to make the defeated Central Empires into good neighbors, nothing to stabilize the new States of Europe, nothing to reclaim
Russia; nor does it promote in any way a compact of economic solidarity amongst the Allies themselves; no arrangement was reached at Paris
for restoring the disordered finances of France and Italy, or to adjust the
systems of the Old World and the New. . . .

It is an extraordinary fact that the fundamental economic problems
of a Europe starving and disintegrating before their eyes was the one
question in which it was impossible to arouse the interest of the Four.
Reparation was their main excursion into the economic field, and they
settled it as a problem of theology, of politics, of electoral chicanery,
from every point of view except that of the economic future of the states
whose destiny they were handling.

A Carthaginian treaty, "if it is carried into effect, must impair yet further, when it might have restored, the delicate, complicated organization,
already shaken and broken by war, through which alone the European
peoples can employ themselves and live." [48]

The Economic Consequences of the Peace is extraordinarily gloomy,
prompting Leonard Woolf to nickname its author Keynessandra. "In
continental Europe the earth heaves and no one but is aware of the rum-
blings," Keynes writes. "There it is not just a matter of extravagance or
'labor troubles'; but of life and death, of starvation and existence, and of
the fearful convulsions of a dying civilization." Part of Keynes's gloom
stems from his sense that it was "not only the war that has made Europe
poorer." Looking backward, Keynes now saw the prewar prosperity as a
fool's paradise.

We assume some of the most peculiar and temporary of our late advantages as natural, permanent, and to be depended on, and we lay our
plans accordingly. On this sandy and false foundation we scheme for social improvement and dress our political platforms, pursue our animosi-

ties and particular ambitions, and feel ourselves with enough margin in hand to foster, not assuage, civil conflict in the European family.

Living standards could not have continued to rise much longer, he maintained. The prosperity of Europe had been based not on the "ingenious mechanism" of competition, an environment friendly to entrepreneurs and ample finance, but rather on a happy historical accident that had temporarily removed certain limits to growth. Thanks to the large exportable surplus of foodstuffs in America, Europe had been able to feed herself cheaply.

The trouble was, Keynes wrote, that American grain *couldn't* stay cheap when US consumption caught up with supply. He reprised an argument by Arthur Jevons, a gifted contemporary of Marshall's, who predicted in 1870 that dwindling coal supplies would choke off England's economic growth. Instead of fuel, the binding constraint for Keynes was wheat. There might be no shortage of wheat in the world as a whole, he acknowledged. But to call forth more supply in the future, he argued, would require England to offer a higher real price. In short, the law of diminishing returns would at last reassert itself, requiring Europe to offer more and more other goods and services to obtain the same amount of bread.

Keynes's bleak economic forecast turned out to be too pessimistic. In the short run, Europe's economy recovered in spite of the war's devastation and the flaws in the treaty. In the long run—starting in the Great Depression and continuing past the end of the twentieth century—food became cheaper, not more expensive, absolutely as well as relative to wages. Keynes's political prediction—that "vengeance . . . will not limp" and that "nothing can then delay for very long that final civil war between the forces of reaction and the despairing convulsions of revolution"—was far more prescient.

World War I and its aftermath set Keynes's intellectual priorities and shaped his thinking about the economy, Skidelsky argues. Henry Wickham Steed, editor of the *Times* of London, characterized Keynes's ideas as a "revolt of economics against politics."[49] Keynes was asserting the importance of something about which generals and prime ministers were only superficially familiar: how the modern world made its living, and that the ability to make a living was a prerequisite if not a guarantor of peace.

Keynes appreciated how specialized the global, especially the European, economy had become, how dependent each part was on the others, how subject to psychological shifts, and, consequently, how easily a breakdown in one could spread to the rest. Keynes had not yet identified policy levers—instruments of mastery—that would let governments exert more control over their economy's course. But he was beginning to think in terms of an "economics of the whole," and of the consequences of government action and inaction.

The war had deepened his distrust of conventional wisdom and had disabused him of any notion that progress was automatic. It was, all in all, a brutal lesson in the destructive powers of governments that willfully ignored economic realities. The Victorian economic miracle had produced the rapid growth of productive power and a dramatic rise in living standards. But the miracle had depended on certain government actions— spreading free trade, enabling the gold standard, upholding the rule of law—as well as untrammeled competition. Having absorbed that lesson, Keynes could not conceive how government could ignore its responsibility to restore prosperity.

In mid-October, Keynes was on the Continent for an international bankers' conference. "There has never been as a big a business transaction as the peace treaty," Melchior's partner Max Warburg had remarked.[50] Now his brother Paul, the American financier, hoped to organize commercial credits, financed mostly by American banks, so that Germany could import raw materials. On a whim, Keynes had invited Melchior by telegram to meet him. Three days later, the two were strolling along Amsterdam's canals in the rain talking freely for the first time and marveling at how "extraordinary [it was] to meet without barriers."[51]

After resigning, the German delegation in protest before the signing of the peace treaty and twice turning down offers to become Weimar's finance minister, Melchior had gone back to his Hamburg bank. He told Keynes that the German president had betrayed Germany's intention to sign the treaty to a British agent ahead of time. Melchior was certain that the tip had led Lloyd George to abandon his efforts to modify the treaty. After lunch, Keynes invited Melchior and Warburg back to his hotel room and read aloud his chapter on President Wilson. Keynes had portrayed the American leader as having raised the world's hopes only to disappoint them:

> With what curiosity, anxiety, and hope we sought a glimpse of the features and bearing of the man of destiny who, coming from the West, was to bring healing to the wounds of the ancient parent of his civilization and lay for us the foundations of the future.
>
> The disillusion was so complete, that some of those who had trusted most hardly dared speak of it. Could it be true? they asked of those who returned from Paris. Was the Treaty really as bad as it seemed? What had happened to the President? What weakness or what misfortune had led to so extraordinary, so unlooked-for a betrayal?

Wilson could preach ringing sermons on his Fourteen Points, but lacked

> that dominating intellectual equipment which would have been necessary to cope with the subtle and dangerous spellbinders whom a tremendous clash of forces and personalities had brought to the top as triumphant masters in the swift game of give and take, face to face in Council.[52]

Warburg, who despised the president, giggled as Keynes read these lines, but Melchior listened solemnly and looked as if he was about to cry.

When the bankers held their meeting, Keynes urged them to support a reduction in reparations, cancellation of Allied war debts, and an international loan for Germany. He and Warburg drafted an appeal to the League of Nations and got a dozen of the conference participants to sign. Thus, the first of many attempts to revise Versailles was drafted before the ink on the treaty had dried.

With his daily quota of a thousand words "fit for the printer" seven days a week, Keynes had piled up sixty thousand words by October. As chapters were finished, he read or sent them to various people, including his mother, Frances, and Lytton Strachey. The whole publishing industry seemed dedicated to churning out books about the peace treaty. Keynes's book was the first out of the gate, appearing two weeks before Christmas. By Easter, a hundred thousand copies had been sold in England and the United States. Keynes's "reparation" to Bloomsbury for having abetted the war was graciously accepted. Lytton Strachey, whose *Eminent Victorians* had been the literary sensation of 1918, called Keynes's argument "crushing" and predicted that "nobody could ignore it." [53] Though grumbling that Keynes had been very indiscreet, Austen Chamberlain confessed to his wife that the book was "brilliantly written" and had given him "malicious pleasure." [54] All reviewers were lavish in their praise of Keynes's style and many were persuaded that it would be impossible for Germany to comply with the treaty.

Keynes's book brought a simmering controversy to the boiling point. Some of the critics argued that Germany could afford to pay much more than Keynes said. Others called him politically clueless. Among the less flattering suggestions were that he was a "dehumanized intellectual" for his lack of partisanship. Predictably, the Tory attack on Keynes questioned his loyalty and suggested that perhaps he deserved an iron cross. A. J. P. Taylor, the historian, succinctly, and not unfairly, summarized the message of *The Economic Consequences of the Peace* as "Precautions should be taken against German grievances, not against German aggression." [55] Captain Paul Mantoux, the Big Four's translator, attacked the book on the grounds that Keynes "had never been present at one of [the Council of Four's] meetings." [56] But the most common criticism was simply that Keynes had missed the point. Wickham Steed, editor of the *Times* of London, noted that

> If the war taught us one lesson above all others it was that the calcula-
> tions of economists, bankers, and financial statesmen who preached the
> impossibility of war because it would not pay were perilous nonsense.
> Germany went to war because she made it pay in 1870–1 and believed
> she could make it pay again.[57]

American reviewers suspected Keynes of advancing British interests under the guise of altruism toward Europe. Thorstein Veblen, the sociologist, scolded him for getting Woodrow Wilson "all wrong."[58] On the first anniversary of the treaty, the *New York Times* called *The Economic Consequences of the Peace* "a very angry book" and claimed that "insofar as American opinion has changed, it is into distrust of all Europe and a desire to break away from entanglement from abroad."[59] Bernard Baruch expressed the administration's position when he claimed that Keynes wanted that "America shall pay instead of Germany."[60]

Some historians now accept that Keynes's criticism of President Wilson was unfair, and consider his condemnation of the French too partisan. If anything, they contend, British claims for reparations were less justifiable than those of the French. On the other hand, Margaret MacMillan's *Paris 1919: Six Months That Changed the World* and other recent histories of the Peace Conference show that Keynes's view that the Allies had blatantly violated their contract with Germany, and should have allowed the losers to negotiate some elements of the peace, is widely accepted now. And few disagree with Keynes's principal point—that no peace based on such shaky economic foundations could possibly last.

Not surprisingly, *Economic Consequences* turned Keynes into a hero in Vienna and Berlin. Excerpts, translations, and new editions poured forth from the presses. Given that no ceiling on the amount of reparations was fixed in the treaty, the view that Keynes had not only voiced the German case but was in a position to influence opinion made perfect sense. Joseph Schumpeter, the former Austrian finance minister, called the book "a masterpiece."[61]

Chapter VIII

The Joyless Street:
Schumpeter and Hayek in Vienna

The alternating boom and bust is the form economic
development takes in the era of capitalism.

—*Joseph Schumpeter*[1]

The 1920s are almost always viewed in a rearview mirror and judged solely
as a preamble to, if not the cause of, the Great Depression, the rise of Fascism, and the triumph of Bolshevism. For the West, it is supposed to have
been a time of decadence, delusions, fake prosperity, and false beliefs. But
seen through the eyes of four individuals—Joseph Schumpeter, Friedrich
Hayek, John Maynard Keynes, and Irving Fisher—it was as inventive, exciting, and genuinely progressive an era as any in the last century.

Keynes and Fisher became economic oracles. They prospered financially. More important, they created new intellectual wealth. The violent
inflations and deflations that followed World War I convinced them that
free markets and democracy could not long survive such pathologies and
focused their minds on systemic causes. Like the doctor in Molière's *Le
Malade Imaginaire,* they shifted their attention from individual parts of
the economic body to its circulatory system. They concluded that inflation and deflation, seemingly polar opposites, were symptoms of the same
underlying disease, and that the system of money and credit creation was
both its source and its transmission mechanism.

Solving the immediate problem of how to revive the interlocking parts of the world economy, some in extremis, required a new framework. Fisher and Keynes nourished the hope that the violent booms and depressions could be avoided. They no longer believed, as Alfred Marshall had, that booms and depressions resulted from random external shocks or, as Karl Marx had, that they were intrinsic to the market economy. Instead of acts of nature, extreme gyrations were man-made disasters capable of being averted. Fisher, Keynes, and Hayek searched for instruments of mastery, confident that these existed and could be made to work—even if the Englishman and the American were prepared to trust the discretion of civil servants while the Austrian, product of a more tragic national history, insisted that governments be bound by rules. Only Schumpeter could be described as fatalistic, as much because of temperament and personal tragedy as because of intellectual conviction.

When Schumpeter was driven from office in the fall of 1919, Austria's fiscal crisis was entering an acute stage. Faced with a ballooning deficit and too fearful of public unrest to impose austerity measures, the cash-strapped government of Karl Renner printed more and more paper money to pay its bills. Ludwig von Mises, the president of the Chamber of Commerce, described the "heavy drone" of the central bank's printing presses: "They ran incessantly, day and night . . . [Meanwhile] a large number of industrial enterprises were idle; others were working part time; only the printing presses stamping out notes were operating at full speed."[2] The more kronen the government issued, the less one krone could buy. Vienna's police chief complained that "every issue reduces the value of the krone."[3] The effect on the krone's exchange value was immediate, and because Austria imported so much of her daily requirements, the plunging exchange rate sent domestic prices spiraling upward. Ironically, the Social Democrats initially welcomed inflation as an economic stimulant, not suspecting how soon it would end in prostration—and political ruin—like any other episode of mania.

Initially, easy credit and rising prices seemed to jolt the paralyzed economy back to some semblance of life. Investment, exports, and employment perked up as inflation slashed the real cost of borrowing and the falling krone let Austrian exporters undercut foreign rivals. But eventually Austria's trading partners began imposing tariffs on her exports, businesses had difficulty restocking inventories, and unemployment began to swell again.

Meanwhile, inflation went from a trot to a canter to a wild gallop. Despite constant renegotiation of union contracts, a worker who had earned 50 kronen a week before the war earned about 400 kronen at the end of 1919. But his new salary let him buy just one-quarter as much food, coal, or clothing as his old one. Instead of an eightfold pay raise, he had actually suffered a 75 percent pay cut. Within a year he would need more than eight weeks' pay to buy a cheap suit and a pair of boots.[4] Civil servants and pensioners found that their weekly incomes afforded them no more than a couple of eggs or loaves of bread. That was just the beginning. At one point, Freud, who was considering moving to Berlin, complained, "One can no longer live here and foreigners needing analysis no longer want to come."[5] By October 1921, prices were rising by more than 50 percent every month on average, marking the beginning of a hyperinflation. By October 1922, the price level was two hundred times higher than a year earlier.

Inflation wiped out the entire savings of the middle class and undermined its faith in democratic government argues historian Niall Ferguson. "All of us have lost 19/20ths of what we possessed in cash," Freud wrote to a friend.[6] Worthless bank notes, like ersatz food and paper suits, created a universal feeling of being cheated. In Stefan Zweig's "The Invisible Collection," a blind art connoisseur believes that his portfolio of old master drawings is intact. In reality, his family has bartered them away and substituted blank sheets of vellum for the missing works. Anna Eisenmenger, the diarist, wrote of feeling betrayed as she surveyed her "remaining 1,000 kronen notes; lying by the side of my food [ration] cards in the writing table drawer . . . Will not they perhaps share the fate of the unredeemed food cards, if the State fails to keep the promise made in the inscription on every note?"[7] As confidence in the krone collapsed, daily commerce reverted to barter. Many peasants and shopkeepers refused to accept cash. For the middle classes, it meant trading a piano for a sack of flour, fifty prewar cigars for four pounds of pork and ten pounds of lard, a gold watch chain or, in Freud's case, a journal article for a few sacks of potatoes.

Until the shelves were bare, one could buy anything in a Viennese shop, including its entire contents, for a few pounds or dollars. *La Peine des Hommes: Les Chercheurs D'Or,* a novel published in 1920 by the French journalist Pierre Hamp, portrays an inner city populated by carpetbaggers who flock to Vienna like vultures. Salzbach, the hero, accuses them of turning misery into gold.[8] Bigger bargains were found in Austria's farmland, mines, railways, ships, power plants, factories, and banks. As the krone depreciated, these too became available at fire sale prices if the buyer paid in pounds, dollars, or another "hard" currency. Foreign takeovers stoked popular anger, one reason that the Kola affair involving Fiat's purchase of Alpine Montan, the iron concern, continued to dog Schumpeter long after he left office.

While war veterans hung around outside dozens of restaurants inside the Ring waiting for scraps, a new class of millionaires drank champagne and dined on delicacies "equal in quality and quantity to that obtained in London."[9] The stark contrast between the newly rich and the newly poor that had disgusted the young Adolf Hitler before the war grew more extreme. Panhandlers, beggars, and refugees seemed to be everywhere. Popular resentment focused on black marketeers, war profiteers, foreigners, and especially Jews. Every surge in food prices was followed by demonstrations against the rising cost of living and outbursts of violence. In December 1921, a huge crowd smashed shop windows, attacked hotels, and looted food shops. One visitor to Vienna wrote to his wife that "hand in hand with the exasperation caused by the continual rise in prices goes a feeling of intense resentment and hate against all those who have made money out of Austria's misfortune, the 'Schiebers,' speculators on the exchange market, and their like 'who are mostly Jews.'"[10]

Inflation turned the old Vienna into a funhouse of inverted, topsy-turvy values. In *The Joyless Street,* Georg Pabst's 1925 film starring Greta Garbo, senior civil servants huddle in dark, unheated apartments, neighbors spy on one another, housewives break the law, girls from good homes become prostitutes, and sober citizens turn into manic stock speculators.

Gilt-edged stock certificates became the inflation hedge of choice. People who had never invested in anything but government bonds suddenly poured what was left of their cash into the stock market, where huge profits were being made.

In her diary, Anna Eisenmenger reports a conversation with her bank manager that captures the helplessness of the middle class in the face of the speculative fever that was attacking the whole population:

> "If you had bought Swiss francs when I suggested, you would not now have lost three-fourths of your fortune."
>
> "Lost?" I exclaimed in horror. "Why, don't you think the krone will recover again?"
>
> "Recover?" He said with a laugh . . . Our krone will go to the devil, that's certain."
>
> "Come into my room for a moment . . ." There he began to explain to me that the monarchy was compelled to issue war loans and that the subscription to these loans was often compulsory. This was done because the State had already used up its gold reserves and had no money left for carrying on the War. With the money from the war loans the War was continued, but there was practically no cover for the notes at present in circulation.
>
> "Just test the promise made on this 20 kronen note and try to get, say, 20 silver kronen in exchange for it," he said, holding out a 20 kronen note . . . "Now you will understand me when I tell you that at the present time it is well to possess a house or [land] or shares in an industry or mine or something else of the sort, but not to possess any money, at least no Austrian or German money. Do you understand what I mean?"
>
> "Yes, but mine are government securities. Surely there can't be anything safer than that."
>
> "But, my dear lady, where is the State which guaranteed those Securities to you? It is dead."[11]

The conversation ended with the bank manager advising Madame Eisenmenger to put her money in stocks. Like countless other Viennese, she did.

. . .

Although his political career was apparently over and he had been forced to return to his university post in Graz, Schumpeter still had friends in high places. To compensate him for his ignominious sacking, conservatives in parliament awarded him a banking charter the following year. The charter was his to sell, use, or sock away. Since there were fewer than two dozen investment banks in Vienna and many banking partnerships were desperate to raise capital by selling shares to the public, a license to start a bank had many potential takers. Parliament's gift to Schumpeter proved a golden parachute of considerable value.

On July 23, 1921, Schumpeter was elected president of Vienna's oldest investment bank, M. L. Biedermann, on the day it went public. He was twenty-nine years old. In return for the use of the charter and his signature on banknotes and such, Schumpeter got a magnificent office, an annual salary of 100,000 kronen (about $250,000 in today's dollars), and enough stock to make him the bank's second-largest shareholder. The biggest perk was a practically unlimited line of credit to invest on his account.

His timing was perfect. The League of Nations was finally cobbling together a rescue package for Austria that bore a striking resemblance to the stillborn Schumpeter plan of 1919. In return for an emergency loan, the government promised to embrace fiscal and monetary discipline by creating a new central bank that would be barred from financing the government's deficits by buying Treasury bills, by balancing its budget by firing a hundred thousand civil servants and closing tax loopholes, and, when Austria's foreign debt had shrunk to a specified level, by returning to the gold standard. The rumor of the impending deal and the simultaneous announcement that the Allied Reparation Commission was renouncing claims on Austria sufficed to halt the krone's decline and brought inflation down from 1,000 percent to 20 percent even before the protocols were signed in August.[12]

The speculative fever did not abate, but instead shifted to gilt-edged stocks. As businesses issued shares instead of taking out loans at higher real interest rates, banks gobbled up the new stock certificates. Soon banks were the largest shareholders in Austrian business. According to the historian C. A. Macartney,

> Austrian banks—a very few conservative concerns of established reputation always excepted—did not confine their investments by considerations of safety, things went on just as merrily on these shares as they had on the exchange. Industry itself, including the most reputable, had become speculative. It passed largely into the hands of the banks, its shares were bandied about and used for the most improbable purposes.[13]

As expected, Schumpeter left the banking to Biedermann's capable longtime chief and became, in effect, a money manager and venture capitalist. He promptly took large stakes in several enterprises, in some cases with a partner who was an acquaintance from the Theresianum. Within months, he was a director of the Kauffman Bank, a porcelain works, and a chemical subsidiary of a German multinational.[14]

The frenzy of deal making, buying, and selling was intoxicating. Schumpeter may have dressed like a bank president, but, as the Viennese press observed snidely, his lifestyle was as extravagant as a lord's. He still owed large personal debts and even larger tax arrears. He had given up his hotel suite and his half of the Palais, but he threw lavish dinners at his apartment and spent prodigiously, whether on his mistresses, horses, or clothes. He was as careless of his reputation as he was of his money. In response to a business associate's warning about appearing in public with prostitutes, "he rode up and down . . . a main boulevard in the inner city . . . with an attractive blond prostitute on one knee and a brunette on the other."[15]

At the beginning of 1924, Schumpeter considered his financial affairs to be "perfectly in order,"[16] his Biedermann line of credit being covered by gilt-edged securities. Then came the spectacular collapse of the Vienna stock exchange on May 9, 1924. Between breakfast and dinner, three-fourths of the value of the "highly marketable securities" that constituted Schumpeter's personal collateral had disappeared in a puff of smoke.[17]

In the frantic days that followed, he was forced to dump the best of his remaining stocks into a falling market. Thanks to a wrong-way bet against the French franc, the Biedermann bank had sustained huge foreign-currency losses. To raise cash, the bank's directors, Schumpeter included, had to sell large numbers of Biedermann shares to a subsidiary of the Bank of England. Over the summer, several of his companies failed, forcing him as a director to compensate their shareholders. His Theresianum partner turned out to be, if not a crook, then guilty of shady dealings, and Schumpeter was named in several lawsuits as well as a criminal inquiry that dragged on for years.

The combination of personal insolvency and an unsavory business associate was too much for Biedermann's British investors, who insisted that Schumpeter resign. By the time he did so in September 1924, amid accusations in the media that he had used his Biedermann connections to do favors for a government minister, nothing was left of his millions. The bank directors granted Schumpeter a severance equal to a year's salary, but his debts were far larger and he had no prospect of recouping his losses. The financial crisis triggered a prolonged recession. Several big banks and hundreds of industrial and commercial firms failed. Ultimately, Biedermann was liquidated, although, amazingly, the investors were all repaid. In the depths of the slump, Ludwig von Mises motioned another economist to his office window and, pointing down to the Ringstrasse, that symbol of Vienna's liberal age, said gloomily, "Maybe grass will grow here because our civilization will end." [18]

If Schumpeter's enemies judged him harshly, they didn't condemn him nearly as severely as he did himself. He plucked a line from Dante's *Inferno*—"Il gran rifiuto" or "the great refusal," a phrase that connotes both a lost opportunity and a failure of nerve—to describe the decade since the start of the war; his entire thirties, more or less. At forty-one, he found more to regret than to look forward to.

The black mood didn't last. The need to defend himself and to find a way to make money energized him. And at the end of his annus horribilis he found a reason to smile again. Like most Don Juans, Schumpeter had been infatuated—even obsessed—countless times, but he had never been truly in love. Annie Reisinger disarmed him because she was young, working class, and vulnerable. She was the twenty-one-year-old daughter of the super in his mother's apartment building. He had known her since she was a baby. When she was eighteen, he had begun a mild flirtation with her, only to be rebuffed. She had been more frightened by his reputation as a womanizer than by the fact that he was a public figure twice her age. He had run into her again on Christmas Day when she paid his mother a visit. She was prettier, more womanly, and more self-possessed than he remembered. Jaded as he was, he found her cheerful good nature and lack of intellectual pretention refreshing.

He was lonely and sore. She was recovering from an unhappy affair with a married man. They were both on the rebound. Schumpeter made a project of their romance. He courted her daily. He swept her off to operas, balls, restaurants, and weekends in the country. He showered her with flowers and expensive trinkets. When he asked her to marry him, he went down on his knees.

Appalled as his mother may have been at the prospect of a shopgirl as a daughter-in-law, she bit her tongue. A man who was as notorious as he was penniless was hardly in a position to make the brilliant match she had craved for him. Besides, he was still legally married to his first wife. Schumpeter had not seen Gladys, who had since resumed the use of her maiden name, since they parted in 1913. It isn't clear whether she had refused to consider a divorce or he simply hadn't bothered to ask for one. What is plain is that they were still legally married and that Gladys, if she wished, could have prevented his remarriage or sued him for bigamy. Luckily for Schumpeter, the Socialist government of Red Vienna had liberalized the divorce laws, and a friendly official granted him a civil waiver to marry Annie. Annie overcame her own and her parents' misgivings and went along.

Meanwhile, Schumpeter's friends were looking for ways to rescue his career. Despite his misadventures in politics and banking, his reputation as a brilliant economic theorist had survived. True, he had made enemies in Vienna and Berlin who would block his appointment at either of those cities' universities, but many others abroad, including the University of

Tokyo, were eager to recruit him. Ultimately, the University of Bonn, the first university out of which Karl Marx had flunked, offered him a chair in public finance. "Schumpeter is a genius," began a letter from one of his supporters to the cultural ministry in Berlin. German universities were completely cut off from contemporary economics, the writer pointed out, and Schumpeter would turn Bonn from a backwater into an important center of theoretical economics.

"Bonn conquered!" Schumpeter telegraphed his fiancée triumphantly in October 1925 when he heard that he had beaten out his Viennese rival, von Mises. Somewhat to his own surprise, he was eager to go. Although his chair was in public finance, he had been promised that he could lecture on pure theory. In early November he and Annie were married in the presence of just two witnesses before embarking on a leisurely tour of luxury spas in northern Italy. They arrived in Bonn just before the start of the spring term.

Schumpeter and his wife soon became the most glamorous couple in Bonn. In a typically grandiose gesture, Schumpeter rented an imposing stucco mansion overlooking the Rhine where Kaiser Wilhelm had lived as a student. By the time Annie attended her first faculty tea, Schumpeter had invented a new identity for her. Instead of a super's daughter who had worked as a bank teller in Vienna and an au pair in Paris, he presented her as the pampered offspring of a prominent Viennese family who had been educated at an expensive French finishing school. Schumpeter's crushing debts forced him to moonlight as a journalist and public speaker, but everyone who knew him agreed that he was happier than he had been in years. Among other things, Annie was pregnant with their first child.

The idyll was not to last. The sudden, unexpected death of his mother in mid-June was a severe blow. For most of his life, she had been "the great human factor," and he often spoke of "his unconditional attachment to her, his unbounded confidence in her."[19] Two weeks after Schumpeter returned from her funeral in Vienna, he suffered a second horrible loss, witnessing Annie's "terrible death" during childbirth.[20] Their baby boy lived less than four hours.

The Biedermann fiasco and the loss of the only two people to whom he felt close scarred Schumpeter permanently. He would need more than a decade just to pay off his debts, and he never got an opportunity to rebuild his fortune. Half a dozen years later, Schumpeter wrote in a letter from Singapore:

> There is no real liberation. I can't get rid of bad memories and premonitions . . . mistakes, failures, hardships, etc. and the year 1924, never stand out so clearly before my eyes as when I am on a beautiful boat, seemingly comfortably safe on a still Ocean. And the feeling of decadence, intellectual and physical often condenses into direct forebodings of death.[21]

Yet on the future of capitalism, Schumpeter remained remarkably sanguine. Israel Kirzner, the economist, observed that the questions that drove research on business cycles in the 1920s were: Can capitalism work?[22] Can an economy with private property and free markets survive? Karl Marx had believed that panics and slumps were generated by the economic system and would eventually destroy it. Alfred Marshall had taken the opposite view, attributing recessions to random shocks that originated outside the economy. Schumpeter stood Marx on his head by viewing the business cycle as intrinsic but essentially benign. As "commonly, prosperity is associated with social well-being, and recession with a falling standard of life. In our picture they are not, and there is even an implication to the contrary."[23]

Despite frequent crises and depressions since 1848, he pointed out, production and living standards had risen by multiples. Growth had occurred in spurts because innovations were not "evenly distributed in time . . . but appear, if at all, discontinuously in groups or swarms."[24] Innovation bred imitators, another burst of investment, and secondary rounds of innovation. Then investment subsided and consumer goods flooded the market, driving down prices and pushing costs higher. The squeeze on profits resulted in recession.

Constant dislocations were the downside to innovation, rising productivity, and higher living standards. In Schumpeter's theory of economic

1

In Jane Austen's lifetime, "nine parts of all mankind" were doomed to dire poverty and life-long drudgery. A generation later, Charles Dickens was convinced that "we are moving in a right direction towards some superior condition of society."

2

3

Henry Mayhew, the first investigative journalist, wanted to learn whether the wages and standard of life of London's poor could improve. In a time of cholera, he scoured London's back streets and alleyways for facts and created an extraordinary portrait of life and labor in the capital of the world. But the answer to his question eluded him.

4

5   6

For Friedrich Engels (*left*), Victorian London was a modern-day Rome and Judgment Day, both inevitable and imminent.

His friend and dependent Karl Marx (*right*) promised to reveal modern society's Law of Motion, but suffered from writer's block. He never learned English or visited a single factory while composing *Das Kapital*.

7

8

A mathematician and missionary manqué from London's lower middle class, Alfred Marshall had an overriding aim to "put man into the saddle," and his deepest conviction was that a proletariat was not a necessity of nature. He and his Cambridge-educated bride, Mary Paley, set out to turn economics into a compass to guide mankind out of poverty.

9   10

Beatrice Potter was born into Britain's governing class but was torn between conflicting desires: to pursue a career as a social investigator or to become the wife of a powerful man, namely the charismatic and domineering Joseph Chamberlain.

11   12

(left): She found a perfect partner in Sydney Webb, the clever son of a London hair-dresser, and together they invented the idea of the welfare state and the "think tank." *(right):* The former Tory and new "thunderer on the Left," Winston Spencer Churchill, picked Beatrice's brain.

13

14

The greatest *American* economic thinker of the last century was a Yankee tinkerer, teeto-taler, and TB survivor. Trained in mathematics but desiring "contact with the living age," Irving Fisher invented the rolodex, the consumer price index, and the economic forecast. By the 1920s, Fisher *(bottom, left)* was America's economic oracle, wellness guru, and stock picker, his celebrity rivaling that of Alexander Graham Bell *(right)*.

In a postgraduate year in London, Joseph Alois Schumpeter rode, fenced, dressed, and talked like one of the Viennese aristocrats he wished to be taken for. He spent most of his time at the British Museum writing a book criticizing economic theory for ignoring how the economy evolved over time.

After marrying impulsively, Schumpeter rushed off to Egypt, the miracle economy of the Belle Epoque, to make his fortune as a lawyer and money manager. In Cairo, he found inspiration for his greatest work, *The Theory of Economic Development.*

15

16

Friedrich von Hayek got interested in how markets and modern economics functioned in the trenches during World War I as a corporal in the Austro-Hungarian army. In the Second World War, Hayek obeyed Wittenstein's injunction by writing *The Road of Serfdom*, a devastating attack on command-and-control economies.

17

18

Datum *Fg. 379. am 30. Juni 1918.*

Unterschrift des Besitzers.

Hayek's cousin, Ludwig Wittgenstein, an aviation engineer turned philosopher, impressed upon young Hayek that the duty of genius was to tell uncomfortable truths and to speak of the unspeakable.

World War I wrecked the foundations of the nineteenth-century economic miracle and bankrupted the governments of victors and vanquished alike, leaving in its wake famine, hyperinflation, and a revolutionary firestorm that spread from the Urals to the Rhine.

As the finance minister of a mutilated, penniless, and starving nation, Schumpeter (*standing, third from left*) tried to convince Austrians that they could recover economically without throwing themselves into the arms of either red Russia or resentful Germany.

21

John Maynard Keynes (*center*), the clever, ambitious, self-confident heir to one of England's intellectual dynasties, defined the good life as the one available to a London gentleman on the eve of World War I. He is shown here with Bloomsbury pals Bertrand Russell, the philosopher (*left*), and Lytton Strachey, the biographer (*right*).

Keynes collected artists and writers as well as, thanks to his speculative genius, art. The great love of his youth was Duncan Grant, the painter (*left*) who, like most of Keynes's other bohemian friends, refused to serve in World War I and urged Keynes to apply for conscientious-objector status.

22

Keynes became the point man in Britain's wartime Treasury for loans from the United States to France and other allies and played a supporting role at the 1919 peace conference. Favoring debt forgiveness among the victors and modest reparations for the losers, he resigned in protest after the Big Four refused to make postwar economic recovery in Europe a priority in the Versailles peace treaty.

23

24

In 1923, Hayek spent a postdoctoral year in New York City, where he met Irving Fisher and wrote a withering critique of monetary reformers who claimed that central banks could tame the business cycle by managing the money supply. He doubted that forecasters could anticipate the economy's ups and downs ahead of time sufficiently reliably to serve as guides to policymakers.

25   26

The postwar slump drew Joan Robinson, the dreamy but driven daughter of a general, to economics, a war-hero husband, and England's celebrity economist, John Maynard Keynes. Self-confident, articulate, uninhibited as a writer, she broke into Keynes's all-male inner circle of disciples, developing a theory of how the rise of big business might lead to an unwelcome combination of higher prices and lower employment. She enlisted the help of her gifted but neurotic lover, Richard Kahn, who served as a go-between with the great man.

To the surprise and disapproval of his Bloomsbury friends, Keynes married the Russian ballerina Lydia Lopokova, a member of Sergei Diaghilev's itinerant Ballets Russes. Her riotous sense of humor, fractured English, and lack of intellectual pretension made her the love of his life.

27

Irving Fisher (*left*) and Joseph Schumpeter (*right*), shown in New Haven in 1932, embraced opposing prescriptions for how to fight the Great Depression but joined forces to promote the use of mathematics in economics.

28

29

Months before D-Day, Franklin Delano Roosevelt called on the Allies to avoid the mistakes made after World War I by focusing on postwar economic recovery.

30

31

Young Milton Friedman (with wife, Rose), one of the legions of young Keynesian support-ers of the New Deal, played a key role in Secretary Henry Morgenthau's wartime Treasury, which was, for all practical purposes, run by the brilliant but devious Harry Dexter White. Keynes (*right*) and White were the principle architects of the Bretton Woods monetary system that paved the way for postwar economic recovery in the West. A Soviet agent of influence and spy, White was taken by complete surprise when Stalin refused to join.

Paul Anthony Samuelson was the most influential American Keynesian of the post–World War II era. With a world view shaped by the collapse of the farm belt, the Florida land bubble, and the Great Depression, he modernized economics with mathematics, Keynes's theories, and numerous original ideas of his own. Postwar generations of Americans, including John F. Kennedy, imbibed the new economics through his textbook and *Newsweek* column, and he is regarded as the guiding spirit behind the 1963 Kennedy tax cut.

32

33

In the 1950s, Joan Robinson, the most famous of Keynes's English disciples, repudiated her brilliant early work and became one of Stalin and Mao's trophy intellectuals. She was a harsh critic of American leadership in mainstream economics. She is shown here, partially hidden, in Beijing in July 1953 with Dr. Chi Chao-ting, Roland Berger, and Harold Spencer at the signing of the first "Icebreaker" trade deal.

34

35

Robinson urged her protégé, Amartya Sen, who came to Trinity College, Cambridge, from Calcutta in 1953, to give up "that ethics rubbish." Democracy and the people's welfare were luxuries that poor countries could not afford, she insisted. Sen ignored her advice to work on famines, economic justice, and the problem of translating individual into social choices.

development, booms were followed by busts—"perennial gales of creative destruction"—but the economy was inherently stable. If the system
was in jeopardy, the threat originated in politics. Marx and Engels saw
recessions as signs of failure and sources of instability. Schumpeter took
the opposite view. Since the cycle produced development, depressions
were healthy, a way to drive out inefficient firms and force companies to
trim costs and rationalize their operations. The death of firms and industries was as inevitable as the death of human beings. Nothing lasted,
Schumpeter observed: "No therapy can permanently obstruct the great
economic and social process by which businesses, individual positions,
forms of life, cultural value and ideals sink in the social scale and finally
disappear." But death also made room for new life. Growth required
managerial talent, labor, and other resources to be shifted from old to new
industries. Thus if nations wanted progress, they had to accept slumps.
Like it or not, he liked to say, "the pattern of boom and bust is the form
economic development takes in the era of capitalism." [25]

Innovations as huge as electricity or as small as toothbrushes are
"primarily responsible" for the recurrent "prosperities" that revolutionize the economic organism and the recurrent "recessions" that are due to
the "disequilibrating impact of the new products or methods." Recessions
produced enormous suffering—rising unemployment, declining wages,
losses, and bankruptcies—but didn't last long. "The phenomena felt to be
unpleasant are temporary," Schumpeter wrote, while "the stream of goods
is enriched, production is partly reorganized, costs of production are
diminished, and what at first appears as entrepreneurial profit finally increases the permanent real incomes of the other classes." [26] He insisted that
constant change was a requirement for economic stability, just as motion
is needed to keep a bicycle upright.

In Bonn, he had plunged into two separate books, cultivated a group
of bright young students, written dozens of newspaper columns, and
spent hundreds of hours on the lecture circuit speaking to German business groups. He had justified his compulsive activity as necessary to pay
off his staggering debt but had used it as an anesthetic. The diary into
which he emptied his battered heart every night was little more than a

catalog of regrets and self-recrimination. Since his mother's funeral, he had never once returned to Vienna.

In the fall of 1927—two years after the deaths of his mother and Annie—Schumpeter accepted an invitation to teach at Harvard and came to the United States for a second time. He was perhaps not as enamored as he had been in 1912, but he was stunned by American opulence, energy, and optimism. A few financial experts were warning of a speculative bubble in the stock market. In an essay written in the spring of 1928, he readily acknowledged that the boom might well be followed by a plunge in stock prices and a period of falling output and high unemployment. But he concluded, "The instabilities, which arise from the process of innovation, tend to right themselves, and do not go on accumulating." Thus, he explained, capitalism was "economically stable, and even gaining in stability." [27]

A tall, dark-haired, slightly shabby young man who vaguely resembled Leon Trotsky sat in the main reading room of the New York Public Library examining yellowed copies of the *New York Times*. He was looking for stories from the final months of the war about the Austro-Hungarian army. Again and again, the blue eyes behind wire-rimmed spectacles widened in surprise. How surreal to come halfway around the world only to learn that everything you thought you knew about an episode in your own life was a fiction.

As cynical as all Viennese were about the Austrian press, Friedrich von Hayek, Ludwig Wittgenstein's cousin and a former corporal in the k.u.k. army, was shocked. Until now he had believed, as the Austrian media had claimed, that the Piave offensive was a bold strategic gamble that failed because of various blunders. It was clear from the *Times* account, however, that American and British war correspondents had unanimously regarded the defeat of the Austro-Hungarian forces as absolutely certain *weeks* before the offensive. In other words, one hundred thousand lives, of which Hayek's might easily have been one, had been squandered for a lie.

In August 1918, Hayek had been swept along by a disintegrating army in chaotic retreat from Italy across the Alps. When he finally reached

Vienna, he had given up an earlier dream of becoming a diplomat and enrolled as a law student at the University of Vienna. He later attributed his interest in social sciences to the war and especially to the experience of serving in a multinational army. How could a society harmonize competing desires and interests without relying on military-style coercion? How could individuals with different languages, cultures, and educations communicate and agree on common actions? The dysfunctional command of the Austro-Hungarian army obviously had not found the answers, but the conduct of trench warfare had left Hayek with time to read. Among the books he read and reread were two turgid volumes on political economy.

At the University of Vienna, which hardly functioned for lack of coal, light, or food, Hayek became best friends with another veteran, a law student named Herbert Furth, who had been gravely wounded at Piave. Furth was the son of a Vienna city councilman and Austria's first suffragette. He introduced Hayek to a sophisticated crowd of left-wing students from assimilated, relatively affluent Jewish families. Furth and his friends hung out at the Café Landtmann across from the opera and argued about Marxism and psychoanalysis. The sons of lawyers, academics, and businessmen, they struck Hayek as considerably more self-confident and cosmopolitan than other young men of his age. He recalled that "what went on in the intellectual world of France and England was to them nearly as familiar as what happened in the German-speaking world." Through them, he discovered Bertrand Russell and H. G. Wells, Proust and Croce, and imbibed "that genuine devotion to things of the spirit need not mean being impractical in the art of getting on in life." [28]

After the war, student politics at the University of Vienna was dominated by virulent Catholic nationalism and violent Communism. Hayek and Furth, who considered themselves Fabian Socialists, found both repellant. Eager to create an alternative, they organized a mildly Socialist organization, the Democratic Students Association, in their first term.

Hayek attended lectures by Friedrich von Wieser, the economist who had served as the monarchy's last finance minister and was Austria's most effective international spokesman. He read the work of Austrian economic thinkers such as Carl Menger and Eugen von Böhm-Bawerk. But as one might expect in a city of ten thousand coffeehouses, a severe apartment shortage, and a surplus of underemployed intellectuals, Hayek's most important education took place in cafés among his peers. In their third year, Hayek and Furth organized a fortnightly seminar that they called the *Geist-Kreis* in jest. *Geist* can refer to the Holy Ghost or to the secular, even demonic, spirits that are channeled at séances. The group's twenty-odd members discussed cultural topics from plays to logical positivism and included the economists Oskar Morgenstern, Gottfried Haberler, and Fritz Machlup, the philosopher Erich Voegelin, and the mathematician Karl Menger (Carl's son), as well as historians, art historians, musicologists, and literary critics.

Hayek completed his doctor of laws degree in the spring of 1922, at the height of the hyperinflation. He immediately took a day job as a minor civil servant in the war claims settlement bureau. Like Einstein's sinecure at the Swiss patent office, Hayek's job was sufficiently undemanding to allow him to earn a second doctorate in political science. A friend of his commented that having one's salary rise from 5,000 kronen to 1 million kronen in the space of nine months, as Hayek's did, was "apt to shape a person's mind."[29] That is probably an exaggeration, but it is safe to say his exploding paycheck and its shrinking purchasing power drew Hayek's attention to the role of money, just as falling asleep in his desk chair at the Bern patent office had drawn Einstein's to the theory of special relativity. Although Hayek preferred collecting old books to investing in stock certificates, he began to daydream about someday becoming president of Austria's central bank.

Another development caught Hayek's attention. The Bolsheviks' "lightning socialization"[30] of 1919 and the Renner government's threat to nationalize key industries had made the most urgent questions for left-wing Viennese intellectuals: Could Socialism work? Could it deliver the goods? Was planning feasible? The German sociologist Max Weber had already weighed in with a blistering "No."[31] Foreign Minister Otto Bauer and Joseph Schumpeter both said "Yes," the affirmative in the latter case being limited to "the right circumstances."[32]

At that point, Hayek's employer and mentor, the liberal economist Ludwig von Mises, propelled the debate to a new intellectual level. In a provocative essay, "Die Gemeinwirtschaft," or "The Collective Economy," Mises essentially reframed the argument by shifting its focus to information. His premise was that an economy was like a computer, a machine for solving a mathematical problem. He argued that a centrally planned economy lacked the necessary data to reduce the number of unknowns to the number of equations and, therefore, lacked the means to calculate prices that brought supply and demand into balance.

Mises allowed that planners could draw up a list of consumer goods and services. But, he asked, then what? How will the authorities assure themselves that the value of, say, an automobile to consumers will equal or exceed the value of the labor, steel, rubber, and other resources that must be sacrificed to produce it? How will they know that the car will be worth more to consumers than the bus that could have been made with those same resources?

To make such calculations in a market economy, Mises said, individual businesses and consumers use price data. Take the question of whether the cost of making the car is more or less than the amount consumers are willing to spend on it. To figure the cost, add up the hours of labor, pounds of steel and rubber, marketing, distribution, and other inputs, multiply by their prices, and add everything up. To figure the value the consumer places on it, take the selling price and multiply by one for one car. Does it make sense to produce cars? If your cost is less than your revenue, you can keep on making them. If it costs more to make them than people are willing to pay, you'll have to reconsider.

The trouble with substituting planners for markets, Mises argued, is that without markets there are no longer market prices to use for making your calculation. Can't you just make some up? Sure, but if no one was producing for, or buying in, markets, they wouldn't be *market* prices. They wouldn't reflect the subjective preferences of the consumers who are demanding a good or the calculations of the businesses deciding whether to supply the good—in real time too. They wouldn't give you the information you need to make a rational decision. You'd have no way of knowing whether you were making the most of your resources or squandering them heedlessly.

The debate over socialization and von Mises's notion of markets as calculators and transmitters of information made an enormous impression on Hayek. It inspired him to write a paper on government rent control. For many families, the severe shortage of housing, another residual of the war, was becoming as pressing a problem as the lack of food or jobs. In 1922, the Social Democrats, among them Furth's father, decided to fix rents at four times the prewar level. Since the consumer price index had risen 110-fold since January 1921, the city council was unwittingly decreeing a virtual rent holiday. As a strategy for ending the housing shortage, it was bizarre. As soon as the controls took effect, new construction ceased, existing buildings became more dilapidated, and overcrowding and homelessness grew worse. Intended to protect the poor, the policy blunder kept people from moving, created more inequality, and reduced the savings available for investment.[33]

Hayek jumped at a chance to spend the academic year 1923–24 at New York University in Greenwich Village as a research assistant to Jeremiah Whipple Jenks, a currency expert on the Allied Reparation Commission whose manners and appearance had confirmed Beatrice Webb's prejudices about Americans. When Hayek arrived in New York with only a few dollars in his pocket, he was aghast to learn that Jenks had gone off to Cornell, where he held a second professorship.

Jenks returned in the nick of time to save Hayek from having to work as a dishwasher at a Sixth Avenue diner. Apart from collecting data for Jenks, Hayek took classes at NYU, started writing a book on how capital goods such as machinery and factory buildings were priced, and finished a long article analyzing the performance of the decade-old Federal Reserve. He met with Irving Fisher, for whom Schumpeter had supplied a letter of introduction. He also crashed the lectures by Wesley C. Mitchell and John Bates Clark at Columbia, the leading center of American research on business cycles.

Hayek's main motive for coming to New York was to learn as much as he could about American thinking about booms and depressions. He was less interested in pursuing the abstract question of whether capitalism could work than in finding out whether economic forecasting could. Was it possible to predict how output or prices would behave six months or a year hence—that is, accurately enough to allow monetary authorities to head off incipient inflations or deflations ahead of time? They were not purely academic questions on Hayek's part. Von Mises, who had recommended him to Jenks, had been talking to Hayek about starting a program of business cycle research and producing economic forecasts at the Vienna Chamber of Commerce.

Hayek would have welcomed the chance to stay in New York for a second year, but by the time the Rockefeller Foundation informed him that its trustees had renewed his grant, he was already sailing back to Europe. By the end of May 1924, he was back in Vienna at his dull job at the reparations office, unhappy and depressed. Before leaving, he had fallen in love with his cousin Helene Bitterlich, who worked in the office as a secretary. He had almost asked her to become engaged to him before he left for New York, but in the end had not. He was furious with himself. In his absence she had married another man.

His spirits were lifted by an invitation from Mises to join his private seminar, "the most important center of economic discussion in Vienna and perhaps in Continental Europe." Along with a dozen or so former members of the *Geist-Kreis*, the group included the economist Steffi Braun, the philosophers Felix Kaufman, Alfred Schutz, and Fritz Schreier, and the historian Friedrich Engel-Janosi. The first paper Hayek delivered at the seminar was on his analysis of rent control in Vienna.

Von Mises had been trying to obtain a position for Hayek at the Chamber of Commerce. When he failed, he raised enough money to create an independent forecasting institute and put Hayek in charge of it. The Austrian Institute for Business Cycle Research was modeled on the academic and private American organizations that Hayek had visited in the United States, and Hayek became its first director. Thus, at thirty, he found himself running a research institute with ties to similar organizations abroad and publishing a monthly forecast for an international audience—though his entire staff consisted of two typists and one clerk.

In 1928, Hayek submitted the book he had started to write in New York, *Monetary Theory and the Business Cycle,* as his "habilitation" to the

University of Vienna. Lionel Robbins, a young working-class Liberal at
the London School of Economics who was looking for intellectual allies,
happened to attend Hayek's trial lecture on "The 'Paradox' of Saving" and
was so impressed that he asked whether he had any interest in coming to
London. Robbins also expressed interest in the institute's latest forecast.
Writing in the February 1929 newsletter, Hayek was predicting that world
interest rates wouldn't fall until the American stock market boom collapsed. "The boom will collapse within the next few months," he warned.[34]

Chapter IX

Immaterial Devices of the Mind: Keynes and Fisher in the 1920s

The world is gradually awakening to the fact of its own improvability. Political economy is no longer the dismal science.

—*Irving Fisher, 1908*[1]

We should be led to control and reduce the so-called "business cycle."

—*Irving Fisher, 1925*[2]

The Great War had postponed the need for Keynes to settle on a career. At one time, he had thought he wanted to run a railroad, but railroads were no longer as glamorous as before the war. That high ground was now occupied by finance. The business of borrowing, lending, and insuring had been transformed by floating currencies, huge war debts, the urgent need for credit, and the vexing issue of reparations. Once a staid if mysterious backwater, finance had become the fastest-growing industry—or, in the eyes of skeptics, a giant casino.

Oswald "Foxy" Falk, a stockbroker friend whom Keynes had brought to the Treasury during the war, introduced him to the City, London's Wall Street. Within a year Keynes found himself chairman of an insurance company. He knew nothing about insurance or the desirability of diversifying an investment portfolio. A life insurance company "ought to have only one investment and it should be changed every day,"[3] he opined at his first board meeting. That Fisher's notion of a trade-off between an investment's risk and its rate of return had not occurred to Keynes is a sign of how novel it was. Like so many ideas that seem too obvious to require discovery, the idea that putting all one's eggs into a single basket was risky was generally as little understood as Einstein's theory of relativity.

Keynes by no means limited himself to running the insurance company. The collapse of the global gold standard, with its fixed exchange rates—something like a single world currency—during the war and its replacement by floating exchange rates had created a foreign exchange speculator's paradise. When his speculation in francs, dollars, and pounds prospered, as in the fall of 1919 and the spring of 1920, Keynes was able to buy paintings by Seurat, Picasso, Matisse, Renoir, and Cézanne. "The affair is of course risky but Falk and I, seeing that our reputations depend on it, intend to exercise a good deal of caution," Keynes assured his father, who, like several of his son's Bloomsbury trust-fund friends, had blithely handed over several thousand pounds for him to manage. Perhaps the son's next thought—"Win or lose this high stakes gambling amuses me"— should have set off warning bells.[4]

In this expansive frame of mind, Keynes took Vanessa Bell and Duncan Grant on a whirlwind tour of the Continent in the spring of 1920. They paid a visit to the American art historian and promoter of Renaissance painters Bernard Berenson. At Berenson's Florentine villa, I Tatti, Keynes and Grant each pretended, to their own but not their host's great amusement, to be the other. But mostly they went shopping. Even Keynes, who tended to be a tightwad where trivial sums were concerned, bought seventeen pairs of leather gloves. In March, around the time Joseph Schumpeter was poised to embark on his own high-stakes gambling spree in Vienna, Keynes had decided to go long in dollars on behalf of his syndicate. Prices were rising faster in Britain—and even more so in Europe—than in the United States, he reasoned, so the pound would be sure to weaken against the dollar. His logic was perfectly sound, his timing, not so much. No sooner had he returned to London than the franc, mark, and lire began, perversely, *appreciating* against the dollar. By the time fundamentals once again prevailed, Keynes was wiped out. Through some reverse alchemy his £14,000 of profits had turned into a loss of more than £13,000. Astonishingly, his investors' confidence in his genius did not falter. His father and friends were convinced that Keynes would soon recoup his and their losses, and his broker agreed to reopen his account if he could put up £7,000. Even more amazingly, these remarkable acts of faith proved to be justified. By the end of 1924, Keynes was a wealthy man.

After his success as a best-selling author, Keynes had turned to journalism to help finance the lifestyle to which he was becoming accustomed. He wrote for the *Manchester Guardian* and Lord Beaverbrook's' London *Evening Standard*, and the American *New Republic*. According to his biographer Robert Skidelsky, Keynes's career in print supplied one-third of his income during the 1920s and culminated in his becoming publisher of the left-wing political weekly founded by the Webbs and G. B. Shaw, the *New Statesman*. Peter Clarke, another of Keynes's biographers, observed that launching "assaults of thoughts upon the unthinking" seemed to bring out the remarkable range of Keynes's talents.[5]

In 1922, his topic of choice was money and banking. Before World War I, monetary economics had been more or less an American obsession. But Irving Fisher, virtually the only American economic theorist taken seriously in Cambridge, had convinced Keynes that money had a far more powerful effect on the "real" economy than accepted theory allowed.[6] As early as 1913, a couple of years after he and Fisher met at George V's coronation, in a speech to a group of businessmen in London, Keynes was echoing Fisher's view that the key to booms and depressions was "the creation and destruction of credit."[7] The economic disorders that followed the war seemed to bear out Fisher's argument.

In 1923, Keynes was so excited by the new ideas that he distilled what he had been thinking and writing about in *A Tract on Monetary Reform*:

> The fluctuations in the value of money since 1914 have been on a scale so great as to constitute, with all that they involve, one of the most significant events in the economic history of the modern world. The fluctuation of the standard, whether gold, silver or paper, has not only been of unprecedented violence, but has been visited on a society of which

the economic organization is more dependent than that of any earlier
epoch on the assumption that the standard of value would be moder-
ately stable.

He tried to show that inflations and deflations made it difficult for investors and businessmen to calculate the effects of decisions and, to a much
greater degree than the public appreciated, distorted decisions to save or
invest. But he also took pains to convey a more general point on which he
and Fisher were of one mind: "We must free ourselves from the deep distrust which exists against allowing the regulation of the standard of value
to be the subject of deliberate decision. We can no longer afford to leave
[things to nature]." The evil of inflation was that it redistributed existing
wealth arbitrarily, pitting one group of citizens against another and, ultimately, undermining democracy. The evil of deflation was that it retarded
the creation of new wealth by destroying jobs and incomes.

> It is not necessary that we should weigh one evil against the other. It
> is easier to agree that both are evils to be shunned. The individualistic
> capitalism of today, precisely because it entrusts saving to the indi-
> vidual investor and production to the individual employer, presumes a
> stable measuring rod of value and cannot be efficient—perhaps cannot
> survive—without one.

Again and again, Keynes stressed his main message, namely, that there
was a remedy: "The remedy would lie . . . in so controlling the standard of
value that, whenever something occurred which, left to itself, would create
an expectation of a change in the general level of prices, the controlling
authority should take steps to counteract this expectation." And failure
to make money the "subject of deliberate decision" would leave a dangerous vacuum in which "a host of popular remedies . . . which remedies
themselves—subsidies, price and rent fixing, profiteer hunting, and excess
profits duties—eventually became not the least part of the evils."

The most famous of Keynes's phrases—"In the long run we are all
dead"—appears in the *Tract* in the following context: "This long run

is a misleading guide to current affairs. In the long run we are all dead. Economists set themselves too easy, too useless a task if in tempestuous seasons they can only tell us that when the storm is long past the ocean is flat again."[8] Later, Schumpeter and other critics interpreted Keynes's flippant phrase to mean that he was indifferent to the inflationary consequences of short-term monetary or fiscal stimulus. But it is clear from the passage that he was attacking the belief that inflation and deflation would cure themselves without active management. His point was, nations had to make deliberate choices between two desirable but incompatible goals. He borrowed the idea from Fisher, whom he called "the pioneer of price stability as against exchange stability."[9] In a world in which capital flowed freely across borders, countries had to choose between stable prices for their imports and exports, on the one hand, and stable prices for their domestically produced goods and services, on the other. They couldn't have both. They had to choose. Keynes left no doubt as to which choice he favored. Domestic price stability was of paramount importance in avoiding socially disruptive transfers of wealth and high unemployment.

World War I had wrecked the gold standard. Since 1875 the British government had guaranteed that £6 could be exchanged at the Bank of England for one troy ounce of gold, and it was the bank's job to see to it that the supply of pounds grew no faster or slower than the rate required to maintain that parity. When other countries pegged their currencies to gold, the effect was, of course, to fix the rate of exchange between all "hard" or gold-standard currencies. For example, since the US government determined that $30 could be exchanged for one troy ounce of gold, £1 equaled $5. In other words, as the economist Paul Krugman has observed, the nineteenth-century gold standard operated almost like a single world currency regulated by the Bank of England.

When the war broke out, one combatant after the other went off gold in order to buy arms and feed their armies. After the war, the holy grail of British politicians and their Chancellors of the Exchequer was the earliest possible return to the gold standard. No politician was a stronger supporter of reinstating the prewar gold standard than Winston Churchill, who had rejoined the Conservative Party and had been appointed Chancellor of the Exchequer by Stanley Baldwin, the leader of the new Tory government.

On March 17, 1925, Keynes attended a fateful dinner with Churchill at which he tried to convince the chancellor that the pound would be grossly overvalued at the prewar parity. While a strong pound would be a boon to Britain's financial industry, it would cripple the old export industries—textiles and coal especially—and result in mass unemployment. This was an argument that he and Irving Fisher had long been making in the press. Keynes did not succeed. As Churchill said afterward, referring to a 1918 campaign promise: "This isn't an economic matter; it is a political decision." [10]

"The Economic Consequences of Mr. Churchill"—as Keynes called a pamphlet he wrote a few months later—were more or less precisely what he, Fisher, and other opponents had predicted. In anticipation of the new policy to raise the foreign exchange value of the pound by 10 percent, the Bank of England had raised its discount rate from 4 percent to 5 percent, a full point above the New York rate, in December 1924. The purpose was to stimulate demand for the pound by attracting short-term American funds to London. As higher interest rates choked off the flow of new credit and the strong pound dampened demand for exports, Britain's heavy industry cratered while unemployment in England's north soared. Keynes blamed the slump on Churchill's failure to take his advice.

Here it is necessary to backtrack slightly. As Keynes succeeded in working out how he was going to make a living and where he would spend his energies, he began to think more about how he wanted to live. He was in his late thirties. Something was missing. For much of 1921 and 1922, he had considered himself "married" to Sebastian Sprott, one of the beautiful undergraduates he met while lecturing at Cambridge. He had also had other affairs. Not only did none of these attachments match the intensity of his relationship with Duncan Grant a decade earlier, but they also intensified his dissatisfaction. They were a reminder that for a variety of reasons, including that homosexuality was both illegal and socially unacceptable, such relationships could never provide him with a partner with whom he could share his rich, varied, and increasingly public life.

Keynes had always been happy in the bosom of his own family. His old Bloomsbury friends were mostly married, living with someone, setting up households, having children. They more or less expected him to do the same, but his choice—a Russian ballerina with a voluptuous body and a droll sense of humor but no obvious intellectual interests—first amazed, then horrified them. Keynes met Lydia Lopokova, who danced comic roles, on an opening night of the Ballets Russes. Their passionate affair commenced in May 1921 when he found an excuse to put her up in the Bloomsbury apartment above his own, belonging to the as yet unsuspecting Vanessa Bell. Four years later, on August 3, 1925, they married in London amid great fanfare and with huge crowds gathered outside. Before the wedding, Keynes purchased a country estate, Tilton, in Surrey, where he strode around in tweeds, inspecting hogs and wheat and behaving like a country squire.

He spent his honeymoon in Russia as a guest at his in-laws' in Saint Petersburg—now named Leningrad—and subsequently as a guest of the Soviet government in Moscow. Along with several other Cambridge dons, he represented the university at the bicentennial of the Russian Academy of Sciences. Keynes's VIP schedule included visits to the economic planning ministry and the state bank, *Hamlet* in Russian, the ballet, and endless banquets. As he wrote to Virginia Woolf, his hosts "embarrassed him with a medal set in diamonds." When he and Lydia turned up at Woolf's house in Surrey after the trip, she found that Keynes had traded his country squire tweeds for an embroidered Tolstoy shirt and Astrakhan fur cap. Afterward she summarized Keynes's impressions of Russia for the benefit of their mutual friends:

> Spies everywhere, no liberty of speech, greed for money eradicated, people living in common ... ballet respected, best show of Cézanne and Matisse in existence. Endless processions of communists in top

hats, prices exorbitant yet champagne produced, & the finest cooking in Europe, banquets beginning at 8:30 and going on until 2:30 . . . then the immense luxury of the old Imperial trains; feeding off the Tsar's plate.

As usual, he displayed his journalist's verve for telling detail, false notes, and delicious contradictions, but he also used his analytical prowess to distinguish appearance from reality. The other VIPs left Moscow incredibly impressed by the relatively well-fed, clothed, and housed Soviet worker, who, apparently, never had to fear unemployment as his Western counterparts did. But Keynes could explain to *New Republic* readers that the Soviet economic "miracle" was a Potemkin village. The typical urban worker did indeed live better than before the war. Indeed, he lived "at a standard of life that is higher than its output justifies," Keynes reported. But the other six in seven Soviet citizens were small farmers who were being exploited even more ruthlessly than under the tsar:

> The Communist Government is able to pamper (comparatively speaking) the proletarian worker who is of course its especial care, by exploiting the peasant . . . The official method of exploiting the peasant is not so much by taxation—though the land tax is an important item in the budget—as by price policy.

Moscow could pay urban workers two or three times what a peasant earned by the simple expedient of forcing peasants to sell their crops to the government at prices far below those of the world market. The result was not just to lower the living standards of the majority of Russians but also to wreck the economy. Farm output, "the real wealth of the country," was falling, farm income was drying up, and an uncontrolled rural exodus was under way. Moscow and Saint Petersburg were full of homeless illegals and had unemployment rates closer to 20 or 25 percent than the official zero. "The real income of the Russian peasant is not much more than half of what it used to be, whilst the Russian industrial worker suffers overcrowding and unemployment as never before," Keynes concluded.[11]

Though he advised his Soviet hosts to reverse their ruinous policies, he conceded that the Soviet economy was not "so inefficient as to be unable to survive," albeit "at a low level of efficiency" and low living standards. And he did not contradict the prediction of Grigory Zinoviev, Stalin's second in command, that ten years hence "the standard of living will be higher in Russia than it was before the war, but in all other countries lower," [12] although only because he had qualms about the West. Perhaps because his in-laws in Saint Petersburg were being persecuted or, more likely, because he was appalled to a greater degree by inefficiency, ugliness, and stupidity than by cruelty, he dismissed the notion that Soviet Russia held the key to the West's salvation:

> How can I adopt a creed which preferring the mud to the fish exalts the boorish proletariat above the bourgeois and intelligentsia and who, whatever their faults, are the quality of life and surely carry the seeds of all human advancement? Even if we need a religion, how can we find it in the turbid rubbish of the Red bookshops?

Displaying his Bloomsbury prejudices, he blamed the "mud" and "rubbish" on "Some beastliness in the Russian nature—or in the Russian and Jewish natures when, as now, they are allied together." [13] When the editor of the *New Republic* asked Keynes to remove the offending sentence for the sake of American readers, he refused.

In late 1925 and early 1926, Keynes was momentarily distracted from monetary issues. Along with the whole country, he was mesmerized by an ugly conflict between coal barons and miners, and the threat of a nationwide strike. The first victim of the stronger pound had been Britain's decaying coal industry, already saddled with excess capacity, outdated technology, high costs, and inept management. After a standoff between owners and unions over pay cuts, the Conservative government had tried to buy time by subsidizing the miners' pay. But when the subsidies were due to expire, the standoff remained and a strike loomed. Keynes's friends in the Liberal Party did not believe, as Conservatives did, that a strike would be the first step toward revolution. Nonetheless, they supported the government, insisting that such an action would be illegal, unconstitutional, and an assault on democracy. Keynes, who sympathized with the miners who were not to blame for Churchill's decision, weighed in with proposals for a compromise. In return for the unions' taking a modest pay cut, and the owners' shutting down their least efficient pits, the government would continue the subsidies. Everyone would win.

It was wishful thinking. The ten-day general strike of May 1926 was a bust. The miners stayed out another six months, until starvation forced them back into the pits on the very terms they had rejected. Meanwhile, however, the Liberal Party had split in two. Keynes wound up siding with his old nemesis Lloyd George, who attacked the government's hard-line response, and against his old friends in the Party. Among Keynes's new friends was Beatrice Webb, whom he met for lunch several times. She attributed his siding with the miners to his recent marriage:

> Hitherto he had not attracted me—brilliant, supercilious, and not suf-
> ficiently patient for sociological discovery even if he had the heart for it,
> I should have said. But . . . I think his love marriage with that fascinating
> little Russian dancer has awakened his emotional sympathies with pov-
> erty and suffering.[14]

Keynes's antipathy to the herd—whether wealthy bankers, trade unions, proletarian culture, or ostentatious patriotism—made him ill suited for politics, Webb thought astutely, although she thought he might be valuable as a cabinet minister.

In September, Keynes was in Berlin giving an informal status report on the general strike as well a formal lecture on "The End of Laissez-Faire." At the University of Berlin, large and excited crowds gave him a warm welcome not usually extended to Englishmen. His attack on the Versailles peace treaty, condemnation of the French seizure of the Ruhr, and support for reparations reductions and foreign loans packages made him a hero there. The latest and most important, the Dawes Plan, had slashed Germany's reparations bill and opened the floodgates to an enormous surge of foreign, mostly American, loans. Awash in money, a magnet for immigrants and foreign visitors, Weimar was in its golden age. Keynes found the atmosphere in Germany's Babylon almost giddy.

He saw his old friend Carl Melchior, who had also gotten married in the interim, again and met Albert Einstein for the first and only time. His reaction to them was tinged with Bloomsbury-ish disgust with money and paranoia that German culture was being endangered by an alien one. "[Einstein] was a Jew . . . and my dear Melchior is a Jew too," he reflected.

> Yet if I lived there, I felt I might turn anti-Semite. For the poor Prussian is too slow and heavy on his legs for the other kind of Jews, the ones who are not imps but serving devils, with small horns, pitch forks, and oily tails . . . It is not agreeable to see a civilization under the ugly thumbs of its impure Jews who have all the money and the power and the brains. I vote rather for the plump Hausfraus and thick fingered Wandering Birds.[15]

His peculiar momentary identification, more propitiatory than sympathetic, with the slow, heavy, and thick masses as opposed to the clever devils that he preferred, reflects his fear of the mob, a theme that he expressed in less objectionable language in his formal talk on "The Death of Laissez-Faire." Governments of democracies risk violence if they are foolish enough to leave the economic circumstances of their citizens to chance.

Keynes continued to lecture at Cambridge throughout the 1920s. One undergraduate recalled him as "more like a stockbroker than a don, a city man who spent long weekends in the country."[16] Nonetheless, his glamour and fame attracted large crowds at his lectures. On Monday nights an invitation-only political economy club met in his rooms at Kings and attracted clever undergraduates and ambitious dons.

"Let us be up and doing, using our idle resources to increase our wealth," Keynes told an assembly of Liberal Party politicians on March 27, 1928.

"When every man and every factory is busy, then will be the time to say that we can afford nothing further." [17] At the time of the general strike, Keynes had assumed that new theories about controlling the business cycle, packaged as a solution to Britain's unemployment problem, might provide an alternative to the high tariffs advocated by the Right and the exorbitant taxes advocated by the Left. Lloyd George, his new ally, had been actively plotting a political comeback and hunting for a new philosophy. Keynes briefly considered running as the Liberal candidate for Cambridge University, but rejected the idea after a few days of agonizing. Instead he became the architect of policies on which Lloyd George campaigned in the spring of 1929. In other words, the germs of Keynes's *General Theory* grew in the Petri dish of a political campaign.

Keynes regarded instability, not inequality, as the great threat to capitalism. The arbitrary windfalls and losses—unrelated to hard work, thrift, or good ideas—not the gap between rich and poor, were what he meant by inequity. "The most violent interferences with stability and with justice, to which the nineteenth century submitted . . . , were precisely those which were brought about by changes in the price level," he wrote, echoing Irving Fisher. So the "first and most important step . . . is to establish a new monetary system." [18] Unlike Webb, Keynes rejected the politics of class war. He was too much of an elitist. Labor "put on an appearance of being against anyone who is more successful, more skilful, and more industrious, more thrifty than the average," he groused. "It is a class party, and the class is not my class . . . I can be influenced by what seems to me to be justice and good sense; but the class war will find me on the side of the educated bourgeoisie." [19]

Lloyd George, whom Keynes had reviled in 1919 as "the devil incarnate," had been forced out of office in 1922 for bartering favors for campaign contributions, womanizing, and a host of other ethical lapses. Yet the "Welsh wizard" retained his hold on the Liberal Party and on Keynes. Essentially unemployed for most of the 1920s, he turned his estate, Churt, into an economic think tank, pouring his energies, time, and a Party fund that he controlled into producing a Liberal program. Now he was planning a comeback on the basis of a plan to fight unemployment. Keynes was the campaign's chief economist.

After 1919, unemployment in Britain never dropped below 1 million, inching up year after year until it reached 10 percent in 1929. At that point Britain had yet to fully recover from World War I. The volume of British exports shrank even as world trade was expanding. In 1913, Britain had been the world's top exporter; by 1929, she had slipped to second place behind the United States.[20] The workshop of the world consisted largely of the old smokestack industries—coal, iron, and steel, textiles, shipbuilding—at a time when the consumers of the world wanted more oil, chemicals, cars, movies, and other products of new industries. Moreover, the national averages hid a sharp cleavage between the prosperous south of England and the chronically depressed industrial north, reviving the old notion, reminiscent of the Hungry Forties in the previous century, of England as two nations estranged from each other; one rich, and the other poor.

On September 25, 1927, Keynes was one of fourteen professors summoned to Churt by Lloyd George for an intimate gathering of "a few trying to lay the foundations of a new radicalism."[21] Keynes coauthored Lloyd George's inquiry "Britain's Industrial Future," backed with £10,000 of the latter's money. The report finally appeared in early February 1928 and quickly took on the moniker of "The Yellow Book," after its yellow cover. Though Keynes wrote to H. G. Wells that he hoped never again "to be embroiled in cooperative authorship on this scale," he conceded that the white paper was a "pretty serious effort to make a list of things in the politico-industrial sphere which are practicable and sensible."[22]

The report gave Keynes his first opportunity to learn something about industrial as opposed to financial companies. He told Liberal candidates that the trend toward bigness in business was driven not just by technology and finance but also by the threat of unsold inventories. Big business had evolved naturally and had to be accepted as such. It was not quite the warm endorsement of giant corporations offered by Schumpeter, but it was distinctly un-Socialist.

"We Can Conquer Unemployment" was the Liberal slogan in the campaign of 1929. On March 1, Lloyd George made a dramatic pledge to reduce unemployment to "normal" proportions within a year.[23] The heart of his program was a huge deficit-financed public works program intended to jump-start the economy. Higher growth was supposed to generate the tax revenue to pay for roads, sewers, telephone lines, electric transmission, and new housing while unemployment insurance would be used to pay workers. Keynes weighed in with a pamphlet titled "Can the Liberal Pledge Be Carried Out?" less than three weeks later. After the Treasury fired back that public works jobs would merely replace private ones, he followed it up with a second, "Can Lloyd George Do It?"

> The fact that many workpeople who are now unemployed would be receiving wages instead of unemployment pay would mean an increase in effective purchasing power which would give a general stimulus to trade. Moreover, the greater trade activity would make for further trade activity; for the forces of prosperity, like those of a trade depression, work with a cumulative effect.[24]

This, Skidelsky points out, was the germ of the idea of a multiplier. Developed two years later by one of Keynes's beautiful young men, Richard Kahn, the idea is that increasing government spending by $1 will generate more than $1 of private spending, since the initial increase in consumption by recipients leads to more hiring and income and another, if smaller, increase in spending, and so on.

Confident as ever before the May 30 general election, Keynes made a bet that the Liberals would win one hundred seats. In fact, they won just fifty-nine, effectively ending Lloyd George's political career, and Keynes had to pay out £160, only partly offset by a £10 bet he collected from Winston Churchill. The campaign also forced him to rewrite large swaths of his *Treatise on Money*. The summer of 1929 was idyllic, taken up with his manuscript, the filming of a five-minute ballet scene for one of the first British "talkies," *Dark Red Roses*, tennis, and a meeting with the government's point man for public works, Oswald Mosley, a rising star in the

Labour Party who would become a Fascist in the 1930s. The only source of irritation was the sorry outcome of Keynes's commodity speculation. He had been long on rubber, corn, cotton, and tin in 1928 when the markets suddenly turned on him and he was forced to liquidate part of his stock portfolio to cover his losses.

Irving Fisher bought his first gasoline-powered car in 1916. The last and most luxurious of the Fishers' electric models, a superdeluxe enclosed Detroit, had had to be driven to a garage every night for recharging and couldn't go faster than twenty-five miles per hour. Now Fisher, who logged thousands of railroad miles every year, hit the road in a brand-new gas guzzler, a Dodge. The highways between New York and Boston were still mostly unpaved, rutted, and dotted with potholes that could swallow a wheel or worse, but for Fisher the new car "opened up almost unlimited vistas."[25] Throughout the 1920s, Fisher got a new car every two years or so, trading up and up as his and the country's fortunes prospered. By the end of the decade, in addition to a Lincoln, he owned a La Salle convertible and a brand-new Stearns-Knight, America's answer to the English Rolls-Royce. And, like Jay Gatsby, he employed an Irish chauffeur.

By 1929, one in five American families had a car. As Fisher had predicted in 1914, the war left the United States with the biggest and strongest economy in the world. Unlike for Britain and France,

> the First World War had not been a cause of unalloyed economic loss; it had on occasions brought economic and social advantages. What is more it had demonstrated to all the combatant powers that it lay in the hands of government to formulate strategic and economic policies which could to some extent determine whether or not a war would be economically a cause of gain or loss; they were not the hopeless prisoners of circumstance.[26]

Thanks to wartime production and exports to the United Kingdom and Europe, the United States overtook Britain in annual output by 1918.[27]

Instead of collapsing, as in Germany or Austria, or being choked off by monetary authorities, as in Britain, America's recovery from the postwar recession started in 1921 and kept going. There were two recessions in the middle of the decade, each a little over a year long, but they were so mild that most Americans—farmers excepted—were unaware of them. For the entire period from 1921 to 1929, the economy expanded at an average rate of 4 percent a year while unemployment averaged less than 5 percent. In 1929, the economy was 40 percent bigger and per capita income 20 percent higher than in 1921, a remarkable performance for any country in any decade and rarely equaled since.[28]

But the averages hardly convey the convulsive changes that new forms of energy brought in their train. They inaugurated a new way of living. The modern era of the car, the suburban house, California, oil, the telephone, daily newspapers, stock quotes, refrigerators and fans and electric lighting, radio and movies, working women and smaller families, declining union membership, and shopping centers took over. The hitherto unknown concept of retirement took hold among men who had reached sixty. "Scientific management" and "Taylorism" became new corporate buzzwords after Louis Brandeis argued successfully that railroads did not have to increase rates in order to pay higher wages, as long as they organized work according to principles pioneered by Frederick Winslow Taylor. RCA and AT&T were the Microsoft and Google of the day. Meanwhile, the old economy of farms, coal mines, woolen mills, and shoe factories—those great sources of American wealth in the nineteenth century—slipped into senescence.

The steamship, railroad, and telegraph had exploded limits on mobility and communication for Alfred Marshall's generation. The automobile and telephone did the same for Fisher's, but in a way that individualized travel and long-distance interaction. Fisher thrilled at his escape from timetables, just as Beatrice Webb gloried in going miles without a chauffeur when she got her first bicycle. Mass production made possible mass ownership of the car, radio, telephone, fan, refrigerator, and prefabricated house, and these, in turn, made life in the suburbs attractive and affordable. Consumers were getting their hands on instruments of mastery that let them turn the dials, flip the switches, and get in the driver's seat.

While Webb absolutely refused to drive a car, and Geoffrey Keynes once called his brother an "anti-motoring motorphobe, giber of all forms of motoring,"[29] Fisher personified America's love affair with cars and also with gadgetry of all kinds. He ordered two wireless sets in March 1922 after giving his first radio speech. It was, he wrote to his son, "perhaps the largest audience I ever addressed." He told "an audience I couldn't see or hear or quite believe existed" that the newly inaugurated transatlantic broadcasts made "the whole world a neighborhood."[30] Not long after a twenty-five-year-old US Airmail pilot named Lindbergh flew a single-engine monoplane nonstop from Long Island to Paris in 1927, Fisher, who was in Paris, took advantage of the new transatlantic telephone service by arranging to have a nine-minute conference call with his wife in Rhode Island, his mother in New Jersey, and his son-in-law in Ohio. Irving Jr. recalled that Fisher "kept his eye on the second hand of his watch."[31] By then, Fisher was handling most of his business correspondence by telephone, doing most of his writing by Dictaphone, and, when he was in a hurry, which was almost always, dictating directly to a typist seated in front of an Olivetti. His home office had long since swallowed up the entire third floor of his New Haven mansion, with filing cabinets and typing tables spilling into hallways and stairwells. His staff included eight to ten "assorted females" who used telephones with glass mouthpieces and typed to the hum of an ozone machine installed to invigorate the office's atmosphere.

Fisher was spending most of his time crusading for the League of Nations, immigration restrictions, environmental conservation, and public health reforms, including universal insurance. He lived by the same precepts. Virtually the whole top floor of Fisher's house was devoted to a home gym, Fisher's "garage for keeping his personal engine in top form." Along with health food and vitamins, he was a sucker for exercise equipment. The gym was crammed with Indian clubs, dumbbells, weight-lifting devices, a rowing machine, an electric cabinet, a sun lamp; a vibrating chaise that his children claimed looked like an electric chair and "an outlandish mechanism for administering all-over rhythmic massage."[32] By 1929, Fisher had a full-time personal physician and a trainer on his payroll.

Again and again, Fisher argued that history was a bad guide to human potential. In a 1926 speech before a public health group,[33] Fisher argued that human beings had no more reached the limit of longevity than they had the limit of consumption. The true limit, he argued, was one hundred. He pointed out that by 1931, the life expectancy of an English boy would be nearly twenty years longer than in 1871.[34] Equally important, seven in ten people were healthy enough to enjoy life and do a day's work. At the end of the war, by contrast, six out of nine had ranged from "infirm" to "physical wrecks" to invalids "with a precarious hold on life."[35] He predicted—accurately as it turned out—that the average life span would increase from fifty-eight to eighty-two by 2000.[36]

Fisher's faith in the improvability of man and the limitless possibilities of science and free enterprise grew in tandem with the twenties boom:

> The world is gradually awakening to the fact of its own improvability. Political economy is no longer the "dismal science," teaching that starvation wages are inevitable from the Malthusian growth of population, but is now seriously and hopefully grappling with the problems of abolition of poverty. In like manner hygiene, the youngest of the biological studies, has repudiated the outworn doctrine that mortality is fatality, and must exact a regular and inevitable sacrifice at its present rate year after year. Instead of this fatalistic creed we now have the assurance of Pasteur that "It is within the power of man to rid himself of every parasitic disease."[37]

Fisher became one of the founders and first president of the American Eugenics Society. Eugenics—the application of genetics to marriage, health, and immigration practices—was by no means only a Fabian cause. Selective breeding of human beings has of course been practiced by most societies in varying forms from Spartan infanticide to the arcane mating rituals of the British aristocracy. In the late Victorian era medical and scientific advances and the spirit of reform endowed eugenics with its name and immense popularity. One of Richard Potter's closest friends,

Charles Darwin's cousin Francis Galton, is regarded as the father of the field. Major Leonard Darwin, Charles Darwin's son, established the International Eugenics Society in 1911. Beatrice and Sidney Webb and, indeed, most prominent Fabians, including G. B. Shaw and H. G. Wells, were enthusiastic eugenicists. Keynes, who served as vice president and board member of the British Eugenics Society as well as treasurer of its Cambridge branch, considered eugenics "the most important, significant and, I would add, genuine branch of sociology."[38] Eugenics was a bipartisan cause. Conservatives such as Arthur Balfour, the Conservative Prime Minister from 1902 to 1905; Winston Churchill; Lord Beveridge, architect of the post-WWII British welfare state; the writers Leonard Woolf and Virginia Woolf; and feminists Victoria Woodhull and Margaret Sanger were all enthusiastic eugenicists.

To be fair, eugenics hardly meant in 1910 or 1920 what it came to signify in the 1970s after it was discredited by association with the Nazi genocide and Jim Crow. The "general spirit" of the first international congress in London in 1912, which Fisher attended, was "conservative."[39] He and Keynes were libertarians, and Fisher in particular was an antiracist who was committed to "eliminating . . . race, prejudice, as well as other antisocial prejudices, such as underlie the Ku Klux Klan."[40] That said, Fisher and the American Eugenics Society were major forces behind the 1924 immigration law aimed not only at, as Fisher put it, "the immigration of the extremely unfit such as formerly were dumped into our population out of the public institutions of Europe"[41] but at radically reducing all immigration from southern and eastern Europe.

Fisher had focused on the evil effects of inflation and deflation on debtors and creditors, the arbitrary redistribution of wealth they caused, and the "vicious remedies" that governments adopted at the behest of victims but that "like the remedies of primitive medicine, they are often not only futile but harmful."[42] He had not yet linked fluctuations in the price level to ups and downs in employment and output, far less assigned them a primary role. Indeed, his *Principles of Economics,* published in 1911, has no index entries for *boom, depression,* or *unemployment.*

The brief but steep recession of 1920–21 focused Fisher's attention on what the government could do to fight unemployment. In 1895, the US federal government had neither the means nor the responsibility to manage the overall level of economic activity. It was small relative to the economy. Taxes were a means of financing government activities, mainly military, and tariffs were a way to aid specific industries. Money creation was left to the banks, and, under the nineteenth-century gold standard, its pace was strictly governed by the rate of growth of the world's gold supply.

Now the United States had a central bank—the Federal Reserve, created in 1913—and more discretionary power to influence the level of economic activity by encouraging or discouraging money creation and lending. The severity of the downturn convinced Fisher that in attempting to roll back wartime inflation, the Fed had slammed the brakes too hard and too long. The widespread distress among farmers—reminiscent of the 1890s—and factory workers convinced him that the greatest evil associated with unstable prices was their effect on output and employment. That chain of causation stretching from money creation to job creation became the focus of Fisher's research during the twenties.

Fisher's concerns were gradually shifting to booms and busts, and the role that money played in the economy's stability or volatility. He suspected that fluctuation in the supply of money and credit not only caused inflation and deflation but also accounted for the ups and downs of economic activity and employment. He was becoming convinced that better monetary management could lead to a "lessening of cyclical fluctuations." [43]

In addition to a steady stream of academic articles, Fisher spent more and more of his time writing for newspapers. Like Keynes and the Webbs, he knew that his best shot at selling his ideas to government policy makers was indirectly and as an outsider. In article after article, he did his best to convince the public that inflation and unemployment had a common monetary cause. He admitted that any connection between the banking system and "a matter as intensely human as the unemployment program" would strike most people as far-fetched. True, commentators had recognized the link between a general decline in the average price level and a rise in unemployment in the severe postwar recession in the United States and Britain. Likewise, inflations were associated with upswings in production and hiring. Yet theories of the "business cycle"—the alternation of boom and bust in output and employment—typically bore no mention of changes in the price level, and other researchers could find no correlation between prices and employment.

As Fisher discovered, other forecasters had missed the empirical link between prices and employment. They had confounded the level of prices with changes in the level—the distinction that had come to him in a flash in the Swiss Alps—a mistake comparable to mixing up the rate at which water flows into a bathtub with the depth of the water in the tub. As Fisher put it, other analysts had "missed the clear distinction between high prices and rising prices and likewise, between low prices and falling prices. In short they scrutinized the price level but not its rate of change."[44] One reason for the confusion was that there were no good gauges of how fast the average level of prices in the economy was changing. Fisher devoted most of the 1920s to developing and publishing accurate price measures that could be used to forecast economic activity and let the public keep track of changes in the dollar's purchasing power.

Fisher was convinced that once the causes of economic cycles were correctly identified, forecasters would be able to "predict business conditions in a truly scientific manner ... much as we forecast the weather." In 1926 he wrote that "monetary theory ought, for instance, to help us analyze and predict the price level." He assumed that once the central bank could forecast prices accurately, it could forestall anticipated price swings and, hence, eliminate or at least moderate booms and depressions. For Fisher, means typically dictated ends. "We should be led to control and reduce the so-called business cycle" instead of ascribing "a sort of fatalistic nature" to depressions and booms, he argued.[45]

In short, by the mid-1920s, Fisher had added business cycles to the list of economic ailments that, far from being untreatable, were shortly to give way to modern cures: "The idea that it's inevitable and unpredictable is entirely false. On the contrary, the causes are well known, in the main, and we know now in large degree to prevent the intensity of these alternate chills and fevers of business."[46] He attributed his confidence to the apparent success with which the Federal Reserve was already achieving a "rough stabilization of the dollar," citing the central bank's efforts to prevent periods of speculation. "We have in our power, as a means of substantially preventing unemployment, the stabilization of the purchasing power of the dollar, pound, lira, mark, crown and many other monetary units."[47] Like Keynes, he insisted that a stable currency was primarily a societal issue. "If our vast credit superstructure is to be kept from periodically falling about our ears," he wrote, "we must regard banking as something more than a private business. It is a great public service."[48]

In a 1925 piece for the Battle Creek Sanitarium's health newsletter, Fisher explained "Why I would rather be a Sanitarium Employee than a Millionaire."[49] Yet while there were many things he valued more than money, he had always secretly wanted someday to become his wife's equal in financial terms. The first of his inventions to achieve commercial potential was the product of his impatience. Having to thumb through boxes of dog-eared index cards drove him mad with frustration, so he fashioned an ingenious device that held the cards in place and kept them visible to the user. Fisher tried to convince a dozen office equipment manufacturers that his nifty gadget was the perfect solution to the increasingly voluminous record-keeping requirements of modern business and that companies would leap at any product that let them organize and store records more efficiently.

Initially, the Rolodex suffered the same fate as many other inventions: the inventor was forced to go into the business himself using his own, or rather his wife's, money. Fisher set up a tiny factory in New Haven with a staff consisting of his brother, a carpenter, and a helper. The firm's capital consisted of a loan of $35,000 from Margaret. A year after the war, Index Visible needed a three-story factory to house its operation, as well as a sales office in the New York Times Building on Nassau Street in downtown Manhattan. Fisher's first big client was New York Telephone, which helped push the company into the black in 1925. Seizing the moment, Fisher engineered a merger with his chief competitor to form the nucleus of Remington Rand. Having by this time poured a total of $148,000 into his start-up, he swapped Index Visible's common stock for $660,000 in cash, a bundle of preferred stocks, bonds, options, and dividends, and a seat on the board of the new entity, Rand Kardex. Afterward, he confessed to his son that paying his own way had been one of his "suppressed desires ever since I was married . . . Inventing offered the one chance I saw of making money without a great sacrifice of time."[50] At fifty, Fisher realized his dream and became a millionaire many times over.

Meanwhile, economic forecasting was really taking off. The boom created a market for economic forecasts. Fisher began writing a syndicated economic outlook column. He also began publishing a weekly Purchasing Power of Money index, one of several price measures that the US government eventually adopted. Before long, he had set up the Index Number Institute and was mailing wholesale price data to dozens of newspapers from its headquarters in his home office at 460 Prospect Street in New Haven. After the sale of Index Visible, Fisher moved his forecasting and data operation into the New York Times Building and his indexes and charts started to appear in the *Philadelphia Inquirer*, the *Journal of Commerce*, the *Minneapolis Journal*, the *Hartford Courant*, and other newspapers.

Always keen to apply his ideas in the real world, Fisher had begun indexing his office workers' pay to inflation during the war. He was probably the first employer to ever grant an explicit, annual, automatic "cost of living" adjustment. Ironically, the experience taught him that indexing was not a practical solution to the problems created by inflation and deflation. He explained:

> As long as the cost of living was getting higher, the Index Visible employees welcomed the swelling contents of their "high Cost of Living" pay envelopes. They thought their wages were increasing, though it was carefully explained to them that their real wages were merely standing still. But as soon as the cost of living fell they resented the "reduction" in wages.[51]

Fisher cited his employees' reaction as proof of the omnipresent "money illusion." He also hazarded a guess that Wall Street traders were as prone as typists to be misled by the false perception that their own currency's value was steady while the price of goods and services, or other currencies, bobbed up and down. A total return on a stock of 10 percent might look like a terrific investment. But if inflation was 11 percent, the investor would actually be losing money. Fisher bet that investors and unions would pay for a yardstick that enabled them to figure their "real" rates of return or whether a pay offer was a "real" increase or not.

Interest in monetary stabilization had led Fisher to an interest in index numbers, and now led to an interest in studying stock returns. The US stock market collapsed in 1921 when the Federal Reserve raised interest rates to quash wartime inflation, but share prices rebounded sharply the following year. By mid-1929, stock prices were three times higher in nominal terms than in 1921 and roughly nineteen times as high as after-tax corporate profits.[52] Fisher's Remington Rand stock had appreciated tenfold in real terms between 1925 and 1929.

As early as 1911, Fisher had argued that a diversified portfolio of stocks was a better long-term investment than bonds. The value of bonds reflected only the government's ability to repay its debt and its willingness to resist inflation. Stocks, on the other hand, could capture the effects of private sector productivity gains on profits and, hence, had far more upside potential. As the twenties boom continued, Fisher grew more and more bullish. By 1927, he had become the New Economy's most prominent promoter and was borrowing hundreds of thousands of dollars to invest on margin. He had a few scares. Once, when he returned from a trip to Paris and Rome that fall, his personal secretary was waiting for him at the New York dock. A plunge in the market had forced her to use $100,000 in his agent's account to repay short-term bank loans. Within a month, however, Fisher was urging Irving Jr. to "risk half of your present holdings by borrowing on it as collateral and using proceeds of loan for buying more. Six months or a year later you could probably sell at substantial advance and then diversify."[53]

In August 1929, unemployment was 3 percent. The tempo of innovation had picked up after the war. More patents had been filed in the previous ten years than in the previous century. Not surprisingly, an economic commission appointed by Herbert Hoover, the newly elected president and former head of the American effort to avert starvation in Europe after World War I, concluded, "Our situation is fortunate. Our momentum is remarkable."[54] When bearish investors such as Roger Babson warned that stock prices had risen too far too fast, Fisher countered that they were not out of line with corporate profits. On another occasion, he listed reasons why corporate profits were likely to keep growing: mergers were increasing scale economies and lowering production costs; companies were spending more on R&D; recycling was on the increase; management was becoming more scientific; automobiles and better roads would increase business efficiency; and the growth of business unionism presaged less industrial strife.

By 1929, Fisher was a director of Remington Rand, an investor in a half dozen start-ups, and the head of a successful forecasting service. Meanwhile, he spent most of that year revising his 1907 masterpiece, *The Theory of Interest*. Reflecting on one of the most spectacular bull markets in the history of the US stock market, Fisher attributed the surge in stock prices to an explosion of innovation since the war and the resulting growth in profitable investment opportunities. He delivered his manuscript in September and immediately began work on a book about stocks. He was scheduled to address a group of loan officers at the Hotel Taft in New Haven on October 29. Two weeks earlier, the *New York Times* reported, Professor Irving Fisher of Yale University had confidently told members of the Purchasing Agents' Association that stock prices had reached "what looks like a permanently high plateau."[55]

Chapter X

Magneto Trouble: Keynes and Fisher in the Great Depression

Men and women all over the world were seriously contemplating and frankly discussing the possibility that the Western system of society might break down and cease to work.

—*Arnold J. Toynbee, 1931*[1]

Keynes spent the first half hour of every day in bed in London reading the financial pages and talking to his broker and other City contacts on the phone. But his daily research turned up no early warnings of the American stock crash of October 1929. The King's College endowment, which he managed as bursar, plunged by one-third, and his personal portfolio fared even worse. The trouble, explains Robert Skidelsky, wasn't that Keynes owned much American stock. Rather, he had gone long in rubber, cotton, tin, and corn in the expectation that the American boom would drive commodity prices higher, and he had done so by borrowing on a ten-to-one margin. When commodity prices began to weaken in 1928, Keynes was forced to sell most of his stock in a falling market to cover his commodity positions. By the end of 1929, his net worth had plummeted from £44,000 to less than £8,000.[2] The experience converted Keynes into a value investor, convincing him that "the right method in investment is to put fairly large sums into enterprises which one thinks one knows something about and in the management of which one thoroughly believes."[3]

In the face of financial calamity and misplaced hopes, Keynes was his usual optimistic self. He was certain that the American monetary authorities would inaugurate "an epoch of cheap money" to head off a severe recession.[4] Three lunches with the new Labour prime minister, Ramsay MacDonald, whose party had soundly defeated both the Tory incumbents and Keynes's own Liberal candidate, Lloyd George, in the general election of May 1929, convinced Keynes that the new government would reject what Churchill had called "orthodox Treasury dogma."[5]

The Treasury's traditional cure for financial crises was to reassert fiscal rectitude by balancing the government's books while the Bank of England raised interest rates to defend the gold value of the pound sterling. Restoring business and investor confidence, the reasoning went, was the shortest route to recovery. Any attempt by government to act as employer of last resort would merely result in less hiring by private employers. As Winston Churchill, the outgoing Tory Chancellor of the Exchequer, reiterated before Parliament, "Whatever might be the political and social advantages, very little additional employment and no permanent additional employment can in fact, and as a general rule be created by State borrowing and State expenditure."[6] Keynes was confident that the Labourites would embrace Liberal proposals for public works spending and lower interest rates, their effect on the government deficit and the gold value of sterling be damned. An invitation the following July to chair MacDonald's Economic Advisory Council, the prime minister's "economic general staff," confirmed his upbeat expectations.[7] "I'm back in favor again," he crowed in a note to Lydia.[8]

Keynes was certain that easier money would stabilize the economy. Unemployment might ratchet up for several months, he wrote in a *Times* of London column, but as long as interest rates fell even faster than prices, business investment would bounce back and commodity prices and farm incomes would recover. He also had faith in the activism of the new president, Herbert Hoover, in contrast to Calvin Coolidge's passivity. Hoover had appointed an energetic Federal Reserve chairman, Eugene Isaac Meyer, the future publisher of the *Washington Post*, and had announced a program to fast-forward federal construction projects. The successful former mining executive and European food aid czar was inviting business bigwigs to the White House for brainstorming sessions. A few weeks after the stock market crash, his treasury secretary, Andrew Mellon, had gone to Congress to ask for a 1 percent tax cut for corporations and individuals.[9] And, as always, Keynes was confident enough to back his forecasts with cash. By September 1930, reports Skidelsky, he was once again buying up large amounts of American and Indian cotton.

Demand for Keynes's opinions soared, and he used his newspaper columns, radio talks, and newsreel interviews to promote monetary activism to fight the slump. In December 1930, he wrote a long piece for the *Nation* that began: "The world has been slow to realize that we are living this year in the shadow of one of the greatest economic catastrophes of modern history." To dispel resignation, he used every public forum to dismiss the popular narrative that cast booms and busts as episodes in a morality play. He vigorously denied the notion that recessions were the inevitable punishment and welcome correctives for extravagance, imprudence, and greed. Instead, Keynes told his readers, "We have involved ourselves in a colossal muddle, having blundered in the control of a delicate machine, the working of which we do not understand."[10]

The problem, in other words, was a technical one. For Keynes, depressions, like car wrecks, were the result of accidents and policy blunders. They involved permanent losses in output that, like time, could never be recouped and were not restoratives but simply a waste. Bad harvests, hurricanes, wars, and other bolts from the blue did sometimes trigger downturns, but the origin of most recessions was bad or erratic decisions by economic policy makers. In principle, that meant that downturns could be minimized or prevented altogether. Keynes was especially eager to rebut the notion that booms, rather than depressions, were the problem. As he put it a few years later, echoing one of Schumpeter's sentiments from *The Theory of Economic Development*, "The right remedy for the trade cycle is not to be found in abolishing booms and thus keeping us permanently in a semi-slump, but in abolishing slumps and thus keeping us permanently in a quasi boom."[11] He insisted that, contrary to the accusations of moralists, the slump meant that past economic gains had been phantasmagorical. Referring to the investment boom of the twenties, he wrote that "the other was not a dream. This is a nightmare, which will pass away with the morning. For the resources of nature and men's devices are just as fertile and productive as they ever were . . . We were not previously deceived."[12]

The economy was suffering from a mechanical breakdown for which there was a (relatively) easy fix. In one column he wrote that there was nothing more profoundly wrong with the economic engine than a case of "magneto" or starter trouble.[13] Prices had fallen so much that farmers and businessmen couldn't sell their products for what it cost to produce them. Hence, they had no choice but to slash production and investment, setting off another round of unemployment and causing prices to fall still further. To break the vicious circle, all the monetary authorities had to do was to lower interest rates by creating more money until business could raise prices and found it worthwhile to begin investing again. He was convinced that easier money would head off anything worse than a garden-variety recession.

Keynes used automotive analogies to make the point that, as Skidelsky put it, immense catastrophes could have trivial causes and trivial solutions. To many ears, however, his message sounded counterintuitive, even flippant. While the eminent mathematician and Marxist G. H. Hardy was ridiculing the notion of mechanical solutions to deep scientific problems— "It is only the very unsophisticated outsider who imagines that mathematicians make discoveries by turning the handle of some miraculous machine"—Keynes was reassuring his readers that once the problem was correctly diagnosed, there was a solution—if only the authorities had the *conviction* to act:

> Resolute action by the Federal Reserve Banks of the United States, the Bank of France, and the Bank of England might do much more than most people, mistaking symptoms or aggravating circumstances for the disease itself, will readily believe . . . I am convinced that Great Britain and the United States, like-minded and acting together, could start the machine again within a reasonable time; if, that is to say, they were ener-

gized by a confident conviction as to what was wrong. For it is chiefly the
lack of this conviction which to-day is paralyzing the hands of authority
on both sides of the Channel and of the Atlantic.

The lack of conviction was partly, or even mainly, intellectual. Keynes
attributed the magnitude of the catastrophe to the fact that "there is no
example in modern history of so great and rapid a fall of prices from a
normal figure as has occurred in the past year." [15] As Keynes knew, old
theories could not be refuted with facts alone. New theories were required.
To add ballast to his editorializing, Keynes hurried his two-volume *Treatise
on Money* into print, finishing the preface in mid-September 1930.

The focus of the *Treatise* was the possibility of controlling the business
cycle by stabilizing prices. When investment exceeded saving, the result
was inflation. When the reverse was true, the results were a falling price
level, slumping output, and rising unemployment—a recession, in other
words. Thus, depressions could be cured by encouraging spending and
discouraging saving, exactly the opposite of the medicine that tradition-
alists such as Churchill extolled. "For the engine which drives Enterprise
is not Thrift, but profit," he argued, asking rhetorically, "Were the Seven
Wonders of the World built by thrift? I doubt it." [16]

His upbeat message was that if deflation was driving farmers, miners,
and businessmen to slash output, the authorities possessed the cure. In his
1921 book *Stabilizing the Dollar,* Irving Fisher had argued that the central
bank could control the quantity of money and credit by manipulating
the interest rate. By raising rates when inflation threatened and lowering
them when deflation loomed, the central bank could restrain or encourage investment, depending on whether it wished to stimulate or slow economic activity. And by controlling investment, the monetary authorities
could keep it in line with saving, and prices in line with costs. This is what
Keynes believed in 1931, when he was still confident that concerted action
to lower interest rates would end the slump.

As Skidelsky observes, Keynes failed to appreciate the economic or-
thodoxy of Socialist politicians. Even though high unemployment had
dominated public concerns for at least nine years, Labour still had no pro-

gram of its own for attacking it. Beatrice Webb was an exception. A vocal critic of the Treasury view, she had criticized "Treasury book-keeping" and annual budget balancing in her controversial 1909 *Minority Report*.[17] In boom times, she had argued, government ought to raise taxes on the rich and create a surplus. In bad times, it should fund public works even if it meant running a budget deficit. But by 1930 she had become convinced that unemployment was intrinsic to capitalism. Ignoring the fact that unemployment in the United States had averaged less than 5 percent for most of the 1920s, she had concluded that it could not be eliminated until private industry had been nationalized.[18]

Most members of the Labour cabinet hewed as steadfastly to the Treasury view as had Winston Churchill. One minister wrote to the prime minister, "The captain and officers of a great ship has run aground on a falling tide; no human endeavor will get the ship afloat until in the course of nature the tide again begins to flow." MacDonald replied that the "letter expresses exactly my own frame of mind."[19] Cutting benefits and raising taxes seemed more prudent than embracing the radical stimulus measures advocated by Keynes and Fisher.

At the end of 1930, Keynes's advisory council of economists came up with a hodgepodge of conventional and radical policies: cut the unemployment benefit, adopt a 10 percent tariff on imports, and implement "a big public works program" to create jobs for the unemployed.[20] They explicitly rejected the view that any additions to government payrolls would merely displace private employment. "We do not accept the view that the undertaking of such work must necessarily cause any important diversion of employment in ordinary industry."[21] But the Labour cabinet, in which Sydney Webb served as colonial minister, adopted only the first measure and rejected tariffs and public works.

By early 1931, reports Skidelsky, Keynes's finances were so strained that he tried to sell his two best paintings, including Matisse's *Deshabille*.[22] He found no buyers at his minimum asking price.

In the summer of 1929 Irving Fisher had not only splurged on his Stearns-Knight but also watched with satisfaction as a crew of workmen finished a lavish renovation of his and Maggie's New Haven house. The best thing about it, he told his son, was that he, not his wife, was footing the bill.

At sixty, Fisher looked fitter and more distinguished than ever, with his thick white hair, trim figure, and a thoughtful gaze that gave no hint that he was blind in one eye. He had borrowed heavily to take advantage of options on Remington Rand stock that came his way as part of his sale of Index Visible. Four years after the sale of Index Visible to Rand, the value of his stock portfolio had multiplied tenfold. His Index Number Institute, still housed in the New York Times Building, had inaugurated a subscriber service for stock indices. Fisher wrote a syndicated weekly column for investors that appeared in newspapers around the country every Monday. In the public's eye, he was identified not only with Prohibition and the wellness craze, but also with the stock market boom and New Era optimism on the economy.

As questions about the durability of the bull market accumulated in 1929, he dismissed the dire warnings of professional stock market bears such as Roger Babson by pointing to the remarkable combination of low inflation and rapid economic growth that had characterized the decade. "We have witnessed probably the greatest expansion in history, within any similar period of time, of the real income of a people," [23] he wrote. In mid-October, according to the *New York Times,* Fisher had predicted that the stock market was poised to go "a good deal higher within a few months." [24]

After the crash, Fisher was by no means convinced that a recession was inevitable. In January 1930 he wrote:

> The fall of paper values was largely a transfer of wealth, not a destruction of physical wealth . . . Physical plans are unimpaired . . . The redistribution of corporate ownership was confined to a very small percentage of the population, and consequently will have little effect upon the purchasing power of the great mass of consumers. [25]

His competitor the Harvard Economic Society agreed that a repeat of the severe 1920–21 recession was not in the cards. Days after the crash, the Harvard forecasters informed their subscribers, "We believe that the present recession both for stocks and business, is not a precursor to a business depression."[26]

Fisher wasted little time bemoaning his losses and instead focused his attention on producing a postmortem of the crash. He wrote much of *The Stock Market Crash—and After* in November and December 1929. He defended his optimism that stock prices would recover by pointing out that they were now only eleven times earnings, below their long-run historical average, and "too low a ratio in view of the expectations of a faster rate of earnings in the future." He rejected the popular explanation that the inflated stock prices were to blame, arguing that "between two thirds and three fourths of the rise in the stock market between 1926 and September, 1929 was justified" by earnings and productivity gains, a conclusion that some recent analyses confirm. At the same time, he explained how investors like him had been lured by a combination of low interest rates and high returns to take on too much debt: "When new inventions give an opportunity to make more than the current rate of interest there is always a tendency to borrow at low rates to make a higher rate from investment." Instead of artificially high stock prices, the problem was excessive borrowing:

> Investors found themselves confronted on the one hand by wonderful opportunities to make money and on the other a low rate for loans. They could borrow at much less than they expected to make. In short, both the bull market and the crash are largely explained by the unsound financing of sound prospects.[27]

Fisher continued to predict a stock market recovery and to deny that the crash had made a depression inevitable. He pointed out that economic activity had begun to decline before the stock market crash and predicted a typical recession. As long as businesses did not succumb to doom and gloom by scaling back production and firing employees, he insisted, the real economy would weather the storm. Month after month for the next year, Fisher maintained that an upturn was around the corner. Like Keynes, he had confidence in Hoover's competence and resolve.

For several months, Fisher's optimism looked plausible. By April 1930, the stock market was back to the level it had reached in early 1929. Prices were not falling as fast, and unemployment was not rising as rapidly, as in 1921. Indeed, as late as June 1930, the unemployment rate was 8 percent. In 1921, it had been 12 percent. Interest rates were extremely low. But as Milton Friedman and Anna Schwartz observe in their magisterial *A Monetary History of the United States, 1867–1960,* instead of the anticipated recovery there was a palpable "change in the character of the contraction."[28]

A further plunge in industrial prices offset any benefit to borrowers from lower interest rates. Billions in assets evaporated in a wave of bank failures in the fall of 1930 and the summer of 1931. Even when Fisher was finally forced to admit the severity of the depression, he insisted that the market and the economy were both bottoming. His optimism, overconfidence, and stubbornness betrayed him, and, like so many others who kept hoping that the tide would turn, he hung on to his stock. Had he adopted Herbert Hoover's cautious formula and paid off his bank loans while Remington Rand stock was climbing to $58 a share in 1928 and 1929, Fisher would still have been a millionaire eight to ten times over. Even if he had sold his stock one year after the crash, he would still have been comfortable. In late 1930 Remington Rand was selling for $28 a share. By 1933, it would fall to $1 a share. By April 1931 Fisher's net worth had shrunk to a little more than $1 million. In August he was forced to shutter the Index Number Institute and disband his staff of economists and statisticians. As if this was not devastating enough, the IRS sued him for $75,000 in back taxes related to sales of Remington Rand stock in 1927 and 1928. He was forced to turn to his sister-in-law Caroline Hazard, the retired president of Wellesley, who eventually turned over the management of the loan to a committee consisting of her lawyer and two nephews.

Public recrimination and ridicule added to the stress and humiliation of financial ruin. The former president of the American Economic Association attacked Fisher in the *New York Times* for "always insisting that all was well and talking of prosperity, a new era and increased efficiency of production as justification of the high stock prices."[29] The paper also reported that "Secretary Mellon, former President Coolidge and Professor

Irving Fisher of Yale were named yesterday as the individuals most responsible for 'continuing and extending the mania'" of speculation which preceded the Wall Street crash.[30] When the CEO of a company in which he had invested heavily was indicted for fraud, Fisher sued. The publicity tarnished his reputation further. His son recalled hearing two strangers discuss the lurid details of the case, which were being reported daily in the *New York Times*. "Gosh, he's supposed to know all the answers, and look how he got burned."[31]

Instead of running its course, the economic slide accelerated and spread across the globe. US industrial output plunged to less than half its 1929 level, and unemployment shot up to 16 percent. The tone of commentary turned panicky: by midyear, newspapers were referring to "the Great Depression."[32] Fisher confessed that "the most important economic event in the lifetime of all of us here" would be "an enigma" for years to come.[33] He and Keynes had both been blindsided, but Fisher had lost his credibility with the public as well.

Keynes and Fisher both spent the first week of July 1931 in the drought-stricken Midwest. Two dozen monetary experts were meeting at the University of Chicago to discuss the government's response to what was now being called the Great Depression. Keynes praised the Hoover administration for cutting taxes and signing off on a raft of building projects, among them the Hoover Dam. He complimented the Federal Reserve for cutting interest rates to record lows to prevent deflation. "The depression must be fought by price-raising, not price-cutting," he told reporters.[34] He was still convinced that lowering interest rates would suffice to end the recession, but prudent enough to recognize that not putting all eggs in one basket—"attacking the problem on a broad front, trying simultaneously every plausible means"[35]—made economic as well as political sense in a situation that no one had foreseen.

Keynes chaired a roundtable that took up the question "Is it possible for Governments and Central Banks to do anything on purpose to remedy Unemployment?"[36] Typical midwestern fiscal conservatives, the Chicago economics faculty nonetheless supported the Hoover administration's policy of more government spending and easier money. Keynes was not the only one to have the insight that shortfalls in demand—the means and desire of households and businesses to spend—caused recessions and that the solution was for the government to make up for them. Indeed, the Chicagoans were decidedly more enthusiastic than was Keynes about Hoover's public works program and business lending initiative. Keynes had less confidence in the organizational capability of American as opposed to British civil servants.

After he returned to London, Keynes lent his name to the Labour government's *Report of the Committee on Finance and Industry,* by Lord Hugh Macmillan, proposing that Britain, the United States, and France join in a concerted effort to expand credit by a number of means, including canceling war debts, making emergency loans, and removing obstacles to trade. Labour's attempt to restore confidence in the pound by proposing £70 million of spending cuts plus £70 million of tax increases was to no avail. By August 1931, the Labour government had split over the policies proposed by the Economic Advisory Board, and Ramsay MacDonald had resigned as prime minister. A few weeks later, the collapse of the largest Austrian bank, Kreditanstalt, triggered a financial crisis on the Continent and a run on the British pound as European investors frantically raised cash by withdrawing sterling from their London accounts. The Bank of England responded by more than doubling the discount rate to 6 percent.

On September 21, Britain finally took the step that Keynes and Fisher had been advocating all along: devaluing the pound by 30 percent and suspending gold payments. Rather than leaving interest rates at their September high to prevent a further outflow of gold and hard currency reserves and defend the gold value of the pound—a measure that would have forced another round of investment and job cuts—the Bank of England lowered the rate from 6 percent to 2 percent in the first half of 1932.[37] In a congratulatory telegram to Prime Minister MacDonald on "the breaking of the gold standard," Fisher assured him that the step was "not something to be ashamed of."[38]

Keynes was reassuring. Vanessa Bell wrote to her sister Virginia Woolf in October, after she and Duncan Grant went to see a movie in London:

Suddenly Maynard appeared on the screen enormously big ... blinking at the lights & speaking rather nervously & told the world that everything was now going to be all right. England had been rescued by fate from an almost hopeless situation, the pound would not collapse, prices would not rise very much, trade would recover, no one need fear anything. In this weather one can almost believe it.[39]

It was too late for the Labour government. The general election in October resulted in a landslide for Tories and Liberals. Ramsay MacDonald retained his prime ministership, but Conservatives once again controlled domestic economic policy.

Despite his financial straits, damaged reputation, and advancing age, the sixty-five-year-old Fisher seemed more energized than depressed by the economic calamity. In 1932 he published an extraordinary number of scientific papers and newspaper pieces. He bombarded the Hoover administration and the Federal Reserve with advice and organized other economists to do the same. His chief objective was to convince President Hoover to take the United States off the gold standard, if not de jure then de facto by having the Federal Reserve do nothing to prevent the foreign exchange value of the dollar from falling. He met with the bankers at the Federal Reserve to urge them to adopt an aggressive program to buy bonds from the banks and the public in order to pump money into the banking system. To his frustration, the "Federal Reserve men thought it would be 'safer' if they waited!" as he later complained. "That waiting, in my opinion, cost the country the major part of the depression."[40]

In January 1932, Fisher attended a second meeting of monetary experts at the University of Chicago. This time, he organized a telegram urging the president to permit the federal budget deficit to rise, pump reserves into the crippled banking system, slash tariffs, and cancel interallied debts. Thirty-two prominent economists from Chicago, Wisconsin, and Harvard universities signed the statement, in which Fisher pointed out that Sweden, Japan, and Britain were recovering after going off gold the previous year. The signatories reflected the extent to which Fisher and Keynes's view of the crisis, with its emphasis on its global nature, monetary causes, forecasts of its future course, and the need for concerted monetary intervention, had gained adherents. On the other hand, theirs was still a minority view. In the same month, two Harvard instructors, Harry Dexter White and Lauchlin Currie, had issued a similar manifesto. Calling the depression "an international calamity," they insisted that the government do more than aid the victims and focus on preventing the slump from worsening:

> With the reparations problem involved, economic distress throughout Europe on the increase, with the progressive mal-distribution of gold reserves, the growing loss of confidence in banks, the mounting trade barriers, disorders in Spain, India, and China, the outlook for recovery in the near future is not encouraging . . . In view of . . . the failure on the part of the government to adopt other than palliative measures there devolves upon the economist the responsibility of recommending a course of action which will hasten the approach of recovery.

Calling for massive public spending, the Harvard dissidents referred derisively to "economists who believe that the course of the depression cannot be checked, that political and economic changes are beyond human control."[41] At Harvard apparently these included the entire senior faculty. The third Harvard signature on the manifesto was also that of an instructor.

By 1932 the depth and global nature of the depression was becoming clear, and Herbert Hoover was on his way to becoming the "most hated man in America." Bombarded with conflicting advice, the president adopted a grab bag of inconsistent policies to combat rising unemployment. Under attack for cutting taxes and raising spending while the budget deficit continued to widen, Hoover reversed course, raising taxes and cutting spending. Bankers, businessmen, and, indeed, the economics community refused to support such unconventional measures. After a meeting with a Treasury undersecretary, Fisher wrote to Maggie, "I told him he and Hoover should choose *some* way and go right after it!"[42]

In truth, there was no consensus anywhere about what government should do. Most governments reacted to falling prices, production, and tax revenues by trying to balance their budgets. The effect of tax increases and spending cuts was to make the slump worse and to trigger further price declines. Banking panics created huge liabilities for governments. Thus, as the economic historian Harold James points out, the action of governments, especially Washington, helped to spread the deflation and depression and made the Great Depression truly global.

Any hope that 1932 would be like 1923, when the American economy had roared back after the steep 1920–21 recession, was soon quashed. Instead of recovering, the economy's slide accelerated. By 1933, stocks were trading at one-fifth of their 1929 values while retail prices had plunged by 30 percent. National output and income had shrunk by one-third. An extraordinary 25 percent of the labor force was out of work. Death by suicide was up sharply, as one might expect. One of the few bright notes was that Americans on the whole were getting healthier and living longer and had a lower chance of dying before their time. Apparently, the 1920s prosperity, with its plethora of opportunities to work and consume, had not been a wholly unalloyed blessing.

By the time Keynes and the American journalist Walter Lippmann conducted their first transatlantic broadcast in real time in July 1933, Franklin Delano Roosevelt was in the White House. Lippmann concluded the broadcast with an observation calculated to win over his interviewer:

> It may be that at the present stage of human knowledge we are not equipped to understand a crisis which is so great and so novel ... Nowhere in the whole world has there been a prophet of whom it can be said that his teachings were comprehensive and prompt and sufficient ... It is also a crisis of the human understanding, and our deepest failures have not been failures arising from malevolence but from miscalculation.[43]

Most economic historians agree that not only did no one predict the Great Depression on the basis of any previous depression, but no one could have predicted it on the basis of any existing theory.[44] In retrospect, modern scholars put the primary blame on mistakes by the Federal Reserve, the collapse in confidence and spending by consumers and business, and the wave of selling into falling markets by increasingly panicky investors. But, as David Fettig at the Federal Reserve Bank of Minneapolis has observed,

> In the end, if the Great Depression is, indeed, a story, it has all the trappings of a mystery that is loaded with suspects and difficult to solve, even when we know the ending; the kind we read again and again, and each time come up with another explanation. At least for now.[45]

For those of a scientific bent, being spectacularly wrong is often the most powerful stimulus to fresh thinking. By late 1932, it had become clear that Keynes and Fisher's theory that price stability was a sufficient condition for economic stability—that is, full employment—was flawed or, at the very least, missing some crucial variable. Neither had a truly satisfactory explanation for the magnitude of the economy's collapse between 1929 and 1933. Without a compelling theory that accounted for the crisis, no government would have the confidence to take strong, consistent action. Thus, both men were driven to examine their earlier assumptions and to look for forces that they had overlooked or misunderstood.

Fisher thought he had discovered the missing variable: debt. He first proposed a new theory to explain the magnitude of the economic collapse by emphasizing the toxic interaction of excessive debt and rapid deflation at a meeting of economists in New Orleans. "Over-investment and over-speculation are often important," he told them, "but they would have far less serious results were they not conducted with borrowed money."[46] Public and private debt levels had exploded since World War I, not only in the United States but worldwide.[47] American households took on debt to buy cars, appliances, and houses while European governments still owed gargantuan sums from the war.

The initial fall in stock prices was enough to rattle the confidence of heavily indebted businesses and households and overextended banks, who rushed to liquidate their debts and shore up their balance sheets. This led to an initial wave of distress selling—"selling not because the price is high enough to suit you, which is the normal characteristic of selling, but because the price is so low it frightens you"[48]—and further declines in stock prices, which in turn caused bank deposits to contract. As the supply of money shrank, prices began to slide downward across the board.

Deflation, as a fall in the overall price level, should, in principle, raise real incomes by increasing the purchasing power of a given nominal wage. As the prices of everything from gasoline to shoes fall, a given wage buys more. In his 1911 book *The Purchasing Power of Money,* Fisher had shown that falling prices could also depress income. The real value of a $1,000 loan is $1,000 divided by the average price level. If prices decline, the real value of the debt increases, impoverishing debtors and enriching creditors. A second effect follows from the redistribution of income from debtors to creditors. Debtors tend to spend more and save less of their income than creditors, one reason they took out a loan in the first place. Thus, their spending falls by more than creditors' spending increases.

If everyone expected prices to fall in the future, Fisher argued, companies would become reluctant to borrow to invest in new factories and equipment, because they would have to repay the banks later in more valuable dollars. As businesses slashed investment plans, spending on capital goods would fall, as would the incomes of capital goods producers and workers. As income slipped, the demand for money and the nominal rate of interest would both fall. But the nominal rate of interest would fall less than the price level, so the real interest rate would wind up higher. In both cases, falling prices would lead to lower production and higher unemployment.

Fisher's point was that the effort of businesses to get rid of debts actually resulted in increasing the debt burdens in real terms, a dramatic instance of actions that were beneficial for an individual but harmful in the aggregate. Even businesses that were debt free would find themselves in trouble as the prices they could charge for their products fell faster than the costs of labor and raw materials. The squeeze on their profits would inevitably result in layoffs and production cuts. The rational attempt by banks and individuals to solve their own difficulties by slashing their debt, he emphasized, had the perverse effect of making things worse.

Fisher had already concluded that the immediate cause of the crisis was "the collapse of the credit system under the weight of these debts."[49] Between 1929 and 1933, three banking panics wiped out billions in business, farm, and personal assets—equal to one-third of the nation's money supply. Yet the Federal Reserve began raising interest rates in the fall of 1931 and did nothing to shore up the banking system, on the grounds that weeding out unfit banks was laying the groundwork for recovery. Fisher blamed lingering war debts, the Smoot-Hawley tariff, and the absence of a strong leader at the Federal Reserve. Benjamin Strong, who as president of the New York Federal Reserve Bank had dominated the Federal Reserve, had possessed a deep knowledge of banking and close ties with the head of the Bank of England. His death at the end of 1928, Fisher was certain, had deprived the relatively untested American central bank of strong leadership—and credibility overseas—just when such leadership was most needed. He told a reporter that "the effect of the economic crisis could have been mitigated 'by at least 90 percent' if the Federal Reserve banks had followed the stabilization policy of former Governor Benjamin Strong of the New York Bank."[50]

Nonetheless, Fisher's optimism that greater understanding would ultimately make preventing and mitigating depressions possible was undimmed:

> The main conclusion of this book is that depressions are, for the most part, preventable and that their prevention requires a definite policy in which the Federal Reserve System must play an important role. No time should be lost in grappling with the practical measures necessary to free the world from such needless suffering as it has endured since 1929.[51]

Judging by newspaper headlines of the early 1930s, popular wisdom viewed economics through a biblical lens: recessions were the wages of sin. When good times lasted too long, businesses and individuals threw caution to the wind and behaved badly. Recessions—periods when output, employment, and income contract instead of expand—occurred when private businesses and households unwound past excesses, wrote off bad investments, and behaved with restraint once again. Recessions, in this view, were regrettable but necessary correctives, like a detox program for a drunk. When they occurred, the government had to prevent business and consumer confidence from being damaged further by balancing the budget and guarding against excessively easy monetary policy. That, of course, is the platform on which Franklin Delano Roosevelt campaigned.

The Brain Trust around FDR was a group of campaign advisors from Columbia University that included Adolph Berle, a law professor and expert on corporate governance; Rexford Tugwell, an agricultural economist; and Marriner Eccles, a millionaire Western banker. Its members distrusted economic radicals such as Keynes and Fisher almost as much as did the British Labourites, considering them inflationists hardly better than William Jennings Bryan and the silverites of the 1890s. This was unfair. Fisher and Keynes advocated that the Treasury and the central bank stop targeting the gold exchange rate and instead target the overall price level. They wanted, in other words, the monetary authorities in the major economies to let their foreign exchange rates depreciate while preventing deflation of domestic prices. For the Brain Trusters, this was a distinction without a difference. Tugwell recalled, "We were at heart believers in sound money." [52] In their way, Roosevelt's advisors were as conservative on money matters and as wedded to the Treasury view as was the British Labour Party.

David Kennedy describes FDR's own brain as "a teeming curiosity shop continuously restocked with randomly acquired intellectual oddments . . . open to all number and manner of impressions, facts, theories, nostrums, and personalities . . . particularly inflation-preaching monetary heretics like Yale's Professor Irving Fisher." [53] Tugwell recalled, "All the old schemes for cheapening money were apparently still alive, and there were many new ones. The Governor [FDR] wanted to know all about them. We shuddered and got him the information." [54]

Inflation's appeal was political. Two-thirds of the Democratic Party consisted of southern and western farmers who were caught between debt and declining crop prices and were hostile to gold. On the other hand, the prospect of inflation inspired more dread among bankers and businessmen than one would suppose in a year when the average price level had dropped by more than 10 percent and one-third of the nation's banks had defaulted. Memories of the violent inflations during and after World War I and the deflations that had been necessary to cure them were still too fresh to ignore. FDR was especially hostile to international cooperation to fight the depression.

Unused to thinking like mathematicians, the Brains Trusters found the notion that huge disturbances might have trivial causes counterintuitive. FDR's economic advisors were more inclined to blame the depression on traditional Democratic nemeses: income inequality, monopolies, and, as had Fisher, the Smoot-Hawley tariff. FDR himself was intrigued by popular theories of overproduction and underconsumption that blamed the depression on either too much wealth or too much poverty. In a speech in May 1932 at Atlanta's Oglethorpe University, the candidate decried the "haphazardness" and "gigantic waste" in the American economy, along with the "superfluous duplication of productive facilities," and called for thinking "less about the producer and more about the consumer." He also predicted that the American economy was nearing its limits and that "our physical economic plant will not expand in the future at the same rate at which it has expanded in the past." [55]

David Kennedy observes that FDR's speech at the Commonwealth Club of San Francisco on September 23, 1932, reflected the "eclecticism and fluidity" of the candidate's views:

> A *mere* builder of more industrial plants, a creator of more railroad systems, an organizer of more corporations is as likely to be a danger as a help. The day of the great promoter or the financial Titan, to whom we granted everything if only he would build, or develop, is over."

Extraordinary as it sounds, at a time when one-third of the nation was destitute, FDR blamed the depression on too *much* rather than too little production:

> It is the soberer, less dramatic business of administering resources and plants already in hand, of seeking to reestablish foreign markets for our surplus production, of meeting the problem of under-consumption, of

adjusting production to consumption, of distributing wealth and products more equitably.[56]

Naturally, FDR's advisors had their own political agendas too. Berle
promoted the notion that the economic crisis had created a unique
window for enacting major social reforms. Kennedy points out that the
economic recovery program on which FDR campaigned "was difficult to
distinguish from many of the measures that Hoover, even if somewhat
grudgingly, had already adopted: aid for agriculture, promotion of industrial cooperation [price fixing], loans to business, support for the banks,
and a balanced budget."[57] The first budget bill FDR sent to Congress cut
the federal budget far more than Hoover had dared.

Keynes and Fisher both considered the candidate's emphasis on social
welfare reforms before the economy had been stabilized wrongheaded and
risky. A few weeks before FDR's inaugural, Keynes sent the president a letter warning against mixing long-run reforms with the recovery program
and advocating "open market operations to reduce the long term rate of
interest."[58] Fisher urged FDR to announce a retreat from the gold standard
on inauguration day, arguing that it "would reverse the present deflation
overnight and would set us on the path toward new peaks of prosperity."[59]
At the end of 1933, Keynes wrote an open letter to FDR, published in the
New York Times, to reiterate his argument. "Even wise and necessary reform may . . . impede and complicate recovery. For it will upset the confidence of the business world and weaken their existing motives to action."[60]
Fisher shared Keynes's reservations about the New Deal:

> It's all a strange mixture. I'm against the restriction of acreage and pro-
> duction but much in favor of reflation. Apparently FDR thinks of them
> as similar—merely two ways of raising prices! But one changes the mon-
> etary unit to restore it to normal, while the other spells scarce food and
> clothing when many are starving and half naked.[61]

The single exception to the continuation of Hoover's policies was a very
large one: FDR's decision to abandon the gold standard. This was the step

that Keynes and Fisher had been urging in one form or another since the 1929 crash. In practical terms, going off gold meant that the Federal Reserve would not push up interest rates to prevent the dollar's exchange rate against the pound and other foreign currencies from falling. The first beneficiaries would be farmers and miners, since a cheaper dollar meant that their grain and ore became more competitive abroad, and then businesses and households that borrowed to buy houses or make capital improvements.

After Roosevelt announced that the United States would go off gold on April 19, 1933, Keynes praised the president for being "magnificently right." Fisher once again let his hopes rise. He wrote to Maggie: "Now I am sure—so far as we ever can be sure of anything—that we are going to snap out of this depression fast."[62] This time, Fisher's economic forecast proved prescient. The US economy hit bottom within a month of Roosevelt's inauguration, marking the beginning of a recovery. On the other hand, Fisher's hope that his personal finances could be mended was not realized. Going hat in hand to his sister-in-law was the least of the humiliations he was to suffer. Had Yale University not agreed to buy his New Haven home and let him live there rent free, he would have been evicted from it. The Fishers' summer cottage at the shore was handed over to Caroline Hazard, who forgave the rest of the debt in her will. Without income from dividends, Fisher had to support himself with directors' fees.

Keynes met FDR for the first time at 5:15 in the evening on May 28, 1934. After days of dawn-to-dusk meetings with cabinet members, Brain Trusters, NRA bureaucrats, and other officials, he had finally gotten in to chat with the president for an hour. Afterward he reported to Felix Frankfurter, now an advisor to FDR, that he had told him that if the government increased federal stimulus spending from $300 million a month to $400 million a month, the United States would have a satisfactory recovery.[63] The president said that he had a "grand talk with Keynes and liked him immensely" but complained that he talked like a "mathematician."[64] The next day, the *New York Times* ran another open letter from Keynes to the president praising the New Deal and calling for deficit spending to the tune of 8 percent of GDP. "This, he promised, might directly or indirectly, increase the national income by at least three or four times this amount . . . Most people greatly underestimate the effect of a given emergency expenditure, because they overlook the Multiplier—the cumulative effect of increased individual incomes, because the expenditure of these incomes improves the incomes of a further set of recipients and so on.[65]

The next evening, Keynes attended a dinner at New York's New School for Social Research with Fisher and Schumpeter.[66] In his talk he spelled out his theory of deficit-financed public works spending, including his notion that the cumulative effect of $1 of such spending could be much greater than $1. Whereas Fisher never departed from his conviction that the Great Depression was the result of monetary blunders, that "of all things tried, monetary policies have succeeded most," and that "the only sure and rapid recovery is through monetary means," Keynes had clearly suffered a crisis of faith in the potency of monetary stimulus.[67] Fisher listened in bemused silence. "His paper was interesting but to me—and I think to everyone else—rather obscure and unconvincing," he wrote to Maggie afterward. "He was very skillful in answering questions and objections but seemed to get nowhere." [68]

As the Great Depression dragged on, Keynes's faith in the effectiveness of monetary policy ebbed further. By the time A Treatise on Money appeared, he was beginning to pose a theory of the causes of unemployment. Cambridge undergraduates were his first audience. The nub of the new theory was that, as he put it in an article published in the American Economic Review in December 1933, "circumstances can arise, and have recently arisen, when neither control of the short-rate of interest nor control of the long-rate will be effective, with the result that direct stimulation of investment by government is a necessary means." [69]

In a severe depression, prices fell even faster than interest rates. So reductions in nominal rates did not prevent real rates from climbing. Once nominal rates fell to zero, there was nothing further that the central bank could do to make borrowing cheaper or to ease debt burdens and thus to end the depression—with incalculable political consequences, what

Keynes called The Liquidity Trap. As he had once observed, "The inability of the interest rate to fall has brought down empires."[70] Once monetary policy was rendered ineffectual, the only option for shoring up demand was getting money into the hands of those who could spend it.

> All past teaching has . . . been either irrelevant, or else positively injurious. We have not only failed to understand the economic order under which we live, but we have misunderstood it to the extent of adopting practices which operate most harshly to our detriment, so that we are tempted to cure ills arising out of our misunderstanding by resort to further destruction in the form of revolution.[71]

Keynes finished the first draft of *A General Theory of Employment, Interest and Money* in 1934 after returning from the United States. He began circulating the manuscript in early 1935. To George Bernard Shaw, he wrote that he believed he was "writing a book on economic theory which will largely revolutionize—not I suppose at once but in the course of the next ten years—the way the world thinks about economic problems."[72]

The prime innovation in the *General Theory* was to show that in severe depressions, monetary policy would not work. Economists grounded in classical models were like

> Euclidean geometers in a non-Euclidean world who, discovering that in experience straight lines apparently parallel often meet, rebuke the lines for not keeping straight as the only remedy for the unfortunate collisions that are occurring. Yet, in truth, there is no remedy except to throw over the axiom of parallels and to work out a non-Euclidean geometry. Something similar is required today in economics.

His innovation has sometimes been misunderstood. It was not that governments should spend more in bad times or run deficits in a slack economy. Beatrice Webb, Winston Churchill, and Herbert Hoover had all embraced deficit spending before Keynes. It was also not that wise behavior on the part of an individual can be self-defeating if everyone behaves similarly. Nor that the classical proposition that excess supply or insufficient demand for labor could always be cured by a fall in wages or interest rates:

> As many of us were forced by the logic of events to realize, the economics of the system as a whole differs profoundly from the economics of the individual; that what is economically wise behavior on the part of a single individual may on occasion be suicidal if engaged in by all individuals collectively; that the income of the nation is but the counterpart of the expenditures of the nation. If we all restrict our expenditures, this means restricting our incomes, which in turn is followed by a further restriction in expenditures.[73]

As Herbert Stein, the economist, pointed out, Keynes asked a very different question from the one posed by Hayek and Schumpeter. In explaining depressions in terms of the preceding booms, the Austrians were trying to figure out how the economy had gotten there. Keynes was less interested in the genesis of slumps than in the more basic puzzle of how high unemployment and slack capacity could persist for long in a free market economy with unrestricted competition.

Not only should unemployment be temporary under standard economic assumptions, but, by and large, it had been. In Fisher's hydraulic machine—as well as in economic models in the heads of Marx, Marshall, and Schumpeter—a bad harvest, a war, a strike, an innovation, or some other "shock" could produce a temporary imbalance between supply and demand that, if large enough relative to the size of the economy, could result in unemployment. But, in that event, competition among workers and among lenders should drive down pay and interest rates until it was once again profitable to hire and invest.

Say's law, which stated that supply creates its own demand, was already considered out of date by the mid-nineteenth century. Based on the truism that every purchase creates an equivalent income, the law presumed that income was earned solely so that it could be spent. But saving was, of course, also an important motive, and even in the Victorian era the saving of working-class households was significant. As soon as the possibility of spending less than one earned was acknowledged, Say's law became obsolete.

What Keynes did, writes Skidelsky, was essentially to avert his eyes from market-clearing equilibrium. Instead he let money flows (such as income) functionally determine other money flows (such as consumption). The denial of supply-demand equilibrium is what Schumpeter simply could not stomach. Thus what made the *General Theory* so radical was Keynes's proof that it was *possible* for a free market economy to settle into states in which workers and machines remained idle for prolonged periods of time—that there were depressions that, unlike the garden-variety ones, were not brief and didn't end of their own accord as a result of falling prices and interest rates, or, at an extreme, that free market economies tended naturally to stagnate even when there were idle workers and machines available. In such depressions, unfreezing credit flows through monetary policy didn't provide a sufficient stimulus, because even zero-percent interest rates could not tempt businesses to borrow while prices were falling and there was reason to think that demand would recover. The only way to revive business confidence and get the private sector spending again was by cutting taxes and letting businesses and individuals keep more of their income so that they could spend it. Or, better yet, having the government spend more money directly, since that would guarantee that 100 percent of it would be spent rather than saved. If the private sector couldn't or wouldn't spend, then the government had to do it. For Keynes, the government had to be prepared to act as the spender of last resort, just as the central bank acted as the lender of last resort.

James Tobin has pointed out that Fisher came close to producing the elements of a general theory in his 1930 book *The Theory of Interest*. He had a theory of investment and savings, as well as how production and prices are determined in the short run. In *Booms and Depressions*, in 1932, he introduced the role of debt in self-reinforcing slumps. But, unlike Keynes, Fisher never combined these separate components into a single unified model that showed how interest rates, the price level, output, and, therefore, employment were determined.

As often happens with novel doctrines, most of the measures urged by Fisher and Keynes, except for the abandonment of gold, were not adopted in either the UK or the United States. Still, in England, the worst was over by August 1932, when the economy began slowly expanding. By 1937, Japan's economy had been growing for a half dozen years. In Germany, where the economic collapse was as bad as in the United States, unemployment had virtually disappeared by 1936. Keynes noted the bitter irony of Nazi Germany and Fascist Italy achieving full employment by engaging in massive deficit spending, repudiating their foreign debts, and letting their currencies depreciate. The same was true of Imperial Japan. Of course, the goal of these governments was to wage war and to pay off their debts by exploiting their victims.

In the United States, however, the depression had come roaring back with a vengeance in 1937—largely, it seems, because of blunders by the administration and especially by the Federal Reserve. In 1936, after three years of recovery, FDR raised taxes and scaled back spending on New Deal programs such as the WPA. A onetime bonus payment for World War I veterans in June 1936 briefly pumped up the federal deficit, but federal spending fell sharply thereafter. Meanwhile, the Social Security Act of 1935 created a payroll tax that began in 1937. Together these two ill-timed actions brought the federal budget into virtual balance by late 1937.

Early in the Depression the Federal Reserve had remained passive in the face of a traumatized banking system and credit markets. The Banking Act of 1935 gave the Fed authority to change reserve requirements. Between August 1936 and May 1937, the Federal Reserve, worried about growing excess reserves and inflationary pressures, abruptly doubled reserve requirements. As excess reserves fell, so did the stock of money. From May 1937 to June 1938, the US economy contracted by one-fifth, industrial output plummeted by one-third, and unemployment, which had fallen to 10 percent, jumped back to 13 percent. The official rate, which excluded temporary government jobs, rose from 15 percent to nearly 20 percent. The stock market plunged too, completing Irving Fisher's financial ruin.

Keynes, who invested heavily in depressed American stock in 1936 and hung on after the 1937 crash, recouped his losses and more. But his heart failed him. Keynes collapsed at his office in London and was diagnosed with a potentially fatal heart condition. He dropped out of public life, seemingly for good. Irving Fisher continued to speak and write but never established the rapport with the Roosevelt administration that he had enjoyed with the Hoover administration. His public reputation was as battered as his stock portfolio.

Hayek's and Schumpeter's predictions that doing nothing would lead to a recovery did not pan out either, and both wound up intellectually isolated and increasingly disheartened by the economic decline and the growing political extremism in Germany and Austria.

But no economist there or anywhere else had a satisfactory theory in the early 1930s to explain the cascading global crisis. In the absence of such a theory, English economists quickly divided into two rival camps: an interventionist group led by Keynes and the "Cambridge Circus," which included Keynes's Communist disciples Piero Sraffa, Joan Robinson, and Richard Kahn, and, on the other side of the divide, a group of young "liberals" at the London School of Economics led by the thirty-year-old Lionel Robbins. One of the few prominent British economists who was the son of a miner or had strong intellectual ties to Continental economics, Robbins had spent considerable time in Vienna with Ludwig von Mises and his circle. Not only did Robbins find Mises's arguments in the debate over Socialism's viability compelling, but he also shared Mises's dismay over the seemingly inexorable trend toward government intervention in the economies of England and America.

Robbins resented the dominance of Cambridge and Keynes in English economics and regarded Keynes, with whom he clashed bitterly on protectionism while serving on Ramsey MacDonald's Economic Advisory Board, as a political opportunist and intellectual bully. Ironically, Robbins's ambition was to turn the London School of Economics, founded and patronized by Fabians, into the liberal counterweight to Cambridge collectivism. In search of potential political allies, Robbins had spotted Hayek, the thirty-one-year-old Austrian protégé of von Mises, and invited him to come to LSE to give a series of lectures in January 1931. Hayek, who was running his business cycle research institute in Vienna and working on a massive history of monetary policy, had impressed Robbins by correctly predicting the collapse of the American boom back in the spring of 1929, when other pundits were issuing sunny forecasts: "The boom will collapse within the next few months."[74] Hayek later recalled that he had said that there was "no hope of a recovery in Europe until interest rates fell, and interest rates would not fall until the American boom collapses, which I said was likely to happen within the next few months."[75]

Mises and Hayek had developed a theory blaming depressions on excessive money creation and overly low interest rates in the preceding boom that led to a massive misallocation of capital—or, as Robbins put it, "inappropriate investments fostered by wrong expectations."[76] Hayek thought the theory explained the Great Depression, which he argued was "due to monetary mismanagement and State intervention operating in a milieu in which the essential strength of capitalism had already been sapped by war and by policy."[77]

If it was true that overinvestment during the boom—not underinvestment in the recession, as Keynes contended—was to blame for the slump, then what was needed was simply "time to effect a permanent cure by the slow process of adapting the structure of production"—in other words, waiting until excess capacity was absorbed or written down and new investment was once again called for. "The creation of artificial demand," Hayek argued, would do nothing to undo the misallocation of capital and therefore would only lead to another burst of inflation and another downturn, as it had in 1921, when Austria suffered a hyperinflation.

Hayek's LSE lectures were "a sensation," according to Robbins. "At once difficult and exciting . . . they conveyed such an impression of learning and analytical invention." William Beveridge, the director of the LSE and the acknowledged father of the English welfare state, was so impressed by the "tall, powerful, reserved" Austrian that he promptly offered him a vacant professorial chair. Hayek had written a stinging review of Keynes's *Treatise on Money* and had engaged in a high-profile debate with Keynes and his disciples. Hayek's grave expression, courtly manners, and reserve that hinted at some private sorrow appealed to his English audience. His enigmatic expression, fearlessness, and ascetic refusal to prescribe easy cures reminded them of his cousin Ludwig Wittgenstein. Hayek had found credible new arguments for the traditional liberal policies of sound money, free trade, and respect for property rights and the view that recessions heal themselves.

Lionel Robbins's 1934 book *The Great Depression* was a skillful application of Hayekian theory to the boom and bust of the interwar period. (Decades later, in his 1971 *Autobiography of an Economist,* Robbins recanted, confessing that he would "willingly see it forgotten."[78]) Hayek supported Robbins's public campaign to counter Keynes's proposals. He was one of the cosigners, with Robbins and other LSE professors, supporting a balanced budget policy in 1932.[79]

Hayek's star did not glitter for long. By 1935, Beatrice Webb said of "Robbins and Co"—the "Co." being Hayek—that "they and their credo are side-tracked, without influence or even relevance to the present state of the world."[80] She was right. By the time Keynes's *General Theory* appeared the following year, the debate was over, and the economics profession had swung solidly to the Keynesian view, which, according to one of Hayek's friends, "fitted the times of deflation and mass unemployment better than Hayek's monetary temperance."[81]

At the time, Hayek was left less embattled than entirely eclipsed. Speculating about Hayek's failure to attack the *General Theory* in print, Bruce Caldwell, editor of Hayek's collected works, hazards a guess that Hayek was simply not invited to review it. Harsh criticisms of the early Hayek— from his adversaries, his erstwhile defenders, and his political allies--are prevalent in the literature. Keynes referred to his 1931 work *Prices and Production* as a "frightful muddle,"[82] and Milton Friedman described himself as "an enormous admirer of Hayek, but *not for his economics.*"[83] Before long, Hayek's exchanges with Keynes were confined to their common passion for antiquarian books.

After three stints as a visiting professor, Schumpeter moved to Harvard for good in 1932. His reasons for leaving Germany had less to do with the rise of left- and right-wing political extremism (the Nazis fared poorly in the 1932 election) than with his failure to obtain a chair in Berlin and his desire to avoid marrying his longtime mistress, Mia Stöckel. Germany had been for him a place of exile, irrevocably associated with the greatest disappointments and tragedies of his life, including the deaths of his beloved second wife, Annie, and his mother.

A severe blow was the publication of Keynes's *Treatise on Money*, which convinced Schumpeter, who had been working on his own book on monetary origins of the business cycle, that his project was "useless." He told one of his students, "The only thing left for me to do now is to throw the money manuscript away."[84] His reaction suggests that his own ideas coincided with those of Keynes and Fisher and that he realized he had little to add. Otherwise, Schumpeter surely would have welcomed a chance to criticize Keynes's theory and contrast his own.

Schumpeter's depression was deepened by the stunning collapse of the German economy after Black Thursday. As American investors rushed to liquidate their foreign holdings and American merchants slashed their imports of German grain, German industrial production fell by 40 percent and unemployment shot to more than 30 percent.[85] The depression in Germany was even deeper than in the United States—deeper, in fact, than in any other major economy.

Twenty years before in the midst of another global economic crisis, Schumpeter and Keynes had advocated similar responses. Now Schumpeter defined his position in opposition to that of Keynes. At the annual meeting of the American Economic Association in December 1930, Schumpeter had attracted a spurt of media attention when he suggested that no politically palatable cure for the depression existed.[86] Joseph Dorfman, the historian of economics, attributed that response to Schumpeter's "somber outlook," which struck many in the United States as "a useful counterbalance to the characteristic optimism of the Anglo-American tradition."[87]

Schumpeter's insistence that monetary expansion was bound to fail intensified over time. It is a bit of a puzzle, especially in light of his praise of Japan's decision to abandon the gold standard in 1931. To be sure,

Schumpeter's theory of the business cycle emphasized causes other than monetary ones far more than Keynes's or Fisher's, particularly the consequences of new technologies, chemical and mechanical, that were revolutionizing farming. Schumpeter also believed that "creative destruction" of obsolete firms or industries was a precondition for long-term growth of productivity and living standards. But had he believed these things any less in 1919? His extreme fatalism struck at least some of his students and colleagues as new.

Schumpeter took part in efforts to find jobs for Jewish economists who were being persecuted by the new Hitler administration. He formed "a Committee [with the American economist Wesley Clair Mitchell] to take care of some of those German scientists who are now being removed from their chairs by the present government on account of their Hebrew race or faith." In a letter written shortly after Hitler became chancellor in Germany's coalition government in March 1933—but before the creation of the Nazi dictatorship—Schumpeter expressed his growing sense of isolation and unhappiness:

> In order to avoid what would be a very natural misunderstanding allow me to state that I am a German citizen but not a Jew or of Jewish descent. Nor am I a thorough exponent of the present German government, the actions of which look somewhat differently to one who has had the experience of the regime which preceded it. My conservative convictions make it impossible for me to share the well-nigh unanimous condemnation the Hitler Ministry meets with in the world at large. It is merely from a sense of duty towards men who have been my colleagues that I am trying to organize some help for them which would enable them to carry on quiet scientific work in this country should the necessity arise.[88]

Schumpeter must have imbibed some of the new attitudes that Hayek brought to the LSE when he gave a series of lectures there on the depression. By the time he arrived at Harvard for good a year later, he was asserting that economists had no business giving advice, although, as his student Paul Samuelson remarked sardonically, "He was always giving advice." He organized an informal seminar with like-minded colleagues, the "Seven Wise Men," who met once a week. The group, which included Wassily Leontief, the Russian-born mathematical economist, eventually published a laissez-faire manifesto attacking the New Deal.

> Recovery is sound only if it does come of itself. For any revival which is merely due to artificial stimulus leaves part of the work of depressions undone and adds, to an undigested element of maladjustment, new maladjustment of its own which has to be liquidated in turn, thus threatening business with another crisis ahead. Particularly, our story provides a presumption against remedial measures which work through money and credit. For the trouble is fundamentally not with money and credit, and policies of this class are particularly apt to keep up, and add to, maladjustment, and to produce additional trouble in the future.[89]

When Keynes's *General Theory* appeared, Schumpeter, who had earlier been on the most cordial terms with Keynes and sympathetic to his views, wrote a singularly splenetic review: "The advice (everybody knows what it is Mr. Keynes advises) may be good. For the England of today it possibly is. That vision may be entitled to the compliment that it expresses forcefully the attitude of a decaying civilization."[90]

Chapter XI

Experiments: Webb and Robinson in the 1930s

The Soviet Union presents a blazing contrast to the rest of Europe.

—*Walter Duranty,* New York Times, *July 20, 1931*[1]

Two experiments on a large scale are actually going on in the world of today—American Capitalism and Russian Communism.

—*Beatrice Webb, April 1932*[2]

The apparent helplessness of Western governments in the face of a global economic calamity seemed to confirm the thesis of the Webbs' 1923 book *The Decay of Capitalist Civilization.* Interpreting Labour's stunning electoral defeat as more of "a victory for the American and British financiers" than a repudiation of the government's shaky response to the slump, Beatrice Webb lost what little remained of her faith in the Fabians' "inevitability of gradualism."[3] Initially hostile to the Bolshevik regime, she now saw the Soviet Union as the only nation that was "increasing the material resources and improving the health and education of its people." Somewhat impulsively, she decided to make this "new social order" the subject of her and Sidney's next magnum opus.[4]

One week after the general election that evicted Sidney from his cabinet post on October 27, 1931, the seventy-eight-year-old Beatrice was asking herself, "How shall we spend our old age?"[5] She wondered if she was strong enough to travel to Russia to collect material, even though her reason for wanting to go was merely to lend "vividness" to her account.[6] She had already made up her mind that the Soviet experiment was working just as surely as the Western one was not, declaring that "without doubt we are on the side of Russia."[7] Before their departure aboard the Russian steamer *Smolny,* she had "summarized the immense book that she and Sidney were to write on their return."[8]

Stalin had not foreseen the worldwide depression any more than Keynes or Fisher had, but he seized the opportunity to recruit Western sympathizers and allies. Prominent fellow travelers were even more prized than more ordinary party members, and extraordinary efforts were expended to cultivate them. A phalanx of official guides, interpreters, and drivers met the Webbs in Leningrad and whisked them off on a strenuous two-month tour of factories, farms, schools, and clinics to inspect what Webb now referred to as a "new civilization."[9]

In London, the dinner invitations, political consultations, and newspaper interviews had dried up after Labour was ousted. In Russia, "We seem to be a new type of royalty," Beatrice observed with pleasure.[10] We now know that while the Webbs were being ferried about in limousines and special trains, Stalin was transforming the Ukraine into a giant concentration camp. Moscow had been selling grain to the West in return for machinery, but the collapse of world grain prices meant having to double the tonnage for export. The Soviet dictator, who was so economically illiterate that he once, after a shortage of small coins developed, had several dozen bank cashiers shot, demanded one-half of the harvest for export. The inevitable famine ultimately claimed at least six million lives, one-quarter of a rural population that was already decimated by forced collectivization.

Once back in England, Webb added her voice to the denials issuing forth from Moscow. She was relying on the testimony of Western correspondents in Moscow like the *New York Times's* Walter Duranty, who insisted, "There is no famine or starvation, nor is there likely to be."[11] But Duranty had not strayed from the capital and was merely echoing the government's disavowals. After Malcolm Muggeridge, a *Manchester Guardian* correspondent who was married to her niece, went to the Ukraine to see for himself, Webb refused to believe his shattering description of starving peasants and official abuse. She dismissed her nephew's reports as "hysterical" and suggested that Soviet Communism had become the innocent target of "poor Malcolm's complexes" and "a well of hatred in [his] nature." Beatrice invited Ivan Maisky, the new Soviet ambassador, and his wife over for the weekend and was "comforted" by their assurances that there was no famine.[12] In *Soviet Communism: A New Civilization,* which was published in 1935, she insisted that "what the Soviet Union was faced with, from 1929 onward, was not a famine but a widespread general strike of the peasantry, in resistance to the policy of collectivization."[13]

Bertrand Russell, who was critical of the Webbs for their "worship of the state" and "undue tolerance of Mussolini and Hitler," was even more appalled by their "rather absurd adulation" of the Soviet government.[14] The historian Robert Conquest faults their naïve faith in official statistics, inclination to depreciate anecdote, and ignorance of history: "They had no background of knowledge, let alone 'feel' for the great slave empires of antiquity, the millenarian sects of the 16th century, the conquerors of medieval Asia."[15] But Keynes probably put his finger on the real source of Webb's infatuation with the Soviet Union when he called Communism a religion "with an appeal to the ascetic in us."[16] In her eighth decade, Webb had found a new faith. As Muggeridge complained, "You couldn't change her mind with facts."[17]

Although Keynes had an "unmitigated contempt for the official Labour Party,"[18] he was an old-fashioned liberal like Russell. He bracketed the Soviet Union with Fascist Germany and loathed Stalin, predicting in 1937 that "an eventual agreement between him and Germany [is] by no means out of the question, if it should happen to suit him."[19] On being asked to contribute to a Festschrift for Webb's eightieth birthday, he replied that "the only sentence which came to my mind spontaneously was that 'Mrs. Webb, not being a Soviet politician, has managed to survive to the age of eighty.'"[20]

Keynes was inclined to see young Communists and fellow travelers in his circle at Cambridge as amateurs whose fanaticism was a harmless eccentricity or a passing phase. He didn't see why ideology should get in the way of friendship or research and, if anything, he admired their idealism and courage. In 1939, he ventured that "there is no one in politics today worth six pence outside the ranks of Liberals except the post war generation of intellectual communists under thirty five." Though deluded, they were "magnificent material," too good to waste.[21]

Joan Robinson, who would become the most famous of Keynes's Cambridge disciples, was almost certainly one of the "intellectual communists" that Keynes had in mind when he wrote that these members of the younger generation were "the nearest thing we now have to the typical nervous non-conformist English gentleman who went to the Crusades, made the Reformation, fought the Great Rebellion, won us our civil and religious liberties and humanized the working classes last century."[22] Robinson's commanding manner, zeal, and combative instincts were bred in the bone. Born Joan Violet Maurice, she came from a long line of military officers, university dons, civil servants, and dissenters. Her mother, the indomitable and perpetually youthful Lady Helen Marsh, was the beneficiary of a trust created by Parliament in 1812 after the assassination of her ancestor the British prime minister Spencer Perceval. Her great-grandfather F. D. Maurice, a famous university radical whom Alfred Marshall had known in the Grote Club, gave up his Cambridge chair rather than agreeing "to believe in eternal damnation."[23] Her father, Major General Frederick Maurice, sacrificed his military career when he publicly accused Prime Minister Lloyd George of lying in World War I, then went on to become a war correspondent, a military historian, the head of two London colleges, and the author of nineteen books. Robinson's maternal uncle, Eddie Marsh, was Winston Churchill's longtime private secretary. He devoted his free time to writing bad poetry and promoting the work of comely young writers and artists, among them Rupert Brooke, Siegfried Sassoon, and Duncan Grant. Robinson's family, her husband, Austin, said, was "a trifle frightening."[24]

Like Webb, Robinson had to reinvent herself. Despite her impressive pedigree, cavernous family mansion, and posh private schooling, she was being groomed to support a husband's career rather than to pursue one of her own. But at fourteen, she was already dreamy, bookish, and introverted. The world of her imagination seemed more vivid than the world around her. She wrote constantly: essays, stories, poetry. She wanted an audience badly enough to declaim her poems at Poet's Corner in Hyde Park.

The Maurice affair, which occupied Parliament in 1918, was a source of pride as well as pain. Even by Edwardian standards, Major General Maurice was an aloof and distant father. All emotion, he believed, was selfish. When he was forced out of the army, he wrote to his children that he was "persuaded that I am doing what is right, and once that is so, nothing else matters to a man," adding that this was what Christ meant when he directed his followers to forsake their parents and *children* for his sake. His son-in-law Austin Robinson observed, "He no more noticed anything irrelevant to his immediate preoccupation than shadows reflected on a wall."[25] On one occasion, Joan's sister Nancy was behind their father on a ski trail when she slipped on a bridge and wound up hanging upside down over the gorge. A passing ski instructor had to rescue her.

Despite her family's numerous connections to Cambridge, Robinson was the only one of the four Maurice sisters to go to university. Higher education was still considered superfluous for an upper-class English girl. And her father's forced retirement may have made it unaffordable had Robinson, as single-minded as her father when she wanted something, not won a teacher's scholarship. She enrolled at Girton College, the oldest women's college at Cambridge, whose mock-medieval architecture and remoteness from the men's colleges prompted the philosopher C. S. Lewis to compare it to the Castle of Otranto in Horace Walpole's Gothic novel.[26]

As a student at St. Paul's School for Girls during the painful and prolonged recession of 1920–21, Robinson had done volunteer work at a London settlement house. When she went up to Cambridge in the late summer of 1922, the downturn was entering its third year. With unemployment in the double digits and the subject of heated political debate, Robinson decided that she would give up history, her favorite subject at St. Paul's, and take up economics instead. As one of her biographers, Marjorie Turner, observed, poverty and unemployment were blemishes of the society in which she and her family occupied a privileged position, and she felt compelled to understand them.

Cambridge in the 1920s may have seemed like a lush suburb of Bloomsbury, where T. S. Eliot, Roger Fry, G. E. Moore, and John Maynard Keynes wandered about, but female undergraduates were forbidden many of its fruits. Countless rules limited intellectual intercourse with resident geniuses, whether dons or students. The one that forbade them to wear gowns to lectures like the men and required them to wear dresses and hats instead was only one of many daily reminders of their inferior status. When Bertrand Russell was scheduled to lecture at Newnham College, the second-oldest women's college, the panicked authorities first threatened to rescind the invitation, then issued an injunction forbidding any young lady "to accompany him from lecture room to door."[27] Robinson and other female students of Arthur Pigou, an eminent economist who held Alfred Marshall's former chair, could only deliver their essays to the porter's lodge, whereas his male students could bring them directly to his rooms, where they might easily be invited to stay and chat The Union, where the undergraduate Keynes had sharpened his debating skills against those of future prime ministers, was off-limits to women, except for the upstairs gallery. So was the Cambridge Conversazione Society, aka the Apostles, where the philosopher Frank Ramsey, who was exactly Robinson's age, came to the attention of his future mentors Keynes and Russell. Keynes's own nursery for future stars, the Monday Political Economy Club, was open—by invitation only—to male but not female undergraduates.

Instead of having one of Cambridge's Olympians as a tutor, Robinson was assigned a smartly dressed daughter of a New York perfume manufacturer. Still in her twenties, Marjorie Tappan had studied economics at Columbia University—although there is no record there of her having received a doctorate, as she claimed—before working for the American economics team at the Paris peace talks for two years. Robinson detested her. Whether her resentment was due to the fact that Tappan was a rich American whose family was in "trade" or simply the fact that Tappan was not one of the luminaries is hard to know. The only thing that seems to have rubbed off on Robinson was Tappan's habit of using a long cigarette holder when she smoked, and gesturing with it while talking with her students.

Robinson attended the lectures of Pigou on economic theory and the less frequent ones of Keynes on current economic issues, but her undergraduate papers gave little hint of her future. "Beauty and the Beast," delivered at the Marshall Society in her third year at Cambridge, was a charming pastiche that proved that she could write and had a firm grasp of Alfred Marshall's *Principles of Economics*. But compared with the problems some of her male peers were solving, it was sophomoric. At twenty-one, Keynes's protégé Frank Ramsey had published a devastating paper on Keynes's probability theory, a forceful critique of Wittgenstein's *Tractatus*, and an article for Keynes's *Economic Journal* showing that a wildly popular economic panacea, the Douglas social credit scheme, was based on a faulty premise.

Despite some early successes, Robinson's undergraduate career ended in tears. She took part one of the economic Tripos in 1924, and part two the following year. Her second-class results on both, which dashed any hope of a college fellowship, were "a great disappointment" to her.[28] Years later she was still fretting over "being so badly educated."[29] Mortified, she moved back home to London, where she spent the fall and winter in a "wretched state" living in a "grubby room" in London's East End and working in a government housing office.[30] She was so miserable that she asked her father to investigate various possibilities in America, among them a scholarship to Harvard's sister college, Radcliffe. But in the spring, she decided to opt for the traditional solution to a female career quandary. On the eve of the General Strike of May 1926, Robinson was in Paris with her sister Nancy shopping for wedding clothes.

Her fiancé was a clean-cut thirty-two-year-old Cambridge don. The son of an impecunious parson, Austin Robinson was a decorated World War I seaplane pilot who was so electrified by Keynes's 1919 lectures on the Versailles peace treaty that he switched from classics to economics. Bright, efficient, and incredibly hardworking, he was invited by Keynes to join the Monday-night Political Economy Club, got a first-class degree in economics, and was elected fellow of Corpus Christi College. By Joan's second year, he was giving lectures on monetary economics. They did not become a couple until Joan left Cambridge for London.

While Austin was besotted, Joan was cooler, refusing him the first time he proposed. He was handsome, intelligent, upright, respected, kind—and seemingly unthreatened by her expressed desire for some money-making occupation. Yet, against the bold canvas of her imagined future life, he lacked color. A dozen years later, when Stevie Smith, one of her many literary acquaintances, invited her to suggest a plot for a novel, Robinson proposed one about a girl who was torn between two lovers, one of whom was a conventional young man with a good job who promised to provide her with an "orthodox life" that she "tries to force herself to want."[31] It was an unpromising start for a marriage.

"I want desperately to stay in Cambridge," Austin confessed to her after they became engaged.[32] But despite Keynes's patronage, his prospects of a salaried university position there or anywhere else in England were far from good. There were simply no academic openings. When Joan learned, from a friend's father, that the old maharajah of Gwalior, India—an Anglophile who insisted on naming his children George and May and importing tutors from Cambridge—had died, leaving behind a ten-year-old heir in urgent need of instruction, she pressed Austin to apply for the post. While they waited for job opportunities to open up at home, she pointed out to Austin he would be earning several times as much as any lecturer in England.

The newlyweds wound up spending the first two years of their married life in an ancient Indian city with "broad streets, beautifully carved balconies, doors and latticed windows, mosques and temples, old and new Palaces,"[33] on the main line between Delhi and Bombay. Although Joan was close to her family, it was delightful for the couple to be on their own. Life in Gwalior involved riding at dawn with the lancers and the boy maharajah, lessons in Hindi at lunchtime, tennis, newspapers, and cocktails at the club before dinner. With a personal staff of a dozen servants, including five gardeners, Joan felt free to teach an economics course at a local secondary school. She worked on a paper that Austin was asked to write on

India's likely future contribution to British tax revenues. Meanwhile, she thought about how she might best help her husband secure a permanent lectureship at Cambridge University, and also about what work she might do. Dorothy Garratt had teased her that if she had not married a minister's son she would "probably be scrubbing lavatory seats in a leper colony or embroidering chasubles for curates."[34] At one point, she thought about opening an import business in Indian handicrafts.

With her husband's three-year tutoring contract due to expire at the end of 1928, Robinson went back to Cambridge on her own that July. Her idea was to personally deliver the report they had written together and to use her connections to pave the way for Austin's return. She was, and would always be, an enterprising and persistent networker. Less than two years later, by May 1930, Austin had his appointment as a permanent, full-time university lecturer. Until then, while Austin wrote his first book, they lived on their considerable savings. Only after Austin's future was assured, say her biographers, did she begin to focus seriously on her own career.

India and marriage had restored her intellectual self-confidence, and Austin gave her access to the university community. Her husband's success and his friendship with luminaries such as Keynes were gratifying. Lacking a college fellowship and a first-class degree, she paid a £5 fee to get a master's diploma and let it be known that she was available to coach undergraduates for a modest wage. She could not help being aware that she was still on the outside, an onlooker instead of a participant in the intellectual feast. High table, fellow's rooms, and clubs were all off-limits to her because of her sex.

Everything changed in the months after the American stock market crash. Two developments were crucial.

While she was waiting for Austin to get his appointment in the 1929–30 academic year, Robinson attended a seminar where she learned about a theoretical challenge that had preoccupied some of Keynes's Cambridge disciples. The seminar had been organized by Piero Sraffa, a brilliant but neurotic autodidact, economist, and Communist who fled Mussolini's Italy in 1927. He had gotten Keynes's attention with an article calling for a revamping of economic theory to reflect the monopoly elements of modern business: the rise of giant corporations, branding, and advertising. Economists assumed competitive markets with large numbers of buyers and sellers selling identical products. Under such circumstances, no single firm could influence the price at which it sold its output, any more than a farmer could influence the price of wheat or a miner the price of silver. But modern businesses mimicked monopolies and spent large sums to influence prices. That invalidated, Sraffa argued, the principle rationale for competition, namely that a free market economy produced maximum output at minimum cost and opened the door to government intervention. What was needed was a theory. He and several others were already working on various approaches.

Robinson also befriended Keynes's "favorite pupil" Richard Kahn, a beautiful, dark-eyed Orthodox Jew who became her ally and helpmeet. Kahn was so gifted that Keynes enlisted him to help him revise A *Treatise on Money* even though he had had less than a year's formal training in economics. It was thrilling to interact with men whose intellect she could worship because it was superior to her own.[35] She started telling Austin that he was a mere plow horse while Sraffa was a tiger, and she was willing to overlook Kahn's immaturity, narcissism, and dysfunction. She was becoming aware of a bigger game, and now she wanted to become a player.

Austin suggested a topic for Sraffa's challenge when he, Joan, and Kahn had lunch one day. With the help and support of her lover from mid-1930 to early 1933, she took up the challenge. She and Kahn developed a theory to show how advertising, branding, and product innovation caused firms in seemingly competitive industries—that is, in industries with lots of buyers and sellers and no barriers to entry—to behave like monopolies. Instead of minimizing prices to consumers and maximizing output and employment, they used their market power to gouge consumers and earn extraordinary profits, depressing employment and lowering wages. In the context of the Great Depression, Robinson saw herself working out an explanation of how, even under ideal circumstances, the free market economy tended toward long-run unemployment, excess industrial capacity, and stagnation.

As Robinson's confidence grew, so did her ambition. In March 1931

Robinson informed Kahn, "I am now toying with the idea of producing a complete book with all this stuff . . . It is not I who am bringing out this book. It is a syndicate of you A + me." [36] Like a general commanding her army, she assigned tasks; Austin would write the introduction, Kahn would pose problems and write the mathematical appendix, and she would draft the book. Six months later, Robinson asked Dennis Robertson, a highly regarded collaborator of Keynes and an expert on the theory of the firm, to write a preface. She told him that she had written five chapters and sketched out another ten. As Aslanbeigui and Oakes observe, Robinson was "clearly planning to publish under her name alone." [37] For the next year and a half, Robinson and Kahn worked intensively on the book, which Robinson soon renamed her "nightmare."

Meanwhile, her collaboration with Kahn let her join Keynes's inner circle. In the first half of 1931, Keynes was grappling with criticisms of *A Treatise on Money*—especially those of Hayek—and working out some of the ideas that would mature into *The General Theory*. Between January and May a group of young Cambridge economists, including Sraffa, Kahn, and Austin, that called itself "the Circus" acted as Keynes's sounding board. Joan attended the weekly meetings and started to send notes to Keynes via Kahn. "Keynes seemed to play the role of God in a morality play," another participant recalled. "He dominated the play but rarely appeared himself on the stage. Kahn was the Messenger Angel who brought messages and problems from Keynes to the Circus and who went back to Heaven with the result of our deliberations." [38] For Robinson, it was an extraordinary opportunity to gain access to Keynes's latest thinking as he tried to understand the worst economic crisis in modern history, as well as to hone her own analytic powers.

Whether her new status was helpful in winning her first formal, if temporary, university teaching post is unclear. In any case, she was appointed junior assistant lecturer. One of her students that year remembered Joan as "young, vigorous and beautiful." He described her lectures: "She addressed us in abstruse terms . . . I understood little but sat spellbound." [39]

Despite the new demands on her time, her own manuscript was nearly complete by October 1932. At that point, any hesitation on her part to claim ownership had disappeared, write her biographers.[40] Husband, wife, and lover seemed to communicate by Cambridge's five-times-a-day post the way modern couples exchange e-mails. Robinson dashed off a triumphant note to Austin:

> I have found out what my book is about. It was quite a sudden revelation which I only had yesterday. What I have been and gone and done is what Piero said must be done, in his famous article. I have rewritten the whole theory of value beginning with the firm as a monopolist. I used to think I was providing tools for some genius in the future to use, and all the time I have done the job myself.[41]

Hitherto she had regarded herself strictly as a teacher. "I used to feel 'I must tell these people what economists think'—now I really feel I am an economist and I can tell them what I think myself."[42] She told Kahn that "AR" would find her "a Changed Woman. I have recovered my self-respect." She left no doubt, however, that she now considered herself first among equals, the original thinker, the guiding genius: "You and Kahn and I have been teaching each other economics intensively these two years. But it was I who saw the great light and it is *my* book." It is hard to miss the note of glee at having beaten the boys.

Meanwhile, Kahn was falling in love with Robinson. By 1931 they were having an on-again, off-again affair, greatly alarming Keynes, who feared for his protégé's career, and made Joan nervous lest a scandal spoil her own imminent academic success. Austin had gone to Africa for six months, and Joan insisted that Kahn also leave Cambridge to cure himself of "lovesickness." He decided to visit America for a year. Alone, under great stress, and feeling that she was on the verge of a breakdown, Joan worked feverishly to finish her book. While she was proofreading her manuscript, Kahn was at the University of Chicago promoting the book, convincing a doctoral student and future Soviet spy, Frank Coe, to incorporate her as-yet-unpublished analysis into his thesis. Then Kahn delivered a bombshell. Edward Chamberlin, a young Harvard professor, was about to publish a book, *The Theory of Monopolistic Competition*, that overlapped with hers and would precede hers by at least six months. In February, Kahn visited Harvard, where he arranged to deliver a lecture one day before Chamberlin's book was released. When he claimed that Robinson's theory and analytical techniques were superior, Chamberlin, who was in the audience, failed to deliver an effective rebuttal. "I feel a viscious [*sic*] pleasure at hearing that Chamberlin is no good," Robinson wrote to Kahn on March 2, 1933, in response to his account of the confrontation. She added that she would "just put in a note" in her preface that she had known nothing of his work. She considered asking Keynes to let her review Chamberlin's book for the *Economic Journal* but realized that "on second thought that would be bad" and that she could "deal with him sometime after I am out."[43]

To Joan's disappointment, Keynes "was not much interested in the theory of imperfect competition" and refused to be convinced that monopoly was a major cause of periodic shortfalls in effective demand.[44] After warning his publishers at Macmillan that they probably wouldn't find the book exciting, Keynes nonetheless urged them to publish it. *The Economics of Imperfect Competition* appeared in the fall of 1933. Robinson's book was an instant critical success, garnering numerous respectful, and even some superlative, reviews. Schumpeter, who had already called her "one of our best men,"[45] responded instantly to Kahn's suggestion that he promote her new book. In his review, Schumpeter praised Robinson for "genuine originality" and concluded that the book gave her "a claim, certainly to a leading, perhaps to the first place" among economic theorists in this area, placing her ahead of Kahn and Sraffa as well as Chamberlin.[46]

Robinson had an enormous edge over Sraffa and Kahn. Both suffered from severe writer's block, and Sraffa was so disabled by severe anxiety that he could not deliver lectures. She, on the other hand, was a superb speaker and writer who, once she found that she had something to say, was one of the most prolific in her discipline. As soon as the final correction had been made on her manuscript, she plunged into a series of articles and reviews.

Less than a year after *Imperfect Competition* was published, Joan gave

birth to her first child. "How well you do things," gushed her friend Dorothy Garratt in May 1934. "A discovery in economics and a baby girl."[47]
Robinson was elated by her *succès d'estime*. That September, when Kahn
went to Tilton to work on Keynes's new book, she wrote to him, asking
cheekily, "Would Maynard like me to write him a preface for the new work
showing in what respects his ideas have altered?"[48] Given that most of
her interactions with Keynes had been via Kahn or by letter, her suggestion was nervy, even more so considering that Kahn was the only member
of the Circus who had made an original contribution (the multiplier) to
Keynes's new theory. Nonetheless, there was no doubt that she had clearly
won Keynes's respect as an economist. A few years later, he acknowledged
that Robinson was "without a doubt within the first half dozen" economists at Cambridge, a group that included Pigou, Sraffa, Kahn, and Keynes
himself.[49]

Andrew Boyle, the Scottish journalist who in 1979 exposed Anthony
Blunt as the fourth member of the notorious Cambridge Five Soviet spy
ring, claims that Robinson was a founding member of the first Communist cell at Cambridge. It was supposed to have been organized by
Maurice Dobb, the economics lecturer who would soon recruit his student and later spy Kim Philby in 1931.[50] But Boyle, who corresponded
with Robinson, gives no sources. Geoffrey Harcourt, who knew Robinson
toward the end of her life, dates her infatuation with Stalin—her "radicalization" as he puts it—to 1936.[51]

That year Robinson's views were unquestionably in a violent state of
flux. When she reviewed John Strachey's *The Theory and Practice of Socialism* in mid-1936, she was critical of Strachey's argument that Soviet-style
central planning was the cure for the Great Depression. She did not call
Strachey's logic "an insult to my intelligence," as Keynes had, but she took
him to task for conflating flaws in mainstream economic theory with fatal
defects in the economic system. "We cannot be recommended to overthrow merely because its economists have talked nonsense about it," she
quipped.[52]

Six months later, Robinson seems to have had a conversion. She described capitalism as "a system which allows effective demand to fall off amongst a population which is overcrowded and underfed, which meets unemployment with schemes to restrict output and can offer no help to distressed areas except orders for armaments." Marxist dogma might be "over simple," she admitted, but at least it didn't stifle "simple common sense." Indeed, she regarded Marxism as an effective vaccine "against the sophistications of laissez faire economics." [53]

In May 1936, her friends the Garratts had introduced Joan to a couple who were visiting Cambridge from Aleppo, Syria, the setting for Agatha Christie's best seller *Murder on the Orient Express.* Dora Collingwood was an English landscape painter whose father was a noted archaeologist, artist, and secretary to John Ruskin, the art historian. Her husband, Ernest Altounyan, was an Anglo-Armenian doctor. Dorothy Garratt described him as "a very strange but attractive person, living at an emotional level which made me feel very suburban." He was in his mid-forties, myopic, graying, but with "a good forehead and nose," [54] an insinuating voice, and all sorts of romantic friends, including Arthur Ransome, the children's author, and T. E. Lawrence, aka Lawrence of Arabia. The latter had recently died in a motorcycle crash, and Altounyan told Robinson that he had hoped to find a publisher for his epic poem celebrating their friendship. Robinson offered to read it and send it to her uncle. Altounyan was terribly impressed and grateful. They began exchanging notes. By the end of the month, he was writing confidentially that she was "by far the loveliest thing that has happened to me in England" and that meeting her had been "intoxicating." [55]

Altounyan loved to dance, and one of his daughters said that "he tried to live his whole life as a kind of dance and got depressed and frustrated if he was prevented from doing so." He was also bipolar. From Aleppo, he began writing Robinson long, rambling love letters. Robinson, meanwhile, was proofreading the poem. Eddie Marsh, Keynes, and a dozen other literary friends pronounced it dreadful, but Robinson persisted until she finally badgered the editor of Cambridge University Press into publishing it.

On March 12 of the following year, one month before the publication of Altounyan's poem, Joan boarded the Orient Express at Victoria

Station. Two months pregnant and traveling alone, she resembled Mary Debenham in Christie's novel: "There was a kind of cool efficiency in the way she was eating her breakfast and in the way she called to the attendant to bring her more coffee, which bespoke a knowledge of the world and of traveling . . . She was, he judged, the kind of young woman who could take care of herself with perfect ease wherever she went. She had poise and efficiency."[56] Joan was reunited with Altounyan in Aleppo before proceeding to Jaffa and Tiberius, in Palestine.

She saw him alone a second time on April 14, on her return trip. By then, seeing him surrounded by an untidy, unhappy household, she may have begun to feel that her lover's appeal had been largely of her own imagining. Reviews were very scarce for his poem, *Ornament of Honor*. The *Palestine Post* hailed him a "Tennyson minor."[57] When she returned to Cambridge, the old ménage à trois with Austin and Richard Kahn again became the emotional pivot in her life. "In another age she would have been on a camel, riding through the desert," Frank Hahn, an economist, once observed. "A part of her personality was simply upper-class refusal to go with the herd; a need to distinguish herself from the herd."[58]

One year after her second baby was born and weeks after Hitler seized Czechoslovakia, Robinson suffered a serious attack of mania. She spent many months in a sanitarium. By the time she got out of the hospital, Austin had been assigned to war work in Whitehall, and a physical separation ensued. One by one her colleagues were enlisted. Eventually, Kahn too had to leave Cambridge. He was eventually posted to Cairo and wound up spending most of the war there. Robinson stayed behind in Cambridge.

Chapter XII

The Economists' War:
Keynes and Friedman at the Treasury

In War we move back from the Age of Plenty to the Age of
Scarcity.

—*John Maynard Keynes, 1940*[1]

The outbreak of war gave Hayek and Keynes an opportunity to make
peace. Both had hoped that war could be avoided, but neither had any illusions about accepting Hitler's "peace" offers. Both hoped and believed that
the United States would enter the war. Otherwise, by the time Germany
collapsed, Hayek said, "the civilization of Europe will be destroyed."[2] Both
saw the war as a defense, not only of Britain, but of the eighteenth-century
Enlightenment. At a benefit performance at the Cambridge Arts Theatre
to raise money for refugees in December 1940, Keynes told the audience
that there were a thousand Germans in Cambridge. There were, he said,
now "two Germanys":

> The presence here of Germany in exile is . . . a sign that this is a war not
> between nationalities and imperialism, but between two opposed ways
> of life . . . Our object in this mad, unavoidable struggle is not to conquer
> Germany, but to convert her, to bring her back within the historic fold
> of Western civilization of which the institutional foundations are . . . the
> Christian Ethic, the Scientific Spirit and the Rule of Law. It is only on
> these foundations that the personal life can be lived.[3]

By the time the blitz began in the summer of 1940, Keynes and Hayek had been exchanging notes for months about the evacuation of the London School of Economics to Cambridge, help for Jewish academics fleeing Nazi-controlled Europe, and efforts to win the release of foreign colleagues as "enemy aliens" in the panicky weeks after the fall of France in June 1940. In October Keynes had arranged rooms and high table privileges at King's College for Hayek. On the long weekends that Keynes continued to spend in Cambridge, they frequented G. David, the antiquarian book dealer around the corner from the Cambridge Arts Theatre, and exchanged historical tidbits.

More surprisingly, the war put Hayek and Keynes on the same side of the economic policy debate. For most of the 1930s, Hayek had dismissed Keynes's proposals to fight the Great Depression with easier money and deficit spending as "inflation propaganda" and once referred to his rival privately as a "public enemy."[4] But by 1939, Hayek was praising Keynes in newspaper articles. Much to the chagrin of some of his left-wing friends and disciples, the war had turned Keynes into an inflation hawk.

What happened? Circumstances had changed. Britain had practically dissolved its army and air force after World War I, so playing catch-up with Hitler's Germany required massive increases in government spending starting in 1937. Partly out of fear that raising taxes would aggravate unemployment, which still hovered at around 9 percent, and partly because rearmament was unpopular, the government of Prime Minister Neville Chamberlain opted not to raise taxes, instead issuing IOUs to the public in the form of bonds. Thus, even before war was declared, Britain's national debt had climbed to dizzying heights. The first war budget, published in September 1939, projected a deficit of £1 billion, or a stunning 25 percent of Britain's annual national income.

Massive deficit spending had a dramatic effect. The economy boomed, especially in the south of England, where ports and bases were being expanded and arms factories were being built. This was, belatedly, the cure that Keynes had advocated in 1933, and it seemed to vindicate the *General Theory.*

One might have expected Keynes to be pleased that the Treasury, having stubbornly resisted his advice in the late 1920s and early 1930s, had finally turned "Keynesian." Instead, writes Skidelsky, he was increasingly worried and disapproving. By running up a huge debt and then printing money to hold down interest rates, the government was sowing the seeds of future inflation. Now that war was certain, things could only get worse. Keynes denied that he was having a change of heart. It was circumstances that had changed. In 1933, the unemployment rate was 15 percent; in 1939 it was below 4 percent and falling, and industrialists were complaining of shortages of skilled mechanics and engineers. Keynes invented the economics of plenty to address a massive shortfall of demand in a depression. Now he was applying the same logic to the opposite condition: namely, an excess of demand during a war.

After World War I, the consequence of inflationary war finance and huge debt burdens had been economic and political chaos. He unveiled the "Keynes Plan" in two articles in the *Times* of London in mid-November 1939.[5] To plug the gap of £400 million to £500 million between spending and tax receipts, he proposed a wartime levy on income. The twist was that the money was to be refunded after the war, enabling Keynes, like Schumpeter in 1919, to call his tax "forced savings." Skidelsky points out that the articles, published a few months later as *How to Pay for the War*, illustrated "Keynes's conception of the budget as instrument of economic policy."[6] One of the warmest endorsements came from Hayek, who seconded Keynes's proposals in a column in the *Spectator* and followed up with a note: "It is reassuring to know that we agree so completely on the economics of scarcity, even if we differ on when it applies."[7]

As Keynes well knew, he was living on borrowed time. A massive heart attack in 1937 had forced him into premature retirement at Tilton. Two years of being cared for by Lydia, a German miracle drug, and Germany's mad dreams of world conquest gave him the opportunity for a third and final act.

On the eve of the Battle of Britain, Hitler's attempt to destroy the RAF on the ground, Keynes was back at the Treasury with "no routine duties and no office hours" but with "a sort of roving commission plus membership of various high up committees."[8] The prime minister, Winston

Churchill, Britain's last lion, paid scant attention to how the war against Hitler would be financed, and even less to postwar economic arrangements. These became the bailiwick of Keynes, who took on the role of Churchill's de facto Chancellor of the Exchequer during World War II. When Keynes wrote his impassioned outburst against the Versailles Treaty in 1919, he had warned that "vengeance, I dare predict, will not limp" if the victors insisted on impoverishing the vanquished. After he was proved tragically right, Skidelsky writes, Keynes's "one overriding aim" was for the Allies "to do better than last time."[9]

After the stunning collapse of France left Britain to face the German juggernaut alone, the Treasury's, and therefore Keynes's, obsession became to raise money to keep fighting. While Hitler's tactic of serial conquest did not require Germany to place her economy on a total war footing, Britain did not have the luxury of waging a limited war. As the aggressor, Hitler could decide when to attack, and his strategy of Blitzkrieg was self-financing insofar as despoiling its victims paid the military bill. Britain's choices boiled down to two: One was accepting Hitler's offer of "peace," which meant sharing France's ignoble fate. While Keynes's old political mentor, Lloyd George, was prepared to become King Edward's Marshal Pétain and the Left was holding peace vigils, that option was a nonstarter with the British electorate. The other choice was to throw fiscal prudence to the wind and wage total war regardless of the postwar consequences. Although Keynes had no doubt that the latter was the correct choice, he never stopped racking his brains for clever ways to soften any negative consequences. Once again he was "interested, geared up, and happy."[10] As he wrote to a friend, "Well here am I, like a recurring decimal, doing very similar work in the same place for a similar emergency."[11]

From August 1940, Keynes spent as many as eighteen hours a day at his desk and, quite often, in the Treasury's deep cellar. Like Hayek, who had insisted on staying in London and commuting to Cambridge during the first phase of the bombing, he ignored the danger, dismissed the possibility of a German invasion, and hoped that his books and pictures would survive. Now that he was an insider with access to "all the innermost secrets" as well as to the chancellor, whose office was next to his own, he had a far bigger hand in shaping British financial policy than during World War I. Insider, yes, but still an iconoclast. Neither middle age, celebrity status, nor bad heart had dimmed his impatience with the inefficiency of the King's College freshmen or the fury expressed in *The Economic Consequences of the Peace.* "To the carpenter with a hammer, everything looks like a nail," goes the old saw. To Keynes, everything looked like a problem that he was better qualified to solve than those who were assigned the responsibility. He meddled in matters from tariffs to beer taxes, often getting the facts wrong and ruffling feathers. He once sent Richard Kahn, now posted in Egypt, a plan for reorganizing Cairo's entire transportation system.

As in the previous war, Keynes's job became to loosen American purse strings. In early May 1941, before America's entrance into the war and at the height of a bitter controversy with the United States over providing navy destroyer escorts for arms shipments to Britain, Keynes spent eleven weeks in Washington, D.C., as Britain's envoy. It was his third visit to the United States—such visits being "considered in the nature of a serious illness to be followed by convalescence"[12]—but this time he eschewed his favorite mode of transatlantic conveyance, the *Queen Mary,* and flew on Pan American's Atlantic Clipper. With German U-boats roaming the North Atlantic sinking British ships at the rate of sixty a month, flying was safer, although not necessarily much faster due to erratic schedules. Stepping onto the tarmac at La Guardia airport, where reporters waited, Keynes first fantasized aloud about a daily shuttle between London and New York, then took aim at American isolationists.

A German victory would mean that America's ties to the Old World would be severed permanently, he pointed out. "The American economy could not function at all on its present basis. It doesn't bear thinking about." Not everyone appreciated his lecture. The arch-isolationist Senator Burton Wheeler of Montana sneered, "The American people resent the fact that these foreigners are trying to involve us in the war by giving us free advice on how to run our country when they've made such a miserable failure with their own."[13] By "miserable failure," the senator meant that Britain couldn't pay her bills. Having converted her economy for total war, Britain was forced to pay for imported matériel with hard currencies, even as her ability to earn hard currencies by exporting evaporated. When Lord Lothian, Britain's ambassador, came right out and said, "Well, boys, Britain's broke. It's your money we want," the US Treasury refused to believe that the British Empire could possibly be short of gold.[14]

Yet American antipathy to sacrificing lives and treasure in fratricidal European wars was so strong after World War I that the United States embraced unilateral disarmament in a period when Germany, Russia, and, belatedly the British and French, were all rearming. Although the United States maintained the world's largest navy, its army was "a tiny skeleton force" of two hundred thousand men, and its entire air force consisted of 150 fighter planes. In 1940, the United States was spending less than 2 percent of its annual income on defense, and all arms sales to foreign governments were restricted by law. The Johnson Act of 1934 was aimed specifically at Britain. It prohibited arms sales to any country that had defaulted on its World War I debts.

The fall of France and the near destruction of the British expeditionary force at Dunkirk in June 1940 provoked a sharp reappraisal. Even in an election year, it was no longer possible to deny that Germany—especially in alliance with the Soviet Union—posed a serious potential threat to the United States. Hitler, who had a huge program to build navy destroyers and aircraft and was badgering the *Caudillo de España,* Francisco Franco, to allow German bases in western Spain, clearly had America in his sights. Congress quickly approved some $4 billion in munitions spending and set a target of 2 million "men under arms" for the end of 1941.

Nonetheless, rearmament was described as being strictly for "hemisphere defense."[15] The overwhelming majority of voters were convinced that Britain could not avoid defeat. Ironically, the historian Alan Milward points out, the American decision to rearm made that dismal prospect somewhat more likely. Britain had ordered some $2.4 billion in munitions from American defense contractors—enough ships, planes, and trucks to keep defense plants busy for several years. Now it risked having its orders bumped by American orders.

Lend-Lease was FDR's inspired strategy for keeping the United States out of the war while keeping Britain in it. Unlike his ambassador in London, Joseph Kennedy, and many of his closest advisors, the president thought that with adequate support from the United States, Britain could and would prevail. Churchill's "we will never surrender" oration during the Dunkirk evacuation convinced him that "there would be no negotiations between London and Berlin" of the kind that antiwar groups from the Communist Party to the America First Committee, two members of the British war cabinet, and Ambassador Kennedy, were demanding.[16]

Arming the British was already reviving the American economy and driving down unemployment. The only trouble was that the flow of arms could not continue on America's cash-and-carry terms, since Britain could no longer earn dollars by exporting—as Churchill explained to the president in his "begging letter," waiting until FDR's reelection in November 1940 to send it.[17] Roosevelt's response was delivered at a press conference where he told reporters that "the best immediate defense of the United States is the success of Great Britain in defending herself."[18] He was not above reminding Americans of the economic benefits of supplying Britain. He illustrated the point with a parable: If your neighbor's house was on fire and you had a water hose, you wouldn't try to sell it to him; you would lend him the hose and tell him to give it back when he had put out the fire. "What I am trying to do . . . is get rid of the silly, foolish old dollar sign," he said.[19] The United States would send Britain whatever arms and supplies she needed, paid for by American taxpayers, in exchange for Britain's promise to repay in kind when the war was won. In a radio "fireside chat" on December 29, the night that German bombers reduced London's financial district to rubble, he declared "We must be the great arsenal of democracy."[20]

The proposal required congressional approval because Roosevelt was asking for an initial appropriation of $7 billion. Opponents argued that Lend-Lease would inevitably drag America into the war by provoking a German attack. Others raised the specter that arms sent to Britain would pass to the Nazis after Britain's inevitable defeat. But the president prevailed and Congress approved the measure, with an amendment that forbade the navy from sending its ships into the war zone, on March 10, 1941.

Churchill hailed Lend-Lease as "the most un-sordid act in the history of any nation," and, indeed, the new arrangement signaled the start of a

$50 billion procession of ships, planes, and food from American factories and farms and a suspension of the traditional American practice of treating loans to allies as strictly business. But, of course, there were strings, and Keynes was determined to loosen them.

The dispute that broke out between Britain and the United States exactly one day after the White House sent the Lend-Lease bill to Congress turned on the fact that the law would cover only orders placed after the bill went into effect, not those placed before. Churchill maintained that down payments on past orders "had already denuded our resources."[21] When he complained that "we are not only to be skinned, but flayed to the bone," he was referring to one particularly onerous condition.[22] To prove that she truly needed help, Britain was supposed to exhaust all of her dollar reserves before tapping Lend-Lease—in effect, to pay for the construction of the American plants that were going to be producing arms for Britain. That meant handing over the country's dwindling gold supplies. The United States actually sent a destroyer to Cape Town, South Africa, to pick up $50 million in bullion that London had placed there for safekeeping. Britain was also required to sell stock in American companies and American subsidiaries of British corporations into a weak market. In the weeks before the passage of Lend-Lease, the British Treasury representative in New York, who was liquidating Britain's stock portfolio at the rate of $10 million a week, detected a jockeying for postwar commercial advantage.

The ever optimistic Keynes was convinced that the United States would never stand by while Britain became another Vichy France, but he failed to appreciate how committed Americans were to staying out of the war. Lend-Lease, of course, was designed to reconcile those goals. Quite apart from his election promise, "I have said this before, but I shall say it again and again and again: Your boys are not going to be sent into any foreign wars,"[23] FDR repeatedly assured Congress that the United States would not fight unless attacked. His critics on the left and the right accused him of secretly maneuvering to create provocations, but recent evidence shows that, until Pearl Harbor, the president continued to hope that he could avoid entering the war. "The time may be coming when the Germans and the Japs will do some fool thing that would put us in," he told his aides. "That's the only real danger of our getting in, is that their foot will slip."[24] One clear sign that the president meant what he said was that when Keynes arrived in Washington, the United States was monitoring encryptions from the Enigma machine, provided by the British in April, not to hunt down German submarines but to *avoid* them.[25]

Keynes accused the United States of "treating us worse than we have ever ourselves thought it proper to treat the humblest and least responsible Balkan country" and argued that Britain had to fight to keep "enough assets to leave us capable of independent action."[26] The point was to limit Britain's dependence on Lend-Lease and thus American control over the British balance of payments. Keynes went to Washington as the chancellor's personal envoy in order to try to work out better financing for Britain's pre-Lend-Lease orders. His target was to replenish Britain's reserves up to $600 million. Building up cash reserves under the cover of Lend-Lease was precisely what the Americans were on guard against.

His initial meeting with Roosevelt's Treasury secretary, Henry Morgenthau, was a disaster. Keynes's condescending professorial manner irritated the secretary. His proposal to the US Treasury to refund $700 million of the previous down payments already made on existing orders ran afoul of the president's assurance to Congress that Lend-Lease would apply only to future orders. Keynes saw Roosevelt twice, the second time in 1941 after Germany broke its pact with Stalin and invaded the Soviet Union. He managed to raise a loan enabling Britain to postpone the sale of its assets at distressed prices by offering prime British properties as collateral and agreeing to a hefty interest rate.

As Keynesianism really took hold in the first year or two of the war. The huge deficit-financed military buildup had accomplished what earlier efforts to fight the Great Depression never did; mopping up the huge residue of unemployment left at the end of the 1930s. After the apparent failure of monetary policy to restore full employment, this struck young economists as a convincing demonstration, in the eyes of young economists, that the economy worked the way Keynes said it did in the *General*

Theory. By 1941, self-identified Keynesians were scattered around the war-time bureaucracy in Washington like raisins in a cake.

A forecasting coup early in the war gave the young Keynesians in the government bureaucracy instant credibility. Most of the businessmen who were consulting for the government's War Production Board were convinced that the economy's productive capacity was "very limited" and skeptical that the output of weapons and matériel could be ramped up as quickly as the president wanted. The Keynesians at the Office of Price Administration disagreed. On one of Keynes's trips to Washington, they had asked their leader his opinion. Keynes displayed his knack for coming up with quick and dirty estimates from just a few facts. "Well, how much was 1929 real output over 1914?" he asked. "Well, that was a fifteen year period and it's been twelve years since 1929, so let's take 12/15ths of that increment ... I think that would be a reasonable goal."[27] The OPA forecasters thought so too. Keynes was reasoning that because World War I through the twenties was a long period of low average unemployment, it was a good indicator of how fast the economy *could* grow when demand wasn't depressed. His and their forecasts proved to be remarkably accurate. As one OPA staffer said, "The Keynesian wing of the U.S. civil service had been vindicated."[28]

By 1941, Keynesians dominated four New Deal agencies: the National Farmers Union, the National Planning Association, the Bureau of the Budget, and the National Resources Planning Board. There was also a group at the Treasury. A few had risen high enough in the Roosevelt administration to influence economic policy. They included John Kenneth Galbraith, deputy chief of the Office of Price Administration; Marriner S. Eccles, chairman of the Federal Reserve; Lauchlin Currie, one of FDR's six administrative assistants; and Harry Dexter White, Treasury Secretary Henry Morgenthau's de facto chief of staff. If old adversaries now found they could make common cause with Keynes, some of his most fanatical fans in Washington were dismayed. At a dinner at the Curries' house, a number of the younger men tried to convince Keynes that the "Keynes Plan" was the wrong prescription for the United States. The official unemployment rate was still in the double digits, and some industries were still saddled with unused capacity. Spending cuts, tax increases, and other austerity measures would only aggravate these and might abort the recovery long before the economy approached full employment. Keynes happened to be right, and in any case he was not swayed. Still, he allowed, "The younger Civil Servants and advisers strike me as exceptionally capable and vigorous." He found, however, "the very gritty Jewish type perhaps a little too prominent."[29]

John Kenneth Galbraith, a farm boy from Canada who looked and sounded like an English lord, liked to say that Keynes's ideas came to Washington via Harvard.[30] But it would be more accurate to say that they had also come by way of the University of Wisconsin, Columbia, the City University of New York, MIT, Yale, and, more often than not, the University of Chicago.

Milton Friedman, a recent Ph.D. from Chicago, did not attend the dinner with Keynes at Lauchlin Currie's house, but in 1941 the future leader of the anti-Keynesian monetarist revival of the Reagan years was nonetheless one of the brightest young Keynesians in the Treasury. And, as it happens, he did more than most to make Keynesianism practically feasible in the United States.

The son of blue-collar Hungarian Jewish immigrants who settled in Brooklyn in the 1890s, Friedman was born just before World War I. He grew up over his parents' store on Main Street in Rahway, a gritty New Jersey factory town on the railway line between New York and Philadelphia, whose main claim to fame was that George Merck had moved his chemical plant there in 1903. Friedman grew up witnessing his parents struggle unsuccessfully to make a go of one business after another, including an ice cream parlor. His mother essentially supported the family, but his father was the one who died of angina at age forty-nine, when Friedman was fifteen. In high school, he read *This Side of Paradise*, F. Scott Fitzgerald's coming-of-age novel about Princeton. Amory Blaine, the protagonist, has "personality, charm, magnetism, poise, the power of dominating all contemporary males, the gift of fascinating all women." If Friedman's being less than five feet tall, wearing glasses, and being poor meant that the resemblance was not perfect, he could at least cultivate the trait Blaine valued most: "Mentally—Complete, unquestioned superiority."[31]

In Friedman's world that meant becoming an actuary. The high school debating champion went to Rutgers, not Princeton, intending to do just that. The Great Depression and a young instructor and future Federal Reserve chairman, Arthur Burns, lured him from accounting to economics. To keep his own economy afloat, the undergraduate sold fireworks, coached other students for exams, and wrote headlines for the student paper. When he graduated in 1932, he took a cross-country road trip before enrolling that fall at the University of Chicago, where the faculty were "cynical, realistic and negative" about reform, yet reformers at heart, and where being a lower-class Jew wasn't a bar to admission.[32] By the end of his first year, he had met Rose Director, the younger sister of one of his professors, taken her to the Chicago World's Fair, and fallen in love.

Three years later, when he had finished his coursework and depleted his savings, the New Deal was "a lifesaver."[33] All during the summer of 1935, he had waited in vain for an offer of a lectureship. Not only was the number of academic openings negligible, but anti-Semitism made the likelihood of his landing one remote. If one of his professors hadn't gotten him a research post in Washington, he might well have abandoned his chosen career and returned to accounting. But his enthusiasm for the New Deal was real—Rose's conservative brother attested to Friedman's "very strong New Deal leanings"[34]—and he went to assist at the "birth of a new order" that promised social change of all kinds.[35]

His new employer, the National Resources Committee, was one of the dozen or so "planning agencies" created during the first Roosevelt administration. "Planning" was then enjoying a great vogue. Proposals for setting agricultural production targets, prices in a host of industries, and minimum wages had their roots not in Stalinist economic doctrine but in the platforms of British Fabians and Labourites. In practice, however, the New Deal planners mostly engaged in constructing national income accounts and forecasting future output and employment. John Maynard Keynes had been badgering the governments of Britain and the United States to create a system of national income accounts analogous to a corporation's annual income statement. Without reliable measures of how much output an economy produced every year, how much income it generated in the form of wages, profits, interest, and rents, or how much and on what households, businesses, and government spent, the government and businesses were operating in the dark. There was no way to detect imbalances between output and demand or to gauge their magnitude. With only desk calculators, constructing national income accounts was an agonizingly labor-intensive, time-consuming project. Thus was born a huge public works program for economics graduate students. Herbert Stein, one of Friedman's Chicago classmates, once estimated that the number of economists in Washington had shot up from a mere one hundred in 1930 to five thousand by 1938.[36]

Friedman was put to work assembling the first large database on consumers and their purchases. Although the labor involved was purely statistical, he later credited the experience for some of his best work, including his "permanent income hypothesis," cited when he won the Nobel Prize in 1976. It explains, among other things, why consumers typically spend a smaller fraction of one-time tax cuts or other windfalls than of permanent tax cuts or other ongoing additions to income.

Two years later, as the far from completed economic recovery that began in 1933 went into reverse, Friedman left Washington for New York and the National Bureau of Economic Research. There he joined a team assembled by Simon Kuznets, a Columbia professor, who was constructing the first complete set of national income accounts for the United States. In addition to filling gaps in the data, Friedman's job was to create detailed estimates of the income of self-employed professionals.

In the course of his research, he was dismayed to discover that despite the huge influx of émigré Jewish physicians after Hitler came to power in 1933, the number of medical licenses had not increased in the intervening five years. Furious at the power of professional groups to prevent outsiders from entering their disciplines, he wrote a scathing indictment of licensing. He bore the brunt of power himself when his study's publication was delayed for three years by a member of the NBER's board of directors with ties to the pharmaceutical industry. Meanwhile, he wondered why he bothered. "The world is going to pieces . . . and we sit worrying about means and standard deviations and professional income," he wrote to his fiancée, the younger sister of Aaron Director, in 1938. "But what the hell else can we do?"[37]

That summer, he married Rose Director, as peppery, energetic, and conservative as her brother. When Friedman returned to Washington the second time, in the fall of 1941, he had finished his doctorate and survived a hellish first academic job at the University of Wisconsin, where sentiment was overwhelmingly pro-neutrality and anti-Semitic. The young couple consoled themselves with the thought that, sooner or later, the United States would have to enter the war. By the time Hitler attacked his Soviet ally, the Friedmans were overjoyed to be going to Washington, where there would be important war work for them to do. Over the summer, Friedman had coauthored a paper, "Taxing to Prevent Inflation," with a public finance professor on the Columbia faculty who recruited him to join the Tax Research Division at the Treasury. In Friedman's first stint in Washington he had come there as a statistician. Now he was poised to play a more influential role in shaping policy.

After Dunkirk, in light of the growing likelihood that the United States would be drawn into the war, the Roosevelt administration had become preoccupied with paying for it. The US economy was already being converted to aid for European allies, and a larger bill was coming due for the military buildup that was under way. One unwelcome side effect of shifting the economy to a wartime footing was that inflation had reappeared. Between 1940 and 1941, consumer prices jumped 5 percent, the largest one-year increase since 1920. While hardly scary by present standards, the surge was enough to revive unpleasant memories of post–World War I inflation and cost-of-living protests, along with the severe recession that followed and was seen as a direct consequence.

During World War I, tax revenues had covered two-thirds of Washington's costs. The rest was financed by issuing bonds. A reasonable inference would be that the government was borrowing to close the gap between revenues and spending—reasonable, but wrong. Most of the "borrowing" was a disguised form of printing more money. The newly created Federal Reserve had urged its member commercial banks to lend their customers money with which to buy war bonds. To increase their reserves commensurately, the banks, in turn, had borrowed from the central bank by discounting the loans at the Federal Reserve—i.e. borrowing from the Federal Reserve on the security of loans for which government bonds served as collateral. As a result, while ... currency and deposits at the Federal Reserve ... increased by $2.5 billion ... only about a tenth of that represented direct purchases of government securities; the remainder consisted of credit extended to member banks.[38]

The result of the massive expansion of the money supply was a surge of inflation. For farmers, miners, and real estate developers inflation had meant a giddy extension of the wartime boom. But when the Federal Reserve jacked up interest rates, wholesale prices plunged by 44 percent and the boom turned into a nasty slump. The political fallout swept Republican Warren Harding, who campaigned on the slogan "A Return to Normalcy," into the White House. For the officials at the Democratic Treasury, how to avoid a repetition of this disaster was Topic A after World War II.

By the time the Friedmans moved into their apartment near Dupont Circle, a short walk from the Treasury building, the Treasury secretary's bulldog assistant, Harry Dexter White, was growling that things weren't going very well. "It's getting away from you," he hissed at Galbraith after one meeting about the inflation problem. "You must get moving."[39] The secretary had already ordered the Tax Division to prepare a restructuring of the federal tax system. Virtually all of the debate in Washington about fighting inflation concerned the relative effectiveness of wage and price controls versus taxation. Ultimately, the Roosevelt administration embraced both.

Selective price controls to avert "price-spiraling, rising costs of living, profiteering and inflation" had already been in effect since April 1941, and the OPA had been created to administer them.[40] After Bernard Baruch told a Congressional committee, "I do not believe in piecemeal price fixing. I think you have first to put a ceiling over the whole price structure, including wages, rents and farm prices ... and then adjust separate price schedules upward or downward, if necessary,"[41] the Office of Price Administration was granted sweeping powers to set prices and wages in most industries.

The Treasury and the OPA had initially been at odds over the tax estimates, since one of Baruch's arguments for more authority over business was that granting it would reduce the need for tax hikes. But once the General Maximum Price Regulation was enacted in 1942, the two agencies were able to agree on taxes. Friedman's first major assignment was to estimate how much taxes had to be raised to contain inflation.

On May 7, 1942, during his first appearance before a congressional committee, Friedman proposed $8.7 billion of additional taxes as "the smallest amount that is at all consistent with successful prevention of inflation."[42] Following Keynes's reasoning in defense of the 1940 Keynes Plan, Friedman pointed out that with government demand and household income soaring, it was essential to restrict consumer spending to prevent a situation in which more money was chasing a fixed output of consumer goods. As Friedman told the committee a trifle pompously, "Taxation is the most important of those measures; unless it is used quickly and severely, the other measures alone will be unable to prevent inflation." Among those other, less potent measures, Friedman listed "price control and rationing, control of consumers' credit, reduction in governmental spending, and war bond campaigns."[43] Nowhere did Friedman mention monetary policy. Looking back on his wartime work in 1953, Friedman attributed the oversight to "the Keynesian temper of the times,"[44] but Friedman numbered among Keynes's American disciples and would do so until the late 1940s.

True to his Keynesian convictions, Friedman was inclined to view the income tax as "more effective in preventing an inflationary price rise and . . . a better distribution of the cost of the war" than a sales tax, which of course was regressive.[45] That summer, he helped develop a proposal for a consumption tax, largely as a measure to avoid raising income tax rates. White, who was very taken with the idea of taxing spending instead of income, proposed combining the consumption tax with Keynes's suggestion for compulsory savings accounts that couldn't be tapped until after the war. After a stormy Treasury meeting that ended with a vote of sixteen to one against the plan, Morgenthau decided to back White and took the proposal to Congress anyway. It was dead on arrival. This contretemps was Friedman's first exposure to the challenges of getting legislation enacted, writing speeches for his superiors, and, eventually, trooping up to Capitol Hill to testify before congressional committees.

Without a doubt, the key to any tax plan was tax *collection*. This is where Friedman placed his stamp on government forever. Before 1942, income taxes were due on the previous year's income in four quarterly installments. It was the taxpayer's responsibility to come up with the money when it was due. That posed no problems, either to taxpayers or to the tax collectors, as long as tax rates were low and only a small fraction of the population paid them. In 1939, fewer than 4 million returns were filed, and the total collected was less than $1 billion, roughly 4 percent of taxable income. The Friedmans' income placed them among the top 2 percent of American households, but their tax bill was just $119, less than 2 percent of their taxable income. They had no trouble paying the whole amount on March 15, the deadline for filing federal taxes before 1955. Under the planned overhaul, their tax bill would be something like $1,704, or 23 percent of their taxable income. It was obvious that if the Treasury wanted to collect more taxes, it would have to find a way to collect the income at the time it was earned, not a year later.

The solution was tax withholding at the source. The Treasury collected taxes from employers when they paid their workers' wages. Recipients of other kinds of income—interest, dividends, money earned by the self-employed—were required to pay taxes quarterly on income earned that year based on advance estimates of liability by the recipient. A major departure from German and British practice, which had relied on collecting taxes at the source for years, was that payments would be treated as tentative and subject to adjustment later. The only serious opposition came from the IRS, which envisioned "an almost insuperable burden" for tax collectors, opposition overcome by having IRS officials visit businesses to study payroll practices so that the mechanics of withholding could be designed with those practices in mind.[46]

Friedman was back on Capitol Hill. This time he got a lesson in getting to the point and keeping things simple. When he started to answer a question by Texas senator Tom Connally, he cleared his throat and said, "There are three reasons. First . . ." Connally cut him off. "Young man, one good reason is enough," said the senator, who was wearing his trademark flowing black neckpiece in place of the usual bow tie.[47] The Treasury secretary, a man of "meager intellectual capacity" in Friedman's opinion, always insisted that his aides explain problems in terms that a high school student like "my daughter Joan" could grasp—even after Joan went off to college.[48]

In his weekly dispatch from the British Embassy, Isaiah Berlin, the historian of ideas, called it "a tax bill of unprecedented dimensions" and reported that the new law was expected to raise $7.6 billion.[49] On the twenty-second of August, he wrote excitedly that "the tax bill will affect more citizens than any ever passed by Congress."[50] For the first time, the United States had a broad-based income tax. A family of four with an income of $3,000 owed no tax in 1939 but owed $275 in 1944; a $5,000 family's taxes went from $48 to $755; a $10,000 family's from $343 to $2,245. Income taxes collected in 1939 equaled little more than 1 percent of personal income; by 1945, the figure had jumped to just over 11 percent. Morgenthau sent the withholding proposal to Congress in early 1942, and the Current Tax Payment Act of 1943 was introduced in the Senate on March 3, 1942.

The most enduring effect of Friedman's wartime efforts was to create "an enormously powerful revenue-raising machine."[51] That machine was so powerful, Herbert Stein pointed out, that revenues would rise faster than GDP for decades after the war because of the interaction between economic growth and progressive tax rates. As incomes rose, more and more taxpayers would be pushed into the higher tax brackets. That dynamic ensured that postwar administrations could keep raising spending while cutting tax rates occasionally without running huge deficits. What's more, withholding rendered taxation far less painful.

It was now possible to manipulate taxes to stabilize the economy. Before the war, Stein observed, taxes were too small a share of national income to leave much scope for stimulating or restraining the economy. More important, large swings in tax collections became automatic. When the economy slumped, tax revenues fell; when it rebounded, the opposite happened. Thus Keynesian stimulus became automatic in recessions, Keynesian restraint in booms. The irony was that Friedman, the future patron saint of low taxes and small government in the Reagan years, made it possible.

Chapter XIII

Exile:
Schumpeter and Hayek in World War II

While history runs its course it is not history to us. It leads us
into an unknown land and but rarely can we get a glimpse of
what lies ahead.

> —*Friedrich Hayek,* The Road to Serfdom, *1944*[1]

For Keynes and many of his disciples who were called to serve their countries, the war was a time of intense engagement, extraordinary intellectual
challenge, and unprecedented influence. For Schumpeter and Hayek, the
Second World War was a time of enforced inactivity, isolation, and exile.
They were out of favor intellectually. As émigrés, they were not asked to
join the war effort. They were left behind in shells of universities populated by the old, disabled, alien, and female. They could not rejoice in the
inevitable Allied victory without also mourning the suffering and devastation on the enemy's side.

As eyewitnesses to—and victims of—the collapse of the Austro-
Hungarian Empire after World War I, they could imagine possibilities
that those who had come of age in the United States or Britain did not
and could not. Keynes was not only determined that the Allies would not
make the same mistakes after the war as in 1919 but also confident that
his voice would be heard and his viewpoint would prevail. Fifty-six when
Britain declared war on the Axis, he was in a position to influence governments and public opinion in ways that he could not at thirty-six. He

was the leader of a revolution in economic thought with many adherents, Churchill's de facto Chancellor of the Exchequer, the chief British financial negotiator in Washington, and one of the architects of the postwar monetary system.

Schumpeter was haunted by a sense of personal failure, depressed by the catastrophe engulfing Europe and Japan, and alienated by prowar fervor. He grew increasingly isolated from his colleagues and students at Harvard. He did not bother to hide his bitterness over the fact that Americans condemned Germany and Japan categorically while embracing the Soviet Union as an ally. As a result, he attracted the attention of the FBI, which investigated him for more than two years.

For Schumpeter, the political triumph of left- and right-wing Socialist parties in Europe after World War I had proved that economic success alone was no guarantee of a society's survival. Capitalism and democracy were an unstable mixture he believed. Successful businessmen would conspire with politicians to bar the entry of new rivals, government bureaucrats would stifle innovation with taxes and regulation, and hostile intellectuals would attack capitalism's moral flaws while singing the praises of totalitarian regimes and even, on occasion, secretly or openly providing aid and comfort to the West's sworn enemies. His fear that bourgeois society was spawning its own gravediggers, as Marx had predicted, had hardened into certainty.

Instead of joining the war effort like other Austrian expatriates in the United States, the fifty-six-year-old Schumpeter poured his premonitions into the book that most shows him as the ultimate ironist that he was. Published in 1942, when faith in free enterprise was dwindling in the West, *Capitalism, Socialism and Democracy* was an encomium disguised as a funeral oration that challenged Keynes's conclusion that capitalism was innately failure-prone. Whatever its shortcomings—financial crises, depressions, social strife—it was in capitalism's nature to deliver the goods to that "nine parts of mankind" who had been enslaved and impoverished throughout human history. "The capitalist engine is first and last an engine of mass production," Schumpeter asserted confidently at a time when American GDP had barely recovered from the Great Depression.[2]

Thanks to that engine, he wrote in an oft-quoted passage, modern working girls could afford stockings that were once too costly for any women, even queens a century earlier. If the United States economy were to grow as fast in the half century after 1928 as in the half century before, he observed in what turned out to be a gross underestimate, the US economy would be 2.7 times bigger in 1978 than in 1928. He wasn't predicting that outcome—the opposite, as it turns out—only impressing his readers with the power of the "ingenious mechanism."

Having argued that competition was an ingenious social contrivance for harnessing creative genius and raising living standards, Schumpeter promptly prophesied the system's demise. To his own rhetorical question "Can capitalism survive?" he replied, "No. I don't think it can."[3] The entrepreneur, the creative force in capitalism's success, was under attack, as was the ideology of economic liberalism, not only in the Soviet Union but in the West. As one reviewer commented, he "predicted the triumph of socialism but proceeded to deliver one of the most passionate defenses of capitalism as an economic system ever written."[4]

Doubtless, the feeling that opportunities for extraordinary individuals were shrinking reflected Schumpeter's middle age and depressive tendencies. He was haunted by thoughts of death and fears that he had become little more than an anachronism himself. At Harvard, his ideas were increasingly regarded as quaint, just like his courtly manner and flowery speech. "A new economics" was needed, he wrote in his diary, but he did not feel up to creating it. In a statement of unconscious irony, he added, "I do not carry weight."[5]

When Friedrich von Hayek and his family had moved to London in the fall of 1931, he had expected to return to Vienna. Within two years, he recognized that his exile would likely be permanent. For several years, Hayek found himself at the head of the liberal economic camp in his adopted country. By the time he became a British subject in 1938, however, his disciples had deserted him. As John Hicks, a prominent Keynesian, recalled in 1967, "It is hardly remembered that there was a time when the new theories of Hayek were the principal rival of the new theories of Keynes."[6]

Hayek's sense of intellectual isolation was compounded by the gloomy developments in Austria. Well before Hitler marched into Vienna and declared *Anschluss* in 1938, Hayek's old associates—including Ludwig von Mises, who had been fired from a university post—had begun to drift abroad to escape growing anti-Semitism. In 1935, he wrote to Fritz Machlup, a Jewish member of his old *Geist-Kreis* seminar, who had informed him of his decision to stay in America permanently. As a Jew, Machlup had had little choice. Hayek agreed, but added that "the mass emigration of intellectuals from Vienna and especially the demise of our school of economic thought pains me deeply."[7] And the following year: "The speed of the intellectual surrender and the corruption of politics (to say nothing of finances) is shattering."[8]

Days after Hitler's troops marched into Vienna to cheering crowds, Hayek was making the rounds of his former *Geist-Kreis* friends, who told him horror stories about Gestapo arrests, firings, and harassments. That year he applied for and got British citizenship. He attacked the Nazi regime in print and condemned anti-Semitism. He became involved in efforts to help Jewish colleagues on the Continent to emigrate.

Hayek's unhappy marriage compounded his misery. He had been pressing his wife for a divorce that she refused. What's more, he had never stopped loving Helene. He had seen her in August 1939, just before the news of the Stalin-Hitler pact signaled the inevitability of war and the impossibility of meeting again until it was over.

By the time war finally came, Hayek's isolation had turned into virtual seclusion. Barely forty, a full decade younger than Keynes, he felt old. He had, among other things, completely lost his hearing in one ear. His deafness epitomized how cut off he had become both from his old world and his adopted one. He had stayed in London during the first six weeks of the blitz to show his loyalty to Britain and his indifference to danger, but eventually he was forced to follow the LSE—shrunken now to a few dozen female students and himself—to Cambridge, where the school remained for the duration of the war. His wife and children went to stay in the country, his old ally Lionel Robbins went to Whitehall, and one by one his other colleagues disappeared to do war work.

The Road to Serfdom was Hayek's contribution to the Allied war effort. He called it "a duty I must not evade."[9] For a few short weeks after war was declared, he had high hopes and expected an assignment in the propaganda ministry. He peppered Lord Macmillan, head of the ministry, with memoranda suggesting possible strategies for German broadcasts— "I am free and anxious to put my capacities to the best use which, after very careful consideration, I believe would be in connection with propaganda work."[10] But it soon became obvious that, because he was foreign-born, he would be shut out of war work. Bitterly, he resigned himself to running the LSE's shrinking economics department, more or less by himself.

Hurt and frustrated, he toyed with the idea of joining his friends in America. "I . . . resent this complete seclusion,"[11] he wrote to Machlup. Still, when Machlup echoed his thought in a subsequent letter, he bristled at any suggestion of jumping ship. "I have given up all thought of going . . . while I am wanted here in any way. It is after all my duty."[12] When the New School offered him a temporary professorship in 1940, he cabled terse, almost haughty regrets.[13] Later, he wrote to another friend, "I envy you a little your chance of doing something connected with the war—when it is all over I shall probably be the only economist who has no such opportunity whatever and shall, *nolens, volens,* have been the purest of pure theoreticians."[14] As always, when faced with disappointment, he shifted his focus to the future. "I seem very early to have lost the capacity quietly to enjoy the present, and what made life interesting to me were my plans for the future—satisfaction consisted largely in having done what I had planned to do, and mortification mainly that I had not carried out my plans."[15]

Paradoxically, the next three years became some of the most productive of his life. "I have . . . done more work this summer than ever before in a similar period."[16] At one point—while the bombs were falling—he was working on no fewer than three different books. Pretty soon he was also filling the pages of *Economica,* LSE's journal, practically single-handedly. "So far the bombing attack is an abject failure," he wrote when he arrived in Cambridge. "What drove me out of London was simply the discomfort of an empty house and of frequent journeys."[17] Still, as a precaution, he mailed chapters of his new book to friends in America for "safe-keeping."

In January 1941, Hayek alluded explicitly for the first time to his ambition to write a book aimed, like Keynes's *The Economic Consequences of the Peace,* at a mass audience: "I am mainly concerned with an enlarged and somewhat more popular exposition of the themes of my *Freedom and the Economic System* which, if I finish it, may come out as a sixpenny Penguin volume."[18] He owed the book to his fellow man: "Since I can do nothing to help winning the war my concern is largely for the more distant future, and although my views in this respect are as pessimistic as can be—much more so than about the war itself—I am doing what little I can to open peoples' eyes."[19]

He worked on *The Road to Serfdom* for two and a half years, from New Year's 1941 to June 1943. "I am a frightfully slow worker," he complained at one point, "and with my interests, as they are at the moment, divided between so many different fields, I shall have to live very long to carry out what I should like to do at the moment."[20]

Hayek began *The Road to Serfdom* by invoking history—its relevance to the present—and his own history of living in two cultures:

> While history runs its course, it is not history to us. It leads us into an unknown land . . . It would be different if it were given to us to live a second time . . . Yet although history never quite repeats itself, and just because no development is inevitable, we can in a measure learn from the past to avoid a repetition of the same process.

Addressing the reader directly, Hayek describes a powerful sense of déjà vu. The drift toward collectivism in England reminded him of Vienna in the aftermath of World War I. "The following pages are the product of an experience as near as possible to twice living through the same period—or at least twice watching a very similar evolution of ideas." He expressed the conviction shared by earlier European observers of English society, from Engels and Marx to Schumpeter, that by moving from one country to another, one may sometimes twice watch similar phases of intellectual development. The senses have then become particularly acute. When one hears for a second time opinions expressed or measures advocated which one has first met twenty or twenty-five years ago, they assume a new meaning . . . They suggest, if not the necessity, at least the probability, that developments will take a similar course.[21]

What opinions, what measures, what works did he have in mind? Of recent books, one was surely Adolf Hitler's *Mein Kampf,* which appeared in an unabridged English edition for the first time in 1939. Another was doubtless the Webbs' 1936 paean to central planning, *Soviet Communism: a New Civilization,* which Hayek reviewed for the Sunday *Times.* Although it was politically far removed from either, he was doubtless also thinking of Keynes's *General Theory.*

Hayek's book was a defense of markets and competition couched in terms of the modern information economy:

We must look at the price system as such a mechanism for communicating information if we want to understand its real function . . . The most significant fact about this system is the economy of knowledge with which it operates, or how little the individual participants need to know in order to be able to take the right action.[22]

It was also a warning. Herbert Spencer had been the first to caution that infringements of economic freedom would lead to infringements of political freedom. Hayek's mentor, Ludwig von Mises, had identified the welfare state as a Trojan horse, "merely a method for transforming the market economy step by step into socialism . . . What emerges is the system of all-round planning, that is, socialism of the type which the German Hindenburg plan was aiming at in the First World War." But Hayek was by no means advocating laissez-faire. In fact, he repudiated benign economic neglect quite explicitly:

There is, finally, the supremely important problem of combating general fluctuations of economic activity and the recurrent waves of large-scale unemployment which accompany them. This is, of course, one of the gravest and most pressing problems of our time. But, though its solution will require much planning in the good sense, it does not—or at least need not—require that special kind of planning which according to its advocates is to replace the market. Many economists hope, indeed, that the ultimate remedy may be found in the field of monetary policy, which would involve nothing incompatible even with nineteenth-century liberalism. Others, it is true, believe that real success can be expected only from the skilled timing of public works undertaken on a very large scale. This might lead to much more serious restrictions of the competitive sphere, and, in experimenting in this direction, we shall have carefully to watch our step if we are to avoid making all economic activity progressively more dependent on the direction and volume of government expenditure.[23]

Later he would tell American audiences in a speech that "You must cease to argue for and against government activity as such . . . We cannot seriously argue that the government ought to do nothing."[24]

Early in 1943, Machlup sent around several chapters to American publishers. The first responses were not encouraging:

Frankly we are doubtful of the sale which we could secure for it, and I personally cannot but feel that Professor Hayek is a little outside the stream of much of present day thought, both here and in England . . . If, however, the book is published by someone else and becomes a bestseller in the non-fiction field, just put it down to one of those mistakes in judgment which we all make.[25]

Harper's dismissed it as "labored" and "overwritten."[26]

In June 1943, Hayek finally signed a contract with Routledge for publication in the UK. It was not until February 1944, shortly before the book was to appear in England, that Hayek heard that the University of Chicago Press had decided to accept it.

Act III

CONFIDENCE

Nothing to Fear

On January 11, 1944, FDR had been in bed for days with the flu. Exhausted from meetings of the Big Three in Cairo and Tehran, suffering from hypertension, hypertensive heart disease, cardiac failure (left ventricle), and acute bronchitis, any of which could kill him, he was too weak to make his customary trip to Capitol Hill to deliver his annual State of the Union message.[1] Knowing that the newspapers couldn't print the full text of his speech, which he had sent by messenger to Congress, he insisted on speaking directly to the American people in a "fireside chat" over the radio. The D-day landing in Normandy was months away and the United States was locked in a life-and-death struggle in the Pacific, but the president urged the country to look beyond the war: "It is our duty now to lay the plans and determine the strategy for the winning of a lasting peace."[2]

Again and again, the president hammered home his theme that the foundation for a lasting peace was not the defeat of gangster regimes alone but also rising living standards. Economic security was the supreme responsibility of democratic governments. He was determined not to repeat the mistakes made by the Allies after World War I that he believed had helped lead to the current war. Maintaining that the welfare state and individual liberty went hand in hand, he warned, "People who are hungry and out of a job are the stuff of which dictatorships are made." Roosevelt called on Congress to support postwar economic recovery at home and abroad.

His major domestic proposal was for an "economic Bill of Rights"—namely, government guarantees of jobs, health care, and old age pensions.[3]

The most radical speech of FDR's presidency, says his biographer James MacGregor Burns, "fell with a dull thud into the half-empty chamber."[4] Congress had a Republican majority, and the president's references to joblessness and hunger did not seem to resonate with millions of Americans gathered around the radio. When Keynes arrived in Washington a few months later, he found that "on this continent the war is a time of immense prosperity for everyone."[5] Not only had the war years shaped up as the best of times, but 60 percent of the population told pollsters that they were "satisfied with the way things were *before* the war."[6]

The war itself was responsible. Even before 1939, intensifying fears of war had resulted in a huge influx of gold into the United States as investors in Europe and Asia sought a safe haven for their savings. As a result, American banks were flush and interest rates remained near zero. And, since 1939, spending by the federal government had soared from 5 percent of GDP to nearly 50 percent, much faster than tax revenues, despite the dramatic increases in income and profits taxes and the imposition of the new Social Security payroll tax. This was deficit spending on a scale that dwarfed the anti-Depression fiscal policies of the first Roosevelt administration.

The combination of massive deficit spending and the accidental monetary stimulus from abroad sparked a boom. With 11 million men and women in uniform, and factories, mines, and farms operating flat out, the official jobless rate had plunged from 15 percent at the end of 1939—11 percent counting "temporary" government workers—to well below 2 percent at the end of 1943. Thanks to the tight labor market, factory pay was up 30 percent after inflation. And after four years of war, the average American household was consuming more, not less, than in 1939.

The United States was supplying planes, ships, and tanks by cranking up production, not by tightening belts. The economy's annual output, or GDP, was growing at a nearly 14 percent annual rate, three times as fast as in the "wild twenties," when, the president said sourly, "this Nation went for a joy ride on a roller coaster which ended in a tragic crash."[7] To be sure, Americans couldn't have new cars, refrigerators, or houses, but they were so confident the dollar would retain its prewar value that they were willing to save nearly one-quarter of their pay to buy them after the war. Nor could they go on their beloved road trips. But they could buy more clothes, food, alcohol, cigarettes, and magazines, listen to more radio and records, and see more movies and ball games. The contrast with Britain, where per capita consumption was down by 20 percent, was extraordinary. As readers of Elizabeth Jane Howard's *Cazelet Chronicles* novels know, the life of English citizens was complicated for years by shortages of housing, clothes, coal, gasoline, and many foodstuffs. Nor did austerity end with the Armistice. As late as 1946, the Labour government was forced to consider, in secret, whether to impose bread rationing. The last of the controls wasn't lifted until 1954.

Although it was clear that the American economic system was hardly on its last legs, the president and his advisors feared that wartime prosperity couldn't last. Among the "economic truths that have become accepted as self-evident," FDR implied in his speech, was that a *new* New Deal would be needed to prevent the Great Depression from roaring back when the troops came home. "A return to the so-called normalcy of the 1920s" after the war would mean that "we shall have yielded to the spirit of Fascism here at home,"[8] he warned melodramatically.

The president's position reflected only one side of a hot debate between Keynesians and anti-Keynesians. The more upbeat the public and businessmen became about postwar prospects, the more American disciples of Keynes worried that the economy would sink into another slump. Public spending would plunge with demobilization. Alvin Hansen, an advisor to the Federal Reserve who was sometimes called "the American Keynes," foresaw "a postwar collapse: demobilization of armies, shutdowns in defense industries, unemployment, deflation, bankruptcy, hard times."[9] Paul Samuelson, a consultant for the main postwar planning agency, warned the administration not to become complacent about unemployment. "Before the war we had not solved it, and nothing that has happened since assures that it will not rise again." They had little faith that business and consumers would pick up the slack. As Samuelson put it, "If a man goes without an automobile for 6 years, he does not then have a demand for six automobiles."[10] Having concluded from the 1930s that business was too timid to invest and that monetary policy was a poor weapon with which to fight recessions, the Keynesians were convinced that the only solution was to slow the cuts in public spending by slowing demobilization and by beefing up spending on infrastructure.

Anti-Keynesians were also worried about stagnation, but of a different type and coming from a different quarter. Schumpeter was worried about the prospects for economic growth—in the longer run. He feared that the economy would no longer produce gains in productivity and living standards—not because of inadequate demand but because of government policy. In an article published in 1943, he agreed that "everybody is afraid of a postwar slump" but argued that the popular fears were overblown: "Viewed as a purely economic problem, the task [of reconstruction] might well turn out to be much easier than most people believe . . . But in any case, the wants of impoverished households will be so urgent and so calculable that any postwar slump that may be unavoidable would speedily give way to a reconstruction boom. Capitalist methods have proved equal to much more difficult tasks."[11]

The real threat to postwar growth, he believed, came from antibusiness policies enshrined in the New Deal. He and Hayek feared that governments would continue their wartime management of production and distribution—including price and wage controls, deficit financing, and high taxes—after the war was won. Such efforts, intended to avert stagnation, might well produce that very result. Schumpeter called it "capitalism in the oxygen tent."[12] Hayek was less concerned about the possible loss of dynamism than he was about the loss of freedom. While the president cautioned that a "return to normalcy" would be tantamount to a victory for Fascism, Hayek warned that continuing wartime management of production and distribution would ultimately result in a radical restriction of economic and political rights as well. Their fears proved more realistic for the UK and Europe than for the United States, where virtually all the wartime agencies were dismantled starting in 1945.

●   ●   ●

Apart from military victory, FDR's top priority was not to repeat the mistakes made by the Allies after World War I that he believed had helped lead to the current war. He pointed to the talks among the Big Three about postwar financial, trade, and political arrangements that were already underway by January 1944 as an example of doing better than last time. Attacking the "ostrich isolationism" of "unseeing moles" who regarded the parleys with suspicion, he lashed out at those who viewed prosperity in the rest of the world as a threat to American economic interests. In Tehran he had extracted Stalin's commitment to a new League of Nations. The "one supreme objective of the future" was collective security, the president insisted, including "economic security, social security, moral security" for the "family of Nations." After bringing the aggressors under military control, "a decent standard of living for all individual men and women and children in all Nations" was essential for peace. "Freedom from fear is eternally linked with freedom from want."[13]

There was no disagreement between Keynesians and anti-Keynesians on the need for international cooperation. On this issue, they had seen eye to eye since 1919. Few believed that a favorable global economic environment would arise spontaneously. The bilateral trading blocs of the interwar era were designed to allow the Soviet Union and Nazi Germany to break away from the world economy. Even Hayek, who by virtue of experience and temperament was more skeptical of the potential for positive government intervention, was convinced that democracies were capable of more competence than they had shown a generation before. That governments had to actively plan and cooperate to ensure the revival of world trade, the resolution of war debts, and the stabilization of currencies this time reflected a consensus.

From Europe, however, FDR's upbeat vision of one world in which the major powers were focused on economic growth instead of expansionist aggression seemed far too rosy. On March 9, 1944, Gunnar Myrdal, the head of one of Sweden's postwar planning commissions, delivered a considerably darker prognosis. The young economist had spent the early part of the war traveling through the American South reporting his classic study of race relations, *An American Dilemma: The Negro Problem and*

Modern Democracy, before returning to his native Sweden—which had retained its status as a nonbelligerent nation despite having supplied the German war machine—in 1942.

Myrdal saw the future through a much darker glass. He feared that autarky, economic stagnation, and militarism—the very pathologies that had helped to breed the second global conflagration within a single generation—had not been defeated, despite four years of unprecedented effort, sacrifice, and suffering. The dream of a single world community— the United Nations—bound together by trade, convertible currencies, and international law was a dangerous illusion, he argued. Dismissing the "overoptimism" of American economists, he predicted that the present wartime boom would turn into a depression more severe than the Great Depression and mass unemployment. A depression in the United States would necessarily have repercussions for the whole world, especially for Sweden and other countries that depended on exports to pay for the imports they needed to survive as modern economies. Inevitably, economic chaos would produce an epidemic of strikes and civil unrest and fuel nationalist rivalries—just as similar economic conditions had done before the war. A general trend of militarism and autarky[14] similar to that which had prevailed in the interwar period would continue. In particular, the world would inevitably break up into three great competing empires— Russian, British, and American—as the conflicting economic and political interests of the Big Three displaced the Allies' common goal of defeating the Axis. In Myrdal's global dystopia, the new imperialism would not only be oppressive but also inherently unstable.

This, of course, is the world of *1984.* George Orwell, who completed his dystopian novel in 1948, pictured a world carved up into three empires—Oceania, Eurasia, and Eastasia—that are locked in a permanent Cold War. Too evenly matched to win or lose, the superpowers use external threats to justify totalitarian rule and economic stagnation. The hero—an everyman named Winston Smith, who "displays flashes of Churchillian courage"—learns that the "splitting up of the world into three great superstates was an event which could be and indeed was foreseen before the middle of the twentieth century."[15]

Ironically, one who viewed the nightmare with satisfaction rather than fear was Stalin. FDR had returned from Tehran convinced that the Allied leaders shared a common interest, once the enemy was defeated, in creating a framework within which all countries could focus on economic growth. He had assured Americans that "All our allies have learned by experience—bitter experience that real development will not be possible if they are to be diverted from their purpose by repeated wars—or even threats of war." [16]

In reality, Stalin was convinced that his capitalist allies were inherently incapable of cooperating for long and that once their common enemy was defeated, the drive for profits would soon set the United States and Britain at each other's throats. In his mind, Anglo-American war was an "inevitability." [17] In that case, he could extract aid and territory from his allies while waiting for the coming crisis to provoke a war and drive their citizens into pseudo-political parties whose first loyalty was to Moscow.

Why did he ignore abundant evidence to the contrary? According to John Lewis Gaddis, the foremost American historian of the Cold War, Stalin was a genuine captive of Lenin's primitive economic theory—a theory based on a false analogy between economic competition and warfare. Instead of FDR's belief that growth in one country would benefit rather than harm its trading partners, Stalin was convinced that trade, like war, was a zero-sum game in which one side's gain was the other's loss. Indeed, Lenin had believed that war was merely a more aggressive form of economic competition.

In *The General Theory*, Keynes had expressed his belief that ideas matter: "Madmen in authority, who hear voices in the air, are distilling their frenzy from some academic scribbler of a few years back." [18] Thanks in no small part to the ideas of Keynes, Hayek, and their followers, those in authority were neither mad nor in the thrall of barbaric relics. They were determined to avert such nightmares.

Chapter XIV

Past and Future:
Keynes at Bretton Woods

Economic diseases are highly communicable. It follows therefore
that the economic health of every country is a proper matter of
concern to all its neighbors, near and distant.

—*FDR, message to delegates at Breton Woods*[1]

Keynes described his and Lydia's crossing on the *Queen Mary* in mid-June
1944, barely two weeks before the international monetary conference at
Bretton Woods, New Hampshire, as "a most peaceful and also a most busy
time."[2] Traveling with Friedrich von Hayek's, and now his, close friend
Lionel Robbins and a dozen other British officials, Keynes presided over
no fewer than thirteen shipboard meetings and had a major hand in writing two "boat drafts" on the two major institutions that were to administer
postwar monetary arrangements: the International Monetary Fund and
the World Bank.[3] In his spare time, he lounged in his deck chair devour-
ing books. Along with a new edition of Plato's *Republic* and a life of his
favorite essayist, Thomas Babington Macaulay, he read Hayek's *The Road
to Serfdom.*

In contrast to his more doctrinaire disciples, Keynes was a genius
capable of holding two opposing truths in his mind: "Morally and philo-
sophically," he wrote in a long letter to Hayek, "I find myself in agreement
with virtually the whole of it; and not only in agreement but deeply moved
agreement." Hayek might not have succeeded in drawing "the line between

freedom and planning satisfactorily,"[4] and therefore might not be a useful guide through the "middle way" of actual policy making, but he was articulating values that Keynes considered essential "for living a good life."[5] Robbins mused that Keynes, "so radical in outlook in matters purely intellectual, in matters of culture he is a true Burkean conservative."[6]

Keynes went on to say that Hayek was too quick to dismiss the possibility that some planning was compatible with freedom, particularly if the planning was done by those who shared their values: "Dangerous acts can be done safely in a community which thinks and feels rightly which would be the way to hell if they were executed by those who think and feel wrongly."[7] He meant that a war economy run by Churchill or FDR was unlikely to lead to a totalitarian state, even though ones run by Stalin and Hitler had.

Keynes and Lydia were whisked to the White Mountains of New Hampshire by private train. The Mount Washington Hotel in Bretton Woods was a turn-of-the-century grande dame meant to recall grande dames such as the Hotel Majestic in Paris, where Keynes had been at the end of the last war—only with 350 rooms, private baths, a ballroom, an indoor pool, and a palm court with Tiffany windows. But the slightly seedy resort, long past her prime, was hardly prepared for the onslaught of 730 delegates from forty-four Allied countries. "The taps run all day, the windows do not close or open, the pipes mend and un-mend and nobody can get anywhere," Lydia wrote to her mother-in-law. They were installed in an enormous suite next to Secretary of the Treasury Henry Morgenthau. Unlike the voyage over, the conference was "a madhouse," Lydia observed, "with most people working more than humanly possible."[8]

FDR had issued the invitations to the conference, and Morgenthau acted as titular host, but the principal architects, planners, and parliamentarians were his aide Harry Dexter White and Keynes. The principals came with different ideas, divergent interests, and, in many cases, hidden agendas. The hotel was crawling with spies. Delegates had no authority to bind their governments. But the organizers recognized that they must guarantee an economic recovery and that no recovery could take place without cooperation. The framers shared the determination expressed by FDR in his State of the Union address not to repeat the mistakes made after World War I, and to take a global, multilateral, "United Nations" approach. The very fact of the conference reflected a radical redefinition— and enlargement—of government's responsibilities. Just as Washington, London, and Paris now accepted responsibility for keeping employment high at home, virtually every government in the West accepted some measure of responsibility for keeping employment high in their trading partners' economies too.

The precise features of the new order reflected a shared view of what had gone wrong the last time and a conviction that getting things right had ramifications that were more than economic. FDR, Churchill, and Keynes and his American disciples believed that economic pathologies— inflation and unemployment—had produced Fascism and fatally weakened many democracies. They believed with equal conviction that the breakup of the pre–World War I global economy—produced by the frantic beggar-thy-neighbor attempts of each nation to insulate itself from the worldwide economic crisis—and the accompanying decline in world trade were partly responsible for world war. Economic rivalry might lead to war. As Cordell Hull, the American secretary of state, put it: "[Un]hampered trade dovetailed with peace; high tariffs, trade barriers and unfair economic competition with war . . . If we could get a freer flow of trade . . . so that one country would not be deadly jealous of another and the living standards of all countries might rise . . . we might have a reasonable chance of lasting peace."[9]

The great innovation of the 1920s and 1930s—the economics of the whole developed by Fisher, Keynes, and, to a lesser extent, Schumpeter and Hayek—taught that what was good for one nation might easily be bad for all. Devaluing one's currency, erecting trade barriers, and clamping controls on capital outflows might be effective for reducing balance-of-payment deficits, stopping the outflow of gold, and pumping up government revenues. But if everybody adopted the same tactics, the eventual result would be universal impoverishment and unemployment.

In the 1930s, world trade fell by half, and trading continued mostly within currency blocs like the pound sterling bloc within the British Empire, the Soviet sphere, and the bilateral trading bloc designed by Hitler's economics minister, Dr. Hjalmar Schacht. It was now commonly acknowledged that keeping free enterprise functioning globally required the visible hand of government. In a way, biographer Robert Skidelsky points out, the new arrangement devised by White and Keynes was Keynesianism applied globally.

The purpose of the Bretton Woods conference was to revive world trade and stabilize currencies and to deal with war debts and frozen credit markets. The war had left much of the world dramatically poorer, and countries had to be able to earn their way back to prosperity. In the broadest sense, salvage meant rebuilding and reconstruction, moving back toward pre-1913 globalization, but without reviving the pre–World War I assumption that the economic machinery worked automatically. For the West, it meant learning from the past in order to avoid the mistakes of the interwar era—the very lesson that Marxists claimed capitalists could not learn—and restoring lost moral and material credibility. Economic stability was a key to political stability, and economic growth was a necessary if not sufficient condition for the long-run survival of the West. Modern societies could not survive if the ingenious mechanism malfunctioned or broke down, any more than great cities could survive without electricity or trains.

Unlike the British thinkers who championed free trade in the 1840s, neither Keynes nor Fisher (nor Schumpeter nor Hayek) believed in an automatic tendency toward peace and progress such as had been cheerily assumed by so many in the Belle Epoque. Governments had to intervene; international cooperation was required. No system was spontaneously generated or self-regulating, as had been taken for granted before 1914. It would require the sole remaining superpower in the West and the once powerful but now humbled European empires to create one. The alternative was unthinkable. White suggested that failure would lead once more to war: "The absence of a high degree of economic collaboration among the leading nations will . . . inevitably result in economic warfare that will be but the prelude and instigator of military warfare on an even vaster scale." [10]

In other words, White and Keynes shared the fears of George Orwell, Gunnar Myrdal, Schumpeter, Hayek, and many others, but they were neither slaves to economic determinism nor radically distrustful of government. They were not prepared to believe that governments could not now be convinced to avert both depression and war by establishing a common framework for cooperation. They believed that democratic governments could learn from past mistakes and rejected both the Marxist notion of historical necessity and the traditional presumption of Great Power rivalry. They certainly did not share Stalin's conviction that war was part of capitalism's DNA.

The real test, of course, was not only whether the West could learn from history but whether, with the help of its ingenious mechanism, the West would draw the *right* lessons.

In 1944 England was fighting for her life at any cost, even if it meant losing much of its empire, cooperating with the Soviet Union, and playing second fiddle to an increasingly assertive United States. All British visions of the postwar world, except for a tiny band of Communists, had in common the overwhelming priority of keeping the Americans engaged in Europe.

At the end of World War I, the United States was already the world's biggest and richest economy, but not a superpower. At the end of World War II, it was the sole superpower. As successive American administrations were to learn, greater wealth and power turned out to involve more rather than less interdependence. At the end of World War I, Woodrow Wilson's argument for America's continued engagement in European affairs fell on deaf ears. In 1944 the argument that the world had to be made safe for the United States no longer seemed far-fetched. Pearl Harbor had shattered, once and for all, the American illusion that two oceans could protect it from foreign security threats.

According to historian John Gaddis, Roosevelt's wartime priorities were supporting the Allies, since the United States could not defeat Japan and Nazi Germany alone; winning their cooperation in shaping postwar settlements, since no lasting peace was possible without Soviet participation; insuring a multilateral approach to security; and preventing another Great Depression. Finally, because the United States was a democracy and politicians had to defer to popular opinion, Roosevelt was committed to convincing the American people that a return to prewar isolationism was unthinkable.

At the Hotel Majestic in Paris in 1919, Keynes had been one of hundreds of technical advisors with little hope of being heard and still less hope of shaping the outcome. At the Mount Washington Hotel in 1944, he was a pooh-bah, to use Lydia's favorite expression. The Allies had learned from experience. They now assumed that peace depended on economic revival. In 1918 that presumption had been shared by only a few— Schumpeter, Keynes, and Fisher among them—but hardly by the leaders of the victorious nations or their electorates.

Britain's bankrupt status and financial dependence on the United States meant that the Americans would largely determine the outcome while putting on an appearance of cooperation. On their side, although Treasury Secretary Morgenthau was nominally in charge, Harry Dexter White, his deputy, was the only one "who knows the complete matter" and "who can prevent a vote on anything he doesn't want voted on." [11] White orchestrated everything from press conferences to having transcripts typed and distributed.

Keynes, typically, took little trouble to disguise the fact that he was ramming his views down the throats of the banking committee that he chaired. Morgenthau had to go around to Keynes's suite and "ask him would he please go slow and talk louder and have his papers in better arrangement." [12] Skidelsky points out that if Keynes was not inclusive, he was at least efficient, and that his haste in rushing through the agenda reflected exhaustion and a growing determination to get away as soon as possible. Keynes gave the final speech at the banquet, his arrival prompting the entire meeting to stand up, silently, until he made his way to the dais and sat down.

• • •

"The Soviet Union is a coming country, Britain is a going country," Harry White told Keynes at one point in their long and difficult negotiations.[13] As Skidelsky points out, Keynes was sometimes puzzled by White's obsession with Russia and often outraged by his hostility to Britain. What he did not apparently suspect was that his most influential American disciples—and, more often than not, adversaries at the negotiating table—were passing government secrets to the Soviet Union and helping the Soviets to spy on him and other delegates. Among the gaggle of government economists White brought with him to Bretton Woods were a dozen or more employees of the Treasury's Monetary Research Division who were members of the "Silvermaster ring" of agents for the KGB.

The wartime alliance, Soviet heroism and sacrifice in defeating Germany, and the role of European Communists in the resistance all explain why the first revelations that the Soviets had set up a large-scale espionage operation seemed at first incredible, and later so shocking. Most disturbing was the Soviets' reliance on a fifth column of American citizens so reminiscent of the highly successful Nazi strategy of relying on a network of sympathizers in Europe. The newly burnished image of the Soviet Union explains not only why FDR and Truman were slow to accept that World War II would be followed by a Cold War, but also what now seems unfathomable: how some of the brightest and best were willing to serve as spies, agents of influence, and apologists for a foreign regime and why most, apparently, had no regrets. They did what they did for the sake of "mankind."

Even in the depths of the Great Depression, the Communist Party of the United States of America (CPUSA) never remotely attained the status of a mass political movement, much less an independent one. Its membership peaked in 1944 at eighty thousand or so, the overwhelming majority of members drifted away in less than a year, and it exerted scant influence beyond a few neighborhoods in the Bay Area, Boston, and New York and a handful of trade unions. The spies were sometimes poor or economically insecure, often first in their family to attend university. Many smarted under casual anti-Semitism and snobbery. The rise of Hitler and Franco, with their explicitly anti-intellectual and militaristic threat to civilization, gave the Party some cachet at universities. Fighting the Great Depression became a political movement, like Civil Rights in the fifties and sixties. Just as physicists at the Manhattan Project saw themselves as part of the war effort, cranking out forecasts at Treasury was part of the fight to defeat fascism.

In the 1930s, Lauchlin Currie had been an instructor at Harvard and had coauthored several prostimulus and New Deal manifestos with his best friend, Harry Dexter White. In 1939 he become one of six adminis-trative assistants on the president's staff and was soon advising Roosevelt on momentous matters such as mobilizing the economy for war, the wartime budget, and Lend-Lease for China. Currie organized the Flying Tigers. He practically ran Lend-Lease for China and was closely involved in US-British and US-Russian loan negotiations, and in the talks leading up to the Bretton Woods conference. Compelling evidence from multiple independent sources shows that Currie and White were not innocent vic-tims of dirty anti–New Deal politics, and certainly not of McCarthyism. The charges against them were made by two independent sources and cor-roborated by Soviet cables captured and encrypted by the US government long before Senator Joseph McCarthy made his sensational claims, and confirmed decades later in material from the KGB archives.

The charge against Currie was that he, and possibly at the behest of the president, pressured the OSS to return purloined Soviet cipher traffic and to suspend encryption operations. The evidence against Harry Dexter White was particularly damning. According to two of his biographers, David Rees and R. Bruce Craig, Whittaker Chambers, a *Time* magazine editor and former agent of the GRU, Russia's foreign intelligence ser-vice, who went to the assistant secretary of state in 1939 with the names of other Soviet agents, volunteered that White and Currie were agents. Chambers produced copies of a Treasury document that White had given him to deliver to the GRU (Chief Intelligence Directorate). His charges were corroborated independently by at least two other ex-agents. One Venona cable, dated November 1944, concerns an offer to White's wife, de-livered by Nathan Gregory Silvermaster, to help with college tuition for the Whites' daughter. Two other cables document unauthorized discussions between White and a KGB general, Vitaly Pavlov, including one in 1941 over lunch in a Washington restaurant.

Although Moscow valued them as spies, Currie's and White's real importance was as agents of influence. Occupying positions of great sensitivity, reach, and authority, they took actions and promoted measures that may or may not have served the interests of their government but were definitely intended to advance those of the Soviet Union. Ironically, they were as clueless about Soviet intentions as the most naïve American politician. Unlike FDR and Truman, whose views shifted sharply after the Yalta conference in 1945, these calculating, hard-nosed, duplicitous men reacted with the shocked incomprehension of jilted lovers when Stalin made fools of them.

The generation that came to economics during or as a direct consequence of the Great Depression seized the message of *The General Theory of Employment, Interest and Money* like drowning men lunging toward a lifeline. Keynes was their hero and they were his disciples—intellectual disciples, that is; the "Keynesian" label did not imply support for Keynes's policy proposals, much less his politics. Some were political conservatives. Some, particularly in Europe, were Socialists. Most fell within the spectrum defined by mainstream parties. That some rose to positions of power and influence and used those positions to pursue hidden agendas out of loyalty to a totalitarian regime says a great deal about them and their times, but very little about Keynesian ideas, much less about Keynes the man— except perhaps that, like everyone else, he could not imagine how such smart men could be so stupid or so bad.

Chapter XV

The Road from Serfdom:
Hayek and the German Miracle

It cannot be said too often—at any rate, it is not being said nearly
often enough—that collectivism is not inherently democratic,
but, on the contrary, gives to a tyrannical minority such powers
as the Spanish Inquisitors never dreamed of. . . .

Since the vast majority of people would far rather have State
regimentation than slumps and unemployment, the drift towards
collectivism is bound to continue if popular opinion has any say
in the matter.

—George Orwell, review of The Road to Serfdom, *1944*[1]

On March 31, 1945, Isaiah Berlin reported in his weekly dispatch from
Washington that *"The Reader's Digest,* which in effect is the voice of Big
Business, has printed a digest of Professor Hayek's notorious work" and
that "the imminent arrival of the Professor himself is eagerly anticipated
by the anti–Bretton Woods party, who expect him to act as the heavy artillery."[2]

Hayek's transatlantic crossing "by slow convoy" in stormy March
weather was considerably less agreeable than Keynes's the previous June,
but when he stepped onto the pier in New York, he was greeted by flashing
cameras and a mob of reporters. Three thousand people turned up at New
York University for his first lecture, and for the next six weeks—four weeks
longer than he had originally planned to stay in the United States—his

schedule of speeches, radio broadcasts, and press interviews was so tightly packed that he could hardly manage a brief late-night rendezvous with his old friend Fritz Machlup, who had been faithfully sending Hayek food parcels with Spam, nuts, prunes, rice, and the like since 1943.

"The voice of Big Business" had turned Hayek into an instant celebrity. A front-page *New York Times* book review by *Newsweek* writer Henry Hazlitt did the rest. The sensational success of *The Road to Serfdom* was partly timing. In the spring of 1945, the recently concluded Yalta conference and the imminent defeat of Nazi Germany by the Red Army had focused American public opinion on postwar settlements and, in particular, on future US-Soviet relations. Among the issues before Congress were a trade bill, a huge loan to the British, and, of course, ratification of the global monetary agreement endorsed at Bretton Woods the previous July—all administration initiatives to which Republicans were strongly opposed. Although most of the references in Hayek's book were to Nazi Germany, not Stalin's Soviet Union, his antistatist message resonated with opponents of the New Deal. As Berlin predicted, American conservatives were ecstatic and rushed to embrace the Viennese professor. But Hayek proved to be an unreliable poster boy. In his next dispatch, Berlin reported with some amusement that the American Bankers Association was wavering in its opposition to the Bretton Woods Treaty, thanks "curiously enough" to a Professor Hayek, who, "at a meeting of influential New York bankers attended by both Winthrop Aldrich and various Morgan partners as well as by Mr. Herbert Hoover and others, argued passionately in favor of Bretton Woods."[3]

A month later, Berlin gloated, "Professor Friedrich von Hayek, upon whom the economic Tories in this country placed so much hope, founded upon the Professor's indubitably anti–New Deal views, has proved a most embarrassing ally to them since his passion for free trade makes him no less hostile to tariffs and monopolies."[4]

Unbeknownst to his Republican sponsors, Hayek had begun to warm to FDR before the war. "I suppose Roosevelt knows what he does," he wrote to Machlup, confessing that Roosevelt's 1938 "Message to Congress on the Concentration of Economic Power" had prompted "a considerable revision of my views about him." [5] Hayek was by no means intimidated by the discomfiture and embarrassment of his supporters. On his final night in Washington, Albert Hawkes, a Republican senator from New Jersey, gave a dinner for him. Bored and disappointed by Hayek's abstract argument and dry delivery, another senator rose to demand his opinion on a piece of pending trade legislation. Hayek responded icily, "Gentlemen, if you have any comprehension of my philosophy at all, you must know that the one thing I stand for above all else is free trade throughout the world. The reciprocal trade program is intended to expend world trade, and so naturally I would be for such a measure."

The *Washington Post* columnist Marquis Childs, who was among the guests, reported gleefully that "the temperature in the room went down at least ten degrees since the Republican Party had decided to take a stand against the extension of the trade program." The cooling-off process continued when, a little later, Hayek repeated that while he did not like many of the features of the Bretton Woods Monetary Agreement, he was in favor of it. The alternative to such an agreement, he said, was "too grim to contemplate." [6]

Congress gave its approval to the Bretton Woods Treaty in July. The British Parliament waited until December, refusing its imprimatur until after Washington finally gave the green light to an $8.8 billion loan to Britain that Keynes had given so much to obtain. The choice between autarky versus globalization, free trade versus protection, had been made. The Russians shocked the Roosevelt administration—and its own moles—by refusing to ratify the treaty. George Kennan, the diplomat and architect of the Truman Doctrine, recalled:

> Nowhere in Washington had the hopes entertained for post-war collaboration with Russia been more elaborate, more naïve, or more tenaciously (one might almost say ferociously) pursued than in the Treasury Department. Now, at long last, with the incomprehensible unwillingness of Moscow to adhere to the Bank and the Fund, the dream seemed to be shattered, and the Department of State passed onto the embassy, in tones of bland innocence, the anguished cry of bewilderment that had floated

over the roof of the White House from the Treasury Department on the other side. How did one explain such behavior on the part of the Soviet government? What lay behind it?[7]

In contrast to Churchill, FDR and Truman had viewed Stalin very much as Neville Chamberlain had viewed Hitler prior to 1938: as a ruler with legitimate grievances and limited aims who would make deals and live up to them if handled properly. They took big-power rivalry and commercial conflicts for granted but assumed that the United States and the Soviets had a common interest in ensuring that those conflicts took place within a cooperative framework. But the view that Stalin could be negotiated with began to crumble even before FDR's death of a cerebral hemorrhage on April 12, 1945, two weeks after Hayek's arrival in America. The dictator's abrupt refusal to join the IMF and the World Bank was one of the decisions that led to a radical reappraisal, beginning with the famous "Long Telegram" sent by George Kennan, the number-two minister in the US Embassy in Moscow, to the secretary of state in February 1946, describing a Soviet Union that did, indeed, resemble the totalitarian empires of George Orwell's imagination.

Keynes and Hayek never fully resolved their long-running debate over how much and what kind of government intervention in the economy is compatible with a free society. Nonetheless, Keynes endorsed *The Road to Serfdom* and nominated Hayek, rather than his disciple Joan Robinson, for membership in the British Academy. When Keynes's heart finally gave out on April 21, 1946, Hayek wrote to Lydia that Keynes was "the one really great man I ever knew, and for whom I had unbounded admiration."[8]

By early 1947, Keynes's hopeful vision of one world was half in ruins. One after the other, Poland, Hungary, and Romania fell to Soviet domination. Churchill had delivered his Iron Curtain speech. Truman announced that the United States would "support free peoples who are resisting attempted subjugation by armed minorities or by outside pressures . . . primarily through economic and financial aid which is essential to economic stability and orderly political processes."[9]

Hayek had avoided returning to Vienna at the end of the war. His closest friends were either dead or in exile abroad. After the Yalta conference, Stalin had postponed the Red Army's assault on Berlin to grab what he saw as a valuable bargaining chip. After heavy aerial bombardment and fierce street-to-street combat, Vienna fell to the Russians. Some of her finest buildings were reduced to rubble. Water, electricity, and gas lines were destroyed. Abandoned by the police and other local authorities, defenseless residents were terrorized by criminal bands. The Soviet assault forces showed some restraint toward the civilian population, but the second wave of troops to arrive in the city engaged in a six-week frenzy of rape, looting, and violence.

During the war Hayek had dreamed of re-creating his old *Geist-Kreis* on the Continent as a way of demonstrating that the ideals of the European Enlightenment were still alive: "The old liberal who adheres to a traditional creed merely out of tradition . . . is not of much use for our purpose. What we need are people who have faced the arguments from the other side, who have struggled with them and fought themselves through to a position from which they can both critically meet the objection against it and justify their views."[10] On his second visit to the United States, the conservative Volker Fund offered to sponsor a conference to found a community of like-minded liberals. Hayek convened the first meeting of the Mont Pelerin Society in Switzerland on a hill overlooking Lake Geneva on April 10, 1947. The majority of attendees were European émigrés from the United States or Britain, including Karl Popper, Ludwig von Mises, and Fritz Machlup. A contingent from the University of Chicago included Milton Friedman and Aaron Director. Henry Hazlitt from *Newsweek* and John Davenport from *Fortune* were there. The assembled individualists could not muster a unanimous vote in favor of the institution of private property, but did so with respect to the principle of individual freedom. They readily agreed that the organization would not publish books or periodicals, engage in political activity, or issue statements, but they rejected Hayek's proposal that they call themselves the Acton-Tocqueville Society after Frank Knight from the University of Chicago objected to naming the group after "two Roman Catholic aristocrats." [11] Ludwig von Mises created a scene during a debate on income distribution by accusing others of harboring Socialist sympathies. Walter Eucken, an economist from Germany, ate his first orange since before the war. When three days of wide-ranging discussion threatened to end without a statement of principles, Lionel Robbins, a veteran of countless committees, managed to draft one that all but Maurice Allais of France felt able to sign. Noting that "freedom of thought and expression, is threatened by the spread of creeds which, claiming the privilege of tolerance when in the position of a minority, seek only to establish a position of power in which they can suppress and obliterate all views but their own," [12] the statement emphasized free enterprise, opposition to historical fatalism, and the obligation of nations as well as individuals to be bound by moral codes and, above all, support for complete intellectual freedom.

As soon as the conference disbanded, Hayek set out for Vienna. The condition of the city and its inhabitants was far worse than anything he had been able to imagine. Under occupation by the four allies for three long years, Vienna was as seedy, demoralized, and dark as it would appear to audiences who saw *The Third Man,* the film noir written by the English novelist Graham Greene, with its immortal line, added by the director and star, Orson Welles: "In Italy for thirty years under the Borgias they had warfare, terror, murder, bloodshed—they produced Michelangelo, Leonardo da Vinci, and the Renaissance. In Switzerland they had brotherly love, five hundred years of democracy, and peace, and what did they produce? The cuckoo clock." [13]

The Russians were still in charge of the eastern suburbs, feared and despised by the Viennese. Hayek protested that the Allies were treating Austria "much worse than Italy or any of the other countries which joined Germany voluntarily." The occupation authorities were applying essentially the same guidelines as in Germany, which meant that virtually all economic activity—except Harry Lime's black market—was banned. Hayek complained, "the Austrians have been prevented from helping themselves to get out of a desperate economic position." [14]

By one of those coincidences that seem to multiply in extraordinary times, Hayek once again ran into his cousin Ludwig Wittgenstein on a train leaving Vienna for Munich. Wittgenstein seemed more morose and angry than ever. He had spent most of his time in the Russian sector, where the Red Army had used the house Wittgenstein had designed and built for one of his sisters as a stable and a garage. Wittgenstein had been a great admirer of the Bolsheviks and had thought seriously of immigrating to Russia in the 1930s.[15] Now, Hayek thought, the philosopher behaved as if he had met the Russians "in the flesh for the first time and that this had shattered all his illusions."

Hayek's visit to Vienna was followed by a tour, arranged by the British Council, of a half dozen German cities. He found Cologne, including its great cathedral, "laid absolutely flat by the war; there didn't seem to be a city left, just great piles of rubble. I climbed through the rubble into an underground big hole to speak." In Darmstadt, he had "my most moving experience as a university lecturer," he wrote to Machlup.

> I didn't have any idea the Germans knew anything about me at that time; and I gave a lecture to an audience so crowded that the students couldn't get in, in an enormous lecture hall. And I discovered then that people were circulating hand-typed copies of *The Road to Serfdom* in German, although it hadn't been published in Germany yet.[16]

Characteristically, Hayek's first thought on returning to London was to organize a drive to collect books published since 1938 that censorship and war had kept out of the hands of Austrian and German scholars. By year's end, the committee had already collected some 2,500 volumes, which were, with great difficulty, eventually shipped to Vienna.

In 1947 the question of how to deal with Germany was still unsettled. Keynes, White, and their respective governments had been embroiled in a bitter debate beginning within weeks of D-day three years before. White was an aggressive advocate of the deindustrialization of Germany, while Keynes argued for economic integration and recovery. Keynes first learned of the Morgenthau Plan from the papers a few weeks later in July 1944. The Versailles Treaty, which he had repeatedly assailed as "Carthaginian" throughout the 1920s and which he blamed for another world war, was punitive. But it was an attempt by the victors to make Germany pay the costs of the war. The Morgenthau Plan was designed to return Germany, a modern economy, to its eighteenth-century preindustrial state. The plan had two strengths, Keynes observed in a letter to the Chancellor of the Exchequer, John Anderson: It was being proposed at a moment of bitter fighting and horrendous casualties when extreme measures—even geno-cidal ones—had become acceptable. It was a plan. The State Department and the War Department had nothing as coherent.

Keynes did not speak out, because he could not afford to alienate Morgenthau or White. He saw that instantly. He eased his conscience by predicting that the plan would never pass Congress. In this he was correct. By the time Eisenhower assumed control of southern Germany in 1945, the Morgenthau Plan had been shelved. But the lack of a positive vision or concrete counterproposal left a vacuum, and Keynes's failure to speak out still had consequences. In the absence of a positive plan, "Morgen-thau principles and Morgenthau men" governed Germany for three full years. As early as June 1945, Austin Robinson, on a fact-finding mission for the Treasury, reported to Keynes that he "felt more worried about the economic system that has completely stopped than about the physical damage." He found "no papers . . . no telephones that operate over long distances, little true communication of any sort." Instead "the Germany of the towns is in ruins, with its factories flat, its houses burnt out or bombed out, and its life dead. The Germany of the country[side] still vigorous, the work of the fields proceeding normally . . . lacking only incentives to sell to the towns that have so little to offer in exchange for food."[17]

The refusal to permit a resumption of economic activity in Germany had two consequences unforeseen by the American authorities. First, the collapse of the German economy prevented the rest of Europe from recovering. Second, the cost of the occupation to American and British taxpayers soared. The price tag had, according to conservative estimates, multiplied by a factor of three. Robinson warned Keynes that if the Russians "or just possibly the French" extracted too much in reparations, Britain "would have to provide and pay for imports to feed and maintain our zone sufficiently to prevent starvation and disaster."[18] Having witnessed the same phenomenon after World War I, Keynes responded immediately: "For goodness sake, see that we don't have to pay the reparations *this* time."[19]

The United States ultimately adopted the Marshall Plan. With Europe starving and in danger of falling into the Communist camp, the Marshall Plan was a natural heir to Bretton Woods and the commitment of Britain and the United States to create institutions that could help promote growth and stability among the free world's economies. The shift from nationalism to a global perspective in economic policy was thus part of the changing perceptions about security and postwar diplomatic and military strategy. The notion that economic collapse had produced totalitarian regimes created American resolve to restore the economic health of Europe that became more urgent when it became clear in 1947 that Europe was not recovering on its own. Economic revival was in the interest of American business, as well as a necessary condition for European self-defense. Truman's rationale helped win over business leaders to massive government spending on aid and the military in peacetime.

Although Germany got relatively little Marshall aid, Germany's recovery was so strong that it was quickly labeled Wirtschaftswunder or economic miracle. In the three years after the currency reform of 1948, per capita output jumped an average of 15 percent every year. By 1950, despite the destruction of the war and the removal of machinery by Russians, it was 94 percent of prewar level.

What happened? Ludwig Erhard, the finance minister, attributed the Wirtschaftswunder to the introduction of a new currency and lifting of price controls in 1948. "More perhaps than any other economy," he recalled, "the German one experienced the economic and supra-economic consequences of an economic and trading policy subjected to the extremes of nationalism, autarchy and government control. We have learned the lesson." The liberalization "awakened entrepreneurial impulses. The worker became ready to work, the trader to sell, and the economy . . . to produce . . . Hitherto there had been a premium on stagnation. Foreign trade moved languidly in a framework provided by allied instructions. Goods were lacking; there was a universal cry for supplies; yet the economic impulse was wanting."[20]

For Hayek, Germany's rise from the ashes was both a vindication of his faith in free markets, free trade, and sound money, and a hopeful portent that the liberal European civilization he loved was not, after all, doomed to extinction.

When he got an invitaion to teach at the University of Chicago, he resigned from the LSE, got a divorce, and married his longtime lover. He indulged his passion for book collecting and intellectual biography by writing a charming account of John Stuart Mill's partnership with Harriet Taylor, and spent his honeymoon retracing Mill's famous pilgrimage from London to Rome.

Hayek's turn as a darling of American conservatives was short-lived. He despised most Republican politicians, all cars, and practically everything else about life in America, including the absence of universal health insurance and government-sponsored pensions. Homesick for Europe and no longer welcome at the LSE, he finally settled at the University of Salzburg.

In 1974, the Swedish Academy of Sciences plucked Hayek out of obscurity by awarding him a Nobel Prize for his "penetrating analysis of the interdependence of economic, social and institutional phenomena." Ironically, he shared it with Swedish socialist Gunnar Myrdal. A few years later, his *Constitution of Liberty* became the bible of Margaret Thatcher's conservative revival. And in the early 1990s, the collapse of the Soviet Union and the spread of free market reforms in Eastern Europe and Asia made him a hero among conservatives around the globe.

Chapter XVI

Instruments of Mastery:
Samuelson Goes to Washington

I don't care who writes the nation's laws—or crafts its advanced
treaties—if I can write its economics textbooks.

—Paul A. Samuelson [1]

Paul Anthony Samuelson, the anonymous mind behind the government
report to which President Roosevelt referred in his "radical" State of the
Union message, had whiled away the first months of the war force-feeding
economics to bored engineering students and producing endless calculations for the army at MIT's Radiation Lab.[2] As early as 1940, Lauchlin
Currie, FDR's economics aide, had suggested to the president that it was
not too early for the United States to begin planning for the postwar era.
The president agreed, and Currie promptly recruited a new class of freshman brain trusters to work at the National Resources Planning Board,
the nation's first and only planning agency, run by the president's uncle
Frederic A. Delano. Samuelson, a twenty-seven-year-old Harvard wun-
derkind, newly minted PhD, and MIT assistant professor, soon became
the titular head of a group of twenty or so economists and a bunch of
graduate students from Johns Hopkins University assigned to calculate
possible trajectories for the postwar economy and propose solutions to
potential problems.[3] To reassure his superiors that the new Keynesian economics was no more subversive than a branch of accounting, Samuelson
made a point of wearing a green eyeshade at White House briefings.

On the morning after Labor Day 1944, for the first time in nearly a year, this foot soldier in the Roosevelt administration's vast wartime army of university consultants was back in Washington, D.C. Short, wiry, and crew-cut, Samuelson had come down from Boston by overnight train. Nattily dressed in a suit and bow tie, he made the rounds of "sweltering temporaries" that had sprung up all over the capital, buttonholing former colleagues and students, pumping them for news and gossip.

Samuelson could "smell cuts in war production."[4] Every office he visited was awash in desk calculators, messy piles of green sheets, and stacks of budget reports. With the end of the war now certain, Washington's attention was shifting from the problems of wartime production to those of conversion to a peacetime economy. Hundreds of bureaucrats were busy calculating how much military procurement could be scaled back, how many GIs could be discharged, how long it would take to convert tank production lines into car production lines. The first round of reductions was slated to begin that fall, perhaps not coincidentally during the 1944 presidential election campaign, which pitted the president against Republican Thomas E. Dewey, who held FDR's old job of governor of New York. As it turned out, the Allied sweep through Europe stalled that fall at the Battle of the Bulge, and the actual reconversion was postponed until early 1945.[5]

Despite the sultry temperature and oppressive humidity, Samuelson found the mood in Washington among "experts," as well as Congress, unexpectedly sanguine. The day before, the New York Times had run a headline: "Boom After War Almost Certain."[6] He was appalled. The potential problems were staggering: 11 million men and women were in uniform, and 16 million—almost a third of the labor force—were working in defense plants. In 1943 the federal government had spent more than $60 billion—nearly half the nation's annual output—and nearly seven times as much as in 1940. The more Samuelson looked beyond the war, the more worried he felt.

His mood coincided with that of other Keynesians who took for granted that American business could increase production, efficiency, and per capita income year in and year out but were less certain that businesses and households could be counted on to spend, rather than save, the profits and wages that all this activity generated. Increasingly, Samuelson leaned toward the view that the tendency of the economy to stagnate was not necessarily a transient illness caused by monetary policy mistakes or external shocks, but rather a chronic disease. David M. Kennedy, the economic historian, observes that the tenor and conclusions of Samuelson's report for the NRPB reflected two sources. One was Keynes's judgment, expressed in his 1940 pamphlet *How to Pay for the War,* of the British economy's poor postwar prospects absent a major and constant infusion of government spending.[7] The other was that of the administration's Keynesian advisors, notably Currie, White, and Alvin Hansen, a Harvard professor and a consultant for the NRPB and the Federal Reserve. It was Hansen who had rallied the conservative department's graduate students and instructors (the "lumpen proletariat," Samuelson liked to say) to the Keynesian banner. If anything, Kennedy points out, Keynes's American disciples were even more pessimistic than their leader. As early as 1938, the year Hansen arrived at Harvard from the Midwest, he published a book, *Full Recovery or Stagnation,* in which he already foresaw a dismal postwar future.

Samuelson, who wrote as fast and breezily as he talked, launched a stellar second career in journalism with a provocative two-part series for the *New Republic* on "the coming economic crisis."[8] His tone was energetic, not fatalistic. Implying that the problem, though dire, was fixable, he urged the same steps as he had in the 1942 NRPB report: slow down demobilization and keep government spending high. The piece radiated confidence that, as New Dealer Chester Bowles once remarked: "We have seen the last of our great depressions for the simple reason that the public [is] wise enough to know that it doesn't have to stand for one."[9]

Samuelson was a child of the Jewish exodus out of Russia to America, the World War I boom in the Midwest, and the go-go twenties. He was born in Gary, Indiana, in 1915, a fact to which he later attributed his lifelong zest for economics and stock market speculation. Gary was not yet an exurb of Chicago. Instead it was a gritty company town of behemoth steel mills and brand-new tenements rising out of the prairie and shrouded in its own special atmosphere of soot, smoke, and money. During World War I, the mills blazed day and night. Steelworkers, mostly immigrants, had the opportunity to work 12/7. When factory hands got sick, they went to the druggist instead of the doctor to avoid losing a day's pay. Frank Samuelson was in the happy position of being one of the town's few pharmacists. A first-generation Jewish immigrant, he spoke Russian and Polish to his customers.

He was also a small-time real estate speculator, as was the typical midwesterner with cash to spare, whether saved or borrowed. The war boom had spilled into the farm economy and sent grain prices into the stratosphere. Farmers, who had never had it so good, borrowed money and poured it into more acreage and machinery. And for several years, they and Frank Samuelson, who invested in property in downtown Gary, prospered. Like Gopher Prairie, the fictional town in Sinclair Lewis's *Main Street,* Gary was full of overachievers like Frank Samuelson and their discontented wives, who despised the town for its ugliness and resented their husbands for marooning them a full day's travel from Chicago. Pretty, vain, and "a great snob," Ella Lipton Samuelson alternately egged on her husband and heaped scorn on him. A woman of uncertain temper and a passionate desire to become a famous hat designer, she longed for daughters. Instead she had three sons whom she farmed out, one after the other, to foster parents not long after they were old enough to walk.

At age seventeen months, the blond, blue-eyed toddler was sent to a farm in Wheeler, Indiana, a crossroads standing amid endless fields of wheat, without electricity, indoor plumbing, a telephone, or an automobile. Later, Samuelson said, "I did experience first hand, in my virtual infancy, the disappearance of the horse economy, the arrival of indoor plumbing and electric lighting. After that radio waves through the air or TV pictures left one blasé." [10] He did not see his mother again until he was ready to start kindergarten.

Maternal abandonment can produce coldness and detachment, but it can also create a longing for attachment and a desire to please. In Samuelson's case, it did a little of both. His foster mother became the first of the many women in his life who adored him: from wives and secretaries to daughters and dogs. Unlike his birth mother, she was ample, warm, kind, and a good cook.

When five-year-old Paul went home again, the armistice had been signed, and the new Federal Reserve was turning off the credit spigot in an effort to reverse wartime inflation. In England and France, the biggest markets for American wheat, central banks were doing the same. In a matter of months, grain prices had fallen by half, the steel mills were standing idle, and banks were failing in droves. "Now, bank failures were not a strange and unfamiliar phenomenon in my part of Indiana," Samuelson recalled. "The farms that were mortgaged up and fully equipped at the peak of the War prosperity were hard hit by the drop in grain prices. And so country banks failed." Inevitably, land prices collapsed, and so did the Samuelsons' financial security.

The economic recovery that began in mid-1921 did little to revive the battered farm economy or the family finances. For four years, Frank Samuelson watched his once-thriving pharmacy business melt away. Finally, in the summer of 1925, lured by delicious visions of warm winters and tropical bounty—oranges at the front door—and tired of his wife's constant scolding, he handed the keys of his drugstore to a new owner. He and Ella got in their car and headed south to Miami, joining tens of thousands of other families in the great Florida land rush. Florida land looked like a sure bet: with 10 percent down, a doubling in price meant a 1,000 percent profit on the original investment. Never mind that the "dream development" was "midway between pine thicket and swamp." [11]

When their parents left Gary, Samuelson, ten, and his twelve-and-one-half-year-old brother, Harold, were back in Wheeler, where they always spent summers. Around Labor Day, they were summoned by their parents. The boys rode from Chicago to Miami in a Pullman. Samuelson recalled that his first sight when he got off the train was not his mother or father but "men in plus-four knickerbockers on the streets buying and selling land." [12]

By mid-1925, the boom had spread all the way north to Jacksonville, a sleepy farm town near the Atlantic Ocean, 350 miles from Miami. It had also attracted an already infamous con man named Charles Ponzi, who sold parcels for $10 that turned out to be sixty-five miles (as the crow flies) from Jacksonville and 1/23 of an acre. In 1926 faith that Florida's streets were lined with gold was beginning to wane, and the influx of new buyers began to tail off. Inevitably, prices did too. Then came two hurricanes, and what looked like a pause in a perpetual upward climb became a plunge. Frank Samuelson lost most of his remaining money and accumulated more of his wife's reproaches. "She didn't hold a lot in," Paul said of his mother, who relished retelling the story of her husband's foolish bets long after his premature death from heart disease at age forty-eight. The nature of the family's economic problem was clear even to a ten-year-old.

Two years later, the Samuelsons were back in the Midwest, settling on Chicago's South Side, then as now a middle-class enclave squeezed between Lake Michigan and an African-American ghetto. The Chicago economy was booming once more. The stench from the stockyards mingled with smog from the steel mills in Gary that came drifting across the lake. Paul entered Hyde Park High School and joined the rest of the country in studying the stock pages daily, often with his high school math teacher.

The cult of F. Scott Fitzgerald, author of *The Great Gatsby,* was at its height. Samuelson wrote stories for the school's literary magazine featuring worldly-wise, cynical youths who fell in and out of love in the time it took them to change their clothes and spit out one-liners like "For the love of Mike, Pat, Pete, and the other seven apostles, shut up!" [13] Living with a mother who was "a screamer," he fantasized about escaping to an eastern college with "a white chapel tower" in a "peaceful green village." [14] By the time Samuelson graduated from high school in 1931 at age sixteen, a Great Depression was settling on Main Streets all over America like a long winter night. Going east for college was no longer in the cards, if it had ever been a realistic possibility. So Samuelson enrolled at the University of Chicago in January 1932, declared a math major, and continued to live at home.

Being trapped in the Midwest had unexpected benefits. Far from the backwater he feared, Chicago was a buzzing hive of intellectual and political activity and a meeting place for economists who wanted Washington to do more to fight the depression. A mix of fiscally conservative midwesterners and Burkean liberals of Central European extraction, the Chicago faculty was alarmed and frustrated by Washington's ineffectual response to the crisis and eager to advise a more activist approach.

Samuelson learned from his freshman tutor that "the world's leading economist," John Maynard Keynes, had spent the previous summer lecturing at the university.[15] His first economics professor was Aaron Director, "a very dry, confident, reactionary economist" and the future brother-in-law of Milton Friedman, who had "quite a big impact" on him. Director's first lecture, on Thomas Malthus's theory of population, got him hooked on economics, he later said. Another professor was Jacob Viner, a Canadian of Romanian extraction with a terrifying reputation as the toughest grader at Chicago. After Roosevelt's inauguration, he became one of Treasury Secretary Henry Morgenthau's closest outside advisors, staffing the Treasury, the Federal Reserve, and the New Deal agencies with dozens of his students. A close friend of Schumpeter and Hayek, Viner became one of the most vocal and influential American critics of Keynes's *General Theory of Employment, Interest, and Money*. He agreed with Keynes on policy and on the need for deficit spending to fight the depression. However, he held that Keynes's theory was not "general" at all but valid only in the short run, and fell apart if applied to longer time frames.

During Samuelson's first month at Chicago, the university hosted a conference at which Irving Fisher, the most famous and simultaneously most notorious American economist, and a bevy of other monetary experts debated how the Hoover administration should fight the depression. Director and Viner both signed Fisher's telegram urging the president to launch an aggressive stimulus plan.

When Samuelson decided three years later that he would make a better economist than mathematician and won a scholarship to graduate school, he chose Harvard over Chicago. The presence of Edward Chamberlin, who had recently published the groundbreaking *The Theory of Monopolistic Competition*, was an attraction, but getting away from home and the fantasy of the "peaceful green village" were far bigger lures. Arriving in Cambridge in the third year of the Roosevelt recovery, Samuelson quickly discovered that Harvard's senior faculty, while politically to the left of Chicago's, was intellectually far more conservative.

A Canadian graduate student who had been attending Keynes's lectures in Cambridge arrived at Harvard during Samuelson's first semester in the fall of 1936. Robert Bryce gave a paper summarizing the ideas in Keynes's as yet unpublished *General Theory.* He emphasized public spending to combat unemployment without fully explaining the underlying theory, leaving Samuelson, who did not regard fiscal activism as a new or uniquely "Keynesian" idea, somewhat puzzled over what the fuss was about. But since the economy was clearly rebounding, he took it for granted that the New Deal was responsible, and he took it on faith that Keynes had a new, rigorous, internally consistent theory explaining how it could be so. "In the end I asked myself why do I refuse a paradigm that enables me to understand the Roosevelt upturn from 1933 'til 1937?" [16]

When Nicholas Kaldor, a Marxo-Keynesian and economic advisor to the Labour Party, visited in 1936, he attended what he thought to be a brilliant talk by a faculty star. "Congratulations, Professor Chamberlin," he prefaced his question to the speaker. The "Professor" turned out to be Samuelson, a first-year graduate student. Samuelson took a class from the mathematician Edwin Bidwell Wilson, Willard Gibbs's last disciple at Yale. He and Schumpeter, who had instantly taken up Samuelson as a protégé, comprised half the students. He took another course with the brilliant Russian émigré and future Nobel laureate Wassily Leontief. Recalled the Japanese economist Tsuru Shigeto, Samuelson's best friend in graduate school, "Leontief, as is well known, was not very eloquent, and he would make a frequent use of a blackboard, drawing a couple of lines which crossed with each other and would start saying: 'You see at this point of intersection. . . .' Thereupon Paul would intervene: 'Yes, that is the point of. . . .' But he cannot finish the sentence, for Leontief would immediately exclaim in approval 'That's right. You see what I mean.' He and Paul both knew each other, but neither of them would reveal it, and the rest of the class had to remain mystified." [17]

The following year, Samuelson became the first economist to be elected to the Society of Fellows, a remarkable Harvard institution inspired by the English university's tradition of high table. It demanded that young scholars from different disciplines suspend work toward their degrees for three years to . . . think. He suddenly found himself in the company of Willard Van Orman Quine, the logician; George Birkhoff, the inventor of lattice theory; Stanislaw Ulam, originator of the Teller-Ulam design for thermonuclear weapons; and other extraordinary mathematical minds.

A heady atmosphere and intellectual thrills were no substitute for a family. Within a year, Samuelson had married a fellow graduate student from Wisconsin, Marion Crawford. By the time the prohibition against finishing his PhD expired in May 1940 on his twenty-fifth birthday, Marion had also finished her PhD, and the young couple had had their first baby.

Like so many young men who came of age in the Great Depression, Samuelson was in a hurry. He horrified his European friends by listening to Beethoven's Ninth Symphony out of order so that he could minimize time wasted in flipping over his seventy-eights. Hoping for a tenure track offer from Harvard, he plunged into his dissertation. Marion did the typing. When he handed it in, it bore the title *Foundations of Economic Analysis*. *Foundations* was inspired partly by Schumpeter's 1931 lament about the crisis in economic theory and bore a family resemblance to Irving Fisher's dissertation. It was an ambitious attack on contemporary economic theory, using "simple arithmetic and logic" to show how much of the theory could be boiled down to simpler, more fundamental propositions. "I felt I was hacking my way through a jungle with a penknife," Samuelson said later. "It was a tangle of contradictions, overlaps, confusions." [18]

Foundations accomplished what Bertrand Russell's *Principia Mathematica* and John von Neumann's *Mathematical Foundations of Quantum Mechanics* sought to achieve—and what, in 1890, Marshall's *Principles of Economics* had achieved. Herbert Stein, a University of Chicago–trained New Dealer, offered the most intuitive explanation of Samuelson's achievement by comparing it to the pre-Fisher, pre-Keynes economics: if people were out of work, you gave them jobs. If people were out of work, you fiddled with something in one corner of the system—say, the money supply or tax rates—on the assumption that it would affect something at the far end of the system: employment. This was the practical implication of the new "economics of the whole," or macroeconomics. This is what was new about Fisher's and Keynes's economics.[19]

The emphasis on links between different parts of the economy and on indirect and secondary effects also explains why the new macroeconomics relied on mathematics. You cannot analyze an integrated system without math. The debate over whether its use to analyze economic problems is a good or bad thing crops up from time to time—as does the debate over the use of computers to prove mathematical theorems. Economists, like engineers, nuclear physicists, and composers, are problem solvers. If they are working on a problem that the old tools aren't quite suited to, they try the new ones. True, the older generation rarely sees the point and often finds it impossible to master new techniques, but to Samuelson's generation that came of age during the Great Depression and World War II, Willard Gibb's point that mathematics is a language seemed perfectly natural. The fear that using mathematics would cause other languages to wither turned out to be overblown. John von Neumann, one of several mathematicians who had a major impact on economics, could translate from German into English in real time and quote verbatim from Dickens. Samuelson's verbal virtuosity was even more pronounced.

It was probably no accident that *Foundations* was a product of the 1930s, an extraordinarily innovative decade. Samuelson, who took his generals at the end of his first year at Harvard, used the three years of his tenure as a Junior Fellow, the academic years 1937 to 1940, to produce the core of *Foundations of Economic Analysis. Foundations* "had no definite moment of conception," he recalled. "Gradually over the period 1936 to 1941, it got itself evolved."[20] When Samuelson defended his dissertation, Schumpeter is said to have turned to Leontief to ask, "Well . . . have we passed?" But like so many ideas and inventions of that pregnant era, *Foundations* was kept off the market by World War II. Unlike von Neumann's and Oskar Morgenstern's *Theory of Games and Economic Behavior,* Samuelson's doctoral dissertation had no influential champions or wealthy patrons. Indeed, Harold Burbank, the chairman of the Harvard Economics Department, was so hostile to it—whether because of an aversion to mathematics or Jews is hard to say—that he had the printing plates destroyed and insisted that Samuelson be offered only a temporary lectureship. When *Foundations* finally appeared in print in late 1947, it was all the more warmly received because the war had made the use of new tools and techniques seem natural. Samuelson won the John Bates Clark Medal, the equivalent of the Fields Medal for the best mathematician under age forty. Schumpeter proclaimed *Foundations* a masterpiece and wrote to his former student, "If I read in it in the evening the excitement interferes with my night's rest."[21]

Americans' fears about the postwar economy were rooted in the belief that the war, not the New Deal, was responsible for the economic recovery. Whereas the British were mostly concerned with preventing an outburst of inflation while rewarding the population for its enormous sacrifices, the worry for most Americans was that unemployment would return when Washington slashed military spending and millions of GIs were demobbed.

The National Resources Planning Board, a precursor to the President's Council of Economic Advisors, was charged with planning the economic transition to peace. Everett Hagen, Samuelson's coauthor on the NRPB report, was responsible for producing the administration's consensus forecast. By mid-1944, a sharp split had developed among Washington's economic experts. The New Dealers tended to be optimistic about postwar prospects. Keynesians tended to be pessimistic. Samuelson admitted that a restocking boom was likely at the end of the war, as business built up depleted inventories and replaced worn-out equipment and consumers took similar steps. But he thought that it would be short lived, overwhelmed by the huge military cuts.

Demobilization occurred even faster than Samuelson expected, but the crisis he predicted did not materialize. After a steep but brief recession in 1947, the economy rebounded rapidly. The onset of the Cold War caused the Truman administration to spend hundreds of millions on America's nuclear arsenal, even as spending on conventional ground forces plunged. But what Samuelson had failed to foresee was the magnitude of pent-up demand by consumers, starved for houses, cars, appliances, and other appurtenances of middle-class life and with plenty of savings in the bank. His embarrassingly wrong prediction slowed the spread of Keynesianism in academe, he always believed. Being disastrously wrong early in one's career was in some ways a salutary experience for someone who hated making mistakes and rarely did. It left Samuelson more skeptical of economic forecasts and more circumspect in the claims he made for policies he favored or opposed.

Demobilization became a bonanza for American colleges, MIT and its embryo economics department included. The only economic bill of rights that Congress passed in the wake of FDR's 1944 exhortation was the GI Bill. But that measure had a large and lasting effect on the postwar economy. In Britain, the Labour government would construct a cradle-to-grave welfare state to compensate the British people for their wartime sacrifices. The GI Bill was the American counterpart. The only serious opposition, David Kennedy points out, came from Samuelson's and Friedman's alma mater, the University of Chicago, and its famous president, Robert Hutchins, who warned, "Colleges and universities will find themselves converted into educational hobo jungles."[22] MIT, which had no graduate program in economics, took a more pragmatic position.

The GI Bill was passed in June 1944, just before demobilization began. Samuelson was begging to be released from his obligations at the Radiation Lab, which he found tedious, to take up new projects. He considered but rejected an offer to ghostwrite a history of the Manhattan Project. Meanwhile, as GIs began streaming into Cambridge, his teaching load increased exponentially. In April 1945, Ralph Freeman, his department chairman, proposed that he write an economics textbook for engineers. "MIT is anxious to have me return to undertake a necessary project that I alone can do," he wrote to the army, which still claimed his time, adding that "the day is approaching when it will no longer be in the national interest to convert a good economist into a mediocre mathematician."[23]

All new MIT students were required to take economics, another sign of changing times. The trouble was, as Freeman confided to Samuelson, for whom it could hardly have been news, "They all hate it." On the day after Japan attacked Pearl Harbor, only one professor had been in his office at the Harvard Economics Department when Basil Dandison, a McGraw-Hill textbook salesman, stopped by. Dandison mentioned to the professor that his company was looking for someone to write an economics textbook and was told about a bright young star who had lately defected to the engineering college at the far end of Cambridge. By the time Japan surrendered, Dandison and the MIT hotshot had struck a deal. "I thought it would do very well," Dandison recalled. The author shrewdly refused an advance and insisted instead on a then unheard-of 15 percent royalty.[24]

Samuelson thought he could knock off the textbook during the summer, provided that the Rad Lab would let him go. But in 1945 he agreed to serve as one of three ghostwriters for Vannevar Bush, an MIT engineer and founder of Raytheon, who headed up a postwar planning group and had been commissioned by FDR to produce a report on research and development, *Science: The Endless Frontier*.[25] *Economics: An Introductory Analysis* wasn't finished until April 1948, although MIT engineering students got previews in mimeographed form.

In *God and Man at Yale: The Superstitions of "Academic Freedom,"* the publishing sensation of 1951, its twenty-five-year-old author, William F. Buckley Jr., leveled a dramatic accusation at his alma mater. "The net influence of Yale economics," he charged, was "thoroughly collectivist," the antithesis of the entrepreneurial values espoused by the university's alumni. As evidence, he cited the textbooks assigned in Economics 10, the introductory course taken on average by one-third of the Yale class.[26] One of the offending texts was Samuelson's *Economics: An Introductory Analysis*. Charging Samuelson with glorifying government and disparaging competition and individual initiative, Buckley was irritated by his "typical glibness . . . and soap opera appeal."[27] He was particularly incensed by the author's suggestion that great fortunes and inheritances were suspect.

The blasphemies in *Economics* were numerous and the bows to traditional wisdom few.[28] Instead of Adam Smith's Invisible Hand, Samuelson invoked the image of a "machine without an effective steering wheel" to describe the private economy.[29] Instead of treating government as a necessary evil, Samuelson called it a modern necessity "where complex economic conditions of life necessitate social coordination and planning,"[30] adding, for emphasis, "No longer is modern man able to believe 'that government governs best which governs least.'"[31] The monetary discipline imposed by the pre–World War I gold standard is breezily dismissed as making "each country a slave rather than the master of its own economic destiny."[32] Samuelson treats budget balancing as a similarly outmoded obsession, assuring students that there is "no technical, financial reason why a nation fanatically addicted to deficit spending should not pursue such a policy for the rest of our lives and even beyond."[33]

Economics was the work of a young man speaking directly to other young men:

> ### TAKE A GOOD LOOK AT THE MAN ON
> ### YOUR RIGHT, AND THE MAN ON YOUR LEFT . . .
>
> [T]he first problem of modern economics: the causes of . . . depression; and other of prosperity, full employment and high standards of living. But no less important is the fact—clearly to be read from the history of the 20th century—that the political health of a democracy is tied up in a crucial way with the successful maintenance of stable high employment and living opportunities. It is not too much to say that the widespread creation of dictatorship and the resulting WWII stemmed in no small measure from the world's failure to meet this basic economic problem adequately.[34]

Capturing the Zeitgeist of big government and bottom-up democracy, Samuelson announced portentously, "The capitalistic way of life is on trial."[35] The book's organization reflected a new set of priorities. Samuelson starts by explaining how the national income is produced, distributed, and spent, and how the government's decisions to tax and spend affect the private economy. These are topics "important for understanding the postwar economic world" as well as "topics people find most interesting." Reversing the usual order, he placed the macroeconomy first, with traditional topics such as the theory of the firm and consumer choice left to the book's second half. Cognizant of the new interest in investing created by wartime saving and purchases of government bonds, and of the need to keep the engineers awake, Samuelson included a chapter on personal finance and the stock market.

Essentially, Samuelson integrated the new Keynesian economics with the economic theory inherited from Marshall, while following Marshall's example of inserting his own insights and techniques. In the fourth edition of *Economics,* Samuelson gave his approach the name of "neo-classical synthesis."[36] Marshall and Schumpeter had emphasized productivity growth as the primary driver of gains in living standards. To this Samuelson added "the importance of preventing mass unemployment."[37]

He described the implications of the new theory by invoking *Alice in Wonderland.* In the world of full employment—in other words, a world of scarcity and substitution in which there were no free lunches and getting more of anything meant giving up something else—the old rules, perhaps restated more precisely in the language of mathematics, applied. In the Keynesian world of abundance and less than full employment, impossible things like getting something for nothing became possible. The best example is the "paradox of thrift."[38] In a full-employment economy, if households save a bigger fraction of their incomes, the total amount of savings goes up. In a depression, saving more actually reduces the total pool of savings because cutting spending causes production and incomes—and hence savings—to fall. At less than full employment, "everything goes into reverse." The same applies to governmental thrift.

The Great Depression was a breakdown not of a single market but in coordination among markets, but Samuelson did not coin the term *macroeconomics* that now refers to effective demand by households, businesses, and government; total amount of unemployment; the rate of inflation; and such. If there was one message that Samuelson meant students to take away, it was that monetary policy no longer worked. The Great Depression was proof of that, he asserted: "Today few economists regard Federal Reserve monetary policy as a panacea for controlling the business cycle."[39] The ideas of the Fed seemed as dusty and dated as flapper fashions. The same could be said about Irving Fisher, who had died the year before, or, indeed, of the pre-1933 Keynes.

. . .

Any impression that the runaway success of *Economics* in university class-
rooms implied an embrace of the new economists in Washington is incor-
rect. Despite the gauzy nostalgia in which the 1950s are wrapped today, the
decade was notable for three recessions, one of which was severe, and toward the end of the decade relatively high unemployment. Historians have
sometimes underestimated the urgency with which Truman, and later
Eisenhower, viewed the need to balance the federal budget and, in particular, to cut military spending. They have also sometimes confused Truman's
hawkish Cold War rhetoric with actual commitments to back words with
resources. But, as Herbert Stein explains, Truman sought major cuts not
just in 1945, but in 1946, 1947, and 1948 as well. The Marshall Plan was an
exception, not the rule.

How to explain the gap between theory and practice? Fiscal prudence,
for one thing. Truman was convinced that a strong defense was predicated
on a healthy economy and attributed Allied victory in no small measure
to America's ability to fulfill its role as the arsenal of democracy. To Truman, who was a Midwestern fiscal conservative and economic conservative (and, in any case, was dealing with a Republican Congress), the top
priority was putting a stop to the run-up in war debt by eliminating the
federal government's annual deficit. What's more, as America's complete
lack of defense in 1940 shows, there was no tradition in the United States
of a large peacetime military. After the defeat of Germany, the pressure for
demobilization was irresistible, and Truman's subsequent proposal for a
universal peacetime draft was overwhelmingly defeated. So, added to the
need to project power globally in order to defend the United States was the
need to do it on a shoestring.

The Keynesian revolution didn't capture Washington until the sixties.
Of all of Samuelson's students, none was more important than John F.
Kennedy, who, shortly before the 1960 presidential election, invited Samu-
elson to give him an alfresco seminar at his family's home in Hyannis Port
on Cape Cod. "I had expected a scrumptious meal," Samuelson later joked.
"We had franks and beans."

On the whole, JFK's cold, calculating, cautious temperament appealed to Samuelson. The new president was hard to sway, but he would stick to his guns once he had made up his mind. Despite a large budget deficit, Kennedy called for a huge tax cut to revive the sluggish economy and his abysmal approval ratings. "The worst deficit comes from a recesion," he told the nation in a televised address, adding that cutting tax rates for individuals and businesses alike was "the most important step we can take to prevent another recession."

The 1963 Kennedy tax cut, passed after the president's assassination, was a huge success. By 1970, President Richard Nixon was insisting that, "We are all Keynesians now," but the tax cut marked the high-water mark for Keynesian theory of managing the business cycle. Samuelson's view was that Keynesianism was toppled by stagflation—that nasty combination of unemployment, inflation, and stagnating productivity that afflicted the world's richest economies in the 1970s and 1980s—rather than a rival theory. But by the late 1950s and early 1960s, Milton Friedman was already mounting a major assault on the reigning paradigm from the University of Chicago, challenging the notion that the government could pick any combination of unemployment and inflation that it wished by fiddling with the government budget. Reviving the legacy of Irving Fisher, and the theory that the supply of money determines the level of economic output, and reinterpreting the Great Depression as a colossal failure of monetary management, Friedman first convinced young economists and later President Jimmy Carter, who appointed Paul Volcker to tame the inflation monster, that money mattered after all. Neither Friedman nor Samuelson ever returned to government, both confident that they could have a bigger impact by teaching and writing than the staff of a president or the Fed.

Chapter XVII

Grand Illusion:
Robinson in Moscow and Beijing

It's very difficult these days to lecture on economic theory because now we have both socialist countries and capitalist countries.

—*Joan Robinson, 1945*[1]

Moscow in April is still frigid, and the snow has not yet melted away, but daylight lingers until almost nine at night, and old women from the country selling mimosa blossoms suddenly appear on street corners. In the spring of 1952, not long after Winston Churchill announced that Britain possessed the atomic bomb, Joan Robinson stared at the golden domes of the Kremlin, feeling that her heart might burst. The sight was both intensely familiar and strangely unreal. "I gaze and gaze," she wrote in her diary, "and wonder if what I see is really there, and if this is really me looking at it."[2]

Later, in the mammoth Hall of Columns, Robinson only half listened to the bombastic speeches, peace resolutions, and "fraternal" greetings from the "women of Scotland." Her mind was taken up with impressions of the new society outside: the farmers' market with its rosy heaps of radishes and piles of chartreuse lettuces; the sparkling shops with plaster hams, sausages, and cheeses in their windows (not because, as in England, the real thing had run out, but to avoid wasting food on a window display); the free day care centers where working mothers dropped off well-dressed, well-fed children; the clever consignment shop where outgrown clothes could be recycled ("What a good idea!"); the "'Swedish' standard of public orderliness and cleanliness"—without the joyless Scandinavian atmosphere. What a contrast to dreary, dirty, dilapidated London.[3]

Robinson luxuriated in her hosts' generosity, so lavish that it almost seemed as if money really had been abolished by the first Socialist Great Power. Four hundred and seventy delegates to the Soviet-sponsored International Economic Conference were being treated like royalty.[4] They were housed in a hotel with "sweeping staircases, chandeliers, malachite columns" grand enough for any sultan.[5] Travel from Prague, Czechoslovakia, was gratis. Each delegate was given 1,000 rubles of pocket money to spend on vodka, furs, and caviar in specially stocked stores. A fleet of one hundred limousines, with uniformed chauffeurs, was on perpetual standby, though Robinson gamely insisted on trying out the subway and trams despite the absence of street maps and her lack of Russian.[6] The best seats at the opera and ballet were always available to the delegates. In contrast to English rations of powdered mashed potatoes and sausages that tasted like wet bread, Moscow dinners were "fabulous." Even the homely act of eating was a reminder of what it meant to be a "coming" rather than a "going" Great Power. After one feast, Joan could almost see "the continent stretching around me, as a Victorian diner might have felt the seaways of the world bearing provisions to his table."[7]

"Oriental lavishness" notwithstanding, Robinson stressed that her Russian hosts displayed "Nordic efficiency" in running the conference. Five hundred interpreters, translators, typists, messengers, and other minions, more than one per delegate, were at the visitors' disposal. Joan was confident that "All the interpreters, cars and guides are not to check our movements, but for our convenience." The promise to refrain from overt propaganda was scrupulously observed. (*Time* reported that the Russians had even removed the ubiquitous life-sized portraits of Stalin that normally hung in every public room.)[8] In postracist Moscow, Robinson exulted, "you can freeze off an Oriental bore just as you would an English one."[9] Here was the reality about which the West was in denial.

Instead of dark forebodings about the future of the West, Robinson was filled with Panglossian optimism about the East. The conference was a Socialist Bretton Woods, a United Nations of Socialists. The conference hall was "cleverly outfitted" with simultaneous translation machinery that seemed to embody the delegates' hopes for a unified global economy and global understanding.[10] A rift had developed in the world economy, thanks to a Cold War that Robinson, like most of the other delegates, assumed was instigated by the world's new imperial superpower, the United States. Lord Boyd Orr, head of the twenty-three-member British delegation, spoke for most of the delegates when he called for East and West to "burst the iron curtain by wagons of goods coming from the East bringing a surplus of goods which the West needs, and wagons of goods going through taking the surplus goods from the West that the East needs."[11] Delegate after delegate insisted that once "artificial barriers" such as the new American ban on strategic exports to the Soviet bloc were removed, the current trickle of East-West trade would become a torrent capable of sweeping away economic ills—from unemployment in the British textile industry, to chronic poverty in India. One delegate from the United States was sure that trade agreements would spark a "spiritual chain reaction of the brotherhood of man" and stave off a nuclear holocaust.

After a week in Moscow, Robinson decided that Stalin was no dictator but a solicitous if stern and somewhat distant father. She recorded a story that she found especially touching: An old cook who had been in service with a Moscow family before the war was assigned to factory work in a rural town after the Nazi invasion. When the war was over, her mistress's family got permission to return to Moscow, but the old servant was left behind. "After trying the regular channels in vain," Robinson noted in her diary, "she wrote to Stalin . . . explaining that factory work did not suit her, that all her village had been wiped out and that she had no friend in the world but her old mistress." According to Joan, "She got a permit within three weeks."[12]

Robinson left Moscow more certain than ever that the Cold War was a mistake rooted in American paranoia rather than in Soviet designs. Her *Conference Sketchbook*, published soon after her return to Cambridge, concluded serenely. "I soak through every pore the conviction that the Soviets have not the smallest desire to save our souls, either by word or sword," she wrote. Without alluding explicitly to the imposition of Soviet rule in Eastern Europe, she was convinced that the Soviets were motivated solely by the fear of Western encirclement. "If they could once be really assured that we will let them alone, they would be only too happy to leave us to go to the devil in our own way," she assured readers. "If our local communists think otherwise, they are the more deceived." [13]

Robinson portrayed herself not as a pilgrim in the new Socialist Mecca but as an objective observer, a truth teller. She insisted that she and the other participants in the conference were not "delegates from anyone but, a job lot of individuals" aware of "the importance of telling the exact truth about all we have seen here." [14] She did not necessarily expect to be believed, however. She wrote to Richard Kahn, "We are steeling ourselves to meet all the dirt that will be slung at us when we get back." [15] Instead of dirt, her lectures on Soviet society drew decent-sized crowds in Cambridge when she returned. "But what about the alleged plot of Jewish doctors to kill Joseph Stalin?" one undergraduate with an American accent had ventured. She didn't miss a beat: "And how about your lynchings in the South?" [16]

By then Robinson was well on her way to becoming one of the Communist bloc's *Parade-Intellektuellen,* or trophy intellectuals, a demanding but rewarding role that involved yearly junkets, photo ops with potentates, a Moscow bank account, and a network of friends consisting largely if not exclusively of government apparatchiks, underground Communists, and spies.

Readers of the *Sketchbook* would have been surprised to learn that the wide-eyed narrator who had tumbled Alice-like into a Socialist Wonderland was, in fact, one of the conference organizers. Robinson was one of two British members of the Initiating Committee, although she insisted that she had signed on merely as a favor to "her old friend Oskar Lange," a Polish economist and central planner who collaborated with the KGB. The British Foreign Office was convinced that she was "well aware of the origins" of the conference, and other committee members commented on her "extreme views," [17] which matched those of the other British delegate, Jack Parry, a Communist Party of Great Britain (CPGB) official as well as a businessman. Alec Cairncross, a member of the British delegation in Moscow, reported that the delegates knew that the conference had originally been conceived as "the next installment of the communist peace campaign" and took for granted that Stalin's main motive in hosting the conference was political; namely, "to drive a wedge between the USA and her European allies."[18] The economists in attendance, including Lange, Jurgen Kuczynski, Piero Sraffa, and Charles Madge, were nearly all party members or fellow travelers.

That is not to say that Robinson had any deeper insight than Harry Dexter White into the true drift of Stalin's thinking. For example, she was probably unaware that he had repudiated the entire premise of the conference just weeks before. In remarks distributed to the Central Committee in early February, Stalin had attacked the very notion of peaceful coexistence and economic convergence with the West that was the gospel of the One Worlders like herself. He accused Soviet Communists who predicted a reconstitution of a single global economy of being misled by the flurry of international cooperation during and immediately after the war. The chief legacy of World War II, he warned, was the permanent division of the global economy into "two parallel world markets." Socialist economies and capitalist ones would evolve in isolation from, and opposition to, one another. The "inevitable" outcome would be deepening economic crisis in the West, intensifying imperialist rivalry, and, ultimately, a fratricidal war between the United States and Britain: "The inevitability of wars between capitalist counties remains in force."[19] All this, Stalin assured committee members, was a matter of scientific law.

He was quite sincere, John Gaddis, the American historian of the Cold War, has concluded.[20] Apparently, Stalin was as devout a believer in a secular apocalypse as Marx or Engels a century before. Had they been widely known, the timing of his pronouncements would have put the Russian conference hosts in an awkward position. On the one hand, they had dangled the prospect of huge orders in front of British textile manufacturers and other businessmen to ensure their attendance. On the other hand, Stalin had gone so far as to claim that the Communist bloc would soon be able to dispense with Western imports altogether. If anything, he insisted, the Soviet Union and her allies would soon "feel the necessity of finding an outside market for their surplus products."[21] However, on the eve of the conference, Stalin espoused the more politic view that the "peaceful coexistence of capitalism and communism" was possible, subject to noninterference with the domestic affairs of other countries and other conditions.[22]

If Robinson felt let down in any way by the proceedings, she gave no sign in either her public accounts or her letters to Kahn. In all likelihood, she and the other foreign delegates had not seen Stalin's remarks to the Central Committee, which Stalin kept from the press until releasing an English translation the following October.[23] The trade deals made at the conference added up to very little, particularly when compared to the inflated rhetoric with which they were presented. An economist estimated that that the volume of East-West trade implied by the proposals was considerably below prewar levels.

Or perhaps Robinson did suspect the truth. At one point, she wandered into some offices at the commerce ministry where abacuses and desk calculators lay side by side on desks. Possibly it was that anomalous juxtaposition of modern and ancient that drew her attention to another incongruity: namely, that the Soviet economists at the conference had "raised not quoting figures to a fine art."[24]

One of Robinson's biographers, Geoffrey Harcourt, an economist at Cambridge, dates the beginning of her political "conversion" to 1936.[25] For British intellectuals, 1936 is associated less with the Great Depression, which was nearly over in Britain, than with the beginning of the Spanish Civil War. When Germany and Italy intervened on behalf of the Nationalists, and the Soviets on the side of the Republicans, the conflict came to be seen as a proxy war between Fascism and Communism. Stalin's willingness to fight the Fascists in Spain enhanced Soviet prestige, while Britain's and America's refusal to engage in the struggle made them seem, at best, pusillanimous.

But in 1936 Joan was infatuated with her poet in Aleppo, Dr. Ernest Altounyan, and intellectually in thrall with Keynes. It was only in 1939, while she was recovering from her breakdown, that she surprised Schumpeter, a regular and admiring correspondent, by taking up Marx (whom Keynes considered a bore). Her political activity during the war consisted of serving on various Labour Party advisory committees, writing Labour Party pamphlets, and working on reports. These included the *Beveridge Employment Report*, which was drafted by her close friend Nicholas Kaldor, the clever Hungarian LSE lecturer who, like Robinson and Hayek, wound up spending the war in Cambridge. Her assumption that the West was doomed to secular stagnation as well as recurring depressions was shared by Keynesians of all political stripes, but in 1943 she had not yet ruled out that the problem was insoluble: "The problem of unemployment overshadows all other post war problems. The economic system under which we are living is on trial. The modern world has seen a great experiment in Socialist planning . . . It remains to be seen if the democratic nations can find a way to plan for peace and prosperity." [26]

Like other Labour Party economists, Robinson advocated a mixture of Socialist planning and Keynesianism demand management through taxes and subsidies. [27] As an advisor to the Trade Unions Congress, she argued for the nationalization of most industries on the grounds that planning required government ownership. [28] Her preferred solution involved government economic planning, government control of investment, and nationalization of key industries, while allowing that "a fringe of small scale private economy might well survive in a controlled economy provided that it did not threaten to encroach too far." [29] All of this was standard for the Labour Party's left wing. "By 1944," one historian commented, "the wartime radicalism had passed its peak, and the proposals advanced by Kaldor and Robinson were noticeably more moderate in tone." [30] When Keynes returned from Washington in December 1945 to announce the terms of the "infamous" American loan—that he had fought so hard to win only to have it attacked furiously by both right and left—Robinson supported him publicly by acknowledging that Britain could not afford to turn down the loan or to alienate the United States.

After Labour swept to power in 1945, Robinson aligned herself with the extreme-left opposition to the leadership. Unlike the Labour government of 1931, the government of Prime Minister Clement Attlee began at once to fulfill its wartime promises to nationalize industry and create a cradle-to-grave welfare state. As unemployment faded away and real wages rose, she became more critical rather than less critical of Labour's leadership, less focused on domestic issues, and increasingly obsessed by American power and the threat of nuclear war. The Labour landslide had not, as expected, resulted in a U-turn away from Churchill's vehement pro-American, anti-Soviet foreign policy. According to the historian Jonathan Schneer, Ernest Bevin, the Labour foreign minister, "did not believe that substantial agreement with Russia about the shape of the postwar world was possible." Bevin's "primary goal, shared by most Conservatives, was to convince the Americans that they must step into the power vacuum in Europe and elsewhere created by Britain's declining strength before the Russians did." [31]

By 1950, Stalin would complain to Harry Pollitt, the British Communist Party boss, that Labour was even more "subservient to the Americans" than the Tories.[32] But his attacks on the Labour Party, which began as soon as the election was over, had the effect of rallying the rank and file around the leadership.[33] The party's left wing resented the allegation that they were no better than Tories while they were waging a furious struggle in Parliament to nationalize heavy industry and create a national health system. Though still leaning toward nonalignment, the left wing was further antagonized by Soviet actions in Bulgaria, Romania, Poland, and East Germany. Already in 1946, the leadership of the Labour Party was convinced that the chief threat to peace came not from the United States but from the Soviet Union.

The hard-core Left opposed the mainstream on the issue of what would today be called human rights. It consisted of no more than a dozen or so activists such as Robinson. The bulk of the Labour Left was far more resolutely anti-Communist than political liberals in the United States. Open Communists such as D. N. Pritt and John Platts-Mills were expelled, and the CPGB's request for affiliation with Labour was denied. As reliably a pro-Soviet figure as Harold Laski—a prominent Marxist political scientist at the LSE who served as Labour Party chairman in 1945—defended the leadership's actions, arguing that Communists "act like a secret battalion of paratroopers within the brigade . . . the secret purpose makes them willing to sacrifice all regard for truth and straight dealing."[34] As far as most of the British Left was concerned, the wartime romance with the Soviet Union was over.

Not for Robinson. Authoritarian by temperament and disdainful of the political compromise that characterizes democracies, she was deterred neither by Stalin's purges at home nor by his fishing in troubled waters abroad—or rather troubling waters so that he could fish. If anything, universal condemnation seemed to heighten his appeal for her. In her mind, the United States was the biggest threat to world peace. "The great question which overshadows everything is whether Russia is planning aggression, for, if not, our whole policy is nonsensical." Accusing the United States of conflating ideological versus military aggression, she argued that "the great boom in America built up on rearmament has gone too far for comfort . . . and yet the prospect of a peaceful détente and a sudden cessation of rearmament expenditure is a menace to their economy . . . The line of least resistance is to keep on with it. That is what seems to me the biggest menace in the present situation."[35]

The Marshall Plan was the bolt from the blue that split the British Left. On June 5, 1947, Secretary of State George C. Marshall gave a speech at Harvard outlining his plan. "The United States should do whatever it is able to assist in the return of normal economic health in the world, without which there can be no political stability and no assured peace." The Marshall Plan eclipsed the IMF, which was "almost inactive," and the World Bank, which was husbanding its resources and refusing to make loans for reconstruction. A 1949 report of the IMF's directors "wrote a poignant epitaph for the wartime hopes of multilateralism," observes Richard Gardner, concluding that, "dependence on bilateral trade and bilateral currencies is far greater than before the war."[36] Within a month, the Soviet foreign minister, Vyacheslav Molotov, publicly rejected the plan at a Paris meeting of Communist bloc countries, calling it an "American plan for the enslavement of Europe."

After the Labour Party welcomed American aid as "an important step toward a united, prosperous Europe," Robinson was quick in her denunciation.[37] On June 25 on the BBC's *London Forum,* she argued that American money would "create a Western anti-communist bloc" and thus increase the chance of war, adding, "I don't think you can say we're going to preserve Western values by accepting dollars and splitting Europe. I think that will imperil Western values."[38] In other words, Britain should reject the offer of American aid, as the Soviets and their Eastern European allies had—a position that put her at odds with virtually the entire British Left, which rallied behind the Labour Party. The only exception was the CPGB, which attacked the Labour government for "selling out to Wall Street."[39]

Robinson's support for Stalin in the 1940s and 1950s was more puzzling—and less conditional—than Beatrice Webb's enthusiasm in the 1930s. It was a bit like her earlier worship of Keynes, whom she seemed to have regarded primarily as an icon.[40] In his 1977 book *The Russia Complex: The British Labour Party and the Soviet Union,* the political scientist Bill Jones estimates that there were no more than twenty or so fellow travelers in the Labour Party in 1946. Robinson's advocacy for the Soviet Union set her apart from Laski—described by George Orwell as "a Socialist by allegiance, and a liberal by temperament"—and most of the Labour Left. It represented a repudiation of her family's traditions, necessarily involving a degree of duplicity as well as complicity in others' deception. "Whereof one cannot speak, thereof one must be silent," Ludwig Wittgenstein had famously concluded in *Tractatus Logico-Philosophicus.* Robinson spoke fearlessly when it came to her opinions yet maintained a cagey silence about the nature of her relationship to the Soviets.

In 1939 she had confessed to Richard Kahn that the "deep rift between my political and tribal loyalty had been a continuous and growing strain all these years."[41] By the time she committed herself to Moscow, her forebodings about Western decline and optimism about the dynamism of the East had become articles of faith, and the strain of divided loyalties greater than ever. Over the summer and fall of 1952, Robinson's elated mood became more fevered and frantic. She wrote that she was discovering great secrets, including the key to her frustrating relationship with Kahn. She developed a conviction that she had discovered a hidden flaw in the foundation of economic theory that would, if people realized its existence, bring down capitalism. By fall, she was no longer sleeping, talking incessantly, obviously delusional. After a three-way consultation among Richard Kahn, Austin Robinson, and Ernest Altounyan, she was once again hospitalized, this time for six months.

Still, she recovered sufficiently to return to Moscow the following spring. Stalin was dead, and Moscow was merely the first stop on an elaborate pilgrimage that took her first to Beijing and then to a string of Russia's third world clients, including Burma, Thailand, Vietnam, Egypt, Lebanon, Syria, and Iraq. She had allowed herself to be appointed vice president of the British Council of International Trade with China, an organization with a board that consisted largely of underground CPGB members and that was suspected of serving as a conduit for CPGB funding. The group's president was Lord Boyd Orr, the food specialist who had headed the British delegation to the Moscow conference and had been a fixture at such events.[42] Possibly it was embarrassment at her role in the so-called Icebreaker Mission that made her hide behind another dignitary almost out of camera range at the "business arrangements signing" ceremony. Milton Friedman, who spent that academic year visiting Cambridge University, was baffled that an economist of Robinson's brilliance "found it possible to rationalize and praise every feature of Russian and Chinese policy."[43]

At forty-nine, Joan Robinson was more formidable than ever, part "magnificent Valkyrie," part houri, part commissar. Imperious, intellectually intimidating, and seductive, she combined Olympian certitude with a fine sarcasm. Although she was not admitted to the British Academy until 1958 and had to wait for Austin to retire in 1965 before being appointed to a university professorship, she stepped into the leadership vacuum that resulted from Keynes's death. She was not the only prominent Keynesian there. But while Sraffa buried himself in collecting and editing the papers of David Ricardo, and Nicholas Kaldor went on to become a political insider in the Labour Party, she defined the agenda. She dominated the men around her.

At a seminar at Oxford run by John Hicks, who later shared the Nobel with the American economist Kenneth Arrow for his work on economic growth, Robinson "kept telling him what he had said," recalled another participant. "He got pinker and pinker and finally said with much stammering, 'I didn't say anything of the sort,' to which she replied that if he didn't say it, that is what he meant to say."[44] Unlike the catholic Keynes, who was anxious not to become too wedded to his own ideas and disliked it when his intellectual offspring became doctrinaire, Joan sought disciples. Her male tutees were either smitten or silenced. One of them recalled,

> Mrs. R. would sit on a hassock, smoking with a long cigarette holder . . . wearing a peignoir, her graying hair pulled into a tight bun in the back, her intelligent eyes set in an expansive brow, focused on me. The scene bore a vague resemblance to Picasso's portrait of Gertrude Stein: the same heavy solidity and presence. But there the resemblance ended. Mrs. R., if not quite a dish, was certainly comely. And the difference between her and Stein was made more evident by a pen sketch which sat on a small table, next to the hassock, of a woman, stark naked, sitting on a hassock, her hands covering her face.[45]

For Robinson, Cambridge, England, became the anti–Cambridge, Massachusetts. Her disdain for mathematics bordered on affectation. She turned down an invitation to become president of the Econometric Society on the grounds that she could not join an editorial committee of a journal she could not read. Arthur Pigou, her old professor, called Joan "a magpie breeding innumerable parrots" and complained that she "propounds the Truth with an enormous T and with such Prussian efficiency that the wretched men become identical sausages without any minds of their own."[46] Michael Straight, whose family owned the *New Republic* and who was recruited by the KGB, called her "the most exciting and brilliant lecturer as far as economics students were concerned."[47]

As a member of the class that had once administered the empire, Joan came of age during British imperialism's terminal decline, and perhaps it was this sense of being on the losing side of history that fueled her determination to side with history's winners. By the time she went to Moscow for the first time, Robinson's new passion was economic growth, and she

was already convinced that she had taken "the wrong turning" intellectually twenty years earlier when she "worked out *The Economics of Imperfect
Competition* on static assumptions."[48] During the Great Depression, she
had striven mightily to answer what she now considered to be the wrong
question. Instead of asking what caused transitory unemployment, she
now realized that she should have focused on what determined the wealth
and poverty of nations. In retrospect, she said, she should have abandoned
"static analysis" and tried instead to "come to terms with Marshall's theory
of development."

The question of long-run growth had originally captured the attention of Keynesians, Robinson included, who were worried about long-run
stagnation in the industrialized West. But several developments caused
them to shift their attention to the "overpopulated, backward countries"—
that is, the former colonies in Asia, Africa, and Latin America.[49] To begin
with, postwar stagnation had not materialized. War-shattered Britain and
Europe rebounded so strongly that by 1950 unemployment had virtually
disappeared and wages were rising rapidly. The Left argued that the arms
race had saved the market economy, but the fact remained that the economic problem was no longer a compelling rationale for Socialism in the
West.

World War II had made decolonization inevitable. Britain's financial
weakness and commitment to building a welfare state at home coincided
with the emergence of indigenous liberation movements. The intensifying
Cold War accelerated the process by improving the third world's bargaining power, and the growing political participation of poor countries in
global organizations, including the United Nations, focused attention on
"underdevelopment" as an economic problem.

The hopeful rhetoric of the Moscow conference sounds absurdly optimistic in retrospect. With one-fifth of the world's population, China had
an average per capita income roughly half that of Africa's in 1952, and a
mere 5 percent of America's. Living standards in India, with 15 percent of
the world's population, were only marginally higher. Had anyone asked
before the war, most economists would have readily conceded that poor
countries could grow rich—eventually. After all, Europe had escaped the

Malthusian trap of universal poverty and life on the edge of starvation by achieving economic growth just 1 or 2 percentage points faster than that of population growth.

But what hope could the European experience offer populous China, India, or the Middle East? Not only was the gulf in material conditions between the populous poor countries and the world's richest countries unimaginably large, but, more disturbingly, the day's poor countries were far poorer than England in the 1840s, before the real wages and living conditions of ordinary Englishmen began their remarkable cumulative rise. "There are today in the plains of India and China men and women, plague-ridden and hungry, living lives little better ... than those of the cattle that toil with them," T. S. Ashton wrote in 1948. "Such Asiatic standards, and such un-mechanized horrors, are the lot of those who increase their numbers without passing through an Industrial Revolution." At the rate at which Britain, Europe, and America had escaped poverty, it would take China and India another hundred years to reach *that* level.

The pros and cons of central planning and state-run enterprises were not the only issue. There was also the question of international trade and investment. Was integration in the global economy or autarky the fastest path? The answer depended on what one thought had caused underdevelopment in the first place. In Victorian England a century before, Friedrich Engels and Karl Marx had maintained that poverty was a new condition, far worse in Victorian than in Elizabethan England. They blamed the rich. Later, Alfred Marshall, Irving Fisher, Joseph Schumpeter, and John Maynard Keynes, among others, took a different view. They pointed out that poverty had been man's fate long before the emergence of the modern economy. The root cause of low living standards was not a lack of resources or unequal distribution of existing incomes but an inability to use existing resources—land, labor, capital, knowledge—efficiently. Now, in most of the globe, the question was whether the poverty of nations was caused by the Western economic system or by local conditions and institutions inimical to economic growth that Western organization could cure.

Schumpeter had called the triumph of Bolshevism in a precapitalist agrarian economy "nothing but a fluke." In her review of *Capitalism, Socialism, and Democracy*, Robinson acknowledged,

> May be so. But in that case the exception seems rather more important
> than the rule. Who knows what flukes may accompany the end of the
> present war? And, even if the Bolshevik fluke remains unique, there
> cannot be much doubt that the existence of a socialist Great Power will
> play at least as important a part in the development in other countries
> (even without any deliberate intervention in their affairs) as the more
> subtle processes of evolution according to the immanent characteristics
> of capitalism.

The Soviet victory over Germany, Europe's leading industrial power, in World War II had apparently convinced Robinson that Socialism was a shortcut to industrialization:

> The grand moral of this thirty years of history is not so much for the
> western industrial countries where the standard of living is already high,
> as for the undeveloped nations. That communism is destined to super-
> sede capitalism is in the nature of a dogma, but it is a proven fact that the
> Soviet system shows how the technical achievements of capitalism can be
> imitated (and in some cases surpassed) by those whom the first indus-
> trial revolution kept as hewers of wood and drawers of water.[50]

In 1951 Robinson wrote a brief introduction to a Marxist classic, *The Accumulation of Capital* by Rosa Luxemburg. Luxemburg was the German Communist leader who was murdered in 1919 and was one of the few first-rate minds among Marx's disciples. Today her reputation rests more on her early criticism of the Bolshevik dictatorship than on her economic theory, but in 1951 Robinson was compelled by Luxemburg's argument that the limits to growth—and the source of the inevitable breakdown—of the global market economy were to be found in the third world.

According to Luxemburg, shrinking investment opportunities at home drove entrepreneurs abroad in search of profits and led, inevitably,

to rivalries. When these imperialists ran out of fresh territory to exploit—
or ran into one another—capitalism had to break down, through either
stagnation or war. Robinson acknowledged that Luxemburg's analysis was
incomplete in that it identified imperialism as the only means by which
capitalism extended its flagging lease on life, omitting any consideration
of technological change or rising real wages: "All the same, few would deny
that the extension of capitalism into new territories was the mainspring
of what an academic economist has called 'the vast secular boom' of the
last two hundred years and many academic economists account for the
uneasy condition of capitalism in the 20th century largely by 'the closing
of the frontier' all over the world." Nonetheless, she concluded, somewhat
inaccurately, that Luxemburg's book "shows more prescience than any orthodox contemporary could claim." [51]

Robinson embarked on her own magnum opus on economic growth,
for which she intended to borrow Luxemburg's title. [52] A hostile 1949
review of Roy Harrod's classic on economic growth makes it clear what
she wanted to accomplish. [53] She castigated Harrod for ignoring conflicts
of interest, history, politics, and especially "the distribution of income or
measures to increase useful investment." [54] A 1952 article for the *Economic
Journal*, written before she left for Moscow, offered a preview of her main
argument: growth, she wrote, was the process of accumulating physical
capital—roads, office buildings, dams, factories, machinery, and the like.
Admittedly, Marx had erred in claiming that free market economies could
not grow indefinitely. She would demonstrate that almost none *would*.
"Perpetual steady accumulation is not inherently impossible," she wrote,
but "the conditions required by the model are unlikely to be found in
reality." [55]

Robinson's first visit to China, in 1953, provided for her "the final
proof that communism is not a stage beyond capitalism but a substitute
for it." [56] She explained later, "Private enterprise has ceased to be the form
of organization best suited to take advantage of modern technology." [57]
The chief obstacle to growth in poor countries was not a lack of capital
or entrepreneurship, she concluded, but interference by the West. North-
south trade was a zero-sum game that produced losers as well as winners,

and inevitably the poor countries wound up as the losers. She discounted the role of education and innovation. "Only when the advanced countries are satisfied that they need not disturb themselves will they tolerate, and so permit, the drastic social changes required to send the colonial and ex colonial and quasi colonial nations on a hopeful path," adding somewhat irrelevantly that "peaceful coexistence is natural and logical."

While Robinson wrote her book, Richard Kahn hosted what he and she called the "secret seminar." It met every Tuesday during the Michaelmas and Easter terms in Kahn's rooms at King's College and served as a testing site for her work in progress. Visitors were invited to drop in but often found it hard to get airtime. Samuelson described a typical meeting as Robinson's friend "Kaldor talking 75% of the time and Joan talking 75% of the time." [58]

When *The Accumulation of Capital* was published in 1956, the book's "heroic scale" and Robinson's lofty stature guaranteed copious reviews. But although reviewers called the book "monumental" and "important," reaction was muted. Some complained of "few new insights," "no propositions [that] can be empirically tested," "a verbal, graphical exposition" of "long familiar results in linear programming." [59] Others criticized her for not understanding the role of consumers, making logical errors, and ignoring recent research. (This was held to be a typically Cambridge, England, vice, with one reviewer pointing out that Piero Sraffa's *Production of Commodities by Means of Commodities*, written during World War II, contained not a single reference more recent than 1913.) Less charitably, Harry Johnson wrote that his former professor "has proved conclusively to her own satisfaction that Capitalism Cannot Possibly Work." [60] Samuelson compared Robinson's theory to Lenin's rule of three: electricity + Soviets = Communism. [61] Abba Lerner called the book a "pearl," not only for redirecting attention to "the causes of the wealth of nations" but for providing graduate students with a host of "errors and . . . ingenious confusions" on which to flex their muscles. [62] Lawrence Klein, who shared Robinson's political views, dismissed her insights as "ordinary sort of results usually derived in economic theory from some maximizing or minimizing principle." [63]

Robert Solow, a Keynesian at MIT who had published a paper on economic growth that same year—one that would earn him a Nobel Prize in 1987—delivered the coup de grace: "I think there's nothing Keynesian about Joanian economics . . . There's nothing in *The Accumulation of Capital* . . . or any of those papers which strikes me as having a genuine root or inspiration in Keynes."[64]

Solow had not only proposed an elegant theory but produced a stunning empirical result: Nine-tenths of the doubling in output per worker in the United States between 1909 and 1949 was due neither to the accumulation of physical capital nor to improvements in the health or education of the labor force, but rather to technological progress. The implication that an economic environment conducive to innovation mattered more than its stock of factories and machines flatly contradicted Robinson's central premise, not to mention that of the widely imitated Soviet model. Solow, who dismissed Schumpeter, rather unfairly, as a pro-German anti-Semite and an intellectual phony, had supplied most compelling evidence that it was not what a nation had but what a nation did with what it had that determined long-run economic success or failure. This, of course, was pure Schumpeter.

Robert Solow and Kenneth Arrow spent the academic year 1963–64 visiting Cambridge, England, and heard Robinson describe her two months touring Chinese communes. Saying she wanted to counter "the malicious misrepresentation of China in the Western press," she dismissed "the critics [who] were shedding crocodile tears over the 'famine'" and claimed that China's communes were "a method of organizing relief" during the three "bitter years" of flood and drought. Echoing Beatrice and Sidney Webb's glowing reports during the 1932 Ukrainian famine, Robinson called the communes "a brilliant invention" and concluded that "the rationing system worked; the rations were tight, but they were always honored."

We now know that an estimated 15 to 30 million peasants in Henan, Anhui, and Sichuan provinces died between 1958 and 1962—ten times the toll in the 1943 Bengal famine—and that forced collectivization, the disastrous Great Leap Forward, and the refusal of Mao Tse-tung's regime to organize relief, not bad weather, were primarily to blame.

That democracy and well-being go hand in hand is now conventional wisdom. For a long time, it was not. Individual rights were thought, by many intellectuals influenced by the utilitarian tradition, to be a luxury that poor nations simply could not afford. Robinson considered democracy a bit of a fraud and politicians both pusillanimous and deceitful. "The notion of freedom is a slippery one," she wrote during World War II, adding, without the slightest hint of irony, "It is only when there is no serious enemy within or without that full freedom of speech can safely be allowed." [65] She was inclined to dismiss democratic reforms as "premature attempts to pluck the low-lying fruit." That blind spot goes a long way in explaining why Robinson, who visited China frequently in the 1950s and 1960s, "failed utterly to detect the biggest famine in modern history," while others—including Bertrand Russell, Michael Foote, Harold Laski, and Harold Macmillan, all of whom were vilified at one time or another as Communist sympathizers or even fellow travelers—saw what was happening and called for international relief.

To be sure, Joan Robinson was hardly the only eminent Western observer to be hoodwinked by Beijing's denials. Lord Boyd Orr, head of the British delegation to the 1952 Moscow economics conference and one of the world's leading experts on food, concluded Mao was ending the "traditional Chinese famine cycle." [66] In fact, the magnitude of the death toll wasn't known outside China until after Mao's death in 1976. But Robinson's willingness to believe a totalitarian regime that forbade free movement, free speech, free press, and free elections was symptomatic of a mind-set—all too common among development economists fifty years ago—that ignored the crucial role of political rights.

Geoffrey Harcourt once remarked that Robinson was "always looking for the next Utopia." Perhaps, but she was also looking for the next Great Leader and, of course, the next worshipful audience. She relished her celebrity, her junkets, the VIP treatment, and bully pulpits. She liked playing the fearless outsider speaking truth to power. Perhaps the Moscow bank account, friendships with Cold War spies, including Solomon Adler, Frank Coe, Donald Wheeler, and Oskar Lange, and the need for veiled allusions and careful elisions gave her a kick as well.

As time went by, Robinson became even more Olympian, imperious, and pessimistic. Her book *Economic Philosophy,* published in 1962, surveys economic ideas since 1700. In his review, George Stigler, Milton Friedman's best friend at the University of Chicago, called Robinson "a superior logician" but accused her of ignoring facts:

> There really isn't a great deal to economics, considered as a logical structure based upon a few indisputable axioms about the world. If one cuts oneself off from two generations of immensely varied and instructive empirical research, and if one thinks economic history had no relevance to economic theory . . . then one is indeed left with a hollow discipline. A logician is a wondrous creature, but he cannot distinguish between the two simple errors: If $A = B$, and $B = C$, then (1) $A = 1.01C$ and (2) $A = 10^{65}C$. An *economist* can.[67]

Chapter XVIII

Tryst with Destiny:
Sen in Calcutta and Cambridge

There haven't been many folk songs written for capitalism, but there have been many composed for social justice.

It is mainly an attempt to see development as a process of expanding the real freedoms that people enjoy. In this approach, expansion of freedom is viewed as both (1) the *primary end* and (2) the *principal means* of development.

—*Amartya Sen*[1]

Joan Robinson wound up her talk at the Delhi School of Economics clutching a copy of Mao's "red book." It was the late 1960s. Her topic was the dismal state of Western economics, but mostly she talked about China and the Cultural Revolution. The audience was in rapture. When the wild applause faded at last, a willowy young man asked a question. His tone implied the mildest and most polite skepticism. Robinson rebuffed him soundly but "with affection."[2] They were, after all, the best of enemies, former professor and favorite student. At Cambridge, she had cultivated students from the third world. One of the most gifted was Amartya Sen, but Sen's interest in human rights and the immediate amelioration of poverty clashed with Robinson's enthusiasm for the Soviet model of industrialization.

Amartya means "destined for immortality." Born into a scholarly and cosmopolitan Hindu family, Amartya Sen grew up amid the horrors of the Bengal famine, communal violence, the collapse of British rule, and partition. As a brilliant student and campus agitator in Calcutta, he overcame a near-lethal bout of cancer, bested one hundred thousand other exam takers, and won admission to the college of Isaac Newton, G. H. Hardy, and the mathematician Srinivasa Ramanujan, Trinity College in Cambridge. Since 1970, Sen has lived mostly in England and America, but his thoughts have never strayed far from India. Drawing on his own experiences, a lifelong study of the disenfranchised, and a deep knowledge of Eastern and Western philosophy, Sen has questioned every facet of contemporary economic thought. Challenging traditional assumptions about what is meant by social welfare and how to measure progress, he has helped restore "an ethical dimension to the discussion of vital economic problems."[3] He is a public intellectual, engaged by issues, from famines and premature female mortality, to multiculturalism and nuclear proliferation. His inspiring journey from impoverished Calcutta in newly independent India to the ivory towers of Cambridge, England, and Cambridge, Massachusetts—and back again—is a triumph of reason, empathy, and a very human determination to overcome incredible odds.

In January 2002, India's Hindu nationalist government of the Bharatiya Janata Party threw a three-day celebration for India's farflung diaspora in Delhi. In a gesture that revealed both how far he had traveled—and how close he had remained to his roots—Sen left that gathering to address an outdoor "hunger hearing" with several hundred peasants and laborers in a chilly dirt field on the far side of town.

One by one, members of the audience went up to the microphone. A scrawny fourteen-year-old from Delhi spoke about going hungry after she lost her dishwashing job. A dark-skinned man from Orissa described how three members of his family had died after a local drought the previous year. Fifty years after independence, a larger fraction of India's population suffered from chronic malnutrition than in any other part of the world, including sub-Saharan Africa. Yet India's government kept food prices high via agricultural price supports and had accumulated the biggest food stockpile in the world, a third of which was rotting in rat-infested government granaries.

When Sen stood up, shivering in his baggy cords and rumpled jacket, he spoke less about the "interest of consumers being sacrificed to farmers" and more about "profoundly lonely deaths." Addressing an audience that seemed plainly awestruck, he conveyed sympathy and encouragement. "Without protests like these," he said, "the deaths would be much more. If there had been something like this, the Bengal famine could have been prevented." Their willingness to speak out, he told them approvingly, was "democracy in action."

Sen is Bengali. Like saying that an American is a southerner, that has very specific connotations. Bengal is a river delta; fish is the mainstay of the Bengali diet; dhoti, chappals, and panjabi are the traditional garb. All Bengalis, Sen says, are great talkers, as he is. The worst thing about dying, Bengalis like to joke, is the thought that the people will keep talking and that you won't be able to answer back.

The Bengali word for public intellectual is *bhadralok,* and Bengal has a long tradition, going back at least two centuries, of learned men with cosmopolitan outlooks who battled social evils such as untouchability and suttee. Sen is part of that tradition. His family is from the old part of Dhaka, an ancient river city 240 kilometers as the crow flies from Calcutta, now the capital of Muslim Bangladesh. In Jane Austen's day, Dhaka was "a big, bustling place of first-rate importance," famous the world over for its fine muslins (called *bafta hawa,* or "woven air").[4] Competition from Manchester brought decline. By 1900, Dhaka's population had shrunk by two-thirds, and, according to a contemporary travel guide, "all round the present city are ruins of good houses, mosques, and temples, smothered in jungle."[5] Thirty-odd years later, when Sen was born, in 1933, Dhaka had regained some of its former importance by becoming a regional administrative center for the British Raj.

Sen was born into that class of English-speaking academics and civil servants who helped run British India. He describes his father, Ashutosh, as "an adventurous man" who got a PhD in chemistry at London University and fell in love with an English Quaker. After returning home to an arranged marriage, he became head of the agricultural chemistry department at Dacca University. The Sens lived in a typical Dhaka house, fifty or sixty feet long, narrow in the front, "the middle being a courtyard open to the sky," with plenty of room for servants and relatives.[6]

Sen began his education at an English missionary school in 1939. Two years later, as the Japanese advanced toward British India, he was sent to live with his maternal grandparents in Santiniketan, just north of Calcutta, "to keep me safe from the bombs." Santiniketan has special connotations for Bengalis—indeed for all Indians—because of its association with Rabindranath Tagore, the poet. After winning the Nobel Prize for literature in 1913, Tagore used his prize money to establish the Visva Bharati University in Santiniketan, where he tried to apply his ideas about education and his notions of merging Eastern spirituality with Western science. Gandhi visited Santiniketan in 1940, and for years India's nationalist elite, including Prime Minister Jawaharlal Nehru, sent their children to study there.

Sen's maternal grandfather, Kshitimohan Sen, a distinguished Sanskrit scholar, was on the faculty of Visva Bharati. Sen attended classes in Tagore's coeducational school under the eucalyptus trees. His free time was spent mostly with his grandfather. "Everyone found him formidable," Sen recalled. "He woke at four. He knew all the stars. He talked with me about the connections between Greek and Sanskrit. I was the only one of his grandchildren who had a sense of academic vocation. I was going to be the one who carried the mantle."

If Santiniketan was a tranquil oasis, it hardly escaped the upheavals of the time. At the time of his death in 1941, Tagore was deeply disenchanted by the West, professing to see little difference between the Allied and Axis powers. The war accelerated the final break with Britain. After Gandhi launched the "Quit India" movement in 1942, the British arrested sixty thousand Congress Socialist Party supporters, including Amartya Sen's uncle; by end of that year, over one thousand people had been killed in anti-British riots. "My uncle was in preventive detention for a very long time," Sen recalled. "Several other 'uncles' also were jailed, including one who died in prison. I grew up feeling the injustice of this."

The 1943 Bengal famine—the consequence of wartime inflation, censorship, and imperial indifference rather than crop failures—destroyed the last remnant of respect for the British. The new viceroy, Lord Wavell, wrote to Churchill, the "Bengal famine was one of the greatest disasters that has befallen any people under British rule and damage to our reputation here both among Indians and foreigners in India is incalculable."[7] Sen later estimated that 3 million people, mostly poor fishermen and landless laborers, perished from starvation and disease.

At the time, for the boy of ten, the famine meant a steady stream of starving villagers who passed through Santiniketan in a desperate attempt to reach Calcutta. His grandfather allowed him to hand out rice to beggars, "but only as much as would fill a cigarette tin" and only one tin per family. Later, as a university student, he reflected on the fact that only the very poor and members of despised castes had starved, while he and his family—and, indeed, their entire class—remained unaffected. That observation was to inform his theory of famines as man-made, not natural, disasters.

Even more traumatic was the eruption of communal violence on the eve of independence. The idea of a multicultural Indian nation was very much alive in Santiniketan, and, traditionally, Muslims and Hindus achieved a higher degree of assimilation in Bengal than in other parts of India. Yet when religious conflict erupted on the eve of independence, it set neighbor against neighbor in a vast pogrom. Ashutosh Sen, along with the other Hindus on the faculty of Dhaka University, were forced to leave Dhaka in 1945.

On one of his last school holidays in his Dhaka home, Sen witnessed a horrific scene. A Muslim laborer named Kader Mia staggered into the family compound, screaming and covered in blood. Stabbed in the back by some Hindu rioters, he died later that day. "The experience was devastating for me," recalled Sen. Mia told Sen's father, who took him to a hospital, that his wife had pleaded with him to stay home that day. But his family had no food, so he had little choice but to go to the Hindu part of town to seek work. The realization that "extreme poverty can make a person a helpless prey," Sen said, was to inspire his philosophical inquiry into the conflict between necessity and freedom.[8] A more immediate effect, however, was a strong distaste for all forms of religious fanaticism and cultural nationalism.

Presidency College, one of the most elite institutions of higher education in India, looks today much as it did in 1951, when Sen enrolled there, and, for that matter, much as it did at the turn of the century when the British founded the Hindoo University. Its faded pink stucco façade with peeling green shutters, the black plaques identifying the different rooms, the dim interiors with their ceiling fans and row upon row of long wooden benches, all evoke a long-bygone era. In the years immediately following independence, though, the college was a political hotbed. Sen arrived thinking he would study physics but quickly found economics of greater urgency and interest.

Thanks to the traditions of Indian higher education, Sen was introduced to classical works like Marshall's *Principles of Economics* as well as new work like Hicks's *Value and Capital* and Samuelson's *Foundations*. (Later, at Trinity, he would be disappointed in the relative lack of mathematical sophistication of his Cambridge dons.) His principal passion, however, was politics, and before his first term ended, he was elected as one of the leaders of the Communist-dominated All India Students Federation. He read voraciously, skipped lectures, and spent most of his time debating Marx with his Stalinist friends in the coffeehouse on nearby College Street, a street that then as now was lined with hundreds of booksellers' stalls.

Later he recalled, "[A]s I look back at the fields of academic work in which I have felt most involved throughout my life . . . they were already among the concerns that were agitating me most in my undergraduate days in Calcutta."[9] Those concerns were crystallized by a life-and-death crisis in his second year at Presidency. Just before his nineteenth birthday, Sen felt a pea-sized lump in the roof of his mouth. A street-corner GP dismissed it as a fish bone that had worked its way under the skin. The lump, however, didn't disappear and, in fact, grew larger. After consulting a premed student who lived next door to him at the YMCA, he learned that cancers of the mouth were fairly common among Indian men. A few hours with a borrowed medical textbook convinced Sen that he was suffering from stage two squamous cell carcinoma.

It took months and the intervention of relatives and family friends to arrange a biopsy at Calcutta's Chittaranjan Cancer Hospital. The biopsy confirmed his suspicions. At that time, a diagnosis of oral cancer was a virtual death sentence. Surgery generally only accelerated the spread of the cancer, and, as a result, most sufferers slowly suffocated as their tumors gradually blocked their windpipes. Radiation, the standard treatment in England and the United States since the turn of the century, was still too difficult and costly to be widely available in Calcutta. After reading about radiation in medical journals, Sen was finally able to locate a radiologist willing to treat him. The radiologist urged Sen to let him use a maximum dose, justifying the risk by saying, "I can't repeat it." For Sen, possible death from radiation sickness seemed preferable to certain death by suffocation.

The treatment was unpleasant, if not as awful as its aftermath. A mold was taken. A leaden mask was made. Radium needles were placed inside the mask. Like the hero of the Victor Hugo novel, Sen sat in a tiny hospital room with the mask screwed down "so there would be no movement." The procedure was repeated every day for one week. "I sat there for four hours at a time and read," Sen recalled. "Out of the window, I could see a tree. What a relief it was to see that one green tree."

The dose was massive, some 10,000 rads—four or five times today's standard dose. After he was sent home—his parents now lived in Calcutta—the effects of the radiation appeared: weeping skin, ulcers, bone pain, raw throat, difficulty in swallowing. "My mouth was like putty. I couldn't go to class. I couldn't eat solids. I lived in fear of infection. I couldn't laugh without bleeding. It brought home to me the misery of human life." That misery lasted for nearly six months. And these were only the immediate effects. Over time, radiation destroys bone and tissue, leads to necrosis and fractures, and destroys the teeth.

Cancer was a defining moment. For one thing, learning that you have a devastating illness—especially one that carries a social stigma, that's taboo—isn't just terrifying, it makes you feel polluted, powerless, outcast. The awful things Sen witnessed growing up were shocking, but they were happening to others. This was happening to him. It produced a lasting identification with others who were also hurting, voiceless, deprived.

Overcoming the cancer was also empowering. His mother, Amita, said, "I gave Amartya to God when he was nineteen." [10] But he has said that taking matters into his own hands left him with enormous confidence in his own instincts and initiative. "Psychologically I was in the driver's seat," he recalled. "I was aggressive. I was the one asking whether I would live. What was best? What could I do? I had a sense of victory."

When he returned to his classes, he said, "I came back with a bang," full of fresh purpose. He promptly got a first, won all sorts of prizes, including a debate prize. He applied to Trinity College in Cambridge, where Nehru had studied. He was rejected initially but, some months later, unexpectedly summoned. His father spent half his slender capital to pay for the journey. The airfare on BOAC proved prohibitive, so in September 1953, just before his twentieth birthday, Sen sailed from Bombay to Liverpool on the same liner as the Indian women's hockey team.

In Cambridge, new miseries—darkness, cold, awful food, dreadful loneliness—awaited Sen. His teeth, addled by radiation, were a chronic source of pain and embarrassment. The landlady of his rooming house, who had begged the college not to send her "Coloreds," fussed at him about such things as drawing the curtains at night. "You can't see out, but they can see you," she would say, as if he were a stupid child.

At the university, Sen encountered a political minefield, split by rancorous rivalries among Keynes's disciples and critics. Indira Gandhi, who studied in Santiniketan for a year, once remarked that she learned an essential survival skill there; namely, "the ability to live quietly within myself, no matter what was happening outside." [11] Sen, too, got by on inner quiet, eagerly engaging with scholars from different sides of the ideological divide but without giving up his independent way of looking at things.

He did, however, fall under the spell of the brilliant and imperious

Joan Robinson. Newly independent India was divided not just along ethnic lines but also between diametrically opposite visions of the future.
Gandhians envisioned a spiritual and rural India of hand-loom weavers.
Followers of Nehru saw Soviet-style central planning and a landscape
dotted with dams and steel plants. Sen's thesis, *The Choice of Techniques*
(1960), criticized government planning in India by underscoring basic
economic principles. After completing a second BA and finishing his thesis
research, he returned to India, first teaching at Jadvapur University and,
subsequently, at the newly formed Delhi School of Economics.

Had Sen stopped writing in the late 1960s, we would know him, if
at all, as one of a generation of Indian development economists who
favored Nehru's formula of heavy industry, state-run enterprises, and
self-sufficiency—a formula that produced disappointing results and that
has since been disavowed by most economists, including Sen. But beginning around 1970, he shifted his intellectual focus sharply and produced
a series of startling philosophical papers on social welfare that account for
much of his influence today.

This burst of creativity followed a second life crisis. In the space of a
year, he accepted a position at the London School of Economics, his father
died of prostate cancer, and he was forced to confront the possibility that
his own cancer had come back. Once in England, he underwent extensive
reconstructive surgery when it turned out that his symptoms had been
due to the delayed effects of his earlier radiation. After a long and difficult convalescence, he left his wife and two young daughters and fell
passionately in love with Eva Colorni, an Italian economist who was the
daughter of a prominent Socialist philosopher killed by Fascist forces in
World War II. Eva encouraged Sen's new philosophical interests and urged
him to apply his ethical insights to urgent issues like poverty, hunger, and
women's inequality. He and Eva lived together in London from 1973 until
her death from stomach cancer in 1985, and had two children together.

When Sen turned to ethics, Robinson advised her star pupil to "give
up all that rubbish." He ignored her counsel. At Eva's urging, he made
a detailed study of what he saw as a particularly grim consequence of
authoritarian rule, notably famines. "I once weighed nearly 250 children

from two villages in West Bengal to check their nutritional status related to income, sex, etc," he said. "If anyone asked me what I was doing, I would have said, I was doing welfare economics." [12]

Famines like the one in Bengal, Sen argued, occurred despite adequate food supplies when higher prices and joblessness robbed the most vulnerable groups in society of their "entitlements" to food and when the lack of elections and a free press stifled public pressure on the government to intervene. By contrast, Robinson applauded draconian policies such as the Great Leap Forward—and, as Sen later pointed out with some bitterness, "failed utterly to detect the biggest famine in modern history," in which an estimated 15 million to 30 million Chinese perished in the aftermath of forced collectivization. He never broke with her publicly, but by the time Robinson died in 1983, they had not corresponded in years.

In the 1970s and 1980s, Sen proposed a general theory of social welfare that attempted to integrate economists' traditional concern for material well-being with political philosophers' traditional concern with individual rights and justice. Objecting to the utilitarian creed of his fellow economists, which called for judging material progress chiefly by the growth of GDP per head—and citing a long tradition from Aristotle to Friedrich von Hayek and John Rawls— Sen argued that freedom, not opulence per se, was the true measure of a good society, a primary end as well as a principal means of economic development. He wished, as he says in his book on India, to "judge development by the expansion of substantive human freedoms—not just by economic growth . . . or technical progress, or social modernization . . . [These] have to be appraised . . . in terms of their actual effectiveness in enriching the lives and liberties of people—rather than taking them to be valuable in themselves." [13]

Sen asked three separate questions to which he proposed answers: Can society make choices in a way that reflects individual citizen's preferences? Can individual rights be reconciled with economic welfare? And, lastly, what is the measure of a just society?

In the 1930s and 1940s, libertarians worried that the West would trade its commitment to political liberalism for economic security. A generation later, Sen worried that India and other third world nations would sacrifice democracy in the race for economic growth. How, he wondered, could conflicts between social action and individual rights be resolved?

When Sen took up the issue in the late 1960s, two powerful challenges had been laid down to the possibility of reconciling the two. One came from Friedrich von Hayek, who feared that "specialists" and specific interests would impose their own preferences on everyone. By substituting government plans for individual plans, he argued, the authorities were imposing a monolithic set of priorities on individuals who would prefer to make their own trade-offs among diverse alternatives.

The other, even more daunting, challenge came from a wholly unexpected quarter: a highly theoretical tract, *Social Choice and Individual Values*, published in 1951 by a politically moderate American economist, Kenneth Arrow. Sen first encountered Arrow's impossibility theorem at Presidency College. The theorem appeared to be a logically unassailable proof that no system of voting could produce results that reflected the preferences of individual citizens. Except when there was complete consensus, all voting procedures yielded outcomes that were, in some sense, undemocratic. Most of Sen's college friends were Stalinists. While Sen shared their enthusiasm for equality, he "worried about political authoritarianism." Was Arrow's theorem a rationale for dictatorship?

Since Arrow's result could not be challenged directly, Sen chose to probe Arrow's seemingly innocuous assumptions—the conditions any democratic procedure had to meet. In *Collective Choice and Social Welfare*, published in 1970, he argued that one of Arrow's axioms—which ruled out comparisons between different citizens' well-being—was not, in fact, essential, and was indeed arbitrary. If such comparisons were allowed, Sen suggested, the impossibility result no longer held. Sen, and researchers inspired by him, went on to pinpoint the conditions that would enable decision-making rules consistent with individual rights to work. In fact, Sen's "comparative metrics of well-being" launched his pursuit of yardsticks that could prod democratic governments to adopt social reforms, and launched a long-running debate over the best ways to define and measure poverty.

Is there a conflict between individual rights and economic welfare? Sen proceeded to mount a much broader attack on utilitarianism, inspired, in part, by John Rawls's magisterial 1971 *A Theory of Justice*, widely seen as a philosophical justification for the modern welfare state. Utilitarians, including most economists, believe that society needs only to take account of the welfare of its citizens. Rights enter their thinking, if at all, only indirectly, as contributors to happiness or satisfaction. In a twist on Jeremy Bentham's rule "the greatest good for the greatest number," Rawls's "difference principle" states that a just society should maximize the welfare of the worst-off group. This, of course, is a very utilitarian idea. But Rawls's primary focus is on individual rights, which take precedence over material well-being, and which economists have traditionally ignored.

In another 1970 journal article, "The Impossibility of the Paretian Liberal," Sen made an urgent case for paying attention to rights as well as welfare, pointing out a potentially serious conflict between the two.[14] Most economists accept a criterion for economic welfare far less demanding than those proposed by Bentham or Rawls. The optimal state, argued the nineteenth-century Italian economist Vilfredo Pareto, is one in which it is no longer possible to make anyone better off without making someone else worse off. In other words, it is a society in which all conflict-free opportunities for improving overall utility have been exploited.

But Sen showed that even this seemingly innocuous standard can run afoul of individual rights. When many people define their own welfare in terms of restricting the freedom of others—Muslim clerics are happier if schooling is prohibited for girls, Catholic nuns feel better if abortion is illegal, parents like the idea of outlawing recreational drugs—free choice can conflict with Pareto optimality.

Suppose, to use an updated version of Sen's original example, "Prude" values the freedom to practice his own religion, but not as much as he would a ban on pornography. "Lewd" values the freedom to read pornography, but not as much as he would a ban on religion. If the government outlawed both pornography and religion, both would be happier—but also less free.

Economics hasn't necessarily come to grips with Sen's message, but economists are now more apt to reflect on what's left out of the equation when they use GDP to measure material gains. In particular, they have become more circumspect in equating GDP with well-being. Sen argues that GDP leaves out individuals' opportunities that may be more important to them than their income, a serious shortcoming. To be sure, one could argue (as does Eric Maskin, a Nobel laureate in economics) that while rights and welfare may sometimes conflict, in general, rights can be seen as a way of protecting welfare. The right to read what you want—as opposed to having people tell you what you can read—usually results in higher incomes, for example. Still, given how polarizing such conflicts are in many societies, it was remarkably prescient of Sen to have pointed it out three decades ago.

In expanding his assault on utilitarianism, Sen argued that growth alone is an inadequate measure of welfare because it doesn't reveal how well or badly deprived individuals are doing, and that utility—based on people's current preferences and satisfaction—is similarly misleading, because deprived individuals often tailor their aspirations to their impoverished circumstances. To get around these and other difficulties, he proposed a new way of thinking about the goals of development. He called it "the capabilities approach."

What creates welfare aren't goods per se, but the activity for which they are acquired, he argued. I value my car for increasing my mobility, for example. You might value your education for giving you the chance to participate in discussions like ours. According to Sen's view, income is significant because of the opportunities it creates. But the actual opportunities (or capabilities, as Sen calls them) also depend on a number of other factors—not just preferences that might be constrained by deprivation—such as life spans, health, and literacy. These factors should also be considered when measuring welfare. He constructed alternative welfare indicators, such as the UN's Human Development Index, in this spirit.

Paralleling his approach to welfare measurement, Sen maintains that individuals' capabilities constitute the principal dimension in which societies should strive for greater equality—though he stops short of saying which capabilities and what degree of equality. He admits, however, that one problem with this definition of justice is that individuals make decisions—whether to work hard or to complete an education—that determine their capabilities at a later stage.

How does postcolonial India measure up in Sen's view? His book with Jean Drèze, *India: Development and Participation,* begins by quoting Nehru's stirring speech at the hour of independence: "Long years ago we made a tryst with destiny, and now the time comes when we shall redeem our pledge." Nehru pledged among other things, "the ending of poverty and ignorance and disease and inequality of opportunity." [15] For Sen, "the ambitious goals . . . remain largely unaccomplished." A student once asked Sen why he hadn't changed the "content" of his thoughts since the 1950s. "Because," said Sen, "the surrounding environment hasn't changed. I'll probably die saying the same things."

To be sure, he points out, much has changed in the third world. Life expectancy has expanded from forty-six to sixty-five, and real per capita income has more than tripled. Many once-poor countries now have more in common with rich ones than with the ones they left behind.

Yet, Sen says, the 1 billion citizens of the world's biggest democracy are still among the world's most deprived. Extreme deprivation, he points out, is now concentrated in just two regions of the world: South Asia and sub-Saharan Africa. Life expectancy is higher in India than in Africa because India has escaped large-scale famine and avoided civil war. But in terms of illiteracy, chronic malnutrition, and economic and social inequality, India does as badly or worse than sub-Saharan Africa, especially with respect to the condition of women.

India and China were comparably poor in the 1940s. Today, however, China's life expectancy is seventy-three versus India's sixty-four. Infant mortality is less than half of India's, seventeen deaths per one thousand births versus fifty. Nutritional yardsticks also show that China is far ahead in eliminating chronic malnourishment. Literacy rates for adolescents are well over 90 percent in China—with no gap between girls and boys—versus much lower, and far more divergent, rates in India. [16] Of course, India's citizens enjoy democratic rights—including a free press—that China's more prosperous citizens can still only dream of. The challenge for Sen and other economists advising India is how to nudge its economy along China's path of globalization without sacrificing the democracy of which Sen and India are so proud.

Robert Solow, who won a Nobel for his theory of economic growth, once called Sen the "conscience of our profession." For a long time, however, Sen's approach to economics was decidedly suspect on both left and right. At Cambridge, Calcutta, and Delhi in the 1950s and 1960s, when Soviet-style planning was in vogue, Sen was persona non grata on the Left. In the 1980s and 1990s, when free markets were once again the rage, the then chairman of the Nobel Prize committee confidently predicted, "Sen will never get the prize." Sen won the Nobel in 1998 "for his contributions to welfare economics."

But times have changed. These days, when he travels to Asia, Sen is treated more like Gandhi than like a professor of economics as he travels about with police escorts. In Santiniketan in January 2002, crowds lined the streets to watch him come and go, and young girls at Visva-Bharati dropped to the ground to touch his feet (something he brusquely discourages). Determined, like the poet who named him, to use his Nobel Prize to draw attention to issues he cares about, he has donated half of his $1 million winnings to establish two foundations, one in West Bengal, the other in Bangladesh, to promote the spread of elementary education in rural areas.

As India's Soviet-style, autarkic, and bureaucratic economy became increasingly dysfunctional, while Japan and the Asian tigers achieved modern standards of living, Sen moved away from the view that Western aid and better terms of trade were the keys to third world growth and closer to the Schumpeterian perspective that local conditions are decisive and that nations do, ultimately, control their own destinies. He embraced deregulation and opening the Indian economy to foreign trade and investment while insisting on government intervention on behalf of the poor, especially in health, education, and nutrition. The argument ended when Mao suspended the Cultural Revolution and introduced economic freedoms. China's remarkable leap into modernity left the Soviet Union in the dust and fatally discredited the Soviet economic model.

Epilogue

Imagining the Future

Most journeys start in the imagination. The grand pursuit to make mankind the master of its circumstances is no exception.

The eighteenth-century founders of economics had a vision of economic organization in which voluntary cooperation would replace coercion. But they assumed that nine out of ten human beings were sentenced by God or nature to lives of grinding poverty and toil. Two thousand years of history convinced them that the bulk of humanity had as much chance of escaping its fate as prisoners of a penal colony surrounded by a vast ocean had of escaping theirs.

Dickens, Mayhew, and Marshall came to economics in Victorian London during a revolution in productivity and living standards. They were animated by a brighter, more hopeful vision. To them, the ocean looked more like a moat. They could imagine humanity on the far side, advancing a step at a time toward an ever-receding horizon. These economic thinkers were driven not only by intellectual curiosity and a hunger for theory but also by the desire to put mankind in the saddle. They were searching for instruments of mastery: ideas that could be used to foster societies characterized by individual freedom and abundance instead of moral and material collapse.

Economic intelligence, they learned, was far more critical to success than territory, population, natural resources, or even technological leadership. Ideas matter. Indeed, as Keynes famously put it during the Great Depression, "the world is ruled by little else."[1] Like Marshall, Keynes thought of economics as an engine of analysis that could separate the wheat of experience from the chaff, and he was convinced that economic ideas had done more to transform the world than the steam engine. Economic truths might be less permanent than mathematical truths, but economic theory was essential for learning what worked, what didn't, what mattered, what did not. Inflation could lift output in the short run but not the long run. Gains in productivity are the primary driver of wages and living standards. Education and a safety net could reduce poverty without producing economic stagnation. A stable currency was necessary for economic stability, a healthy financial system is essential for innovation. As Robert Solow observed, "The questions keep changing and the answers to even old questions keep changing as society evolves. That doesn't mean we don't know quite a bit that is useful, at any given moment."[2]

Economic calamities—financial panics, hyperinflations, depressions, social conflicts and wars—have always triggered crises of confidence, but they have not come close to wiping out the cumulative gains in average living standards. The Great Depression put economics as well as the modern decentralized economy on trial. World War II ended on a note of gloom and self-doubt with Keynesian economists anticipating a twilight age of stagnation and disciples of Hayek fearing the triumph of socialism in the West. Instead, growth rebounded and living standards shot up. Governments achieved some success in managing their economies. Since World War II, history has been dominated by the escape of more and more of the world's population from abject poverty. Defeated Germany and Japan rose phoenixlike from the ashes in the 1950s and 1960s. China launched its remarkable growth spurt around 1970. More recently, India has emerged from decades of stagnation.

Reality has mostly outstripped imagination. Even Schumpeter could not have imagined that the world's population would be six times greater but ten times more affluent. Or that the fraction of the earth's citizens who lived in abject poverty would dwindle by five-sixths. Or that the average Chinese lives at least as well today, if not better, than the average Englishman did in 1950. Only Fisher would not have been surprised to learn that the average lifespan has risen to two and one-half times that of 1820 and continues to edge higher. Remarkably, even the Great Recession of 2008 to 2009, the most severe economic crisis since the 1930s, did not reverse the prior gains in productivity and income. Life expectancy kept going up. The world financial system did not collapse. There was no second great depression.

Madmen in authority from the Kaiser to Hitler, Stalin, and Mao have repeatedly tried—still try—to ignore or even suppress economic truths. But the more nations escape poverty and make their own economic destinies, the less compelling the rationalizations of dictators become. Rather than overtaking the West, the Soviet Union collapsed in 1990.

There is no going back. Nobody debates any longer whether we should or shouldn't control our economic circumstances, only how. Asked about their fondest hope for the future, protestors in Cairo named economic improvement. The men and women on the streets of Tunisia, Syria, and other Middle Eastern nations in 2011 represent the latest wave of citizens to imagine an economic future characterized by growth, stability, and a business climate favorable to entrepreneurship. Once such a future can be imagined, returning to the nightmare of the past seems increasingly impossible.

Acknowledgments

I've accumulated a staggering number of debts while researching and writing this book.

The largest are owed to three individuals without whom *Grand Pursuit* would never have been started, sustained, or completed: My editor, Alice Mayhew, who showed me, patiently and with extraordinary dedication, how to turn economics, history, and biography into a story; my agent, Kathy Robbins, who launched the whole enterprise with her customary elan; and my eldest daughter, Clara O'Brien, who helped bring the project to its conclusion.

Many individuals and institutions generously supported my research. Topping the list are Amartya Sen, Emma Rothschild, Eric Maskin, Philip Griffiths, Alan Krueger, Orley Aschenfelter, and Eric Wanner. I am grateful to the Institute for Advanced Study, Russell Sage Foundation, Churchill and Kings Colleges at the University of Cambridge, the Yaddo Foundation, and the MacDowell Colony for stimulating and productive visits.

At Columbia, I got some of my best ideas from the extraordinary Bruce C. N. Greenwald. My journalism colleague Jim Stewart was a constant source of support and sage advice. And I can't thank my teaching partner, Ed McKelvey, enough for giving his all to our students for the past two years, to my benefit as well as theirs.

I had the incredible good fortune to work with a remarkable team at Simon & Schuster. Special thanks to Jonathan Karp, Richard Rhorer, Roger Labrie, Rachel Bergmann, Irene Kheradi, Gina DiMascia, John Wahler,

Nancy Inglis, Jackie Seow, Ruth Lee-Mui, Tracey Guest, Danielle Lynn, Rachelle Andujar, and the imperturbable Phil Metcalf.

For granting me interviews and sources, I am grateful to William Barber; Peter Singer; Harold James; Bruce Caldwell; Meghnad Desai; Marina Whitman; Peter Dougherty; Geoffrey Harcourt; Prue Kerr; Frances Stewart; Francis Cairncross; Barbara Jeffrey; Dutta Jayasri; Avinash Dixit; Lawrence Hayek; Luigi Pasinetti; Bill Gibson; Laurie Kahn-Leavitt; Jim Mirlees; Hans Jörg Hennecke; Hans Jörg Klausinger; Nils Eric-Sahlin; Geoffrey Heal; the family of Margaret Paul; Harold Kuhn; Hugh Mellor; Peter Passell; Edmund Phelps; Jagdish Bhagwati; Andrew Scull; Ruth and Carl Kaysen; Peter Boettke; Guido Hulsmann; William Barnett; Vernon Smith; Peter Temin; Elizabeth Darling; Robert Skidelsky; Andrew Scull; Mark Whitaker; Ray Monk; Amartya Sen; Paul Samuelson, his wife, Risha, and longtime assistant, Janice Murray; Robert and Anita Summers; Robert and Bobbie Solow; Milton and Rose Friedman; and Kenneth Arrow.

Ruth Tenenbaum waged a ruthless but always good-natured campaign against errors and omissions. Alexandra Saunders, Louise Story, Jonathan Hull, Barry Harbaugh, Melanie Hollands, Rachel Elbaum, Catherine Viette, and Tori Finkle provided helpful research assistance at various points. I am especially thankful to Bill Gibson for spotting logical and other lapses in the final galleys.

Most of the research for this book was done in archives and libraries, and I would especially like to thank the staffs of the following for their kindness and expert guidance: Marshall Library, University of Cambridge, Trinity College Archive, Kings College Archive, City of Cambridge Archive, Harvard University Archive, London School of Economics Archive, MIT Archive, Hoover Institution Archive. My gratitude extends, naturally, to the creators of Google Books, J-Stor, Lexis-Nexis, the Marx-Engels Archive, and numerous online archives and libraries that have revolutionized historical research.

The last word is, as always, for my children, Clara, Lily, and Jack, and my dear friends. They know that it's all about the journey . . . and who travels with you.

Notes

NOTES ON SOURCES

In researching *Grand Pursuit* I consulted and read hundreds of inspiring and informative works of biography, history, and economics. But the following are the books on which I especially relied for facts, ideas, and understanding:

Preface: Claire Tomalin, *Jane Austen: A Life*, (New York: Knopf, 1997); Gregory Clark, *A Farewell to Alms: A Brief Economic History of Modern Britain* (Princeton: Princeton University Press, 2009); Bradford DeLong, unpublished economic history of the twentieth century; Harold Perkin, *The Origins of Modern British Society* (London: Routledge, 1990); Angus Maddison, *The World Economy: A Millennial Perspective* (Paris: OECD Publishing, 2006) and *The World Economy: Historical Statistics* (Paris: OECD Publishing, 2006); Mark Blaug, *Economic Theory in Retrospect* (Cambridge: Cambridge University Press, 1983); T. W. Hutchison, *A Review of Economic Doctrines 1870–1939* (London: Clarendon Press, 1966); W. W. Rostow, *Theorists of Economic Growth from David Hume to the Present* (Oxford: Oxford University Press, 1992); Niall Ferguson, *Cash Nexus* (New York: Basic Books, 2001).

Act I Prologue: Kitson Clark, "Hunger and Politics in 1842" (*Journal of Modern History*, 24, no. 4 (December, 1953); James P. Henderson, " 'Political Economy Is a Mere Skeleton Unless . . .' : What Can Social Economists Learn from Charles Dickens" (*Review of Social Economy*, 58, no. 2 (June, 2000); Michael Slater, *Charles Dickens* (New Haven: Yale University Press, 2009).

Chapter I: David McLellan, *Karl Marx: Interviews and Recollections* (New York: Barnes & Noble, 1981); Gustav Mayer, *Friedrich Engels: A Biography* (Berlin: H. Fertig, 1969); Steve Marcus, *Engels, Manchester and the Working Class* (New York: Norton, 1974); Gertrude Himmelfarb, *The Idea of Poverty: England in the Early Industrial Age* (New York: Alfred A. Knopf, 1984) and *Poverty and Compas-*

sion: The Moral Imagination of the Late Victorians (New York: Random House, 1991); David McLellan, *Karl Marx: His Life and Thought* (London: Macmillan, 1973); Isaiah Berlin, *Karl Marx: His Life and Environment* (London: Thornton Butterworth, 1939); Francis Wheen, *Karl Marx: A Life* (New York: W. W. Norton & Co., 1999); Dirk Struik, *Birth of the Communist Manifesto* (New York: International Publishers, 1986); Anne Humphereys, *Travels into the Poor Man's Country: The Work of Henry Mayhew* (Athens: University of Georgia Press, 1977); Francis Sheppard, *London 1808–1870: The Infernal Wen* (London: Seeker and Warburg, 1971); Asa Briggs, *Victorian Cities* (Berkeley: University of California Press, 1993); Gareth Stedman Jones, *Outcast London* (London: Penguin Books, 1982).

Chapter II: Mary Paley Marshall, *What I Remember* (Cambridge: Cambridge University Press, 1947); J. M. Keynes, "Alfred Marshall 1842–1924," in Arthur Pigou, ed., *Memorials of Alfred Marshall* (London: MacMillan, 1925); Gertrude Himmelfarb, *Poverty and Compassion: The Moral Imagination of the Late Victorians* (New York: Alfred A. Knopf, 1991); Peter Groenewegen, *A Soaring Eagle: Alfred Marshall 1842–1924* (London: E. Elgar, 1995); Mark Whitaker, *Early Economic Writings of Alfred Marshall, Vols. 1–2* (London: The Royal Economic Society, 1975); Mark Whitaker, *The Correspondence of Alfred Marshall, Vols. 1–3* (Cambridge: Cambridge University Press, 1996); Tizziano Raffaeli, Eugenio F. Biagini, Rita McWilliams Tullberg, eds., *Alfred Marshall's Lectures to Women: Some Economic Questions Directly Connected to the Welfare of the Laborer* (Aldershott, UK: Edward Elgar Publishing Company, 1995).

Chapter III: Barbara Caine, *Destined to Be Wives: The Sisters of Beatrice Webb* (Oxford: Clarendon Press, 1986); Carole Seymour Jones, *Beatrice Webb: Woman of Conflict* (Chicago: Ivan R. Dee, 1992); Royden Harrison, *The Life and Times of Sidney and Beatrice Webb: The Formative Years, 1858–1903* (London: Palgrave, 1999): Kitty Muggeridge and Ruth Adam, *Beatrice Webb: A Life, 1858–1943* (New York: Alfred A. Knopf, 1968); Margaret Cole, *Beatrice Webb* (New York: Harcourt Brace, 1946); Michael Holroyd, *Bernard Shaw* (London: Chatto and Windus, 1997); William Manchester, *The Last Lion: Winston Spencer Churchill: Visions of Glory, 1874–1932* (New York: Little Brown, 1983); Gertrude Himmelfarb, *Poverty and Compassion: The Moral Imagination of the Late Victorians* (New York: Random House, 1991); Elie Halevy, *A History of the English People in the Nineteenth Century, Vol. 6, The Rule of Democracy (1905–1914)*, (London: Ernest Benn Ltd., 1952); Jeanne and Norman MacKenzie, *The Diary of Beatrice Webb*, vols. 1–4 (London: Virago, 1984); Norman MacKenzie, *The Letters of Sidney and Beatrice Webb*, vols. 1–3 (Cambridge: Cambridge University Press, 2008).

Chapter IV: Muriel Rukeyser, *Willard Gibbs* (New York: Doubleday, Doran and Co., 1942), William J. Barber, ed., *The Works of Irving Fisher*, vols. 1–17 (London: Pickering and Chatto, 1997); Irving Norton Fisher, *My Father: Irving Fisher* (New York: Comet Press, 1956); Muriel Rukeyser, *Willard Gibbs: American Genius*

(New York: Doubleday, Doran and Co., 1942); Robert Loring Allen, *Irving Fisher: A Biography* (Cambridge: Blackwell Publishers, 1993); Richard Hofstadter, *The Age of Reform: From Bryan to FDR and Social Darwinism in American Thought* (New York: George Braziller, Inc., 1969); Jeremy Atack and Peter Passell, *A New Economic View of American History* (New York: W. W. Norton, 1994); Perry Mehrling, "Love and Death: The Wealth of Irving Fisher," *Research in the History of Economic Thought and Methodology*, Warren J. Samuels and Jeff E. Biddle, eds. (Amsterdam: Elsevier Science, 2001; New York: Harcourt Brace Jovanovich, 1992), 47–61.

Chapter V: Seymour Harris, *Joseph Schumpeter: Social Scientist* (Cambridge, Mass.: Harvard University Press, 1951); Wolfgang F. Stolper, *Joseph Alois Schumpeter: The Public Life of a Private Man* (Princeton: Princeton University Press, 1994); Robert Loring Allen, *Opening Doors: The Life and Works of Joseph Schumpeter*, vol. I (New Brunswick: Transaction Publishers, 1991); Richard Swedberg, *Joseph A. Schumpeter: His Life and Work* (Cambridge, UK: Polity Press, 1991); Thomas K. McCraw, *Prophet of Innovation: Joseph Schumpeter and Creative Destruction* (Cambridge, Mass.: Harvard University Press, 2007); Charles A. Gulik, *Austria from Habsburg to Hitler*, vol. I (Berkeley: University of California Press, 1948); David F. Good, *The Economic Rise of the Hapsburg Empire 1750–1914* (Berkeley: University of California Press, 1990); Joseph Schumpeter, *History of Economic Analysis* (Cambridge, Mass.: Harvard University Press, 1954).

Act II Prologue: Charles John Holmes, *Self and Partners (Mostly Self): Being the Reminiscences of C. J. Holmes* (London: Macmillan, 1936); Anne Emberton, "Keynes and the Degas Sale," *History Today*, December 31, 1995; Ray Monk, *Ludwig Wittgenstein: The Duty of Genius* (New York: Penguin Books, 1991); Ray Monk, *Bertrand Russell: The Spirit of Solitude 1872–1921*, vol. I (New York: Simon & Schuster, 1996); Hugh Mellor, *Frank Ramsey: Better Than the Stars* (London: BBC, 1994); Henry Andrews Cotton, with a Foreword by Adolf Meyer, *The Defective, Delinquent and Insane: The Relation of Focal Infections to Their Causation, Treatment and Prevention, Lectures delivered at Princeton University, January 11, 13, 14, 15, 1921* (Princeton: Princeton University Press, 1922).

Chapter VI: Eduard Marz, *Joseph A. Schumpeter: Forscher, Lehrer und Politiker*, Munchen: R. Oldenbourg, 1983); Eduard Marz, "Joseph Schumpeter as Minister of Finance in X Helmut Frisch, in *Schumpeterian Economics* (New York: Praeger, 1981); F. L. Carsten, *The First Austrian Republic* (Aldershot, UK: Wildwood House, 1986); F. L. Carsten, *Revolution in Central Europe: 1918–1919*, Aldershot, UK: Wildwood House, 1988); David Fales Strong, *Austria (October 1918–March 1919)* (New York: CUP, 1939); Norbert Schausberger, *Der Griff nach Oesterreich: Der Anschluss* (Wien, Muenchen: Jugend und Volk, 1988); Otto Bauer, *The Austrian Revolution*, (London: Parsons, 1925); Eduard Marz, *Austrian Banking and Financial Policy: Creditanstalt at a Turning Point, 1913–1923* (New York: St. Martin's Press, 1984); Christine Klusacek and Kurt Stimmer, *Dokumentation zur Oesterreichische Zeitgeschichte 1918–1928* (Wien und Muenchen: Jugend und Volk, 1984); Joseph A. Schumpeter, *Aufsatze zur Wirtschaftspolitik*, Wolfgang F. Stolper and Christian Seidl, eds. (Tuebingen: JCB Mohr, 1985); Joseph A. Schumpeter, *Politische Reden*, Seidl and Stolper, eds. (Tubingen: JCB Mohr, 1992).

Chapter VII: D. E. Moggridge, ed., *The Collected Writings of John Maynard Keynes*, vols. 1–30 (London: Macmillan, 1971–1989); Paul Mantoux, *The Carthaginian Peace or The Economic Consequences of Mr. Keynes* (Oxford: Oxford University Press, 1946); Robert Skidelsky, *John Maynard Keynes, Vol. 1, Hopes Betrayed* (New York: Viking, 1986); Donald E. Moggridge, *Maynard Keynes: An Economist's Biography* (London: Routledge, 2009); Margaret MacMillan, *Paris 1919: Six Months That Changed the World* (New York: Random House, 2002).

Chapter VIII: Peter Gay, *Freud: A Life of Our Time* (New York: W. W. Norton, 1988); F. L. Carsten, *The First Austrian Republic* (Aldershot: Wildwood House, 1986); Otto Bauer, *The Austrian Revolution* (London: Parsons, 1925); Eduard Marz, *Austrian Banking and Financial Policy: Creditanstalt at a Turning Point, 1913–1923* (New York: St. Martin's Press, 1984).

Chapter IX: Robert Skidelsky, *John Maynard Keynes, Vol. 2: The Economist as Savior 1920–1937* (London: Macmillan, 1992); D. E. Moggridge, *Maynard Keynes: An Economist's Biography* (London, Routledge, 1992); Irving Norton Fisher, *My Father: Irving Fisher* (New York: Comet Press, 1956), Robert Loring Allen, *Irving Fisher: A Biography* (Cambridge: Blackwell Publishers, 1993); Milton Friedman, *Money Mischief: Episodes in Monetary History* (New York: Harcourt Jovanovich Brace, 1992).

Chapter X: Robert Skidelsky, *John Maynard Keynes, Vol. II: The Economist as Savior 1920–1937* (London: Macmillan, 1992); D. E. Moggridge, *Maynard Keynes: An Economist's Biography* (London, Routledge, 1992); Irving Norton Fisher, *My Father: Irving Fisher* (New York: Comet Press, 1956), Robert Loring Allen, *Irving Fisher: A Biography* (Cambridge: Blackwell Publishers, 1993); Milton Friedman, *Money Mischief: Episodes in Monetary History* (New York: Harcourt Brace Jovanovich, 1992).

Chapter XI: Nahid Aslanbeigui and Guy Oakes, *The Provocative Joan Robinson: The Making of a Cambridge Economist* (Durham, N.C.: Duke University Press, 2009); Marjorie Shepherd Turner, *Joan Robinson and the Americans* (Armonk, N.Y.: ME Sharpe, 1989).

Chapter XII: Robert Skidelsky, *John Maynard Keynes, Vol. 3: Fighting for Freedom, 1937–1946* (New York: Viking, 2001); David Kennedy, *Freedom from Fear: The American People and in Depression and War* (Oxford: Oxford University Press, 1999); Milton Friedman and Rose Friedman, *Two Lucky People* (Chicago: University of Chicago Press, 1998), Herbert Stein, *Presidential Economics: The Making of Economic Policy from Roosevelt to Clinton* (Washington, D.C.: American Enterprise Institute, 1994); Stephen Kresge and W. W. Bartley III, eds., *The Collected Works of F. A. Hayek*, vols. 1–17 (Chicago: University of Chicago Press, 1989).

Chapter XIII: Seymour Harris, *Joseph Schumpeter: Social Scientist* (Cambridge, Mass.: Harvard University Press, 1951); Wolfgang F. Stolper, *Joseph Alois Schumpeter: The Public Life of a Private Man* (Princeton: Princeton University Press, 1994); Robert Loring Allen, *Opening Doors: The Life and Works of Joseph Schumpeter,* vol. I (New Brunswick: Transaction Publishers, 1991); Richard Swedberg, *Joseph A. Schumpeter: His Life and Work* (Cambridge: Polity Press, 1991); Thomas K. McCraw, *Prophet of Innovation: Joseph Schumpeter and Creative Destruction* (Cambridge, Mass.: Harvard University Press, 2007).

Act III Prologue: James McGregor Burns, *Roosevelt: The Soldier of Freedom, 1940–1945* (New York: Harcourt Brace Jovanovich, 1970).

Chapter XIV: Robert Skidelsky, *John Maynard Keynes, Vol. 3: Fighting for Freedom* (New York, Viking, 2000).

Chapter XV: Alan Ebenstein, *Hayek's Journey* (Chicago: University of Chicago Press, 2005); Hans Jorg Hennecke, *Friedrich von Hayek* (Hamburg: Junius Verlag GmbH, 2010); Werner Erhard, *Germany's Comeback in the World Market* (New York: Macmillan, 1954).

Chapter XVI: Richard Reeves, *President Kennedy* (New York: Simon & Schuster, 1993); Herbert Stein, *Presidential Economics: The Making of Economic Policy from Roosevelt to Clinton* (Washington, D.C: American Enterprise Institute, 1994).

Chapter XVII: John Lewis Gaddis, *The Cold War: A New History* (New York: Alfred A. Knopf, 2009); Marjorie Shepherd Turner, *Joan Robinson and the Americans* (Armonk, N.Y.: ME Sharpe, 1989).

Chapter XVIII: Amartya Sen, *Development as Freedom* (New York: Alfred A. Knopf, 1999); Amartya Sen, *The Idea of Justice* (Cambridge, Mass.: Harvard University Press, 2009).

PREFACE: THE NINE PARTS OF MANKIND

1. John Kenneth Galbraith, *The Affluent Society* (Boston: Houghton Mifflin, 1958).
2. Edmund Burke, "A Vindication of Natural Society Or, a View of the Miseries and Evil Arising to Mankind from Every Species of Artificial Society, In a Letter to Lord **** by a Late Noble Writer, 1756," *Writings and Speeches* (New York: Little Brown and Co., 1901), 59.
3. Patrick Colquhoun, *A Treatise on the Wealth, Power, and Resources of the British Empire* (London: Jay Mawman, 1814(1812)), 49.

4. James Heldman, "How Wealthy is Mr. Darcy—Really? Pound and Dollars in the World of *Pride and Prejudice*," *Persuasions* (Jane Austen Society), 38–39.

5. Author's calculation based on data from Colquhoun, *Wealth, Power, and Resources*; Harold Perkin, *The Origins of Modern British Society* (London: Routledge), 20–21; and Roderick Floud and Paul Johnson, *Cambridge Economic History of Modern Britain* (Cambridge: Cambridge University Press, 2004), 92.

6. Jane Austen to Cassandra Austen, *Jane Austen's Letters*, Deirdre le Fay, ed. (Oxford: Oxford University Press, 1995) and Anonymous, *How to Keep House! Or Comfort and Elegance on 150 to 200 a Year* (London: James Bollaert, 1835, 14th edition).

7. Claire Tomalin, *Jane Austen, A Life* (New York: Knopf, 1997).

8. Burke, *Vindication*, 59.

9. Gregory Clark, *A Farewell to Alms: A Brief Economic History of the World* (Princeton: Princeton University Press, 2009).

10. James Edward Austen Leigh, *A Memoir of Jane Austen* (London: Richard Bentley & Son, 1871), 13.

11. Clark, *A Farewell to Alms.*

12. Robert Giffen, *Notes on the Progress of the Working Classes (1883) and Further Notes on the Progress of the Working Classes, Essays in Finance* (London: Putnam & Sons, 1886), 419.

13. Burke, *Vindication*, 60.

14. Tomalin, *Jane Austen*, 96.

15. Patrick Colquhoun, *A Treatise on Indigence* (London: J. Hatchard, 1806).

16. Leigh, *A Memoir of Jane Austen*, 13.

17. Giffen, 379.

18. Alfred Marshall, *The Present Position of Economics: An Inaugural Lecture* (1885), 57.

19. John Maynard Keynes, "Economic Possibilities for our Grandchildren," *Essays in Persuasion* (London: Macmillan, 1931), 344.

20. John Maynard Keynes, Toast on the occasion of his retirement from the editorship of *The Economic Journal*, 1945, quoted in Roy Harrod, *The Life of John Maynard Keynes* (London: Harcourt Brace, 1951), 193–94.

ACT I: PROLOGUE: MR. SENTIMENT VERSUS SCROOGE

1. G. Kitson Clark, "Hunger and Politics in 1842," *Journal of Modern History*, 24, no. 4 (December 1953), 355–74.

2. Thomas Carlyle, *Past and Present* (London: Chapman and Hall, 1843), 26.

3. Charles Dickens, *Daily News* (London), January 21, 1846.

4. Asa Briggs, ed., *Chartist Studies* (London: Macmillan, 1959).

5. Carlyle, *Past and Present*, 335.

6. Thomas Carlyle to John A. Carlyle, Chelsea, London, March 17, 1840. The Carlyle Letters Online, 2007, http://carlyleletters.org (accessed January 2, 2011).

7. John Stuart Mill to John Robertson, London, July 12, 1837 in *The Earlier Letters of John Stuart Mill*, vol. 1, *1812–1848*, ed. Francis E. Mineka (University of Toronto Press, 1963), 343 (paraphrasing Carlyle's description of Camille Desmoulins in *The French Revolution: A History*, [1837]).

8. Quoted in Michael Slater, *Charles Dickens: A Life Defined by Writing* (New Haven, Conn.: Yale University Press, 2009), 143.

9. Thomas Carlyle, "Occasional Discourse on the Negro Question," *Fraser's Magazine for Town and Country* 40 (February 1849), 672.

10. Edmund Burke, *A Vindication of Natural Society: or, a View of the Miseries and Evils Arising to Mankind from Every Species of Artificial Society* (1756), Frank N. Pagano, ed. (Indianapolis: Liberty Fund, Inc., 1982), 87.

11. Thomas Robert Malthus, *An Essay on the Principle of Population, as It Affects the Future Improvement of Society with Remarks on the Speculations of Mr. Godwin, M. Condorcet, and Other Writers* (London: J. Johnson, 1798), 30.

12. Ibid., 139.

13. Ibid., 31.

14. Leviticus 19:18, Romans 13:9.

15. Charles Dickens, *Oliver Twist*, vol. 1 (London: Richard Bentley, 1838), 25.

16. Nicholas Bakalar, "In Reality, Oliver's Diet Wasn't Truly Dickensian," *New York Times*, December 29, 2008.

17. Charles Dickens, *American Notes for General Circulation*, vol. 2 (London: Chapman and Hall, 1842), 304.

18. Charles Dickens to Dr. Southwood Smith, March 10, 1843, in *The Letters of Charles Dickens*, vol. 3, *1842–1843*, eds. Madeline House, Graham Storey, Kathleen Mary Tillotson, Angus Eanon, Nina Burgis (Oxford: Oxford University Press, 2002), 461.

19. James P. Henderson, "'Political Economy is a Mere Skeleton Unless . . .': What Can Social Economists Learn from Charles Dickens?," *Review of Social Economy*, 58, no. 2 (June 2000): 141–51.

20. Charles Dickens, *A Christmas Carol; in Prose: Being a Ghost Story of Christmas* (London: Chapman Hall, 1843).

21. Henderson, "Political Economy," 146.

22. Dickens, *A Christmas Carol*, 96.

23. Thomas Malthus, *An Essay on the Principle of Population: Or, a View of Its Past and Present Effects on Human Happiness: With an Inquiry Into Our Prospects Respecting the Future Removal or Mitigation of the Evils Which It Occasions*, 2nd ed. (London: J. Johnson, 1803), 532.

24. Dickens, *A Christmas Carol*, 94.

25. Michael Slater, introduction and notes to Charles Dickens, *A Christmas Carol and Other Christmas Writings* (London: Penguin, 2003), xi.

26. Anthony Trollope, *The Warden* (London: Longman, Brown, Green, and Longmans, 1855), chap. 15.

27. Charles Dickens, "The Bemoaned Past," *All the Year Round: A Weekly Journal, With Which is Incorporated Household Words*, no. 161 (May 24, 1862).

28. Sir Robert Peel to Sir James Graham, August 1842, quoted in Clark, "Hunger and Politics in 1842."

29. Charles Dickens, "On Strike," *Household Words; A Weekly Journal* no. 203 (February 11, 1854).

30. Ibid.

31. Joseph A. Schumpeter, *The Economics and Sociology of Capitalism*, ed. Richard Swedberg (Princeton: Princeton University Press, 1991), 290. Schumpeter coined this phrase to describe Alfred Marshall's view that economics "is not a body of concrete truth, but an engine for the discovery of concrete truth." Alfred Marshall, *The Present Position of Economics: An Inaugural Lecture* (London: Macmillan and Co., 1885), 25.

32. John Maynard Keynes, introduction to *Cambridge Economic Handbooks*, I (London: Nesbit and Co. and Cambridge: Cambridge University Press, 1921).

I: PERFECTLY NEW: ENGELS AND MARX IN THE AGE OF MIRACLES

1. Walter Bagehot, *Lombard Street: A Description of the Money Market* (New York: Scribner, Armstrong & Co., 1873), 20.

2. Friedrich Engels to Karl Marx, November 19, 1844, Marxists Internet Archive, www.marxists.org/archive/marx/works/1844/letters/44_11_19.htm.

3. Ibid.

4. Friedrich Engels to Arnold Ruge, June 15, 1844, quoted in Steven Marcus, *Engels, Manchester and the Working Class* (New York: Random House, 1976), 82.

5. Friedrich Engels, writing as "X," four-part series on political and economic conditions in England, *Rheinische Zeitung*, December 8, 9, 10, and 25, 1842.

6. Edwin Chadwick, *Report on the Sanitary Condition of the Labouring Population of Great Britain* (1842).

7. Friedrich Engels, *Rheinische Zeitung*, December 8, 1842.

8. Charles Dickens, *Nicholas Nickleby*, chap. 43.

9. Friedrich Engels, *The Condition of the Working Class in England in 1844, With a Preface Written in 1892*, trans. Florence Kelley Wischnewetzky (London: Swan Sonnenschein & Co., 1892).

10. Quoted in David McLellan, *Friedrich Engels* (New York: The Viking Press, 1977), 22.

11. Friedrich Engels, "Outlines of a Critique of Political Economy," *Deutsch-Französiche Jahrbücher* 1, no. 1 (February 1844).

12. Karl Marx, preface to *A Contribution to the Critique of Political Economy* (1859) in Karl Marx and Friedrich Engels, *Selected Works* (Moscow: Foreign Languages Publishing House, 1951).

13. Karl Heinzen, *Erlebtes* [Experiences], vol. 2 (Boston: 1864), 423–24.

14. Isaiah Berlin, *Karl Marx: His Life and Environment,* London: Thompson Butterworth, 1939), 26.

15. George Bernard Shaw, "The Webbs," in Sidney and Beatrice Webb, *The Truth About Soviet Russia* London: Longmans Green, (1942).

16. Arnold Ruge to Ludwig Feuerbach, May 15, 1844, in Arnold Ruge, *Briefwechsel und Tagebuchblatter aus den Jahren 1825–1880* [Correspondence and Diaries from the Years 1825–1880], vol. 1 (Berlin: Weidmannsche Buchhandlung, 1886), 342–49.

17. Karl Marx to Arnold Ruge, July 9, 1842, in ed., *Marx/Engels Collected Works,* vol. 1, 398–91.

18. Karl Marx, "A Contribution to the Critique of Hegel's Philosophy of Right," *Deutsch-Französische Jahrbücher* 1, no. 1 (February 1844).

19. Karl Marx to Arnold Ruge, September 1843; *Deutsch-Französische Jahrbücher* 1, no. 1 (1844), www.marxists.org/archive/marx/works/1843/letters/43_09-alt.htm.

20. Gertrude Himmelfarb, *The Idea of Poverty: England in the Early Industrial Age* (New York: Alfred A. Knopf, 1984), 278.

21. Friedrich Engels to Karl Marx, November 19, 1844, in *Der Briefwechsel Zwischen F. Engels und K. Marx,* vol. 1 (Stuttgart, 1913), Marxist Internet Archive, www.marxists.org/archive/marx/works/1844/letters/44_11_19.htm.

22. Friedrich Engels to Karl Marx, January 20, 1845, in *Der Briefwechsel Zwischen F. Engels und K. Marx,* vol. 1 (Stuttgart, 1913), Marxist Internet Archive, www.marxists.org/archive/marx/works/1845/letters/45_01_20.htm.

23. Engels, *Condition of the Working Class in England,* 296.

24. Friedrich Engels to Karl Marx, Paris, January 20, 1845. Marxist Internet Archive, http://www.marxists.org/archive/marx/works/1845/letters/45_01_20.htm (accessed March 15, 2011).

25. Karl Marx, Preface to *Das Kapital* (1867), Friedrich Engels, ed., trans. S. Moore and E. Aveling (New York: Charles H. Kerr & Company, 1906), 14.

26. Henry Mayhew, letter 47, *The Morning Chronicle,* April 11, 1850. *The Morning Chronicle Survey of Labour and the Poor: The Metropolitan Districts,* vol. 4 (Sussex or London: Caliban Books, 1981), 97.

27. Asa Briggs, *Victorian Cities* (Berkeley: University of California Press, 1993), 311.

28. William Lucas Sargant, "On the Vital Statistics of Birmingham and Seven Other Large Towns," *Journal of the Statistical Society of London* 29, no. 1 (March 1866): 92–111.

29. Roy Porter, *London: A Social History* (Cambridge, Mass.: Harvard University Press, 1998), 187.

30. Engels, *Condition of the Working Class in England,* 23.

31. Charles Dickens, *Dombey and Son* (London: Bradbury and Evans, 1846–1848).

32. Niall Ferguson, *The House of Rothschild*, vol. 1 (New York: Penguin Books, 2000), 401.

33. Bagehot, *Lombard Street*, 4.

34. Ferguson, *The House of Rothschild*, vol. 12, 65.

35. Peter Geoffrey Hall, *The Industries of London* (London: Hutchison, 1962), 21.

36. Francis Sheppard, *London 1808–1870: The Infernal Wen* (London: Secker and Warburg, 1971), 158–59.

37. George Dodd, *Dodd's Curiosities of Industry* (Henry Lea's Publications, 1858), 158.

38. Hall, *The Industries of London*, 6.

39. Henry Mayhew, *The Daily Chronicle*, October 19, 1849, in *The Unknown Mayhew: Selections from the* Daily Chronicle *1849–1850* (London: Penguin Books 1884), 13.

40. John Maynard Keynes, *The Economic Consequences of the Peace* (London: Macmillan, 1919), 9.

41. Henry James, *Essays in London and Elsewhere* (New York: Harper and Brothers, 1893), 19.

42. George Augustus Sala, *Twice Around the Clock; or the Hours of the Day and Night in London* (London: Richard Marsh, 1862), 157.

43. Henry Mayhew and John Binney, *The Criminal Prisons of London and Scenes of Prison Life* (London: Griffin, Bohn and Co., 1862), 28.

44. *The Economist*, May 19, 1866.

45. Harold Perkin, *The Origins of Modern English Society 1780–1880* (London: Routledge and Kegan Paul, 1969), 91. Sala, *Twice Around the Clock*, 157.

46. Mayhew and Binny, *The Criminal Prisons of London*, 28.

47. Ibid., 32.

48. Henry James, "London," *Century Illustrated Magazine*, December 1888, 228.

49. Charles Dickens, *Bleak House* (London: Chapman and Hall, 1853), 1.

50. Friedrich Engels to Karl Marx, Paris, November 23–24, 1847. Marxist Internet Archive, http://www.marxists.org/archive/marx/works/1844/letters/ 44_11_19.htm (accessed March 14, 2011). Friedrich Engels, "Introduction to English Edition of *The Communist Manifesto*," (1888), in Karl Marx and Friedrich Engels, *The Communist Manifesto*, Gareth Stedman Jones, ed. (London: Penguin Books, 2002).

51. David McLellan, *Karl Marx: His Life and Thought* (London: Macmillan, 1973), 169.

52. Friedrich Lessner, quoted in David McLellan, ed., *Karl Marx: Interviews and Recollections* (London: Barnes & Noble, 1981), 45.

53. *The Rules of the Communist League*, adopted by the Second Congress of the Communist League in December 1847, in Karl Marx and Friedrich Engels, *The Communist Manifesto* (London: Lawrence & Wishart, 1930).

54. Friedrich Engels, "The Book of Revelation" (1883), in *Marx and Engels on Religion* (Moscow: Foreign Languages Publishing House, 1957), 204.

55. Karl Marx, preface to *The Poverty of Philosophy* (1847), trans. H. Quelch (Chicago: Carles H. Kerr & Company, 1920).

56. Anonymous [Robert Chambers], *Vestiges of the Natural History of Creation* (London: John Churchill, 1844).

57. Marx and Engels, *Communist Manifesto*, 223.

58. Friedrich Engels, "The English Constitution," *Vorwaerts!*, no. 75 (September 1844).

59. Angus Maddison, *Statistics on World Population, GDP and Per Capita GDP, 1–2008 AD*, www.ggdc.net/maddison/.

60. Marx and Engels, *Communist Manifesto*, 224.

61. Gregory Clark, *A Farewell to Alms: A Brief Economic History of the World* (Princeton, N.J.: Princeton University Press, 2007); Roderick Floud and Bernard Harris, "Health, Height and Welfare: Britain 1700–1800," in *Health and Welfare During Industrialization*, eds. Richard H. Steckel and Roderick Floud (Chicago: University of Chicago Press, 1997), 91–126.

62. Charles H. Feinstein, "Pessimism Perpetuated: Real Wages and the Standard of Living in Britain During and After the Industrial Revolution," *Journal of Economic History* vol. 58, no. 3 (September 1998), 630.

63. Thomas Carlyle, *Past and Present* (London: Chapman and Hall, 1843), 4.

64. Arnold Toynbee, *Lectures on the Industrial Revolution of the Eighteenth Century in England* (London: Rivingtons, 1884), 84.

65. John Stuart Mill, *The Subjection of Women* (London: Longmans, Green, Reader, and Dyer, 1869), 29–30.

66. John Stuart Mill, *Principles of Political Economy*, vol. 2 (London: John W. Parker, 1848), 312.

67. Marx and Engels, *Communist Manifesto*, 233, 258.

68. McLellan, *Karl Marx*, 35.

69. Charles Dickens, "Perfidious Patmos," in *Household Words; A Weekly Journal* 7, no. 155 (March 12, 1853).

70. *Times* (London), October 26, 1849.

71. Anne Humpherys, *Travels into the Poor Man's Country: The Work of Henry Mayhew* (Athens: University of Georgia Press, 1977), 203.

72. Henry Mayhew, "A Visit to the Cholera Districts of Bermondsey," *The Morning Chronicle*, September 24, 1849.

73. E. P. Thompson and Eileen Yeo, eds., *The Unknown Mayhew* (London: The Merlin Press Ltd., 2009), 102–3.

74. Quoted in Humpherys, *Travels*, 31.

75. Charles Dickens, *Oliver Twist* (London: Richard Bentley, 1838), 252.

76. Gareth Stedman Jones, *Outcast London: A Study in the Relationship Between Classes in Victorian Society* (New York: Penguin Books, 1984).

77. Henry Mayhew, letter 11, *The Morning Chronicle,* November 23, 1849.
78. Ibid.
79. Ibid., letter 15, December 7, 1849.
80. Henry Mayhew, "Needlewomen Forced into Prostitution," letter 8, *The Morning Chronicle,* November 13, 1849.
81. Thomas Carlyle, "The Present Time," *Latter Day Pamphlets,* issue 9 (February 1, 1850).
82. Douglas Jerrold to Mary Cowden Clarke, February 1850.
83. Henry Mayhew, *London Labour and the London Poor,* no. 40, September 13, 1851.
84. John Stuart Mill, "The Claims of Labor," *Edinburgh Review,* April 1845.
85. Quoted in James Anthony Froude, *Thomas Carlyle: A History of the First Forty Years of His Life (1795–1835)* (Montana: Kessinger Publishing, 2006), 298.
86. Ibid., 282.
87. Thomas Carlyle, "Chartism," *Latter Day Pamphlets,* London, December 1839.
88. John Stuart Mill to Macvey Napier, November 9, 1844.
89. H. G. Wells, "Men Like Gods," *Hearst's International* 42, no. 6 (December 1922); David Ricardo, *On the Principles of Political Economy and Taxation* (London: John Murray, 1817).
90. Mill, *Principles of Political Economy,* vol. 3, ch. 1.
91. Thomas Carlyle, "Occasional Discourses on the Negro Question," *Fraser's Magazine,* 1849.
92. *Archiv für die Geschichte des Sozialismus und der Arbeiterbewegung* [Archive for the History of Socialism and the Workers' Movement] (1922), 56ff 10, quoted in McLellan, *Karl Marx,* 268–69.
93. Karl Marx to Joseph Weydemeyer, London, August 2, 1851, in Saul K. Padover, ed., *The Letters of Karl Marx* (Englewood Cliffs, N.J.: Prentice-Hall, 1979), 72–73.
94. John Tallis, *Tallis's History and Description of the Crystal Palace, and the Exhibition of the World's Industry in 1851* London and New York: John Tallis and Co., 1852), quoted in Jeffrey A. Auerbach, *The Great Exhibition of 1851,* (1999).
95. "The Revolutionary Movement," *Neue Rheinische Zeitung,* no. 184, January 1, 1850.
96. Ibid.
97. Karl Marx and Friedrich Engels, *Neue Rheinische Zeitung,* May–October, 1850.
98. Marx and Engels, *Communist Manifesto,* chap. 1.
99. Karl Marx to Ludwig Kugelmann, December 28, 1862.
100. Ibid.
101. Marx and Engels, *Communist Manifesto,* chap. 1.

102. Marx, *Das Kapital,* 671.

103. John Stuart Mill, *Essays on Some Unsettled Questions of Political Economy* (London, 1844), 94.

104. Mark Blaug, *Economic Theory in Retrospect* (Cambridge, UK: Cambridge University Press, 1997).

105. Marx, *Das Kapital,* 711.

106. Robert Giffen, "The Recent Rate of Material Progress in England," *Opening Address to the Economic Science and Statistics Section of the British Association* (London: George Bell and Sons, 1887), 3.

107. R. Dudley Baxter, *National Income, the United Kingdom* (London: Macmillan, 1868), B1.

108. E. J. Hobsbawm, "The Standard of Living During the Industrial Revolution: A Discussion," *Economic History Review,* New Series, vol. 16, no. 1 (1963), 119–34.

109. Charles H. Feinstein, "Pessimism Perpetuated: Real Wages and the Standard of Living in Britain During and After the Industrial Revolution," *Journal of Economic History* 58, no. 3, 625–58.

110. Gareth Stedman Jones, introduction to Marx and Engels, *Communist Manifesto.*

111. Marx, *Das Kapital,* 264–65, note 3.

112. Egon Erwin Kisch, *Karl Marx in Karlsbad* (Weimar, Germany: Aufbau Verlag, 1968); Saul Kussiel Padover, *Karl Marx: An Intimate Biography* (New York: McGraw-Hill, 1978).

113. Karl Marx to Friedrich Engels, July 22, 1859. Reviews appeared in *Das Volk,* no. 14, August 6, 1859, and no. 16, August 20, 1859.

114. Berlin, *Karl Marx,* 13.

115. Ibid.

116. Karl Marx, "The Right of Inheritance," August 2 and 3, 1869, endorsed by the General Council on August 3, 1869. Marxist Internet Archive, www.marxists.org/archive/marx/iwma/documents/1869/inheritance-report.htm.

117. Karl Marx to Eleanor Marx, quoted in McLellan, *Karl Marx,* 334.

118. Karl Marx to Ludwig Kugelmann, December 28, 1862.

119. Fyodor Dostoyevsky, *Winter Notes on Summer Impressions* (Illinois: Northwestern University Press, 1988).

120. Author's calculation.

121. *The Bankers Magazine,* vol. 26 (1886), 639; *Illustrated London News,* May 19, 1866; *Times* (London), May 12, 1866.

122. *New York Times,* May 26, 1866.

123. Sidney Pollard and Paul Robertson, *The British Shipbuilding Industry, 1870–1914* (Cambridge, Mass: Harvard University Press, 1999), 77–79.

124. Marx, *Das Kapital,* 733–34.

125. J. H. Clapham, *An Economic History of Modern Britain,* vol. 3, *Machines and National Rivalries (1887–1914) with an Epilogue (1914–1929)* (Cambridge: Cambridge University Press, 1932), 117.

126. Karl Marx to Friedrich Engels, April 6, 1866.

127. Friedrich Engels to Karl Marx, May 1, 1866.

128. Karl Marx to Friedrich Engels, July 7, 1866.

129. Marx, *Das Kapital,* 715.

130. William Gladstone, "Budget Speech of 1863, House of Commons," *Times* (London), April 16, 1863.

131. Honore de Balzac, *The Unknown Masterpiece* (1845), www.gutenberg.org/files/23060/23060-h/23060-h.htm.

132. John Maynard Keynes, *Essays in Persuasion* (W. W. Norton and Co., 1963), 300.

II: MUST THERE BE A PROLETARIAT? MARSHALL'S PATRON SAINT

1. Ralph Waldo Emerson, "Ode, Inscribed to William H. Channing," in *Poems* (London: Chapman Bros., 1847).

2. Alfred Marshall, "Speech to the Cambridge University Senate," in John K. Whitaker, ed., *The Correspondence of Alfred Marshall,* vol. 3, *Towards the Close, 1903–1924* (Cambridge: Cambridge University Press, 1996), 399.

3. *Morning Star,* quoted in Karl Marx, *Das Kapital* (1867), Modern Library edition. 734; W.D.B, "Distress in Poplar," letter to the editor, *The Times* (London), January 12, 1867; "Able-Bodied Poor Breaking Stones for Roads, Bethnel Green London," *Illustrated London News,* February 15 (or 16?); "The Distress at the East End: A Soup Kitchen in Ratcliff Highway," *Illustrated London News,* February 16, 1867; "The Distress at the East End: A Soup Kitchen in Ratcliff Highway," *Illustrated London News,* February 16, 1867.

4. Sara Horrell and Jane Humphries, "Old Questions, New Data, and Alternative Perspectives: Families' Living Standards in the Industrial Revolution," *Journal of Economic History* 52, no. 4 (December 1992): 849–80.

5. Florence Nightingale to Charles Bracebridge, January 1867, in Lynn McDonald, ed., *The Collected Works of Florence Nightingale,* vol. 6, *Florence Nightingale on Public Health Care* (Ontario: Wilfred Laurier University Press, 2002).

6. Francis Sheppard, *London: 1808–1870* (London: Secker & Warburg, 1971), 340.

7. *Times* (London) May 6, 1867.

8. Robert Giffen, "Proceedings of the Statistical Society," *Journal of the Statistical Society of London* 30, no. 4 (December 1867), 564–65.

9. Henry Fawcett, *Pauperism: Its Causes and Remedies* (London: Macmillan, 1871), 1–2.

10. Edward Denison, *A Brief Record: Being Selections from Letters and Other Writings of Edward Denison*, ed. Sir Bryan Baldwin Leighton (London: E. Barrett and Sons, 1871), 46.

11. Alfred Marshall, in John Maynard Keynes, "Alfred Marshall, 1842–1924," in Arthur Pigou, ed., *Memorials of Alfred Marshall* (London: Macmillan, 1925), 358.

12. Alfred Marshall, "Lecture Outlines," in Tiziano Raffaelli, Eugenio F. Biagini, Rita McWilliams Tullberg, eds., *Alfred Marshall's Lectures to Women: Some Economic Questions Directly Connected to the Welfare of the Laborer* (Aldershott, UK: Edward Elgar Publishing Company, 1995), 141.

13. Ronald H. Coase, "Alfred Marshall's Mother and Father," and "Alfred Marshall's Family and Ancestry," in *Essays on Economics and Economists* (Chicago: University of Chicago Press), 1994.

14. Charles Dickens, *Great Expectations* (London: Chapman and Hall, 1861).

15. *The Times* (London), October 8, 1859.

16. Anthony Trollope, *The Vicar of Bullhampton* (London: Bradbury and Evans, 1870).

17. K. Theodore Hoppen, *The Mid-Victorian Generation 1846–1886* (Oxford, UK: Clarendon Press, 1998), 40.

18. Anthony Trollope, *The Warden* (London: Longman, Brown, Green, and Longmans, 1855), 289.

19. Peter D. Groenewegen, *A Soaring Eagle: Alfred Marshall: 1842–1924* (London: E. Elgar, 1995), 51.

20. David McLellan, *Karl Marx: His Life and Thought* (New York: Harper and Row, 1974).

21. William Dudley Baxter, *National Income: The United Kingdom* (London: Macmillan, 1868), *Global Prices and Income History Website*, http://gpih.ucdavis.edu.

22. Groenewegen, *A Soaring Eagle*, 107.

23. John Maynard Keynes, "Alfred Marshall," in *Essays in Biography* (New York: W. W. Norton, 1951), 126.

24. Mary Paley Marshall, quoted in Keynes, "Alfred Marshall, 1842–1924," 37.

25. Ibid.

26. Groenewegen, *A Soaring Eagle*, 62.

27. Leslie Stephen, *Sketches from Cambridge by a Don* (London: Macmillan and Co., 1865), 37–38.

28. Alfred Marshall to James Ward, in John King Whitaker, ed., *The Correspondence of Alfred Marshall*, vol. 2, *At the Summit, 1891–1902* (Cambridge: Cambridge University Press, 1996), 441.

29. Mary Paley Marshall, quoted in Keynes, "Alfred Marshall, 1842–1924," 37.

30. Alfred Marshall, "Speech to Promote a Memorial for Henry Sidgwick," in Whitaker, ed., *Correspondence*, vol. 2, 441.

31. Groenewegen, *A Soaring Eagle*, 3.
32. Alfred Marshall, preface to *Money, Credit and Commerce* (London: Macmillan, 1923).
33. Beatrice Webb, *My Apprenticeship* (London: Macmillan, 1926).
34. Alfred Marshall to James Ward, September 23, 1900, in Whitaker, ed., *Correspondence*, vol. 2.
35. Gertrude Himmelfarb, "The Politics of Democracy: The English Reform Act of 1867," *Journal of British Studies* 6, no. 1 (November 1966): 97.
36. Henry James, preface to *The Princess Casamassima* (New York: Charles Scribner's Sons, 1908 [1886]), vi.
37. Keynes, "Alfred Marshall, 1842–1924," 37.
38. Marshall to Ward, September 23, 1900.
39. Henry Sidgwick, *Principles of Political Economy* (London: Macmillan and Co., 1883), 4.
40. John E. Cairnes, *The Character and Logical Method of Political Economy; Being a Course of Lectures Delivered in the Hilary Term, 1857* (London: Longmans, Brown, Green, Longmans and Roberts, 1857), 38.
41. John Ruskin, *Unto This Last: Four Essays in the First Principles of Political Economy* (London: Smith Elder, 1862).
42. Gertrude Himmelfarb, *The Idea of Poverty: England in the Early Industrial Age* (New York: Alfred A. Knopf, 1984).
43. Leslie Stephen, *The Life of Henry Fawcett* (London: Smith, Elder and Co., 1886), 222.
44. Ruskin, *Unto This Last*, 20.
45. J. E. Cairnes, *Some Leading Principles of Political Economy* (London: University College London, 1874), 291.
46. John Stuart Mill, *Principles of Political Economy* (London: Longmans, Green and Co., 1885), 220.
47. Francis Bowen, *The Principles of Political Economy Applied to the Condition, the Resources, and the Institutions of the American People* (Boston: Little, Brown and Co., 1859) 197.
48. Millicent Garrett Fawcett, *Political Economy for Beginners* (London: Macmillan, 1906), 100.
49. John Francis Bray, *Labour's Wrongs and Labour's Remedy, or the Age of Might and the Age of Right* (Leeds, UK: David Green Briggate, 1839).
50. Alfred Marshall, *Alfred Marshall's Lectures to Women, Some Economic Questions Directly Connected to the Welfare of the Labourer* (Aldershot, UK: Edward Elgar, 1995), lecture 5, 119.
51. Ibid., 156.
52. Ibid., quotes from April and May 1873 notes by Mary Paley, 47, 53, and 54.
53. Joseph Schumpeter, *The History of Economic Thought* (Cambridge, Mass.: Harvard University Press, 1954), 290.

54. Arnold Toynbee, *Lectures on the Industrial Revolution of the Eighteenth Century in England* (London: Rivingtons, 1884) 175.

55. Marshall, *Lectures to Women*. May 9, 1873.

56. Ibid.

57. Mary Paley Marshall, *What I Remember*, 9.

58. Winnie Seebohm in Martha Vicinus, *Independent Women: Work and Community for Single Women 1850–1920* (Chicago: University of Chicago Press, 1985), 151.

59. W. S. Gilbert and Arthur Sullivan, *Princess Ida*, 1884.

60. Mary Paley Marshall, *What I Remember*, 16.

61. George Eliot, *The Mill on the Floss* (London: William Blackwood and Sons, 1860).

62. Mary Paley Marshall, *What I Remember*, 20–21.

63. Lord Ernle, *English Farming Past and Present*, 3d ed. (London: Longmans, Green and Co., 1922), 407.

64. *The Cambridge Chronicle*, April 11, 1874.

65. Alf Peacock, "Revolt of the Fields in East Anglia," *Our History* (London: Communist Party of Britain, 1968).

66. *Times* (London), April 13, 1874.

67. George Eliot, *Middlemarch* (Edinburgh: William Blackwood and Son, 1874).

68. *The Cambridge Chronicle*, April 25, 1874, and May 8, 1874.

69. *The Cambridge Independent Press*, May 16, 1874.

70. Alfred Marshall, "Beehive Articles," 1874; in R. Harrison, "Two Early Articles by Alfred Marshall," *Economic Journal* 73 (September 1963): 422–30.

71. Alfred Marshall, quoted in *The Cambridge Independent Press*, May 16, 1874.

72. Alfred Marshall to Rebecca Marshall, Niagara Falls, July 10, 1875, in John K. Whitaker, ed., *The Correspondence of Alfred Marshall, Economist, vol. 1, Climbing, 1868–1890* (Cambridge: Cambridge University Press, 1996), 68–70.

73. Ibid., Alfred Marshall to Rebecca Marshall, Springfield, Mass., June 12, 1875.

74. Ibid.

75. Ibid., Alfred Marshall to Rebecca Marshall, Boston, June 20, 1875, 54.

76. Ibid., Alfred Marshall to Rebecca Marshall, Cleveland, July 18, 1875, 71.

77. Alfred Marshall, "Some Features of American Industry," November 17, 1875, lecture to the Cambridge Moral Sciences Club, in John K. Whitaker, ed., *The Early Economic Writings of Alfred Marshall, 1867–1890*, vol. 2 (London: The Royal Economic Society, 1975), 369.

78. Alfred Marshall to Rebecca Marshall, Cleveland, July 18, 1875, in Whitaker, *Correspondence*, vol. 1, 72.

79. Keynes, "Alfred Marshall: 1842–1924," *Essays in Biography* (New York: W. W. Norton and Co., 1951), 142.

80. John K. Whitaker, "The Evolution of Alfred Marshall's Economic Thought and Writings Over the Years," in Whitaker, *Early Economic Writings*, 57.

81. Alfred Marshall, "Some Features of American Industry," in Whitaker, *Early Economic Writings*, 354.

82. *Reminiscences of America in 1869 by Two Englishmen* (London: Sampson, Low and Son and Marston, 1870).

83. Mary Paley Marshall, *What I Remember*.

84. Marshall, "Some Features of American Industry," 357.

85. Alfred Marshall to Rebecca Marshall, Lowell, Mass., and Cambridge, Mass., June 22, 1875, in Whitaker, *Correspondence*, vol. 1, 58.

86. *Reminiscences of America*, 86.

87. Samuel Bowles, *The Pacific Railroad—Open: How to Go, What to See* (Boston: Fields, Osgood and Co., 1869).

88. Marshall, "Some Features of American Industry," 357.

89. Alfred Marshall to Rebecca Marshall, Springfield, Mass., June 12, 1875, in Whitaker, *Correspondence*, vol. 1, 44.

90. *Reminiscences of America*, 242.

91. Marshall, "Some Features of American Industry," 359.

92. Alfred Marshall, *Principles of Economics* (London: Macmillan, 1890).

93. Marshall, "Some Features of American Industry," 353.

94. Alfred Marshall to Rebecca Marshall, Cleveland, July 18, 1875, in Whitaker, *Correspondence*, vol. 1, 71.

95. Ibid., June 5, 1875.

96. Marshall, "Some Features of American Industry," 372.

97. Karl Marx, *Das Kapital* (1887), Friedrich Engels, ed., trans. S. Moore and E. Aveling (New York: Charles H. Kerr & Company, 1906), 709.

98. Marshall, "Some Features of American Industry," 375.

99. Alfred Marshall to Rebecca Marshall, June 5, 1875, in Whitaker, *Correspondence*, vol. 1, 36.

100. Mary Paley Marshall, *What I Remember*, 19.

101. Phyllis Rose, *Parallel Lives: Five Victorian Marriages* (New York: Alfred A. Knopf, 1983).

102. Mary Paley Marshall, *What I Remember*, 23.

103. Alfred Marshall, testimony, December 1880, Governmental Committee on Intermediate and Higher Education in Wales and Monmouthshire, quoted in J. K. Whitaker, "Marshall: The Years 1877 to 1885," in *History of Political Economy* 4, no. 1 (Spring 1972): 6.

104. Mary Paley Marshall, *What I Remember*, 24.

105. Marion Fry Pease, "Some Reminiscences of University College, Bristol" (University of Bristol Library, Special Collections, 1942).

106. John Maynard Keynes, "Mary Paley Marshall," in *Essays in Biography*.

107. Marshall, in Whitaker, *Early Economic Writings*, 355.

108. Alfred Marshall, "The Present Position of Economics," in Whitaker, ed., *Early Economic Writings,* 51.

109. Marshall, *Principles of Economics,* 1.

110. Mill, *Principles of Political Economy,* vol. 2.

111. Mary Paley Marshall, unpublished notes, Marshall Archive, Cambridge University.

112. Charles Dickens, *Hard Times,* 1854, chap. 5.

113. Marx, *Das Kapital,* 462.

114. Alfred Marshall, in Whitaker, *Correspondence,* vol. 1, 59.

115. Alfred and Mary Marshall, *The Economics of Industry* (London MacMillan, 1879).

116. Mary Paley Marshall, *What I Remember,* 24.

117. Edwin Cannan, "Alfred Marshall, 1842–1924," *Economica* 4 (November 1924): 257–61.

118. Alfred Marshall to Macmillan, June 1878, in Whitaker, *Correspondence,* vol. 1, 97.

119. Henry George, *Progress and Poverty* (New York: Appleton, 1879).

120. *Jackson's Oxford Journal,* March 15, 1884. An account of the meeting is reprinted in an appendix to George Stigler, "Three Lectures on Progress and Poverty by Alfred Marshall," *Journal of Law and Economics* 12, no. (April 1969): 184–226.

121. Ibid., 186.

122. Ibid., 188.

123. Ibid., 208.

124. Ibid.

125. Ibid.

III: MISS POTTER'S PROFESSION:
WEBB AND THE HOUSEKEEPING STATE

1. George Eliot, *Middlemarch* (Edinburgh: William Blackwood and Son, 1874).

2. Daniel Pool, *What Jane Austen Ate and Charles Dickens Knew . . .* (New York: Simon & Schuster, 1993), 50–56.

3. Beatrice Webb, *My Apprenticeship* (London: Longmans, Green and Co., 1926), 48.

4. Michelle Jean Hoppe, "The London Season," *Literary Liaisons,* accessed March 14, 2011, www.literary-liaisons.com/article024.html.

5. Norman and Jeanne MacKenzie, eds., *The Diary of Beatrice Webb,* vol. 1, *1873–1892: "Glitter Around and Darkness Within"* (Cambridge, Mass.: Harvard University Press, 1982), 90 (July 15, 1883).

6. Ibid., 75 (February 22, 1883).

7. Ibid., 76 (February 26, 1883).

8. Ibid., 74 (January 2, 1883).
9. Beatrice Webb, *My Apprenticeship,* 157.
10. Henry James, preface to *The Portrait of a Lady* (New York: Charles Scribner's Sons, 1908).
11. Margaret Harkness to Beatrice Potter, n.d., 2/2/2 Papers of Beatrice and Sidney Webb, Passfield Archive, British Library of Political and Economic Science, London School of Economics and Political Science.
12. Henry James, *The Portrait of a Lady,* vol. 1 (London: Macmillan and Co., 1881), 193.
13. MacKenzie, *Diary of Beatrice Webb,* vol. 1, 80 (March 31, 1883).
14. Ibid., 54 (July 24, 1882).
15. Eliot, *Middlemarch,* 61.
16. Barbara Caine, *Destined to Be Wives: The Sisters of Beatrice Webb* (Oxford, UK: Clarendon Press, 1986), 12.
17. Webb, *My Apprenticeship,* 39.
18. Ibid., 42.
19. MacKenzie, *Diary of Beatrice Webb,* vol. 1, 4.
20. Norman and Jean MacKenzie, eds., *The Diary of Beatrice Webb,* vol. 2, *1892–1905: All the Good Things of Life* (Cambridge, Mass.: Harvard University Press, 1983), 132 (n.d. [March 1883]).
21. Herbert Spencer, *An Autobiography,* vol. 1 (New York: D. Appleton and Co., 1904), 298.
22. Webb, *My Apprenticeship,* 10.
23. MacKenzie, *Diary of Beatrice Webb,* vol. 2.
24. Spencer, *An Autobiography,* vol. 1, 298.
25. Ibid.
26. Webb, *My Apprenticeship,* 10.
27. MacKenzie, *Diary of Beatrice Webb,* vol. 1, 112 (April 8, 1884).
28. Ibid., 16 (March 6, 1874).
29. Webb, *My Apprenticeship,* 25 (emphasis added).
30. Kitty Muggeridge and Ruth Adam, *Beatrice Webb: A Life, 1858–1943* (New York: Alfred A. Knopf, 1968).
31. Ibid.
32. MacKenzie, *Diary of Beatrice Webb,* vol. 1, 19 (September 27, 1874).
33. Webb, *My Apprenticeship,* 56, 106, 112; MacKenzie, *Diary of Beatrice Webb,* vol. 1, 74 (January 2, 1883).
34. Webb, *My Apprenticeship,* 112–13.
35. MacKenzie, *Diary of Beatrice Webb,* vol. 1, 77 (March 1, 1883).
36. Ibid.
37. Ibid., 81 (March 31, 1883).
38. Ibid., 88 (May 24, 1883).
39. Ibid., 79 (March 24, 1883).

40. Helen Dandy Bosanquet, *Social Work in London, 1869–1912: A History of the Charity Organization Society* (New York: E. P. Dutton, 1914), 95.

41. MacKenzie, *Diary of Beatrice Webb*, vol. 1, 85 (May 18, 1883).

42. Ibid., 89 (July 7, 1883).

43. Ibid., 81 (March 31, 1883).

44. J. L. Garvin, *The Life of Joseph Chamberlain*, vol. 1 (London: Macmillan, 1932), 202.

45. MacKenzie, *Diary of Beatrice Webb*, vol. 1, 90–91 (July 15, 1883).

46. Ibid., 88 (June 3, 1883).

47. Ibid., 89 (June 27, 1883).

48. Ibid., 91 (July 15, 1883).

49. Ibid., 111 (March 16, 1884).

50. Ibid., 95 (September 22, 1883).

51. Ibid., 94 (September 26, 1883).

52. Ibid.

53. "The Bitter Cry of Outcast London," *The Pall Mall Gazette*, October 16, 1883 (issue 5808), 11.

54. Andrew Mearns, *The Bitter Cry of Outcast London: An Inquiry into the Condition of the Abject Poor* (London: James Clarke and Co., 1883), 5, 7; Earl Grey Pamphlets Collection (1883), Durham University Library, www.jstor .org/stable/60237726 (accessed January 13, 2011); Gertrude Himmelfarb, *Poverty and Compassion: The Moral Imagination of the Late Victorians* (New York: Alfred A. Knopf, 1991).

55. MacKenzie, *Diary of Beatrice Webb*, vol. 1, 137 (August 22, 1885).

56. Webb, *My Apprenticeship*, 150.

57. Ibid., 152.

58. MacKenzie, *Diary of Beatrice Webb*, vol. 1, 101 (December 31, 1883).

59. Ibid.

60. Ibid., 100 (December 27, 1883).

61. Ibid., 102–3 (January 12, 1884).

62. Ibid.

63. Webb, *My Apprenticeship*, 23.

64. Terence Ball, "Marx and Darwin: A Reconsideration," *Political Theory* 7, no. 4 (November 1979), 469–83.

65. Herbert Spencer, *The Man Versus the State* (London: Williams and Norgate, 1884), vii.

66. Arnold Toynbee, "Progress and Poverty: A Criticism of Mr. Henry George— Mr. George in England," London, January 18, 1883, in *Lectures on the Industrial Revolution of the 18th Century in England: Popular Addresses, Notes and Fragments by the Late Arnold Toynbee*, 6th ed. (London: Longmans, Green, and Co., 1902), 318.

67. MacKenzie, *Diary of Beatrice Webb*, vol. 1, 91 (July 15, 1883).

68. Beatrice Webb to Anna Swanwick, London, 1884 (not sent), in MacKenzie, ed., *The Letters of Sidney and Beatrice Webb*, vol. 1 (Cambridge: Cambridge University Press, 1978), 23.

69. MacKenzie, *Diary of Beatrice Webb*, vol. 1, 115 (April 22, 1884).

70. Webb, *My Apprenticeship*, 138.

71. MacKenzie, *Diary of Beatrice Webb*, vol. 1, 105–12 (March 16, 1884).

72. Joseph Chamberlain, "Work for the New Parliament," Birmingham, UK, January 5, 1885, in *Speeches of the Right Honorable Joseph Chamberlain, M.P.*, Henry W. Lucy, ed. (London: George Routledge and Sons, 1885), 104.

73. MacKenzie, *Diary of Beatrice Webb*, vol. 1, 117 (May 9, 1884).

74. Ibid., 119 (July 28, 1884).

75. Ibid. (August 1, 1884).

76. Webb, *My Apprenticeship*, 272.

77. MacKenzie, *Diary of Beatrice Webb*, vol. 1, 145 (December 19, 1885).

78. Ibid., 153 (January 1, 1886).

79. Ibid., 154 (February 11, 1886).

80. "London Under Mob Rule," *New York Times*, February 8, 1886.

81. Ibid.

82. Ibid.

83. "London's Recent Rioting," *New York Times*, February 10, 1886.

84. "The Rioting in the West-End," *Times* (London), February 10, 1886.

85. Queen Victoria to William Ewart Gladstone, Windsor Castle, February 11, 1886, in *The Letters of Queen Victoria; Third Series: A Selection of Her Majesty's Correspondence and Journal Between the Years 1886 and 1901*, vol. 1, George Earle Buckle, ed. (New York: Longmans, Green and Co., 1932), 52.

86. Ibid.

87. Margaret Harkness [John Law], *Out of Work* (London: Swan Schonnenschein, 1888).

88. Webb, *My Apprenticeship*, 273.

89. MacKenzie, *Diary of Beatrice Webb*, vol. 1, 154.

90. Beatrice Webb, "A Lady's View of the Unemployed at the East," *Pall Mall Gazette*, February 18, 1886.

91. Joseph Chamberlain to Beatrice Potter, February 25, 1886, 2/1/2 Passfield Archive.

92. Joseph Chamberlain to Beatrice Potter, February 28, 1886, 2/1/2 Passfield Archive.

93. Ibid.

94. Beatrice Potter to Joseph Chamberlain, Bournemouth, n.d. [March 1886], in *Letters*, ed. MacKenzie, vol. 1, 53–54.

95. Joseph Chamberlain to Beatrice Potter, March 5, 1886, 2/1/2 Passfield Archive.

96. Royden Harrison, *The Life and Times of Sidney and Beatrice Webb: The Formative Years, 1858–1903* (London: Palgrave, 1999), 125.

97. MacKenzie, *Diary of Beatrice Webb*, vol. 1, 160 (April 4, 1886).

98. Webb, *My Apprenticeship*, 212.

99. MacKenzie, *Diary of Beatrice Webb*, vol. 1, 164 (April 18, 1886).

100. Charles Booth, "The Inhabitants of Tower Hamlets (School Board Division), Their Condition and Occupations," Royal Statistical Society, London, May 17, 1887, in *Journal of the Royal Statistical Society*, vol. 50 (London: Edward Stanford, 1887), 326–91.

101. MacKenzie, *Diary of Beatrice Webb*, vol. 1, 164 (April 17, 1886).

102. Ibid., 173 (July 2, 1886).

103. Ibid.

104. Ibid., 174 (July 18, 1886).

105. Ibid., 213 (n.d.).

106. Webb, *My Apprenticeship*, 300.

107. MacKenzie, *Diary of Beatrice Webb*, vol. 1, 241 (April 11, 1888).

108. Beatrice Potter, "Pages from a Work-Girl's Diary," *The Nineteenth Century: A Monthly Review* 24, issue 139 (September 1888): 301–14.

109. MacKenzie, *Diary of Beatrice Webb*, 249 (April 13, 1888).

110. "The Peers and the Sweaters," *Pall Mall Gazette*, May 12, 1888.

111. MacKenzie, *Diary of Beatrice Webb*, vol. 1; 261 (September 14, 1888).

112. Ibid., 264 (November 8, 1888).

113. Ibid., 269 (December 29, 1888).

114. Ibid., 250 (April 26, 1888).

115. Ibid., 274 (March 8, 1889).

116. Webb, *My Apprenticeship*, 341.

117. Review of *Labour and Life of the People*, ed. Charles Booth, *The Times* (London), April 15, 1889, 9.

118. Webb, *My Apprenticeship*, 374.

119. MacKenzie, *Diary of Beatrice Webb*, vol. 1, 321 (February 1, 1890).

120. Ibid., 328 (March 29, 1890).

121. Ibid., 321 (February 1, 1890).

122. Ibid., 310 (November 26, 1889); Beatrice Potter to Sidney Webb [December 7, 1890], in *Letters*, vol. 1, ed. MacKenzie, 239.

123. *Letters*, vol. 1, ed. MacKenzie, 70.

124. Webb, *My Apprenticeship*, 390.

125. Muggeridge and Adam, *Beatrice Webb: A Life*, 123.

126. MacKenzie, *Diary of Beatrice Webb*, vol. 1, 184 (October 31, 1886).

127. Ibid., 324 (February 14, 1890).

128. Sidney and Beatrice Webb, *The History of Trade Unionism* (London: Green and Co., 1907), 400.

129. G. M. Trevelyan, *British History in the Nineteenth Century (1782–1901)* (London: Longmans, Green and Co., 1922), 403.

130. Sidney Webb to Edward Pease, London, in *Letters,* vol. 1, ed. MacKenzie, 101; Sidney Webb, *Socialism in England* (London: American Economic Association, 1889), 11, 20.

131. Sidney Webb, "Historic," in *Fabian Essays in Socialism,* ed. G. Bernard Shaw, 30–61 (London: The Fabian Society, 1889), 38.

132. MacKenzie, *Diary of Beatrice Webb,* vol., 322 (February 1, 1890).

133. William Harcourt, Speech to the House of Commons, August 11, 1887. *Parliamentary Debates,* 3rd series, vol. 319.

134. MacKenzie, *Diary of Beatrice Webb,* 330 (April 26, 1890).

135. Beatrice Potter to Sidney Webb, Gloucestershire, May 2, 1890, in *Letters,* vol. 1, ed. MacKenzie, 133.

136. Ibid., Sidney Webb to Beatrice Potter, April 6, 1891, 269.

137. MacKenzie, *Diary of Beatrice Webb,* vol. 1, 354.

138. Beatrice Potter to Sidney Webb, Gloucestershire, in *Letters,* vol. 1, ed. MacKenzie, 281.

139. MacKenzie, *Diary of Beatrice Webb,* vol. 1, 357 (June 20, 1891).

140. Friedrich August Hayek, review of *Our Partnership* by Beatrice Webb, eds. Barbara Drake and Margaret I. Cole (London: Longmans, Green and Co., 1948); *Economica,* New Series 15, no. 59 (August 1948): 227–30.

141. MacKenzie, *Diary of Beatrice Webb,* vol. 1, 371 (July 23, 1892).

142. Ibid., vol. 2, 37 (September 17, 1893).

143. Michael Holroyd, *Bernard Shaw: The One-Volume Definitive Edition* (London: Chatto and Windus, 1997), 164.

144. George Bernard Shaw to Archibald Henderson, June 30, 1904, in Archibald Henderson, *George Bernard Shaw: His Life and Works* (Cincinnati: Stewart and Kidd Company, 1911), 287.

145. George Bernard Shaw, preface to *Mrs. Warren's Profession: A Play in Four Acts* (London: Constable, 1907), xvii.

146. George Bernard Shaw to the editor of the *Daily Chronicle,* April 30, 1898, in *Bernard Shaw: Collected Letters, 1874–1897* (New York: Dodd, Meade and Company, 1965), 404.

147. H. G. Wells, *The New Machiavelli* (New York: Duffield and Co., 1910), 194–95.

148. James A. Smith, *The Idea Brokers: Think Tanks and the Rise of the New Policy Elite* (New York: Free Press, 1991), xiii.

149. Wells, *The New Machiavelli,* 199.

150. Ibid., 197.

151. A. G. Gardiner, *The Pillars of Society* (London: James Nisbet, 1913); Wells, *The New Machiavelli,* 195.

152. Wells, *The New Machiavelli,* 194.

153. Ibid., 190.

154. MacKenzie, *Diary of Beatrice Webb,* vol. 2, 262 (November 28, 1902), 325 (June 8, 1904).

155. Gardiner, *The Pillars of Society,* 204, 206.

156. Wells, *The New Machiavelli,* 196.

157. Richard Henry Tawney, *The Webbs in Perspective: The Webb Memorial Lecture Delivered 9 December 1952* (London: The Athlone Press, 1953), 4.

158. MacKenzie, *Diary of Beatrice Webb,* vol. 3, 69 (March 22, 1907).

159. Wells, *The New Machiavelli,* 196.

160. Wells, *The New Machiavelli,* 191.

161. MacKenzie, *Diary of Beatrice Webb,* 287 (July 8, 1903).

162. Ibid., 321 (May 2, 1904), 326–27 (June 10, 1904).

163. Elie Halevy, *A History of the English People in the Nineteenth Century,* vol. 6, *The Rule of Democracy (1905–1914),* 2nd ed. (London: Ernest Benn Limited, 1952), 267.

164. Edward Marsh, *A Number of People: A Book of Reminiscences* (New York: Harper and Brothers, 1939), 163; Winston Churchill and Henry William Massingham, introduction to *Liberalism and the Social Problem: A Collection of Early Speeches as a Member of Parliament* (London: Hodder and Stoughton, 1909).

165. Winston S. Churchill, "H. G. Wells," in *The Collected Essays of Sir Winston Churchill,* vol. 3, *Churchill and People,* ed. Michael Wolff (London: Library of Imperial History, 1976), 52–53.

166. Marsh, *A Number of People,* 150.

167. William Manchester, *The Last Lion: Winston Spencer Churchill, Visions of Glory (1874–1932)* (Boston: Little, Brown and Company, 1983), 403.

168. Peter de Mendelssohn, *The Age of Churchill,* vol. 1, *Heritage and Adventure, 1874–1911* (New York: Alfred A. Knopf, 1961), 365.

169. *Never Give In! The Best of Winston Churchill's Speeches,* Winston S. Churchill, ed. (New York: Hyperion, 2003), 25.

170. Beatrice Webb, *Our Partnership,* eds. Barbara Drake and Margaret I. Cole (London: Longmans, Green and Co., 1948), 149.

171. Sidney and Beatrice Webb, *Industrial Democracy,* vol. 2 (London: Longmans, Green, and Co., 1897), 767.

172. Sidney and Beatrice Webb, *The Prevention of Destitution* (London: Longmans, Green and Co., 1911), 1.

173. Ibid., 17, 97.

174. Ibid., 5.

175. Ibid., 90.

176. Ibid., 285.

177. MacKenzie, *Diary of Beatrice Webb,* vol. 3, 95 (July 27, 1908).

178. Webb, *Our Partnership,* 481–82.

179. George Bernard Shaw, "Review of the Minority Report," quoted in Holroyd, *Bernard Shaw,* 398.

180. Webb, *Our Partnership,* 481–92.

181. MacKenzie, *Diary of Beatrice Webb,* February 10, 1908.

182. Ibid., October 16, 1908.

183. Ibid., April 18/20, 1908.

184. John Grigg, *Lloyd George: The People's Champion, 1902–1911* (London: Eyre Methuen, 1978), 100.

185. Charles Frederick Gurney Masterman to Lucy Blanche Masterman, February 1908.

186. Roy Jenkins, *Churchill: A Biography* (London: Hill and Wang, 2001), 143–44.

187. Winston S. Churchill to H. H. Asquith, March 14, 1908, quoted in Martin Gilbert, *Churchill: A Life* (New York: Henry Holt and Company, 1991), 193.

188. Churchill to Asquith, December 29, 1908.

189. MacKenzie, *Diary of Beatrice Webb,* vol. 3, 100 (October 16, 1908), 118 (June 18, 1909).

190. Ibid., June 18, 1909.

191. Ibid., vol. 3, 90 (March 11, 1908).

192. Manchester, *The Last Lion,* 371.

193. Himmelfarb, *Poverty and Compassion,* 378.

194. Baron William Henry Beveridge, *Power and Influence* (London: Hodder and Stoughton, 1953), 86.

IV: CROSS OF GOLD: FISHER AND THE MONEY ILLUSION

1. David A. Shannon, ed., *Beatrice Webb's American Diary* (Madison: The University of Wisconsin Press, 1963), 72. Remark made by Professor H. Morse Stephens to Beatrice Webb during a tour of Cornell University in May 1898.

2. Norman and Jeanne MacKenzie, eds., *The Diary of Beatrice Webb,* vol. 2, *1892–1905: All the Good Things of Life* (Cambridge, Mass.: Harvard University Press, 1983), 137.

3. Beatrice Webb, *Our Partnership* (London: Longmans, Green and Co., 1948), 146.

4. Niall Ferguson, *Empire: The Rise and Demise of the British World Order* (New York: Basic Books, 2004), 242.

5. See, for example, the following articles in *The Manchester Guardian:* "An American Invasion," June 21, 1871 (rumors of Susan B. Anthony's trip to Ireland with the American Woman's Rights League); "From Our London Correspondent," October 21, 1890 (American girls invade the market for Britain's eligible noblemen); "Cycling Notes," October 29, 1894 (American-made bicycles threaten to dominate the British market); "By-ways of Manchester Life, XI. An American Invasion," April 9, 1898 (American firm builds a grain elevator on the Manchester Ship Canal).

6. Frederick Arthur McKenzie, *The American Invaders: Their Plans, Tactics and Progress* (London: Grant Richards, 1902), 142–43.

7. William Ewart Gladstone, *Gleanings of Past Years,* vol. I, *1843–78: The Throne and the Prince Consort; The Cabinet and the Constitution* (London: John Murray, 1879), 206.

8. Angus Maddison, *The World Economy: A Millennial Perspective* (Paris: OECD, 2001), 265.

9. Ferguson, *Empire,* 242.

10. Dudley Baines, *Migration in a Mature Economy: Emigration and Internal Migration in England* (Cambridge: Cambridge University Press, 2003), 63, table 3.3.

11. William Ewart Gladstone, "Free Trade" in Gladstone et. al., *Both Sides of the Tariff Question by the World's Leading Men* (New York: Alonzo Peniston, 1890), 44.

12. Jeremy Atack and Peter Passell, *A New Economic View of American History from Colonial Times to 1940* (New York: W. W. Norton, 1994), 468.

13. Shannon, *American Diary,* 27 (April 12, 1898).

14. Ibid., 136 (July 2–7, 1898).

15. Ibid., 137–50 (July 2–7 and July 10, 1898).

16. Ibid., 89, 90–91 (May 24, 1898), and 92–93 (May 29, 1898).

17. Beatrice Webb to Catherine Courtney, Chicago, May 29, 1898, in Norman McKenzie, ed., *The Letters of Sidney and Beatrice Webb,* vol. 2, *Partnership: 1892–1912* (Cambridge: Cambridge University Press, 1978).

18. Norman and Jean MacKenzie, eds., *The Diary of Beatrice Webb,* vol. 2, *1892–1905: All the Good Things of Life* (Cambridge, Mass.: Harvard University Press, 1983), 159 (May 16, 1889); Charles Philip Trevelyan to Beatrice Webb, Chicago, April 19, 1898, quoted in Shannon, *American Diary,* 88, note 4.

19. Shannon, *American Diary,* 60 (April 29, 1898), 10 (April 1, 1898), May 24, 1898, and 68 (May 7, 1898).

20. Milton Friedman, *Money Mischief: Episodes in Monetary History* (New York: Harcourt Brace Jovanovich 1992), 37.

21. Henry James, *The Ambassadors* (New York: Harper and Brothers Publishers, 1903), 257.

22. Alfred Marshall to Rebecca Marshall, St. Louis, August 22, 1875, in John K. Whitaker, ed., *The Correspondence of Alfred Marshall, Economist,* vol, 1, *Climbing, 1868–1890* (Cambridge: Cambridge University Press, 1996), 73.

23. Henry Seidel Canby, *Alma Mater: The Gothic Age of the American College* (New York: Farrar Reinhart, 1936), 71, 32.

24. Irving Norton Fisher, *My Father: Irving Fisher* (New York: Comet Press, 1956), 21, 26–27, 29–30, 33.

25. Muriel Rukeyser, *Willard Gibbs: American Genius* (New York: Doubleday, Doran and Co., 1942), 158.

26. Edward Bellamy, *Looking Backward: 2000–1887* (London: George Routlege and Sons, 1887).

27. Rukeyser, *Willard Gibbs,* 146.

28. Ibid., 231.

29. Paul A. Samuelson, "Economic Theory and Mathematics—An Appraisal," in Joseph E. Stiglitz, ed., *The Collected Scientific Papers of Paul A. Samuelson,* vol. 2 (Cambridge, Mass.: The M.I.T. Press, 1966), 1751.

30. Irving Fisher to William G. Eliot, Jr., Berlin, N.J., May 29, 1886, in Irving Norton Fisher, *My Father,* 25–26.

31. Irving Fisher to Will Eliot, Fisher to Eliot, Jr., Pittsfield, Mass., July 25, 1886, in Irving Norton Fisher, *My Father,* 26.

32. Arthur Twining Hadley, *Economics: An Account of the Relations Between Private Property and Public Welfare* (New York: G.P. Putnam's Sons, 1896), iv.

33. Richard Hofstadter, *Social Darwinism in American Thought* (New York: George Braziller, Inc., 1959), 8.

34. Albert Galloway Keller, introduction to *War and Other Essays by William Graham Sumner,* Keller, ed. (New Haven, Conn.: Yale University Press, 1911), xx, xxiv; Hofstadter, *Social Darwinism,* 51.

35. Fisher to Eliot, Peace Dale, R.I., September 1892, in Irving Norton Fisher, *My Father,* 52.

36. William James to Thomas W. Ward, Berlin, n.d. [November 1867], in Henry James, ed., *The Letters of William James,* vol. 1 (Boston: Atlanta Monthly Press, 1920), 118.

37. Irving Fisher, "Mathematical Investigations in the Theory of Value and Prices (April 27, 1892)," in William J. Barber, ed., *The Works of Irving Fisher,* vol. 1 (London: Pickering and Chatto, 1997), 162.

38. Ibid., 68.

39. Ibid., 145.

40. Ibid., 4.

41. Francis Ysidro Edgeworth, review of "Mathematical Investigations in the Theory of Value and Prices" by Irving Fisher, *Economic Journal,* vol. 3, no. 9 (March 1893), 112.

42. Alfred Marshall, *Principles of Economics,* 3rd ed. (London: Macmillan, 1895), 450, 148 (note 1).

43. Barbara W. Tuchman, *The Proud Tower: A Portrait of the World Before the War, 1890–1914* (New York: Macmillan and Co., 1966).

44. *Narragansett Times,* June 23, 1893, quoted in Irving Norton Fisher, *My Father,* 60.

45. *New York Times* wedding announcement, June 18, 1893.

46. Daniel T. Rogers, *Atlantic Crossings: Social Politics in a Progressive Age* (Cambridge, Mass.: Harvard University Press, 1998).

47. Irving Fisher to Ella Wescott Fisher.

48. Fisher, Jr. *My Father,* 69.

49. Douglas Steeples and David O. Whitten, *Democracy in Desperation: The Depression of 1893* (New York: Greenwood, 1998).

50. Reverend T. De Witt Talmage, sermon delivered in Washington on September 27, 1896, quoted in William Jennings Bryan, *The First Battle: A Story of the Campaign of 1896* (Chicago: W. B. Conkey Company, 1896), 474.

51. Albro Martin, *James J. Hill and the Opening of the Northwest* (Minneapolis: Minnesota Historical Society Press, 1975), 428.

52. Bryant, *The First Battle,* 439.

53. Paxton Hibben and Charles A. Beard, *The Peerless Leader: William Jennings Bryan* (Whitefish, MT: Kessinger Publishing, 2004), 189.

54. Bryan, *The First Battle,* 485–86.

55. Ibid.

56. Ibid.

57. "Bryan's Backers Are Shy," *New York Times,* September 27, 1896; Canby, *Alma Matter,* 27; Martin L. Fausold, *James W. Wadsworth, Jr.: The Gentleman from New York* (Syracuse, N.Y.: Syracuse University Press, 1975), 17.

58. "Yale Would Not Listen," *New York Times,* September 25, 1896, 15.

59. Fisher to Eliot, summer 1895, quoted in Irving Norton Fisher, *My Father,* 71.

60. Fisher to Eliot, July 29, 1895, quoted in Barber, *Works of Irving Fisher,* 10.

61. Fisher to Eliot, summer 1895, quoted in Irving Norton Fisher, *My Father,* 71.

62. Fisher to Eliot, New Haven, November 1865, quoted in Irving Norton Fisher, *My Father,* 71.

63. William Graham Sumner, *The Absurd Effort to Make the World Over,* in Keller, *War, and Other Essays,* 195–210.

64. Fisher to Eliot, summer 1895, quoted in Irving Norton Fisher, *My Father,* 71.

65. Irving Fisher, "The Mechanics of Bimetallism," *Economic Journal,* 4 (September 1894), 527–36; Irving Norton Fisher, *My Father,* 187.

66. Harold James, *The End of Globalization: Lessons from the Great Depression* (Cambridge, Mass.: Harvard University Press, 2001), 24–25.

67. Walter Bagehot, *Lombard Street: A Description of the Money Market* (New York: Scribner, Armstrong, 1873), 123.

68. Fisher, *Mathematical Investigations,* in Barber, *Works of Irving Fisher,* 147.

69. Katherine Ott, *Fevered Lives: Tuberculosis in American Culture Since 1870* (Cambridge, Mass.: Harvard University Press, 1996), 113.

70. Ibid.,79.

71. Irving Fisher, May 1901, "Self Control," a talk given at the Thacher School in Ojai, California, a high school founded by William L. Thacher.

72. Fisher to Eliot, Saranac, December 11, 1898, in Irving Norton Fisher, *My Father,* 75.

73. Fisher to Margaret Hazard Fisher, Battle Creek, Michigan, December 31, 1904, in ibid., 108.

74. Irving Fisher, "Memorial Relating to the Conservation of Human Life," S. Doc. No. 493, at 7–8 (1912).

75. Irving Fisher, "Why Has the Doctrine of Laissez Faire Been Abandoned?" Address at the Fifty-fifth Annual Meeting of the American Association for the Advancement of Science, New Orleans, December 1905-January 1906.

76. Perry Mehrling, "Love and Death: The Wealth of Irving Fisher," in Warren J. Samuels and Jeff E. Biddle, eds., *Research in the History of Economic Thought and Methodology,* vol. 19 (New York: Elsevier Science BV, 2001), 47–61.

77. Fisher, "Why Has the Doctrine of Laissez Faire Been Abandoned?"

78. Ibid.

79. Ibid.

80. Ibid.

81. Fisher to Bert, Peace Dale, Rhode Island, January 1, 1903, in Irving Norton Fisher, *My Father,* 84–85.

82. Irving Fisher, *The Rate of Interest: Its Nature, Determination and Relation to Economic Phenomena* (New York: The Macmillan Company, 1907), 326.

83. Ibid., 327.

84. Ibid., 288.

85. Ibid.

V: CREATIVE DESTRUCTION:
SCHUMPETER AND ECONOMIC EVOLUTION

1. Rosa Luxemburg, *The Accumulation of Capital* (1913) (London: Routledge and Keegan Paul, 1951), 458.

2. National Bureau of Economic Research, UK Bank Rate, www.nber.org/databases/macrohistory/rectdata/13/m13013.data.

3. Felix Somary, *Erinnerungen aus Meinem Leben* [Memories from My Life] (Zurich: Manesse Verlag, 1959).

4. Oszkár Jászi, *The Dissolution of the Habsburg Monarchy* (Chicago: University of Chicago Press, 1929), 210.

5. Carl Schorske, *Fin de Siècle Vienna* (New York: Knopf, 1979).

6. Erich Streissler, "Schumpeter's Vienna and the Role of Credit in Innovation," in H. Frisch, ed., *Schumpeterian Economics* (New York: Praeger, 1981), 60.

7. Joseph Roth, *The Radetzky March,* trans. Geoffrey Dunlop (New York: Viking, 1933), 212.

8. "Opening of the International Exhibition of Electricity at Vienna," *Manufacturer and Builder,* vol. 15, no. 9 (September 1883), 214–15; "An Electric Exhibition," *New York Times,* August 12, 1883.

9. Quoted in Roman Sandgruber, "The Electrical Century: The Beginnings of Electricity Supply in Vienna," trans. Richard Hockaday, in Mikulas Teich and Roy Porter, eds., *Fin de Siècle and Its Legacy* (Cambridge, UK: Cambridge University Press, 1990), 42.

10. Richard L. Rubenstein, *The Age of Triage: Fear and Hope in an Overcrowded World* (Boston: Beacon Press, 1983), 8; Raymond James Sontag, *Germany and England: Background of Conflict, 1848–1894* (New York: Russell & Russell, 1964), 146.

11. David F. Good, *The Economic Rise of the Habsburg Empire, 1750–1914* (Berkeley: University of California Press, 1984), 256.

12. Gottfried Haberler, *Quarterly Journal of Economics,* vol. 64, no. 3 (August 1950), 338.

13. Arthur Smithies, "Memorial: Joseph Alois Schumpeter, 1883–1950," *American Economic Review,* vol. 40, no. 4 (September 1950), 628–48.

14. Marcel Proust, *Swann's Way,* trans. C. K. Scott Moncrieff (London: Chatto and Windus, 1922), 73.

15. Joseph A. Schumpeter, "Preface to the Japanese Edition of *The Theory of Economic Development,*" in Schumpeter, *Essays on Entrepreneurs, Innovations, Business Cycles, and the Evolution of Capitalism,* Richard Clemence, ed. (New York: Transaction Publishers, 1951), 166.

16. Alfred Marshall, *Principles of Economics,* vol. 1, 5th ed. (London: Macmillan, 1907), xxix, 820.

17. Joseph A. Schumpeter, "Review of *Essays in Biography* by J. M. Keynes," *Economic Journal* 43, no. 172 (December 1933), 652–57.

18. "Wills and Bequests," *Times* (London), January 12, 1933.

19. Richard Swedberg, "Appendix II: Schumpeter's Novel Ships in Fog (a Fragment)," in *Schumpeter, a Biography* (Princeton, N.J.: Princeton University Press, 1991), 207.

20. W. W. Rostow, *Theorists of Economic Growth from David Hume to the Present,* 234–35.

21. Anthony Trollope, *The Bertrams* (London: Chapman and Hall, 1859), 465.

22. Rosa Luxemburg, *The Accumulation of Capital (1913)* (London: Routledge and Keegan Paul, 1951), 434.

23. Quoted in Alexander D. Noyes, "A Year After the Panic of 1907," *Quarterly Journal of Economics* 23 (February 1909); 185–212.

24. "The Progress of the World," *American Monthly Review of Reviews,* vol. 35, no. 1 (January 1907).

25. Evelyn Baring Cromer, *The Situation in Egypt: Address Delivered to the Eighty Club on December 15th, 1908 by the Earl of Cromer* (London: Macmillan, 1908), 9.

26. William Jennings Bryan, "The Government of Egypt Beyond Definition," in *The Old World and Its Ways* (St. Louis: Thompson, 1907), 323.

27. "Railroad Up Cheops," *Los Angeles Times,* February 12, 1907, II.

28. Quoted in Noyes, "A Year After the Panic," 202.

29. "Cotton Crops and Gold in Egypt," *New York Times,* January 5, 1908, AFR 28.

30. Harry Boyle to Lord Rennell, April 21, 1907, in Clara Boyle, *A Servant of the Empire: A Memoir of Harry Boyle with a Preface by the Earl of Cromer* (London: Methuen, 1938), 107.

31. "Egyptian Finance," *New York Times*, December 8, 1907, 54.

32. Noyes, "A Year After the Panic," 202–3.

33. Ibid., 194.

34. Desmond Stewart, "Herzl's Journeys in Palestine and Egypt," *Journal of Palestine Studies* vol. 3, no. 3 (spring, 1974), 18–38.

35. Wassily Leontief, "Joseph A. Schumpeter," *Econometrica*, vol. 8, no. 2 (April 1950).

36. Quoted in Trevor Mostyn, *Egypt's Belle Époque, 1869–1952: Cairo and the Age of the Hedonists* (London: Quartet Books, 1989), 154.

37. Douglas Sladen, quoted in Max Rodenbeck, *Cairo: The City Victorious* (New York: Alfred A. Knopf, 1999), 138.

38. Joseph A. Schumpeter, *Das Wesen und Hauptinhalt der Theoretischen Nationalekonomie* (Altenburg: Stefan Geibel, 1908), 621, trans. by Bruce McDaniel as *The Nature and Essence of Economic Theory* (New Brunswick, N.J.: Transaction Publishers, 2010), x.

39. Ibid., 621.

40. Smithies, "Memorial," 629.

41. Joseph A. Schumpeter, *The Theory of Economic Development: An Inquiry Into Profits, Capital, Credit, Interest and the Business Cycle,* (1911) trans. Redvers Opie (New York: Transaction Publishers, 2004), 91.

42. *The Norton Anthology of English Literature,* vol. 2, *The Age of Victoria* (New York: Norton, 2000).

43. Joseph Schumpeter, *History of Economic Analysis* (Cambridge, Mass.: Harvard University Press, 1952), 571.

44. Alfred Marshall, "The Social Possibilities of Economic Chivalry," *Economic Journal* 17, no. 5 (March 1907); 7–29.

45. Angus Maddison, "GDP per Capita in 1990 International Geary-Khamis Dollars," *The World Economy: Historical Statistics* (Paris: OECD Publishing, 2003).

46. Jeffrey Williamson, "Real Wages and Relative Factor Prices in the Third World Before 1940: What Do They Tell Us About the Sources of Growth?" October 1998, Conference on Growth in the 19th and 20th Century: A Quantitative Economic History, December 14–15, 1998, Valencia, Spain, 37, table 2, www.economics.harvard.edu/pub/HIER/1998/1855.pdf; Michael D. Bordo, Alan M. Taylor, Jeffrey G. Williamson, *Globalization in Historical Perspective* (Chicago: University of Chicago Press, 2005), 285.

47. Joseph A. Schumpeter, *Capitalism, Socialism and Democracy,* 87.

48. Karl Marx and Friedrich Engels, *The Communist Manifesto* (1848), trans. Samuel Moore, introduction and notes by Gareth Stedman Jones (London: Penguin Books, 1967), 222.

49. Marshall, *Principles.*

50. Schumpeter, *Theory of Economic Development,* 95.

51. Beatrice Webb, *My Apprenticeship* (1926) (Longmans, Green, 1950), 380.

52. Schumpeter, *Capitalism, Socialism and Democracy,* 132.

53. Schumpeter, *Theory of Economic Development,* 85.

54. Schumpeter, *Capitalism, Socialism and Democracy,* 132.

55. Friedrich von Wieser, *The Theory of Social Economics* (New York: Augustus M. Kelly, 1927 and 1967).

56. Joseph A. Schumpeter, "The Communist Manifesto in Sociology and Economics," *Journal of Political Economy* (June 1949), 199–212.

57. Ibid.

58. David Landes, *Bankers and Pashas: International Finance and Imperialism in Egypt* (Cambridge, Mass.: Harvard University Press, 1980), 57.

59. Joseph A. Schumpeter to David Pottinger, June 4, 1934, in Swedberg, *Schumpeter,* 219.

60. Edwin A. Seligman, Professor of Economics at Columbia, to Nicholas Murray Butler, President of the University, October 22, 1913, quoted in Robert Loring Allen, *Opening Doors: The Life and Work of Joseph Schumpeter* (New Brunswick: Transaction Publishers, 1991), 130.

ACT II: PROLOGUE: WAR OF THE WORLDS

1. Irving Fisher, "The Need for Health Insurance," *American Labor Legislation Review* 7 (1917): 10.

2. Norman and Jeanne MacKenzie, eds., *The Diary of Beatrice Webb* vol. 3, *1905–1924: The Power to Alter Things* (Cambridge, Mass.: Harvard University Press, 1984), 204.

3. Ibid., August 5, 1914.

4. Ibid., November 4, 1918.

5. George Bernard Shaw, "Common Sense About the War," 1914.

6. Bertrand Russell, quoted in Niall Ferguson, *The Pity of War* (New York: Basic Books, 1999), 318.

7. Robert Skidelsky, John Maynard Keynes: *Hopes Betrayed,* vol. I (New York: Viking, 1986).

8. John Maynard Keynes to Neville Chamberlain.

9. Richard Shone with Duncan Grant, "The Picture Collector," in Milo Keynes, *Essays on John Maynard Keynes* (Cambridge: Cambridge University Press, 1975), 283.

10. Charles John Holmes, *Self & Partners (Mostly Self): Being the Reminiscences of C. J. Holmes* (London: Macmillan, 1936); Anne Emberton, "Keynes and the Degas Sale," *History Today,* December 31, 1995.

11. John Maynard Keynes to Florence Keynes.

12. Vanessa Bell to Roger Fry.

13. Sigmund Freud, in Peter Gay, *Sigmund Freud: A Life of Our Time* (New York: W.W. Norton, 1988).

14. Friedrich Hayek, "Remembering My Cousin Ludwig Wittgenstein (1889–1951)," *Encounter,* August 19, 1977, 20–21, and Ray Monk, *Ludwig Wittgenstein: The Duty of Genius* (New York: Penguin Books, 1991)

15. Hayek, "Remembering My Cousin," 20.

16. D. H. Mellor, "Better than Stars: Portrait of Frank Ramsey," BBC; D. H. Mellor (1995), "Cambridge Philosophers, vol. I: F. P. Ramsey," *Philosophy 70* (1995), 259.

17. "National Society to Conserve Life," *New York Times,* December 30, 1913; Irving Fisher and Eugene Lyman Fisk, Preface to *How to Live: Rules for Healthful Living Based on Modern Science,* 2nd ed. (New York: Funk & Wagnalls Company, 1915).

18. Henry Andrews Cotton, *The Defective, Delinquent, and Insane: The Relation of Focal Infections to Their Causation, Treatment, and Prevention, by Henry A. Cotton, lectures delivered at Princeton University, January 11, 13, 14, 15, 1921,* with a foreword by Adolf Meyer (Princeton, N.J.: Princeton University Press, 1922).

19. Bette M. Epstein, New Jersey State Archives, to author.

20. Irving Fisher, *American Labor Legislation Review,* p. 10.

21. MacKenzie, *Diary of Beatrice Webb,* vol. 3, 324 (November 17, 1918).

22. Ibid., 318 (November 11, 1918).

23. Ray Monk, *Bertrand Russell: The Spirit of Solitude 1872–1921, Vol. I* (New York: Simon & Schuster, 1996).

VI: THE LAST DAYS OF MANKIND: SCHUMPETER IN VIENNA

1. Joseph A. Schumpeter, *Politische Reden* [Political Speeches], Wolfgang F. Stolper and Christian Seidl, eds. (Tubingen: J.C.B. Mohr, 1992).

2. Francis Oppenheimer, *The Stranger Within: Autobiographical Pages* (London: Faber, 1960).

3. Norman and Jeanne MacKenzie, eds., *The Diary of Beatrice Webb,* vol. 3, *1905–1924* (Cambridge, Mass.: Harvard University Press, 1982–84), November 11, 1918.

4. Sigmund Freud, quoted in Peter Gay, *Freud: A Life of Our Time* (New York: W. W. Norton and Co., 1988), 382.

5. F. L. Carsten, *Revolution in Central Europe: 1918–1919* (Aldershot, UK: Wildwood House, 1988), 41.

6. Karl Kraus, *The Last Days of Mankind: A Tragedy in Five Acts* (New York: Unger, 2000).

7. Edmund von Glaise-Horstenau, "The Armistice of Villa Giusti 1918," in *The Collapse of the Austro-Hungarian Empire* (London: J. M. Dent and Sons, 1930).

8. Sigmund Freud, quoted in Gay, *Freud.*

9. F. O. Lindley, British high commissioner, quoted in Carsten, *Revolution in Central Europe,* 11–12.

10. Friedrich Wieser, "The Fight Against Famine in Austria," in *Fight the Famine Council, International Economic Conference* (London: Swarthmore Press, 1920), 53.

11. *The Memoirs of Herbert Hoover,* vol. 1, *Years of Adventure 1874–1920* (New York: Macmillan, 1951), 392.

12. Ibid.

13. Stefan Zweig, *The World of Yesterday: An Autobiography* (Lincoln: University of Nebraska Press, 1984), 289.

14. Ludwig von Mises, "The Austro-Hungarian Empire," *Encyclopedia Britannica,* 1921.

15. Quoted in Gay, *Freud,* 378.

16. Felix Salten, *Florian, the Emperor's Horse* (New York: Aires Scribner Sons, 1934).

17. "Austria Willing to Pawn Anything," *New York Times,* January 22, 1920.

18. Carsten, *Revolution in Central Europe,* 37.

19. Joseph Schumpeter, *Die Arbeiter Zeitung,* November 22, 1919, in *Dokumentation zur Oesterreichischen Zeitgeschichte, 1918–1928.* [Documentation of Austrian History, 1918–1928], eds. Christine Klusacek, Kurt Stimmer (Vienna: Jugend und Volk, 1984).

20. Sir T. Montgomery-Cuninghame, *Dusty Measure* (London: John Murray, 1939), 309.

21. SHB to ASB, December 30, 1918, quoted in William Beveridge, *The Power and Influence,* 153.

22. Karl Kautsky, *The Social Revolution and On the Morrow of the Social Revolution* (London: Twentieth Century Press, 1907), part 2, 1.

23. Felix Somary, *Erinnerungen aus Meinem Leben* [Memories from My Life] (Zurich: Manesse Verlag, 1955), 171.

24. Eduard Bernstein

25. Otto Bauer, *The Austrian Revolution* (London: Parsons, 1925).

26. Albert Einstein to Hedwig and Max Born, January 15, 1919, *Albert Einstein, Collected Papers,* vol. 4.

27. Joseph Schumpeter, quoted in Eduard Marz, *Joseph A. Schumpeter: Forscher, Lehrer und Politiker* [Researcher, Teacher, and Politician] (Munchen: R. Oldenbourg, 1983).

28. Somary, *Erinnerungen,* 172.

29. Karl Corino, *Robert Musil* (Hamburg: Rowolt, 2003), 598.

30. Friedrich von Wieser, *Tagebuch* Gertrud Enderle-Burcel, Staatsarchiv Wien Nachlass Wieser in the Haus-, Hof- und Staatsarchiv Extracts in Seidl, *Politische Reden,* 10–12.

31. Wolfgang F. Stolper, *Joseph Alois Schumpeter: The Public Life of a Private Man* (Princeton, N.J.: Princeton University Press, 1994), 123.

32. Karl Kraus, *Die Fackel,* April 1919.

33. Joseph Schumpeter, *Politische Reden.*

34. Otto Bauer, *The Austrian Revolution* (London: Parsons, 1925).

35. Gabor Betony, *Britain and Central Europe 1918–1933* (Oxford, UK: Clarendon Press, 1999), 10.

36. Joseph Schumpeter, "The Sociology of Imperialism," in Richard Sweds, *The Economics and Sociology of Capitalism* (Princeton: Princeton University Press, 1991), 156–57.

37. Joseph Schumpeter, *Politische Reden.*

38. Joseph Schumpeter, *Politische Reden.*

39. David Lloyd George, "Fontainebleau Memorandum," March 25, 1919, www.fullbooks.com/Peaceless-Europe2.html.

40. Winston Churchill, House of Commons, May 29, 1919, http://www.winstonchurchill.org; Randolph Spencer Churchill and Martin Gilbert, *Winston S. Churchill,* vol. 4, *The Stricken World* (New York: Houghton Mifflin, 1966), 308.

41. Bauer, *The Austrian Revolution,* 106.

42. *The Memoirs of Herbert Hoover,* vol. 1, *Years of Adventure 1874–1920* (New York: Macmillan, 1951); Bauer, *The Austrian Revolution,* 103.

43. Hans Loewenfeld-Russ, *Im Kampf Gegen den Hunger* [In the Fight Against Hunger] (Munich: R. Oldenburg, 1986).

44. T. Montgomery-Cuninghame, *Dusty Measure,* (London: John Murray, 1939).

45. Ellis Ashmead-Bartlett, *The Tragedy of Central Europe* (London: Thornton Butterworth, 1924), 159.

46. Ibid.

47. Friedrich von Wieser, *Tagebuch,* Gertrud Enderle-Burcel, Staatsarchiv Wien Nachlass Wieser in the Haus-, Hof- und Staatsarchiv Extracts in Seidl, *Politische Reden,* pp. 10–12.

48. Eduard Marz, *Austrian Banking and Financial Policy: Creditanstalt at a Turning Point, 1913–1923* (New York: St. Martin's Press, 1984), 333.

49. "Entretien avec le Docteur Schumpeter," De notre envoye spécial, Vienne, Mai, *Le Temps,* June 2, 1919, translated and quoted in W. F. Stolper, *Joseph Alois Schumpter, The Public Life of a Private Man* (Princeton: Princeton University Press, 1994), 219.

50. Bauer, *The Austrian Revolution,* 110.

51. Ibid., 257.

52. Schumpeter, *Politische Reden.*

53. Ibid.

54. Francis Oppenheimer to John Maynard Keynes, May 18, 1919, Kings College Archive.

55. Francis Oppenheimer, *The Stranger Within: Autobiographical Pages* (London: Faber, 1960), 369.

56. Bauer, *The Austrian Revolution.*

57. Ibid.

58. Joseph Schumpeter, *Neue Freie Presse,* June 24, 1919, in Klusacek et al., eds., *Dokumentation.*

59. Joseph Schumpeter, *Neue Freie Presse,* June 28, 1919. "Es ist nicht leicht ein Volk zu vernichten. Im allgemeinen ist es sogar unmöglich. Hier haben wir aber einen der seltenen Fälle for uns, wo es möglich ist."

60. Friedrich Wieser, "The Fight Against Famine in Austria," in *Fight the Famine Council, International Economic Conference* (London: Swarthmore Press, 1920), 53.

61. Quoted in Stolper, *Joseph Alois Schumpeter.*

62. Richard Kola, *Rückblick ins Gestrige: Erlebtes und Empfundenes* [Looking Back to Yesterday: Experiences and Perceptions] (Vienna: Rikola, 1922).

63. Schumpeter, *Politische Reden.*

64. Somary, *Erinnerungen.*

65. Richard Swedberg, *Joseph A. Schumpeter, His Life and Work* (Cambridge, UK: Polity Press, 1991).

66. Ibid., 144–45.

67. Friedrich von Wieser, *Tagebuch,* November 19, 1919: "Es scheint, dass Schumpeter in der Meinung aller Parteien und aller gebildeten Menschen völlig abgewirtschaftet hat. Wie mir Kelsen erzählte, auch unsere jüngeren Nationalökonomen, die ihn als ihren Führer betrachteten, sind von ihm abgekommen und geben ihn wissenschaftlich auf, es sei nichts mehr von ihm zu erwarten."

68. Eduard Marz, "Joseph Schumpeter as Minister of Finance," in Helmut Frisch, ed., *Schumpeterian Economics* (New York: Praeger, 1981).

VII: EUROPE IS DYING: KEYNES AT VERSAILLES

1. Frances Oppenheimer, *The Stranger Within: Autobiographical Pages* (London: Faber, 1960), 374.

2. Lord William Beveridge, *Power and Influence* (New York: Beechhurst Press, 1955), 149–50.

3. David Lloyd George to Woodrow Wilson, April 1919.

4. John Maynard Keynes to Vanessa Bell, March 16, 1919, Keynes Papers, King's College Archive.

5. Harold Nicolson, *Peacemaking 1919: Being Reminiscences of the Paris Peace Conference* (Boston: Houghton Mifflin, 1933), 44.

6. Ibid., 275–76.

7. David Lindsay, *The Crawford Papers: The Journals of David Lindsay, Twenty-seventh Earl of Crawford and Tenth Earl of Balcarres (1871–1940), During the Years 1892 to 1940,* April 9, 1919.

8. Robert Skidelsky, *John Maynard Keynes,* vol. 1, *Hopes Betrayed* (New York: Viking, 1986), 304.

9. John Maynard Keynes, "My Early Beliefs," September 9, 1938, in *Essays in Biography* (London: MacMillan St. Martin's Press for the Royal Economic Society, 1972), 436.

10. John Maynard Keynes to Lytton Strachey, November 23, 1905, quoted in Skidelsky, *Keynes,* vol. 1, 166.

11. John Maynard Keynes to Lytton Strachey, November 15, 1905, Skidelsky, 165.

12. "A Key for the Prurient: Keynes's Loves, 1901–15," Donald E. Moggridge, *Maynard Keynes: An Economist's Biography* (London: Routledge, 1992), annex 1.

13. C. R. Fay, "The Undergraduate," in Milo Keynes, ed., *Essays on John Maynard Keynes* (Cambridge: Cambridge University Press, 1975), 36.

14. Lionel Robbins, *Autobiography of an Economist* (London: Macmillan, 1971).

15. Winston Churchill to Clementine Churchill, *Speaking for Themselves: The Personal Letters of Winston and Clementine Churchill,* ed. Mary Soames, (London and New York: Doubleday, 1998).

16. Elizabeth Johnson, "Keynes' Attitude Toward Compulsory Military Service," *Economic Journal* 70, no. 277 (March 1960): 160–65.

17. David Lloyd George, *Memoirs of the Peace Conference,* vol. 1 (New Haven, Conn.: Yale University Press, 1939), 302.

18. William Shakespeare, *A Midsummer Night's Dream* (New York: Palgrave, 2010).

19. Lloyd George, *Memoirs of the Peace Conference,* vol. 1, 302.

20. John Maynard Keynes to Florence Keynes, quoted in Skidelsky, *Keynes,* vol. 1, *Hopes Betrayed,* 353.

21. John Maynard Keynes to Florence Keynes, Keynes Papers, King's College Archive.

22. Quoted in Macmillan, *Paris 1919,* 60.

23. John Maynard Keynes, "Dr. Melchior: A Defeated Enemy," in *Essays in Biography,* 210.

24. Max Warburg, "Aus Meinem Aufzeichnungen" [From My Records], quoted in *Collected Writings of John Maynard Keynes,* vol. 16, *Activities 1914–1919, The Treasury and Versailles* (Cambridge: Cambridge University Press), 417.

25. Keynes, "Dr. Melchior," 214.

26. Ibid., 216.

27. Ibid., 218.

28. Ibid., 221.

29. Ibid., 223.

30. George Allerdice Riddell, *Lord Riddell's Intimate Diary of the Peace Conference and After, 1918–1923* (New York: Reynal & Hitchcock, 1924), 30.

31. Keynes, "Dr. Melchior," 231.

32. Thomas W. Lamont, "The Final Reparations Settlement," *Foreign Affairs,* 1930.
33. Nicolson, *Peacemaking 1919,* 86.
34. Peter Rowland, *David Lloyd George* (London: Macmillan, 1975), 485–86.
35. Nicolson, *Peacemaking 1919,* 78.
36. Skidelsky, 367.
37. Jan Smuts, quoted in Skidelsky, *Keynes,* vol. 1, *Hopes Betrayed,* 373.
38. *The Memoirs of Herbert Hoover,* vol. 1, *Years of Adventure 1874–1920* (New York: Macmillan, 1951), 461–62.
39. John Maynard Keynes to Florence Keynes, in Skidelsky, *Keynes,* vol. 1, *Hopes Betrayed,* 371.
40. John Maynard Keynes to Florence Keynes, Keynes Papers, King's College Archive.
41. John Maynard Keynes, *The Economic Consequences of the Peace* (London: Macmillan and Co., 1920), 233 (note 1).
42. John Maynard Keynes to Duncan Grant, May 14, 1919.
43. Rowland, *David Lloyd George,* 480.
44. John Maynard Keynes to Austin Chamberlain, June 5, 1919.
45. Alec Cairncross, "Austin Robinson," *Economic Journal* 104 (July, 1994): 903–15.
46. Ibid.
47. Jan Smuts, quoted in Skidelsky, *Keynes,* vol. 1, 373.
48. John Maynard Keynes, *The Economic Consequences of the Peace* (London: Macmillan, 1920).
49. Henry Wickham Steed, "A Critic of the Peace," "The Candid Friend at Versailles," "Comfort for Germany," *John Maynard Keynes: Critical Responses,* ed. Charles Robert McCons (London: Taylor and Francis, 1998), 51–60.
50. Quoted in Niall Ferguson, *Paper and Iron* (Cambridge: Cambridge University Press, 1995), 206.
51. Keynes, "Dr. Melchior," 234.
52. Keynes, *The Economic Consequences of the Peace,* 39.
53. Lytton Strachey to John Maynard Keynes, quoted in Michael Holroyd, *Lytton Strachey* (London: Heineman, 1978), 374.
54. Austin Chamberlain to Ida Chamberlain.
55. A. J. P. Taylor, *The Origins of the Second World War* (London: Penguin Books, 1964), 26.
56. Paul Mantoux, *The Carthaginian Peace or the Economic Consequences of Mr. Keynes* (Oxford: Oxford University Press, 1946).
57. Wickham Steed, "A Critic of the Peace," "The Candid Friend at Versailles," "Comfort for Germany," *John Maynard Keynes: Critical Responses* (Charles Robert McCann, ed. (London: Taylor & Francis, 1998), 51–60.

58. Thorstein Veblen, "Review of J. M. Keynes' *The Economic Consequences of the Peace*," *Political Science Quarterly* 35 (1920): 467–72.

59. "Europe a Year Later," *New York Times*, May 16, 1920.

60. "Solution of Europe's Disorder, as Seen by Baruch," *New York Times*, April 20, 1920.

61. Joseph A. Schumpeter, *History of Economic Analysis* (London: Allen & Unwin, 1954), 39.

VIII: THE JOYLESS STREET: SCHUMPETER AND HAYEK IN VIENNA

1. Joseph A. Schumpeter, *The Theory of Economic Development* (Oxford: Oxford University Press, 1961), 215.

2. Ludwig von Mises, "The Austro-Hungarian Empire," *Encyclopedia Britannica*, 1921.

3. Schober, quoted in F. L. Carsten, *The First Austrian Republic* (Aldershot, UK: Wildwood House, 1986), 41.

4. Ibid., 45.

5. Peter Gay, *Freud: A Life of Our Time* (New York: W. W. Norton and Co., 1988), 386.

6. Ibid., 382.

7. Anna Eisenmenger, *Blockade: The Diary of an Austrian Middle-Class Woman, 1914–1924* (London: Constable Publishers, 1932), 149.

8. Pierre Hamp, *La Peine des Hommes: Les Chercheurs D'Or* [The Pain of Men: The Seekers of Gold], 1920.

9. Quoted in Carsten, *The First Austrian Republic*, 13.

10. Charles A. Gulik, *Austria from Habsburg to Hitler*, vol. 1 (Berkeley: University of California Press, 1948), 248.

11. Eisenmenger, *Blockade*, 149.

12. Ibid.

13. C. A. Macartney, *The Social Revolution in Austria* (Cambridge, UK: Cambridge University Press, 1926), 215.

14. Alois Mosser and Alice Teichova, "Investment Behavior of Joint Stock Companies," in *The Role of Banks in the Interwar Economy*, Harold James, Hekan Lindgren, Alice Teichova, eds. (Cambridge, UK: Cambridge University Press, 2002), 127.

15. Quoted in Richard Swedberg, *Joseph A. Schumpeter: His Life and Work* (Cambridge, UK: Polity Press, 1991), 68.

16. Quoted in Wolfgang F. Stolper, *Joseph Alois Schumpeter: The Public Life of a Private Man* (Princeton, N.J.: Princeton University Press, 1994), 3.

17. Charles A. Gulik, *Austria from Hapsburg to Hitler*, vol. 1 (Berkeley: University of California Press, 1948), 251.

18. Fritz Machlup, *Tribute to Mises, 1881–1973* (Chislehurst, UK: Quadrangle, 1974).

19. "Ships in Fog," a fragment of a novel Schumpeter started in the 1930s, in Swedberg, *Joseph A. Schumpeter*, appendix 2.

20. Thomas K. McCraw, *Prophet of Innovation: Joseph Schumpeter and Creative Destruction* (Cambridge, Mass.: Harvard University Press, 2007), 140.

21. Quoted in Robert Loring Allen, *Opening Doors: The Life and Work of Joseph A. Schumpeter*, vol. 1, *Europe* (New Brunswick, N.J., and London: Transaction Publishers, 1991), 274.

22. Israel Kirzner, "Austrian Economics," lecture at Foundation for Economic Education, July 26, 2004.

23. Joseph A. Schumpeter, *Business Cycles: A Theoretical, Historical and Statistical Analysis of the Capitalist Process* (New York: McGraw-Hill Company, 1939).

24. Joseph A. Schumpeter, *The Theory of Economic Development: An Inquiry into Profits, Capital, Credit, Interest and the Business Cycle* (New Brunswick, N.J.: Transaction Publishers, 1934).

25. Ibid.

26. Ibid., 245.

27. Joseph A. Schumpeter, *Essays on Entrepreneurs, Innovations, Business Cycles, and The Evolution of Capitalism*, ed. Richard Clemence (New York: Transaction Publishers, 1951), 71–72.

28. Friedrich A. Hayek, *Hayek on Hayek: An Autobiographical Dialogue*, ed. Stephen Kresge (Chicago: University of Chicago Press, 1984).

29. Fritz Machlup to Barbara Chernow, June 12, 1978.

30. Gulik, *Austria from Hapsburg to Hitler*, vol. 1, 134–35.

31. Max Weber, "Der Sozialismus" (1918), in *Gesammelte Aufsätze zur Soziologie, Economy and Society*

32. Otto Bauer, "Der Weg zum Sozialismus" [The Way to Socialism], 1921, serialized in *Arbeiter Zeitung*, January 1919.

33. *Hayek on Hayek*, 54–59.

34. Friedrich Hayek, *Austrian Institute for Economic Research Monthly*, February 1929.

IX: IMMATERIAL DEVICES OF THE MIND: KEYNES AND FISHER IN THE 1920s

1. Irving Fisher, et al, *Report on National Vitality Bulletin 30 of the Committee of One Hundred on Public Health* (Washington, D.C.: Government Printing Office, 1908), 1.

2. Irving Fisher, "Unstable Dollar and the So-called Business Cycle," *Journal of the American Statistical Association*, vol. 20, no. 150 (June, 1925), 179–202.

3. John Maynard Keynes, quoted in Robert Skidelsky, *John Maynard Keynes*, vol. 2, *The Economist as Savior, 1920–1937* (London: Macmillan, 1992).

4. Ibid.

5. Peter Clarke, *Keynes; The Rise, Fall, and Return of the 20th Century's Most Influential Economist* (New York: Bloomsbury, 2009).

6. John Maynard Keynes, "Alternative Theories of the Rate of Interest," *Economic Journal* 47 (June 1937).

7. John Maynard Keynes, "How Far Are Bankers at Fault for Depressions?," 1913, quoted in Angel N. Rugina, "A Monetary and Economic Dialogue with Lord Keynes," *International Journal of Social Economics* 28, vol. 1, No. 2, 200, www.emeraldinsight.com/journals.htm?articleid=1453937&show=html.

8. John Maynard Keynes, *Tract on Monetary Reform*, 1923.

9. Ibid.

10. Quoted in D. E. Moggridge, *Keynes: An Economists' Biography* (London: Routledge, 1992), 429.

11. John Maynard Keynes, *A Short View of Russia* (London: Hogarth Press, 1925).

12. Ibid.

13. Ibid.

14. Norman and Jean MacKenzie, eds., *The Diary of Beatrice Webb*, vol. 4, *1924–1943: The Wheel of Life* (Cambridge, Mass.: Harvard University Press, 1985) (August 9, 1926).

15. John Maynard Keynes, "My Visit to Berlin," *Collected Writings of John Maynard Keynes*, vol. 10, 383–84; "Das Ende des Laissez-Faire, Ideen zur Verbindung von Privat und Gemeinwirtschaft" [The End of Laissez-Faire: Ideas for Combining the Private and Public Economy], *Zeitschrift für die Gesamte Staatswissenschaft* 82 (1927): 190–91. A review of a lecture given by Keynes in Berlin. In papers: October 1925–June 1926 correspondence, autograph manuscript "My Visit to Berlin," June 23, "The General Strike," June 24, given to Berlin University; Conditions in Germany; Keynes at Melchior's apartment in Berlin for dinner, 1926 visit; source: Felix Somary, *Erinnerungen Aus Meinem Leben*, (Zurich: 1926), 199.

16. *The Letters of Virginia Woolf*, vol. 3.

17. John Maynard Keynes addressing the National Liberal Federation, March 27, 1928, quoted in Robert Skidelsky, *John Maynard Keynes*, vol. 2, *The Economist as Savior, 1920–1937* (London: Macmillan, 1992), 297.

18. Skidelsky, *Keynes*, vol. 2, *The Economist as Savior*, 231.

19. Ibid., 232.

20. Charles Loch Mowat, *Britain Between the Wars, 1918–1940* (London: Methuen and Co., 1956), 262.

21. Skidelsky, *Keynes*, vol. 2, *The Economist as Savior*, 258.

22. John Maynard Keynes to H. G. Wells, January 18, 1928.

23. Mowat, *Britain Between the Wars*, 349.

24. Skidelsky, *Keynes*, vol. 2, *The Economist as Savior*, 302.

25. Irving Norton Fisher, *My Father: Irving Fisher* (New York: Comet Press, 1956), 171.

26. Alan Milward, *War, Economy and Society, 1939–1945* (Berkeley: University of California Press, 1979), 17.

27. Angus Maddison, "Statistics of World Population, GDP, per Capita GDP, 1–2008 AD," www.ggdc.net/maddison/.

28. Joseph Schumpeter, "The Decade of the Twenties," *American Economic Review, 1946* and "Business Cycle Dates," National Bureau of Economic Research.

29. Geoffrey Keynes, quoted in D. E. Moggridge, *Maynard Keynes: An Economist's Biography* (London: Routledge, 1992), 103.

30. Irving Norton Fisher, *My Father: Irving Fisher,* 200.

31. Ibid., 232.

32. Ibid., 117–18.

33. Irving Fisher, address to the American Public Health Association, October 23, 1926.

34. Irving Fisher et al., *Report on National Vitality,* bulletin 30 of the Committee of One Hundred on Public Health (Washington, D.C.: GPO, 1908), 1.

35. Irving Fisher, *Stabilizing the Dollar* (New York: Macmillan, 1920), 75.

36. Irving Fisher, *The Purchasing Power of Money: Its Determination and Relation to Credit Interest and Crises* (New York: Macmillan, 1912).

37. Irving Fisher, "Our Unstable Dollar and the So-Called Business Cycle," *Journal of the American Statistical Association* (June 1925): 181.

38. John Maynard Keynes, "Opening remarks: The Galton Lecture," *Eugenics Review,* vol. 38, no. 1 (1946), 39–40.

39. See Robert W. Dimand, "Economists and 'the Other' Before 1912," *The American Journal of Economics and Sociology,* July 2005, http://findarticles.com/p/articles/mi_m0254/is_3_64/ai_n15337798/?tag=content;col1, and *New International Year Book* (New York: Dodd Meade & Co., 1913).

40. Irving Fisher, "Lecture on The Irving Fisher Foundation," *Collected Works,* vol. I (1997), 35.

41. Ibid.

42. Irving Fisher, "Our Unstable Dollar and the So-Called Business Cycle," 197.

43. Irving Fisher, "Depressions and Money Problems," April 4, 1941.

44. Irving Fisher, "I Discovered the Phillips Curve: 'A statistical relation between unemployment and price changes'" *Journal of Political Economy* 81, no 2; 496–502, reprinted from *International Labour Review,* 1926.

45. Irving Fisher, *New York Times,* September 2, 1923.

46. Irving Fisher, "The Unstable Dollar and the So-called Bisiness Cycle" (1925). 179–202.

47. Irving Fisher, "A Statistical Relation Between Unemployment and Price Changes" (1926), 496–502.

48. Ibid.
49. Irving Fisher, *Battle Creek Sanitarium News*, 25, 7, July 1925.
50. Irving Norton Fisher, *My Father: Irving Fisher*, 57.
51. Ibid., 192, from autobiographical appendix in *Stable Money, A History of the Movement*.
52. Jeremy Siegel, *Stocks for the Long Run* (New York: McGraw-Hill, 2008).
53. Irving Norton Fisher, *My Father: Irving Fisher*, 264.
54. *Recent Economic Changes in the United States* (Chicago: National Bureau of Economic Research, 1929), xii.
55. "Fisher Sees Stocks Permanently High," *New York Times*, October 16, 1929.

X: MAGNETO TROUBLE: KEYNES AND FISHER IN THE GREAT DEPRESSION

1. Arnold J. Toynbee, *Journal of International Affairs*, 1931, 1.
2. David Fettig, "Something Unanticipated Happened," in *The Region* (Minneapolis: Federal Reserve Bank of Minneapolis, 2000).
3. John Maynard Keynes to F. C. Scott, August 15, 1934.
4. John Maynard Keynes, "A British View of the Wall Street Slump," *New York Evening Post*, October 25, 1929.
5. Charles A. Selden, "Big British Labor Gains; Third of Vote Counted; Tory Control Seems Lost," *New York Times*, May 31, 1929, 1.
6. Winston Churchill, "Disposal of Surplus," *Hansard 1803–2005*, April 15, 1929, Commons Sitting, Orders of the Day, www.hansard.millbanksystems .com/commons/1929/apr/15/disposal-of-surplus.
7. Lionel Robbins, *Autobiography of an Economist* (London: Macmillan, 1971), 151.
8. John Maynard Keynes to Lydia Keynes, 1929.
9. Joseph J. Thorndike, "Tax Cuts, Confidence, and Presidential Leadership," September 8, 2008, www.taxhistory.org/thp/readings.nsf/.
10. John Maynard Keynes, "The Great Slump of 1930," *The Nation & Athenæum*, December 20, 1930, and December 27, 1930, www.gutenberg.ca/ ebooks/keynes-slump/keynes-slump-00-h.html.
11. John Maynard Keynes, *The General Theory*, book 6, chapter 22, section 3 (London: Macmillan, 1936), 322.
12. Keynes, "The Great Slump," *Nation*.
13. Ibid.
14. Godfrey Harold Hardy, "Mathematical Proof," in Raymond George Ayoub, *Musings of the Masters: An Anthology of Mathematical Reflections* (New York: American Mathematical Association, 2004), 59.
15. Keynes, *The Great Slump of 1930*.
16. Robert Skidelsky, *John Maynard Keynes*, vol. 2, *The Economist as Savior, 1920–1937* (London: Macmillan, 1992), 333.
17. *Minority Report*, 35, 507n, 657–59, 660, 661, 662.

18. Skidelsky, *Keynes,* vol. 2, *The Economist as Savior,* 32.

19. Sir John Anderson to Ramsay MacDonald, July 31, 1930.

20. October 20, 1930.

21. Ross McKibbin, "The Economic Policy of the Second Labour Government, 1929–1931," *Past and Present* 65 (1975); 95–123.

22. Skidelsky, *Keynes,* vol. 2, *The Economist as Savior,* 524.

23. Irving Fisher, September 2, 1929, quoted in Kathryn M. Dominguez, Ray C. Fair, Matthew D. Shapiro, "Forecasting the Depression: Harvard Versus Yale," *American Economic Review* 78, no. 4 (September 1988); 607.

24. "Fisher Sees Stocks Permanently High," *New York Times,* October 16, 1929, 8.

25. Irving Fisher, January 6, 1930, *Collected Works,* ed. Robert Barber, vol. 14, 4.

26. Harvard Economic Society, *Weekly Letter,* vols. 8 and 9 (Cambridge, Mass.: Harvard University Press, 1929), quoted in Dominguez et al., "Forecasting the Depression," 606.

27. Irving Fisher, The *Stock Market Crash and After* (New York: Macmillan, 1930).

28. Milton Friedman and Anna Jacobson Schwartz, *A Monetary History of the United States, 1867–1960* (Princeton, N.J.: Princeton University Press, 1971).

29. "Scores Coolidge in Market Slump," *New York Times,* January 12, 1930.

30. Robert W. Dimond, "Irving Fisher's Monetary Macroeconomics," in *The Economics of Irving Fisher* (London: Elgar, 1999).

31. Irving Norton Fisher, *My Father, Irving Fisher,* 263.

32. "Harvard Group Sees Debt Plan Benefits: Believes Moratorium Will Balance Exchanges and Remove Pressure on Commodities," *Wall Street Journal,* July 17, 1931, 20; "The 1929 Speculation and Today's Troubles: Controversy as to How Far the 'Great Boom' Caused the Great Depression," *New York Times,* January 1, 1932, 33.

33. Irving Fisher, "The Stock Market Panic in 1929," *Proceedings of the American Statistical Association,* 1930.

34. June 22–23, 1931, quoted in Skidelsky, *Keynes,* 391.

35. John Maynard Keynes, typewritten notes, King's College Archive.

36. John Maynard Keynes, discussion leader, typewritten notes, King's College Archive.

37. Bank of England rate of discount, 1836–1939, National Bureau of Economic Research Macro Data Base, www.nber.org/databases/macrohistory/rectdata/13/m13013.dat.

38. Irving Fisher to Ramsay MacDonald, December 1931.

39. Vanessa Bell Skidelsky, *Keynes,* vol. 2, *The Economist as Savior,* 430.

40. Irving Fisher to Henry Stimson, November 11, 1932, quoted in Fisher, 273.

41. Lauchlin Bernard Currie, *Memorandum Prepared by L. B. Currie, P. T. Ellsworth, and H. D. White* (Cambridge, Mass., 1932), reprinted in *History of Political Economy* 34, no. 3 (Fall 2002): 533–52.

42. Irving Fisher to Margaret Fisher, quoted in Irving Norton Fisher, *My Father: Irving Fisher*, 267.

43. Walter Lippmann, *Interpretations 1933–1935* (New York: Macmillan, 1936), 15.

44. K. M. Dominguez, R. C. Fair, and M. D. Shapiro, "Forecasting the Great Depression: Harvard Versus Yale," *American Economic Review*, 78 (September, 1988), 595–612.

45. David Fettig, "Something Unanticipated Happened," (Minneapolis Fed, 2000).

46. Irving Fisher, *Booms and Depressions: Some First Principles* (New York: Adelphi, 1932).

47. Irving Fisher, "Cancellation of War Debts," Southwest Foreign Trade Conference Address, July 2, 1931, quoted in Giovanni Pavanelli, "The Great Depression in Irving Fisher's Thought," *Fifth Annual Conference of the European Society for the History of Economic Thought*, February 2001.

48. Irving Fisher, *The Depression: Causes and Cures* (Miami: Committee of One Hundred, March 1, 1932).

49. "Economists Urge Release of Gold," *New York Times*, October 28, 1931.

50. *New York Times*, December 9, 1931.

51. Irving Fisher, *Booms and Depressions*, viii.

52. R. G. Tugwell, *Brains Trust* (New York: Viking, 1964), 97.

53. Kennedy, *Freedom from Fear*, 113.

54. Tugwell, 98.

55. Franklin Delano Roosevelt, *Oglethorpe University Commencement Speech*, May 22, 1932, http://georgiainfo.galileo.usg.edu/FDRspeeches.htm.

56. Franklin Delano Roosevelt, *Address to Commonwealth Club*, September 23, 1932, San Francisco, in *Great Speeches* (New York: Courier Dover, 1999).

57. Kennedy, *Freedom from Fear*, 123.

58. John Maynard Keynes, *The Means to Prosperity* (London: Macmillan, 1933).

59. Irving Fisher, George Warren of Cornell, and John Commons of the University of Wisconsin to Franklin Roosevelt, February 25, 1933.

60. *The New York Times*, December 31, 1933.

61. Irving Fisher to Irving Norton Fisher, August 15, 1933.

62. Irving Fisher to Margaret Hazard Fisher, quoted in Irving Norton Fisher, *My Father, Irving Fisher*.

63. Skidelsky, *Keynes*, vol. 3, 506.

64. Ibid.

65. *The New York Times*, May 29, 1933.

66. D. E. Moggridge, *Maynard Keynes: An Economists' Biography* (London: Routledge, 1992), 584.

67. Irving Fisher to Howe (FDR's secretary), May 18, 1934.

68. Irving Fisher to Margaret Hazard Fisher, June 7, 1934.

69. John Maynard Keynes, *American Economic Review*, 1933.

70. John Maynard Keynes, *Lecture Notes*
71. Quoted in Skidelsky, *Keynes,* 503.
72. John Maynard Keynes to George Bernard Shaw, January 1, 1935.
73. Marriner S. Eccles, *Fortune,* April 1937, reproduced in *The Lessons of Monetary Experience: Essays in Honor of Irving Fisher Presented to Him on the Occasion of His 70th Birthday* (New York: Farrar and Rhinehart, 1937), 6.
74. Friedrich Hayek, Austrian Institute of Economic Research Report, February 1929.
75. Friedrich A. Hayek, interview. *Gold and Silver Newsletter* (Newport Beach, Calif.: Monex International, June, 1976).
76. Lionel Robbins, *The Great Depression,* 1934.
77. Ibid.
78. Robbins, *Autobiography of an Economist,* 154.
79. Skidelsky, *Keynes,* vol. 2, *The Economist as Savior,* 469.
80. Beatrice Webb, quoted in José Harris, *William Beveridge: A Biography* (Oxford: Clarendon Press, 1977), 330.
81. Fritz Machlup to Barbara Chernow, June 12, 1978.
82. John Maynard Keynes "The Pure Theory of Money: A Reply to Dr. Hayek," *Econometrica,* vol. 11 (November, 1931), 387–97.
83. Alan Ebenstein, *Friedrich Hayek: A Biography* (New York: Palgrave, 2001), 81.
84. Erich Schneider, *Joseph A. Schumpeter: Leben und Werk eines grossen Sozialekonomenen* [Life and Work of a Great Social Scientist]
85. Harold James, *The German Slump: Politics and Economics, 1924–1936* (Oxford: Clarendon Press, 1986), 6.
86. Joseph Schumpeter, "The Present World Depression: A Tentative Diagnosis," in American Economic Association, *Proceedings,* March 31, 1931.
87. Joseph Dorfman, *The Economic Mind in America,* vol. 4, 168.
88. Joseph Schumpeter, to Rev. Harry Emerson Fosdick at Riverside Church, April 19, 1933.
89. Douglas V. Brown, *The Economics of the Recovery Program* (New York: McGraw-Hill, 1934), reprinted in Joseph Schumpeter, *Essays: On Entrepreneurs, Innovations, Business Cycles, and the Evolution of Capitalism* (New York: Transaction Publishers, 1989).
90. Joseph Schumpeter, review of Keynes's *General Theory of Employment, Interest and Money, Journal of the American Statistical Association* (December 1936), 791–95.

XI: EXPERIMENTS: WEBB AND ROBINSON IN THE 1930s

1. Walter Duranty, *New York Times,* July 20, 1931, 1.
2. Beatrice Webb to Arthur Salter, April 12, 1932, Norman and Jeanne MacKenzie, eds., *The Letters of Sidney and Beatrice Webb* (Cambridge, Mass.: Harvard University Press, 1978).

3. Norman and Jean MacKenzie, eds., *The Diary of Beatrice Webb*, vol. 4, *1924–1943: The Wheel of Life* (Cambridge, Mass.: Harvard University Press, 1985), September 23, 1931, and October 10, 1931.

4. Ibid.

5. Ibid., 272.

6. Ibid., May 14, 1932.

7. Ibid.

8. Ibid., September 2, 1931.

9. Ibid.

10. Ibid.

11. Walter Duranty, *New York Times*, November 13, 1932, 1.

12. MacKenzie, *Diary of Beatrice Webb*, vol. 4, 299–301, 315, 328 (March 29, 1933; March 30, 1933; October 21, 1933; February 22, 1934).

13. Beatrice and Sidney Webb, *Soviet Communism: A New Civilization* (London: Longmans, Green and Co., 1935), 265.

14. Bertrand Russell, *Autobiography* (London: George Allen and Unwin, 1967), 74–75.

15. Robert Conquest, *Reflections on a Ravaged Century* (New York: W. W. Norton and Co., 2001), 148.

16. John Maynard Keynes, *Collected Writings*, vol. 23, *Activities 1940–1943* (London: Macmillan, 1979), 5.

17. Malcolm Muggeridge, *Chronicles of Wasted Time*, vol. 1, *The Green Stick* (New York: William Morrow, 1973), 207.

18. MacKenzie, *Diary of Beatrice Webb*, vol. 4, 371 (June 19, 1936).

19. John Maynard Keynes to Kingsley Martin, 1937, in *The Collected Writings of John Maynard Keynes*, vol. 28, *Social, Political and Literary Writings* (London: Macmillan, 1928), 72.

20. John Maynard Keynes, quoted in Muggeridge, *Chronicles*, 469.

21. John Maynard Keynes, "Democracy and Efficiency," *New Statesman and Nation*, January 28, 1939.

22. Ibid.

23. Rita McWilliams Tullberg, "Alfred Marshall and Evangelicalism," in Claudio Sardoni, Peter Kriesler, Geoffrey Colin Harcourt, eds., *Keynes, Post-Keynesianism and Political Economy* (London: Psychology Press, 1999), 82.

24. Austin Robinson to Joan Robinson, Robinson Papers, Kings College Archive.

25. Major General Sir Edward Speers, "Forward," in Sir Frederick Maurice and Nancy Maurice, *The Maurice Case* (London: Archon Books, 1972), 95–96.

26. Quoted in Marjorie Shepherd Turner, *Joan Robinson and the Americans* (New York: M. E. Sharpe, 1989), 13.

27. Margaret Gardiner, *A Scatter of Memories* (London: Free Association Books, 1988), 65.

28. Interview with Geoffrey Harcourt, Jesus College, University of Cambridge, 2000.
29. Joan Robinson to Richard Kahn, n.d., November 1930.
30. Joan Robinson to Stevie Smith
31. Ibid.
32. Austin Robinson to Joan Robinson, n.d., April 1926.
33. *Diary of Beatrice Webb.*
34. Dorothy Garratt to Joan Robinson, January 26, 1932.
35. Joan Robinson to Richard Kahn, March 1931.
36. Ibid.
37. Nahid Aslanbeigui and Guy Oakes, *The Provocative Joan Robinson: The Making of a Cambridge Economist* (Durham, N.C.: Duke University Press, 2009).
38. James Meade, quoted in George R. Feiwell, *Joan Robinson and Modern Economic Theory* (New York: New York University Press, 1989), 917.
39. Ibid., 916.
40. Aslanbeigui and Oakes, *The Provocative Joan Robinson.*
41. Joan Robinson to Austin Robinson, October 11, 1932.
42. Joan Robinson to Richard Kahn, Michaelmas term, 1932; Joan Robinson to Austin Robinson, October 11, 1932; Richard Kahn to Joan Robinson.
43. Joan Robinson to Richard Kahn, March 2, 1933.
44. Joan Robinson, introduction to *The Theory of Employment* (London: Macmillan, 1969), xi.
45. Richard Kahn to Joan Robinson, March 1933.
46. Joseph Schumpeter, "Review of Joan Robinson's Theory of Imperfect Competition," *Journal of Political Economy,* 1934.
47. Dorothy Garratt to Joan Robinson, May 25, 1934.
48. Joan Robinson to Richard Kahn, September 5, 1934.
49. John Maynard Keynes to Richard Kahn, February 19, 1938.
50. Andrew Boyle, *Climate of Treason* (London: Hutchinson, 1979), 63, 453 (note 4).
51. Geoffrey Harcourt, "Joan Robinson," *Economic Journal.*
52. Joan Robinson, "Review of *The Nature of the Capitalist Crisis* by John Strachey," *Economic Journal* 46, no. 182 (June 1936): 298–302.
53. Joan Robinson, "Review of *Britain Without Capitalists*," *Economic Journal* (December 1936).
54. Taqui Altounyan, *Chimes from a Wooden Bell* (London: I. B. Taurus and Co., 1990) and *In Aleppo Once* (London: John Murray, 1969).
55. Ernest Altounyan to Joan Robinson, May 30, 1936.
56. Agatha Christie, *Murder on the Orient Express* (New York: Collins, 1934), 17.
57. Quoted in Altounyan, *Chimes from a Wooden Bell.*
58. Interview with Frank Hahn, Churchill College, University of Cambridge, 2000.

XII: THE ECONOMISTS' WAR:
KEYNES AND FRIEDMAN AT THE TREASURY

1. John Maynard Keynes, *How to Pay for the War* (London: Macmillan, 1940), 17.
2. Friederich von Hayek to Fritz Machlup, October 1940.
3. Robert Skidelsky, *John Maynard Keynes*, vol. 3, *Fighting for Freedom, 1937–1946* (New York: Viking, 2001), 51.
4. Friedrich Hayek to Fritz Machlup, March 19, 1934 (Machlup Papers, box 43, folder 15).
5. John Maynard Keynes, "Paying for the War I: The Control of Consumption," *Times* (London), November 14, 1939, 9, and "Paying for the War II: Compulsory Savings," *Times* (London), November 15, 1939, 9.
6. Skidelsky, *Keynes*, vol. 3, *Fighting for Freedom*, 142.
7. John Maynard Keynes to F. A. Hayek, guoted in Skidelsky, ibid., 56.
8. John Maynard Keynes to J. T. Sheppard, August 14, 1940.
9. Skidelsky, *Keynes*, vol. 3, 179.
10. Winston Churchill to Clementine Churchill, July 18, 1914, in Mary Soames, *Winston and Clementine: The Personal Letters of the Churchills* (New York: Houghton Mifflin Harcourt, 2001), 96.
11. John Maynard Keynes to Russell Leffingwell, July 1, 1942.
12. John Maynard Keynes to P. A. S. Hadley, September 10, 1941.
13. "Wheeler Doubts President Will Order Convoys," *Chicago Daily Tribune*, May 10, 1941.
14. Sir John Wheeler Bennet, *New York Times*, November 24, 1940, 7.
15. Alan Milward, *War, Economy and Society, 1939–1945* (Berkeley: University of California Press, 1979), 49.
16. Gerhard L. Weinberg, *A World at Arms: A Global History of World War II* (Cambridge: Cambridge University Press, 2005); David Kennedy, *Freedom from Fear: The American People in Depression and War* (Oxford: Oxford University Press, 1999), 446.
17. Winston Churchill to Franklin D. Roosevelt, December 7, 1940, Great Britain Diplomatic Files.
18. Franklin D. Roosevelt, press conference, White House, December 17, 1940, http://docs.fdrlibrary.marist.edu/ODLLPc2.html.
19. Ibid.
20. Franklin Roosevelt, "Fireside Chat" radio address, White House, December 29, 1940, http://docs.fdrlibrary.marist.edu/122940.html.
21. Winston S. Churchill to Franklin D. Roosevelt, December 31, 1940, in Martin Gilbert, ed., *The Churchill War Papers* (New York: W. W. Norton and Co., 2000), 3:11.
22. Winston S. Churchill to Sir Kingsley Wood, March 20, 1941, in Gilbert, *The Churchill War Papers*, 3:372.

23. Franklin D. Roosevelt, campaign address, Boston, October 30, 1940, www .presidency.ucsb.edu.

24. Franklin D. Roosevelt, conversation in the Oval Office with unidentified aides, October 4, 1940, White House Office Transcripts, 48–61:1, Franklin D. Roosevelt Presidential Library and Museum, Hyde Park, New York, http:// docs.fdrlibrary.marist.edu:8000/transcr7.html.

25. Weinberg, *A World at Arms*, 240.

26. John Maynard Keynes, quoted in Skidelsky, *Keynes*, vol. 3, *Fighting for Freedom*, 102.

27. Paul A. Samuelson in *The Coming of Keynesianism*, 170.

28. Ibid.

29. Quoted in Skidelsky, *Keynes*, vol. 3, *Fighting for Freedom*, 116.

30. John Kenneth Galbraith, *A Life in Our Times,*

31. F. Scott Fitzgerald, *This Side of Paradise* (New York, 1920).

32. Milton Friedman and Rose Friedman, *Two Lucky People* (Chicago: University of Chicago Press, 1998).

33. Ibid.

34. Ibid.

35. Ibid.

36. Herbert Stein, *Presidential Economics: The Making of Economic Policy from Roosevelt to Clinton* (Washington, D.C.: American Enterprise Institute, 1994).

37. Friedman and Friedman, *Two Lucky People.*

38. Ibid., 107

39. Galbraith, *A Life in Our Times,* 163.

40. Ibid. Galbraith was assistant, then deputy, chief of the Price Division. Richard Gilbert, George Stigler, Walter Salant, and Herbert Stein belonged to OPA's economics staff.

41. Quoted in ibid., 133. The General Maximum Price Regulation of 1942 went into effect on April 28.

42. Friedman and Friedman, *Two Lucky People,* 113. See also Milton Friedman and Walter Salant, *American Economic Review* 32 (June 1942); 308–20; Milton Friedman, "The Spendings Tax as a Wartime Fiscal Measure," *American Economic Review* (March 1943); 50–62.

43. Friedman and Friedman, *Two Lucky People.*

44. Ibid., 113

45. Ibid.

46. Withholding was first imposed on 1943 income, but the Ruml Plan, the subject of the 1942 debate, called for it to be imposed on 1942 income. The Revenue Act of 1942 passed on October 21, 1942; the Current Tax Payment Act of 1943, on June 9, 1943.

47. Friedman and Friedman, *Two Lucky People*.
48. Ibid., 116.
49. Isaiah Berlin, March 3, 1942, *Washington Dispatches*, 25.
50. Ibid.
51. Herbert Stein, *Presidential Economics*, 68.

XIII: EXILE: SCHUMPETER AND HAYEK IN WORLD WAR II

1. Friedrich Hayek, *The Road to Serfdom* (Chicago: University of Chicago Press, 1944).
2. Joseph Schumpeter, *Capitalism, Socialism and Democracy* (New York: Harper and Co., 1942).
3. Ibid.
4. Joseph Schumpeter to Irving Fisher, February 18, 1946.
5. Joseph Schumpeter, Diary, October 30, 1942.
6. John Hicks, "The Hayek Story," in *Critical Essays in Monetary Theory* (Oxford, UK: Oxford University Press, 1967).
7. Friedrich Hayek to Fritz Machlup, January 1935.
8. Friedrich Hayek to Fritz Machlup, May 1, 1936.
9. Friedrich Hayek to Fritz Machlup.
10. Friedrich Hayek to Lord Macmillan, September 9, 1939.
11. Friedrich Hayek to Fritz Machlup, December 14, 1940.
12. Friedrich Hayek to Fritz Machlup, June 21, 1940.
13. Friedrich Hayek to Alvin Johnson, August 8, 1940.
14. Friedrich Hayek to Alfred Schutz, September 26, 1943.
15. Friedrich Hayek to Fritz Machlup.
16. Friedrich Hayek to Fritz Machlup, June 21, 1940.
17. Friedrich Hayek to Herbert Furth, January 27, 1941.
18. Friedrich Hayek to Fritz Machlup, January 2, 1941.
19. Friedrich Hayek to Fritz Machlup.
20. Friedrich Hayek to Fritz Machlup, July 31, 1941.
21. Friedrich Hayek, *The Road to Serfdom*.
22. Ibid.
23. Ibid., 135.
24. Friedrich Hayek, "The Road to Serfdom: Address Before the Economic Club of Detroit, April 23, 1945," typescript, Hoover Institution.
25. Quoted in Fritz Machlup to Friedrich Hayek, January 21, 1943.
26. Ordway Tead to Fritz Machlup, September 25, 1943.

ACT III: PROLOGUE: NOTHING TO FEAR

1. James MacGregor Burns, *Roosevelt: The Soldier of Freedom, 1940–1945* (New York: Harcourt Brace Jovanovich, 1970), 424.

2. Franklin Delano Roosevelt, "Economic Bill of Rights," State of the Union Address, January 11, 1944, transcript, Franklin D. Roosevelt Presidential Library and Museum, Hyde Park, New York, http://www.fdrlibrary.marist.edu/archives/stateoftheunion.html.

3. Ibid.

4. James McGregor Burns, *Roosevelt: The Soldier of Freedom*, vol. 2 (New York: Harcourt Brace Jovanovich, 1970), 426.

5. John Maynard Keynes to Sir J. Anderson, August 10, 1944, quoted in Robert Jacob Alexander Sidelsky, *John Maynard Keynes*, vol. 3, Fighting for Freedom (New York: Viking Press, 2001), 360.

6. Gunnar Myrdal, "Is American Business Deluding Itself?," *Atlantic Monthly* (November 1944), 51–58.

7. Roosevelt, State of the Union Address, January 11, 1944.

8. Ibid.

9. Alvin H. Hansen, "The Postwar Economy," in Seymour E. Harris, ed., *Postwar Economic Problems* (New York: McGraw-Hill Book Company, 1943), 12.

10. Paul A. Samuelson, "Full Employment After the War, in Harris, *Postwar Economic Problems*, 27, 52.

11. Joseph A. Schumpeter, "Capitalism in the Postwar World," in Harris, *Postwar Economic Problems*, 120–21.

12. Ibid.

13. Roosevelt, State of the Union Address, January 11, 1944.

14. Myrdal, "Is American Business Deluding Itself?"

15. George Orwell, *Nineteen Eighty-Four* (London: Penguin Classics, 2009), 231.

16. Roosevelt, State of the Union Address, January 11, 1944.

17. John Lewis Gaddis, *The Cold War: A New History* (New York: Penguin, 2006), 14.

18. John Maynard Keynes, *The General Theory* (1936; repr. London: MacMillan & Co., 1954), 383–84.

XIV: PAST AND FUTURE: KEYNES AT BRETTON WOODS

1. FDR, Message to Delegates at Bretton Woods, July 1944.

2. John Maynard Keynes to Florence Keynes, June 28, 1944.

3. Robert Skidelsky, *John Maynard Keynes*, vol. 3, *Fighting for Freedom 1937–1946* (New York: Viking, 2000), 343.

4. John Maynard Keynes to Friedrich Hayek, July 1944.

5. John Maynard Keynes, "My Early Beliefs," in *Essays in Biography*.

6. Lionel Robbins, *Autobiography of an Economist* (London: Macmillan, 1976).

7. John Maynard Keynes to Friedrich Hayek, July 1944.

8. Lydia Keynes quoted in Liaquat Ahmed, *Lords of Finance: The Bankers Who Broke the World* (New York: Penguin, 2009).

9. Cordell Hull, *The Memoirs of Cordell Hull* (New York: Macmillan, 1948), 1:81.
10. Papers of Harry Dexter White, Princeton University Archive.
11. Skidelsky, *Keynes,* vol. 3, *Fighting for Freedom,* 348.
12. Ibid.
13. Ibid.

XV: THE ROAD FROM SERFDOM: HAYEK AND THE GERMAN MIRACLE

1. George Orwell, review of *The Road to Serfdom* (1944).
2. Isaiah Berlin, March 31, 1945, *Washington Despatches, 1941–1945: Weekly Political Reports from the British Embassy* (Chicago: University of Chicago Press, 1981).
3. Berlin, *Despatches,* May 6, 1945.
4. Berlin, *Despatches,* June 10, 1945.
5. Friedrich Hayek to Fritz Machlup, and *Message to Congress on the Concentration of Economic Power,* April 29, 1938.
6. Marquis Childs. "Washington Calling: Hayek's 'Free Trade,'" *Washington Post,* June 6, 1945, http://www.proquest.com.ezproxy.cul.columbia.edu/ (accessed February 10, 2011).
7. George Kennan, *Memoirs 1925–1950* (New York: Atlantic Monthly Press, 1967), 292.
8. Friedrich Hayek to Lydia Keynes, April 21, 1946.
9. Harry S. Truman, March 12, 1947, transcript of the Truman Doctrine (1947), http://www.ourdocuments.gov/; Robert A. Pollard, *Economic Security and the Origins of the Cold War, 1945–1950* (New York: Columbia University Press, 1985), 123, http://questia.com.
10. Friedrich Hayek, "Opening address to a conference at Mont Pelerin," 1947, P. G. Klein, ed., *The Collected Works of F. A. Hayek, Volume IV: The Fortunes of Liberalism,* (Chicago, Ill.: University of Chicago Press, 1992), 238.
11. Friedrich A. Hayek, *Nobel Prize Winning Economist Friedrich A. von Hayek* (Los Angeles: University of California at Los Angeles Oral History Program, 1983), http://www.archive.org/stream/nobelprizewinnin00haye#page/n11/mode/2up.
12. *Statement of Aims,* Mont Pelerin Society, https://www.montpelerin.org/montpelerin/mpsGoals.html.
13. Orson Welles's contribution to *The Third Man,* 1949 in Robert Andrews, *The Columbia Dictionary of Quotations,* (New York: Columbia University Press, 1993), 888.
14. Quoted in Kurt R. Leube, "Hayek in War and Peace," *Hoover Digest,* no. 1, 2006.
15. Ray Monk, *Wittgenstein: The Duty of Genius* (New York: Penguin Books), 518.
16. Friedrich Hayek, *Hayek on Hayek: An Autobiographical Dialog,* Stephen Kresge, ed. (Chicago: University of Chicago Press, 1994), 105–6.

17. Austin Robinson, *First Sight of Postwar Germany, May–June, 1945* (Cambridge: The Canteloupe Press, 1986).

18. Ibid.

19. John Maynard Keynes to Austin Robinson, June, 1945.

20. Ludwig Erhard, *Germany's Comeback in the World Market* (New York: Macmillan, 1954).

XVI: INSTRUMENTS OF MASTERY: SAMUELSON GOES TO WASHINGTON

1. Quoted in Philip Saunders and William Walstead, *The Principles of Economics Course* (New York: McGraw-Hill, 1990), ix.

2. Paul A. Samuelson, *The Samuelson Sampler* (Glen Ridge, N.J.: Thomas Horton & Co., 1973), vii.

3. Paul A. Samuelson with Everett Hagen, "Studies in Wartime Planning for Continuing Full Employment" (Washington, D.C.: National Resources Planning Board, 1944); Paul A. Samuelson et al., *After the War 1918–1920* (Washington, D.C.: National Resources Planning Board, 1943); and Paul A. Samuelson et al, (Washington, D.C.: National Resources Planning Board, 1942).

4. Paul Samuelson, Godkin Lecture I.

5. Alan Millward, *War, Economy and Society, 1939–1945* (Berkeley: University of California Press, 1980).

6. Will Lissner, *New York Times*, September 3, 1944, 23.

7. Paul Samuelson, "Unemployment Ahead and the Coming Economic Crisis," *New Republic*, September, 1944.

8. Quoted in Polenberg, 94.

9. Interview, Paul Samuelson.

10. Paul A. Samuelson and William Nordhaus, *Economics: The Original 1948 Edition*, 573.

11. Robert Summers, father of Lawrence Summers. He and Harold Samuelson, Paul Samuelson's older brother, changed their names to "Summers" in an attempt to avoid anti-Semitism.

12. Florence Wieman, South Chicago, *The Scroll*, May, 1930.

13. Paul A. Samuelson, "Reflections on the Great Depression," typescript.

14. Ibid., p. 58.

15. Paul A. Samuelson, "How Foundations Came To Be," *Journal of Economic Literature* (1998), 1376.

16. Tsuru Shigeto, "Reminiscences of Our 'Sacred Decade of Twenties,'" *The American Economist* (Fall 2007).

17. Samuelson, "Reflections on the Great Depression."

18. Herbert Stein, *Presidential Economics*.

19. Paul A. Samuelson, interview.

20. Joseph Schumpeter to Paul A. Samuelson, November 3, 1947.

21. Robert Maynard Hutchins, quoted in David Kennedy, *Freedom from Fear: The American People in Depression and War* (Oxford, UK: Oxford University Press, 2001).

22. Paul A. Samuelson to F. Wheeler Loomis, director, M.I.T. Radiation Laboratory, April 26, 1945.

23. Kenneth Elzinga, "The Eleven Principles of Economics," *Southern Economic Review* (April 1992).

24. Stanley Fisher, interview with Paul A. Samuelson, typescript transcript.

25. William F. Buckley, *God and Man at Yale* (Washington, D.C.: Regnery Gateway, 1951).

26. Ibid., 49.

27. Ibid., 60.

28. Ibid., 81.

29. Paul A. Samuelson, *Economics* (New York: McGraw-Hill, 1948), 412.

30. Ibid., 434.

31. Ibid., 152.

32. Ibid., 380.

33. Ibid., 433.

34. Ibid., 3.

35. Ibid., 584.

36. Paul A. Samuelson, *Economics,* 4th ed. (New York: McGraw-Hill), 209–210.

37. Samuelson, *Economics,* 1st ed., 607.

38. Ibid., 271.

39. Ibid.

XVII: GRAND ILLUSION: ROBINSON IN MOSCOW AND BEIJING

1. Joan Robinson, lecture, Cambridge University, quoted in Harry G. Johnson, *On Economics and Society* (Chicago: University of Chicago Press, 1975), 110.

2. Joan Robinson, *Conference Sketch Book, Moscow, April 1952* (Cambridge: W. Heffer and Sons, 1952), 19.

3. Ibid., 6, 21, 23–24.

4. Alec Cairncross, "The Moscow Economic Conference," *Soviet Studies* 4, no. 2 (October 1952), 114.

5. Robinson, *Conference Sketch Book,* 5.

6. Robinson, *Conference Sketch Book,* 7–8; Cairncross, "The Moscow Economic Conference," 119.

7. Robinson, *Conference Sketch Book,* 23.

8. "Russia: Two Faces West," *Time,* April 14, 1952.

9. Robinson, *Conference Sketch Book,* 11.

10. Committee for the Promotion of International Trade, *International Economic Conference in Moscow April 3–12, 1952* (Moscow, 1952); Oleg Hoeff-

ding, "East-West Trade Possibilities: An Appraisal of the Moscow Economic Conference," *American Slavic and East European Review*, 1953; Richard B. Day, *Cold War Capitalism: The View from Moscow, 1945–1975* (Armonk, NY: M. E. Sharpe, 1995), 79.

11. Committee for the Promotion of International Trade, *International Economic Conference*, 85.

12. Robinson, *Conference Sketch Book*, 28.

13. Ibid.

14. Ibid., 3, 5.

15. Joan Robinson to Richard Kahn, April 4, 1952, Papers of Richard Ferdinand Kahn, RFK/13/90/5, King's College, University of Cambridge.

16. Paul Samuelson, "Remembering Joan," in G. R. Feiwell, ed., *Joan Robinson and Modern Economic Theory* (London: Macmillan, 1989), 135.

17. Paul Preston, Michael Partridge, and Piers Ludlow, "British Documents on Foreign Affairs: Reports and Papers from the Foreign Office Confidential Print" (Lexis Nexis, 2006).

18. Cairncross, "The Moscow Economic Conference," 113, 118.

19. *Economic Problems of Socialism in the U.S.S.R.* (New York: International Publishers, 1952), 26, 30. Stalin's "Remarks on Economic Questions in Connection with Discussion of November 1951" were distributed around February 7, 1952, to Central Committee members working on Stalin's textbook on Soviet economic theory. "Remarks" was published later that year as *Economic Problems*.

20. John Lewis Gaddis, *We Now Know: Rethinking Cold War History* (New York: Oxford University Press USA, 1997), 195.

21. Stalin, *Economic Problems of Socialism*, 27.

22. Richard B. Day, *Cold War Capitalism: The View from Moscow, 1945–1975* (Armonk, NY: M. E. Sharpe, 1995), 76.

23. Ethan Pollock, "Conversations with Stalin on Questions of Political Economy," July 2001, Working Paper No. 33, Cold War International History Project, Woodrow Wilson International Center for Scholars, http://www.wilsoncenter.org/topics/pubs/ACFB07.pdf.

24. Robinson, *Conference Sketch Book*.

25. Geoffrey Colin Harcourt, "Some Reflections on Joan Robinson's Changes of Mind and Their Relationship to Post-Keynesianism and the Economics Profession," in *Capitalism, Socialism and Post-Keynesianism: Selected Essays of George Harcourt* (Cheltenham, UK: Edward Elgar, 1995), 111.

26. Joan Robinson, *The Problem of Full Employment: An Outline for Study Circles* (London: Workers Educational Association, 1943).

27. Stephen Brooke, "Revisionists and Fundamentalists: The Labour Party and Economic Policy During the Second World War," *Historical Journal* (March 1989), 158.

28. Elizabeth Durbin, *New Jerusalems: The Labour Party and the Economics of Democratic Socialism* (London: Routledge and Keegan Paul, 1985), 164.

29. Quoted in C. W. Guillebaud, "Review of Joan Robinson, *Private Enterprise or Public Control: Handbook for Discussion Groups*," *Economica* 10, no. 39 (August 1943), 265.

30. J. E. King, "Planning for Abundance: Joan Robinson and Nicholas Kaldor, 1942–1945," in European Society for the History of Economic Thought, *Political Events and Economic Ideas* (London: Elgar), 307.

31. Jonathan Schneer, "Hopes Deferred or Shattered: The British Labour Left and the Third Force Movement, 1945–1949," *Journal of Modern History* (June 1984), 197.

32. Joseph Stalin, *Meeting Between Comrades Stalin and H. Pollitt 31st May 1950*, transcript, Russian State Archive of Social and Political History, 4.

33. Eric Shaw, *Discipline and Discord in the Labour Party* (Manchester, UK: University of Manchester Press, 1988).

34. Harold Laski, *The Secret Battalion*, a 1946 pamphlet defending the Labour Party's rejection of the Communist Party of Great Britain's application for affiliation.

35. Joan Robinson, "Preparation for War," *Cambridge Today*, October 1951, reprinted in *Monthly Review*, no 2 (1951), 194–95.

36. Richard Gardner, *Sterling Dollar Diplomacy: Anglo-American Collaboration in the Reconstruction of Multilateral Trade* (London: Clarendon, 1956), 298.

37. Schneer, "Hopes Deferred or Shattered."

38. Joan Robinson, BBC, *London Forum*, June 25, 1947, quoted, ibid., 221.

39. "Why the CP Says Reject the Marshall Plan," July 5, 1947, quoted in Keith Laybourn, *Marxism in Britain: Dissent, Decline and Re-emergence, 1945–c.2000* (New York: Taylor and Francis, 2006), 35.

40. Robert Solow, quoted in Marjorie Shepherd Turner, *Joan Robinson and the Americans* (Armonk, NY: M. E. Sharpe, 1989), 143.

41. Joan Robinson to Richard Kahn, King's College Archive.

42. Christopher Andrew, *Defend the Realm: The Authorized History of MI5* (New York: Alfred A. Knopf, 2009), 400; Marjorie S. Turner, *Joan Robinson and the Americans*, 86; Percy Timberlake, *The 48 Group: The Story of the Icebreakers in China* (London: 48 Group Club, 1994).

43. Milton Friedman and Rose Friedman, *Two Lucky People: Memoirs* (Chicago: University of Chicago Press, 1998), 245–46.

44. Robert Clower, quoted in Turner, *Joan Robinson and the Americans*, 133.

45. Alvin L. Marty, "A Reminiscence of Joan Robinson," *American Economic Association Newsletter*, (October 1991), 5–8.

46. Arthur Pigou to John Maynard Keynes, June 1940, King's College Archive.

47. Michael Straight, quoted in Turner, *Joan Robinson and the Americans*, 56.

48. Brian Loasby, "Joan Robinson's Wrong Turning," in Ingrid H. Rima, ed., *The Joan Robinson Legacy* (London: M. E. Sharpe, 1991), 34.

49. Joan Robinson, "Mr. Harrod's Dynamics," *Economic Journal* (March 1949), 81.

50. Joan Robinson, "Review of Joseph Schumpeter, *Capitalism, Socialism and Democracy,*" *Economic Journal*, 1943.

51. Sidney Hook, "Review of Rosa Luxemburg, *The Accumulation of Capital, with a Preface by Joan Robinson,*" 1951,

52. Joan Robinson, *The Accumulation of Capital* (London: MacMillan, 1956).

53. Roy Forbes Harrod, *Towards a Dynamic Economics* (London: Macmillan, 1948).

54. Robinson, "Mr. Harrod's Dynamics," 85.

55. Joan Robinson, "Model of an Expanding Economy," *Economic Journal* (March 1952).

56. Joan Robinson, *Letters from a Visitor to China* (Cambridge: Students' Bookshop, 1954), 8.

57. Joan Robinson, "Has Capitalism Changed?" *Monthly Review*, 1961.

58. Samuelson, "Remembering Joan," 121–43.

59. Stanislaw H. Wellisz, review, *Review of Economics and Statistics* 40, no. 1 (February 1958): 87–88.

60. Elizabeth S. Johnson and Harry G. Johnson, *The Legacy of Keynes* (Oxford: Basil Blackwell, 1978).

61. Samuelson, "Remembering Joan."

62. Abba Lerner, "*The Accumulation of Capital,*" *American Economic Review* (September 1957): 693, 699.

63. L. R. Klein, "*The Accumulation of Capital* by Joan Robinson," *Econometrica* 26, no. 4 (October 1958), 622, 624.

64. Robert Solow, "Technical Change and the Aggregate Production Function," *Review of Economics and Statistics* 39, no. 3 (August 1957); 320; and Robert Solow, quoted in Turner, *Joan Robinson*, 143.

65. Joan Robinson, *Private Enterprise or Public Control* (London: English University Press Ltd.), 13–14.

66. Quoted in Jason Becker, *Hungry Ghosts: Mao's Secret Famine* (London: Macmillan, 1998), 292.

67. George J. Stigler, review of *Economic Philosophy* by Joan Robinson, *The Journal of Political Economy* 71, no. 2 (April 1963), 192–93 (emphasis added).

XVIII: TRYST WITH DESTINY: SEN IN CALCUTTA AND CAMBRIDGE

1. Amartya Sen, *Development as Freedom* (New York: Alfred A. Knopf, 1999), 36.

2. Sankar Ray, "The Third World Apologist Finally Strikes," *Calcutta Online*, October 15, 1998, http://www.nd.edu/~kmukhopa/cal300/sen/art1014m.htm.

3. The Royal Swedish Academy of Sciences, "The Prize in Economics 1998—Press Release," news release, October 14, 1998, http://nobelprize.org/nobel_prizes/economics/laureates/1998/press.html.

4. John B. Seely, *The Road Book of India* (London: J. M. Richardson and G. B. Whittaker, 1825), 12: "Dacca ... is celebrated for the manufacture of the finest and most beautiful muslins." Muslin was a favorite topic of Jane Austen's letters to her sister Cassandra. In *Northanger Abbey* (1818), a potential suitor wows a chaperone with the "prodigious bargain" he got on a gown for his sister made of "true Indian muslin."

5. William Sproston Caine, *Picturesque India: A Handbook for European Travellers* (London: George Routledge and Sons Limited, 1891), 367.

6. Amartya Sen, interview by the author. Except where otherwise noted, quotes of Mr. Sen are from discussions and interviews with the author.

7. Archibald Percivel Wavell to Winston Churchill, telegram, February 1944, in Penderel Moon, ed., *Wavell: The Viceroy's Journal* (Oxford University Press, 1973), 54.

8. Amartya Sen, "Autobiography," http://nobelprize.org/nobel_prizes/economics/laureates/1998/sen-autobio.html.

9. Ibid.

10. Amita Sen, interview by the author.

11. Indira Gandi, *Selected Speeches and Writings of Indira Gandi,* vol. 5, *January 1, 1982–October 30, 1984* (Delhi: Publications Division, Ministry of Information and Broadcasting, Government of India, 1986), 457.

12. Arjo Klamer, "A Conversation with Amartya Sen," *Journal of Economic Perspectives* 3, no. 1 (Winter 1989), 148.

13. Jean Drèze and Amartya Sen, *India, Development and Politics* (Oxford University Press, 2002), 3.

14. Amartya Sen, "The Impossibility of a Paretian Liberal," *Journal of Political Economy* 78 (1970): 152–57.

15. Drèze and Sen, *India, Development and Politics,* 2.

16. World Bank World Development Indicators (accessed April 13, 2011), http://data.worldbank.org/indicators.

EPILOGUE: IMAGINING THE FUTURE

1. John Maynard Keynes, *The General Theory of Employment, Interest and Money* (New York: Harcourt, Brace, 1936), 383.

2. Robert Solow, "Faith, Hope and Clarity" in David Colander and Alfred William Coats, eds., *The Spread of Economic Ideas* (Cambridge, Mass.: Cambridge University Press, 1993), 37.

Index

C

W

Photo Credits

Mary Evans Picture Library: 1, 2, 4, 10, 12

Hulton Archive/Getty Images: 3

Collection International Institute of Social History, Amsterdam: 5, 6

Courtesy of the Marshall Library of Economics, University of Cambridge: 7, 8

Courtesy of the Library of the London School of Economics and Political Science, reference number 00042: 9

©The National Portrait Gallery, London: 11, 21

Manuscripts & Archives, Yale University: 13

University of Albany, State University of New York: 14

Harvard University Archives, call # HUGBS 276.90p (2): 15

Mary Evans Picture Library / Thomas Cook Archive: 16

Courtesy of Michael Nedo and The Wittgenstein Archive, Cambridge: 17, 18

Mary Evans Picture Library / Robert Hunt Collection: 19

Courtesy of the Austrian State Archives: 20

"Photograph of Duncan Grant and Maynard Keynes at Asheham House in Sussex, the home of Leonard and Virginia Woolf"—Vanessa Bell ©Tate, London 2011: 22

About the Author

SYLVIA NASAR is the author of the bestselling *A Beautiful Mind,* which won the National Book Critics Circle Award for biography. She was an economics correspondent for *The New York Times* and is the John S. and James L. Knight Professor of Business Journalism at the Columbia University Graduate School of Journalism. She lives in Tarrytown, New York.